Human Societies

An Introduction to Macrosociology

Twelfth Edition

Patrick Nolan
University of South Carolina at Columbia

Gerhard Lenski
University of North Carolina at Chapel Hill

New York   Oxford
OXFORD UNIVERSITY PRESS

Oxford University Press is a department of the University of Oxford.
It furthers the University's objective of excellence in research, scholarship,
and education by publishing worldwide.

Oxford   New York
Auckland   Cape Town   Dar es Salaam   Hong Kong   Karachi
Kuala Lumpur   Madrid   Melbourne   Mexico City   Nairobi
New Delhi   Shanghai   Taipei   Toronto

With offices in
Argentina   Austria   Brazil   Chile   Czech Republic   France   Greece
Guatemala   Hungary   Italy   Japan   Poland   Portugal   Singapore
South Korea   Switzerland   Thailand   Turkey   Ukraine   Vietnam

For titles covered by Section 112 of the US Higher Education
Opportunity Act, please visit www.oup.com/us/he for the
latest information about pricing and alternate formats.

Published in the United States of America by
Oxford University Press
198 Madison Avenue, New York, NY 10016
http://www.oup.com

Library of Congress Cataloging-in-Publication Data
Nolan, Patrick, 1947–
    Human societies : an introduction to macrosociology / Patrick Nolan, University of South Carolina
at Columbia, Gerhard Lenski, University of North Carolina at Chapel Hill. -- Twelfth Edition.
        pages cm
    Includes bibliographical references and index.
    ISBN 978-0-19-938245-3
    1. Macrosociology. 2. Social evolution. 3. Social systems--History. I. Lenski, Gerhard, 1924- II. Title.
    HM490.N65 2015
    301--dc23
                                                                                        2014024611

Printing number: 9 8 7 6 5 4 3 2 1

Printed in the United States of America
on acid-free paper

For Lou and Ann

BRIEF CONTENTS

CONTENTS

Change—*extremely rapid social change*—is the most important fact of life today. Today's world is a vastly different place from the world of just twenty-five or fifty years ago, and the world of the next half century will almost certainly be greatly changed from our world today. Yet this will be the world in which most of today's students will find themselves. This means that the most important things they should be learning are the things that can help them anticipate and prepare for the changes that lie ahead.

Human Societies attempts to address this need in two ways. First, it offers students a framework for understanding human societies, and more especially for understanding the forces responsible for the more fundamental kinds of social change. To do this, we begin in Chapters 1 to 4 with an examination of the basic elements of this framework as found in ecological-evolutionary theory. We then show that this theoretical framework helps to explain the emergence, development, and, in some cases, the extinction of the various types of societies that men and women have created over the centuries and millennia. We believe that this broadly comparative and historical approach offers students a fresh and far more challenging perspective than is provided by texts that focus almost entirely on the students' own society.

Second, *Human Societies* offers students a model of how to use evidence to evaluate the validity of ideas and opinion. We do not ask students to accept our views on societies and social change because we claim to be authorities, but rather because we present a systematic body of evidence to support our claims. We believe it is important for students to understand the role of empirical evidence in evaluating ideas and opinions about the social world. In this vein, we encourage instructors and students alike to become acquainted with the data sources identified in the text and in the accompanying *Instructor's Manual* and to use these sources to test their own ideas about human societies or to challenge ours.

NEW TO THIS EDITION

This is the twelfth edition of *Human Societies,* and the first to appear with Oxford University Press. Although no chapter is entirely unchanged in the present edition, in the early chapters (1–8), on preindustrial societies, with few exceptions, the changes are stylistic or refinements; but in the later chapters (9–15), on industrial and contemporary developing societies, the changes are substantive, significant, and widespread. Virtually all the data in them have been updated or replaced. Noteworthy changes are indicated below.

The opening of Chapter 1 has been rewritten to make students more aware of how unusual contemporary societies are and how dependent their lifestyle is on technology and inanimate energy. There is also a new boxed insert, Good Parents, Bad Kids?, illustrating an aspect of the complex relationship between human genetics and socialization. In Chapter 4, Figure 4.1, showing societal levels of technological development and common paths of evolution, now also displays data on the amounts of energy produced and expended in them. In Chapter 5 there is a new boxed insert, Neandertals Among Us? discussing the continued presence of Neandertal genes in modern populations. In Chapter 6, the discussion of the origins of plant cultivation has been updated, and Table 6.4, Incidence of Warfare, now reports more complete data based on Nolan's 2003 *Social Theory* paper. There also is a new boxed insert in Chapter 7, Women's Power in a Man's World, that summarizes Rae Lesser Blumberg's research on an interesting subset of agrarian societies that have mitigated the more typical pattern of patriarchy and male domination.

In Chapter 9, data in Table 9.2, on the current distribution of gross world product has been updated, as has data in Table 9.3, on gross domestic product per capita in contemporary societies. The data, tables, and discussions throughout Chapters 10 through 15 have been substantially revised, updated, and, in many cases, extended.

Data on materials production, growth in GDP and per capita GDP—Tables 10.1, Productivity of American Agriculture; 10.2, regarding changing employment patterns in the United States; 10.3, which documents changes in union membership in industrial societies; 10.5, about oligopoly in U.S. industries; 10.6, Government Spending as a Percentage of GDP; and 10.7, Trade as a Percentage of GDP—have all been extended and updated.

In Chapter 11, Table 11.1, Percent in Industrial Societies Certain God Exists, is new, and the discussion centers now on the trend in belief over recent decades. Also, the increasingly dated Tables 11.2 and 11.3 were dropped, but their basic historical data have been incorporated into the text. Figure 11.2, U.S. Government Employment, and boxed inserts Changing Catholic Belief and Practice in France and the United States, and Money and Politics have all been updated; and data on political spending incorporates data from the 2012 elections. In addition, the discussions of mass media and views of government have been largely rewritten to incorporate more current data and surveys.

Chapters 12 and 13, on inequality and the family, respectively, in addition to being thoroughly updated, have been largely rewritten and reoriented, in part, to account for the dramatic changes that have occurred in them but also to show, more clearly, the long-term trends in them.

Tables 12.1, Fifteen Wealthiest Individuals in the World, and 12.2, which breaks down income shares in industrial societies, have been updated; and the new Table 12.3 reports changes in U.S. income *shares* and *income* from 1967 to 2012. Subsequent Tables (now renumbered) 12.4, Distribution of Adult Population among Occupational Classes in the United States; 12.5, Ratio of Women and Men's Wages; and 12.6, Quality of Life in Industrial Societies have been updated as have Figures 12.1, U.S. Family Income Inequality; 12.4 (extending William J. Wilson's data on), Percentage of African-Americans in Middle-Class Occupations; and 12.5, Ratio of Women's to Men's Incomes.

In Chapter 13, Tables 13.1, Death Rates for Communicable Diseases in the U.S.; 13.2, Total Fertility Rate in Industrial Societies; and Table 13.4, Percentage of Degrees Awarded to Women have been updated, as has data on international migration; and Table 13.5 now reports the current percentage of women in parliaments in industrial societies (not Proportion of Elite Positions Held by Women). Figures 13.1, Female Labor Force Participation, and Figure 13.2, Married Couple Income have also been updated. The most important change is the new Table 13.3 that reports the dramatic changes in the size and composition of U.S. households and families that has occurred over the last half century, and its discussion in the new subhead Changing Structure of Households and Families.

Tables 14.1, on trade commodity concentration; 14.2, on economic and population growth; 14.3 and 14.4, on average levels of freedom and perceived corruption, respectively; 14.5, Mean Income Share and Standardized Income; 14.6, Quality of Life Index; 14.7, on school enrollment; and 14.8, on perceptions of a women's right to employment have all been updated. The (outdated) boxed insert on the recent presence of slavery in the world has been dropped, but contemporary data, on its continuance, has been incorporated into the text.

The first part of Chapter 15, looking back over societal evolution has been refined but is largely unchanged. On the other hand, the latter part, examining current social problems, technological advances, and consideration of future prospects and developments has been substantially rewritten based on more recent data and expert opinion. Table 15.1, Mathematical Literacy Scores, has been updated.

Finally, the "Teaching and Learning Supplement," with Jack Goldstone and Joel Cohen's prognostications on future world prospects and problems, and the assignments based on them, have been dropped from this edition.

All the changes are also identified and discussed in the *Instructor's Manual* (available on request from Oxford University Press), and we strongly recommend that instructors who have used previous editions, as well as those who are using *Human Societies* for the first time, consult it before preparing their course materials or making class assignments. We invite your comments, reactions, and suggestions regarding *Human Societies*. You can send them to Patrick Nolan at the Department of Sociology, the University of South Carolina, Columbia, SC 29208, or e-mail pnolan747@gmail.com.

ACKNOWLEDGMENTS

It is not possible to acknowledge adequately all our intellectual debts in the brief space available here. But many who read this volume will recognize our debt to Adam Ferguson, John Millar, Thomas Malthus, Charles Darwin, Herbert Spencer, Karl Marx, Max Weber, Albert Keller, William Ogburn, V. Gordon Childe, George Peter Murdock, R. H. Tawney, Sir Julian Huxley, George Gaylord Simpson, Leslie White, Julian Steward, Amos Hawley, Marvin Harris, William H. McNeill, George Kingsley Zipf, Jonathan Turner, Alexandra Maryanski, George Orwell, Sir Karl Popper, and Bruce Mayhew, among others. The citations that appear at the end of this volume should be regarded as further acknowledgments of our indebtedness and appreciation.

We would also like to thank the following reviewers commissioned by Oxford University Press: Timothy J. Bertoni, Tri-County Technical College; George H. Conklin,

North Carolina Central University; Wenqian Dai, University of South Dakota; Steven Pfaff, University of Washington; and Linda Scola, Bethune-Cookman University.

Many social scientists and a few biologists have been kind enough to provide critical comments on, and suggestions for, one or more of the eleven editions of *Human Societies* thus far. The social scientists include Brian Aldrich, Francis R. Allen, E. Jackson Baur, Bill Breedlove, Rae Lesser Blumberg, Steve Borgatti, William Brustein, Brad Buchner, Woody Carlson, Robert Carroll, William R. Catton Jr., Ronald Cosper, Timothy Crippen, David Featherman, Thomas Feucht, George Furniss, Eric Godfrey, Walter Goldschmidt, Robert Bates Graber, J. Patrick Gray, Gareth Gustafson, Thomas D. Hall, Amos Hawley, Paul Heckert, John Hofley, Joan Huber, Holly Hughes, Larry Hunt, Donald Irish, Sangmoon Kim, Peter Kivisto, Philip Marcus, Robert Miller, Donald Millman, François Nielsen, Peter Peregrine, Ross Purdy, Leo Rigsby, Ellen Rosengarten, Tom Rotollo, David Rowlee, Tim Schwartz, Norman Storer, Jacek Szmatka, Theodore H. Tsoukalas, Wout Ultee, Charles K. Warriner, Norbert Wiley, and Everett K. Wilson. The biologists include Alfred E. Emerson, Richard E. Lenski, and Edward O. Wilson. We extend sincere thanks to each of them for valuable suggestions, but we remind readers that the final responsibility for the contents is ours alone.

Patrick Nolan
Gerhard Lenski

Theoretical Foundations

CHAPTER 1

The Human Condition

Outline
Human Societies: Their Place in Nature
Understanding Human Societies: Basic Assumptions
Human Societies: The Basic Model
Excursus: A Brief History of Sociology

We live in a remarkable age. It's difficult for most of us to imagine life without electricity, for example, and all the devices and conveniences that it powers—from our computers, televisions, and microwaves to our hair dryers and hot water. We occasionally get a glimpse of what such a life would be like when a wind or ice storm knocks out our power, but that experience is mediated by our expectation that it is only temporary and by our access to a number of alternatively powered substitutes.

Yet this source of power and the life-enhancing devices dependent on it only became available in the late nineteenth century and were not widespread until the middle of the twentieth. Thus they were not available to humans for more than 99.9 percent of our time on earth and are still not available to over a billion people in the world today![1] As we shall show in the following chapters, its effects on our lifestyle and quality of life have been nothing short of revolutionary.

Today, we take continuous change in our technology and lives as ordinary and normal. We expect that the automobile, computer, or smartphone that we buy today is already scheduled to be superseded by something more sophisticated and more powerful tomorrow. Nothing stays the same for long. Yet this too is a very recent and unusual development.

To see the dimensions of these fundamental changes, let us imagine a huge photo album filled with pictures of human life beginning 100,000 years ago, each of its 1,000 pages providing a record of life in a different century.

Beginning with photographs of life in the Stone Age long, long ago, the pages would be terribly repetitive. And after the initial shock of our ancestors brutally primitive lifestyle faded, you would find them tiresome and boring. In fact, throughout the first half of the album and beyond, hundreds of pages, representing thousands of years, would be filled with the same kinds of pictures—scenes of people physically indistinguishable from ourselves, though naked or clad in animal skins, huddled around fires in front of caves or beside rude shelters made of branches and leaves;

3

fashioning simple tools and weapons from stone, wood, and bone; hunting with wooden spears; foraging for edible plants; nursing infants; and performing a limited number of other basic tasks. Fascinating though the first of these pictures might be, you would soon tire of the repetitiveness and might begin to flip pages in search of something new and different.

Roughly halfway through the volume, if you were still paying attention, you would gradually begin to see occasional indications of innovation and change. For example, you might see for the first time a photograph of people burying someone who had died. Later, you would slowly find increasing evidence of other new activities. Occasionally, you might see a photograph of people painting on the walls of caves or engaging in strange new rituals unlike anything you had seen before. Other innovations would gradually appear, especially new kinds of tools and weapons—spoons, saws, needles, bows and arrows, oil lamps, even crude dugout canoes. Shortly before page 900, you would begin to see people trapping and netting fish, harvesting wild grains with stone sickles, weaving baskets, taming wild dogs and sheep, and, yes, even drinking beer.

Not until the last hundred pages, however, would you find the first photographs of people farming, and it would be another twenty or thirty pages before you would see any real towns. A little after page 950, you would find views of the construction of the great pyramids of Egypt, and later still, you would begin to see the first pictures of individuals whose names you would recognize: Moses on page 967, Aristotle on 976, Cleopatra on 979, Jesus on 980, Mohammed on 986.

Although signs of innovation and change would be growing, you would not find evidence of really rapid social and cultural change of the kind to which we are accustomed until you got to the end of the album. There, crowded into the *last three pages,* you would see for the first time everything from the first steam engine to the first jet engine, the first computer, the first television, and the first nuclear weapons—all those inventions and discoveries that are so important in our lives today.

This journey through the past is bound to raise questions in the mind of any thoughtful person. Why, for example, did the Stone Age last so long? Was life so satisfying that people had no interest in finding different ways of doing things? But, if that was true, why did they eventually begin to change?

The historical record also raises questions about the more recent past and about conditions today and in the years ahead. What has caused the explosive acceleration of the rate of change in the recent past, and should we expect even more rapid change in the years ahead? If so, what kind of world awaits us in the rest of the twenty-first century?

There are other questions, too. Has all the change of the recent past been worth it? Are we better off today than our forebears were a century or more ago, or have the costs outweighed the benefits? Finally, and most important of all, can we do anything to control the process of change and to maximize its benefits and minimize its costs?

Questions like these force us to recognize how much we are like poorly prepared astronauts on a fleet of spaceships, hurtling at fantastic speeds on an uncharted course filled with unknown hazards. Our ships are the societies in which each of us lives—American society, Canadian society, Dutch society, Chinese society, Polish society,

Nigerian society, Brazilian society, and all the rest. Each of these extraordinarily complex social systems is moving rapidly into new and uncharted realms, and most of us, like ill-prepared astronauts, have as yet only the most limited understanding of these systems on which our survival and well-being depend.

Presidents, prime ministers, and other leaders continually assure us that they understand the situation and have matters firmly under control. But a moment's reflection reminds us that neither they nor their predecessors planned or willed the world that exists today. Like the rest of us, they have repeatedly been caught off guard and swept along by unanticipated changes and developments.

In a world like this, all of us have a vested interest in learning all that we can about the societies in which we live and the others with which we share the planet. Above all, we need to prepare ourselves for the changes that lie ahead.

Fortunately, we are not without resources. A branch of modern science known as sociology* has made the study of human societies its chief concern. Its basic aim is to understand human societies and the forces that have made them what they are. Although many important questions remain to be answered, considerable progress has already been made, and the aim of this volume is to provide a summary of, and introduction to, what has been learned thus far.

Much of the work of sociologists is devoted to the study of one or another of the many different component parts of societies (e.g., individuals, families, communities, classes) and to their specific features and problems (e.g., crime, race relations, religion, politics). The study of these components and features of societies is sometimes called *micro*sociology.

*Macro*sociology, in contrast, focuses on human societies themselves. Although it, too, is concerned with individuals, families, classes, social problems, and all the other parts and features of societies, it analyzes them *in relation to the larger social systems— the societies—of which they are part.* The difference between macrosociology and microsociology is much the same as the difference between the study of complex mechanical systems, such as spaceships, and the study of one of their component parts, such as their booster engines or life-support systems.

This volume takes the *macro*sociological approach. Our primary concern, and the focus of our analysis, will be human societies themselves. This does not mean that we will ignore their components; that would be impossible. It does mean, however, that when we consider their component parts and various features, *we will treat them as what they are: parts of larger and more inclusive social systems.*

Two other characteristics of this book should be noted. First, its approach to the study of human societies is *historical* and *evolutionary.* We must examine societies over an extended period of time if we are ever to understand the critical processes of societal change and development. Experience has shown, moreover, that the longer the span of time we consider, the better we can understand the most basic processes of change in human life.

Second, our approach to the study of human societies is *comparative.* Comparison is the basis of all science. An understanding of anything depends on comparing it

---

*For definitions of this and other terms used in this volume, see the Glossary, pp. 409–416.

with other things. To understand an individual chimpanzee, for example, scientists compare it with other chimpanzees. To understand chimpanzees as a species, they compare them with other apes, and to understand apes, they compare them with other primates and other mammals. In every comparison both the similarities and the differences are used to draw inferences about why things are as they are. Only by repeated comparisons are we likely to build a reliable store of knowledge about the world of nature and all that it contains. This is true whether our concern is with atoms, galaxies, viruses, chimpanzees—or human societies.

In making comparisons, the most important task for scientists is to discover *differences that make a difference*. In medicine, for example, the aim is to discover the actual causes of diseases, not just their symptoms. The same is true in other sciences: The goal is to discover the *causes* of things.

This search for the causes of things leads to the development of theory. *Scientific theories* are explanations of various aspects of the world of nature; they are explanations of why things are as they are. Theories also provide a coherent set of principles that form the basic frame of reference for a field of inquiry.

One of the most important characteristics of scientific theories is that they are *falsifiable.* This means that they are stated in such a way that they can be tested and shown to be wrong, if indeed they are wrong. To win acceptance in the scientific community, a theory must withstand repeated tests and must be supported by a substantial body of observations that are consistent with its explanation of relationships.

Sometimes it seems as though science is merely the patient accumulation of facts. But facts by themselves are meaningless; they explain nothing. For scientists, the collection of facts is the means to a much more important end, namely, the development and testing of theories designed to explain some aspect of the world of nature.

Our study of human societies in this volume is guided by such a theory—*ecological-evolutionary theory.* As its name suggests, this theory is concerned with two things. First, it is concerned with the relations among the parts of societies, and with the interactions between societies and their environments. Second, the theory is concerned with the evolution of societies—how and why they change and how these changes create differences among societies.

HUMAN SOCIETIES: THEIR PLACE IN NATURE

Often in the past, and still today, many people have thought of human societies as though they stood apart from the world of nature that science studies. This is easy to do, because modern industrial societies are much like giant cocoons that insulate us from the surrounding environment. As a result, we seldom encounter anything that has not been processed and transformed by human actions. Nevertheless, the first premise of ecological-evolutionary theory is that *human societies are a part of the global ecosystem and cannot be adequately understood unless this fact is taken fully into account.*[2]

As many scholars have observed, the world of nature is structured like a system of wheels within wheels. Larger things are made up of smaller things, and these in turn are made up of still smaller things. Figure 1.1 provides a greatly oversimplified view of the structure of the world of nature as understood by modern science. Subatomic

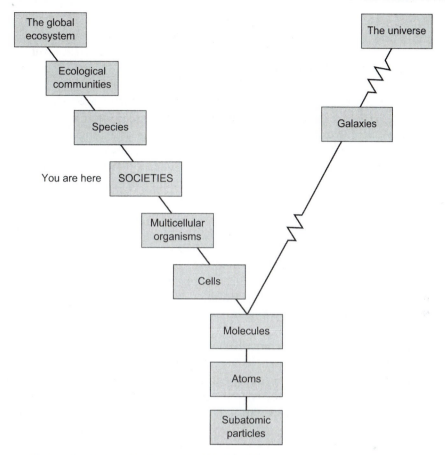

Figure 1.1. Levels of Organization in the World of Nature.

particles, such as quarks and leptons, form the lowest level. These are combined in various ways to form atoms, such as carbon and radium. Atoms in turn are organized into molecules, such as water, salt, amino acids, and proteins.[†]

Once we go beyond the level of molecules, we encounter the important division between living and nonliving things. Since our concern is with human societies, there is no need to consider *all* the levels of nonliving matter. Suffice it to note that the structure leads by degrees to the level of the giant galaxies that wheel through space and ends with the universe itself.

Societies, however, are part of the biotic world: they are one of the ways in which *living* things are organized. More specifically, they are a form of organization found in many species of multicellular organisms.

[†]Though Figure 1.1 does not show it, molecules constitute multiple levels in the hierarchy, because some of the simpler molecules, the amino acids, for example, are building blocks for more complex and more inclusive molecules such as proteins.

This brings us to the question of why some species are organized into societies while others are not.

Societies as Adaptive Mechanisms

The development of the societal mode of organization has been called "one of the great steps in evolution, as important as the emergence of the cell, the multicellular organism, and the vertebrate system."[3] Actually, societies evolved not once but a number of times, independently, and in widely scattered parts of the animal kingdom. According to the biologist E. O. Wilson, four groups of animals are especially noteworthy with respect to the development of social organization: (1) the colonial invertebrates (such as corals, sponges, and Portuguese man-of-wars); (2) the social insects (ants, termites, and many species of wasps and bees); (3) many species of nonhuman vertebrates, especially mammals, birds, and fish; and (4) humans.[4]

Why did so many and such diverse species develop this particular mode of organization? Quite simply, because being organized in this way helped the members of these species survive—the societal mode of life became common in the animal kingdom for the same reason that wings, lungs, and protective coloring became common: They are all valuable *adaptive mechanisms.*

But societal organization is different from adaptive mechanisms that enable species to perform some *specific* activity—the way wings, for example, enable creatures to fly, or lungs enable them to obtain oxygen from the air. What distinguishes social species from all the rest is a characteristic that has the potential for being used in a great *variety* of ways—an enhanced capacity for cooperation.

To those who study animal behavior, "cooperation" means simply that the individuals in a given species associate with and interact with one another for their mutual benefit. It does not mean they cooperate in every activity, nor does it imply an absence of competition and conflict.

The types of cooperative activities in which the various social species engage include reproduction, nurture of their young, securing food, and defense against predators and other dangers.[‡]

Some social species rely on cooperative behavior in almost every area of life; others are less involved in, or less dependent on, social activities. But every *social species* benefits substantially from the fact that its members are genetically programmed to solve at least some of their problems by acting together instead of individually.

A Definition of Human Societies

Once we recognize that human societies are adaptive mechanisms involving cooperative activities among their members, we are close to a definition of these important entities. There is, however, one other essential consideration that must be taken into account.

---

‡Even nonsocial animals display cooperative activity in the area of reproduction (i.e., they reproduce sexually). But a species is not classified as "social" if its cooperative activity is limited to this single, though important, area.

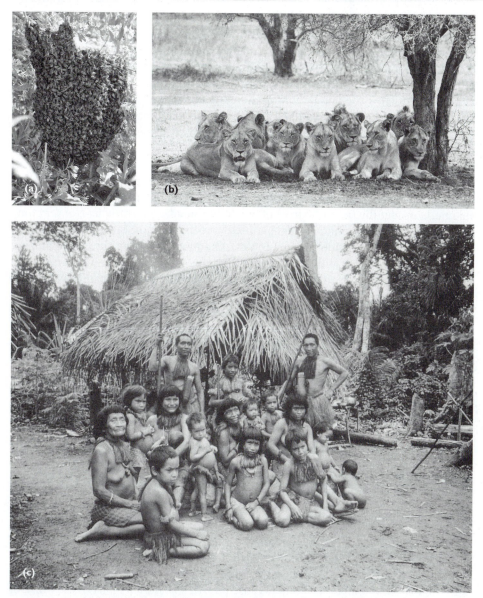

Societies Evolved Not Once but a Number of Times, Independently, and in Widely Scattered Pats of the Animal Kingdom: (a) Honeybee Swarm, (b) a Pride of Lions, and (c) Yagua Society in Brazil.

Human societies have within them many kinds of smaller groups, such as families, communities, political parties, and religious groups, and these subgroups are also adaptive mechanisms involving cooperative activities among their members. Thus, our definition needs to specify that human societies are *autonomous* groups—groups that are not subject to the political authority or control of any larger, more inclusive group.§ In short, *a human population is considered a society to the degree that it is politically autonomous and its members engage in a broad range of cooperative activities.*

This definition obviously applies to American society, Russian society, or Brazilian society, but not to an American labor union, Russian Jews, or the city of Rio de Janeiro. None of the latter is autonomous; each is subordinate to the larger society of which it is a part. Similarly, the population of Germany constitutes a society, but German-speaking people as a whole, scattered among several societies (e.g., Germany, Austria, Switzerland), do not; the population of Saudi Arabia constitutes a society, but Arabs as a whole and Muslims do not.

Sometimes unusual circumstances make it difficult to say whether a group of people is or is not a society at a particular point in its history. Uncertainty is most likely to arise when a small society is gradually absorbed by a larger and more powerful one. Consider the Inuit (Eskimo) of northern Canada, for example. Not very long ago these people lived in numerous small settlements, each one largely self-sufficient, and each one free of outside political control. Gradually, however, the Canadian government began asserting authority over these groups. At the same time, the Inuit were becoming increasingly involved in economic relationships with Canadians and were drawn into the complex web of cooperative ties that is Canadian society. Because these developments occurred slowly over an extended period, it is impossible to say precisely when a given Inuit group ceased being a society and became, instead, part of Canadian society. Then, many years later, there was a rare reversal in this common pattern of large societies swallowing smaller ones; the Inuit were granted their own homeland, Nunavut (Our Land), and thereby regained much of their lost autonomy from the Canadian government.[5]

UNDERSTANDING HUMAN SOCIETIES: BASIC ASSUMPTIONS

That human societies are part of the larger world of nature is not simply a truism to be acknowledged and then forgotten; it is a fundamental fact that must be reckoned with and taken fully into account in any serious effort to understand them. At the same time, however, human societies are not merely one more kind of society with a few new wrinkles added. On the contrary, many of their most important characteristics are unique.

In studying human life and human societies, it is easy to emphasize one of these aspects of the human condition to the neglect of the others. Ecological-evolutionary theory, the theory that guides our study of human societies, avoids this by starting with three basic assumptions. First, because human societies are part of the world of nature, they are all influenced by their *environments* in a variety of ways. Second, because human societies are part of the world of nature, their members, like the members of every other species, are endowed with a *genetic heritage* that profoundly influences their actions. Third, this genetic heritage enables the members of human

---

§Clearly autonomy is a matter of degree. For instance, in today's global economy no society is completely free of the economic influences of other societies. Nonetheless, they still maintain considerable political autonomy, especially over their domestic affairs.

societies—and them alone—to *create* symbolic cultural heritages, and it is *this* that gives human life its unique qualities. If we neglect or ignore any of these three factors, our understanding of human societies will necessarily be flawed.

Human Societies and the Environment

To say that every human society is dependent on its environment and that this environment profoundly influences it raises an important question. Exactly what does the term *environment* mean?

This term refers to *everything that is external to a specified population and that has any effect on it.* Thus, for whales, the oceans and the varied forms of life they contain, together with the air above them, the ships that sail on them, and the toxic wastes that pour into them, constitute the environment, just as tropical forests and the countless species of plants and animals they contain make up the environment of monkeys.

For a human society, the environment includes such things as the soil, mineral and water resources, climate, terrain, plants, animals, and other features of the territory it occupies. In addition, its environment includes any other human societies with which its members come into contact or which influence it in any way. In other words, every human society must adapt not only to a *biophysical* environment but to a *human social* environment as well. Its welfare and even its survival depend on its success in adapting to both.

In thinking about the environment, we need to recognize at the outset that it presents both opportunities and threats. Thus, while a society depends on its environment for all the material necessities of life (i.e., food, water, shelter, etc.), that same environment also harbors deadly enemies. The biophysical environments of some human groups have contained many kinds of large and deadly predators, and the environments of even the most technologically advanced modern societies continue to harbor countless species of harmful viruses, bacteria, insects, and rodents. Moreover, the efforts of human groups to cope with their environments, can, in turn, alter those environments and create new problems. Societies can hunt valuable animals into extinction, and they can pollute their air and water.

The social environment also poses both opportunities and threats. Contact between societies can produce mutually beneficial exchanges of goods and information, or it can produce death and destruction. We live today in a global economy where goods, services, and people literally flow around the world, but in the twentieth century alone, hundreds of millions of people lost their lives, were wounded, or were driven from their homes as a result of war. And even when war is avoided, societies can be threatened and harmed by other societies through other means, such as disease, atmospheric pollution, economic competition, or political subversion.

Human Societies: Their Genetic Heritage

In the efforts of societies to cope with the challenges of their environments, their most basic resource has always been the vast store of information contained in the genes of their members. For *genes*, within which each of us is endowed at the moment of conception, contain the information that is essential for life itself and for everything we do from breathing and walking to learning and communicating.

Until the past century, however, no one even knew of the *existence* of genes and far less imagined the enormous influence they exert on every living thing from the simplest one-celled animals to humans. Even today many people fail to recognize, or badly underestimate, their importance.

As biologists have discovered, every species has a genetic heritage uniquely its own. This heritage is the product of an evolutionary process that has been going on for more than three billion years. Because of it, each member of a species is endowed with a vast store of *chemically coded information* that it receives from its parents or parent.**

Individuals have no control over the information stored in their genes. Yet this information guides and shapes the life of every living thing, in much the same way that the information built into the design of a computer influences the computer's operations, and the same way that information stored in our brains affects our feelings and our actions.

Like every other species, we humans possess a unique and distinctive heritage that influences every aspect of our lives. Like the information we carry in our brains, the information stored in our genes is a *product of experience.* Unlike the kinds of information *we* learn, however, it does not result from our personal experience. Rather, it is the result of the experiences of countless generations of our *ancestors.* Through the interaction of the biological processes of mutation, sexual recombination, and natural selection, every species gradually accumulates its own distinctive store of genetic information.

To understand our species' genetic heritage, we need to bear in mind the nature of our ancestry. We are members of the anthropoid suborder (which also includes the great apes and monkeys), which is part of the *primate order,* which is part of the mammalian class, which, in turn, is part of the vertebrate division of the animal kingdom. This means that we are more closely related and genetically more similar to other *anthropoids* than to the rest of the primate order, to other primates than to other mammals, to the rest of the mammalian class than to other vertebrates, to the rest of the vertebrate division than to other animals, and to other animals than to plants. It also means that our basic adaptations resemble those of primates and mammals more closely than those of other, less closely related species.

When we compare ourselves with the other anthropoids and especially with our closest kin of all, the great apes (e.g., chimpanzees and gorillas), the range of common traits is striking (see Table 1.1). To begin with, there are the many traits that we and they share with most other mammals, such as warm-bloodedness, body hair, lungs, four limbs, a relatively elaborate brain, the ability to learn and communicate, and, in the female, mammary glands that secrete milk for the nurturance of offspring. In addition, we and the other anthropoids share to varying degrees such physical traits as upright posture, flexible arms and hands, separated fingers and opposable thumbs, prolonged immaturity of offspring, greater reliance on stereoscopic color vision than on smell, and a high order of intelligence, as well as such behavioral similarities as the abilities to deceive one another, form coalitions, and play.[6]

One cannot compare humans with other species in this way without recognizing the extent to which basic patterns of human life are rooted in our genetic system.

**Some species reproduce asexually and these individuals therefore have only a single parent.

Good Parents, Bad Kids?

Recent research provides yet another striking example of how human life is shaped by the *interaction* of genetics and environment. The question it addressed was why is it the case that good parenting sometimes produces ill-behaved, unhappy children, and bad parenting sometimes produces well-behaved, cheerful children? To find out, researchers ran three different experiments with 1,874 children aged eight to sixteen. Their results indicated that the much-investigated 5-HTTLPR gene that controls the mood-altering chemical serotonin in the brain might provide the answer.

What they found was that about one in five children inherit the *short* version, or allele, of the 5–HTTLPR serotonin-transporter gene from *both* of

their parents and this makes them especially sensitive to good or bad parenting. The other 80 percent were much less influenced by the quality of their parenting.

Other studies have found this gene may affect moral judgments, risk of depression, and anxiety. Together they add to the growing body of evidence that the "nature" "nurture" argument was based on a false dichotomy. Human life—both individually and collectively—is shaped by the *combined* influence or interaction of genetics, or heredity, and environment, and that neglect of either can only impoverish our understanding of human life.

Source: *Los Angeles Times,* October 4, 2011, based on a report in the journal *Translational Psychiatry* of the same date.

Table 1.1 Physical Characteristics Shared by Primates, Including Humans

- Independent mobility of fingers and toes
- A wraparound first digit in both hands and feet (thumb, big toe)
- Replacement of claws by nails to support the digital pads of the last phalanx of each finger and toe
- Teeth and digestive tract adapted to an omnivorous diet
- A semierect posture that enables hand manipulation and provides a favorable position preparatory to leaping
- Center of gravity positioned close to hind legs
- Well-developed hand-eye motor coordination
- Optical adaptations that include overlap of the visual fields that provide precise three-dimensional information on the location of food objects and tree branches
- Bony orbits that protect the eyes from arboreal hazards
- Shortening of the face accompanied by reduction of the snout
- Diminution of the sense of smell in those active in daylight
- Compared to practically all other mammals, a very large and complex brain in relation to body size

Source: Adapted from Monroe Strickberger, *Evolution* (Boston: Jones and Bartlett, 1990), p. 384.

For it is not just a matter of similarities between our anatomy and physiology and that of the other primates: it is also a matter of behavioral tendencies and predispositions. If we humans are capable of cooperation and live in societies, it is not because we *choose* to be social creatures, but because of our genetic heritage. Similarly, if we rely on learning as a basic mode of adaptation to the world we live in, it is not because we decided it was the best thing to do, nor did we invent learning. Rather, it is an expression of our mammalian and primate heritage.

The Adaptive Value of the Ability to Learn is Greatly Enhanced When Animals Live Together in Groups. This Gives the Individual More Opportunity to Observe, and to Communicate with, Others of Its Kind. A Chimpanzee Family Considering a Problem.

Learning is the process by which an organism acquires, through experience, information with behavior-modifying potential.[7] This means that when it comes to solving problems, an animal that can learn is not completely dependent on *instinct* (i.e., the behavioral repertoire provided by its genetic heritage). Instead, its own experiences become a factor shaping its behavior. In the case of humans and some of the higher primates, the evolution of the forebrain has reached the point where they are able to store such a wide range of memories that they can learn by *insight*; in other words, they can analyze a situation in their minds and thereby potentially avoid the time-consuming, costly, and often painful process of trial and error.[8]

The adaptive value of the ability to learn is greatly enhanced when animals live together in groups. This gives the individual more opportunity to observe, and to communicate with, others of its kind. In effect, social animals benefit from the experience of their fellows as well as from their own individual experience. Social life thus multiplies the amount of information available to a population. In the words of two leading students of primate life, "The [primate] group is the locus of knowledge and information far exceeding that of the individual member. It is in the group that experience is pooled."[9]

The adaptive value of the ability to learn is also greatly enhanced among primates by the prolonged physical immaturity of their young. The young of most species are genetically equipped to fend for themselves from the moment of birth or shortly thereafter. For mammals, however, there is a period during which the young depend on sustained contact with one or both parents. In the case of the anthropoids, this period of dependence is especially prolonged, a fact that is linked both with their enhanced capacity for learning and with their dependence on the societal mode of life.

But what makes us so different from those anthropoid apes—chimpanzees and gorillas—with whom we share nearly 99 percent of our genes?[10] After all, only we build skyscrapers, set off nuclear explosions, philosophize, compose symphonies, and travel in space. The explanation is that at some point in the evolution of one anthropoid line there occurred a series of genetic changes that, although few in number, had revolutionary consequences for behavior. *The most critical changes altered the structure of the brain and shifted the center of vocalization to the neocortex, or newer part of the brain, where learning takes place and learned information is stored.*[11] Thus, thanks to relatively minor genetic changes, our remote ancestors acquired the capacity to create a radically new mode of adaptation—*symbolic culture.*[††]

Human Cultures: A New and Unique Mode of Adaptation and a New and Unique Kind of Heritage

Over the years, zoologists have observed that among many species of animals, local groups develop distinctive patterns of behavior that appear to have been learned through individual experience and then shared within the group. These shared patterns of behavior and the stores of information on which they are based are commonly referred to as "cultures."

Human societies also have cultures, but their cultures are much more complex, and vastly more important to the well-being and survival of the group, than the cultures of any other species. The key to understanding this difference lies in the fact that *the cultures of nonhuman societies depend entirely on information that is shared by means of (genetically programmed) signals or is learned from direct observation,*[12] whereas the cultures of human societies are based on information that is shared primarily by means of *symbols.*

Why have symbols been so important? After all, *signals* and *symbols* are both methods of communicating information. There is, however, one critical difference: the meaning of signals is wholly or largely determined by the genetic makeup of the individuals who use them; the meaning of symbols is not.

The best way to understand this distinction is to look at examples of the two kinds of information conveyers, beginning with signals.[13] Animals signal with movements, sounds, odors, color changes, and so on, and the signals they produce vary greatly in the amount of information they convey. The simplest type of signal is one that is used in only a single context and that has only one possible meaning—the sexually attractive scent released by a female moth, for example. In contrast, some species are able to transmit more complex information by varying the frequency or intensity of a signal or by combining different signals simultaneously or in sequence. Thus, a foraging

---

[††]This is a classic example of what is known as the "threshold effect," in which a small change in one thing has a big effect on something else—as when someone walks for miles in a pouring rain without any improvement in his situation and then takes one or two additional steps and enters a building and completely escapes the downpour.

Fifteen Ways to Say "I Love You"

Because the connection between the sounds people make and their meaning is arbitrary, different languages use different combinations of sounds to express the same idea. Thus, every language has its own distinctive way of saying "I love you." In some languages, the phrase varies slightly when a woman addresses a man; these variants are shown in parentheses.

Arabic: Ana b'hibbik (Ana b'hibbak)
Cambodian: Bon sro lanh oon
Chinese: Wo ai ni
Danish: Jeg elsker Dig
English: I love you

French: Je t'aime
German: Ich liebe dich
Hebrew: Ani ohev otakh (Ani ohevet otkhah)
Hindi: Maiñtumheñ piyar karta huñ
Hungarian: Szeretlek
Italian: Ti voglio bene
Japanese: Watakushi-wa anata-wo aishimasu
Korean: Tangsinul sarang hä yo
Navaho: Ayór ánosh' ní
Russian: Ya tebya liubliu

Source: Charles Berlitz, *Native Tongues* (London: Panther, 1984), p. 54.

honeybee returns to her hive and performs the "waggle dance" to direct fellow workers to the food source she has located.[14] By varying the movements and vibrations that comprise the dance, she communicates enough information about direction and distance to enable her sisters to land remarkably near the target, and at the same time adds a comment on the quality of the food supply and the state of the weather.

In some species, especially birds and mammals, the use of and response to signals are partially learned. The young of certain species of birds, for example, must learn some elements of their territorial songs from adults.[15] We, too, learn to modify and use genetically based signals in different ways. Thus, we learn to pretend to yawn to indicate boredom. But whether simple or complex, and whether or not learning is involved, *a signal is an information conveyer whose basic form and meaning are genetically determined.*

Symbols, by contrast, are *not* genetically determined. The *ability* to create and use symbols does depend on genetics, but the form of a symbol and the meaning attached to it do not. Thus, a symbol is *an information conveyer whose form and meaning have developed within a community of users.*

Humans share with no other species the ability to create symbols. Various kinds of animals from plow horses to circus seals have been trained to recognize, respond to, and even use, after a fashion, a number of symbols. Chimpanzees and gorillas have proved to have a remarkable ability in this regard, perhaps learning to use as many as 750 different symbols, and even combining a few of them to convey more complex meanings.[16] None of these animals, however, has ever *created* a symbol system, and they show not even the rudiments of language development in the wild.[17] Thus, while their accomplishments are impressive, they cannot compare with humans. For we not only quickly master, without special training, the language of the group into which we are born, but we are also capable at a very early age of devising new symbols and even entire symbol systems. Small children invent names for their stuffed animals and

With Symbols, Every Society Has Developed Its Own Rich and Distinctive Heritage to Supplement Its Genetic Heritage: The Flag of Canada.

sometimes go on to make up "secret codes." And there are cases where twins apparently have invented entirely original and complex languages by which they communicated with one another.[18]

We can appreciate the significance of symbols only when we understand the degree to which symbolic meanings have been unleashed from our species' genetic endowment. Take the sound of the third letter of the English alphabet, for example. That sound is used to refer to the act of perceiving (to see), to a bishop's jurisdiction (a see), and to a large body of water (a sea), as well as to the letter itself. Spanish-speaking people, meanwhile, use it to say "yes" and "if," and French-speaking people to say "yes," "if," "whether," and "so." Obviously there is no *logical or necessary* connection between these various meanings, nor is there any genetically determined connection between the meanings and the sound. They are simply *arbitrary* usages adopted by the members of certain societies.

Further evidence that symbols are determined by their users and not by genes is the ease with which we alter them. When English people of the thirteenth century said, "Fader oure that art in heve, i-halged bee thi nome," they meant to say—in fact they did say—"Our Father who art in heaven, hallowed be Thy name,"[19] and when Chaucer wrote, "Hir nose tretis, hir yen greye as glas," he meant to say—in fact, he did say—"Her nose well-formed, her eyes gray as glass." English-speaking people have simply altered many of their symbols since his day. Slang is created by the reverse procedure: the symbol itself remains unchanged, but it is given a new meaning. The words "bread" and "dough," for example, have both come to be used to refer to money.

The Difference between a Human Mind without Symbols and the Same Mind with Them Is Eloquently Described in Helen Keller's Account of Her Early Life.

Although linguistic symbols are the most basic and important, they are not the only kind we use. Anything to which humans assign a meaning becomes a symbol. Thus, the cross has become a symbol of Christianity; the maple leaf is a symbol of Canada. Every nation in the world today has a flag to represent it, and standardized symbols communicate basic traffic directions on highways.

Because they are not genetically determined, symbols can be combined and recombined in countless ways to form symbol systems of fantastic complexity, subtlety, and flexibility. The only limits are set by the physical characteristics of those who use them, that is, by the efficiency and capacity of the human brain and nervous system and the accuracy of our senses. And symbol systems help overcome even these limitations. For example, our species' memory (i.e., its capacity for storing information) has been greatly increased by the use of written symbols and written and digital records.

In the final analysis, the importance of symbol systems lies not in what they are, but in what they have made it possible for our species to *become*. Although we are all born into the human family, we become fully human only through the use of symbols. Without them, we are unable to develop the unique qualities we associate with humanness. For symbols are more than a means of communication: They are tools with which we think and plan, dream and remember, create and build, calculate, speculate, and even moralize.

The difference between a human mind without symbols and that same mind with them is eloquently described in Helen Keller's account of her early life.[20] She became both deaf and blind before she learned to talk. By the age of seven, after years without meaningful communication with other people, she had become very much like a wild animal. Then, a gifted teacher, Anne Sullivan, began trying to communicate with her by spelling words into her hands. Helen learned several words, but she did not yet comprehend the real significance of symbols. Finally, in a moment that both women later described in moving terms, Helen suddenly realized that *everything* had a name, that *everything* could be communicated with symbols! In her own words, she felt "a thrill of returning thought." At last, the world that exists only for symbol users began to open to her.

Miss Keller's experience helps us understand why the ancients, in their accounts of creation, so often linked the beginning of language with the beginning of the world. One of the oldest written texts from Egypt, for example, tells how Ptah, the creator of the world and the greatest of the gods, "pronounced the names of all things" as a central part of his act of creation.[21] Language also figures prominently in Chinese and Hindu creation myths. The book of Genesis tells us that the first thing Adam did after he was created was to name all the beasts and birds; and the Gospel according to St. John opens with the lines: "In the beginning was the Word, and the Word was with God, and the Word was God." Significantly, the original Greek for "word" was *logos,* which meant not merely word, but meaning and reason. And *logos* is the root of our own word "logic," and of the suffix *-logy,* used to denote science, as in biology or sociology.

The German scientist Alexander von Humboldt once said, "No words, no world," and it is true that the human world, the world of human societies, would not exist without words. Without words and other symbols, human societies and human cultures would differ little from those of other primates. *With* symbols, every human society has developed a rich and distinctive heritage.

In the chapters that follow, we will explore in detail the impact of these unique symbolic heritages and see how they have influenced human life. First, however, we need to pull together the several elements of our analysis to this point.

HUMAN SOCIETIES: THE BASIC MODEL

The aim of ecological-evolutionary theory, as we have seen, is to understand *why* human societies are the way they are. Like every theory, it starts with certain assumptions. It assumes that human societies are both part of the world of nature and, at the same time, unique in a number of fundamental ways.

One of the tools that can help us analyze societies and construct theories about them is a technique known as *modeling,* which expresses hypothesized cause-and-effect relationships in a detailed and explicit manner. Modeling compels us to be precise about the relationships involved in a theory—more precise than we might otherwise be. One way of doing this is to construct models in the form of mathematical equations that express these relationships. This method is used widely in physics and economics, and sometimes also in sociology. Another method, and one that is especially well suited to *macro*sociology, expresses relationships by means of *visual* diagrams.

In the chapters that follow, we will present a number of models in diagrammatic form as a means of summarizing various aspects of ecological-evolutionary theory. Since some of the relationships involved are complex, some of the models will also be complex.

Our first model, however, is quite simple. But it is extremely important because it identifies the most basic determinants, or causes, of the characteristics of human societies as understood by ecological-evolutionary theory. As Figure 1.2 indicates, this theory asserts that all of a society's characteristics are ultimately due to just three things: (1) the influence of its biophysical and social environments, (2) the influence of

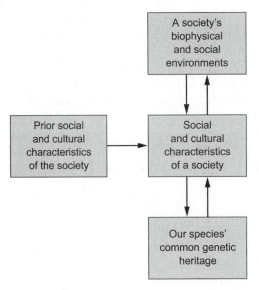

Figure 1.2. Basic Ecological-Evolutionary Model of the Determinants of the Characteristics of Human Societies.

our species' genetic heritage, and (3) the influence of prior social and cultural characteristics of the society itself. The double arrows in the model also indicate that human societies are not just affected by, but also affect, the environment and our species' genetic heritage.[22]

In the chapters that follow, we will *amplify and extend* this basic model, adding greater detail. In Chapter 2, for example, we will examine the middle box on the right side of Figure 1.2 to see just what those characteristics are. In Chapter 3 we will see why and how human societies change. This will provide us with the information we will need in Chapter 4 to "map" the principal types and varieties of societies that have evolved over the course of the last 100,000 years.

From that point on we will examine each of the major types of societies and see how the forces of change have transformed human societies over the course of history. Throughout the process, we will gradually extend our basic model by incorporating into it, and into our theory, the more interesting features and complexities of human life.

One point to bear in mind is that ecological-evolutionary theory, like all theories, is subject to refinement and modification as new facts become known and new evidence is uncovered. For example, while we know that our species' genetic heritage influences human societies in countless important ways (e.g., symbolic cultural systems could not exist without it), it is still impossible at this point to determine many of its more specific effects (e.g., whether differences in mathematical ability between men and women are genetically determined), and opinions often differ. Recent advances in the science of genetics, however, promise to clarify our understanding of this issue in the years ahead, and research in various other areas will almost certainly lead to other refinements and improvements.

EXCURSUS: A BRIEF HISTORY OF SOCIOLOGY

Before going further in our analysis of human societies, we will pause and take a closer look at sociology itself—its origins and history, its recent trends and current status. This brief excursus also provides an opportunity to consider the relationship between sociology and the other social sciences.

Though sociology is a relatively recent addition to the scholarly world, its roots can be traced back to the writings of Plato and Aristotle. Philosophers were already then speculating about societies—comparing one with another and trying to understand the forces that shaped them.

The more immediate origins of modern sociology, however, lie in the sixteenth, seventeenth, and eighteenth centuries. This was a period in which the peoples of western Europe, especially the educated minority, were confronted with a tremendous amount of new information that could not be assimilated into traditional belief systems. They learned that the earth was not, as they had long supposed, the center of the universe. And they also learned, through the discovery of whole new continents populated by peoples with cultures radically different from their own, that western Europe was not the center of the earth. At the same time, European societies were themselves changing. The Protestant Reformation had divided western Europe, and the bitter religious wars that followed undermined much of the moral and intellectual authority of the clergy. Meanwhile, urban populations were growing in size and influence. All this led to the questioning of older theories and to renewed speculation about the nature of human life.

Among the consequences were two more or less independent developments, which laid the foundation for modern sociology. The first of these was the revival of interest in the systematic study of man and society, fostered by writers such as Thomas Hobbes, John Locke, A. R. J. Turgot, Jean-Jacques Rousseau, Adam Ferguson, John Millar, Adam Smith, and Thomas Malthus. Before the eighteenth century ended, these men and others had established the independence of social theory from theology and had laid the foundations of the modern social sciences. Some of them even went so far to identify the phenomenon of sociocultural evolution—long before Darwin's day— and to formulate explanations for it.[23]

During the nineteenth century, others began making systematic, quantitative studies of various social phenomena. Birth and death rates were an early object of research; later there were studies of class, family income, jury verdicts, election results, and a variety of other phenomena. Sometimes those who were involved in developing theory were also involved in research, though usually this was not the case. By the end of the century, the quantitative tradition was firmly established; ties to theory were still imperfectly developed, but a basis had been established for the eventual integration of these two essentials of science: theory and research.[24]

The term *sociology* first appeared in the 1830s in the writings of a Frenchman, Auguste Comte. He originally wanted to call it "social physics," but that term had been used by the Belgian social statistician Adolphe Quetelet, for what we would today call demography. Since he gave it its name, Comte is often referred to as the founder of modern sociology. This is an unmerited honor, however, since his writings were in an already established tradition and his own contributions were not that important.

The most famous nineteenth-century sociologist, and the most influential in his own day, was an Englishman, Herbert Spencer. Through his writings, which were translated into nearly all the major languages, he brought sociology to the attention of the educated classes throughout the world. Like others before him, Spencer was profoundly interested in sociocultural evolution, though he saw it as merely one manifestation of a universal cosmic process linking the physical, biotic, and human worlds. Interest in evolution was stimulated even more in that period by the writings of Charles Darwin, a contemporary of Spencer.

In hindsight, Karl Marx is seen as another major contributor to the study of human societies in the nineteenth century. Unlike Spencer, he stood apart from the emerging discipline of sociology, with the result that the relevance of his work to the discipline went unrecognized for many years. With the passage of time, however, this changed. One reason was the belated appreciation of the importance of the material base of human life—people's need for food, shelter, and the like, and the techniques for meeting these needs. Marx also called attention to the ubiquity of conflict in human societies and its role in producing social change.

Ironically, despite its European origins, sociology found more rapid acceptance in the United States. A number of leading American universities established professorships before the end of the century, and, by the early decades of the twentieth century, many institutions had established full-fledged departments of sociology. During the period between the two world wars, sociology continued to expand in the United States but declined in Europe, partly because of attacks by totalitarian governments, especially in Germany and the Soviet Union, partly because of greater resistance to change and innovation by the faculties of European universities. As a result, sociology became primarily an American enterprise.

Following World War I, sociology underwent a number of important changes. Under American leadership the discipline became increasingly parochial, concerned mainly with contemporary American society. Interest in other societies declined, as did interest in the historical dimension of human experience. To a large extent these changes reflected the desire of a new generation of sociologists to make the discipline more scientific. The result was a greatly heightened interest in field research, especially studies of local communities and their problems—crime, poverty, divorce, juvenile delinquency, illegitimacy, prostitution, the problems of immigrants, and so forth.

With this shift in interest, sociologists gradually abandoned the earlier evolutionary approach. In part, this was because of criticisms leveled against it, but primarily it was because the older approach seemed irrelevant to the concerns of the newer generation. Sociologists were forced to find a substitute for evolutionary theory—some new theoretical approach that could organize the growing but diffuse body of information on American society. By the late 1930s, *structural-functional* theory emerged as the apparent successor to evolutionary theory.

Structural-functional analysis is, in effect, the sociological counterpart of anatomy and physiology in biology. Like anatomists, structural-functionalists are concerned with the identification and labeling of the many different parts of the things they study and with the structural relations among them (e.g., the structural patterns formed within business organizations, families, etc.). Like physiologists, they are interested in the functions each part performs. Just as physiologists are concerned with the functions of organs, such as the liver, heart, and spleen, structural-functionalists are interested in the functions of institutions, such as the family, and of moral rules, such as the taboo against incest. The theory has been criticized, however, for its emphasis on order and stability, and its relative neglect of conflict and change.

Since World War II, sociology has grown substantially not only in the United States but also in Europe, Japan, South Korea, Latin America, and Canada, and it has begun to take root in other areas as well. During the Stalin era, sociology was outlawed throughout the communist world. Later, however, restrictions were removed and there is now a lively interest in the subject throughout eastern Europe and in China. This growth of sociology in other countries has reduced the unhealthy concentration of the discipline in the United States that characterized the decades of the 1930s and 1940s.

Another notable development has been the movement of sociology beyond the confines of the academic community. Prior to the 1940s, sociologists were employed almost entirely by universities and colleges. Beginning in World War II and continuing to the present, there has been a growing demand for their services by government, industry, and other kinds of organizations.

Several research traditions are active in sociology today. These include: (1) social psychology/symbolic interactionism/constructionism; (2) structural-functionalism; (3) Marxist/conflict; and (4) ecological-evolutionism. The first is primarily concerned with microsociological issues and focuses on interaction, decision making, and the means by which individuals make sense of their social situations. The second, as we have already noted, is primarily concerned with the mutual interdependence of the parts of societies. Marxist/conflict theorists, on the other hand, emphasize societal conflict and the role it plays in transforming societies. Ecological-evolutionary theory, the theory that guides this book, focuses on the relationships between the parts of society and how the relationships of societies to their environments (both social and biophysical) are affected by, and affect, their development.

Our advocacy of the ecological-evolutionary perspective is based, in part, on the fact that it incorporates valuable elements from each of the other perspectives. It is concerned with interdependence and order (structural-functionalism) as well as conflict and change (Marxist/conflict), and it provides an understanding of the changing social *context* within which people interact and create a meaningful world (social psychology/symbolic interactionism/constructionism). More important, it provides an *integrative* framework that enables one to see the relations among all the varied aspects of human societies. In fact, as will become apparent in the following chapters (especially Chapters 10 through 15), one of its distinguishing characteristics is its view of industrial societies and their future prospects; it is neither as pessimistic about present social conditions nor as optimistic about their future possibilities as are many Marxist/conflict theories.[‡‡]

[‡‡]The chapters that follow contain both descriptions and explanations. It is worth noting that even where there is some disagreement among scholars about *why* or *how* certain features exist or develop, there is general agreement about *what* features exist. Therefore, although different theories may provide different explanations of "facts," theorists generally agree on what the "facts" are.

Despite continuing disagreements, sociology has made substantial progress. In our view, two of the more important developments have been the increasing use of quantitative techniques and the revival of interest in *macrosociology.* The first of these was a natural outgrowth of efforts to achieve greater precision in describing social phenomena and greater rigor in analysis. This trend was given an enormous boost by the invention and continuing advance of computers, which enable researchers to handle large amounts of data and carry out complex statistical analyses that would otherwise be impossible.

The revival of interest in macrosociology has come about for a number of reasons. Above all, there is a growing recognition that the most pressing problems of our time—war, the distress of third world nations, the problem of poverty, environmental degradation—are all macroorganizational problems that require macrosociological theory and research if solutions are to be found. Moreover, there is a growing recognition that many microorganizational problems and developments—the changing role of women, the changing nature of the family, globalization, immigration and cultural diversity in industrial societies—cannot be understood adequately, or dealt with effectively, unless they are viewed within the *context* of broader societal trends. One response to this renewal of interest in macrosociology has been a revival of interest in societal development and change and the formulation of ecologically oriented developmental theories of the kind that provide the foundation and framework for the present volume.[25]

Sociology and the Other Social Sciences

The study of human societies has never been exclusively a sociological concern. All the social sciences have been involved in one way or another. Most of the others, however, have focused on some *particular* aspect of the subject. For example, economics and political science limit themselves to a single institutional area; human geography studies the impact of the physical and biotic environments on societies; and social psychology is concerned with the impact of society on the behavior and personality of individuals.

Only sociology and anthropology have been concerned with human societies per se. That is to say, only these two disciplines have interested themselves in the full range of social phenomena, from the family to the nation and from technology to religion. And only these two have sought to understand societies as entities in their own right.

In matters of research, there once was a fairly well-established division of labor between sociology and anthropology. Sociologists studied industrial societies; anthropologists studied preliterate societies. This division of labor made good sense, since the skills needed to study a remote tribe in the mountains of New Guinea are very different from those needed to study a modern industrial society.

From the standpoint of teaching and the development of theory, however, the separation of sociology and anthropology has been much less satisfactory. Many problems, especially those involving long-term evolutionary processes, require the contributions of both disciplines. Ignoring either leads to incomplete analyses and biased interpretations. As a consequence, there has been a long tradition of intellectual "borrowing" between sociology and anthropology, and this volume stands in that tradition.

With the revival of evolutionary theory, scholars in these fields came to recognize that both disciplines were neglecting agrarian (i.e., farming) societies—those societies that occupy the middle range in the evolutionary scale between preliterate societies and modern industrial societies. More recently, therefore, both sociologists and anthropologists have undertaken research on these societies in Southeast Asia, the Middle East, and Latin America.

The growing concern with agrarian societies has also led to increased cooperation between sociologists and historians. Since history is the study of written records of the past, historians are the experts on agrarian societies of earlier centuries. Much of the older work by historians, with its heavy emphasis on the names and dates of famous people and events, is of limited value to students of human societies. But that discipline has been changing too, and historians today are much more concerned with the *social processes* and patterns that underlie the more dramatic, but often less significant, events on which their predecessors focused. As a result, history and sociology have become more valuable to each other.

This trend toward interdisciplinary cooperation is evident today in all the social sciences and even beyond. Scholars are coming to recognize that no discipline is sufficient unto itself. To the degree that any field cuts itself off from others, it impoverishes itself intellectually. Conversely, to the degree that it communicates with other disciplines, it enriches itself and them.

CHAPTER 2

Human Societies as Sociocultural Systems

Outline
Human Societies as Systems
The Five Basic Components of Human Societies
The World System of Societies

One of the fascinations of *human* societies is their diversity. In any other social species (e.g., bees, lions), despite some variation caused by differences in their environments, one society is remarkably like the next in size, complexity, and the activities of its members. This is hardly surprising, of course, in view of the fact that one society is also remarkably like the next in its genetic heritage and that this heritage determines the great majority of the species' characteristics.

Why, then, are human societies, which *also* have similar genetic heritages, so different from one another in so many ways? Why are some huge and organizationally complex, while others are small and simple? And why are the activities of their members often so varied? Why, for example, are the members of some societies aggressive and warlike, while the members of others are relatively more passive and peaceful? Why are some puritanical regarding relations between the sexes, while others are much more permissive?

The explanation of the tremendous variations among human societies is simply that their common genetic heritage enables them to develop very different *cultural* heritages. Without their symbolic cultures, human societies, too, would all be essentially alike. But with *symbolic culture* comes an extraordinary potential for diversity.

Because our societies, unlike those of other species, have both a social *and* a symbolic cultural dimension, sociologists and other social scientists often refer to them as *sociocultural* systems. This contraction of the two words is partly a convenience. But it is more than that: it is a reminder that the social and cultural aspects of human life are inextricably intertwined.

HUMAN SOCIETIES AS SYSTEMS

The term *system,* which we have just linked with "sociocultural," and which appears frequently in sociological writing, is a simple word with a *profound* meaning. It can be

The Computer Is a Familiar Example of a Complex Modern Electronic System: Printed Computer Motherboard.

applied to a wide variety of things, many of them in the world of nature. There are physical systems, such as the solar system, star systems, weather systems, and systems of lakes and rivers. Every living organism is a system. And there are systems *within* organisms (digestive, reproductive, etc.), systems *of* organisms (populations, societies), and systems that include organisms and their environments (ecosystems). Then there are the systems created by humans: mechanical systems (cars, pianos), political systems, linguistic systems, mathematical systems, irrigation systems, and transportation systems. In every instance, "system" refers to *an entity made up of interrelated parts*.

The key word in this definition is "interrelated." In the words of one expert, a system is a "bundle of relations."[1] For this reason, what happens to one of the component parts of a system has implications for other parts and for the system as a whole. Too much beer in the stomach has repercussions for the brain, for example, just as the alignment of an automotive system's wheels affects its steering. Francis Thompson, the poet, captured the systemic qualities of the universe itself in his line, "Thou canst not stir a flower without troubling of a star."[2]

The meaning of the concept *system* is best understood, however, if we focus on a smaller, more specific "bundle of relations," such as a desktop computer. In working order, this entity is an electronic system. Each of its components (chips, cables, mouse, keyboard, etc.) is also an entity—and each remains an entity even if the computer is dismantled. But when the relations among these components have been destroyed, the entity that is *the system* ceases to exist. A system, then, is clearly more than the sum of its parts: it is the sum of its parts *plus all the relations among them*.

Systems vary greatly in the *degree* to which the functions of the parts are co-ordinated with one another and with the functioning of the system as a whole. Using this as a criterion, mechanical systems are some of the most tightly organized, nearly "perfect" systems known. Consider a watch mechanism or the gears of an automobile transmission. Each component exists, and each functions, for one purpose only: the purpose for which *the system* exists and its functions (i.e., to mark the passage of time, or move the vehicle). Moreover, each component relates only to the other parts of its own system, and its operation is totally dependent upon theirs.

It should come as no surprise, then, to note that, insofar as *systemic* qualities are concerned, the societies of some species resemble a watch more than they resemble human societies. The activities that go on in the honeybee's social system, for example, are as beautifully coordinated as gears and dials: they all serve the interests of the system (i.e., the society as a whole) and demonstrate a nearly total interdependence among the parts. The bee's genetic heritage is clearly a blueprint for a harmonious social system.*

The situation is quite different in human societies. For one thing, the coordination among their component parts is often weak. For another, their components do not always function in ways that are conducive to the well-being of the system itself (i.e., the society). For example, their members are individualistic and often self-assertive, resist efforts to coordinate and control their behavior, and do not readily subordinate their needs to the needs of the group. In short, a genetic blueprint that is very different from the honeybee's, but just as compelling, *prevents* human societies from achieving the strict ordering of relations that characterizes some systems.

There must, however, be enough *cooperation* among the members of a human society, and the various parts of the system must mesh smoothly enough, for *the basic needs of the system itself* to be met. The alternative is the dissolution of that "bundle of relations" that is the society.

This creates problems, because the needs of the system and those of its members are not necessarily the same. For example, an individual does not have to have children in order to satisfy his or her basic survival needs, but a *society* is doomed if it fails to produce new members to replace each older generation as it dies off. Similarly, individuals can violate their society's laws and moral codes and often survive, even prosper; but no society can long endure unless it resists such violations and keeps antisocial and disruptive behavior under control.

In response to the multiplicity of needs of both individuals and societies, untold numbers of social and cultural answers have evolved. Although these answers have always been imperfect, they are fascinating in their diversity and complexity.

---

*Virtually all members of bee, ant, and wasp (*Hymenoptera*) societies are sisters who, because of their reproductive process, share three-fourths of their genes. Thus their individual biological interests (preserving and passing on their genes) are largely indistinguishable from their collective interest (survival of the group). In contrast, the most closely related humans (other than identical twins)—parents and their children, and siblings—share only one-half of their genes, aunts/uncles and nieces/nephews one-quarter, cousins one-eighth, and others even less. It is not surprising, therefore, that there is a greater divergence of "interests" and a greater potential for conflict in human societies.

THE FIVE BASIC COMPONENTS OF HUMAN SOCIETIES

To understand how these social and cultural answers develop, we need to consider the five basic components that are present in every human society: (1) population, (2) culture, (3) material products, (4) social organization, and (5) social institutions and institutional systems. Although we will examine each one separately, these components cannot truly be understood in isolation. Because they exist only in interaction with one another in a society, it is impossible to discuss any one of them without reference to the rest. We will, however, disentangle them as best we can.

Population

Population, the first basic component of society, is a term that refers to *the members of a society considered collectively*. In analyzing human societies, there are three aspects of population that must be taken into account: (1) the genetic constants, (2) the genetic variables, and (3) the demographic variables.

Genetic Constants

The genetic constants of a population are those characteristics that reflect our species' *common genetic heritage*. As the word *constants* implies, these traits are the *same* for every society and, for all practical purposes, the same from one generation to the next.

Specifying the genetically based traits that are shared by people everywhere is not an easy task. First, there is simply no way that scientists can observe and study the biological component of human life without cultural influences getting in the way.

The second problem in drawing up a list of our common genetic traits lies in the complexity of genetics itself. Although the Human Genome Project has completed its mapping of our species' genes, scientists are still a very long way from fully understanding their interplay and effects. One thing that is clear, however, is that most observable traits—for example, physical characteristics or behavioral tendencies—do not result from the action of a single gene but rather from the interaction of *a number of different genes*. Any given gene, meanwhile, usually affects not just a single trait but a *number of different traits*. To compound the problem further, the influence of genes on development, apparently, can be modified by environmental factors.

Several illustrations may help make the complexity of the problem clear. First, despite much debate it is still not clear whether the difference in performance of men and women on certain kinds of aptitude tests (e.g., spatial reasoning) is the result of early cultural influences, of genetics, or of some combination of the two. Similarly, sexual orientation, long considered to be entirely the product of cultural influences, is now suspected of being, at least in part, the result of genetics and hormonal influences on the fetus during pregnancy. And schizophrenia, autism, and other mental and emotional problems once blamed entirely on poor parenting and other cultural factors may have a basis in genetics and fetal development.[3]

Obviously, there is a great deal we do not understand about the influence of genes on human life. We know enough, however, to put to rest the once-popular *tabula rasa* hypothesis.[4] Proponents of this view claimed that newborn infants were like "blank slates" or "empty cabinets," totally devoid of content, and that all

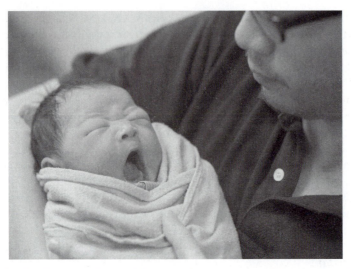

Human Babies Are Born in a State of Extreme Immaturity and Helplessness Compared with Most Other Animals: A Father and His Infant.

human thought and action were due *entirely* to social and cultural influences experienced after birth.

This idea has long had great appeal because if it were true, it should be possible for careful social planning to eliminate most of the ills of the world. If societies can make people selfish, cruel, and aggressive, they should also be able to make them kind, compassionate, and caring.

Today, however, after more than a century of disappointments resulting from efforts to fundamentally alter human behavior, and because of insights provided by the new sciences of genetics and primatology, it is clear that people and their societies are profoundly influenced by the genetic heritage of our species *as well as* by their cultures.[5] The unattractive aspects of human life, no less than the attractive ones, inevitably reflect this ancient evolutionary heritage and seem destined to remain a part of the human scene for a long time to come.[†]

With these cautions and considerations in mind, what can be said about the genetic constants?

First, *all humans have the same basic needs.* These include obvious physical requirements such as the need for food, water, sleep, warmth, and oxygen—needs that must be satisfied for people merely to survive. Individuals also need to have some social contact or be a part of *some* group or society. This is especially important during the early formative years: Human babies are born in a state of extreme immaturity and helplessness compared with most other animals. In fact, during the first year their

---

[†]This does not mean, of course, that nothing can be done about the unpleasant aspects of human behavior. Every society takes steps to discourage and suppress them, but both modern history and our knowledge of genetics indicate that there are limits to what societies can achieve in this regard.

physical development includes processes such as brain growth and bone hardening that are part of the *fetal* development of other primates.[‡6] Maturation proceeds at an unusually slow pace, and humans require a much longer time than members of other species to reach maturity and the greater "self-sufficiency" that adulthood brings. But even as adults, they are *still* dependent on society.

In addition, there are a variety of other genetically based *drives* whose satisfaction, while not essential for survival, motivate the actions of individuals. These vary in importance and intensity from individual to individual and from stage to stage within the life cycle.

They include such things as our sexual drive, our need for play, the need for new experience, and the need for respect and affection from others.[§8]

Second, *the members of every society have the same basic physiological resources for satisfying their needs and desires.* These include such obvious things as eyes, ears, hands, legs, teeth, bowels, heart, brain, and so on. The brain is an especially impressive resource: it provides us with the means of recording information equivalent to the content of 1,000, twenty-four-volume sets of the *Encyclopaedia Britannica* and is far more densely packed with information than any computer.[10] In addition, we are genetically programmed for the automatic performance of a variety of activities (e.g., digestion, ovulation, circulation, growth) and have many invaluable reflexes and response sets (e.g., we automatically draw back without conscious thought when touching something hot).

Third, because of their genetic heritage, *humans are motivated to optimize pleasurable experiences and minimize painful and unpleasant experiences.* This is a trait that we share with the rest of the animal world. Although an individual's definition of pleasure and of pain may be modified to some degree by experience (see point 5 below), the extent to which this is possible is usually quite limited.

Fourth, in their activities, *humans economize most of the time, seeking the optimal return for their expenditure of resources.*[11] This is because their needs and desires almost always exceed their resources. Thus, to maximize the satisfaction of needs and desires, economizing is essential, especially when the costs involved are high. Failure to observe this basic principle can only lead to frustration, disappointment, and unfulfilled needs and desires.

Fifth, *humans have an immense capacity for learning and for modifying their behavior in response to what they learn.* Learning is not merely a process of remembering what happened and when; it is also a process of evaluation based on the association of things and events with experiences of pleasure and pain. Patterns of action that prove painful tend not to be repeated while those that are pleasurable tend to be reinforced. Because of

---

[‡]The reason humans enter the world in this immature state is apparently due to brain size. At birth the human brain is only 23 percent of its adult size, whereas for chimpanzees and rhesus monkeys it is 41 percent and 65 percent, respectively.[7] If human infants were to develop in the womb the additional months it would take for them to become more mature, their greater head size would make birth impossible.

[§]Newborn infants, for example, have a decided preference for visual variety and contrast in their surroundings and a "bias to explore" that is manifest from the moment of birth. Newborns also have such a powerful need for social contact and the stimulation it provides that when this is denied, their health often suffers and they may even die.[9]

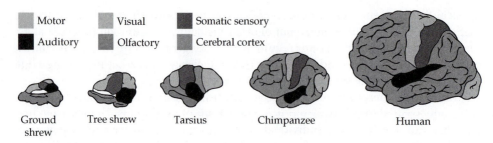

Figure 2.1. The Human Brain Is an Impressive Resource: It Can Record as Much Information as 1,000, Twenty-Four-Volume Sets of the *Encyclopaedia Brittanica*. Compare the Size of the Cortex of Humans with That of Other Primates.
Source: J. R. Napier, *Nature* 196: 409–11.

their remarkable capacity for learning, humans enjoy far more freedom from the constraints imposed by genetically programmed behaviors that so restrict the lives of most animals. Thus, they are able to devise alternative patterns of action for most of the situations that confront them—a fact that has proved both a blessing and a curse.

Sixth, *humans everywhere develop a variety of derivative needs and desires that reflect their experiences as members of society.* Because these experiences vary from society to society and from individual to individual within a given society, the nature and intensity of our derivative needs also vary. All of us, however, tend to develop, at a minimum, the need or desire to possess things, to give and receive affection, to express ourselves, to be respected, to have emotional and aesthetic experiences, and to discern order and meaning in our lives.

Seventh, *humans have the capacity to create and use symbol systems and to develop cultures.* This *uniquely human ability* is dependent on a variety of genetically based attributes, including such organs of speech as lips, tongue, palate, sinuses, and vocal cords. Equally important, however, are peculiarities of the human brain, specifically those areas of the cerebral cortex that control speech and abstract thought (see Figure 2.1).[12] Most linguists now believe that, despite the many differences among the 3,000 spoken languages humans employ, there is a single underlying structure that is shared by all and is part of our common genetic heritage.[13]

Eighth, *our species' heritage includes powerful emotions and appetites inherited from distant prehuman ancestors.* The structure of our brain reflects its long evolutionary heritage. This is because as new components developed they did not *replace* but were *entwined with and added on to* existing ones. Thus, the highest level, the cerebral cortex, which houses our ability to reason, is layered around and interconnected with the more primitive levels, which house our emotions. The precise nature of the relations between these components is still being investigated, but it is obvious that our actions and thoughts are often powerfully influenced—both positively and negatively—by such emotions as fear, love, and rage.**[14]

**This helps explain why advertisements for everything from automobiles and beer to presidential candidates so often appeal to emotions rather than to reason. Advertisers and candidates are literally betting millions that emotions have the power to override reason when people make purchasing and voting decisions.

Ninth, and finally, *humans have a highly developed sense of self and are powerfully motivated to put their own needs and desires ahead of those of others, especially when the stakes are high.*[15] In part, especially early in life, this is instinctive and genetic, but it is also a product of learning.[*] No two individuals can possibly share exactly the same set of experiences over the course of their lives, and since experience shapes both our values and our perceptions of ourselves, a highly developed awareness of self and self-serving behavior become unavoidable. As recognition of this gradually penetrates our consciousness, the distinction between self and others grows increasingly salient. Meanwhile we are discovering that actions that are pleasurable to others are not always pleasurable to ourselves, and *vice versa.*

Because of this divergence of interests, competition and conflict are endemic in human societies, though their form, intensity, and nature vary depending on circumstances. This does not prevent us from cooperating with one another, since most of us discover in infancy and early childhood that the benefits of cooperation usually exceed the costs. Thus, *enlightened* self-interest ensures a substantial amount of cooperation in every human society.

As many great novelists and poets have recognized, however, a powerful tension is built into the very fabric of human life: *Homo sapiens* is, by nature, both a social animal and an individualistic, self-centered animal. It is this more than anything else that creates the drama in human life, and the uncertainties. And it is this which justifies one early sociologist's characterization of human societies as systems of "antagonistic cooperation."[16]

Genetic Variables

In addition to the core of traits which all humans share and which make up the major portion of everyone's genetic heritage, each of us also has thousands of genes that are absent, or occur in somewhat different forms, in other individuals. Because these genes are not distributed equally among societies and their populations, there are *variable* aspects to the genetic heritage of human societies. These include skin color, hair texture, eye shape, blood type, incidence of color blindness, taste sensitivity, and susceptibility to various diseases, to name a few of those that have been identified thus far.[17] The *direct* impact of these variables on the life of human societies appears to have been of limited importance. However, because of social and cultural *responses to them*, such as ethnic stereotyping and prejudice, their indirect effects have often been substantial.

Although prior to the modern era, many human populations in different regions of the world had no direct contact with one another and, therefore, could not interbreed for long periods, *no fully human group was ever isolated long enough or became genetically differentiated enough to become a separate species.* During prolonged periods of isolation, however, human populations did become genetically differentiated in a number of highly visible ways, such as skin, hair, and eye color; hair type; body build; and shape of face and head. These differences, which tend to be interrelated,

---

[*]The genetic basis of this becomes obvious when we compare human societies with the societies of the social insects.

Human Populations Became Genetically Differentiated in a Number of Highly Visible Ways During Prolonged Periods When Interbreeding Was Not Possible: Compare the Height, Body Build, Hair Type, and Skin Color of the Eskimo with the Masai Tribesman from Kenya.

eventually became the basis of our modern concept of race. A *race* is simply a part of the human population in which some combination of these highly visible traits occurs with a frequency that is appreciably different from that of other parts of the human population. Racial differences, it may be noted, are found in many species, not just in humans.[18]

Members of modern societies often have difficulty appreciating the adaptive value of racial characteristics, *because we no longer depend on them for our survival or well-being.* When we encounter unpleasantly strong sunlight, for example, we adapt *culturally:* we create artificial shade or we apply artificial "pigment" to our eyes (sunglasses) and to our skin (sunscreen). Throughout most of human history, however, a population's *genetic* attributes were its primary means of adapting to the hazards of its environment, and even minor variations in relevant characteristics, such as the ability to store body fat as an insulation against extreme cold, could determine which individuals survived and which did not.

This explains why many genetic variables, from skin color to body and facial form, are not randomly distributed across the globe, but occur in discernible geographical patterns.[19] For example, the pigment in our skin determines how dark it is and protects underlying cells from exposure to ultraviolet light. Darker skin is universal in hot, sunny regions, with the heaviest pigmentation of all in the African Sudan, where solar radiation is the most intense and constant.[20] In contrast, light pigmentation in countries with limited sunshine facilitates the synthesis of vitamin D, which protects a person against rickets.[21]

The "sickling gene," found chiefly in populations of Africa, the Middle East, and India, in areas where a particularly deadly form of malaria occurs, provides a somewhat different illustration of the adaptive value of genetic variables. An individual who inherits this gene from *both* parents will develop sickle-cell anemia, a disease that is normally fatal before adulthood. But a far greater number of people in the population inherit the gene from only *one* parent, develop only mild symptoms of the anemia, and are highly *resistant* to certain virulent forms of malaria. As a result, in areas with a high incidence of malaria, the sickling gene has had great adaptive value: more individuals derive a benefit—resistance to malaria—than suffer a cost—death from sickle-cell anemia—and the trait, therefore, persists in the population.[22]

Most genetic variables are not as easy to identify as the ones we have discussed so far. This is because most of our characteristics result from the action of more than one gene and are not determined by genes alone. Genes provide the potential, but the reality is determined by the interaction of genes and environment. Complicating matters, environment also includes the intrauterine environment of the prenatal period, even the preconception experience of sperm and egg. This interaction of genetics and environment has been dramatically illustrated many times, as in the case of Jewish children born in Israeli kibbutzim and Japanese children born in America who, because of better diets, towered over parents born in the ghettos of Europe and in Japan. It is clear that most biological characteristics, from longevity to musical aptitude, are shaped by both genes and environment. But so far, at least, efforts to separate the two and measure their relative influence have proved frustrating and unprofitable.

One thing has been clarified, however: the relation between racial and nonracial genetic variables. Studies have been made, for example, of color blindness and blood characteristics, which are variables that can be precisely identified and are minimally affected by environmental factors, and whose gene frequency in a population can therefore be accurately calculated. When the distributions of these genes are plotted geographically, they cut across racial lines. For example, the frequency of the gene for type B blood is essentially the same among the south Chinese, Russians, and west Africans.[23] Findings like these make it clear that the *traits used to define race are an extremely limited set of variables that are not correlated to any appreciable degree with other genetic variables that have been carefully analyzed.*[24]

Demographic Variables

The demographic properties of a population include such things as its size, its density, how it is dispersed or concentrated (e.g., to what extent its members are concentrated in a few areas or spread out more evenly over its entire territory), the patterns of migration into and out of the society, its composition in terms of age and sex, and its birth and death rates. These characteristics, like certain clusters of genes, vary from one society to another. But these variations, unlike most genetic variations, have direct, demonstrable, and far-reaching consequences for human societies.

Population size is the most variable of the demographic properties of human societies, which have ranged in numbers from twenty members or less (in some preliterate societies of the recent past) to more than 1.4 billion (China's current estimated population). Variations in other demographic characteristics often appear insignificant beside such variations in size. For example, two societies with stable populations (i.e., neither growing in size nor declining) and with annual death rates of 14 per 1,000 and 40 per 1,000, respectively, may not seem very different. But this variation actually means that the average life expectancy at birth of the members of the first society is seventy-one years and of the second only twenty-five years!

In later chapters we will have frequent occasion to consider demographic variables, since they play an important part in the evolution of human societies. By contrast, we will have very little to say from here on about the genetic variables discussed in the previous section, since there is little to indicate that they have played a significant role in societal evolution.

Culture

The second basic component of every sociocultural system is *symbolic culture*: *a society's symbol systems and the information they convey.*[‡‡] As we saw in Chapter 1, *symbols* are information conveyers that enable humans to handle information in ways that are impossible for other creatures. We can *extract* more information from an experience (i.e., learn more) because symbols permit us thought processes denied other species. We can also *share* more information, because symbols enable us to express so much of the subtlety, complexity, and diversity of our experiences. We can, in fact, do more with information *whatever* is involved: In recording it, accumulating it, storing it, processing and combining it, or applying it, symbol users have a fantastic advantage over signal users.

The symbol systems and store of information that comprise a society's culture are like a foundation laid down by previous generations. Because each new generation has this base on which to build, it can avoid repeating many of the experiences of earlier generations. If a group has already learned how to make and use fire, or invented the plow, or devised a system of numbers, its members need not repeat the time-consuming and often difficult process by which that particular element of culture was first acquired. Instead, they can address new challenges, which may result in further enrichment or modification of their culture.

We will examine both of the basic parts of culture in some detail, beginning with symbol systems.

[‡‡]We emphasize the symbolic component of human culture over its imitative and "behavioral" aspects, in part, because it is what distinguishes human cultures from that of all other animals, but also because it dwarfs the other components in both extent and influence.

Symbol Systems

The most basic symbol systems in any society are its spoken *languages*.[§§] No matter how many other symbol systems a society creates, these are the ones that bear the major burden of transmitting information among them.

At the heart of every spoken language is an enormous set of social conventions, or customary practices, that constitute its vocabulary and grammar. The vocabulary is a set of sounds with meanings attached to them, and the relationship between a sound and its meaning is embedded in the history of its use by those who share that language. To those who speak English, the word "bed" means a place to sleep, not because of any logical or necessary connection between the sound and the activity, but because this is the convention that has evolved in English-speaking populations. Similarly, grammatical conventions tell us how words must be combined if they are to be meaningful and intelligible to others. Thus, it means one thing to say, "The bear ate Jack," something quite different to say, "Jack ate the bear," and nothing at all to say, "The ate bear Jack."

Until we study a foreign language, most of us have the impression that there is something natural—even inevitable—about the way our own society and its language separate experience and thought into the bits of meaning we call words, and that learning another language is only a matter of learning the sounds another society applies to those same "units of experience." Yet as people conversant in two or more languages are well aware, *words in one do not necessarily have a simple equivalent in the other.*

Americans and Russians were reminded of this some years ago during talks between President Kennedy and Chairman Khrushchev during the Cold War. Kennedy repeatedly said that the Russians should not *miscalculate* the will and intentions of the American people, and every time the word "miscalculate" was translated, Khrushchev flushed angrily. Kennedy later learned that the Russian language has no precise equivalent of this word, and the translator had seized on a Russian word, normally applied to a small child or uneducated person, meaning "unable to count." Khrushchev naturally assumed that Kennedy was implying he was not very bright![***][25]

One reason languages separate experience into different units is because the experiences of the people who *create* and *use* the languages are so different. For example, gauchos, the famous horsemen of the Argentine prairies, distinguish among 200 different colors of horses, but use only four words for all the plants known to them: *pasto,* fodder; *paja,* bedding; *cardo,* wood; and *yuyos,* all others.[27] Meanwhile, the Inuit (Eskimo) use numerous expressions to refer to the various phenomena that we call

---

[§§]Many societies have, or have had, two or more languages. Even those with a single language have often had multiple dialects that were mutually unintelligible.

[***]In another incident during the Cold War, tensions between the Soviet Union and the United States were very high and focused on the city of Berlin, where many feared World War III might break out at any moment. To assure citizens of Berlin that he and the United States supported them, President Kennedy said, "Ich bin ein Berliner," thinking he was saying "I am a Berliner." Unfortunately inserting the article "ein" into the sentence changed its meaning, and what he said, literally, was "I am a jelly doughnut"![26]

simply "snow." For instance, they distinguish among dry-wind-driven snow, dry-packed-suitable-for-cutting-into-blocks-and-building-igloos snow, and ice-crust-surface snow.[†††28] In yet another part of the world, the Dugum Dani, Stone Age horticulturists on the island of New Guinea, have seventy different words that refer to sweet potatoes, their staple crop;[30] and in the Middle East, Arabic is reputed to have a thousand expressions for "sword," indicative of that culture's stress on poetry and emphasis on synonyms and figures of speech.[31] English is a language rich in numbers and units of measurement, well-suited for describing and recording mathematical and scientific data. In short, a language reflects the needs, concerns, and experiences of those who use it.

Another reason languages differ in the way they categorize and classify experience is the haphazard and spontaneous manner in which they evolve. Consider the evolution of the word "bureau," for example. A bureau was originally something made of baize, a thick green cloth. Because these bureaus were often put on writing tables and chests of drawers, the word was eventually extended to mean the furniture as well as the cloth. Later, because many government offices were equipped with bureaus, or writing tables, the offices themselves came to be known by that term (e.g., the Federal Bureau of Investigation).[32]

This process of change in language is so much a matter of chance that it is unlikely that the same pattern would occur in two societies. Even if two societies begin with the same language, as when a small group separates from the parent group to settle a new territory, linguistic differences are bound to develop unless an extremely high level of communication is maintained between them. There is no better example of this in the modern era than in the differences between English as it is spoken in England, Australia, Canada, Jamaica, and the United States. Australians, for example, refer to someone who is lazy or borrows money without intending to repay it as a "bludger," and describe something as "dinkum" or "fair dinkum" to indicate that it is really true or genuine. Australians even have a distinctive word for their version of English; they call it "Strine," which is a contraction of the word "Australian" as that word sounds when spoken by them.[33]

So far we have discussed spoken language as if it were merely a neutral and passive vehicle for transmitting information. But as political leaders, propagandists, and advertisers have long recognized, individual words often acquire, through the process of association, powerful emotional connotations that enable them to convey more than is embodied in their formal definitions. Words like "communist," "racist," and "sexist," for example, have such strong negative associations for many Americans that they respond unthinkingly to the emotional content of these symbols. Words can also acquire strong positive associations, and these, too, may be used to manipulate emotions. For example, linking kinship terms with organizations, as in "Mother Russia," "Mother Earth," or "Uncle Sam," can stimulate warm feelings of affection.

[†††]It is worth noting that these are not really different words but complex combinations of terms.[29] The point being made, however, is simply that these differences in snow are of considerable importance for Inuit life, whereas they attract little attention in a society practicing a different technology.

Two Sides of a Limestone Tablet Found in Iraq, Bearing Some of the Oldest Known Writing (about 3500 B.C.). Included Are Symbols for Head, Hand, Foot, Threshing Sledge, and Several Numerals.

Supplementing its spoken language, every society uses conventional gestures and facial expressions whose meanings are evident to members of the group. This second kind of symbol system, *body language,* should not be confused with such facial expressions and body movements as our involuntary reaction when we touch something hot, or the way we pucker up when we taste something bitter. These are genetically determined signals. True body language is *symbolic,* just as words are, for the form and meaning of the gestures and expressions are determined by those who use them. Consider, for example, the shrug of the shoulders. Various groups use it to convey indifference, uncertainty, or a lack of information on the subject in question, with the specific meaning indicated by the context in which it is used.[34]

A third kind of symbol system in many societies is *written language,* a relatively recent development in human history. Some of the oldest written records in existence today were prepared thousands of years ago by temple authorities in Mesopotamia to enable them to keep a record of business transactions.[35] These priests were stewards of their god's resources, and when they loaned out his animals or grain, it was imperative to get them back. Even though the priest who made a loan might die, the god expected it to be repaid. To keep track of their god's property and thereby avoid his wrath, the priestly community devised a primitive system of writing that involved a mixture of numerals, pictographs, and ideograms.

The arbitrary and symbolic nature of this writing is clear. Even when a pictograph (essentially a picture) was used to represent a bull, it was a stylized representation that excluded many of the animal's features that might have been included. Moreover, the same features were used consistently, indicating that conventional forms of notation had already been established. From a very early date, the pictograph of a jar came to represent a certain quantity of grain, rather than the jar itself. And finally, among these early examples of writing are a number of ideograms, which are "pure" symbols, since they are completely arbitrary and based solely on convention. They lack any visual resemblance to the objects they represent, just as the dollar sign bears no resemblance to the currency it symbolizes.

As new uses for writing were discovered, new efforts were made to translate spoken language into written form. At an early date, kings and princes recorded their military triumphs for posterity, and priests their sacred rites and traditions. At first, as the Mesopotamian priests' experience makes clear, a society's written symbols could express only a small part of what was possible with its spoken symbols. Gradually, however, written languages developed until they were able to convey the same information as spoken ones, and writing came into its own as a means of storing information; for communication across the barriers of space and time; and, eventually, as a medium of artistic expression, education, and entertainment.

As societies have acquired more information, it has often become necessary to go beyond such basic symbols as letters and numerals. Thus, new symbol systems have evolved that greatly facilitate the handling of specialized kinds of information. For example, musicians devised musical notation so they could express the information that they create and use, and mathematicians and scientists developed a wide variety of symbol systems to express abstract ideas, complex numbers, and so on. The specialized symbol systems now found in modern societies include languages for the deaf, the blind, engineers, stenographers, computer scientists, and others too numerous to mention.

Over the course of history, the relative importance of the three basic types of language—body, spoken, and written—has altered considerably. Body language, including symbolic gestures and facial expressions, may well have been dominant among our very early ancestors, declining only when true speech evolved. Then, until quite recently, spoken symbols remained the primary means of transmitting information from one person to another and from one generation to the next. With the invention of movable type and the subsequent spread of literacy, written language steadily increased in relative importance, largely because it could overcome space and time, the historic barriers to communication. During the last century, thanks to such devices as the telephone, radio, movies, and television, spoken language, too, has overcome those barriers, altering the balance once again. And in the most recent, most dramatic development of all, a great variety of languages have been created for computers, enabling them to handle fantastic amounts of information of diverse kinds. More important than these shifts in the relative importance of different types of language, however, is the fundamental trend that has persisted from early prehistoric times: *The continuing expansion of old symbol systems and the creation of new ones have steadily increased the capacity of human societies to store and process information.*

Information

Cultural information is *knowledge acquired through experience and largely conveyed through symbols.* A society's information is, in effect, a product of its experience: its experiences in the remote past and in the recent past; its experiences with its environment and within itself. Needless to say, no society's culture preserves *every* experience of every member throughout its entire history. Rather, societies tend to preserve those elements that their members—especially their more influential members—have found useful.

Because every society has a unique past, every culture is unique. We can say this another way: Out of diverse experience, diverse information emerges. This means that human societies not only have different amounts of information on a given subject; they frequently have different "facts" as well. Since we know that human senses and intellect are limited and fallible, this should be no surprise. Even hard scientific "facts" must often be revised in the light of later research.

Cultural information is not limited to the kinds of ideas whose truth or accuracy is capable of being proved or disproved, however. It includes a group's total perception of reality: its ideas about what is real, what is true, what is good, what is beautiful, what is important, what is possible. When we discussed symbol systems, we saw that they, too, are so rooted in subjective experience that even individual symbols may become "units of experience"—which explains why a word like "mother" can be so emotionally charged. We also saw that the kind of information conveyed by symbol systems ranges from historical and statistical data to concepts of deity, attitudes toward horses and plants, characteristics of snow, poetic inclinations, even music itself. Cultural information includes, quite literally, *everything humans are capable of experiencing and able to convert into symbolic form.*

Because all human societies have certain fundamental kinds of experiences in common, because their members all have the same basic needs to satisfy, and because all societies have the same system needs, all cultures include information on certain basic subjects:

- Every culture has a substantial store of information about the biophysical environment to which the society must adapt, including its plant and animal life, its soils and terrain, its mineral resources and water supply, and its climate and weather conditions.
- Every culture includes information about the group's social environment; the other human societies with which the group has contact.
- Every culture contains information about the society itself: its origin, its people, its heroes, its history.
- Every culture contains information that seeks to explain the ultimate causes of things and events.
- Every culture has information that enables the members to cope with recurring problems, from feeding themselves to resolving intragroup conflict.
- Every culture contains information that guides individuals in making judgments about what is good, what is true, and what is beautiful.
- Every culture has information created solely to satisfy culturally activated and intensified needs, such as the desire for artistic expression, for example, or for ritual.

Although this list is neither exhaustive nor detailed, it conveys something of the breadth of culture.

Much of the information contained in cultures is ideological in nature and results from efforts to make sense out of human experience.[36] For *ideology is information used to interpret experience and help order societal life.* Because humans are users of symbols and creatures of culture, life can be overwhelming. We think, feel, hope, enjoy, and suffer as no other creatures can. We imagine what we cannot know and yearn for what may not exist. We live simultaneously in three worlds: the past, the present, and the future. We alone, apparently, live out our lives aware that death is inevitable. To make things more difficult, we create for ourselves a profusion of cultural alternatives, in the face of which our genetic heritage is an inadequate guide. It is not surprising, therefore, that as individuals we need help in interpreting experience, finding meaning,

All Cultures contain Information Created Solely to Satisfy Culturally Activated and Intensified Needs, Such as the Desire for Artistic Expression and Social Rituals: Balinese Dancers Performing the Scared Dance Drama of the Witch and the Dragon.

and making choices. And, as we have seen, societies need help in regulating and ordering their collective life.

Medieval Christianity is a good example of a highly developed and comprehensive ideology, the kind that answers virtually all of these individual and societal needs. At its center was a vision of a universe inhabited by many kinds of spiritual beings (seraphim, cherubim, humans, demons, devils, etc.) mostly under the dominion of God. God was perceived as the king above all earthly kings, but because His authority was challenged by Satan, the prince of evil, people were confronted with a choice as to which to serve. Those who chose God (who would ultimately prevail) were obliged to accept the Church's doctrines and conform to its code of morality. The latter enjoined Christians to be charitable to one another, honest, sober, hardworking, monogamous (better yet, celibate), obedient to all in authority, and regular in devotions and worship. Since no one could adhere perfectly to these requirements, the Church provided opportunities for people to confess their sins, do penance, and obtain absolution.

When we look closely at medieval Christianity, we find the three basic elements that comprise *every* ideology. First, there is a system of *beliefs* about the kind of world we inhabit. Second, there is a system of general *moral values* that emanate from, or are justified by, those beliefs. Finally, there is a system of *norms* that apply those general values to specific situations and spell out how the members of the group are to act in various circumstances, that is, what they should and should not do.

There are two basic kinds of norms, and they have evolved in very different ways. Some are part of official or legal codes of conduct that are enforced by an authority, such as a government, a church, or other organization. We refer to such norms as *laws, regulations,* or *rules,* and they are sometimes accompanied by explicit statements of the sanctions that will be used to punish those who violate them. A city ordinance, for example, may specify a fine of twenty-five dollars for littering streets or sidewalks.

In contrast, many norms are informal and unofficial, and violations of them are not officially sanctioned. Thus, every society and every subgroup in a society, from corporations to families, have many informal rules, or *customs,* which define for the members acceptable and unacceptable behavior. Customs apply to such diverse things as modes of dress, hairstyles, food preparation, the selection of marriage partners, the performance of various tasks, proper grammar, and attitudes toward children or older people—to name only a few. These informal norms are as important in shaping behavior as more formal ones. Norms and their related *sanctions* (i.e., rewards and punishments) are basic components of every system of social control.

Sometimes it is difficult to determine, or even to imagine, how certain elements of ideology originated, or what they can possibly tell us about the past experience of a society. This is true, for example, of one of the central beliefs of Hinduism, the belief in the sacredness of the cow. The boxed insert (below) explains how this seemingly strange belief has, for centuries, helped the members of Indian society cope with some of their basic and recurring problems in a highly adaptive way.

India's Sacred Cows: The Adaptive Value of an Ideology

In a society where tens of millions of people go to sleep hungry every night, devout Hindus, who constitute the vast majority of India's population, would not dream of killing any of that country's fifty-four million cows. To a devout Hindu, even the killing of a human being is not thought to be as great a sacrilege as is the killing of a cow.

Marvin Harris, a leading proponent of ecological-evolutionary theory, examined this seeming paradox in an effort to find a rational explanation. He rejected the view that an ideology evolves arbitrarily, unrelated to the rest of societal life or to the experiences of its members in the past. Rather, he suspected that any belief that has been as widespread and as persistent as the Indian taboo against slaughtering cows for food must have significant adaptive value for the society.

In a book titled *Cows, Pigs, Wars and Witches: The Riddles of Culture,* Harris reported the results of an analysis of this subject. He found that the cow is of enormous economic value to the members of Indian society. A peasant's cow is, in effect, a factory that provides food (milk, butter); fertilizer; fuel for cooking (dried manure is excellent for this purpose, producing a clean, low heat); flooring material (a paste of manure and water hardens into a smooth surface that holds down dust and can be swept clean); and, most important of all, oxen to pull the peasant's plow. Harris also found that less than 20 percent of the food consumed by Indian cattle is edible by humans. In short, the cow converts substances of little worth to the peasant into extremely valuable products.

Although Indian peasants recognize that a living, productive cow is vastly more valuable to them and to their children than the same cow consumed as food, it would be only natural for them to ignore this fact when they are desperately hungry. The religious taboo against killing cows is a powerful cultural mechanism that helps protect these animals even in times of famine and thereby preserves an invaluable resource. In short, Hinduism's conception of the cow as sacred is based on the experience of countless generations of the Indian people, and it has served them well.

In very small societies, all the members usually have common beliefs and values. In larger and more complex societies, however, this is rarely the case. People in different occupational groups, different kinds of communities, and different classes have different interests and different experiences, and these inevitably lead to different beliefs, different values, and different norms. Not infrequently, these differences cause conflicts between the people involved. In extreme cases, as in parts of the Middle East today or in the United States at the time of the Civil War, such conflicts may threaten the very existence of a society.

Another crucial body of information in every culture is *technology*. This is *information about how to use the material resources of the environment to satisfy human needs and desires.* Compared to ideology, technology seems rather prosaic and uninteresting. Historians and social scientists have tended to ignore it,[37] and until recently people seldom came to blows over the relative merits of different technologies. As we will see in coming chapters, however, the influence of technological information on the course of history and on the process of societal change and development has been greatly out of proportion to the recognition usually accorded it.

In every society, a large component of technological information concerns *food*: where and how to grow it or get it, and how to process it for consumption or storage. There is also information about the other material resources available to the society and how they may be converted into useful forms—into fuel for heat, cooking, and other purposes; into clothing and shelter; into tools, weapons, ornaments, houses, factories, toys; and other things the group or its members need or value.

Because a distinctive body of information tends to build up in response to each set of human needs, we sometimes speak of various technologies in the same society, such as a military technology or a communications technology. Often, however, we speak of a society's technology in the singular, because there is an underlying unity to this store of information. The basic principles of *metallurgy*, for example, are used in virtually every area of technological activity in a modern industrial society.

Material Products

The third component of human societies consists of *the things they produce or obtain through trade*. These products of technology range from perishable items that are consumed within days or even hours, as with many foods, to things that endure for centuries, such as pyramids, cathedrals, and plastic containers. They range, too, from utilitarian objects like hammers and houses to frivolous items like Xboxes and Frisbees.

Energy is easily the most vital product of societal activity, since without a continuous input of it, all activity would come to a halt: even thought requires energy! Food is the most basic source of energy. In societies today the energy resources of food are supplemented by energy obtained from animals, from wind and water, and, in modern industrial societies, from mineral sources (coal, petroleum, natural gas, and uranium).

Many of the material products of human labor are meant only for consumption. Some, however, are created to facilitate the *production* of other products. These are known as *capital goods* and are a major determinant of a society's wealth. The more capital goods a society possesses, the more goods it is able to produce.

The first capital goods were simple tools and weapons made of stone, wood, and bone which enabled our early ancestors to produce such essentials as fire, food, shelter, and more tools and weapons. Later, as the store of cultural information increased and as new environmental resources became available, the character of tools changed. Metals became especially important because they combined strength and durability with malleability. With the domestication of animals, an important new kind of capital good was created. In more recent times, new and enormously productive capital goods have been created in the form of large industrial complexes that utilize sophisticated machines and instruments powered by *inanimate forms of energy*.

Social Organization

The fourth component of every society is *the network of relationships among its members*. These relationships make it possible for members to satisfy both their own individual needs and the needs of the society as a whole. The latter include the need to replace members who die or leave the group and to equip their successors with the many skills needed to make them productive, contributing members of the group; the need to produce and distribute essential goods and services; the need to hold in check conflicts within the group so that vital relationships can be maintained; and the need to protect members from external threats, whether from the biophysical environment or from other human societies.

Systems of social organization are influenced to some extent by biological differences among the members. *Social relationships in all mammalian societies, for example, are organized to take account of age and sex differences.* Human societies, however, rarely stop there. In most instances they go much further, developing elaborate kinship networks and other complex social arrangements that reflect cultural influences. Thus, when we think of social organization we must think of it as a product of the interaction of culture and people.

Individuals

Every society must cope with a constant turnover in its membership. Older members die and are replaced with newborn infants.[‡‡‡] This creates a major problem: Although these infants have the same basic genetic resources as the individuals who died, they lack their *cultural* resources. In other words, none of them knows anything about their society's store of information on matters ranging from religion to technology. *Everything* must be learned. To put it another way, raw, ignorant "recruits" must somehow be transformed into productive and responsible people who can work cooperatively with others and make a contribution to the group's welfare.

The means by which societies do this is known as the *socialization* process. This is a complex process that begins as soon as the infant is capable of discerning that its actions generate reactions by others, and that some of those reactions are pleasant while others are not. Sometimes these reactions are conscious, purposive efforts by

---

[‡‡‡]To varying degrees, membership turnover also involves individuals who migrate from one society to another. Emigration and immigration, however, do not alter the basic nature of the problem of member turnover discussed in this section.

parents and others to influence or train the child. But often they are unintended, unplanned, and unconscious—a parent losing his temper in a traffic jam or holding a door open for a stranger burdened with packages.

Over time, even very young children begin to anticipate the responses of other people and to adjust their behavior accordingly. At this point, they have begun to absorb the culture of their society and to *internalize* its norms and values. This process continues throughout an individual's life, and comes to include the conscious acquisition of countless skills that can range from brushing one's teeth to programming computers.

The socialization process is never entirely successful in any society. The "concern for self" which is part of our genetic heritage, together with the individuating nature of learning, combine to limit the extent to which people are able to subordinate their personal interests to those of society. All of us are able to rationalize at least some violations of our society's norms. ("It was just a little white lie." "Everybody drives five miles over the speed limit here.")

Most of the time, however, most individuals, by the time they reach adulthood, conform to their society's standards, partly because of their desire to obtain the rewards and avoid the penalties that can otherwise be expected, and partly because they have come to accept their society's standards as their own. In short, they have become contributing members of their society; individuals who are able to fulfill their duties and meet their responsibilities.

Social Positions, Roles, and Statuses
Individuals who occupy positions in a social structure are expected to fulfill a number of social roles. These roles emerge and develop in response to recurring needs and problems in societies. Young children, for example, require care and attention, and the roles of mother and father have evolved in response to this need. In large and complex societies, there is a continuing need for political leadership, and a variety of roles, ranging from school board member to president or prime minister, have developed in response.

Roles in society, like roles in the theater, *have distinctive behavioral expectations and requirements attached to them.*[38] Thus, just as a woman may play the role of Juliet on the stage, so she may "play" the roles of wife, mother, and doctor in her home and community. In both instances, people expect her to act in certain ways and not in others, simply because of the social positions she occupies. When she meets those expectations, she is applauded or rewarded. When she fails to meet them, she is criticized, or worse.

The behavioral requirements and expectations that are attached to "real life" roles are the *norms* we discussed on page 42. As we saw then, they may be quite formal, as in the laws forbidding theft and murder, or they may be informal, as in a neighborhood's expectations concerning property maintenance. They may involve fundamental moral issues, or they may involve the fine points of etiquette. Norms also vary in their scope. Some apply to everyone, as in laws forbidding murder; others apply to only a few, as in rules governing the conduct of members of the Canadian Parliament.

As we will see in later chapters, roles change as societies change. New roles are added and older ones disappear. Even when roles persist, their content often changes.

Thus, prior to the development of modern technology, the feeding of infants was entirely the work of women. Today, this is a responsibility often shared with men.

It is also important to recognize that roles differ greatly with respect to the prestige or social honor accorded them. For instance, people in industrial societies hold the occupational role of medical doctor in higher esteem than that of garage mechanic.[39] Successful hunters and good storytellers are held in similarly high regard in hunting and gathering societies. Such rankings are referred to as *statuses,* and, as we will see later, status differences are important in motivating people to fill certain roles in societies, and they can affect people's access to scarce and valued social resources.

Groups

In most societies, individuals are organized into a variety of units we call groups. These range from small family units and *cliques* to giant corporate entities of various kinds. In popular usage, the term "group" is often applied to any *aggregation* of people, regardless of their other characteristics. Sociologists, however, try to limit the term to an aggregation whose members (1) cooperate to satisfy common, or complementary, needs; (2) have shared norms; and (3) have a sense of common identity.

As this definition suggests, human aggregations differ in their degree of "groupishness." While some aggregations clearly qualify as groups (e.g., Jehovah's Witnesses) and others just as clearly do not (e.g., all redheads in the United States), many are borderline (e.g., Americans of Irish descent). This last example reminds us that the degree of "groupishness" of an aggregation is not permanently fixed. Aggregations may take on more of the qualities of a group, or they may lose some. Their members may come to work together more closely; develop new, stronger, and more generally shared norms; and acquire a stronger sense of common identity; or just the opposite may occur, as has happened with Irish Americans during the last hundred years.

Even after we exclude such aggregations as redheads, the concept "group" still includes such a wide variety of organizations that it is necessary to differentiate among them. The most familiar way of doing this is by their basic function in society. Thus, we differentiate between families, churches, schools, political parties, and so forth.

Sociologists have also found it useful to differentiate among groups on the basis of their size and the intensity of the social ties among their members. Small groups in which there are face-to-face relations of a fairly intimate and personal nature are known as *primary groups.* Primary groups are of two basic types, families and friendship groups (*cliques*). In other words, they are organized around ties of either kinship or friendship. Larger, more impersonal groups are known as *secondary groups.*

Classes

Inequality is a fact of life in every human society. Some individuals may control more of the society's resources than others do and enjoy more than their share of its benefits, or be more highly valued or respected by peers. Human societies differ greatly, however, in the amount of inequality present among their members. In some it is minimal and is a matter primarily of differences in prestige or respect, but in others it is enormous and involves differential access to material resources. In larger and more complex societies, where inequality is always substantial, individuals can be divided into *classes,* or *strata,* on the basis of their relationship to various social and cultural resources,

Roles in Society Are Like Roles in the Theater: Both Have Distinctive Behavioral Expectations Attached to Them. Scene from Shakespeare's *Hamlet,* Performed in Moscow by Actors of the Central Academic Theater of the Russian Army.

such as political office, wealth, occupational skills, education, and legal status (e.g., free persons versus slaves). Taken together, all the classes on a given dimension constitute a *class system.*[40]

Sociologists and others often find it is enough simply to distinguish between the upper, middle, and lower strata of a society, or the haves and have-nots. For some purposes, however, more precise distinctions are needed. Thus, in discussing societies of the past, we often distinguish between nobles and commoners or between free persons and slaves. Similarly, in discussing contemporary societies, we often refer to the working class, the professional class, political elites, and others. In each instance the class or stratum is defined on the basis of *some important attribute* (e.g., legal status, type of job, education) *that is the same for all members of the class and that influences their access to power, privilege, and prestige.*

Stratification

Viewed as a whole, all the statuses and class systems of a society constitute its system of stratification. And, as we will see in the following chapters, stratification systems vary dramatically in a number of important ways. For instance, in some societies the differences in wealth, power, and prestige between those at the top and those at the bottom of the stratification system are quite small, while in others they are enormous. In some the great majority of people are concentrated near the bottom, while in others more are in the middle range. In some the people who are privileged with respect to one dimension of inequality are privileged with respect to all dimensions, while in others, people who are high on one dimension may be at the middle or near the bottom on others.

Not surprisingly, stratification is one of the major sources of conflict within societies. No system of distribution can satisfy *everyone*, since there is no obviously "right" or "fair" way to distribute power, privilege, and prestige. For example, it is equally reasonable, in the abstract, to assert that a given product should be distributed on the basis of (1) how much a person needs it, (2) how much effort a person invests in producing it, or (3) how much skill a person contributes in producing it, to name only three of the possibilities.

Even if the members of a society employed just one of these principles in allocating its rewards, disputes would still be likely. If members applied the principle of effort, for example, they would have to measure and compare effort. Should it be calculated by the hours spent on the job, by the foot-pounds of energy expended, or by how hard a person tries? Or if the group used the skill criterion, then they would have to measure and compare such dissimilar skills as those of a nurse, a computer programmer, and a diplomat. In brief, there is no obviously "right" way to allocate rewards in human societies, and conflict over the rules and results of distribution, therefore, is virtually inevitable.

Because of systems of stratification, not everyone has an equal voice in decision making within societies. On the contrary, in many societies a few individuals have vastly more influence on societal policies than others. We need to keep this in mind whenever we discuss the policies and actions of such societies: While leaders make decisions on behalf of, and in the name of, the entire society, most members of the society have usually never been consulted. This is true even in societies with multiparty representative political systems and free elections.

Social Institutions and Institutional Systems

Social institutions and *institutional systems* are the last of the five basic components of human societies. These differ from the other components we have considered in one important respect: they are *combinations of the other four components*. In other words, they bring together population, culture, the material products of culture, and social organization (see Figure 2.2).

A British sociologist once described social institutions as "frozen answers to fundamental questions."[41] Although it is an exaggeration to call them "frozen" answers, institutions are durable and persisting elements of sociocultural systems. For purposes of definition, we may think of them as *durable answers to important and persistent problems*.

One reason for their durability is that their value to society is impressed on individuals at an early age. Thus, we grow up thinking of them as *natural* and *inevitable*. Another reason for their durability is that the different elements of institutional systems are intricately intertwined, and it is often impossible to change one element without being compelled to change countless others, making the cost of, and resistance to, change too great.

All societies develop numerous "durable answers." Among those found in modern industrial societies are such things as: marriage, the jury system, secret-ballot elections, private property, religion, and rights of privacy.

Figure 2.2. Relations Among the Basic Components of Human Societies. Each Major Institutional System Brings Together People, Culture, the Material Products of Culture, and Social Organization.

For many purposes, sociologists are less interested in specific social institutions than in institutional *systems*. As the name implies, *institutional systems are systems of interrelated institutions.* Five such systems are of major importance in the study of human societies, and much of our analysis in later chapters, especially Chapters 5 to 14, will be organized around them.

The first is *kinship,* which structures such things as the obligations and responsibilities among relatives, marriage choices, and relations between spouses. The second is the *economy,* which centers on the production and distribution of valued goods in a society. The third is the *polity,* which focuses on the distribution of power and the governance of society. The fourth is *religion,* that is, societal beliefs and practices regarding things considered sacred. Fifth, and finally, *education* is the system that prepares people to assume productive roles in society.

These are like major slices of the sociocultural "pie." Each provides answers to a set of interrelated, important, and persistent problems that confront every society. Kinship is the oldest of these systems, but all of them have existed for thousands of years and all seem likely to continue for as long as human societies endure.

THE WORLD SYSTEM OF SOCIETIES

Before we conclude this discussion of human societies as sociocultural systems, there is one more system that needs to be considered. Every human society is, itself, part of a larger and more inclusive sociocultural system that sociologists have come to call the *world system of societies.*

Throughout history, human societies have established and maintained relations with one another. They have met at waterholes, traded goods, exchanged ambassadors, sent out missionaries, fought wars, translated books, exacted tribute, spied on one another, and in countless other ways developed and maintained a network of social and cultural ties. During much of the past, direct ties were limited to neighboring societies, since direct relations with distant societies were not possible. But even then, *indirect* relations often existed. Society A maintained ties with society B, which, in turn, maintained ties with society C, and so on throughout the system. No society was *ever* totally cut off from the world system of societies, since even the most isolated societies had occasional contacts with others. With advances in transportation and communication during the last 5,000 years, however, relations between societies increased greatly, and direct relations have been established between societies far removed from one another. As a result, the world system of societies has grown more integrated and more complex and has come to exercise an ever-increasing influence on the life of individual societies.

The Evolution of Human Societies

Outline

*E*volution is a term that refers to long-term directional patterns of change that scientists have discovered throughout the world of nature. Today different groups of scientists are engaged in the study of cosmic evolution (the evolution of the universe as a whole), biological evolution (the evolution of living organisms), and sociocultural evolution (the evolution of human societies).

Sociocultural evolution, like biological evolution, is a complex process involving three basic sets of forces: (1) forces of *continuity* that act to preserve from generation to generation much of the existing store of information and many or most existing arrangements; (2) forces of *innovation* that produce new information and new arrangements; and (3) forces of *selection* that determine which elements survive and which are eliminated.*

After we examine each of these forces individually in some detail, we will consider the interplay among them and the directional changes they have produced in the world system of human societies of the past 10,000 years.

FORCES PROMOTING SOCIAL AND CULTURAL CONTINUITY

Evolutionary change in a society is a *cumulative* process. Even in a society that appears to be changing rapidly, most elements of culture and social organization remain unchanged for extended periods. In modern industrial societies, for example, where rates of change are among the highest the world has ever known, many elements of culture are hundreds of years old, and some, such as the alphabet, the calendar, the numeral system, certain religious beliefs and practices, and basic techniques of farming and

---

*See the excursus at the end of this chapter for a more detailed comparison of sociocultural and biological evolution.

Although Rates of Change in Modern Industrial Societies Are Among the Highest the World Has Ever Known, Many Elements of Their Cultures Are Hundreds or Even Thousands of Years Old: Jewish Boy Reading from Scriptures More than 2,000 Years Old.

metallurgy, are thousands of years old. The same is true of many elements of social organization, such as the roles of prime minister, king, queen, priest, and rabbi, and the even older roles of mother, father, husband, wife, child, cousin, and grandparent.

There are a number of reasons for the persistence of social and cultural elements in a society.

One major reason is that, in the absence of a clearly better alternative, people will continue to do what works. For instance, in simple societies, through generations of experience, people have developed effective tools, technologies, and strategies for coping with their environments. Any alternative or change, therefore, is likely to be *less effective* than what it would replace, and diminished results would quickly lead any potential innovators to return to "tried and true" ways.

Cultural elements are also preserved if they are perceived by enough people as useful in answering their individual or personal needs.[†] This explains the persistence of many elements of art, music, literature, and religion, and the persistence of a great variety of customs and norms, including even such antisocial patterns of behavior as speeding or illicit drug use.

In more complex societies, there are additional reasons. For example, in class-stratified societies, fundamental technological or social change is likely to affect the amount and distribution of valued goods. As a result, classes and groups that would

---

[†]This does not mean that human societies strive to satisfy the needs and desires of all their members equally or impartially. On the contrary, as we have seen (p. 49), all societies are more responsive to the needs of some of their members than to the needs of others.

lose benefits are likely to resist, and since they generally have more power and more resources than those that would gain, they are often able to delay or prevent change from taking place.‡

Sometimes elements of culture are preserved, not because they are superior solutions to problems, but simply because they ensure *standardized behavioral responses* in situations where these are essential. For example, although driving a car on the right side of the road is inherently neither safer nor easier than driving on the left, this choice cannot be left to individuals. Every society must have a norm to ensure that all of its drivers follow the same procedure.

Another cause of continuity is the *cost involved in changing.* Change can be expensive; it would cost billions of dollars, for example, for Americans to change to the metric system. Change can also be costly in terms of time and energy, since it takes both to learn new rules and techniques and new ways of relating to others and performing one's job.

The *socialization process* is also a tremendous force for continuity within societies. As we saw in Chapter 2, this is the process by which individuals learn the culture of their group and acquire the skills that enable them to become functional members of their society. Through this process the members of a society acquire the belief that their culture is a precious resource and worth preserving. During their prolonged immaturity, children are obliged to master many of the most basic elements of their culture. This is essential for their survival, and their only road to any degree of independence. Before they learn to talk, for example, children are almost totally dependent on other people; after they master their society's language, they have an invaluable tool to help them get what they want. The same is true of other elements of culture: it pays the child to master them. Thus, the desire of members of the adult generation to preserve their culture by transmitting it to their offspring is more than matched by their offspring's eagerness to learn it, especially during the formative years. Since this cycle necessarily repeats itself as each generation matures, the result is a tremendous force for continuity.

These efforts to pass culture on to the next generation are reinforced by *ideologies.* One of the chief functions of ideology is to preserve valued insights of the past. Since these insights usually include the belief that the existing social order is a moral order that ought to be preserved, a society's values, norms, and leadership acquire an aura of the sacred and thus become less vulnerable to efforts to alter them. Ironically, even revolutionary ideologies, like Marxism, eventually acquire a sacred and conservative character: Once they win acceptance, they too become a force for continuity and for resistance to change.

Finally, *the systemic nature of human societies* is a major force for continuity. This is because most of the elements in a sociocultural system are linked to other elements in such a way that change in one area often makes change in other areas necessary. As a result, the members of a society do not adopt change casually, especially when they are aware of how extensive—and expensive—that change may ultimately be. When

---

‡We will also see that in complex stratified societies, the potential for innovation is affected by the distribution of information in societies (e.g., see Chapter 7).

Sweden shifted to driving on the right-hand side of the road, for example, this "simple" change meant not only that cars and other vehicles had to be redesigned, but also that traffic signals and road signs throughout the country had to be relocated, traffic laws revised, and the deeply ingrained habits of millions of people altered. Similarly, as more women with young children have become employed in many societies, it has been necessary to create expensive new child care systems.

FORCES PROMOTING SOCIAL AND CULTURAL CHANGE

In spite of the strength of the forces promoting social and cultural continuity, some change occurs in every society. Even in the simplest and most tradition-minded societies, gradual changes occur in such things as the pronunciation of words, and legends are altered inadvertently as they are transmitted by word of mouth from one generation to the next. Social and cultural change is of two basic types. Sometimes it involves the addition of new elements to the existing system; sometimes it involves a new combination of existing elements.

Forms of Innovation

Social and cultural innovation takes various forms. Often it takes the form of borrowing from other societies, a process known as *diffusion*. This occurs more often than most of us realize. In fact, there is good reason to believe that most elements in most sociocultural systems have been borrowed from other societies.

Many innovations, of course, are independently produced within society. These are of several types. *Alterations* are the least important. These are innovations whose adaptive value is no greater than that of the things they replaced, as in new styles of dress or new musical fashions. Alterations are often unintentional, as in gradual changes in the pronunciation of words or inadvertent errors in the transmission of stories and legends.

Discoveries and inventions are much more important types of innovations. *Discoveries* provide the members of a society with new information that has adaptive value, while *inventions* are new combinations of already existing information.[1] Thus, Columbus was a discoverer, while Gottlieb Daimler, who built the first automobile, was an inventor. What Daimler did was to combine in a new way a number of things that were already part of the technological heritage of Western societies (e.g., the gasoline engine, the carriage body, running gears, the drive shaft, brakes). The "only" thing that was new about the automobile was the automobile itself. As we will see shortly, we must understand the nature of inventions if we are to understand why societies differ in their rates of innovation and change, and why these rates have changed over the centuries.

Causes of Innovation

Persius, a Roman poet, once wrote of hunger as "the teacher of the practical arts and the bestower of invention." Plato put the matter even more succinctly when he described necessity as the mother of invention.

One does not need to be a social scientist to recognize the stimulus that *hunger and other human needs* provide. Throughout the ages, men and women, prodded by unfulfilled needs and desires, have dreamed of ways of satisfying them. Most dreams have remained just dreams, but sometimes individuals have transformed them into realities and something new and useful has been added to the sum of human knowledge.

Because of culture, human needs and desires seem limitless. Each problem that is solved and each need that is satisfied seem to generate new needs and new desires as people come increasingly to take the satisfaction of their former needs and desires for granted. This is the basis of the so-called revolution of rising expectations that was such a striking feature of life in the twentieth century. Despite the fact that standards of living rose more in the last century than in any previous century, discontent and dissatisfaction have probably never been greater. Recognition of this important aspect of human nature has led some observers to note that while Plato was certainly correct in his observation that necessity is the mother of invention, it is also true that *invention is the mother of necessity*. In other words, the process of innovation and change seems to feed on itself so that once it is set in motion it tends to continue and even to accelerate.

While most of us have no trouble recognizing how unsatisfied needs influence the innovative process, we are likely to overlook the role of *chance*, or accident. Based on our experience as members of a modern industrial society, we tend to think of inventions and discoveries as products of planning and forethought. Yet from earliest times to the present, chance has been an important factor in the innovative process. Thus, in a primitive society, someone with a high fever may dream of a visit by a long-dead grandmother and awaken to find the fever abated. Nothing would be more natural under the circumstances than for the individual to assume that the "visit" was the cause of the cure and, in future illnesses, to pray to the grandmother for help. Should such prayers sometimes be followed by cures, the practice might well spread and eventually become a permanent feature of the society's culture.

Chance has also played an important role in *technological* innovation. Random strikes by lightning, for example, were almost certainly an important part of the

"If This Doesn't Result in One or Two First-Class Inventions, Nothing Will."

process by which humans first learned about fire and became aware of its uses and dangers. More recently, the great scientist Louis Pasteur discovered the principle and technique of immunization only after he accidentally injected some animals with a stale bacterial culture of chicken cholera. When the animals unexpectedly survived, it occurred to Pasteur that weakened bacteria might immunize against the very disease that the bacteria, at full strength, were responsible for. Similarly, a key problem in the development of modern photography was solved when Louis Daguerre put a bromide-coated silver plate into a cupboard where, unknown to him, there was an uncovered container of mercury. When he returned the following day, he found that a latent image had begun to develop and correctly surmised that fumes from the mercury were responsible.[2]

While these and many other examples illustrate the role that chance has played in the innovative process, it would be a mistake to suppose that chance *alone* is responsible in most of these cases. Conscious, purposive action is also involved. Not just anyone could have made the discoveries made by Pasteur and Daguerre. Each man was already working on a problem about which he was highly knowledgeable, and each was a member of a society that already possessed a substantial store of relevant information.

Many changes in human societies arise in response to *changes in either their biophysical or social environments.* Archaeologists have found, for example, that changes in climate in the past (e.g., global warming following the last Ice Age) led to changes in diet, in technology, and probably in other societal characteristics as well.[3] Similarly, changes in the social environment (e.g., increasing contacts among societies or the rise of expansionistic and militaristic neighbors) can create new problems for societies and lead to social and cultural innovations of various kinds.

Finally, one often overlooked cause of change has been *human fecundity.* Human populations, like other populations, are able to produce many more offspring than environmental resources can sustain. In other species, this merely leads to high death rates among the young, except in those rare instances when a genetic mutation or environmental change enables a population to utilize some new resource. Human societies, however, are able to respond to population pressures with cultural innovations. *Ideological* changes in customs or in laws, for example, may cause people to delay the age at which they marry or legitimate such practices as abortion. Alternatively, *technological* changes may provide the population with better methods of contraception or enable them to produce more food to keep a growing number of children alive and well.

Variations in the Rate of Innovation

When we compare different societies, we find that they produce innovations at greatly different rates. Some, such as American society, have had extremely high rates of innovation. In many others, the rate of innovation has been negligible.

There are a number of reasons for such variations, but one of the most important is *the amount of information a society already possesses.*[4] One of the most important forms of innovation—invention—is the act of combining already existing elements of culture. This means that a society's potential for invention is a mathematical function of the number of elements, or amount of information, already present. Table 3.1 illustrates this

Table 3.1 Number of Combinations Possible for Various Numbers of Units

No. of Units	Total Number of Combinations									Total
	2 at a Time	3 at a Time	4 at a Time	5 at a Time	6 at a Time	7 at a Time	8 at a Time	9 at a Time	10 at a Time	
2	1	0	0	0	0	0	0	0	0	1
3	3	1	0	0	0	0	0	0	0	4
4	6	4	1	0	0	0	0	0	0	11
5	10	10	5	1	0	0	0	0	0	26
6	15	20	15	6	1	0	0	0	0	57
7	21	35	35	21	7	1	0	0	0	120
8	28	56	70	56	28	8	1	0	0	247
9	36	84	126	126	84	36	9	1	0	502
10	45	120	210	252	210	120	45	10	1	1,013

principle. It shows how various numbers of units, or elements, of information can be combined. Although two units can be combined in only one way, three units can be combined in four ways, and four units in eleven ways. In other words, *the addition of each new unit more than doubles the number of possible combinations*. Thus, a mere five-fold increase in the number of units from two to ten leads to a *thousandfold* increase in the number of possible combinations, and when the number of units reaches twenty, over a million combinations are possible!

Of course, not all elements can be combined in a useful way. It is difficult, for example, to imagine a useful combination of the hammer and the saw. The number of potential combinations, therefore, is much greater than the number of fruitful ones. This does not affect the relationship between the number of units and the number of combinations, however.

One indication of the importance of the existing store of information is the frequency with which two or more individuals sharing the same body of information, but working entirely independently, have made the same invention or discovery at about the same time. Nearly a century ago, two sociologists compiled a list of 148 such inventions and discoveries, and there have been more since then.[5] Some interesting examples are listed below.

Sunspots: Fabricius, Galileo, Harriott, Scheiner, 1611
Logarithms: Napier, 1614; Buergi, 1620
Calculus: Newton, 1671; Leibnitz, 1676
Nitrogen: Rutherford, 1772; Scheele, 1773
Oxygen: Priestley, Scheele, 1774
Water as H_2O: Cavendish, Watt, 1781; Lavoisier, 1783
Telegraph: Henry, Morse, Steinheil, Wheatstone and Cooke, 1837
Photography: Daguerre and Niepce, Talbot, 1839
Natural selection: Darwin, Wallace, 1858
Telephone: Bell, Gray, 1876

A second cause of variations in the rate of innovation is population size.[6] Because every member of a society has somewhat different needs and abilities, the more people there are, the more new ideas and information are likely to be produced. Larger populations are also likely to generate problems, and, because they tend to be organizationally more complex, are likely to generate more varied patterns of social interaction, leading to more new customs, norms, laws, and other kinds of information required to control and regulate relationships. In the case of technological innovations, the more people who are aware of a problem and looking for a solution, the more quickly it will be found, other things being equal. Since societal populations vary so greatly in size, this is another factor of considerable importance.

Third, the stability and character of a society's environment can also affect the rate of change. There is greater pressure for social and cultural change in an unstable or changing environment than in a stable one. This is true with respect to both the biophysical and the social environment.[§] Any change in the latter that upsets the balance of power among societies (e.g., large-scale migrations, empire building, a new weapons system) is an especially potent force for further innovation and change.

The potential for development and change can also be severely limited by environmental factors. For example, desert and arctic societies have been unable either to develop the techniques of plant cultivation themselves or to adopt them from others. The absence of vital resources, such as an adequate water supply or accessible metallic ores, can also hinder innovation, as can endemic diseases and parasites that deplete people's energy.[7] Topography has played an important role in shaping patterns of intersocietal communication. Oceans, deserts, and mountain ranges have all prevented or seriously impeded the flow of information between societies, while navigable rivers and open plains have facilitated it. Considering the importance of diffusion, enormous differences in the rate of innovation can be explained by this factor alone.

A fourth factor influencing the rate of innovation in a society is *the extent of its contact with other societies*. The greater its interaction, the greater its opportunities to appropriate their innovations. In effect, contact enables one society to take advantage of the brainpower and cultural information of other societies through the process of *diffusion*. The importance of diffusion was beautifully illustrated some years ago by an anthropologist, Ralph Linton, who wrote:

> Our solid American citizen awakens in a bed built on a pattern which originated in the Near East but which was modified in Northern Europe before it was transmitted to America. He throws back covers made from cotton, domesticated in India, or linen, domesticated in the Near East, or wool from sheep, also domesticated in the Near East, or silk, the use of which was discovered in China. All of these materials have been spun and woven by processes invented in the Near East. He slips into his moccasins, invented by the Indians of the Eastern woodlands, and goes to the bathroom, whose fixtures are a mixture of European and American inventions, both of recent date. He takes off his pajamas, a garment invented in India, and

---

[§]It is worth repeating that change in the biophysical environment is often the result of previous human activities.

washes with soap invented by the ancient Gauls. He then shaves, a masochistic rite which seems to have been derived from either Sumer or ancient Egypt.

Linton followed this individual as he went through his daily round of activities using cultural elements most of which originated in other societies. As the day comes to a close and "our friend has finished eating," Linton wrote:

> He settles back to smoke, an American habit, consuming a plant domesticated in Brazil in either a pipe, derived from the Indians of Virginia, or a cigarette, derived from Mexico. If he is hardy enough he may even attempt a cigar, transmitted to us from the Antilles by way of Spain. While smoking he reads the news of the day, imprinted in characters invented by the ancient Semites upon a material invented in Germany. As he absorbs the accounts of foreign troubles, he will, if he is a good conservative citizen, thank a Hebrew deity in an Indo-European language that he is 100 per cent American.[8]

A fifth factor influencing the rate of innovation is *the systemic nature of sociocultural systems*. Because the various components of these systems are interdependent, a change in any one of them generates pressure for change in others. The invention of the automobile, for example, created the need for many new laws and for the construction of a vast new highway system. More important still, it led to the transformation of cities by encouraging the growth and spread of suburbs and the construction of thousands of new suburban shopping centers, which often have weakened or destroyed older business districts in the centers of cities. In addition, the automobile spawned a tremendous number of other changes in the business world, including the fast-food industry, motels, and the trucking industry, to name but three. The negative consequences of widespread automobile use have also spurred innovations.** For example, the noxious by-products of gasoline combustion have encouraged development of a number of pollution-control devices, and leaking underground gas tanks from abandoned gasoline stations have led to new (microbiological) methods of decontaminating underground water.

Not all cultural innovations generate the same degree of pressure for change in the rest of the system. Some create very little pressure for further change, while others generate tremendous pressure. A new style of painting, for example, may have no impact on society outside a small circle of artists and critics. A new political movement, on the other hand, can have far-reaching consequences, depending on the number of people who join it and the seriousness with which they take it. But one kind of innovation that never fails to have far-reaching consequences is change in a society's *basic subsistence technology*. For reasons that will become clear shortly, changes in subsistence technology have ramifications that are felt in almost every other area of life.

Sixth, the rate of innovation is greatly influenced by *"fundamental" innovations*. Not all discoveries and inventions are of equal importance: a few pave the way for thousands more, while the majority have little effect.[10] The invention of the plow and the steam engine and the discovery of the principles of plant cultivation, animal

---

**This is not unusual. In fact, many technological innovations are the direct result of problems caused by the adoption of earlier technological innovations (e.g., see Chapter 9).[9]

domestication, and metallurgy were all fundamental innovations. So, too, were the inventions of writing and money.

Sometimes a fundamental innovation will cause the rate of innovation to rise because it involves a principle that can be applied, with minimum effort and imagination, in hundreds, even thousands, of different areas. This was true, for example, of the steam engine, metallurgy, printing, and the silicon chip. Sometimes, however, an invention or discovery is considered "fundamental" because it so drastically alters the conditions of human life that hundreds or thousands of other changes become either possible or necessary. This was the case with the principle of plant cultivation, which, as we shall see in a later chapter, led to revolutionary changes in every area of human life.

A seventh factor influencing the rate of innovation is *the society's attitude toward innovation*. In many societies there has been such a powerful ideological commitment to tradition that innovation of any kind has been discouraged.[11] In contrast, most modern societies have a strongly positive attitude toward innovation and change.

Though the problem has not been studied as carefully as it deserves, a society's attitude toward innovation seems to be greatly influenced by its prior experience. A society that has benefited from change in the past is usually more receptive to innovation than a society that has not. Attitudes toward innovation also vary according to the nature of the dominant ideology in a society. Some ideologies generate a very conservative outlook and oppose change; Confucianism is an example of such an ideology. Capitalism, in contrast, has been much more supportive of innovation and change.

Before we leave the subject of the rate of innovation, it is important to note a tendency that is especially evident where technological innovation is concerned: it tends to occur at *an accelerating pace*. Figure 3.1 illustrates this speedup for human societies

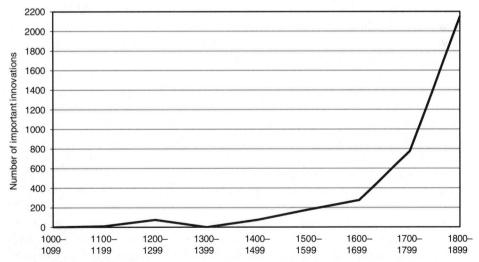

Figure 3.1. The Number of Important Technological Innovations by Century, A.D. 1000 to A.D. 1900. Technological Innovation Tends to Occur at an Accelerating Rate, Because Each New Element Increases the Probability of Acquiring More. See also Table 5.1, page 94.
Source: Adapted from Ludwig Darmstaedter and Rene DuBois-Reymond, *4000 Jahre Pionier-Arbeit in den Exakten Wissenschaften* (Berlin: Stargardt, 1904).

as a whole during the period from A.D. 1000 to A.D. 1900. The majority of societies have never experienced such an acceleration. But those that have experienced it have influenced human history out of all proportion to their numbers.

The explanation of the acceleration is that *each new bit of useful technological information acquired by a society increases the probability it will acquire still more.* This is partly a function of the potential of technological elements for being recombined in new ways. But more than that, technological advance tends to reinforce several of the other basic factors that influence the rate of innovation. Throughout history, for example, advances in a society's subsistence technology, themselves engendered by increasing population and population density, have led to further growth in population size. This growth in population, in turn, often elicited further innovations. Similarly, technological advance and population growth have led to increased intersocietal contact, resulting in greater diffusion and thus enhancing the rate of technological innovation.

In short, technological innovation and advance tend to make *further* innovation and advance increasingly likely. It is hardly surprising, therefore, that societies in which this happens come to be increasingly different from societies in which it does not.

FORCES OF SELECTION
Intrasocietal Selection

Selection operates at two levels in sociocultural evolution: *within* societies and *among* them. *Intrasocietal selection* occurs when members of a society choose one way of doing things rather than another. For instance, in the distant prehistoric past, our ancestors began to cultivate plants and domesticate animals and gradually abandoned their earlier practices of foraging for wild fruits and vegetables and hunting wild animals. Although such choices are generally based on what appear at the time to be rational considerations, they are always made on the basis of limited and imperfect knowledge, and therefore sometimes produce disastrous and unintended consequences in the future. This was certainly the case when wealthy Romans chose to use lead, instead of pottery, for their cooking utensils, dishes, and water piping, and when Europeans adopted the Native American practice of smoking tobacco.

Because of social and cultural innovations, societies are often faced with choices between competing alternatives. Earlier in this century, for example, the members of many societies were confronted with a choice between the horse and carriage and the new "horseless carriage." Gradually, the horseless carriage, or automobile, as it came to be known, replaced the older means of transportation.

The process of selection is like the process of innovation in that it too can be rational and deliberate, as in the adoption of the automobile and the rejection of the horse and buggy. But, again, as in the process of innovation, chance, limited information about long-term consequences, and irrational factors may play a part.

Although it is, of course, the members who make the choices which shape and alter their society, everyone does not have an equal voice. "Who decides" depends on the kind of decision involved and the nature of the power structure involved. For example, members of an industrial society may choose, at one level, which songs become hits, but, despite some notable exceptions, their range of choices has already been substantially narrowed by the people who control the music industry. Similarly, all the members of a democratic society may have equal opportunities to cast their votes

Intrasocietal Selection Often Occurs Imperceptibly, as One Element of Technology Gradually Replaces Another. In the Early Decades of the Previous Century, the Horseless Carriage Gradually Replaced the Horse-Drawn Carriage in Industrial Societies.

for public officials, but the choice among candidates has already been substantially narrowed by elites in the mass media and the political system.

This raises the question of whether a society's culture and social organization can be considered optimally adaptive. While much of it *is* adaptive for the society as a whole (i.e., it helps satisfy basic needs of the system or its members), many elements have been selected by and for the benefit of special segments of the society and are "adaptive" only, or largely, for them. Thus, the process of selection may result in the retention of many elements that are *nonadaptive* or even *maladaptive* for the society as a whole. Drug pushers and users select elements which they find rewarding, but which create serious problems for society as a whole (e.g., crime and illness). Similarly, others make decisions to use maladaptive or harmful products, such as sugar-coated cereals, tobacco, and alcohol.

Intersocietal Selection
Intersocietal selection occurs when a society ceases to exist as an autonomous entity. This can be the result of conquest or absorption by a more powerful society, or disintegration as a result of a natural disaster, environmental change, food crisis, or epidemic

Table 3.2 The Great Paradox Illustrated: While the Majority of Societies Have Remained Unchanged Throughout Their Existence, the World System of Societies Has Changed Tremendously

Society	Population Size			
	Time 1	Time 2	Time 3	Time 4
A	100	1,000	2,000	5,000
B	100	500	1,000	2,500
C	100	100	100	100
D	100	100	100	100
E	100	100	100	*
F	100	100	100	*
G	100	100	*	*
H	100	100	*	*
I	100	*	*	*
J	100	*	*	*
World system total	1,000	2,100	3,400	7,700

*This society no longer exists.

disease. Throughout human experience, but especially over the past 10,000 years, societal extinction has been the result of contact and conflict among societies, and warfare and disease, either singly or in concert, have played the most important role.[12] As a result, larger, more technologically advanced and militarily powerful, and more disease-experienced societies have prevailed, and they have come to constitute an ever larger proportion of the world system of societies.

The key to the major changes that have occurred in the world system of societies in the last 10,000 years is the process of intersocietal selection that has drastically reduced the number of societies.[13] Were it not for this process, in which the units that survive (or become extinct) are entire societies, human life would not have changed nearly as much as it has.

The process of intersocietal selection presupposes the existence of differences among societies. Such differences were inevitable once the human population began to spread out geographically and occupy new and different kinds of environments. Chance also contributed to the process of societal differentiation, so that even when two societies confronted similar environmental challenges, they did not respond in exactly the same way. Differences in vocabulary provide a good example of this: even when all societies were confronted with identical experiences, such as birth and death, or the differences between males and females, they created different symbols to represent them. More important still, different beliefs developed to explain and interpret these experiences, and varied norms evolved to guide behavioral responses.

Not all the differences that have developed among societies have been equally important from the standpoint of intersocietal selection. Differences that influenced societal growth and development have been especially important, because *societies that have grown in size and developed in complexity and military power have been much more likely to survive and transmit their cultures and institutional patterns than*

The Great Paradox

Despite the tremendous changes that have occurred in human life during the last 10,000 years, the majority of societies changed very little during their entire existence. In other words, contrary to what we might infer from the changes that have occurred in the world system of societies—or from our own experience—rapid social and cultural change has been the exception rather than the rule until recently. In most societies, life changed very little from one generation to the next or even from one century to the next.

When first considered, this paradox seems to be a contradiction, but actually it is not.* A system can change greatly even if most of its parts do not change—if the parts that fail to change are simply eliminated from the system.

This is exactly what has happened in the world system of societies. The great majority of individual societies changed very little during the course of their existence, but almost none of those societies survived into the present century. Almost all the societies that *have* survived have been that small minority that have changed, and changed greatly.

Table 3.2 provides a simplified illustration of what has happened in the last 10,000 years. Of the ten hypothetical societies in the illustration, only two changed from Time 1 to Time 4. During the course of

their existence, the other eight did not change at all in terms of size. Nevertheless, as the bottom line of the table shows, the size of this hypothetical world system steadily increased, and by Time 4 it was almost eight times larger than it had been in Time 1.

As this illustration suggests, *a process of selection has been at work in the world system of societies, favoring larger, more powerful societies at the expense of smaller, less powerful ones.* As we will see later in this chapter and elsewhere, this process has favored those societies that have been most successful in accumulating useful information relevant to subsistence activities. When societies have come into conflict with one another over territory and other vital resources, those that have been technologically more advanced have usually prevailed.[†] Thus, even though the vast majority of individual societies have resisted social and cultural change, the world system of societies has been dramatically transformed.

It is obvious, therefore, that we have to consider both change and continuity (i.e., the absence of change) if we are to understand human societies. Both have been profoundly important in the evolution not only of the world system of societies but of individual societies as well.

---

*It should be noted that this is the nature of a paradox; it is an *apparent* or *seeming* contradiction, rather than an actual one.

[†]There have been exceptions, of course, as when more-advanced societies have waged wars far from home and when their vital interests were not involved. This happened in the American war in Vietnam, for example.

---

societies that have preserved traditional social and cultural patterns and minimized innovation (see Figure 3.2).

The reasons for this are obvious. To survive, societies must be able to defend their populations and territories against a variety of threats. These include the ravages of epidemics, natural disasters of other kinds, and, above all, threats from other societies. One only need consider the history of the United States, Canada, Australia, Brazil, or Russia to see what happens to smaller and less developed indigenous societies (i.e., the American Indians, the Australian aborigines, and various tribal groups in Siberia) when they compete for territory with larger and more technologically developed societies. Larger societies have greater manpower and can more easily absorb military casualties. In addition, their more advanced technology has military applications, so that their soldiers have more deadly weapons, better logistical support, and greater

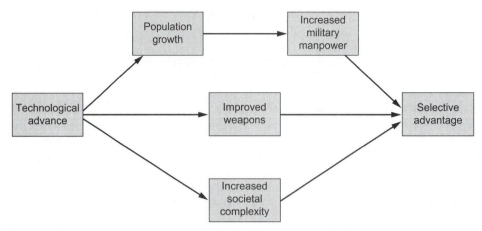

Figure 3.2. Model of the Effects of Technological Advance on the Process of Intersocietal Selection.

mobility. Finally, their more complex patterns of social organization can easily be adapted to military needs and this, too, provides an important competitive advantage. Thus, while it would be a mistake to suppose that more developed societies always prevail over their less developed rivals, the odds are strongly in their favor.

Intersocietal selection is not always a violent process. Sometimes societies collapse simply because of insufficient support from their members. This is especially likely to occur when a less developed society comes into contact with one that is much more highly developed.[††] Many members of the less developed society become impressed with the wealth and power of the more advanced society and either migrate to it or begin to adopt its customs. If these tendencies become widespread, the institutional fabric of the less developed society begins to fray and a process of societal disintegration begins. There are a number of well-documented cases of this in India, where tribes in the hill country have simply disintegrated and their former members have been absorbed into Indian society.[14]

SOCIETAL GROWTH AND DEVELOPMENT

Most societies change little during the course of their existence. Occasionally, however, significant changes have occurred. Some societies have grown substantially. Some have shifted from a nomadic way of life to permanent settlements in villages, and some have shifted from a predominantly rural mode of life to a predominantly urban one. Such changes have usually been accompanied by important changes in social organization—substantial increases in organizational complexity, marked increases in the division of labor, and significant increases in social inequality. In short, some societies have experienced a process of substantial growth and development while most have not.

How can we explain such a profound difference in the experience of societies?

[††]This can also be the result of the spread of an epidemic disease which breaks down and disrupts the operation of the other society (e.g., the Aztecs after contact with the Spanish).

We have already considered the basic factors that cause innovation in a society and those that affect the rate of innovation. Now we need to look at cultural innovation from a somewhat different angle and ask the further question, Do all kinds of new information have the same potential for societal growth and development, or do certain kinds of innovations have a greater potential than others?

Subsistence Technology's Role in Sociocultural Evolution

Technology, as we have seen, is that part of a society's store of cultural information that enables its members to convert the resources available in their environment into the material products they need or desire—food, clothing, shelter, and all the rest. But information alone is not enough: *Energy* is also needed if natural resources are to be converted into things that humans need.[15] In fact, without some source of energy, information is useless, since even the least physically demanding of activities, such as thinking, require energy.

Subsistence technology is the term used to refer to those elements of a society's store of information that enable it to obtain the energy its members require, and it is no exaggeration to say that subsistence technology provides the key to understanding societal growth and development. Specifically, *advances in subsistence technology are a necessary precondition for any significant increase in either the size or the complexity of any society.*

Societies that depend on hunting and gathering as their chief means of subsistence cannot sustain populations nearly as large as those that depend on farming; and those that depend on slash-and-burn horticulture, a more primitive method of farming, cannot sustain populations as large as those that depend on plow agriculture. These differences in the limits set on the size of a society by its subsistence technology are matched by differences in the limits set on other aspects of societal development, such as the extent of the division of labor, the degree of social inequality, the size and complexity of communities, the wealth of the society and its standard of living, and the power of the society over its biophysical environment and over other societies. In short, *technology defines the limits of what is possible for a society.*[16]

Within the range of options made possible by its technology, a society's choices are often influenced by the relative economic costs of the various alternatives. China's technology, for example, makes the production of automobiles and the construction of a highway system possible, but until recently its decision makers opted instead for less costly solutions to their society's transportation needs: mass public transport and private bicycles. In a world in which resources are never sufficient to meet all the demands for goods and services, differences in cost can never be ignored by societies, and they are compelled to adopt one of the less expensive solutions much of the time. Thus, in addition to determining the limits of the possible for a society, *technology also affects the choices that are made by influencing the costs of various alternatives.*

Advances in a society's subsistence technology are also important because *they stimulate advances in other kinds of technology.* For example, advances in subsistence technology tend to be accompanied or followed by advances in other productive technologies and in the technologies of transportation, communication, and defense, all of which contribute to societal growth and development (see Figure 3.3).

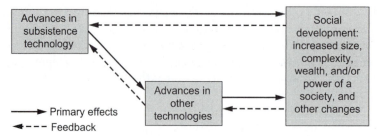

Figure 3.3. Model of the Effects of Advances in Subsistence Technology on Other Technologies and on Societal Development.

Technology's critical role in societal growth and development is not surprising when we consider that a society's tools and machines are, in effect, the functional equivalent of improvements in the basic organs with which its members are endowed—eyes, ears, voice box, arms, legs, brain, nervous system, and the rest. Microscopes, telescopes, and television all extend the range of our vision, just as telephones and radios extend the range of our hearing, and bicycles, automobiles, and airplanes increase our mobility. Where technological advances have occurred, they have enabled the members of societies to act as if they had acquired a new and improved genetic heritage—improved sight, more acute hearing, new powers of locomotion, and so forth. Thus, technological advances—especially advances in subsistence technology—are functionally equivalent to the important kinds of changes that occur in the course of biological evolution.

One important feature of the process of societal development that should not be overlooked is indicated by the feedback loops shown in Figure 3.3. Feedback is a special kind of causal relationship. It is one in which a part of the effect produced by the initial cause or event reverts back to, and alters, its source. For example, illness may cause a loss of appetite, and the resulting failure to eat may then aggravate the illness. Advances in subsistence technology stimulate advances in other technologies and lead to growth in the size and complexity of a society. But these developments, once they have occurred, usually increase the probability of further advances in subsistence technology.[‡‡] Population growth, for example, increases the number of potential innovators and, although few individuals ever make an invention or discovery of practical value, the greater the number of potential innovators in a society, the greater tends to be the rate at which innovations occur. Thus, as this example suggests, *once the process of societal development is set in motion, it can become self-sustaining*. While this is not inevitable, the probabilities of continued development clearly increase.

Societal growth and development, while advantageous to societies in many ways, are not unmixed blessings. They create new problems and these often lead to changes that many members of society would prefer not to make—changes in beliefs and values, changes in patterns of social organization, changes in institutional arrangements. Among preliterate societies, for example, technological advance often leads to population growth, and population growth necessitates changes in social organization. Such

---

[‡‡]There are exceptions, as we will see in Chapter 7.

societies must choose either to split up into smaller independent groups in order to preserve their traditional kin-based system of governance or to remain united but adopt a more authoritarian political system that is dominated by a small elite minority. Not surprisingly, they will generally continue to "fission" into smaller groups until they are prevented from doing so.[17]

Ideology's Role in Sociocultural Evolution

Whenever its technology presents a society with a range of options, its beliefs and values—the core elements of ideology—always come into play. These often have little or no effect on societal growth and development, as when people choose one style of clothing in preference to another, one form of entertainment rather than another, or even one form of marriage over another. Sometimes, however, ideologies do have a substantial effect, as when they dispose people to accept and even welcome change or, conversely, to view it negatively.[18] Western capitalism, for example, has been far more supportive of new ideas and innovations of many kinds than was Soviet Marxism.

When the beliefs and values involved are felt to be sufficiently important, a society may reject the most economic solution to its needs in favor of a solution that is ideologically preferable. The United States, for example, has chosen to make private automobiles and an extensive interstate highway system a major part of its solution to its transportation needs, reflecting not only the influence of powerful trucking, petroleum, concrete, and automotive lobbies, but also the individualism of its members and their desire for ease and freedom of movement as well.

Ideologically based decisions that affect a society's basic institutions may have extremely grave consequences. In Eastern Europe, for example, countless decisions by communist leaders over the years eventually led to a political and economic crisis of such proportions that the members of these societies rose up in mass revolt. And in a number of third world societies, deeply ingrained beliefs about the value of large families continue to promote high rates of population growth that make it virtually impossible for the living conditions of all but a small minority of the people to improve.

Since one of the important consequences of technological advance is that it increases the range of options available to societies and their members, such advance leads to greater scope for the exercise of beliefs and values. Advanced societies today have far more choices available to them than societies of the past, and they are much freer to apply diverse ideologies in making their decisions. This does not guarantee happy results, of course, as the bitter experiences of Nazi Germany and the Soviet Union remind us.

A MODEL OF THE EVOLUTION
OF THE WORLD SYSTEM OF SOCIETIES

We can now construct a model of the evolutionary process that explains the basic trends in the world system of societies in recent millennia. Numerous cultural traits—occasionally augmented by discoveries, diffusion from other societies, and inventions—pass through the filter of intrasocietal selection. Items that people continue to use and pass on are preserved; those that are abandoned or superseded become extinct. In addition, whole societies and their streams of cultural traits pass through a filter of intersocietal

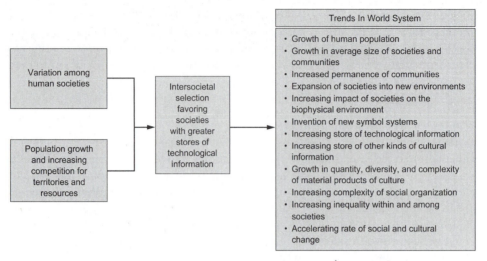

Figure 3.4. Model of the Causes of the Evolution of the World System of Societies.

selection. Societies that effectively cope with their biophysical and sociocultural environments continue to exist as autonomous systems, those that don't either break up or are incorporated into other systems. Although societies with large effective bodies of cultural information are more likely to survive and pass on their traits, as the earlier citation from the anthropologist Ralph Linton showed, diffusion allows much of the cultural information of systems that fail to survive to be preserved and passed on within the world system of societies.

Because technologically advanced societies have had the advantage in this process of intersocietal selection, *their characteristics have increasingly come to be the characteristics of the world system as a whole* (see Figure 3.4). Thus, because technologically advanced societies tend to be larger than other societies, the average size of societies has been increasing for the last 10,000 years. Similarly, because technologically advanced societies are structurally more complex than other societies, the trend in the world system has been in the direction of increasingly complex societies. The same logic applies to all the trends shown in Figure 3.4.

There is, of course, nothing inevitable or unalterable about these trends. A number of factors could disrupt them. For example, a deadly new disease could sweep through human societies and, in a short period of time, reverse many of the trends of the last 10,000 years. The black plague of the fourteenth century had this effect in a number of societies, and it is not inconceivable that something comparable could happen on a global scale.[§§] An unpredictable catastrophe involving the biophysical environment could also reverse the trends of history, as could a war fought with modern military

---

[§§]Although the plague caused immeasurable human misery, the dramatic depopulation of Europe produced by its cyclical recurrences may actually have fostered economic change and technological innovation. For instance, since the plague killed people but did not destroy property, it increased *per capita* wealth among the elite. It also greatly reduced population pressure on the land and other resources, increased the bargaining power and earnings of surviving peasants, and helped spur a number of labor-saving innovations, such as firearms.[19]

technology. Both nuclear and biochemical warfare have the potential for producing a global catastrophe, and there is no technological antidote for either. Ecological-evolutionary theory clearly provides no grounds for complacency regarding the future.

Although we cannot predict the future, we can say that, so far, the process of intersocietal selection has favored technologically advanced societies. Like the old game of musical chairs, it has eliminated first one, then another, of the less developed societies. The result is a world system that, with the passage of time, increasingly consists of what were once the exceptions—innovative and developing societies.

EXCURSUS: A COMPARISON OF BIOLOGICAL AND SOCIOCULTURAL EVOLUTION

In recent decades, our understanding of biological evolution and sociocultural evolution has advanced dramatically. It is now clear for the first time that *both types of evolution are based on records of experience that are preserved and transmitted from generation to generation in the form of coded systems of information.* In the case of biological evolution, the record of experience is preserved and transmitted by means of the genetic code. In sociocultural evolution, the record is preserved and transmitted by means of symbol systems. Both the genetic "alphabet" and symbol systems provide populations with the means of acquiring, storing, transmitting, and using enormous amounts of information on which their welfare and, ultimately, their survival depend. Thus, *symbol systems are functional equivalents of the genetic alphabet.*

It is hardly surprising, therefore, that there is a fundamental similarity in the way the two evolutionary processes operate. Both processes involve random or "blind" variation and "selective retention."[20]

Despite these similarities, there are a number of important differences in the way the two systems of evolution operate. Some of these are of special significance for students of human societies, such as the difference that results from the way information is transferred and spread in the two evolutions. The only way genetic information can be transmitted is through the process of reproduction. Because different species cannot interbreed, they cannot share genetic information with one another.*** Thus, biological evolution is characterized by continued differentiation and diversification, a process much like the branching of a tree or shrub. Cultural information, by contrast, is easily exchanged between the members of different societies. Not only can human societies exchange information, but two or more can merge into a single system—the equivalent, were it possible, of the merging of separate species in biological evolution. Thus, sociocultural evolution is likely to eventuate in even fewer and less dissimilar societies than exist today.

This is related to a second important difference. In biological evolution, the emergence of more complex species of plants and animals has not had the effect of eliminating, or reducing the number of, simpler species. One-celled organisms thrive alongside, and indeed *inside,* complex multicellular organisms. In sociocultural evolution, on the other hand, the emergence of new and more complex kinds of societies has usually led

---

***Closely related species do occasionally interbreed, as when lions and tigers produce "ligers" or "tiglons." These hybrids are usually sterile, however, at least in the animal kingdom, and therefore their importance in the process of biological evolution has been minimal.

to the extinction of older, simpler ones, as illustrated by the destruction of thousands of small American Indian societies since 1492. Thus, while biological evolution produces the pattern of a richly branched shrub, sociocultural evolution approximates the pattern of a pine tree that gradually loses its lower branches as new, higher branches appear and overshadow them.

A third important difference involves a population's ability to incorporate into heritable form the useful information its members have acquired through the process of individual *learning*. In sociocultural systems, this is easily done; it is, as we have seen, the basis of their evolution. But it has no counterpart in biological evolution. Prior to Darwin, biologists believed that something analogous *did* occur in the biotic world. Jean-Baptiste Lamarck, Darwin's most famous predecessor, argued that if an organism continually repeated a certain action this would not only produce structural change in the organism, but the change would also be inherited by its offspring.[21] It has long since become clear that biological evolution does not work that way: giraffes do not have long necks because their ancestors stretched day after day to reach high leaves, but because short necks were a liability in their ancestors' environment; animals with the genes for short necks were unable to survive and reproduce. In the cultural world, however, a kind of Lamarckian evolution *does* occur. Just about anything a population learns and considers worth preserving can be incorporated into its cultural heritage.

Springing from the easy flow of cultural information among societies and the ease with which it is incorporated into heritable form is yet another way in which sociocultural evolution differs from biological: it has given rise to much higher rates of change in our species. An evolution whose mechanism is genetic change is necessarily a slow process in a species that has a long generation span and relatively few offspring. But cultural information, relative to genetic, can be rapidly acquired, exchanged, recombined, and accumulated, with the result that substantial alterations in a society's culture may occur within a single generation. Moreover, sociocultural evolution does not require that every society go through step-by-step sequential stages of development, as in biological evolution. Rather, a society may compress or even skip stages.[22] In developing societies today, for example, some nations (e.g., Afghanistan) have gone directly to satellite and cell phones, bypassing the long and expensive process of physically wiring telephones that was part of the evolutionary experience of those societies in which the newer methods of communication were first developed.[23]

Finally, sociocultural evolution may have a greater potential than biological evolution for being brought under rational human control. So far, however, this process has hardly begun. One of humanity's most urgent tasks in the years ahead is to increase our understanding of the dynamics of sociocultural evolution so that we can find ways to control its direction and make it more responsive to human needs and ideals.

CHAPTER 4

Types of Human Societies

Outline
Classifying Human Societies
Societal Types through History
Differences among Types of Societies
Societal Types: What They Are and What They Are Not

The basic aim of science, as we have seen, is to explain how the world works. To this end, scientific research—whether it is focused on butterflies, galaxies, or human societies—looks for patterns and regularities in the world around us. This requires countless observations designed to reveal how things resemble one another, how they differ, and why—*a process of systematic comparison.*

CLASSIFYING HUMAN SOCIETIES

Over the years this process of comparison has given rise to many systems of classification in the various sciences. The periodic table in chemistry and the Linnaean taxonomy and its successors in biology are two of the more familiar. Such systems help us make sense of the wealth of data generated by research and serve as guides to scientists, suggesting new comparisons for study and new lines of research. But most important of all, these systems of classification have stimulated the development of theories that explain the patterns and regularities that have been discovered.

The system of classification that we will use in studying human societies is based on the *subsistence technologies* they employ. The origin of this system, like the origin of ecological-evolutionary theory itself, lies in the work of seventeenth- and eighteenth-century European scholars who responded to the discovery of less developed societies in the New World, Africa, and Asia by rethinking age-old questions about human origins and history. This led some of them to compare societies and try to classify them. A number of them even recognized the crucial importance of subsistence technology and based their systems of classification on it.[1]

The system of classification used in this volume grows out of that early work. It divides human societies into nine basic categories, with individual societies classified on the basis of their *primary mode of subsistence:*[2]

Hunting and gathering societies
Simple horticultural societies

Advanced horticultural societies
Simple agrarian societies
Advanced agrarian societies
Industrial societies
Fishing societies
Maritime societies
Herding societies

A system of classification is most useful when it is simple, reliable, and objective,* so that the classification of cases is as unambiguous as possible. A society is classified as a hunting and gathering society only if the hunting of wild animals and foraging for uncultivated plant foods are its *primary* means of subsistence. Horticultural societies are societies that cultivate plants but do not have plows.[3] Advanced horticultural societies use metal tools and weapons, while simple horticultural societies have only wood and stone ones. Agrarian societies also cultivate plants but in addition have and use plows. Advanced agrarian societies use iron tools and weapons, while simple agrarian societies use only copper and bronze, which are softer and less plentiful metals (see Table 4.1).

Industrial societies are the newest type of society and technologically the most advanced. The distinguishing feature of these societies is their heavy dependence on machine technology and on the *inanimate* sources of energy—coal, petroleum, natural gas, and nuclear power—that drive the various machines. Because of their highly advanced technology, industrial societies are the most powerful and productive societies the world has ever seen (see Figure 4.1).

Over the course of history, the majority of people have lived in one or another of the six kinds of societies described above. Some, however, have lived in societies that do not fall neatly into any of these categories. For example, many today in Asia, Africa, and Latin America live in what are commonly referred to as "less developed" or "developing" societies. These are, in effect, *hybrid* societies, combining elements of modern industrial technology with traditional horticultural or agrarian technology.

Table 4.1 Criteria for Classifying Primary Types of Human Societies*

Type of Society	Plant Cultivation*	Metallurgy*	Plow	Iron*	Inanimate Energy
Hunting and gathering	−	−	−	−	−
Simple horticultural	+	−	−	−	−
Advanced horticultural	+	+	−	−	−
Simple agrarian	+	+	+	−	−
Advanced agrarian	+	+	+	+	−
Industrial	+	+	+	+	+

*The symbol + means that the trait is widespread in the type of society indicated; the symbol − means it is not.

---

*Objective and reliable in the sense that different observers, using the classification criteria, would place cases in the same categories.

Members of a Twentieth-Century Society of Hunters and Gatherers: Australian Aborigines Singing Sacred Songs in Preparation for an Important Ritual Ceremony.

Finally, in addition to all the others, there are three kinds of societies that have evolved in response to special or unusual environmental conditions. In semiarid regions, for example, as in the Middle East and North Africa, farming has not been possible, and, in order to survive, people have been forced to rely on the herding of livestock (sheep, goats, camels, etc.) as their basic means of subsistence. Elsewhere, peoples who have lived along the shores of rivers, lakes, or oceans have often found it advantageous to adopt fishing or overseas trade and commerce as their principal means of subsistence.

As Figure 4.1 indicates, the various societal types differ from one another, not merely in terms of the kind of subsistence technology they employ but also in their overall level of technological development: agrarian and maritime societies, for example, are technologically on about the same level of development, and both are far more advanced technologically than hunting and gathering societies.

In the chapters that follow, we will examine each of the major types of societies. In Chapters 5 through 7, we examine in turn hunting and gathering, horticultural, and agrarian societies. In Chapter 8, we consider more briefly the environmentally specialized types of societies. In Chapters 9 through 13, we examine in considerable detail modern industrial societies; and, finally, in Chapter 14, we examine two kinds of hybrid societies, industrializing horticultural societies and industrializing agrarian societies.

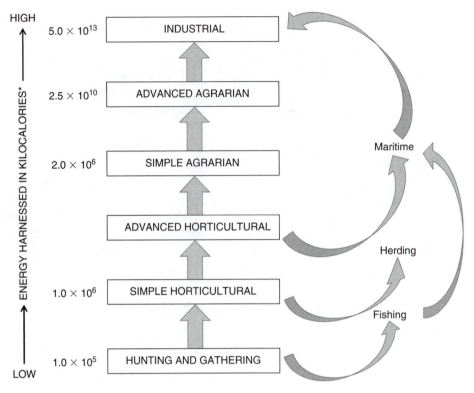

*Energy estimates from Marvin Harris, *Cultural Materialism* (New York: Random House, 1979), p. 67

Figure 4.1. Levels of Technological Development and Patterns of Evolution.
Source: See Appendix, pp. 417–418.

SOCIETAL TYPES THROUGH HISTORY

Throughout most of human history, everyone lived in hunting and gathering societies. This period of relative social and cultural uniformity ended only within the last 10,000 to 12,000 years.

Fishing societies were the first new type of society to emerge (see Figure 4.2). Though the practice of fishing seems to have begun thousands of years earlier, fish-hooks, nets, traps, boats, and paddles had to be invented before any society could make the shift from hunting and gathering to fishing as its *primary* means of subsistence.[4]

Simple horticultural societies probably came next; they first appeared in the Middle East between 10,000 B.C. and 8000 B.C. and were well established 10,000 years ago.[5] Though people began to use copper within the next 1,500 years,[6] it was not until nearly 4000 B.C. that metal tools and weapons became common enough in any of these societies to permit us to call them *advanced* horticultural.[7]

The plow was invented late in the fourth millennium, and this innovation also occurred in the Middle East.[8] By 3000 B.C. it was used widely enough by societies in Mesopotamia and Egypt to justify labeling them simple agrarian.

Iron was discovered early in the second millennium B.C. but, like copper, did not become the dominant material in tools and weapons for a long time.[9] Thus, the

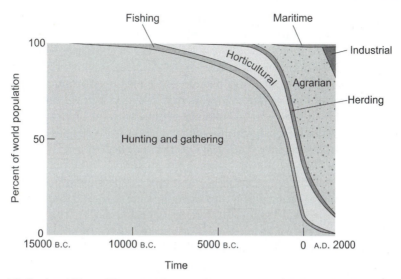

Figure 4.2. Societal Types Through History: Changes in Size Reflect the Growth or Decline in Numbers of Each of the Societal Types.

first advanced agrarian societies did not appear until the early years of the first millennium B.C.

The origin of herding societies remains something of a mystery. Evidence of the domestication of sheep and goats dates from about 9000 B.C., but evidence from the earliest site suggests a hybrid technology.[†10] While we cannot say for certain when any society first came to depend on herding as its chief means of subsistence, it was probably sometime after horticultural societies appeared.

Minoans on the island of Crete, around 2000 B.C., were apparently the first people to rely on overseas commerce as their basic means of subsistence.[12] Maritime societies also flourished in Europe during the Middle Ages.

The last major societal type is industrial. The inventions that mark the beginning of the modern technological revolution occurred in the eighteenth century. But it was not until early in the nineteenth that Britain, which pioneered industrialization, reached the point where it could be classified as a truly industrial society. Since then, nearly thirty others have followed Britain's lead.

Historical Eras

As Figure 4.2 makes clear, the types of human societies in the world system have changed greatly in the last 10,000 to 12,000 years. There was a time when every society was at the hunting and gathering level of development; we have recently had everything from hunting and gathering to industrial societies.

To understand a given society, past or present, it is not enough to know what type of society it is or was. It is equally important to know *when* it existed, since this tells us

---

[†]Earlier—sometime between 22,000 and 10,000 B.C.—the dog achieved the distinction of being the first animal domesticated by humans.[11]

a great deal about its *social* environment. For example, the situation of hunting and gathering societies in the last hundred years has been far more precarious than it was 10,000 years ago. Such groups have found themselves in the unenviable position of interacting with far more advanced and far more powerful societies. No matter where hunting and gathering societies have been located, members of industrial societies have penetrated, using vast resources in ways that have transformed the conditions of life for less advanced groups. This has often been done with the best of intentions—as in the establishment of medical, educational, or religious missions—but good intentions have made little difference. The ultimate effect has been to transform and eventually destroy the social and cultural systems of technologically primitive peoples.

In studying a society, therefore, it is important to specify the historical era involved. The various eras are named according to the type of society that was politically and militarily dominant at the time. Thus, the long period in which all human societies were hunting and gathering societies is designated as the hunting and gathering era, while the period in which we live today is the industrial era.

From the standpoint of ecological-evolutionary theory, the four major eras in human history have been:[‡]

1. The hunting and gathering era: from human beginnings ~ 200,000 B.C. to about 8000 B.C.
2. The horticultural era: from about 8000 B.C. to about 3000 B.C. (advanced horticultural from about 4000 B.C. to 3000 B.C.)
3. The agrarian era: from about 3000 B.C. to about A.D. 1800 (advanced agrarian from about 1000 B.C. to about A.D. 1800)
4. The industrial era: from about A.D. 1800 to the present.

The best way to understand what sociocultural evolution has meant is to examine in sequence the four types of societies whose dominance in successive eras has defined the upper limits of technological advance. In them we can trace all the basic trends in population, culture, the material products of culture, social organization, and social institutions.

The reason for these trends *is that the rise of technologically more advanced societies contributed directly to the decline of those less advanced.* For when horticultural societies appeared, the chances for survival of neighboring hunting and gathering societies were substantially reduced unless they too adopted the new technology. The same was true for both hunting and gathering and horticultural societies after agrarian societies appeared. The less advanced societies lacked both the numbers and the weapons needed to defend themselves against the more advanced societies that coveted their territories and other resources. Those that managed to survive did so only in remote and isolated areas protected by oceans or other geographical barriers, or in territories judged undesirable by members of the more advanced societies (e.g., deserts, tropical rain forests, mountainous areas). In recent times, the pattern of military conquest and expansion has greatly declined, but the pattern of cultural

---

[‡]These dates are for the world as a whole. In many parts of the world, the horticultural and agrarian eras began later. For example, the agrarian era did not begin in the New World until the sixteenth century A.D., after European colonization and settlement.

Science and Measurement

Science requires the precise and accurate comparison of phenomena. In most cases, it is not enough simply to say, for example, that X is larger than Y, or that it is hotter, or faster, or growing more rapidly. For this reason, scientists in every field use quantitative tools to measure and describe things, and to analyze relationships among them.

Sociology is no exception. In comparing human societies, for example, it is not enough to say merely that one type of society is larger than another; this could mean that it is 1 percent larger or a thousand times larger. Such imprecise statements fail to clarify the nature of relationships that exist among phenomena and thus hamper the search for patterns and their explanation.

Sociologists and other social scientists make great use of a set of quantitative tools known as *statistics,* the most basic of which are called summary measures. A summary measure reduces a number of different measurements to a single measure that represents them all. The most widely used are *measures of central tendency*—or what are popularly known as "averages."

The most familiar measure of central tendency is the arithmetic mean. The *arithmetic mean* is determined by adding the measurements of the individual units and dividing the sum by the number of units. For example, if 5 hunting and gathering societies have 25, 32, 39, 48, and 56 members respectively, the sum of the individual measurements is 200; when this is divided by the number of societies—5—we obtain a mean of 40.

Another widely used measure of central tendency is the *median*. We determine the median by arranging the individual measurements in order and identifying the one that is in the middle. In the example above, the median is 39. The median is often a more meaningful measure of central tendency than the mean, because it minimizes the effect of a single, highly discrepant case. If the sizes of the 5 societies in the example above had been 25, 32, 39, 48, and 156 (instead of 56), we would have obtained a mean of 60, which would have been a poor "summary" of the situation. The median, however, would still have been 39, a truer reflection of the size of most of the societies.

penetration by technologically more advanced nations has increased tremendously, as we will see in later chapters.

DIFFERENCES AMONG TYPES OF SOCIETIES

One of the most important propositions in ecological-evolutionary theory asserts that advances in subsistence technology are a necessary condition for any significant increase in the size and complexity of a society (see p. 67). Beginning in Chapter 5, we will put this proposition to the test as we examine each of the major types of societies.

Before plunging into the detailed evidence that bears on this proposition, it may be helpful to consider a much more limited body of evidence that was assembled over a period of years by George Peter Murdock with the aid of his students and colleagues. Together they assembled and codified a tremendous amount of information on hundreds of societies. These data enable us to classify most of these societies in terms of the taxonomy described earlier in this chapter and to compare the various types of societies in a number of important ways.[13] Since the societies differ considerably in their levels of technological advance, we will be able to see whether they also differ in some of the ways that ecological-evolutionary theory says they should.

Size of Societies

One of the most important consequences of technological advance, according to ecological-evolutionary theory, is an increase in the size of societies. Table 4.2 confirms this. Technologically more advanced types of societies have, on average, much larger populations. Thus, the median size (see "Science and Measurement" box) of industrial societies is larger than the median size of agrarian societies, which is larger than the median size of horticultural societies, which is larger than the median size of hunting and gathering societies.[14] The median sizes of fishing and herding societies are also about what one would expect in view of their places in the taxonomy of societies (see Figure 4.1). Fishing societies are larger, on average, than hunting and gathering societies, but much smaller, on average, than horticultural societies. Herding societies are roughly the same size as advanced horticultural societies.

Permanence of Settlements

Ecological-evolutionary theory also predicts that technological advances lead societies to establish more permanent settlements.[15] Because the hunting of wild animals and the gathering of uncultivated vegetable products soon deplete the supply of foodstuffs in the immediate area surrounding human settlements, hunter-gatherers are forced to move about with considerable frequency. In contrast, societies that practice horticulture or agriculture should, according to our theory, be able to establish more permanent settlements.

Murdock's data confirm this. Of the 167 hunting and gathering societies for which data were available, *only 10 percent* were reported to have permanent settlements, and all of these enjoyed unusually favorable environmental conditions or partial reliance on horticulture, fishing, or other more advanced technologies. In contrast, *94 percent* of the 507 horticultural and agrarian societies had permanent settlements.

Societal Complexity

A third important prediction of ecological-evolutionary theory is that technological advance is linked to greater complexity of the social system. Murdock's data permit us to test this hypothesis in two ways. First, we can compare societies on the basis of *the amount of occupational specialization* found in them. Second, we can compare them

Table 4.2 Median Size of Societies, by Type of Society

Type of Society	Median Size of Society	No. of Societies
Hunting and gathering	40	46
Simple horticultural	1,500	53
Advanced horticultural	5,250	69
Agrarian	Over 100,000	38
Industrial*	10,500,000	27
Fishing	90	16
Herding	5,750	19

Sources: See Appendix, pp. 417–418; and World Bank, *World Development Indicators* online database, http://data.worldbank .org.
*The mean is 36.4 million.

Table 4.3 Frequency of Craft Specialization, by Type of Society (in Percentages)

Type of Society	Metal-Working	Weaving	Leather Working	Pottery	Boat Building	House Building	Average
Hunting and gathering	0	0	0	0	0	0	0
Simple horticultural	0	1	1	0	8	4	2
Advanced horticultural	96	5	12	14	4	2	22
Agrarian	98	34	24	24	5	18	34
Industrial	100	100	100	100	100	100	100
Fishing	7	0	0	0	5	2	2
Herding	44	3	6	0	0	1	9

Source: See Appendix, pp. 417–418.

on the basis of *the complexity of their status systems.* Thus, we can test the complexity of both the horizontal and the vertical dimensions of social organization.

Table 4.3 shows the frequency with which several kinds of occupational specialists are found in seven different types of societies. In hunting and gathering societies, technologically the least advanced, there are no specialists in the six areas indicated. Specialization in those areas occurs in a tiny minority of simple horticultural societies but becomes considerably more common in advanced horticultural and agrarian societies. In *every* industrial society, there are specialists in *all* of these fields. In fishing societies, the level of occupational specialization is comparable to that in hunting and gathering and simple horticultural societies, while herding societies occupy an intermediate position between simple and advanced horticultural societies.

Figure 4.3 shows the relationship between subsistence technology and the complexity of status systems. Once again, as ecological-evolutionary theory would lead us to expect, there is a steady progression from hunting and gathering to industrial societies, with no complex status systems found in the former but universally present in the latter.[§] The two environmentally specialized types of societies—fishing and herding societies—rarely had complex status systems, which is what ecological-evolutionary theory predicts. None of the fishing societies and only 3 percent of the herding societies had status systems that could be classified as complex.

Ideology

Finally, there are a number of reasons to suspect that advancing technology will change the way people view the world and their place in it (e.g., see Chapter 11). One important aspect of this is the structure of their religious beliefs. Do they believe in one god or many? Does that god, or do those gods, encourage moral behavior? Again Murdock's data allow us to explore this question.

As Figure 4.4 indicates, belief in a god who created the world and who is concerned with the moral conduct of humans has been found in only a small minority of technologically less advanced societies—hunting and gathering, simple horticultural,

---

[§]Complex status systems are those which distinguish a large number of distinct levels or strata.

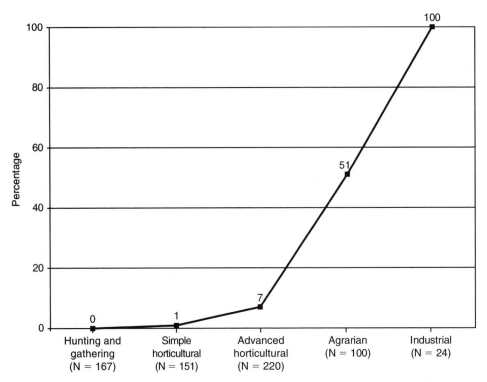

Figure 4.3. Percentage of Societies having Complex Status Systems, by Type of Society.
Source: See Appendix, pp. 417–418.

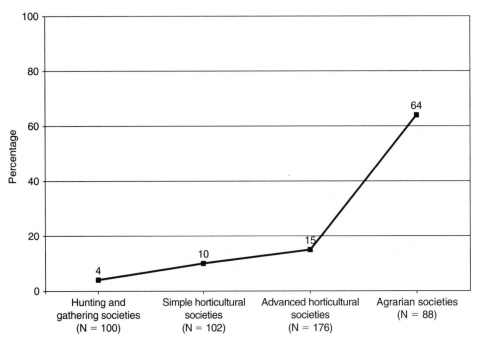

Figure 4.4. Percentage of Societies with Belief in a Creator God Concerned with the Moral Conduct of Humans, by Type of Society.
Source: See Appendix, pp. 417–418.

and advanced horticultural—but it is found in the majority of agrarian and in almost all industrial societies.**[16]

SOCIETAL TYPES: WHAT THEY ARE AND WHAT THEY ARE NOT

By now it should be clear that the societal types with which we will be concerned throughout this volume are sets of societies in which individual societies resemble others of their type more than those of other types. The societies of one type are not identical, however. They differ from one another in many ways. Often, in fact, a number of societies of one type resemble some of the societies of another type *in certain respects* more than they resemble the majority of societies of their own type. For example, as Figure 4.4 indicates, the religious beliefs of a small minority of hunting and gathering societies (4 percent) resemble those of the majority of agrarian societies more than they resemble the beliefs of other hunting and gathering societies.

The differences between societal types are something like the differences between age categories within a population. Every society finds it useful—even necessary—to make distinctions between children and adults, and many societies go further and differentiate between infants, children, adolescents, young adults, the middle-aged, and the elderly. These distinctions reflect real and important differences within the population, but we recognize that the characteristics of all the individuals in a category are not identical. For example, a few elderly people will be in better physical condition than many middle-aged ones, and some adolescents may already be employed while some adults are still students in school. But these exceptions do not keep us from using age categories as tools that help us understand and anticipate the different ways individuals respond to various situations.

The reason we find age categories useful is because the physiological process of development and aging has such a profound impact on the daily lives of individuals. It sets limits on what is possible for individuals at various ages, and within those limits it makes some patterns of action more likely than others. Furthermore, the physiological process of development and aging has a similar impact on everyone who is at the same stage in the life cycle: this is why the members of a given age category resemble one another more than they resemble the members of other age categories. This is also why the members of adjacent categories resemble one another more than they resemble members of more distant categories (e.g., why adolescents resemble children or young adults more than they resemble babies or the elderly).

Obviously, however, the physiological process of development and aging is not the only force that shapes our lives and personalities. This is why all the members of a given age category are not exactly alike and why there are always differences among them.

Societal types are much like age categories in all these ways. The reason they are so valuable is because subsistence technology has such a profound impact on the life of societies. It sets limits on what is possible for individual societies at every stage of development, and within those limits it makes certain social and cultural patterns more likely than others. Furthermore, it is a force that has a similar impact on all

---

**The clear exception is Japan, where Shintoism was once the dominant belief.

societies that share a common mode of subsistence: this is why societies of a given type tend to resemble one another more than they resemble societies of other types. This is also why societies of adjacent types (see Figure 4.1) resemble one another more than they resemble societies of more distant types (e.g., why simple horticultural societies resemble hunting and gathering societies more than they resemble industrial societies).

But subsistence technology is not the only force that influences the nature of societies, any more than the physiological process of development and aging is the only force that influences individual health, personality, and behavior. This is why there are differences among societies within a given societal type just as there are differences among individuals in the same age category.

In summary then, societal types are valuable analytical tools that help us understand societies, both individually and collectively. They are sets of societies that share a single common characteristic, subsistence technology. But subsistence technology is not just any characteristic chosen at random from the almost endless list of societal characteristics. On the contrary, it appears to be *the single most powerful force responsible for the most important differences among human societies.*

Technological Determinism Rejected

Today, as in the past, efforts to understand the role of technology in human life are hindered by those who take extreme positions on the subject.

Over the years, a few scholars have argued that technology explains almost every sociocultural pattern.[17] To combat this exaggerated view and to uphold the importance of ideological and organizational factors, other scholars have minimized or even denied the importance of technology.[18] Unfortunately, the unreasonableness of *both* positions has escaped many social scientists, with the result that sociology and anthropology have both been slow in coming to a realistic assessment of technology's role in the evolutionary process.

Much of the confusion results from a failure to think in *probabilistic* and *variable* terms. Few, if any, significant social patterns are determined by a single factor. Where human societies are concerned, one can rarely say that A and A alone causes B. Usually B is due to the combined effect of a number of factors, and, although A may be the most important, it is not likely to be strong enough to dictate the outcome. The most we can say, as a rule, is that if A is operative, then B will occur with *some degree of probability.*

The problem is further complicated because so many of the B's we deal with are not *categorical* variables—things that are either present or absent, or true or false; they are *continuous* variables—things that vary by degree. For example, as we noted in Chapter 2, when we examine a society's population, we are not interested merely in noting that it exists; we are interested in its many graduated properties, such as its relative size, wealth, or military power. The same is true of most of the other things we are concerned with—the *degree* of occupational specialization, the *frequency* of warfare, the *extent* of the authority exercised by leaders, and so forth. To think in categorical, either-or terms about such matters is bound to be misleading.

While ecological-evolutionary theory emphasizes the tremendous importance of technology and technological innovation in the life of human societies, it does not

A Number of Third World Societies Today Contain Elements of Advanced Technology Side by Side with Features of Their Traditional Technologies: Camels Graze in Front of a Modern Oil Refinery in Iran.

claim that technology can explain everything in sociocultural evolution. It recognizes that other forces have also played a part—often an important part. Its view of technology's role in human affairs can best be summarized in the following propositions:

1. Because subsistence technology sets limits on what is possible within a society, an advance in subsistence technology is a necessary precondition for substantial growth or development in terms of size, complexity, power, and wealth; this is true both for individual societies and for the world system.
2. Because subsistence technology sets limits on what is possible within a society and greatly influences the relative cost of each of the options within those limits, it is the single most important cause of the *totality of differences* among societies (but not of each individual difference).
3. Because societies that have grown substantially in size, complexity, wealth, and power enjoy a great advantage in intersocietal competition and are therefore more likely to transmit their social and cultural characteristics to future generations, the nature of the world system has been increasingly shaped by the process of technological advance and increasingly reflects the characteristics of those societies that are technologically the most advanced and most innovative.

If these propositions are correct, students of human societies can ill afford to ignore or neglect subsistence technology and the role it plays in human life. In fact, these propositions indicate that the first step in analyzing any society should be to identify its primary subsistence technology. This will ensure that we take into account from the outset the most powerful of the variables affecting it.

Our basic task for the rest of this volume will be to apply these principles in a broadly comparative study of human societies. We will examine each of the major societal types that have emerged in the course of history, seeing how technological advance has influenced its social institutions and how these institutions have, in turn, reacted to technology and influenced its development. We will, for obvious reasons, give special attention to the industrial and industrializing societies of our own day. Our ultimate goal is to achieve a better understanding of the forces that influence human societies, in the hope that this will help us understand and perhaps eventually control the process of change that is such a striking, and at times threatening, feature of the contemporary world.

Preindustrial Societies

CHAPTER 5

Hunting and Gathering Societies

Outline

The Emergence of *Homo sapiens sapiens* Prior to 40,000 B.C.:
   Establishing a Genetic Foundation for Cultural Evolution
Hunting and Gathering Societies 40,000 B.C. to 8000 B.C.:
   Cultural Evolution Takes Over
Hunting and Gathering Societies of the Recent Past
Hunting and Gathering Societies in Theoretical Perspective

Throughout most of their history, our hominid ancestors* were foragers, gathering fruits and vegetables wherever they could find them and hunting wild animals or scavenging the remains of those that had died or been killed by others. Only in the last 10,000 to 12,000 years, or the last small fraction of 1 percent of hominid history, have farming and other modes of subsistence and other types of societies evolved. Thus, hunting and gathering societies served humankind long and well.

Despite their longevity, hunting and gathering societies, are now, or soon will be extinct. They simply have not been able to compete for territories and other vital resources with technologically more advanced societies. As a result, in recent centuries hunting and gathering societies have survived only in remote and isolated regions. And now in the twenty-first century, with the development of new and more powerful technologies and their growing appetite for material resources, more advanced societies have penetrated even into these areas. Thus, few, if any, hunting and gathering societies are likely to survive much longer.

Fortunately, from the standpoint of our understanding of these societies and their way of life, missionaries, colonial administrators, anthropologists, and others have had opportunities in the last several centuries to observe dozens of surviving societies of hunters and gatherers and in many cases have provided detailed descriptions of their way of life. In addition, archaeologists have developed a substantial body of information about prehistoric hunters and gatherers from the excavation and analysis of the bones and artifacts they left behind.

---

*The term, *hominid*, refers to genetically modern humans (*Homo sapiens sapiens*) and to other human-like species that evolved after the ancestral lines of modern humans and chimpanzees separated five to seven million years ago.[1]

Neandertals Among Us?

The first remains of a Neandertal, discovered some 200 years ago in the Neander valley of Germany (hence the name), were of an aged, arthritic, man. The immediate impression it gave was that these creatures, though similar to modern humans in some ways, were unintelligent heavy-browed brutes.

But as our knowledge of them has grown, a very different picture has emerged. Evidence indicates that they created art, used medicinal plants, practiced a form of religion, and may have spoken a sophisticated language. It is even believed that they may have invented a tool that was later adopted by their "cousins," modern humans.

If all of this is so, why did they apparently disappear some 30,000 to 40,000 years ago?

Although climate change undoubtedly played a role (they were highly adapted to a cold climate), scientists have been divided over whether they were out-competed or perhaps killed off by modern humans, or whether their small population was absorbed into, and "swamped" by, the much larger population of modern humans—as anthropologist John Hawks put it: Did they "make love or war?"

The recently completed mapping of the Neandertal genome suggests an answer. It shows evidence of limited, but prolonged, interbreeding among Neandertals and modern humans. In fact, about 3 percent of the genes found in a random sample of non-sub-Saharan African modern humans today, are Neandertal in origin! Thus, John Hawks and Zachary Throckmorton calculate that if you were to take all the Neandertal genetic material from the six billion people who carry it today, you would have enough material to make up 180 million Neandertals.

Thus, far from being brutes who disappeared from the planet tens of thousands of years ago, Neandertals, or at least some of their genetic material, walks among us today!

Sources: April Halloway, "Were Neanderthals More Sophisticated Than Currently Believed?" *Ancient Origins*, July 11, 2013, http://www.ancient-origins.net/news-evolution-human-origins/were-neanderthals-more-sophisticated-currently-believed-00644; "Find Indicates Neanderthals Capable of Making Sophisticated Bone Tools," UPI, August 12, 2013; and John Hawks, "New Denisova and Neandertal DNA results reported," May 17, 2013, http://johnhawks.net/weblog/reviews/neandertal_dna; and "Neandertal night on PBS," May 14, 2013, http://johnhawks.net/weblog/reviews/tv/neandertal-night-pbs-2013.html.

Viewed individually, any single one of these accounts has serious limitations, but collectively the various sources provide a surprisingly rich and informative picture of the basic features of life in societies in which hunting and gathering were the primary means of subsistence. In the pages that follow, we will examine first the archaeological record and then turn to the evidence from more recent times.

THE EMERGENCE OF *HOMO SAPIENS SAPIENS* PRIOR TO 100,000 B.C.: ESTABLISHING A GENETIC FOUNDATION FOR CULTURAL EVOLUTION

The story of the evolution of genetically modern humans (*Homo sapiens sapiens*) is long and complex, and much of it need not concern us here. Some developments, however, are critical to an understanding of why human life today is as it is and why it is so different from the life of every other species, even that of our closest surviving kin, the chimpanzees.

If, somehow, we could look across the great expanse of space and time to a grass-covered plain in Africa five million years ago, we would see that our ancestral line was already developing in several increasingly distinctive ways. Fossil evidence indicates

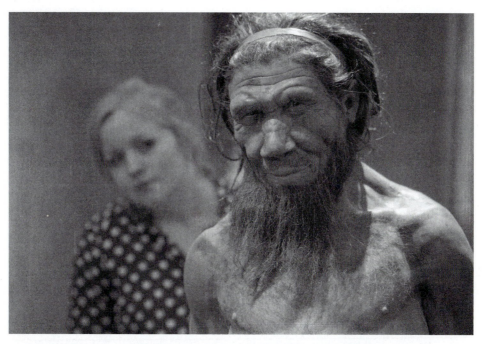

It Is Estimated That about 3 Percent of the Genes Found in a Random Sample of Non-Sub-Saharan African Modern Humans Today Are Neanderthal in Origin. An Employee of the Natural History Museum of London Looks at a Model of a Neanderthal Male in His Twenties, on Display at the Museum's "Britain: One Million Years of the Human Story" Exhibition That Opened on February, 13, 2014.

that these distant ancestors had given up their forebears' arboreal and largely herbivorous way of life for a bipedal, terrestrial, and omnivorous lifestyle. In other words, these early ancestors had come out of the trees and were walking about on two legs much as we do today; also, they were increasingly eating meat obtained by hunting small animals or by scavenging the remains of carcasses of larger animals they found.[2]

This set of behavioral changes was linked to equally important anatomical and genetic changes, especially changes in the skull, mouth, hips, and limbs. The most critical of these was the new upright stance, for this meant that hands were no longer needed to propel their bodies through trees or over ground but were freed for other kinds of activities, such as examining sticks, stones, and other objects and sometimes using them as tools.[3] It is hard to exaggerate the importance of this development, because much of the subsequent evolution of the human brain appears to have been a response to what these early hominids did with their hands.

Throughout hominid evolution, the attributes that were selected as elements in their genetic heritage developed more or less in concert. These included greater overall brain size, especially an enlarged cerebral cortex (see Figure 2.1, p. 32), larger physical size (the earliest hominids appear to have weighed only about fifty pounds), improved hand-eye coordination, various other advances in the nervous system, and an increased capacity for communication and cooperation.

Interestingly, the shift to an omnivorous diet seems to have contributed to several important new elements in early hominid society. For example, the increasing dependence on meat seems to have led to the beginnings of a division of labor between the sexes. Because of the demands of pregnancy, lactation, and care of the young, females were disadvantaged in hunting activities (see "Why Were Women Not the Hunters?" p. 106). This appears to have led at an early date to the beginnings of the pattern found in every hunting and gathering society in modern times in which males have had primary responsibility for providing meat and females for providing vegetables, fruits, shellfish, and other foods that are more easily collected or "gathered." This opinion is supported by evidence that as early as two million years ago, hominid hunter-scavengers in east Africa carried meat from the place where they obtained it to an "eating place" somewhere else.[4] This practice, which is unlike that of any other species of primate living today, suggests a division of labor in acquiring food and the organization of activities around a "home base."

This division of labor along sexual lines may well lie behind yet another development that distinguishes modern humans from almost all other primates: the formation of durable bonds between males and females. Most other primate societies are organized around mothers and their offspring, with adult males not maintaining sustained contact with these groups.[5] Thus, the nuclear family with its pattern of sustained association between the sexes that has been such a fundamental feature of human life may well have had its origin in that ancient innovation in hominid diet.

The scavenging, and later hunting, of larger animals confronted hominids with another problem, how the meat should be distributed. This was almost certainly important, because observations of chimpanzees in the wild have shown that the time when they communicate most intensely is when they are dividing up meat.[6] Thus, the increasing dependence on meat was very probably an early factor in stimulating increased use of body language and rhythmic grunts, as means of communication.

As the ages passed, hominids gradually came to be more and more like modern humans in both appearance and behavior, but the rate of change was extremely slow. Archaeologists speak of the "almost unimaginable slowness of change" during this period.[7] Eventually, however, as a consequence of their increasing use of tools and the further evolution of their brains, hominids reached a point where, as the "brainiest" of the mammals, they began to make new and more effective use of the resources of their environment.

One manifestation of this was the beginning of big-game hunting, an activity with numerous repercussions on hominid life. For example, the pursuit of larger animals would have required a greater capability for planning, maneuvering, remembering, communicating, and cooperating; and the males that did these things best were the most likely to survive and reproduce. Thus, there appears to have been an important link between this activity and the continuing evolution of the human brain, especially in its development of greater memory capacity and more interconnecting nerve cells.[8] The beginning of big-game hunting almost certainly also led to a strengthening of social ties between adult males, since this type of hunting with primitive weapons requires the cooperation of a group of hunters.

As social bonds among adults of both sexes were strengthened, both the opportunities and the need for increased communication developed. Studies have shown that the use of signals is widespread among modern primates as a means of communicating varied emotional states ranging from fear and anger to affection and sexual arousal, and the same was almost certainly true of early hominids.[9] Full-blown speech employing verbal symbols, however, appears to have been a relatively recent evolutionary development, probably emerging only in the last 35,000 to 40,000 years. This view is based on evidence of the rapid increase in the rate of technological innovation in this period (see Table 5.1). Scholars today believe that the use of spoken language evolved slowly from an earlier system of rhythmic grunts and other sounds used to express various emotions.[10]

The use of fire was another significant early innovation. Fire was the first important natural force to be brought under control. Although early hominids were probably not able to generate fire for a long time, they could preserve it after it was ignited by natural causes. And fire did far more than just provide warmth: it set hominids apart from all other species, giving them a measure of control over the cycle of day and night, and providing them with a powerful weapon for driving off predators.

At some point, our hominid ancestors also discovered the use of fire as a means of cooking meat and other materials. It may have been involved, too, in the beginnings of religious experience as an object of worship. But most important, fire strengthened the network of interrelations within societies, drawing the group together at the end of a day to communicate, to remember, and to plan.

HUNTING AND GATHERING SOCIETIES 40,000 B.C. TO 8000 B.C.: CULTURAL EVOLUTION TAKES OVER

No one can say with any certainty when *Homo sapiens* first appeared, but the best available evidence indicates that it was probably only a little more than 100,000 years ago.[11] If we look for some dramatic change in hominid societies at this point, however, we are in for a disappointment. Though the archaeological record for this period is sparse, there is nothing to suggest that there were any dramatic new developments. Living remained precarious, and life expectancy short. For example, one study of the skeletons of forty individuals who lived as recently as 50,000 to 100,000 years ago found that only one individual had reached the age of fifty, and half had died before their twentieth year.[12]

Beginning about 40,000 years ago, however, the rate of innovation and change quickened appreciably. Over the next 30,000 years, the rate of technological innovation appears to have increased more than tenfold (see the final column in Table 5.1).

The clearest indication of this was the rapid proliferation of new and improved tools and weapons. For example, hunters developed the spear-thrower (see Figure 5.1), a device which applies the principle of the lever and doubles the distance a spear can be hurled.[13] At the other end of the spear, they began adding sharpened bone points to increase the penetrating power and barbs that created a more serious wound.[14]

The most important innovation in weapons, however, was the bow and arrow. Applying the principle of the concentration of energy, hunters created a weapon of great usefulness and versatility. Its effective wounding range is roughly four times that of the spear and twice that of the spear thrown with the aid of a spear-thrower.[15] Furthermore, an arrow travels two and one-half to three times faster than a spear. This is important not only because of the time advantage it affords the hunter, but also

Table 5.1 The Rising Rate of Technological Innovation: 4,000,000 B.C. to 8,000 B.C.

Time Periods and Their Major Technological Innovations Years		No. of Major Innovations	Innovations per Thousand
4,000,000 to 100,000 B.C.		6	0.0015
Hand ax	Wooden spear		
Use of fire	Constructed shelters		
Fire-hardened spear point	Colored pigments		
100,000 to 40,000 B.C.		4	0.0667
Use of bone for tools	Skin clothing (probable)		
Built-in handles on tools	Harpoon heads		
40,000 to 10,000 B.C.		21	0.7000
Spear-thrower	Bow and arrow		
Lamps	Pins or awls		
Fish gorgets	Cord		
Needles with eyes	Antler hammers		
Shovels or scoops	Mattocks		
Stone saws	Graving tools		
Spoons	Stone ax with hafted handle		
Jewelry	Pestles and grinding slabs		
Separate handles	Musical instruments		
Boats	Figurative art		
Domestication of dog			
10,000 to 8000 B.C.		16	8.0
Beer	Fishhooks		
Fish traps	Fishnets		
Adzes	Sickles		
Plant cultivation	Domestication of sheep		
Basketry	Cloth		
Grinding equipment	Leather-working tools		
Paving	Sledge		
Ice picks	Combs		

Sources: This table is based on data in Grahame Clark and Stuart Piggott, *Prehistoric Societies* (New York: Knopf, 1965); S. A. Semenov, *Prehistoric Technology* (New York: Barnes and Noble, 1964); John Pfeiffer, *The Emergence of Man,* 3d ed. (New York: Harper & Row, 1978); Jacquetta Hawkes, *Prehistory, UNESCO History of Mankind,* vol. 1, part 1 (New York: Mentor, 1965); Alexander Marshak, *The Roots of Civilization* (New York: McGraw-Hill, 1972); P. S. Bellwood, "The Peopling of the Pacific," *Scientific American,* 243 (Nov. 1980), pp. 174–185; Bruce Bower, "When the Human Spirit Soared," *Science News,* 130 (Dec. 13, 1986), pp. 376–379; and "Site Surrenders Fabric of Prehistoric Life," *Science News,* 144 (July 24, 1993), p. 54; Robin Dennell, "Needles and Spear Throwers," *Natural History* (Oct. 1986), pp. 70–78; John Putnam, "In Search of Modern Hunters," *National Geographic,* 174, no. 4 (Oct. 1988), p. 449; Paul Mellars, "Major Issues in the Emergence of Modern Humans," *Current Anthropology,* 30 (1989), pp. 349–385; "The Dawn of Creativity," *U.S. News and World Report* (May 20, 1996); Naama Goren-Inbar, Nira Alperson, Mordechai E. Kislev, Orit Simchoni, Yoel Melamed, Adi Ben-Nun, Ella Werker, "Evidence of Hominid Control of Fire at Gesher Benot Ya'aqov, Israel" *Science,* 304 (April 30, 2004), pp. 725–727; John Wilford, "Art Among Earliest Known Is Found in Cave in Germany," *New York Times,* Dec. 18, 2003; and Nicolas Wade, "What a Story Lice Can Tell," *New York Times,* Oct. 5, 2004.

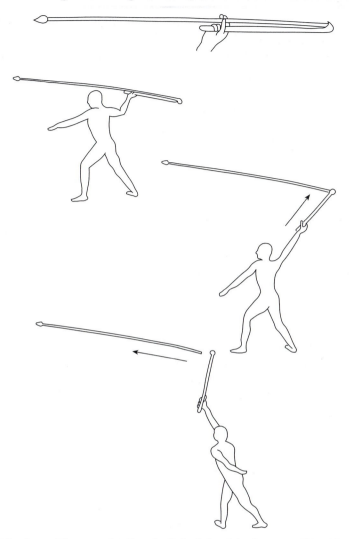

Figure 5.1. The Spear-Thrower Applies the Principle of the Lever and Doubles the Distance a Spear Can Be Hurled.
Source: After John Purcell, *From Hand Ax to Laser: Man's Growing Mastery of Energy* (New York: Vanguard Press, 1982). Illustrated by Judy Skorpil.

because the force of the blow is a function of the missile's velocity. Finally, unlike the spear, the bow and arrow permit the hunter to sight the missile at eye level, thus greatly increasing the accuracy of his aim.

Other technological improvements, though less dramatic, were no less important. As one writer puts it, people of this era "began to make the tool fit the task with an altogether new precision."[16] Innovations included such diverse tools as pins or awls, needles with eyes, spoons, graving tools, axes, stone saws, antler hammers, shovels or scoops, pestles and grinding slabs (for grinding minerals to obtain coloring materials), and mattocks (a type of pickaxe).

In colder regions, people frequently lived in caves, but this was not always possible and, as archaeologists have found, in some areas people began building earthen houses.[17] The discovery of such settlements has provided us with information about the size of human societies in this era. In general, they were quite small, many with as few as six to thirty people. The largest settlement of prehistoric hunters and gatherers ever found was spread out along a two-mile stretch of river in France and may have contained as many as 400 to 600 people, but this was quite exceptional and appears to have been only a temporary assemblage of a number of normally separate societies taking advantage of a rich seasonal salmon run.[18]

Perhaps the best-known innovation of this period was its art. The drawings on the walls of caves are world famous (see photo of Famous prehistoric rock painting of Tassili N'Ajjer, Algeria), but they are only one of the new art forms developed at this time. There was sculpture of various kinds as well as bone and ivory carvings, often on the handles of weapons and tools.

These artistic remains provide us today with important evidence of the evolution of human thought. Drawings of men dressed to resemble animals and of men standing before animals with heads bowed and in a nonthreatening posture suggest magical or religious practices. Sympathetic magic, which is based on the belief that something done to an image of a person or animal will affect that person or animal, is strongly suggested by the fact that many of the drawings have spears or darts drawn or scratched into the animals' flanks.[19] Sympathetic magic was apparently also used in attempts to induce fertility in both humans and animals; at least this is the generally accepted explanation for the numerous female figurines that have been discovered with exaggerated indications of pregnancy (see photo of the Venus of Willendorf). Most scholars think that it is no coincidence that the artists usually ignored the facial features and focused on the symbols of fertility. In short, the art of this era reveals the growth of human consciousness and the effort of prehistoric hunters and gatherers to understand and control their environment.

Viewed as a whole, developments in this period raise an important question: Why this sudden and explosive growth in culture at this particular time? Why not at some much earlier time, or why not much later?

The growing consensus today is that this cultural revolution (for it was a revolution) resulted from critical advances in language.[20] While symbol use almost certainly began much earlier than this, earlier symbol systems were probably much more primitive and much less effective as instruments for learning, remembering, and sharing information. According to proponents of this view, the relatively modest genetic changes that were involved in the transition to *Homo sapiens sapiens* (fully modern man) paved the way for the explosive growth of culture that occurred at the end of the Old Stone Age, and for all the revolutionary social and cultural changes that followed. In other words, there was a critical "threshold effect" involved: until a certain point was reached in biological evolution, the development of full-fledged symbol systems was impossible. But once that point was reached, the development of language could proceed rapidly.

The striking advances in technology at the end of the hunting and gathering era coincided with, and were probably the cause of, an equally striking growth in the size of the human population. According to estimates based on recent archaeological research, the rate of growth of the human population increased substantially after

Famous Prehistoric Rock Painting of Tassili N'Ajjer, Algeria.

The Venus of Willendorf, Germany (about 25,000 B.C.) This Is the Oldest Sculpture of a Human Figure Found Thus Far.

Table 5.2 The Growth of Human Population during the Hunting and Gathering Era

Approximate Date	Estimated Human Population	Average Percentage Increase in Human Population Worldwide per Thousand Years*
1,800,000 B.C.	400,000	
150,000 B.C.	800,000	0.04
40,000 B.C.	1,200,000	0.40
8000 B.C.	8,500,000	6.10

Source: Adapted from Fekri Hassan, *Demographic Archaeology* (New York: Academic Press, 1981), Table 12.3.
*These figures are authors' calculations.

40,000 B.C. (see Table 5.2). This growth of population then would have increased the need for food and also increased the number of people looking for ways of providing it, thus contributing to the rising rate of innovation.

Despite the rapid increase in the rate of growth during this period, the human population at the end of the hunting and gathering era still numbered less than ten million, and its rate of growth was still less than 0.1 percent per year (compared with 1.1 percent per year today). The reason for this was the inability of societies to provide adequately for their members and to protect them against disease and other dangers. A recent study of more than 300 skeletons of adults from Europe and Africa during this period indicates that the average age at death was just thirty-three years for men and twenty-eight for women.[21] Thus, the reproductive years for women were far fewer than they are today. With the high rates of infant mortality that also prevailed,[22] it is no wonder that the rate of growth of the human population was still extremely low at the end of the hunting and gathering era.

Handle of Spear-Thrower, France.

HUNTING AND GATHERING SOCIETIES OF THE RECENT PAST

Even after the emergence of more advanced types of societies, hunting and gathering societies continued to flourish in many parts of the world. A hundred years ago there were still large numbers of them in both the New World and Australia, and smaller numbers in southwest Africa, in parts of the rain forest in central Africa, in certain remote areas in southeast Asia and neighboring islands, and in Arctic Asia.[23] As recently as 1788, there were probably 5,000 hunting and gathering societies in Australia alone,[24] and almost certainly as many in North America. Although the settlement of these areas by Europeans and the spreading influence of industrialization are now destroying the last of them, we have detailed descriptions of many of these groups.

There is considerable variation among the 174 societies in Murdock's data bank (see Appendix). For example, 12 percent of them relied on hunting and gathering for their *entire* subsistence, while 13 percent relied on these techniques for only about half. Most groups (81 percent) depended on fishing to some extent, and a few (15 percent) obtained nearly half their food from this source. A minority (28 percent) derived part from horticulture, and a few (less than 5 percent) almost half. In short, a few were pure hunting and gathering societies, but most of them incorporated limited elements of fishing or horticulture or both.

Population

Size and Density

Despite these variations in subsistence technology, modern hunting and gathering societies have a lot in common.[†] For example, none supports a large or dense population: Nearly 80 percent have less than one person per square mile.[25] Communities, therefore, are necessarily small. And, since communities are almost always autonomous, societies are equally small. The average size of those that survived into the modern era has been approximately forty (see Table 4.2).[26] As ecological-evolutionary theory would lead us to expect, the more completely societies depend for their subsistence on hunting and gathering, the smaller they tend to be, while those that incorporate fishing, horticulture, or herding as secondary means of subsistence are larger (see Table 5.3).

Table 5.3 Average Size of Hunting and Gathering Societies, by Percentage of Food Supply Obtained through Hunting and Gathering

Percentage of Food Supply Obtained through Hunting and Gathering	Median Size	Number of Societies
86–100*	29	34
50–85*	49	71

Source: See Appendix, pp. 417–418.
*These figures are estimates made by Murdock and his associates, based on nonquantitative statements in ethnographic sources.

[†]When referring to "modern" hunting and gathering societies, we mean those that survived into the modern era (i.e., the last several hundred years). In writing about these societies, the present tense is usually used for convenience even though most of the studies were conducted some years ago.

The rate of population growth in hunting societies is usually very low.[‡] In many cases, the number of births is virtually matched by the number of deaths. In part, this is because of high death rates from natural causes, such as accidents and disease.[27] But it is also the result of physiological responses to the diet and nomadic lifestyle of hunters and gatherers. For example, prolonged nursing of infants and low levels of body fat both reduce fertility, and high levels of maternal mobility increase the risks of miscarriage.[28] Furthermore, since the braking effects of these variables rise and fall with the availability of food, they help to promote a rough balance between population size and environmental resources.[29]

Nonetheless, the most important factors producing equilibrium between births and deaths are probably cultural. Delayed marriages and postpartum sex taboos reduce the number of children a woman will give birth to, and we cannot ignore the fact that infanticide and abortion are widespread in these societies. One study revealed that infanticide was practiced in eighty of eighty-six hunting and gathering societies examined, while another study found that abortion was practiced in thirteen of fifteen societies.[30] Some scholars estimate that between 15 and 50 percent of all live births end in infanticide in societies at this level of development.[31]

The members of hunting and gathering societies are not, of course, less loving than the members of other societies. Their norms and values, like those of every society, simply reflect the past experience of the group. And this has taught them that any other course of action can be disastrous. When a mother already has one child at the breast, and may have to keep it there for several years because there is no safe alternative source of nourishment,[32] another baby can mean death for both children. This is especially likely to be true if the food supply is variable, that is, if hunting and gathering provide a glut of food at some times and shortages at others. If, in addition, the mother must participate regularly in the search for food and watch over her children at the same time (see photo of !Kung San mother), and if she must carry all her possessions as well as her children to a new campsite every few weeks or months the logic of abortion and infanticide becomes obvious. They are simply measures that ensure the health and survival of mothers and children, and thus the survival of the society.

Nomadism

Modern hunting and gathering societies are usually nomadic. Some groups are reported to remain in an area for periods as short as a week.[33] In contrast, a few occupy permanent settlements, but all of these either rely on fishing or horticulture as important secondary sources of subsistence or are located in areas with unusually high concentrations of game and other food resources.[34]

The nomadic character of most hunting and gathering groups is an inevitable result of their subsistence technology. One anthropologist described the basic problem when he said of a group of African Pygmies with whom he had lived that "after a month, as a rule, the fruits of the forest have been gathered all around the vicinity of the camp, and the game has been scared away to a greater distance than is comfortable

---

[‡]Rapid population growth occurs in these societies only when they are able to expand into new (uninhabited) territories or gain access to new sources of food.

!Kung San Mother Carrying Infant While Digging Roots.

for daily hunting."[35] He went on to say that since "the economy relies on the day-to-day quest, the simplest thing is for the camp to move."

Hunters and gatherers may also change campsites for other reasons. A study of the Hadza in east Africa, for example, indicates that they often move to the place where a large animal has been killed simply to avoid carrying the meat.[36] Since their possessions are few, such a move requires little effort. The Hadza also move to a new site when someone dies, or even when a member becomes sick or has a bad dream, because these are regarded as bad omens.

Many hunting and gathering groups disperse for a part of the year, with individual families striking out on their own. This pattern has been observed in such widely scattered groups as the !Kung San[37] of southwest Africa, the Eskimo, and the Australian aborigines. Sometimes seasonal changes in flora and fauna make it more advantageous for the group to split up and do their hunting and foraging in smaller groups. Sometimes the splitting up of the group seems to be a response to controversies and conflicts that require a cooling-off period—after which the desire for more social interaction serves to bring the group together again.[38]

Despite their nomadism, hunters and gatherers usually restrict their movements to a fairly well defined territory. When the society moves, it usually settles in or near some former campsite. There may even be a regular circuit of sites that the group uses year after year. A group is usually deterred from entering new territories because they are already occupied by others. Moreover, hunters and gatherers normally have a strong attachment to their traditional territory, which has often acquired a sacred character that is maintained through song and legend.

Kinship

Ties of kinship are vitally important in most hunting and gathering groups. It is hard for members of modern industrial societies to appreciate the tremendous significance of these ties, because so much of our own social interaction is organized independently of kinship, in terms of roles such as teacher and student, clerk and customer, or friend and friend.

In contrast, social interaction in hunting and gathering societies is usually organized around kinship roles. A student of the Australian aborigines reports that "in a typical Australian *tribe* it is found that a man can define his relations to every person with whom he has any social dealings whatever, whether of his own or of another tribe, by means of the terms of [kinship]."[39] Another writer says of these people that "every one with whom a person comes in contact is regarded as related to him, and the kind of relationship must be ascertained so that the two persons concerned will know what their mutual behavior should be."[40] He adds that kinship ties are the anatomy and physiology of aboriginal society and "must be understood if the behavior of the aborigines as social beings is to be understood." Though there are exceptions, kinship is usually the basic organizing principle in hunting and gathering societies.[41]

Viewed in evolutionary perspective, the family has often been described as the matrix, or womb, from which all other social institutions have evolved. This points to a basic truth: in hunting and gathering societies, kin groups perform many of the functions that are performed by schools, business firms, governmental agencies, and other specialized organizations in larger, more advanced, and more differentiated societies.

Kin groups in hunting and gathering societies are of two types, nuclear and extended families. A nuclear family includes a man, his wife or wives, and their unmarried children; an extended family contains multiple nuclear families linked by a parent-child relationship (e.g., parents of a married couple or their married children).[42] *Polygyny,* marriage of a man to two or more women, is widespread; only 10 percent of the hunting and gathering groups in Murdock's data set are classified as monogamous. It does not follow, of course, that 90 percent of the families in this kind of society are polygynous: this is impossible, given the roughly equal numbers of men and women. Usually only one or two of the most influential men have more than one wife, and they seldom have more than two or three. This limited polygyny is possible because girls usually marry younger than boys, and some men are obliged to remain bachelors. Multiple wives appear to be an economic asset in these societies and, to some extent, a status symbol as well.

Divorce is permitted in virtually all hunting and gathering societies and is fairly common in some.[43] In others, however, it is made relatively difficult. The most we can say is that there is great variability in this matter.

The nuclear family is usually part of a larger and more inclusive kin group known as the extended family.[44] In the majority of modern hunting and gathering societies the extended family includes both maternal and paternal relatives—a pattern that is not found in the majority of horticultural, herding, and agrarian societies. Compared with extended family systems that emphasize ties with either maternal or paternal kin, this bilateral, or two-sided, system effectively doubles the number of people to whom an individual can turn for help in time of difficulty, an arrangement that appears to have considerable adaptive value in societies that are so small.[45]

The extended family is also important because the ties of kinship among its members encourage the practice of sharing. When the daily acquisition of food is uncertain, as it is in many hunting and gathering societies, a nuclear family could easily starve if it had to depend exclusively on its own efforts. A family might be surfeited with food for a time and then suddenly have nothing. Or all the adult members of the family could become ill or injured at the same time. In either case the family would be dependent on the generosity of others. Although sharing can, and does, take place between unrelated persons, kinship ties strengthen the tendency. In this connection it is interesting to note that many hunting and gathering peoples create what we would call fictional ties of kinship when there is no "real" relationship by blood or marriage. These ties are just as meaningful to them as "true" kinship ties, and they serve to strengthen the bonds uniting the group—much like the role of godparent in some more developed societies.

Through marriages with people in nearby groups (a practice known as *exogamy*), a society gradually establishes a web of kinship ties with neighboring groups. According to one anthropologist, "One of the important functions of exogamy is that of opening up territories so that peaceful movements can take place among them, and particularly so that any large temporary variations in food resources can be taken advantage of by related groups."[46] This is also the explanation for the custom of wife lending, practiced by hunting and gathering peoples as diverse as the Eskimo and the Australian aborigines.[47] As in the case of exogamy, the purpose seems to be to strengthen, restore, or create bonds between the men involved. Thus, if two individuals or two groups have had a quarrel, they may settle it by lending one another their wives. The practice is predicated on the assumption that women are prized possessions that one does not share with everyone. It would be a mistake to suppose, however, that women are merely property in these societies; they often have considerable influence in the life of the group and are by no means mere chattels.

The Economy

Economic institutions are not very complex in hunting and gathering societies. One reason is that the combination of a simple technology and a nomadic way of life makes it impossible for most hunting and gathering peoples to accumulate many possessions (see photo on p. 105). In describing the !Kung San of southwest Africa, one ethnographer explains, "It is not advantageous to multiply and accumulate in this society. Any man can make what he needs when he wants to. Most of the materials he uses are abundant and free for anyone to take. Furthermore, in their nomadic lives, without beasts of burden, the fact that the people themselves must carry everything puts a sharp limit on the quantity of objects they want to possess."[48] The minority of hunting and gathering groups that are able to establish permanent settlements may accumulate more possessions, but even they are severely limited by their simple technology.[49]

The quest for food is obviously a crucial activity in every hunting and gathering society. Since most of these societies have no way to store food for extended periods, the food quest must be fairly continuous. Moreover, unlike the situation in more advanced societies, every adult member of the group, except some of the elderly, participates and makes a contribution in this most basic part of the economy.

Prior to the last quarter century, most studies of hunting and gathering societies emphasized the uncertainty of the food supply and the difficulty of obtaining it.[50] A number of more recent studies, however, paint a brighter picture. Reports from the Pygmies of the Congo, the aborigines of Australia, and even the !Kung of the Kalahari Desert in southwestern Africa indicate that they all secure an ample supply of food without an undue expenditure of time or energy.[51] This has led some anthropologists to swing to the opposite extreme and refer to hunters and gatherers as "the most leisured people in the world" and to their way of life as "the original affluent society."[52]

Neither view does justice to the diversity and unpredictability of the situations reported by the numerous observers who have lived among these peoples. Conditions vary considerably from group to group, and within a group they may vary from season to season. For example, the Indians of northern California usually had an abundance of food, and yet even they occasionally encountered a shortage so severe that some of them starved.[53]

A very few societies do not practice hunting. For the rest, hunting usually provides less food, in terms of bulk, than gathering. According to one estimate, the gathering done by women accounts for 60 to 80 percent of the food supply of hunters and gatherers, except in arctic regions.[54] Yet hunting is valued more highly than gathering in virtually all these groups for several reasons. For one thing, meat is generally preferred to vegetables.[55] Whether this reflects a genetically based need or preference, we do not know; certainly not everyone feels this way. In some groups, preference for meat may simply reflect its scarcity. Hunting may also be valued because it requires greater skill and involves more uncertainty regarding the outcome. Added to all this is the fact that meat, unlike vegetables, is commonly shared beyond the immediate family, so success in hunting may be rewarded by widespread respect and deference. One leading anthropologist even suggests that sharing meat "is basic to the continued association of families in any human group that hunts."[56]

Because of the primitive nature of its technology, the division of labor in a hunting and gathering economy is largely limited to distinctions based on age and sex (i.e., sex or gender roles). Almost all hunting and military activities fall to the males, as do most political, religious, ceremonial, and artistic activities. The collection and preparation of vegetables and the care of children are women's responsibilities.[57] Some activities, such as constructing a shelter, may be defined as either men's or women's work, depending on the society.[58] Still other activities may be considered appropriate for both sexes. Further division of labor results because both the very young and the aged are limited in their capabilities.

There are no full-time occupational specialties in hunting and gathering societies, although there is usually some part-time specialization. For example, most groups

Home and Possessions of Paiute Family in Southern Utah in the 1870s.

have at least a *headman* and a *shaman* or medicine man. When their services are required, they function in these specialized capacities, but, as one writer says of the headmen of the Bergdama and the !Kung, "when not engaged on public business they follow the same occupations as all other people."[59] He adds that this is most of the time.

Within hunting and gathering societies, the family or kin group is normally the only significant form of economic organization. Sometimes, when the practice of sharing is widespread and hunting and gathering are carried on as communal activities, even the kin group ceases to be economically important.

With respect to subsistence, each society is virtually self-sufficient. Trade between societies often occurs, but except where contacts have been established with more advanced societies, the bartered items tend to be nonessentials—primarily objects with status or aesthetic value. Such exchanges usually involve things that are scarce or nonexistent in one group's territory but present in the other's (e.g., certain kinds of shells, stones, or feathers).

Why Were Women Not the Hunters?

The revival of the women's movement in recent decades and its claim that biological differences between the sexes should be irrelevant in the division of labor invite the question of why men were the hunters and women the gatherers in hunting and gathering societies. Why not the reverse, or perhaps a sharing of responsibilities?

In recent years, a number of social scientists have reexamined these questions and concluded that the biological differences between the sexes made a role reversal, or even a sharing of responsibilities, impossible in technologically limited societies such as these. Hunting with bows and spears requires speed, agility, and upper-body strength, and women, *on average,* are biologically disadvantaged in all three respects.

These disadvantages are linked to the special role of women in the reproductive process. The later stages of pregnancy, for example, reduce the speed and agility of women in obvious ways. But the requirements of reproduction have other, more subtle consequences. Because of the physiological demands of pregnancy and lactation on a mother's body, women have a higher ratio of fat to muscle than men. On average, about 21 percent of their weight consists of fatty tissue compared to 15 percent for men. This provides women with nutritional reserves on which they can draw during food shortages, both for their own sustenance and for that of a fetus or nursing infant. But less muscle tissue means reduced upper-body strength. Tests by the U.S. Army indicate that, *on average,* women have 42 percent less upper-body strength than men and 30 percent less lower-body strength.

With training, women can obviously develop their muscles to a level that exceeds that of the average man. For example, when Candy Csencsits placed second in the 1983 Ms. Olympia Contest, she was down to 7 percent body fat (champion male bodybuilders have even less, 3 to 5 percent). But when women drop below 15 percent body fat, they often cease to ovulate and become infertile. Thus, muscular development in women appears to conflict with the role of childbearing. In other words, if there ever were societies that used women extensively in hunting, they probably did not survive because of low birthrates.

In addition to all this, women in most hunting and gathering societies must nurse their babies for at least two to four years, because of the lack of a safe and adequate substitute for mother's milk. And since nursing infants need to be fed often, mothers are not able to roam as widely or as fast as hunting requires. Finally, in most of these societies, women in the prime of their lives are usually either pregnant or lactating and thus have little opportunity to develop and maintain the many complex skills required in hunting. The end result, therefore, has been the classic division of labor in which men hunt and women gather.

Sources: Ernestine Friedel, *Women and Men* (New York: Holt, Rinehart, and Winston, 1975); Joan Huber and Glenna Spitze, *Sex Stratification* (New York: Academic Press, 1983); Janet Saltzman Chafetz, *Sex and Advantage* (Totowa, N.J.: Rowman and Allanheld, 1984); Michael Levin, "Women as Soldiers—The Record So Far," *The Public Interest,* 76 (Summer 1984), pp. 31–44; Blythe Hamer, "Women Body Builders," *Science 86,* 7 (March 1986), pp. 74–75; and U.S. Army Research Institute of Environmental Medicine, AP, Jan. 31, 1996.

Trade with advanced societies is more likely to involve economically important items. For example, many groups obtain metal tools and weapons this way.[60] In the past, these imports were seldom on a scale sufficient to alter the basic character of hunting and gathering societies.[61] In the last century, however, as contacts with industrialized and industrializing societies have increased, the volume and importance of such items have often greatly distorted traditional patterns of economic life and done much to undermine the sociocultural system as a whole.

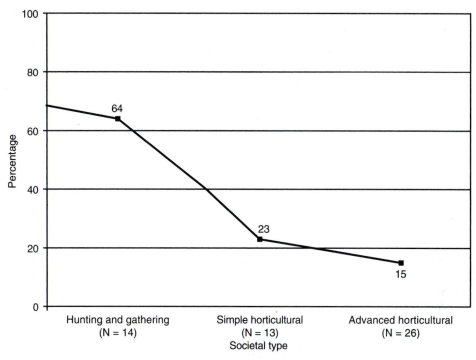

Figure 5.2. Percentage of Societies in Which Political Leaders Rely on Persuasion (by Societal Type).
Source: Appendix, pp. 417–418.

The Polity

The political institutions of modern hunting and gathering societies are very rudimentary. As we have seen, most local communities are autonomous and independent entities (i.e., they are societies as well as communities) even though they have populations of fewer than fifty people. Because they are so small, hunting and gathering societies have not developed political mechanisms of the kind required to control and coordinate large or diverse populations.

The primitive nature of the political systems of these societies can be seen clearly in their limited development of specialized political roles and in the equally limited authority given to people in those roles. In most cases there is simply a headman who provides minimal, largely ceremonial or symbolic, leadership for the group (see Figure 5.2).[62] Allan Holmberg, who lived among the Siriono of eastern Bolivia, wrote a description of their headmen that, except for details, is a portrait of the "typical" headman in a hunting and gathering society.

> Presiding over every band of Siriono is a headman, who is at least nominally the highest official of the group. Although his authority theoretically extends throughout the band, in actual practice its exercise depends almost entirely upon his personal qualities as a leader. In any case, there is no obligation to obey the orders of a headman, no punishment for nonfulfillment. Indeed, little attention is paid to

what is said by a headman unless he is a member of one's immediate family. To maintain his prestige a headman must fulfill, in a superior fashion, those obligations required of everyone else.

The prerogatives of a headman are few. . . . The principal privilege . . . if it could be called such, is that it is his right to occupy, with his immediate family, the center of the [communal] house. Like any other man he must make his bows and arrows, his tools; he must hunt, fish, collect, and [so forth]. He makes suggestions as to migrations, hunting trips, etc., but these are not always followed by his [people]. As a mark of status, however, a headman always possesses more than one wife.

While headmen complain a great deal that other members of the band do not satisfy their obligations to them, little heed is paid to their requests. . . .

In general, however, headmen fare better than other members of the band. Their requests more frequently bear fruit than those of others because headmen are the best hunters and are thus in a better position than most to reciprocate for any favors done them.[63]

There are similar reports on headmen in most other hunting and gathering societies.[64] In a number of instances it is said that the headman "held his place only so long as he gave satisfaction."

Occasionally the headman enjoys a bit more power and privilege. Among the Bergdama of southwest Africa, for example, the headman "is treated with universal respect, being specified as a 'great man' by adults and 'grandfather' by children; he usually has the most wives (sometimes three or more); he has the pick of all wild animal skins for clothing himself and his family, and only his wives wear necklaces or girdles of ostrich eggshell beads; and he receives portions of all game killed in the chase, and tribute from men finding honey."[65]

At the opposite extreme are a number of hunting and gathering societies, including 12 percent of those in Murdock's data set, that do not even have a headman. In these societies, decisions that affect the entire group are arrived at through informal discussions among the more respected and influential members, typically the heads of families.[66]

The limited development of political institutions in hunting and gathering societies contrasts markedly with the situation in more advanced societies. The small size and relative isolation of these societies make it possible for them to handle their political problems very informally. Consensus is achieved much more readily in a small, homogeneous group of a few dozen people (of whom only the adults, and often only the adult males, have a voice) than in larger, more heterogeneous communities with thousands of members. A headman is valuable to such a small group only if he contributes special knowledge, insight, or skills.

Even if the leader of a hunting and gathering band were ambitious and eager to increase his power, he would not get very far. Unlike leaders in more technologically advanced societies, he would find it impossible to build and maintain an organization of dependent retainers to do his bidding or to obtain a monopoly on weapons. The materials for making weapons lie ready at hand, and every man is trained to make and use them. If a person becomes unhappy with the group, he or she can usually leave it and join another.[67] Thus, there are no opportunities for building political empires, even on a small scale.

Given the rudimentary nature of political institutions in hunting and gathering societies, one might suppose that there are few restrictions on people. In one sense this is true; there are few rules imposed by political authorities—no courts, no police, no prisons. Individuals are hardly free, however, to do as they wish. No society is indifferent to the actions of its members, and even in the absence of formal constraints, the group controls their conduct through informal norms and sanctions.

Though there are minor variations from one hunting and gathering society to another, similar patterns of social control have developed in groups as far apart as the Kaska Indians of the Canadian Northwest, the Andaman Islanders of southeast Asia, and the !Kung of southwest Africa.[68] First, there is the custom of blood revenge, whereby the injured party, aided, perhaps, by his kinsmen, punishes the offender himself. As one student of the !Kung put it, "when disputes arise between the members of the band . . . there is no appeal to any supreme authority [since] . . . there is no such authority. . . . The only remedy is self-help."[69] This mode of social control is usually invoked only when the victim of the offense is a single individual or a family. In contrast, when an entire band suffers because of a member's actions, group pressure is brought to bear on the individual. For example, if a man refuses to do his part in providing food, he is punished by losing the respect of others.[70] In the case of more serious offenses, the penalty may be ostracism or even banishment. The third method of control is a deterrent that applies primarily to violations of ritual proscriptions. In such cases, the group's fear of supernatural sanctions provides the needed restraint. The !Kung, for example, believe that girls who fail to observe the restrictions imposed on them at puberty turn into frogs.[71] All three methods of social control are very informal and would not work except in small, homogeneous groups in which ties among the members are intimate and continuous, and contradictory ideas are absent.

Stratification

The rudimentary nature of the political system and the primitive nature of the economic system contribute to yet another distinctive characteristic of modern hunting and gathering societies: minimal inequality in power and privilege. Differences between individuals are so slight, in fact, that a number of observers have spoken of a kind of "primitive communism." To some extent this is justified. As we have seen, political authority with the power to coerce is virtually nonexistent. Differences in influence exist, but only to the degree permitted by those who are influenced, and only as a result of their respect for another individual's skills or wisdom. When individuals lose this respect, they also lose their influence.

In most hunting and gathering societies, differences in wealth are very minor. Many factors are responsible for this. For one thing, as we have seen, the nomadic way of life prevents any substantial accumulation of possessions. In addition, the ready availability of most essential resources (e.g., wood for bows, flint for stone tools) precludes the need to amass things, while technological limitations greatly restrict what can be produced. Finally, there is the widespread practice of sharing in most of these groups.

As a general rule the concept of private property has only limited development among hunting and gathering peoples. Things that an individual uses constantly, such as tools and weapons, are always recognized as his own, but fields and forests are the common property of the entire society (see Table 5.4). These territorial rights are often

Table 5.4 Private Ownership of Land, by Societal Type

Societal Type	Percentage of Societies in Which Private Ownership of Land Is		Number of Societies
	Absent	Present	
Hunting and gathering	83	17	100
Simple horticultural	22	78	81
Advanced horticultural	7	93	204
Agrarian	3	97	86

Source: See Appendix, pp. 417–418.

taken quite seriously, and outsiders are frequently obliged to ask permission to enter another group's territory to seek food.[72] Animals and plants are normally considered common property until they are killed or gathered, at which time they become the property of those who killed or gathered them. Even then, however, use of them is hedged about by the rule of sharing.[73]

A successful hunter does not normally keep his kill for himself alone or even, in most cases, for his family.[74] The reason for this seems to be the same as that which underlies insurance systems in industrial societies: it is an effective method of spreading risks. As we have seen, poor hunting conditions, ill health, or just a streak of bad luck can render any individual or family incapable of providing for itself, and sharing food greatly enhances everyone's chances of survival.

Despite near equality in power and wealth, there is inequality in prestige in most hunting and gathering societies. The interesting thing about this, from the viewpoint of members of industrial societies, is the extent to which prestige depends on the personal qualities of an individual rather than on impersonal criteria, such as the offices or roles he occupies or the possessions he controls. This is, of course, a natural consequence of the limited development of specialized offices and roles and the limited opportunities for accumulating possessions and wealth. But it sharply differentiates these societies from more advanced ones.

The Andaman Islanders accord honor and respect to three kinds of people: (1) older people; (2) people endowed with supernatural powers; and (3) people with certain personal qualities, notably "skill in hunting and warfare, generosity and kindness, and freedom from bad temper."[75] Men are apparently more likely than women to become honored members of the group. Similar types of people are accorded honor and prestige in most other hunting and gathering societies, and skill in oratory is often honored as well.[76]

Because personal characteristics are so important, systems of stratification in these groups have an openness about them not often found in more advanced societies. Almost no organizational or institutional barriers block the rise of talented individuals. For example, even where the office of headman is inherited, as it is in approximately half the societies,[77] others may surpass him in achieving honor. The study of the Siriono Indians cited earlier tells of a headman who was a very poor hunter and whose status, as a result, was low. The importance attached to age also contributes to the openness of the system. Almost anyone who lives long enough usually ends up with a fair degree of honor and respect.

Religion

In almost every carefully studied hunting and gathering society of the modern era, there is evidence that its members have grappled with the problem of explaining the world around them, especially those aspects of it that influence their own lives. Up to a point, their explanations and their interpretations of reality are the same as ours: animals run when they are frightened, people become hungry when they do not have enough to eat, and serious illness can cause death.

Because their store of information is so much more limited than ours, however, members of these societies quickly reach the limits of their ability to explain things in naturalistic terms. Insufficient food causes hunger; but why is there insufficient food? Illness is the cause of a death; but what caused the illness? To answer questions such as these, members of hunting and gathering societies, like people in every society confronted with what they do not fully understand, have developed their own sets of explanations. These explanations form the basis of a type of religion known as animism.[78]

The central element in animism is the belief that spirits inhabit virtually everything in the world of nature: rocks, trees, lakes, clouds, and other inanimate things, as well as animals and humans. These spirits are constantly intervening in human affairs, sometimes helping, sometimes harming. They cause the arrow to strike the deer, or they warn the animal so it bolts; they enter the body to heal a wound, or they settle

!Kung San Shaman in Trance, Southwest Africa.

in the intestines to twist and burn them. Furthermore, these spirits can be influenced by humans who know the proper rituals, sacrifices, and magic charms. Some humans, however, are more skillful at this than others, and when people fail in their efforts to appease a spirit, as when a sick child fails to recover, they turn to the expert in such matters, the medicine man or shaman.

Shamans are not specialists in the strict sense of the term, any more than headmen are specialists. They are individuals who spend most of their time doing the same things as others of their sex (most shamans are men, but some are women), serving in their more specialized role only when the need arises.

While a shaman uses his powers in various ways, one of the most common is in healing. He may also use them to ensure the success of hunting expeditions, to protect the group against evil spirits and other dangers, and generally to ensure the group's well-being. Shamans do not always use their special powers for the benefit of others, however. Sometimes they employ them to punish people who have offended them.[79]

Because of their role, shamans usually command respect and often are more influential than the headman.[80] Sometimes, as with the Northern Maidu in California, the headman "was chosen largely through the aid of the shaman, who was supposed to reveal to the older men the choice of the spirits."[81] The role of shaman also tends to be profitable, since others are usually happy to offer gifts in exchange for help or to maintain goodwill.[82]

Education

Socialization of the young in hunting and gathering societies is largely an informal process in which children learn both through their play and through observing and imitating their elders. At a relatively early age, boys are allowed to join the men on the hunt, participating in any activities of which they are capable. Fathers commonly make miniature bows as soon as their sons can handle them, and encourage the boys to practice. Girls assist their mothers in their campsite duties and in gathering vegetables and fruits. Thus children prepare for their future roles.

This informal socialization is often supplemented by a formal process of initiation that marks the transition from childhood to manhood or womanhood.[83] Initiation rites vary considerably from one society to another, though girls' ceremonies are usually linked with their first menstruation. The rites for boys commonly involve painful experiences (e.g., circumcision, scarification, or knocking out a tooth), which prove their courage and thus their right to the privileges of manhood. As a rule, these rites are also the occasion for introducing young men to their group's most sacred lore, and this combination of experiences helps impress on them its value and importance.

Compared with horticultural and agrarian societies, hunting and gathering societies put more stress on training the child to be independent and self-reliant, less on obedience (see Table 5.5). This is apparently a cultural response to a subsistence economy in which it is imperative to have venturesome, independent adults who take initiative in finding and securing food.[84] In contrast, venturesomeness and independence are less valuable and less often encouraged in technologically more advanced horticultural and agrarian societies. Rather, it is important that children in those societies learn to conform to the established norms of planting, cultivating, and harvesting, and the other proven routines of farming.

Table 5.5 Emphases in Child Rearing, by Societal Type (in Percentages)

Societal Type	Self-Reliance Stressed More than Obedience	Self-Reliance and Obedience Stressed Equally	Obedience Stressed More than Self-Reliance	N
Hunting and gathering	63	13	23	19
Simple horticultural	34	20	46	26
Advanced horticultural	24	13	63	39
Agrarian	12	7	82	15

Source: See Appendix, pp. 417–418.

Note: The values in this table are arithmetic averages of four separate sets of data for (1) young boys, (2) older boys, (3) young girls, and (4) older girls. Controlling for age, greater emphasis was placed on self-reliance for boys than for girls in all types of societies. Controlling for sex, greater emphasis was placed on self-reliance for older boys than for younger, but no consistent pattern was observed among girls.

The Arts and Leisure

Modern hunting and gathering peoples have produced a variety of artistic works. Some are strikingly similar to the cave drawings and carvings of hunters and gatherers of prehistoric times. The motivation behind these efforts is not always clear, but in some cases it is plainly religious, in others, magical.[§][85] And sometimes it appears to be purely aesthetic.

Music, too, plays a part in the lives of most, if not all, hunters and gatherers. In Pygmy hunter festivals, songs and the music of a primitive wooden trumpet are central.[86] These festivals have great religious significance and express the people's devotion to, and trust in, the forest in which they live and on which they depend. And, as with the visual arts, music may be used purely for aesthetic purposes, self-expression, and enjoyment.[87] Dancing is another valued feature of life in many of these societies, and, again, the motives for it are varied.

Another popular leisure activity is storytelling. Pygmies are said to be blessed with a lively imagination.[88] Stories range from accounts of the day's hunt (often embellished to hold the listeners' attention) to sacred myths and legends passed down over many generations. Legends commonly deal with the origins of the world and of the group. Stories about the exploits of great heroes of the past are popular and are often used to explain the group's customs. Sacred myths and legends, as we have seen, frequently enter into initiation rites, especially for boys, and they are sometimes accompanied by music and dance. This complex interweaving of art, religion, entertainment, and education provides a strong foundation for tradition and for sociocultural continuity.

Hunters and gatherers, like people everywhere, enjoy gossip, small talk, and other nonessential activities. Games are played in virtually all of these societies, but it is interesting to note that games of strategy are absent, while games of chance are more

---

[§]A key difference between religion and magic is that in the former the objects of attention are valued for their *intrinsic* worth, whereas in the latter they are valued only as a *means* toward some (usually material) end. That is, they can be manipulated for human purposes.[86]

Table 5.6 Types of Games, by Societal Type

Type of Society	Percentage of Societies Having Games of			
	Physical Skill	Chance	Strategy	N
Hunting and gathering	97	81	0	129
Simple horticultural	78	34	10	67
Advanced horticultural	90	37	57	60
Agrarian	97	74	71	35
Fishing	97	61	3	33
Herding	92	39	54	13

Source: See Appendix, pp. 417–418.

common than in other types of societies (see Table 5.6). Since a society's games, like the rest of its culture, reflect its experiences, the absence of games of strategy suggests that hunters and gatherers feel less sense of control over the events in their lives than the members of more advanced societies.

Tribal Ties: Links between Societies

As we have noted a number of times, each band or local group of hunters and gatherers is usually autonomous. Rarely are even two of them brought together under a single leader, and when this does happen, it usually involves groups that are no longer completely dependent on hunting and gathering.

Cave Art by Contemporary Australian Hunters and Gatherers: The Water Snake and Turtle Are Important Figures in the Religion of These People.

Despite the virtual absence of formal political organizations encompassing different communities, there are often informal social and cultural ties. The most inclusive of these, and one that is nearly universal, is the tribe—a group of people who speak a distinctive language or dialect, share a culture that distinguishes them from other peoples, and know themselves, and are known, by a distinctive name.[89] Unlike a society, a tribe is not necessarily organized politically. On the contrary, among hunting and gathering peoples almost none are.

Most tribes appear to have been formed by the process of societal fission or division. When the population of a hunting and gathering band grows too large for the resources of the immediate area, it divides. Division may also occur because of conflict within a band.[90] In either case, although a new group is formed, its members will naturally continue to share the culture of the parent group. Normally the new group locates somewhere near the old one, if only because its technology and accumulated experience become less relevant the farther it moves and the more the environment differs from the one its members have been used to. If this process of fission is repeated a number of times, a cluster of autonomous bands with the same language and similar stores of information develops, and a tribe emerges.

As this suggests, among hunters and gatherers the tribe is more important as a cultural unit than as a social unit. One writer, describing the !Kung, reports that the tribe "has no social solidarity, and is of very little, if any, importance in regulating social life. There appears to be no tribal organization among the [people], nothing in the nature of a central authority whose decisions are binding on all the members of the tribe, nor is collective action ever taken in the interests of the tribe as a whole."[91] Sometimes, as in Australia, an entire tribe assembles periodically for rituals and ceremonies, but this is not typical.

From the organizational standpoint the chief significance of these tribal groupings lies in their evolutionary potential: with technological advance, they may become political units. Even among societies still on the hunting and gathering level, there is some evidence of movement in this direction. In a few of the more favorably situated sedentary groups, for example, several villages have been brought together under the leadership of a single individual.[92] This development is greatly facilitated by their common cultural heritage.

HUNTING AND GATHERING SOCIETIES IN THEORETICAL PERSPECTIVE
Archaeological and Ethnographic Evidence Compared

Now that we have completed our review of both the archaeological and the ethnographic evidence, we can consider the relationship between prehistoric hunting and gathering groups and those of the modern era. Though indiscriminate comparisons of the two can be misleading, our evidence indicates that careful comparisons can be extremely valuable.[93] To begin with, we must recognize that we cannot equate hunters and gatherers of the modern era with early hominid hunters and gatherers of a million or more years ago—before the process of human biological evolution had produced *Homo sapiens sapiens* and before the basic tools and weapons of modern hunters and gatherers had been invented. We can, however, reasonably compare hunters and gatherers of the recent past with others who have lived during the last 15,000 years.

We can see why, now that we are familiar with both sets of evidence. The similarities between these two sets of hunters and gatherers are many and basic; the differences are fewer and less important. The societies of the two periods are similar in such crucial matters as subsistence technology, size, relative equality,** and minimal occupational specialization. In addition, similarities in art suggest similarities in religious belief and practice.

The differences are largely of three types. First, in many hunting and gathering societies of the modern era there are some elements that originated in more advanced societies (e.g., metal tools and some religious ideas). Second, modern hunters and gatherers have had no opportunity to move into new unoccupied territories. Prehistoric hunters and gatherers were not always subject to this harsh restriction. Finally, technologically advanced societies have often forced modern hunters and gatherers out of territories that were suitable for farming and herding.***

As we have seen, the archaeological record is much less complete than the ethnographic, being silent on many subjects about which the latter provides a wealth of information. Therefore, when the ethnographic record shows patterns that are consistent for all or most modern groups and when these patterns do not depend on conditions peculiar to the industrial era, archaeologists now tend to regard them as applicable to most of the hunting and gathering societies of the last 15,000 years. This reflects the growing awareness of the limiting nature of a hunting and gathering technology,[94] and the realization that the range of variation in the basic characteristics of societies that depend on that technology will inevitably be small. In short, except where relevant conditions have changed significantly, we can probably assume substantial similarity between the advanced hunting and gathering societies of late prehistoric times and those of recent centuries.[††]

A Model of Limited Development

In Chapter 2 we saw that human societies are systems of interrelated parts. In Chapters 3 and 4 we identified subsistence technology as the single most powerful variable influencing the other characteristics of these systems. Now that we have completed our analysis of the first of the major societal types, we are in a better position to appreciate both the systemic nature of societies and the critical role of technology.

Figure 5.3 portrays the systemic qualities of a hunting and gathering society, and the relationships among its most important characteristics. The key element is the subsistence technology on which members of these societies depend for their survival

---

**This is indicated by the absence of differentiation in the burial remains of prehistoric hunters and gatherers. In contrast, in technologically more advanced societies of later eras one finds clear evidence of distinctions between rich and poor, the former having rare and costly objects buried with them.

***Hunters and gatherers in both the New World and Australia, however, still occupied good farming and herding lands until fairly recently, so we are not entirely without information on societies that existed under such conditions.

††Archaeological evidence indicates that the societies of !Kung hunters and gatherers were not fundamentally altered by their contact with technologically more advanced societies over the past 2,000 years or so. In fact, the tools and diet of the !Kung in the 1960s apparently were not much different from those of 40,000 years earlier.[95]

and well-being. Because of their dependence on hunting and gathering, most of these groups are destined to be nomadic and to have a low level of productivity and a limited store of other kinds of information.

These characteristics lead in turn to other, second-order effects. Nomadism and the low level of productivity combine to limit possibilities for the accumulation of possessions. The low level of productivity and the limited store of other technological information, especially information relevant to transportation and communication, combine to keep hunting and gathering societies small. The limited development of these technologies also limits contacts with other societies. These characteristics combine with the small size of these societies to keep the rate of technological innovation low. The limited store of information about natural phenomena also contributes to the development of animistic beliefs.

Finally, these second-order effects, individually and collectively, produce a series of third-order effects. These include the low level of inequality that is characteristic of hunting and gathering societies, their limited division of labor, the kinship basis of social organization, and their ideological conservatism and low rates of social and cultural change. The latter, through a process of feedback, reinforces the dependence of these societies on hunting and gathering as their basic mode of subsistence. Thus, the system tends to be self-perpetuating.

The causal linkages indicated in Figure 5.3 may actually understate the degree to which the various characteristics of a hunting and gathering society are interrelated: some arrows that should have been included may have been omitted. The important point, however, is not the completeness of the model but the way it illustrates the systemic nature of these societies and shows the consequences of technology for every major component of the system, including basic beliefs and values.

Ecological-evolutionary theory, as we have seen, asserts that technology limits "the range of the possible" for a society, and in the case of hunting and gathering societies it

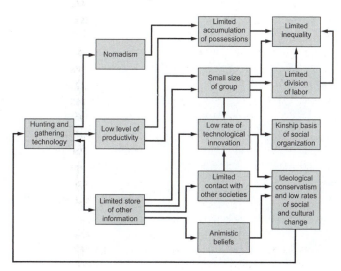

Figure 5.3. Model of Relationships Among the Characteristics of Hunting and Gathering Societies.

is clear that that range is remarkably narrow. We do, of course, find differences among these societies, but not in their most basic characteristics. Many of these differences, as in modes of dress and housing, simply reflect variations in the environments to which these societies must adapt. Some differences, however, do not appear to be related to environmental conditions, and we have to assume that they reflect unknown and unknowable past experiences of the groups, experiences that led them to adopt dissimilar practices. We can see this, for example, in the case of marriage practices, which vary among societies at this level of development. It is clear that the limits set by a hunting and gathering technology are fairly broad with respect to this relationship. As a result, ideology—the information that helps people order societal life—comes into greater play.

But where the basic characteristics and development of hunting and gathering societies are concerned, technology sets strict and seemingly inviolable limits. These limits are less restrictive when the technology is applied to a particularly favorable environment. A society's biophysical environment, for example, may be especially rich in the resources on which the society depends, or its social environment may not provide much competition for those resources. But the only way the limits set by its technology can be expanded is for a hunting and gathering society to increase its store of technological information, as some of them have done by incorporating elements of fishing and horticulture.

The Last Hunting and Gathering Societies

In the summer of 1975, death came to the last full-blooded member of the Ona, a tribe of hunters and gatherers that had inhabited the southern tip of South America since at least the days of Ferdinand Magellan, the famed sixteenth-century explorer, and probably for centuries or even millennia before that.[96] It is estimated that in Magellan's day there were 2,000 Ona, divided into about thirty societies. The Ona survived the remoteness and harshness of their homeland only to be destroyed by their contacts with

One of the Last Photographs of the Ona of Terra del Fuego, a Tribe of Hunters and Gatherers That Is Now Extinct.

technologically more advanced societies. Disease, loss of territory, and loss of members to other societies all took their toll. The last Ona *society* died long ago; now even the last *Ona* is also dead.

The experience of the Ona has been the experience of tens of thousands of hunting and gathering societies during the 10,000 years since hunters and gatherers first began competing for territories and other resources with technologically more advanced societies. Hunters and gatherers have had only one defense: retreat to lands that other groups regarded as worthless or inaccessible.

Today, even this defense is crumbling and the last outposts of this ancient way of life are doomed. The speed of the process is demonstrated by the experience of an anthropologist who pioneered in the study of the !Kung of the Kalahari Desert in southwest Africa. She reports that to reach them in 1951 required an arduous trip across the desert by truck, lasting eight days from the final outposts of civilization until contact with the !Kung was made.[97] There was no road of any kind, not even a track across the sand and bush country. When she returned in 1962, only eleven years later, she reached them in one day over a well-cleared track. As they came more and more in contact with, and under the influence of, more advanced societies, their traditional way of life was doomed. Today, few, if any, !Kung, or other "indigenous peoples," are still relying on hunting and gathering for subsistence.[98]

Thus, in a few short years the last hunting and gathering society will probably have vanished—and with it an irreplaceable link to our past. For thousands of years these societies maintained a remarkably stable relationship with their environments and a highly satisfying way of life. Relying entirely on cultural information that they had accumulated over centuries, hunters and gatherers adapted to a wide variety of biophysical environments; and, until the advent of societies with larger populations and more sophisticated technologies, they also adapted successfully to their social environments. The process of change in each part of those sociocultural systems occurred so slowly that answering changes could occur in other parts without serious social unrest or upheaval. Today, this way of life, which served our species extremely well for so many years, is no longer viable.

Horticultural Societies

Before the hunting and gathering era ended 10,000 to 12,000 years ago, human societies had accumulated substantial stores of information about plants and animals. People were as familiar with the behavior patterns of some animals as they were with their own and probably understood them almost as well. They had also identified hundreds of varieties of edible plants and had become familiar with their processes of reproduction and growth. Some hunters and gatherers in the Middle East were even harvesting wild grains with stone sickles and hunting cattle, sheep, goats, and pigs.[1] Clearly the shift from hunting animals to herding them and from gathering plants to cultivating them was not as great or as difficult a step as one might imagine.

But what induced societies to take that step? Why, after hundreds of thousands of years of hunting and gathering, did the members of some societies abandon that ancient, time-hallowed way of life? Above all, why did they do it when the new mode of production meant more work and less freedom?

CAUSES OF THE SHIFT FROM HUNTING AND GATHERING TO HORTICULTURE

Until recent decades, scholars tended to assume that, because of human intelligence and unsatisfied human needs, technological innovation and societal development are normal and natural and require no special explanation. By shifting from hunting and gathering to horticulture, they reasoned, societies assured themselves of a greater and more stable supply of food, and the members of any society would naturally make such a shift once the principles of plant cultivation came to be understood. Furthermore, it was generally assumed that horticulture required less labor than hunting and gathering. Thus, by adopting horticulture—that is, farming without plows—societies traded a precarious and onerous way of life for a more secure and satisfying one. Or so it seemed.

More recently, however, doubts have been cast on these explanations. To begin with, a growing body of archaeological research indicates that the members of many hunting and gathering societies understood and occasionally applied the basic principles of plant cultivation thousands of years before horticulture became their primary mode of subsistence. In addition, ethnographic studies of modern hunting and gathering societies have made it clear that their members place a high value on their way of life: they cherish the challenge and excitement of the hunt and the freedom and other benefits their way of life affords. Finally, it has also become clear that most societies have not shared the positive view of innovation and change that prevails in industrial societies today. On the contrary, they place a high value on tradition and continuity.

As a result, most scholars now doubt that hunters and gatherers abandoned hunting and gathering and adopted horticulture unless they were compelled to do so by circumstances beyond their control. Instead, they have come to believe that the gradual growth of human population over millions of years (see Table 5.2) and changing climate eventually created a situation in which it became imperative for societies to increase the supply and reliability of food resources. This was probably done gradually, with plant cultivation and animal domestication initially serving only as a minor means of supplementing the food resources obtained by hunting and gathering. But changing diet and a sedentary lifestyle led to still larger populations and greater dependence on domesticated plants and animals. Eventually, after hundreds or thousands of years, the point would have been reached where horticulture replaced hunting and gathering as the dominant mode of subsistence. But the whole process would have been so gradual that the people involved may have been largely unaware of the significance and irreversibility of the changes that were occurring.

Although their relative importance varied in different regions, three things are now generally thought to have contributed to the transition from hunting and gathering to plant and animal domestication: (1) environmental change, (2) population growth, and (3) growth in cultural information and technology.[2]

Global warming in the period between 15,000 and 8,000 years ago changed the climate greatly in many areas, raised ocean levels, and altered the habitat of a number of important animals and plants.* Shrinking habitats reduced the supply and changed the migration patterns of a number of large game animals. This forced societies either to follow surviving animal populations into new territories or to find substitute foods. It also permitted wild cereals to spread into areas where they became available first for gathering and then for domestication.[3] In addition, the cumulative effects of population growth (see Table 5.2) meant that even though population densities were not high by modern standards, more people were competing for a shrinking resource base. Under these circumstances periodic food and resource shortages would have been especially acute.

---

*Later climatic shifts also affected developmental trends in horticultural and agrarian societies.

The importance of the first two causes is attested to by the fact that domestication of a variety of species of plants occurred independently in the same approximate latitudes around the world—southwest Asia (barley, wild einkorn, and wild emmer wheat), India (fruits, herbs, and possibly rice), southeast Asia (various tubers), China (millet, rice, and soybeans), North and South America (maize, beans, squash, cocoa, and quinoa)—in the short period between 8500 and 3000 B.C.[4] It is also supported by the fact that many of the plants first domesticated, the ancestors of wheat, barley, millet, and rice, were "third choice" foods in the wild.[5] In all likelihood, then, they were domesticated not because people had a special appetite for them per se, but because they constituted a reliable and storable source of *additional* food.

During this same time period, a variety of animal species were also domesticated (see Figure 6.1). For example, sheep and goats were domesticated in southwest Asia, cattle in Turkey and Greece, pigs in southwest Asia, and llamas and guinea pigs in South America.[6]

Overall, domestication generally occurred gradually, but in some areas at least, the pressures to adopt horticulture may have been intensified by earlier advances in weapons technology that led to the rapid depletion and extinction of many species of big-game animals that previously had been important sources of food.

The shift from hunting and gathering to horticulture, although seemingly a change in only one aspect of technology, was destined to have profound and far-reaching consequences for human life as a whole. We will examine the more immediate consequences in the present chapter and the longer-term consequences in Chapters 7 through 15. Before doing this, however, we must first consider the new technology itself.

THE TECHNOLOGY OF HORTICULTURE

The practice of horticulture is referred to as *swidden cultivation,* or sometimes it is known as *slash-and-burn cultivation.* Both of these terms refer to the widespread practice of clearing new gardens by cutting and then burning existing vegetation, especially shrubs and small trees.[†] Larger trees are often left standing but are killed by girdling them, or cutting away a circular strip of bark all the way around the tree, thereby stopping the flow of nutrients from the roots to the branches.

After existing vegetation has been burned away, the resulting layer of ash provides fertilizer for the crops that are planted. Good yields can be expected for a year or two, but after that, as the nutrients in the ash are consumed, yields decline. Also, because there are no plows to dislodge them, weeds eventually take over. Thus, gardens must be abandoned and new plots cleared after only a few years.

The length of time a garden can be cultivated by horticulturalists varies considerably, depending on environmental conditions and on the length of time since the land was last cultivated. The longer the land remains uncultivated, the greater the amount of vegetation that grows on it and the thicker the layer of ash and nutrients when it is burned. Allowing the land to revert to jungle or forest is especially important because

---

[†]This too appears to be an extension of, rather than a decisive break with, practices of the past. Archaeological and ethnographic evidence indicates that hunters and gatherers around the world used fire to clear trees and encourage the growth of plants (e.g., grasses and legumes), which would attract desired game animals.[7]

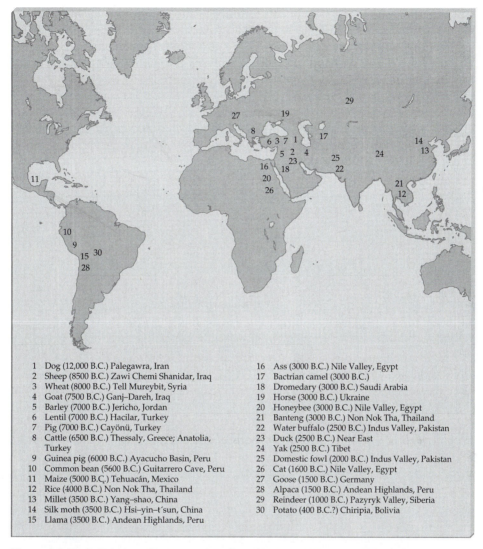

1	Dog (12,000 B.C.) Palegawra, Iran	16	Ass (3000 B.C.) Nile Valley, Egypt
2	Sheep (8500 B.C.) Zawi Chemi Shanidar, Iraq	17	Bactrian camel (3000 B.C.)
3	Wheat (8000 B.C.) Tell Mureybit, Syria	18	Dromedary (3000 B.C.) Saudi Arabia
4	Goat (7500 B.C.) Ganj–Dareh, Iraq	19	Horse (3000 B.C.) Ukraine
5	Barley (7000 B.C.) Jericho, Jordan	20	Honeybee (3000 B.C.) Nile Valley, Egypt
6	Lentil (7000 B.C.) Hacilar, Turkey	21	Banteng (3000 B.C.) Non Nok Tha, Thailand
7	Pig (7000 B.C.) Cayönü, Turkey	22	Water buffalo (2500 B.C.) Indus Valley, Pakistan
8	Cattle (6500 B.C.) Thessaly, Greece; Anatolia, Turkey	23	Duck (2500 B.C.) Near East
9	Guinea pig (6000 B.C.) Ayacucho Basin, Peru	24	Yak (2500 B.C.) Tibet
10	Common bean (5600 B.C.) Guitarrero Cave, Peru	25	Domestic fowl (2000 B.C.) Indus Valley, Pakistan
11	Maize (5000 B.C.) Tehuacán, Mexico	26	Cat (1600 B.C.) Nile Valley, Egypt
12	Rice (4000 B.C.) Non Nok Tha, Thailand	27	Goose (1500 B.C.) Germany
13	Millet (3500 B.C.) Yang–shao, China	28	Alpaca (1500 B.C.) Andean Highlands, Peru
14	Silk moth (3500 B.C.) Hsi–yin–t´sun, China	29	Reindeer (1000 B.C.) Pazyryk Valley, Siberia
15	Llama (3500 B.C.) Andean Highlands, Peru	30	Potato (400 B.C.?) Chiripia, Bolivia

Figure 6.1. Early Evidence for Domestication of Selected Plants and Animals.
Source: Adapted from Robert J. Wenke, *Patterns in Prehistory: Humankind's First Three Million Years* (New York: Oxford University Press, 1990).

this destroys the weeds that spring up when land is cleared and that then choke out cultivated plants.

Because of the need to allow the land periodically to revert to wilderness, horticulturalists are able to cultivate only a small fraction of the territory they occupy. Thus, horticultural societies seldom achieve the high levels of population density typical of agrarian societies. Nevertheless, their mode of subsistence is much more productive than hunting and gathering in terms of yield per acre, and their societies, as a result, almost always have larger and denser populations.

In the horticultural system of cultivation, men are usually responsible for clearing the land when new gardens are needed, while women are responsible for planting, tending, and harvesting the crops. This division of labor is almost certainly linked to the earlier division of labor in hunting and gathering societies, where

Women Planting Taro in a Simple Horticultural Society in New Guinea. Note the Tree Stumps in the Cultivated Area: Horticulturalists Do Not Clear the Land as Thoroughly as Agriculturalists, Who Use Plows.

women were responsible for providing the vegetable materials that people consumed. Men continue to hunt in many horticultural societies, but hunting is a much less productive activity since the ratio of game animals to humans is much lower (partly because of the growth of human population, partly because game animals tend to avoid areas of more permanent human settlement). Overall, men's contribution to subsistence is often much less than that of women in horticultural societies and requires much less time. Thus, men in these societies often have substantial amounts of time at their disposal—a fact that has had important consequences, as we will see.

In our analysis of horticultural societies, we will use the same format we used in the last chapter. We will first examine the archaeological and ethnographic evidence on simple and advanced horticultural societies, and then, at the end of the chapter, we will return to ecological-evolutionary theory to help us formulate a coherent model of horticultural societies.

SIMPLE HORTICULTURAL SOCIETIES IN PREHISTORIC ASIA AND EUROPE

In Asia Minor, Palestine, Syria, and the hill country east of the Tigris River, archaeologists have found the remains of ancient settlements dating from about 10,000 to 8000 B.C., in which horticulture appears to have been the primary means of subsistence.[8] In traditional archaeological usage, the period in which simple horticultural societies were dominant in a region was called the Neolithic era, or New Stone Age. This name was chosen because in early research in Europe and the Middle East, excavated sites often yielded stone axes, adzes, and hammers that, unlike earlier stone tools, had been smoothed by grinding or polishing. Before radiocarbon dating, these tools were the best indicators of the relative age of excavated materials and of their place in evolutionary history.

As research progressed, however, and more and more sites were excavated, it became increasingly clear that these tools were not the most distinctive feature of Neolithic societies, and certainly not their greatest technological achievement. Rather, their most important innovations were in the area of subsistence technology. For the first time in history, groups of people were primarily dependent on horticulture, and hunting and gathering was relegated to a secondary role. In this connection, it is important to recognize that these early horticultural societies were not based on a single resource or activity. Horticulture was their primary means of subsistence, but it was supplemented by herding, fishing, hunting, and gathering in various combinations.[9] The presence of livestock in many of these early societies was especially important, as we will soon see.

The First Great Social Revolution

Although many scholars today describe the emergence of horticultural societies as the first great social revolution in human history, it would be wrong to assume that the rate of change *seemed* revolutionary to those involved. As far as we can judge, the process was so gradual that the changes occurring during a lifetime were neither very numerous nor overwhelming. For example, hunters and gatherers in the Middle East had been using wild grains for a thousand years or more before the horticultural era began. Techniques of harvesting, storing, grinding, and cooking these grains were well-known even before the techniques of cultivating them were adopted. Furthermore, as we have noted, hunting, and to some extent gathering, continued to play a part in the lives of early horticulturalists. There was almost certainly considerable continuity in other areas of life as well, especially in kinship, religion, and politics. The survival of fertility cults, indicated by the widespread presence of female figurines in Neolithic remains, is one evidence of this.[10] Our use of the term "revolutionary" in connection with the rise of horticultural societies, therefore, is based primarily on the *long-term consequences* of the change.

Permanence of Settlements

One immediate and very important consequence of the shift to horticulture was the greater permanence of settlements. No longer did a group of people have to move about constantly in quest of food; on the contrary, the practice of horticulture forced them to stay in one place for extended periods.‡ In the Middle East and in southeastern Europe, many truly permanent settlements seem to have been established. In most areas, however, simple horticulturalists usually have had to move their settlements every few years.[11] Why this was not necessary in the Middle East and southeastern Europe is still a mystery, since only continuing fertilization (by flooding or by human activity), the use of the plow, and crop rotation permit land to be kept under continuous cultivation,[12] and so far there is no evidence of any of these practices at that time. We do know, however, that these early horticulturalists kept livestock, and so it is possible that the value of manure as fertilizer was discovered at an early date.[13] This practice may not have spread because, in other areas, there was more arable land available.

In any case, the shift from hunting and gathering to horticulture substantially increased the permanence of human settlements, thereby enabling people to accumulate many more possessions than ever before. This is evident in the archaeological remains left by horticulturalists of the Neolithic era. Tools and weapons are much more numerous and varied than in older sites, and for the first time there are large, bulky objects such as stone cups and bowls and pottery.[14] Dwellings also became more substantial. Some buildings contained several rooms and a small courtyard and were made of materials like sun-dried clay blocks, capable of lasting for as long as two generations.[15] Even more noteworthy is the appearance of such things as religious shrines or ceremonial centers, village walls, and occasional paved or timbered (corduroy style) roadways or alleys; though none of these is typical of simple horticultural communities, they are not rare.[16]

The change from hunting and gathering to horticulture also resulted in larger settlements and denser populations (see Table 6.1). Jerf el Ahmar, one of the oldest horticultural villages yet discovered, had about forty houses and a population of possibly 240, or six times that of the average hunting and gathering band.[17] Neolithic

---

‡As noted earlier, in extremely supportive environments some hunters and gatherers established relatively permanent settlements. Indeed, there is evidence that some of the hunters and gatherers in southwest Asia lived in permanent settlements in the millennium *before* they domesticated the cereal grains they were gathering and the animals they were hunting. Nonetheless, according to Murdock's data only about 10 percent of hunters and gatherers are sedentary, whereas more than 91 percent of simple horticulturalists and 95 percent of advanced horticulturalists are.

Table 6.1 Median Density of Population, by Type of Society

	Persons per Square Mile	N
Hunting and gathering	0.6	27
Simple horticultural	13.8	35
Advanced horticultural	42.7	38
Agrarian	100.0+	27

Source: See Appendix, pp. 417–418.

Figure 6.2. Early Horticultural Societies in Southwest Asia. The "Fertile Crescent" Is Outlined, and Its Extensions into Turkey Are Indicated by the Dashed Lines.
Source: Adapted from Robert J. Wenke, *Patterns in Prehistory: Humankind's First Three Million Years* (New York: Oxford University Press, 1990), and Luigi Luca Cavalli-Sforza and Francesco Cavalli Sforza, *The Great Human Diasporas: The History of Diversity and Evolution* (New York: Addison-Wesley, 1995).

villages in Europe had from eight to fifty houses, suggesting populations ranging up to 300.[18] In several cases there were even more striking concentrations of population. One was a town located on the site of Jericho 5,000 years before the days of Joshua of biblical fame. Excavations there have uncovered a community that apparently housed 2,000 to 3,000 inhabitants.[19] More recent excavations of Çatal Hüyük,[§] in what is now Turkey, revealed a community occupying an even larger area with a population estimated between 4,000 and 6,000 in 6000 B.C.[21]

[§]Pronounced "Chatal Huooyook."[20]

Artist's Conception of Farmhouse in Denmark During the Horticultural Era There (about 2700 B.C.). Compare This with the Dwelling of the Family of the Paiute Hunter on Page 105.

Growth of Trade and Commerce

These two communities, though obviously exceptional, illustrate another development associated with the rise of horticultural societies—the rapid expansion and growing importance of trade and commerce.[22] Modern scholars believe that the "great" size of Jericho and Çatal Hüyük was not due merely to the practice of horticulture. As one writer put it, "It is . . . most unlikely that [horticulture] should have flourished more at Jericho, 200 metres below sea level, than elsewhere in Palestine. Some other resource must have existed, and this was probably trade."[23] As he points out, Jericho, because of its location on the Dead Sea, had easy access to salt, bitumen,** and sulfur, all of which were valuable materials in simple horticultural societies and not available everywhere. This view of Jericho as an early center of trade is supported by the discovery there of products such as obsidian from Asia Minor and cowrie shells from the Red Sea. In the case of Çatal Hüyük, obsidian[††] seems to have been the key local resource responsible for its growth. Even in remote villages, there is evidence of trade. For example, shells from the Mediterranean have been found in the sites of horticultural villages and in graves in northern Europe, and obsidian from Çatal Hüyük has been found throughout the Middle East and in what is now Turkey and Cyprus.[24]

**Bitumen was used to fix blades in handles, mend pottery, etc.

††Obsidian, or volcanic glass, was much sought after for use in weapons and cutting tools.

The growth in trade and commerce, combined with the increasing quantity of material products, may well have led to the beginnings of formal record keeping. Archaeologists have found a variety of clay tokens in horticultural sites from modern Turkey to Iran, but until recently no one could identify their use. Then it was discovered that the markings on many of the tokens were remarkably similar to symbols later used in early forms of writing for such words as "sheep," "wool," "cloth," "bread," "bed," and a variety of numerals.[25] This strongly suggests that the tokens were used to represent those same objects and numbers. Since these tokens were often stored in small clay jars, they were probably records of early business transactions, such as loans. But whatever their precise use in the societies of the time, these tokens tell us of a major breakthrough in the ability of human societies to store information.

Another probable consequence of the growth in trade and commerce was an increase in occupational specialization, at least in the chief commercial centers. Direct evidence of this has been found at several sites. For example, excavation of a community south of Jericho revealed a number of small workshops where specialized craftsmen, such as a butcher, a bead maker, and a maker of bone tools, worked.[26] This kind of specialization, however, was limited.[27] Most communities were still largely self-sufficient, and most families still produced nearly everything they used.[28] Innovations continued in the domestic arts, with the invention of pottery and weaving being especially important.[29]

Increase in Warfare

There is little evidence of warfare in early horticultural societies. Graves rarely contain weapons, and most communities had no walls or other defenses.[30] Some, it is true, had ditches and fences, but these were more suitable for protection against marauding animals than against human enemies. *Later in the horticultural era the picture changed drastically and warfare became increasingly common.* In this period, battle-axes, daggers, and other arms are found in the graves of all adult males, reflecting the impact of technological advance, specifically metallurgy. The causes of this increase in warfare are not clear, but some scholars think it was linked with the growth of population and the resulting scarcity of new land suitable for horticulture. It may also have been related to declining opportunities for hunting, a traditional male activity. Warfare, with its demands for bravery and skill in the use of arms, would be a natural substitute, and if women were doing much of the work of tending the gardens, as is the case in most horticultural societies of the modern era, men would have had plenty of time to spend in this activity.[31] Moreover, the frictions created by growing pressure for land would provide a strong motivation. Finally, some experts suspect that the increase in warfare was linked with the increase in wealth, especially in the form of cattle, which could be easily stolen.[32]

One consequence of horticulture was that, as more and more societies adopted the new technology, it became increasingly difficult for other societies in the same area to continue hunting and gathering. As the population grew in a horticultural society, new settlements would form on the outer fringes. When they moved into territory occupied by hunters and gatherers, the horticulturalists would, by remaining in one place for a number of years, deplete the supply of game to the point that it could no longer support the hunters. If the hunters were tempted to fight for their "rights," they would usually find themselves badly outnumbered, if the population sizes of contemporary groups are any indication.[33]

Paris in the Horticultural Era

Discoveries have indicated that human settlement in what is now the city of Paris is much older than previously supposed. Excavations during an urban renewal project on the banks of the Seine in southeastern Paris have uncovered 50,000 objects, including perfectly preserved fragments of ceramic bowls; a millstone; a polished ax; a wooden bow; a fish hook; a tomb containing two children; and eleven wooden canoes, each carved from a single oak log, some large enough to hold six people.

Careful dating of the canoes indicates that they were hewn around 4500 B.C., or 6,500 years ago. This is 1,500 to 2,000 years earlier than any previous evidence of human settlement in the Paris area.

Other remains from the horticultural era were found in the 1980s under the courtyard of the Louvre in central Paris, but these were not as numerous or as exciting as the canoes and other recent finds. Since their discovery, the canoes have undergone an expensive process of preservation to stabilize the wood, and are now on display at the Carnavalet Museum.

Source: Associated Press, Sept. 15, 2000.

SIMPLE HORTICULTURAL SOCIETIES IN THE MODERN ERA

In recent centuries simple horticultural societies have been confined almost entirely to the New World and the islands of the Pacific. All of these societies have practiced some version of slash-and-burn horticulture. In most matters where comparisons are possible these societies are strikingly similar to simple horticultural societies of prehistoric times.[34] As with hunting and gathering societies, ethnography provides a richer source of information than archaeology. It answers many questions that would remain unanswered if our knowledge of horticultural societies were limited to what can be gleaned from the archaeological record.

Population and Economy

As we saw in our brief introduction to the various types of societies in Chapter 4, horticultural societies of the modern era have been substantially larger than hunting and gathering societies. Where the average hunting and gathering society of the recent past has had a population of approximately forty people (including children), the average simple horticultural society has had about 1,500 and the average advanced horticultural society more than 5,000 (see Table 4.2). Their larger numbers have given horticultural societies a substantial advantage when they have competed with hunting and gathering societies for territory, and this was almost certainly a major factor in the considerable decline in the number of hunting and gathering societies during the horticultural era (see Figure 4.2).

The larger populations of horticultural societies are due primarily to their greater economic productivity. The clearest indication of this is the greater population density that horticultural societies have been able to sustain. As Table 6.1 indicates, simple horticultural economies have been able to support more than twenty times as many people per square mile of territory as hunting and gathering economies, and advanced horticultural economies have supported even denser populations.

Increased productivity has not been the whole story, however. The larger populations of horticultural societies also reflect the emergence of *multicommunity* societies.

The Chinese Experience

The horticultural societies of China are of special interest because the shift to the new mode of subsistence began late enough there, and writing developed early enough, that some memory of the horticultural era was preserved in legends that were eventually written down. For a long time scholars thought this material was entirely fictional, but modern archaeological research has substantiated enough of it that it is now regarded as a mingling of fact and fiction.[35]

According to the legends, China's earliest inhabitants were hunters, but the growth of population eventually forced a shift to horticulture. As one source recounts, "The ancient people ate meat of animals and birds. At the time of Shen-nung [an early legendary ruler and cultural hero] there were so many people that the animals and birds became inadequate for people's wants and therefore Shen-nung taught the people to cultivate."[36] Other legends relate that Shen-nung introduced pottery and describe the era as a period of peace and self-sufficiency. "During the Age of Shen-nung people rested at ease and acted with vigor. They cared for their mothers, but not for their fathers. They lived among deer. They ate what they cultivated and wore what they wove. They did not think of harming one another." This preference for mothers is especially intriguing, because it is contrary to the later Chinese tradition and yet conforms to one of the distinctive features of contemporary horticultural societies (see p. 132). Finally, there is a legend that describes the Age of Shen-nung as the last era in which people were free from coercive political authority. "People were administered without a criminal law and prestige was built without the use of force. After Shen-nung, however, the strong began to rule over the weak and the few over the many."

Among hunters and gatherers, as we have seen, each community is usually politically independent, and thus a separate society in its own right. In horticultural societies, however, a number of communities are usually united under a single leader. The typical simple horticultural society consists of slightly more than ten communities, the average advanced horticultural society of seventeen.[37]

This widespread occurrence of multicommunity societies at the horticultural level and their virtual absence at the hunting and gathering level support the conclusion based on archaeological evidence (see pp. 125–126) that this shift in subsistence technology was the critical step that made possible the production of *a stable and dependable economic surplus.* Hunters and gatherers may produce surpluses for brief periods, but a complex institutional system cannot be built on such an uncertain foundation. Full-time occupational specialization involving priests, kings, craftsmen, and soldiers is possible only when an economy becomes productive enough so that some individuals regularly produce more of the necessities of life than they and their families require. In addition, they must be persuaded or forced to part with enough of this surplus to free others to perform tasks unrelated to basic subsistence. An economic surplus, therefore, is an essential precondition both for the emergence of full-time occupational specialization and for the development of complex social institutions.

One other noteworthy feature of the economies of horticultural societies is *the continuing importance of women's productive activities.*[38] For those whose ideas about farming are based on agricultural practices, it usually comes as a surprise to discover that in many horticultural societies women—not men—do most of the work of plant cultivation (see Table 6.2). As we will see shortly, the relative freedom of men from

Table 6.2 The Division of Labor between the Sexes in Horticultural and Agrarian Societies

Type of Society	Percentage Distribution				
	Cultivation Primarily a Female Responsibility	Both Sexes Share Equally	Cultivation Primarily a Male Responsibility	Total	N
Horticultural	39	33	28	100	389
Agrarian	8	33	59	100	100

Source: See Appendix, pp. 417–418.

time-consuming economic responsibilities in these societies has had interesting, important, and, sometimes, quite unpleasant, consequences.

The Continuing Importance of Kinship

As with hunting and gathering societies, the ethnographic record not only supports the view provided by archaeology but also broadens and extends it. For example, ethnographic studies show that kinship ties have been extremely important in simple horticultural societies of the modern era. In most instances, these ties provide the basic framework of the social system.[39] This is hardly surprising in view of the small size of these groups: almost everyone is related in some way to almost everyone else. Kinship obligations must constantly be considered in relations between individuals. The virtual absence of competing social organizations (e.g., craft guilds, political parties) further enhances the importance of kinship.

Kinship systems in these societies are sometimes very complex, with intricate systems of rules governing relations among numerous categories of kin. Extended kin groups, or *clans,* are common and usually very important, since they perform a number of essential functions for their members.[40] Above all, they function as *mutual aid associations,* providing individuals with protection against enemies and with economic support. Although both functions are important, the former is critical, for the political system is too limited in these societies to provide police services. Clans also perform important regulatory functions in the area of marriage, and they sometimes have important religious functions as well. Finally, the most powerful or respected clan often assumes leadership of an entire community, with its head serving as its headman, or even as tribal chief.

In horticultural societies, both simple and advanced, the concept of the kin group includes the dead as well as the living. This manifests itself in many ways, but especially in religious rituals designed to appease the spirits of dead ancestors. Nowhere is ancestor worship more common than in horticultural societies (see Figure 6.3).

The reason for such a high incidence of ancestor worship among horticulturalists, relative to hunters and gatherers, is probably tied to the greater permanence of their settlements. Because of this, the living remain in close physical proximity to their buried dead and carry on their daily activities in the very same settings in which their ancestors lived. Under such circumstances, ancestors are more likely to be remembered and honored. In agrarian societies, more awesome and more powerful polytheistic and monotheistic deities usually displaced ancestors from the central position they occupied in most horticultural societies, though ancestor worship continued to be important in many of them (e.g., China, Rome).

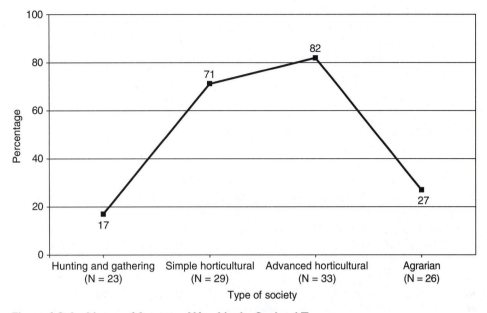

Figure 6.3. Incidence of Ancestor Worship, by Societal Type.
Source: Adapted from Dean Sheils, "Toward a Unified Theory of Ancestor Worship: A Cross-Cultural Study," *Social Forces*, 54(1975), 427–40, appendix, part B.

Another distinctive feature of kinship systems in horticultural societies is the importance many of them attach to ties with the mother's side of the family. This can be seen in Murdock's data, where the percentage of societies having *matrilineal* kin groups (i.e., descent traced through the maternal line) is as follows:[41]

Hunting and gathering societies	7 percent
Simple horticultural societies	24 percent
Advanced horticultural societies	12 percent
Agrarian societies	4 percent

This unusual pattern appears to be linked to the relative contributions men and women make to subsistence. For in those horticultural societies where men also make a substantial contribution, the matrilineal pattern is not as likely to develop (see Table 6.3). Nonetheless, two very different interpretations of this connection are possible. On the one hand, it may indicate recognition of the *importance* of women's economic contribution to these societies, while on the other, it may be a consequence of the long-term *absence of men* who are off hunting or fighting. In the latter case, matrilineal kinship would put control of the absent men's property in the hands of their *sisters*—members of their own kin group—rather than wives—who by the rules of exogamy are members of another kin group.[42]

Developments in Polity, Stratification, and Warfare
The power of political leaders has been quite limited in nearly all simple horticultural societies. Even in the larger, multicommunity societies, local villages have virtual autonomy except in matters of war and relations with other societies. Both the village

Table 6.3 Matrilineality among Simple Horticultural Societies, by Percentage of Subsistence Obtained from Hunting and Herding

Percentage of Subsistence Obtained by Hunting and Herding	Percentage of Societies Matrilineal	N
26 or more	14	29
16 to 25	24	54
15 or less	30	60

Source: See Appendix, pp. 417–418.

headman and the tribal chief (i.e., leader of the multicommunity society) depend more on persuasion than on coercion to achieve their goals (see Figure 5.2). This is partly because of the limited development of the governmental system; a leader has few subordinates so dependent on him that they are obliged to carry out his instructions. Also, since men still make their own weapons, no one can monopolize them and thereby dominate the others. The absence of weapons that only a few can afford limits the growth of political inequality.

In some simple horticultural societies, shamans also serve as headmen or chiefs because of the awe or respect in which they are held.[43] In others, secular leaders assume important religious functions and become quasi-religious leaders. As one writer notes, a "chief's influence is definitely enhanced when he combines religious with secular functions."[44] In short, in many simple horticultural societies of the modern era, just as

In Horticultural Societies, Combat Appears to Provide a Psychic Substitute for the Excitement, Challenge, and Rewards That Hunting Once Provided. Yanamamö Men Intoxicated on Ebene, a Hallucinogenic Drug, Prepare for a "Friendly" Duel with Men from a Neighboring Village. Such Duels Often Turn Violent and Lead to War.

in the prehistoric past, "church" and "state" are closely linked and sometimes almost become one.

The only other important basis of political power in these societies is membership in a large and prosperous kin group. As we noted earlier, the senior member and leader of the largest, most powerful or most respected clan often becomes the village headman or tribal chief.[45] He can usually count on the support of his kinsmen, and that is a substantial political resource in this kind of society.

Social and gender inequality is generally rather limited in most *simple* horticultural societies of the modern era. Although extremes of wealth and political power are absent, substantial differences in prestige are not uncommon. Political and religious leaders usually enjoy high status, but this depends far more on personal achievements than on mere occupancy of an office. Other bases of status include military prowess (which is highly honored in nearly all horticultural societies), skill in oratory, age, kinship ties, and in some cases wealth in the form of wives, pigs, and ornaments.[46] Each society has its own distinctive combination of criteria.

The more advanced the technology and economy of one of these groups, the greater social inequality tends to be. Societies that practice irrigation, own domesticated animals, or practice metallurgy for ornamental and ceremonial purposes are usually less egalitarian than groups without these characteristics. We see this clearly when we compare the villagers of eastern Brazil and the Amazon River basin with their more advanced neighbors to the north and west who, in pre-Spanish days, practiced irrigation and metallurgy. Hereditary class differences were absent in the former, but common in the latter, where a hereditary class of chiefs and nobles was set apart from commoners.[47]

Ethnographers have found warfare to be more common among horticulturalists than among hunters and gatherers (see Table 6.4). This finding parallels the findings of archaeology, where the evidence indicates that warfare increased substantially during the horticultural era. Now, as in the past, combat appears to serve as a psychic substitute for the excitement, challenge, and rewards that hunting previously provided and that were so important in the lives of men in hunting and gathering societies.

Warfare may also function as an important mechanism of population control in these groups. In addition to the direct loss of life in combat, warfare is a stimulus to the development of a "warrior complex" which often reduces the status of women and promotes female infanticide, which provides an even greater check on population growth.[48] In societies in which warfare is the normal state of affairs, it is imperative that the group be able to field the largest possible number of warriors, and female infanticide seems to be a common method of accomplishing this. By reducing the

Table 6.4 Incidence of Warfare, by Societal Type (in Percentages)

Type of Society	Present	Rare or Absent	Total	No. of Societies
Hunting and gathering	61	39	100	23
Simple horticultural	70	30	100	27
Advanced horticultural	86	14	100	35
Agrarian	83	17	100	30

Source: Patrick D. Nolan, "Toward an Ecological-Evolutionary Theory of the Incidence of Warfare in Preindustrial Societies," *Sociological Theory*, 21 (March 2003) pp. 18–30.

number of girls, the group can devote its resources to the care and nurture of its boys. A survey of studies of 609 "primitive" societies found that the sex ratio among the young was most imbalanced in those societies in which warfare was current at the time of the study and most nearly normal in those societies in which warfare had not occurred for more than twenty-five years.[49] In the former, boys outnumbered girls by a ratio of seven to five on the average, indicating that nearly 30 percent of the females born in these societies had died as a result of female infanticide or neglect.

As warfare grows in importance in a society, several new patterns tend to develop. Above all, there is the cult of the warrior, which heaps honors on successful fighters. Record keeping and publicity are as important to these warrior heroes as to modern athletes, and, in the absence of statisticians and sportswriters, they devise techniques of their own—especially trophy taking. Trophies include such things as skulls and shrunken heads, which are preserved and displayed like modern athletic trophies.[50]

The high incidence of warfare in simple horticultural societies helps keep the channels of vertical mobility open. Almost every boy becomes a warrior and thus has

Record Keeping and Symbols of Success Are No Less Important to Warriors in Horticultural Societies than They Are to Modern Athletes. The Jivaro Indians of South America Collected Heads as Trophies and Developed a Technique for Shrinking and Preserving Them for Purposes of Display.

a chance to win honor and influence. Nevertheless, the channels of vertical mobility are somewhat more restricted in horticultural societies than in hunting and gathering societies, because status advantages can more easily be passed from parent to child. This is partly due to the greater amount of private property in horticultural societies, and its increased importance. In addition, there are the beginnings of inequality among kin groups: it is a distinct advantage to be born into a large, powerful, and wealthy clan. Finally, the institutional structures of these societies frequently evolve to

Ceremonial Cannibalism

Ceremonial cannibalism, a widespread practice in simple horticultural societies, may have developed as a by-product of trophy collecting. Utilitarian cannibalism, or the eating of other humans to avoid starvation, is an ancient practice, traceable to distant prehistoric times, but ceremonial cannibalism seems to be a more recent innovation. The basic idea underlying it is that one can appropriate the valued qualities of a conquered enemy by eating his body. Ceremonial cannibalism is usually surrounded by a complex, and often prolonged, set of rituals, as the following account from South America indicates.

The prisoners taken by a Tupinamba war party were received with manifestations of anger, scorn, and derision, but after the first hostile outburst, they were not hampered in their movements nor were they unkindly treated. Their captors, whose quarters they shared, treated them as relatives. The prisoners generally married village girls, very often the sisters or daughters of their masters, or, in certain cases, the widow of a dead warrior whose hammock and ornaments they used. They received fields for their maintenance, they were free to hunt and fish, and they were reminded of their servile condition by few restrictions and humiliations.

The period of captivity lasted from a few months to several years. When, finally, the date for the execution had been set by the village council, invitations were sent to nearby villages to join in the celebration. The ritual for the slaughter of a captive was worked out to the most minute detail. The club and cord which figured prominently in the ceremony were carefully painted and decorated in accordance with strict rules. For three days before the event, the village women danced, sang, and tormented the victim

with descriptions of his impending fate. On the eve of his execution a mock repetition of his capture took place, during which the prisoner was allowed to escape but was immediately retaken; the man who overpowered him in a wrestling match adopted a new name, as did the ceremonial executioner.

The prisoner spent his last night dancing, pelting his tormentors, and singing songs which foretold their ruin and proclaimed his pride at dying as a warrior. In the morning he was dragged to the plaza by old women amidst shouts, songs, and music. The ceremonial rope was removed from his neck and tied around his waist, and it was held at both ends by two or more men. The victim was once more permitted to give vent to his feelings by throwing fruit or potsherds at his enemies. The executioner, who appeared painted and dressed in a long feather cloak, derided the victim, who boasted of his past deeds and predicted that his relatives would avenge him.

The actual execution was a cruel game. The prisoner was allowed sufficient freedom of movement to dodge the blows aimed at him; sometimes a club was put in his hands so that he could parry the blows without being able to strike back. When at last he fell, his skull shattered, everyone shouted and whistled. Old women rushed in to drink the warm blood, children were invited to dip their hands in it, and mothers smeared their nipples so that even infants could have a taste. While the quartered body was being roasted on a babracot the old women, who were the most eager to taste human flesh, licked the grease running from the sticks. Certain delicate or sacred portions, such as the fingers and the grease around the liver, were given to distinguished guests.[51]

the point where they can, to some extent, supplement the personal attributes of their leaders. *No longer does a headman have to be the best man in the group; he need only be competent, because he now has assistants who will support and help him.* As a consequence, the headmanship is more likely to be inherited than is the case in hunting and gathering societies. This growth in the heritability of status, though modest in scope and of limited importance in simple horticultural societies, marked the beginning of a trend that was destined to become tremendously important in more advanced societies.

ADVANCED HORTICULTURAL SOCIETIES
IN PREHISTORIC ASIA AND EUROPE

Each of the inventions and discoveries of the horticultural era increased to some degree the ability of societies to utilize the resources in their environments. But none had such far-reaching effects as *the manufacture and use of metal weapons and tools.* This is why metallurgy is used as the criterion for differentiating between simple and advanced horticultural societies. Societies are classified as advanced horticultural only if the use of metal weapons and tools was widespread. Societies in which this was rare, or in which metals were used only for artistic and ceremonial artifacts (as in a number of pre-Columbian South and Central American Indian societies where gold was the only metal known), are better classified as simple horticultural, since the impact of metallurgy on societal life was limited.

The Shift from Stone to Metals

To a person who is not technically inclined, the shift from stone to metal may suggest a radical break with the past and the introduction of something completely new. Actually, however, the use of metals evolved from the use of stone by a series of surprisingly small steps.

For thousands of years people had been aware of differences among rocks and stones. They knew that some were better for tools and weapons because they were harder and held a cutting edge longer. They were also aware of the colors in rocks and used the more unusual ones for beads and other ornaments, and as a source of pigments for paint.

This interest in unusual rocks undoubtedly attracted people to copper. In its native form, copper appears as a purplish green or greenish black nugget which, when scratched or rubbed, shows a yellowish kernel of pure unoxidized copper. At first, copper was simply hammered cold into small tools and ornaments such as awls, pins, and hooks. A few articles made by this method have been found in Middle Eastern sites dating from about 7000 B.C.[52] Later, between 5000 and 4000 B.C., the technique of annealing was discovered.[53] By alternately heating and hammering copper, it was made less brittle and thus could be used for a wide variety of purposes. The heat from a simple wood fire was sufficient. Later still, people discovered techniques for extracting copper from ore by means of smelting, and they also found ways to melt copper and cast it in molds.[54]

These discoveries illustrate again the cumulative nature of technological progress. Since both smelting and melting copper require higher temperatures than a simple wood fire can produce, these important discoveries must have come after the invention of pottery and the pottery kiln.[55] And these inventions in turn came after the establishment of permanent communities where heavy and bulky objects could be

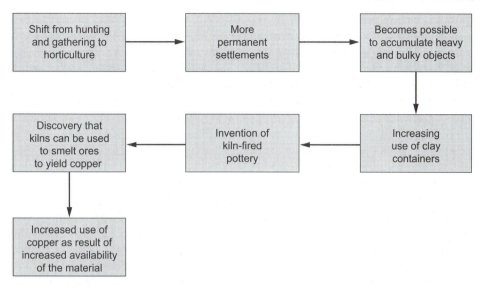

Figure 6.4. Model of the Chain of Causes Leading from the Adoption of Horticulture to the Widespread Use of Copper in the Manufacture of Tools, Weapons, and Other Artifacts.

accumulated. Figure 6.4 summarizes the complex chain of causation involved and reminds us again of the systemic nature of human societies.

As far as we can judge, the use of copper tools and weapons increased rather slowly for a variety of reasons.[56] For one thing, until smelting was discovered, the supply of copper was extremely limited; even then, the ore often had to be carried some distance by primitive and costly methods of transportation. In addition, metalworking (particularly smelting and casting) was probably mastered by only a few specialists, who may have treated their skills as a kind of magic (as smiths in contemporary horticultural societies often do) to protect a lucrative monopoly. Finally, since any man could make his own tools and weapons out of stone, people were undoubtedly reluctant to switch to the costlier product.[57] Thus, although copper was discovered as early as 7000 to 6000 B.C., no truly advanced horticultural society (i.e., one in which metal tools and weapons were widespread) seems to have developed until about 4000 B.C.[58]

To see what the widespread adoption of metal tools and weapons meant for the life of a horticultural society, we will turn to China, where the archaeological record is unusually rich and informative.

Social Consequences of Metal Tools and Weapons
Advanced horticultural societies flourished in China from the middle of the second millennium B.C. to the middle of the first.[59] The plow, for reasons that are unclear, was slow to appear in China, thus delaying the emergence of agrarian societies. This prolonged horticultural era was undoubtedly a major reason that the overall level of technological development in China's advanced horticultural societies surpassed that in most others of that type.

One indication of this is the fact that the dominant metal in China during most of this era was not copper, as in the Middle East and Europe, but bronze. This is significant because bronze,‡‡ which represents an important advance in metallurgy, is much harder than copper and can be used for many purposes for which copper is unsuitable. In the Middle East the technique of making bronze was not really mastered until some time *after* the first agrarian societies had made their appearance.[61] Variations in the sequence of such major innovations as bronze and the plow warn us of the inadequacy of *unilinear* theories of evolution, which assume that all societies follow exactly the same evolutionary path. Some variation is the rule, not the exception.

When the advanced horticultural era in China is compared with the simple horticultural period, the differences are striking. During the earlier era northern China was covered with many small, mostly self-sufficient, autonomous villages. But in the later period the villages were no longer autonomous and a few had become urban centers of some size and substance.

The emergence of these urban centers was largely the result of the military success of villages that had one important advantage: *bronze weapons.* As one scholar described this period, "In the course of a few centuries the villages of the plain fell under the domination of walled cities on whose rulers the possession of bronze weapons, chariots, and slaves conferred a measure of superiority to which no [simple horticultural] community could aspire."[62]

The importance of this development can hardly be exaggerated. For the first time in Chinese history, people found that the conquest of other people could be a profitable alternative to the conquest of nature. Much the same thing happened in other parts of the world at this same stage of societal development. Thus, beginning in advanced horticultural societies and continuing in agrarian, we find almost as much energy expended in war as in the more basic struggle for subsistence. One might say that *bronze was to the conquest of people what plant cultivation was to the conquest of nature: both were decisive turning points in sociocultural evolution.*

From the military standpoint China's advanced horticulturalists enjoyed a great advantage over simple horticulturalists. Excavated burial remains show that their warriors wore elaborate armor, including helmets. They also carried shields and were equipped with spears, dagger-axes, knives, hatchets, and reflex bows capable of a pull of 160 pounds.[63] In addition, they used horse-drawn chariots carrying teams of three men.

These societies also enjoyed substantial *numerical* superiority over simple horticultural societies and every victory brought more people under their control, enabling them to enlarge their armies still further.[64] This could not have been accomplished by a hunting and gathering society, whose simple technology would make it impossible for conquerors to incorporate a defeated people into the group. At that level of development, the *economic surplus* (i.e., production in excess of what is needed to keep the producers healthy and productive) was small and unpredictable. But with the introduction of horticulture the situation changed dramatically. *For the first time, the conquest, control, and exploitation of other societies had become not only possible, but economically profitable.* All that was needed to transform this possibility into a reality was an advance in military technology that would give one society a definite advantage over its neighbors. That advance was bronze. It tipped the balance of military power decisively in favor of advanced horticulturalists.

---

‡‡Bronze involves the important technique of *alloying,* the combining of two or more metals—in this case, copper with tin.[60]

Chariots, Together with Bronze Weapons, Gave the Advanced Horticulturalists of China a Great Advantage Over Their Simple Horticultural Neighbors. Burial Remains of a Warrior with His Horses and Chariot, Eleventh Century B.C.

The earliest advanced horticultural society in China of which we have any knowledge was established around 1600 B.C., and its structure was basically feudalistic.[65] In most regions, especially those that were some distance from the capital, power was in the hands of a warrior nobility that ruled the people in their immediate area. They paid tribute to the king and supported him militarily, but otherwise were essentially independent.[66] They were so independent, in fact, that they often waged war among themselves.

Marked social inequality was the rule in these societies. There were two basic classes: a small warrior nobility, and the great mass of common people.[67] The warrior nobility were the governing class and lived in walled cities that served as their fortresses. It was they who enjoyed most of the benefits of the new technology and the new social system. The chief use of bronze was to manufacture weapons and ceremonial objects for the benefit of this elite class. Almost none of this scarce material was made available to the common people for farm tools.[68] The situation was much the same in the Middle East and Europe for 2,000 years or more. As one writer put it, this was a world in which metals played a major role in the military, religious, and artistic spheres but not in subsistence activities.[69]

Kinship was extremely important in the political systems of advanced horticultural China. Membership in the governing class was largely hereditary, and as far as possible leading officials assigned the major offices under their control to kinsmen.[70]

The Great Wall of China: This 1,500-Mile-Long Fortification, Begun Late in China's Horticultural Era, Illustrates the Growing Power of Political Elites and Their Ability to Mobilize Labor on a Massive Scale.

The origins of these noble families are unknown, but they were probably descendants of early conquerors and their followers.

The walled towns where the aristocracy lived, though small by modern standards, were nonetheless an important innovation. One recently excavated town, probably the capital of an early state, covered slightly over one square mile, or twenty times the area of Çatal Hüyük.[71] The size of the walled areas, however, does not tell the full story of these towns, especially in the earlier period, for many of the common people had their homes and workshops outside the protected area and cultivated nearby fields.

The walled area, while basically a fortress and place of residence for the governing class was also a political and religious center. Religious activities were quite important and were so closely tied to the political system that one writer describes the state as "a kind of theocracy."[72] Though this may be an overstatement, ancient inscriptions prove that the ruler performed major religious functions and was what we today would call the head of both church and state.

The physical structure of those early urban centers was impressive and reflected the evolution of the *state* and its newly acquired ability to mobilize labor on a large scale. One scholar estimates, for example, that it required the labor of 10,000 men working eighteen years to build the wall around the capital of one early state. Such massive undertakings apparently utilized large numbers of captives taken in war, many of whom were used later as human sacrifices.[73]

Not much is known about the daily life of the common people, but their chief functions were obviously to produce the economic surplus on which the governing

---

class depended and to provide workers and soldiers for various projects and military campaigns. Not all labor was of the brute, physical type, however. Some people were craft specialists who provided the new and unusual luxury goods that the governing class demanded for display and for ceremonial purposes; others produced military equipment.[74] Although many of these specialists were probably also part-time farmers, the increase in occupational specialization was undoubtedly accompanied by a significant growth in trade.

Despite their increasingly exploitative character, the advanced horticultural societies of China made important advances in a number of areas. The more important innovations included writing, money, the use of the horse, probably irrigation, and the manufacture of iron at the very end of the horticultural era. In addition, there were lesser innovations too numerous to mention, some of them Chinese inventions or discoveries, others products of diffusion. In most cases, it is impossible to determine which were which.

ADVANCED HORTICULTURAL SOCIETIES IN THE MODERN ERA

For several centuries advanced horticultural societies have been limited to two parts of the world, sub-Saharan Africa and southeast Asia. Until recently they occupied most of sub-Saharan Africa. In southeast Asia, on the other hand, agrarian societies have occupied most of the land, and horticulturalists have been confined to the hill country.

These advanced horticulturalists of modern times differ in one important respect from those of prehistoric times: the dominant metal in their societies has been iron rather than copper or bronze. This is important, because iron ore is so much more plentiful than copper and tin that it can be used for ordinary tools as well as weapons. However, because it is much more difficult to separate iron from the ore, the manufacture of iron was a later development.

The history of Africa proves once again that the evolutionary process does not compel all societies to follow exactly the same pattern of development. Bronze was never the dominant metal in most of Africa below the Sahara. During the period when bronze was dominant in the Middle East, cultural contacts between Egypt and the territories to the south were minimal. By the time there was sufficient contact to permit diffusion of specialized skills like metallurgy, iron had become dominant.[75] *Thus, most of Africa seems to have moved directly from the Stone Age to the Iron Age.*

Increased Size and Complexity

Compared with hunting and gathering or simple horticultural societies, advanced horticultural societies are usually larger and more complex. Table 4.2 summarizes the evidence from Murdock's data set: On average, advanced horticultural societies are three and a half times the size of simple horticultural and 130 times the size of hunting and gathering societies. Table 4.3 shows that craft specialization is much more common in advanced horticultural societies than in either simple horticultural or hunting and gathering societies. Murdock's data also show that social inequality increases markedly at this level of societal development. Slavery, for example, is found in 83 percent of advanced horticultural societies, but in only 15 percent of simple (see Figure 6.5). And finally, complex status systems are reported in 7 percent of advanced horticultural societies and in only 1 percent of simple (see Figure 4.3).

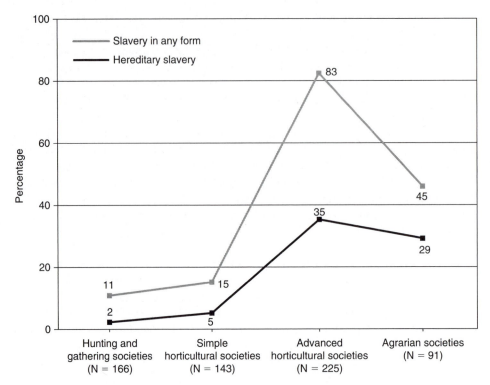

Figure 6.5. Percentage of Societies with Slavery, by Type of Society.
Source: See Appendix, pp. 417–418.

One consequence of the more highly developed economy and stratification system in advanced horticultural societies is their increased emphasis on the economic aspect of marriage. In almost every one of these societies, marriageable daughters are viewed as a valuable property, and men who want to marry them must either pay for the privilege or render extended service to their prospective in-laws. Fortunately for young men with limited resources, extended kin groups usually view marriage as a sensible investment and are willing to loan suitors part of the bride price. This economic approach to marriage is much more common in advanced horticultural societies than in either hunting and gathering or simple horticultural societies.

Political Development
The growth in social inequality is closely linked with the growth of government. A generation ago, one of the pioneers in the study of African political systems argued that most traditional African societies fell into one of two basic categories: those "which have centralized authority, administrative machinery, and judicial institutions— in short, a government—and in which cleavages of wealth, privilege, and status correspond to the distribution of authority," and those which have none of these attributes.[76] Though studies suggest that this twofold division was an oversimplification, they confirm that African societies differ in the ways described and that there is

a strong relationship between the development of the state and the growth of social inequality.[77]

African societies afford a valuable opportunity to study the early stages of political development. A leading student of east African political systems suggests that a critical step in the process occurs when the head of a strong clan begins to take on, as retainers, men who are not related to him, thereby overcoming one of the traditional constraints on power and its expansion.[78] These retainers are usually individuals who have been expelled from their own kin group for misconduct or whose group has been destroyed in war or by some natural disaster, and they offer their allegiance and service in exchange for protection and a livelihood.

Since there is a natural tendency for men in this position to turn to the strongest extended family in their society, power begins to accumulate. This is reinforced by the wealth of such a family, which permits it to buy more wives to produce more sons and warriors, and by the development of myths that attribute the group's success to the magical powers of its leader. The final link in this chain of state building is forged when less powerful families, and even whole communities, are brought under the control of the head of a strong kin group—either by conquest or by the decision of weaker groups to put themselves under the strong group's protection. When this happens, each of the subordinate groups is usually allowed to retain its land, and its leader his authority within his own group, but the group is compelled to pay tribute. The leader of the dominant group then uses these revenues to support his kinsmen and retainers, thereby increasing their dependence on him and, he hopes, their loyalty as well.

Trade and Commerce Are Much More Important in Horticultural Societies than in Hunting and Gathering Societies: The Marketplace in Ouagadougou, Burkina Faso.

Sometimes this state-building process is stimulated by feuds that get out of hand. Where strong political authority is lacking, feuds can be a serious matter. Individuals and families are forced to settle their own grievances; this often sets off a deadly cycle of action and reaction. More than one east African group has voluntarily put itself under the authority of a strong neighboring leader just to break such a cycle and reestablish peace among its members.

One might imagine that these processes, once set in motion, would continue until eventually all Africa came under a single authority. But powerful countervailing forces have prevented this. Technological limitations, especially in transportation and communication, were most important. Advanced horticulturalists in Africa, as in the New World, had no knowledge of the wheel and did not have draft animals until contact with Europeans. As a result, the farther a ruler's power was extended into outlying areas, the weaker it became. Not only were these areas vulnerable to attack by other societies, but even more serious, they were likely to revolt. From the territorial standpoint, Songhay was probably the largest kingdom that ever developed in sub-Saharan Africa. In the early fourteenth century, it controlled approximately 500,000 square miles in the western Sudan (i.e., twice the size of present-day France).[79] Most African kingdoms, however, were much smaller.

By the standards of modern industrial societies, the governments of Africa's advanced horticultural societies were extremely unstable. Revolts were a common occurrence, not only in outlying provinces but even in the capitals. These were seldom, if ever, popular uprisings. Rather, they were instigated by powerful members of the nobility, often the king's own brothers. This pattern was so common that

In Almost Every Politically Advanced Society of Horticultural Africa There Was a Sharp Cleavage between Nobles and Commoners: Early Bronze Casting of Dahomean Chief and His Entourage of Relative and Retainers. Note the Fine Workmanship.

the Zulus had a proverb that "the king should not eat with his brothers lest they poison him."[80]

In virtually every politically developed society of horticultural Africa there was a sharply defined cleavage between a hereditary nobility and the mass of commoners. Historically, this distinction grew out of the state-building process.[81] Nobles were usually descendants of past rulers and their chief officers, or hereditary leaders of subordinated groups. They comprised a warrior aristocracy supported by the labor of the common people. Below the commoners there was often a class of slaves, many of them captives taken in war, and, as in other horticultural societies, they were frequently slaughtered as human sacrifices.

In horticultural Africa, as in the New World and elsewhere, religion and politics were intimately related. In many instances the king was viewed as divine or as having access to divine powers.[82] This served to make tyrannical and exploitative practices legitimate. It also helps explain why no efforts were made to establish other kinds of political systems: given their ideological heritage, any alternative was inconceivable. These beliefs did not protect a ruler against attacks from his kinsmen, however, because they shared his special religious status and thus were qualified to assume the duties and privileges of the royal office—if they could seize it.

A comparison of the politically complex societies of horticultural Africa with those that remained autonomous villages shows that the former were more developed in other ways as well. They were far more likely to have full-time craft specialization, for example, and they were also more likely to have urban or semiurban settlements— a few with populations of 20,000 or more.[83]

Horticultural Societies in Southeast Asia

Before concluding this discussion of advanced horticultural societies in the modern era, a brief comment on those in southeast Asia is necessary. The striking feature of these societies is their organizational simplicity, especially in terms of political development. In most instances, villages have been autonomous; and when multicommunity societies have developed, they have invariably been small.[84] Urban or semiurban settlements have been absent.

The reason appears to be ecological. Centuries ago, after this region came under the domination of more powerful agrarian societies, horticultural societies survived only in hill country where transportation was difficult and the land unsuited to the plow and permanent cultivation. This combination of more powerful neighbors and the deficiencies of their own territories apparently prevented all but the most limited development and caused these groups to be looked down upon, and often exploited, by their agrarian neighbors.

Ecological factors of a different type had a similar effect in certain parts of Africa: political development was quite limited in the tropical rain forests. Apparently the dense vegetation and other hindrances to the movement of armies and goods made it impossible to build and maintain extensive kingdoms.[85]

HORTICULTURAL SOCIETIES IN THEORETICAL PERSPECTIVE

Few events in human history have been as important as the shift from hunting and gathering to horticulture. It is no exaggeration to say that *the adoption of horticulture in the realm of technology was comparable to the adoption of symbol use in the realm of*

The El Castillo Pyramid of Kulkulcán at Chichén Itzá. Several Horticultural Societies in the New World Achieved a Level of Technological Advance Approaching That of Ancient Egypt and Mesopotamia in the First Centuries After They Became Agrarian Societies.

communication: each was a decisive break with the mammalian and primate world. Hunting and gathering, like the use of signals, are adaptations our species inherited from its prehuman ancestors. In contrast, horticulture and symbols are more peculiarly human.[§§]

Of all the changes in human life that resulted from the horticultural revolution, the most fundamental—the one with the most profound consequences—was the creation of a *stable economic surplus.* Hunting and gathering societies were rarely able to create such a surplus: food producers and their dependents usually consumed within days all they were able to provide. With nothing left over to support *non*producers of food, except children and the aged, only the most limited occupational specialization was possible. There could be no governmental or religious institutions staffed by full-time officials and priests, nor could there be full-time artisans and merchants. And this, in turn, ruled out the development of towns and cities, since these are based on populations that are freed from the necessity of producing their own food.

[§§]It is worth noting that although symbols do appear to be uniquely human, plant cultivation and animal husbandry really are not. Ants, too, have accomplished these feats. In fact, a number of traits associated with humans and human societies have parallels in ant societies. In addition to plant and animal domestication, various species of ants have developed organized warfare, a division of labor, caste-like stratification, slavery, and even drug addiction![86]

The shift from hunting and gathering to plant cultivation provided societies for the first time with the means of establishing an economic surplus, but only if the growth in productivity was not consumed by a corresponding growth in population. *To translate the potential for a stable surplus into a reality required an ideology that would motivate the producers of food to turn over part of their harvest to an individual in authority who could dispense it as he saw fit.*

Traditional religious beliefs often answered this need. In a number of societies people were already accustomed to offering sacrifices, and nothing was more natural than that they should continue this practice as they shifted to plant cultivation, giving part of their yield to priests. With greater productivity, rituals became more elaborate and more frequent, and priestly activities became full time, for one man at first and eventually for others. In this way, small proto-urban communities began to develop around important shrines—communities that could exist only if a stable economic surplus was maintained.

In other societies the development of a stable surplus appears to have evolved out of a tradition of turning over to the headman part of the fruits of the hunt to distribute to the families of unsuccessful hunters. Here too the increase in productivity that resulted from the shift to plant cultivation made full-time employment possible, first for a headman, later for his aides. Thus, the foundation was laid for the emergence of the state.

In either case, the outcome was the same: the potential for a stable, dependable economic surplus became a reality, opening up important new possibilities for the organization of societal life. The possibilities would not all be realized in horticultural societies, however. The most dramatic and the most revolutionary would be realized only in agrarian and industrial societies, where the economic surplus would be many times larger.

It is important to note that in horticultural societies we see, for the first time, ideology playing a recognizable role in societal development. In hunting and gathering societies, the limits set by technology are so narrow that ideology's role in the developmental process is negligible.*** But the picture changed with the shift to horticulture, where ideological differences sometimes gave rise to significant differences in societal development.

Figure 6.6 summarizes the effects of the shift from hunting and gathering to horticulture. Not all of these consequences occurred in every horticultural society, but the model indicates *the possibilities* inherent in the new subsistence technology.

At a minimum, the shift to horticulture meant more food and more permanent settlements, and frequently more free time for men. More food meant population growth and, when combined with certain traditional beliefs concerning the role of headmen and shamans, created the possibility of a stable economic surplus. The increase in free time for men often led to increased warfare and the emergence of the cult of the warrior. More permanent settlements made it feasible for people to accumulate far more possessions than was possible when frequent moves were necessary. Also, more permanent settlements, in combination with the emergence of the cult of

***This is not to say that these societies do not have a rich cultural life, but simply that differences in cultural beliefs have minimal effects on their material life.

Horticulture in the New World:
Testing Ground for Ecological-Evolutionary Theory

No one knows for certain when humans first settled the New World. There is convincing evidence that humans were in the Americas by 12,000 to 14,000 years ago, but some archaeologists believe they were here much earlier, perhaps as much as 50,000 years ago.[87] The original settlers appear to have been hunters and gatherers who migrated from Asia by means of the land bridge that once connected Siberia and Alaska.

When the last Ice Age ended and the waters locked in the glaciers melted, the level of the oceans rose and the land bridge was submerged. As a result, the inhabitants of the New World were cut off from the inhabitants of the Old World during the horticultural revolution. Thus, there was no way information about the techniques of plant cultivation could have spread from Asia to the Americas.[88]

Despite this, horticultural societies did develop in the New World, and some of them achieved a level of technological advance comparable to that of early agrarian Mesopotamia and Egypt. Space limitations prevent us from tracing these developments in detail, and much of the account would be repetitive if we did. But in the New World, as in the Old, the shift from hunting and gathering to horticulture was preceded by the growth of population and led to more permanent settlements, more substantial dwellings, increased wealth and possessions, greater inequality, the development of pottery and later of metallurgy, the beginnings of full-time craft specialization, the appearance of permanent markets and increased trade, the beginnings of urbanism, the establishment of permanent religious centers, the construction of massive temples and temple complexes (see p. 148), and a marked increase in both militarism and imperialism.[89]

There were also some differences: New World horticulturalists were not as successful in domesticating animals, for example, nor was their metallurgy as advanced, although some evidence indicates that copper smelting was independently developed and practiced on an extensive scale in Peru about A.D. 500.[90] On the other hand, they developed a numerical

system that included the concept of zero centuries before this was invented in the Old World. Overall, however, the similarities far outweigh the differences.

The fact that horticulture developed at all in the isolated New World is the important point, for it provides an independent test of some basic ideas. For a long time scholars debated whether the striking similarities in patterns of societal development in the Middle East, China, and Europe were due to the independent operation of the same basic laws of sociocultural evolution or were simply the result of the diffusion of ideas from a single source. Despite the fact that different species of plants and animals were involved, the issue would have been impossible to resolve as long as only Old World societies were involved, because the possibility of diffusion could never be ruled out. The New World, however, is a different matter. Its contacts with the Old World ended several thousand years before horticulture began, and contact was not resumed until about A.D. 1000, when Leif Ericson briefly visited Vinland, somewhere on the northeast coast of North America.*

In short, the New World has been a kind of "Second Earth," where ideas about sociocultural evolution suggested by studies of the Old World can be put to the test.[92] The remarkable parallels between developments in the New World and the Old strongly suggest that there are limits to the amount of variation that is possible in the sequence of basic technological innovations. People must know certain things about both fire and rocks, for example, before metallurgy is possible, and a society must be familiar with the hoe before it can invent the plow. In addition,

---

*Although attempts have been made to prove other contacts, they have not been successful. Moreover, careful studies of plant cultivation in the New World convince scholars that this was entirely an indigenous process. For example, the transformation of maize, or corn, from a wild plant to a cultivated plant took much longer than one would expect if the process had been guided by information on the techniques of plant cultivation brought from the Old World.[91]

major technological innovations have fairly predictable consequences for other aspects of sociocultural systems—especially for social organization, the demographic variables, and material production.[93]

This is not to say that sociocultural evolution compels societies to march in lockstep. But much is predictable about the critical early stages of societal development. Marvin Harris, a major contributor to ecological-evolutionary theory, put the matter as well as anyone: *"Similar technologies applied to similar environments tend to produce similar arrangements of labor in production and distribution, and these in turn call forth similar kinds of social groupings, which justify and coordinate their activities by means of similar systems of values and beliefs."*[94]

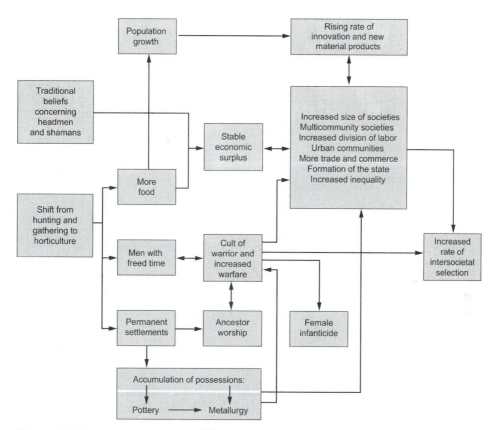

Figure 6.6. Model of the Potential Effects of the Shift from Hunting and Gathering to Horticulture.

the warrior, frequently led to the practice of ancestor worship, and the greater frequency of warfare contributed to the practice of female infanticide.

The development of a stable economic surplus was especially important since it paved the way for growth in the size of societies, the formation of multicommunity societies, an increased division of labor, urban communities, increased trade and commerce, the formation of the state, and greatly increased inequality. Several of these developments, especially the formation of multicommunity societies, the formation of the state, and increased inequality, were also stimulated by the increase in warfare, the increasing accumulation of possessions, and the production of new material products of many kinds. Finally, all of these developments, but especially the increase in warfare and the increasing differences in the military might of societies (many of which remained at the hunting and gathering level), *contributed to a substantial rise in the rate of intersocietal selection.*

In several instances, boxes in Figure 6.6 are connected by two-headed arrows. These indicate that a process of feedback was operating, with the paired developments mutually stimulating one another. The most important of these is the two-headed arrow linking a stable economic surplus with the important set of changes in social organization in the large box to the right. In other words, once the creation of a stable economic surplus had given rise to an increased division of labor, urban communities, multicommunity societies, the formation of the state, and so forth, these developments in social organization tended to stabilize and ensure the continued production of an economic surplus. New institutional arrangements ensured that priests, political and military leaders, merchants, craftsmen, and other specialists would get a share—and usually a disproportionate share—of the goods and services produced in the society. These

Kano, a City in Northern Nigeria, Has Been an Important Commercial and Political Center for More than 500 Years. The Style of Architecture Remains Much as It Was Centuries Ago.

Technological Advance but Moral Regress?

For years, many anthropologists presented an idyllic view of life in simpler societies, making them seem like the last remnants of the Garden of Eden. But as numerous scholars have noted, it is one of the great ironies of evolution that progress in technology and social organization has often been linked with ethical regress. Horticultural societies provide several striking examples. Some of the most shocking, by the standards of modern Western societies, are the emergence and spread of head-hunting, human sacrifice, and cannibalism.

There is also evidence that rates of homicide rise to unprecedented levels. For example, a recent study of simple horticulturalists in New Guinea found that nearly a third of all deaths over a forty-year period were due to homicide. In fact, the rate of homicide in this society was *more than 50 times* that in the United States, which for many years has had the highest rate of any modern industrial society. Evidence from other simple horticultural societies indicates that this is not an isolated instance but reflects a relatively widespread tendency in societies at this level of development.

In addition, there is a precipitous decline in the practice of sharing, a marked increase in inequality, and a dramatic increase in the frequency and scale of warfare. As Figure 6.5 shows, more than eight out of ten of the advanced horticultural societies in Murdock's data set practiced some form of slavery, and in more than one-third of them slavery was an inheritable condition. Warfare is also much more likely than it was in hunting and gathering societies (see Table 6.4). Since war captives constituted the great majority of slaves, the parallel increases in warfare and slavery are not unrelated. Trophy taking, human sacrifice, and cannibalism are also linked to warfare; war captives apparently often faced the unenviable fates of either death or servitude. Horticulture and warfare are also associated with the development of female infanticide and the rise of patriarchal systems in which women are dominated and, in many cases, physically abused by men.

These startling developments and sobering patterns serve to remind us that technological advance does not necessarily imply or entail moral progress.

Sources: Bruce Knauft, "Reconsidering Violence in Simple Human Societies," *Current Anthropology*, 28 (Aug.–Oct. 1987), p. 462; Marvin Harris, *Cannibals and Kings: The Origins of Culture* (New York: Random House, 1987), chap. 6; Napoleon Chagnon, *Yanamamö: The Fierce People* (New York: Holt, Rinehart, Winston, 1977); Mark Sevenson, "Pre-Hispanic Reports of Brutality Confirmed," *Associated Press*, Jan. 23, 2005; Kristin M. Romey, "Watery Tombs," *Archaeology* 58, no. 4 (July–Aug., 2005), pp. 42–49.

---

specialists would have the first claim on food and other essentials. Thus, in order to survive, farmers were obliged to produce more than they and their families required.

The rise in the rate of intersocietal selection is another feature of Figure 6.6 that merits attention. It is a reminder that the horticultural revolution meant dramatic change not only for individual societies but also for the world system of societies. If Figure 6.6 is compared with Figure 3.4, the similarity in trends is striking. This is no coincidence, since the shift from hunting and gathering to horticulture was the first major step along the road that has led to the modern world system.

EXCURSUS: RACE, ENVIRONMENT, AND SOCIETAL DEVELOPMENT

After the first explorers returned to Europe from Africa, the Americas, and Asia, Europeans were intrigued by differences in the level of development of societies in various parts of the world. Interest in these differences led quite naturally to efforts to explain them.

The apparent association between differences in physical appearance and levels of technological development gave rise to a number of racialist explanations. Racialist explanations assert that societies differ in their level of development and in other ways because the members differ in their culture-building abilities.[95] Translated into modern scientific terminology, these theories assert that societies differ in their levels of development because of differences in the genetic heritages of their populations.

These theories have had great appeal because they seem to fit the evidence rather well. During the last several hundred years, societies dominated by Europeans have been technologically the most advanced and organizationally the most complex and powerful. Societies dominated by Asians have ranked next, while societies dominated by Africans have been the least developed technologically and organizationally. Since the level of societal development is obviously not responsible for the race of a population, racialist theorists have argued that the race must be responsible for the level of development.

Racialist theories can be quite compelling if one does not have an ecological and evolutionary perspective. If one adopts such a perspective, however, those theories prove to have a number of fatal flaws.

To begin with, we find that the recent ranking of societies in terms of development has not always prevailed. For thousands of years Middle Eastern societies—not European societies—were the most highly developed.[96] Also, for many centuries China equaled or surpassed northwestern Europe. Finally, for several centuries before and after the start of the Christian era, the center of civilization was in the Mediterranean basin, and North African societies, such as Carthage and Egypt, were much more advanced than the barbarian societies of northwest Europe; also, there is some evidence that steel was being produced in Africa 1,900 years before this capability was developed in Europe.[97] While there have been some changes in the racial composition of some populations during this period (e.g., in ancient times the proportion of fair-haired and fair-skinned individuals in Greek and Roman societies seems to have been appreciably higher than today), they do not appear to have been great enough to cause the substantial changes that have occurred in the relative level of societal development.

If, then, the evolutionary record undermines the credibility of racialist theories, where do we look for an explanation? Here the ecological perspective comes to our aid. It suggests that environmental differences offer a promising alternative. Recent research has shown that many tropical and semitropical regions are poorly suited to plow agriculture.[98] Although the lushness of tropical rain forests suggests rich and fertile soils, modern research has found the opposite: The soils of tropical rain forests are among the poorest in the world. While it is possible to clear small and temporary gardens in these forests, as horticulturalists have done for centuries, it is not possible to clear permanent fields and cultivate them continuously as agriculturalists do. The fertility of these soils is quickly exhausted, and worse yet, some of the soils harden and become compacted to the point where cultivation of any kind is impossible. In addition, large-scale clearing of the rain forest appears to break the hydrological cycle and rainfall declines. In short, indigenous development beyond the level of horticultural societies seems to have been impossible in much of sub-Saharan Africa and much of Latin America.

In addition, research has shown that human populations in tropical regions are exposed to many more tiny predators than are populations in temperate regions.[99] In fact, the number, variety, and seriousness of the parasites (bacteria, viruses, worms, etc.) that prey on human populations seem to increase steadily as one moves from polar regions to the tropics. In the tropics, the problems created by these micropredators have often been overwhelming. Large portions of the population have been affected by debilitating diseases of one kind or another—diseases such as malaria, onchocerciasis (which causes blindness), and schistosomiasis (which causes people to become listless and lack energy).

Prior to the invention of the microscope, the causes of such diseases were not only unknown but also *unknowable*. Societies afflicted by them were badly handicapped, but they had no method of overcoming their handicap. Thus, the most serious challenges that confronted horticulturalists in the tropics were profoundly different from those that confronted horticulturalists in temperate areas such as Europe. In the latter, the basic challenge was to increase the food supply, and this could be achieved through the gradual improvement of tools of various kinds—in other words, through the exercise of ordinary human intelligence. In contrast, in tropical regions this was impossible. Because of environmental constraints that were beyond human control, the usual course of evolution, from horticulture to agriculture, was impossible in most tropical societies, and human health and vitality were constantly undermined by forces that would remain unknowable until the technological development elsewhere (in temperate regions) and in other societies of the microscope and other elements of modern medical technology—a late stage in an evolutionary process that presupposes an earlier agricultural stage.

Thus, the adoption of an ecological and evolutionary perspective provides quite a different explanation of the relationship of race and societal development than that provided by earlier racialist theories. Moreover, because the former explanation fits more of the facts than the latter, it has greater scientific credibility. Although it would be premature to suggest that we now fully understand the causes of the complex relationship between race and societal development, it appears that ecological-evolutionary theory substantially advances our understanding of it.

Agrarian Societies

Outline

"The thousand years or so immediately preceding 3000 B.C. were perhaps more fertile in fruitful inventions and discoveries than any period in human history prior to the sixteenth century, A.D."[1] So wrote V. Gordon Childe, one of the most influential archaeologists of the twentieth century. The innovations of the period he wrote about included the invention of the wheel and its application both to wagons and to the manufacture of pottery, the invention of the plow, the harnessing of animals to pull wagons and plows and their use as pack animals, the harnessing of wind power for sailboats, the invention of writing and numerical notation, and the invention of the calendar.[2]

Collectively, these innovations transformed the conditions of life for societies in the Middle East, and eventually for societies throughout the world. With these new cultural resources, societies expanded their populations, increased their material wealth, and developed social organizations far more complex than anything known before.

SIMPLE AGRARIAN SOCIETIES
Technology
Although all the innovations mentioned above were important, the plow had the greatest potential for social and cultural change. To a modern city dweller, the plow may not sound very exciting, yet without it we would still be back in the horticultural era. To appreciate its importance, we need to recognize two basic problems that confront farmers everywhere: controlling weeds and maintaining the fertility of the soil.[3] With traditional horticultural tools and techniques, both problems become more severe the longer a plot of ground is cultivated. Weeds multiply faster than horticulturalists with hoes can root them out; and unless periodic flooding or fertilization replenishes them, the soil's nutrients seep deeper into the ground, below the reach of

Hoeing the ground.

Plow drawn by men.

Plow drawn by oxen.
2242. Tools in the sculptures on a Theban tomb.

Intensification of Cultivation in Ancient Egypt from Horticulture to Agriculture. Note the Humans Pulling the Plow in the Middle Panel. Drawing from a Tomb in Thebes.

plants and too deep to be brought back to the surface with hoes and other simple tools. Within a few years the yield from such a garden usually becomes so small that the farmer is forced to abandon it and clear a new one.

The plow, if it did not eliminate these problems, at least reduced them to manageable proportions. Because it turns the soil over to a greater depth than the hoe, the plow buries weeds, not only killing them but also adding humus to the soil. Deeper cultivation also brings back to the surface the nutrients that have seeped below root level. Thus, the plow made more permanent cultivation possible in a greater variety of soils,* and thereby led to the widespread replacement of horticulture (from the Latin *horti cultura,* or the cultivation of a garden) by agriculture (from *agri cultura,* the cultivation of a field).

The invention of the plow also facilitated the harnessing of animal energy.[5] As long as the digging stick and hoe were the basic tools of cultivation, men and women supplied the energy. But a plow could be pulled, and it did not take long for people to discover that oxen could do the job better than people. The importance of this discovery can hardly be exaggerated, since it established a principle with broad

*Before the plow and systems of fertilization, permanent cultivation was only possible in a few very limited areas, such as alluvial flood plains.[4]

applicability. In Childe's words, "The ox was the first step to the steam engine and the [gasoline] motor."[6]

More immediately, however, the harnessing of animal energy led to greatly increased productivity. With a plow and a pair of oxen, a farmer could cultivate a far larger area than was possible with a hoe.[7] In addition, the use of oxen led, in many societies, to feeding them in stalls, and this in turn led to the use of manure as fertilizer.[8] In short, the shift from hoe to plow not only meant permanently cultivated fields and larger crops; it also meant the potential for a larger economic surplus and new and more complex forms of social organization.

The earliest evidence of the plow comes from Mesopotamian cylinder seals and Egyptian paintings dating from a little before 3000 B.C.[9] Modern research indicates that the plow, like so many other innovations in the last 10,000 years, presupposed certain earlier inventions and discoveries—underlining again the *cumulative* nature of technological change. The first plows of the Mesopotamians and the Egyptians were, in fact, simply modified versions of the hoe, the basic farm implement of all advanced horticultural societies. In the earliest period, the plow was pulled by men (see Figure 7.1), but before long, cattle and oxen were used. These plows, like all plows in simple agrarian societies, were made of wood, though sometimes the plowshare (i.e., tip) was made of bronze for greater strength.

The plow and related techniques of agriculture apparently spread by diffusion until agrarian societies were eventually established throughout most of Europe and much of North Africa and Asia. (See Figure 7.1.) The plow did not spread to sub-Saharan Africa until the period of European colonialism, and in the New World, too, it was unknown until introduced by Europeans.

The full impact of the new technology was not felt immediately in either Mesopotamia or Egypt. Even so, the shift to agriculture was followed quickly by further development of a number of trends that started with plant and animal domestication. For example, the simple "tokens" that were used as early as 8000 B.C. to record the quantities and types of commodities produced and exchanged evolved into systems of counting and writing,[10] urban communities increased in size and complexity and became recognizable as "cities," and empire building occurred on a greatly expanded scale (which in Egypt led to the unification of the entire country under a single ruler for the first time in history). This was the period that historians refer to as "the dawn of civilization."

Similar developments occurred (though at later dates) in horticultural societies in China and Mesoamerica, indicating that the plow is not a necessary precondition for literacy, urbanism, and imperialism.[†] But the rarity of these developments in *horticultural* societies and their frequency in agrarian societies demonstrates that the shift to agriculture, by increasing productivity, greatly increased the *probability* of their occurrence.

[†]In the New World, empires based on horticulture developed in the Valley of Mexico, Central America, and along the west coast of South America. With the exception of the Peruvian civilizations, which had an accounting system based on knots, all of them had written languages and numerical systems. Furthermore, the capital of the Aztec empire, Tenochtitlán, may have had a permanent population of more than 200,000 prior to contact with the Spanish.[11]

Figure 7.1. The Early Diffusion of Plant Cultivation into Europe.
Source: After Luigi Luca Cavalli-Sforza and Francesco Cavalli-Sforza, *The Great Human Diasporas: The History of Diversity and Evolution* (New York: Addison-Wesley, 1995), p. 135.

Religion and the Growth of the Economic Surplus

In the earliest agrarian societies, religion was an extremely powerful force. Mesopotamian societies believed that "man was . . . created for one purpose only: to serve the gods by supplying them with food, drink, and shelter so that they might have full leisure for their divine activities."[12] Each temple was believed to be, quite literally, the house of a particular god, and each community had its own special deity. Priests and other attendants constituted the god's court or household, and their chief task was to minister to his needs. Another responsibility was to mediate between the god and the community, trying to discover his will and appease his anger. In order to perform these tasks, temples and their staffs had to be supported by a steady flow of goods. Over the years the temples were continually enlarged and became increasingly costly. In fact, they became, in many respects, substantial business enterprises, a development that apparently provided the stimulus for the *invention of true writing,* which was originally a means of recording the business activities of temples.[13] Many scholars have described the early Mesopotamian city-states as theocracies, since the local deity was regarded as the real ruler and the king merely as his "tenant farmer."[14]

Egypt was also a theocracy, but of a different type. The ruler was himself believed to be a god.[15] To his subjects he "was the incarnation, the living embodiment, of the god of any district he happened to be visiting; he was their actual God in living form, whom they could see, speak to, and adore."[16] Like the gods of the Mesopotamian city-states, he was the owner of all the land and entitled to a portion of all that was

The Temple of Luxor, Egypt, Built about 1400 B.C.

produced; as in Mesopotamia, these revenues supported a small army of specialists (e.g., officials, craftsmen, soldiers).

In later years there was a secularizing trend, especially in Mesopotamia.[17] By then, however, these societies had developed other institutional arrangements—notably political ones—to ensure the continued transfer of the economic surplus from the peasant producers to the governing class. Nevertheless, religion continued to play an important role as a legitimizing agency. It provided a rationale to justify the operation of the political system and its often harsh economic consequences.

The experience of Mesopotamia and Egypt thus supports the impression gained from horticultural societies concerning the importance of religion in the formation of an economic surplus. *Technological advance created the possibility of a surplus, but to transform that possibility into a reality required an ideology that motivated farmers to produce more than they needed to stay alive and productive, and persuaded them to turn that surplus over to someone else.* Although this has sometimes been accomplished by means of secular and political ideologies, a system of beliefs that defined people's obligations with reference to the supernatural worked best in most societies of the past.

Population: Growth in Size of Communities and Societies
In the first few centuries after the shift to agriculture, there was striking growth in the size of a number of communities, especially in Mesopotamian societies.[18] For example,

the population of the city of Uruk, which was already an impressive 10,000 in 3800 B.C., increased to 50,000 by 3000 B.C.[19] The largest cities were the capitals of the most prosperous societies, and, although it is impossible to determine exactly the size of the cities and towns of 3000 and 2000 B.C., scholars believe that one or more of them had a population of at least 100,000.[20]

Egypt was the largest of the simple agrarian societies of ancient times and politically the most stable. It enjoyed the unique distinction of being a united and independent nation throughout most of the time it was a simple agrarian society. This achievement was due to its unique environmental situation: no other society had such excellent natural defenses (i.e., it was bounded by desert, mountains, and the sea) and was so little threatened by other societies.

In the second half of the second millennium, Egypt embarked on a program of expansion that extended its boundaries to Syria and the Sudan. There were also other important empires in this era, especially those established by the Babylonians in the eighteenth century B.C. and the Hittites in the thirteenth century B.C. Babylonia succeeded briefly in uniting most of Mesopotamia, while the Hittites conquered much of what is now Turkey and Syria.

The Polity: Growth of the State

These conquests posed serious organizational problems for the rulers of early agrarian societies. Traditional modes of government based on kinship ties were no longer adequate for administering the affairs of societies whose populations now sometimes numbered in the millions. Though rulers continued to rely on relatives to help them govern, they were increasingly forced to incorporate others. One solution was to subsume a conquered group as a subdivision of the conquering society, leaving its former ruler in charge but in a subordinate capacity. Eventually all of the more successful rulers found it necessary to create new kinds of governmental structures that were no longer solely based on kinship ties.

We can see these newer patterns evolving in both military and civil affairs. For example, the first armies in agrarian societies, like those in horticultural, were simply militias made up of all the able-bodied men in the society.[21] During this period, wars did not last long and were fought only after the harvest was in. In fact, the period following the harvest came to be known as the "season when kings go forth to war." These limitations were necessary because, with the shift to agriculture, men's responsibilities in farming, with a few notable exceptions (e.g., see "Women's Power in a Man's World") were much greater than they had been in horticultural societies (see Table 6.2).

As long as wars were brief and limited to skirmishes with neighboring peoples, militias were adequate. But once rulers became interested in empire building, a new system was necessary. As early as the middle of the third millennium, would-be empire builders in Mesopotamia established small but highly trained *professional armies.* For example, Sargon, the famous Akkadian king, had a standing army of 5,400 men.[22] As far as possible, recruits were sons of old soldiers, and thus a military caste was gradually created. The Egyptians followed a similar policy except that they relied chiefly on foreign mercenaries. These new armies were *royal,* rather than national, armies. Their expenses were paid by the king out of his enormous revenues, and the profits resulting from their activities were his also. Not only were these armies useful in dealing with foreign enemies, they also served as a defense against internal threats.[23]

In civil affairs, too, the casual and informal practices of simpler societies proved inadequate. As states expanded and the problems of administration multiplied, new kinds of governmental positions were created and governmental *bureaucracies* began to take shape.[24] In addition to the many officials who comprised the royal court and were responsible for administering the king's complex household affairs, there were officials scattered throughout the countryside to administer the affairs of units ranging from small districts to provinces with hundreds of villages and towns (see Figure 7.2). Each official had a staff of scribes and other lesser officials to assist him, and written records became increasingly important as administrative problems grew more complex.[25]

Throughout most of the history of the simple agrarian societies of antiquity, writing was a complex craft mastered by only a few individuals after long apprenticeships.[26] This is not surprising, considering the complex systems of writing then in use. Even after a 2,000-year process of simplification, Mesopotamian cuneiform script still had between 600 and 1,000 distinct characters. Before a person could learn to read or write, he had to memorize this formidable array of symbols and learn the complex rules for combining them. The Egyptian hieroglyphic and hieratic scripts were equally complicated. Thus, those who could write formed a specialized occupational group in society—the scribes—and their services were much in demand. For the most part, this occupation was filled by the sons of the rich and powerful, since only they could afford the necessary education.[27] Because of the political importance of their skill and the limited supply of qualified personnel, most scribes were at least members of the middle class.

One consequence of the growth of empires and the development of bureaucracy was the establishment of the first formal legal systems. Over the centuries every society had developed certain concepts of justice, as well as informal techniques for implementing them. The most common solution, as we saw in our survey of hunting and gathering societies, was to rely on blood revenge by the injured party and his relatives. Because of the anarchic tendencies in such a system, people began to seek settlement by arbitration, and to help them in this they would turn to the most respected and powerful members of the community. In this way, headmen and other political leaders gradually acquired judicial powers (i.e., the power to administer justice). Later, as empires grew, peoples of diverse cultures were brought within the framework of a single political system. In many instances the official appointed to rule over an area was not a native and was therefore unfamiliar with local conceptions of justice (which varied considerably from place to place). This generated pressure to clarify and standardize judicial practice, which eventually led to the *first formal codes of law*. The most famous of these was the Code of Hammurabi, named for the great Babylonian conqueror and empire builder of the early second millennium.

The Economy: The First Monetary Systems and the Growth of Trade

Money as we know it was absent in the first simple agrarian societies. There were, nevertheless, certain standardized media of exchange. Barley served this function in

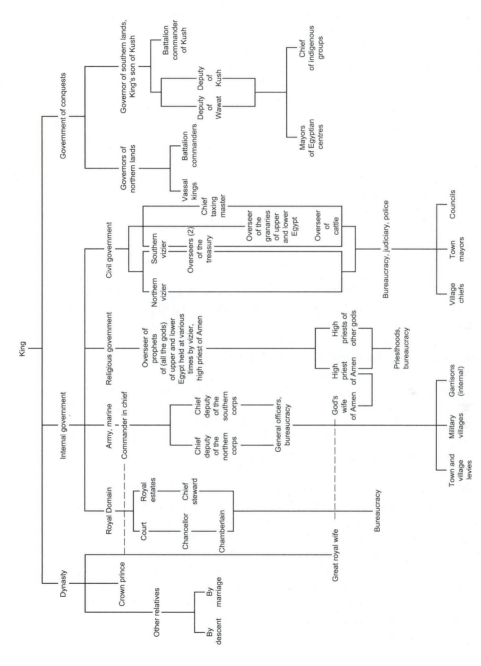

Figure 7.2. The Organizational Chart of the Government of Egypt Illustrates the Extent to which Bureaucratic Organization in Agrarian Empires Replaced Earlier Systems of Organization Based on Kinship.
Source: David O'Connor, *Ancient Egypt: A Social History* (Cambridge: Cambridge University Press, 1983). Reproduced by permission of the publisher.

ancient Mesopotamia, wheat in Egypt. Wages, rents, taxes, and various other obligations were paid in specified quantities of these grains.[28]

As media of exchange, grains were less than ideal because they were both perishable and bulky. So, from a fairly early date, various metals, particularly silver and copper, were adopted as alternatives.[29] Initially, they were circulated in the form of crude bars of irregular size and weight, and their use was restricted to major transactions, since metal was still scarce. Later, as the production of metals increased, smaller units were introduced in local trade and sizes and weights were gradually standardized. As a final stage in the process, governments assumed the responsibility for manufacturing metallic currencies and full-fledged monetary systems took shape. This did not occur, however, until the very end of the simple agrarian era.

The growth of monetary systems had enormous implications for societal development. *Money has always facilitated the movement, the exchange, and ultimately the production of goods and services of every kind.* The establishment of a monetary system greatly expands the market for the things each individual produces, because, unlike barter, use of a "universal" medium of exchange means it is no longer necessary to find a mutually agreeable exchange of goods between individuals. Thus the demand for goods and services is increased.

Model of a Royal Granary, Found in an Egyptian Tomb (About 2000 B.C.). Note the Scribes Sitting by the Door Recording the Deliveries of Grain.

One immediate consequence of the emergence of a monetary system is the growth of opportunities for *merchants,* or middlemen, who purchase goods that they do not want for themselves but which they know are in demand by others. Once a class of merchants has come into being, it serves not only to better satisfy existing demands but also to create new ones. By displaying new and unusual articles, merchants generate new needs and desires and thereby stimulate economic activity.

In the long run, a money economy subverts many of the values of simpler societies, especially the cooperative tendencies of extended kin systems. It fosters instead a more individualistic, rationalistic, and competitive approach to life and lays a foundation for many of the attitudes and values that characterize modern industrial societies.[30]

All of these tendencies were still quite limited, however, in the simple agrarian societies of the ancient Middle East. The newly emerging money economies barely penetrated the rural villages, where most people lived. Even in the cities and towns, the role of money was quite limited compared with what we are accustomed to. Fully developed cash economies still lay far in the future.

Stratification: Increasing Inequality

In most simple agrarian societies of the ancient world, newly emerging or expanding social and cultural differences created internal divisions within society, and sometimes conflict as well. Three cleavages were especially serious. First, there was one between the small governing class and the much larger mass of people who had no voice in political decisions and who had to hand over all or most of the surplus they produced to the governing class. Second, there was a division between the urban minority and the far more numerous rural population. Finally, there was a cleavage between the small literate minority and the illiterate masses.

Because these three lines of cleavage tended to converge, their impact was greatly magnified. The small and often literate urban governing class lived in a strikingly different world from that of the illiterate, rural, peasant majority—despite the fact that they were members of the same society. Each group had its own distinct subculture.[31]

The subculture of the common people was a mixture of primitive superstition and the practical information they needed in their daily lives. It was extremely parochial in outlook and knew little of the world beyond the village. The subculture of the governing class, in contrast, incorporated the refinements we identify with "civilization," such as philosophy, art, literature, history, and science. It also included contempt for physical labor of any kind and for those who engaged in it.

In many respects the differences *within* simple agrarian societies were greater than differences *among* them. Apart from the problems of language, an Egyptian peasant could have adapted far more easily to the life of a Babylonian peasant than to the life of a member of the governing class of his own society. As this gulf widened, members of the governing class found it increasingly difficult to recognize the ignorant, downtrodden peasants as fellow human beings. The scribes of ancient Egypt were fond of saying that the lower classes lacked intelligence and had to be driven like cattle, with a stick.[32]

Slowdown in the Rate of Technological Innovation

Another significant development in these societies was a surprising slowdown in the rate of technological innovation and progress, beginning within a few centuries after the shift from horticulture to agriculture. V. Gordon Childe described the change this way:

> Before the [agrarian] revolution comparatively poor and illiterate communities had made an impressive series of contributions to man's progress. The two millennia immediately preceding 3,000 B.C. had witnessed discoveries in applied science that directly or indirectly affected the prosperity of millions of [people] and demonstrably furthered the biological welfare of our species by facilitating its multiplication. We have mentioned the following applications of science: artificial irrigation using canals and ditches; the plow; the harnessing of animal motive-power; the sailboat; wheeled vehicles; orchard husbandry; fermentation; the production and use of copper; bricks; the arch; glazing; the seal; and—in the earliest stages of the revolution—a solar calendar, writing, numerical notation, and bronze.
>
> The two thousand years after the revolution—say from 2,600 to 600 B.C.—produced few contributions of anything like comparable importance to human progress. Perhaps only four achievements deserve to be put in the same category as the fifteen just enumerated. They are: the "decimal notation" of Babylonia (about 2000 B.C.); an economical method for smelting iron on an industrial scale (1400 B.C.); a truly alphabetic script (1300 B.C.); aqueducts for supplying water to cities (700 B.C.).[33]

Childe went on to note that two of these four innovations, the smelting of iron and the development of the alphabet, "cannot be credited to the societies that had initiated and reaped the fruits of the [agrarian] revolution" but rather were the products of somewhat less advanced neighboring societies.[34]

At first glance this slowing of the rate of cultural innovation seems an unlikely development. Larger populations, increased intersocietal contacts, and the greater store of information available to potential innovators should have produced higher rates of innovation, especially in technology.[‡] The fact that they did not poses an interesting problem.

To explain this unusual development, we need to return to the concept of *feedback*. This, as we have seen, is when the effects of, or response to, a change affects the pressure for future change. Until now, we have only seen examples of *positive* feedback, in which the effect of the original change *enhanced* or *strengthened* the original impetus for change. This is the type of feedback that has been involved in all the major social and cultural changes we have examined so far. Now we are seeing one of the relatively rare instances in sociocultural evolution in which major technological advances generated *negative* feedback. In other words, this is a case in which the results of technological change *diminished* or *weakened* the impetus for future technological change.

---

‡To avoid misunderstanding, it is worth emphasizing that we do not assume that innovation is necessary or automatic, only that *under these conditions* its rate should have increased, not decreased (e.g., see Chapter 3).

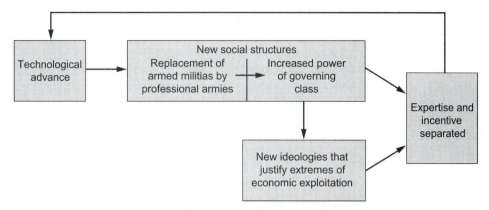

Figure 7.3. Model of the Causes of the Decline in the Rate of Technological Innovation During the First Two Millennia of the Agrarian Era. Negative Feedback Is Indicated by the Minus Sign Over the Arrow to Technological Advance.

As Figure 7.3 indicates, changes in social organization and ideology that were themselves consequences of technological advance had the effect of *slowing* the rate of technological innovation and advance. As the older system of a militia that included all of a society's able-bodied men was replaced by a professional army, there was a substantial increase in the power of the governing class, which controlled the new army. New beliefs and values emerged that justified and legitimized the new system of exploitation and thereby made it even worse. Thus, the governing class found it easier to extract economic surplus from the peasants, leaving them with little more than the bare necessities of life.[35]

As a result, the peasants lost the incentive for innovation, knowing that any benefits that resulted from their inventions and discoveries would simply be appropriated by the governing class, whereas losses—which could be devastating given the peasant's narrow margin of survival—would be borne by themselves.[§] At the same time, the governing class, though it had a vested interest in a more productive economy, no longer had the necessary knowledge of, and experience with, subsistence technology and thus was in no position to make creative innovations. In short, *expertise and incentive were inadvertently divorced,* with disastrous results for technological progress.

Under the circumstances it is hardly surprising that members of the governing class turned increasingly to warfare and conquest, practices that first became profitable with the advent of horticulture, as the best ways to increase their wealth. Warfare was something they understood; moreover, in their system of values, waging war was one of the few occupations considered appropriate for members of their exalted class. More than ever before, the resources of societies were turned from the conquest of nature to the conquest of people.[36] And this, due to the new, more productive technology,

---

[§]It is possible that the process was even more complicated and that the health and mental capacities of many peasants may have been impaired by protein-deficient diets, parasites, debilitating chronic diseases, and by environments not conducive to learning in early childhood. In short, the basic intelligence and creative potential of many peasants may have been permanently impaired.

could be a highly profitable enterprise. With vast numbers of peasants producing more than they needed to survive and remain productive, there was a large economic surplus that could be extracted by means of taxes, tribute, tithes, and rents and used to support the host of servants and artisans who catered to the whims of the governing class and the army of soldiers and officials who ensured the flow of revenues.

These developments help explain the growing complexity of social organization during this period. Having cut themselves off from the gritty world of work and having turned their efforts instead to conquest, members of the governing class found new challenges for their creative talents in the field of social organization. The exercise of power and the manipulation of others were activities in keeping with their dignity. Moreover, they were rewarding: the better organized an army or government, the greater its chances of success in struggles with other groups.[37]

By the end of the period when simple agrarian societies were dominant, substantial changes had occurred in societies that had adopted the new technology. The largest of them were substantially larger than any horticultural society had ever been, and substantially more complex. There was a much greater division of labor within them, and social inequality had also increased. But as impressive as they were, these changes were only a prelude to what was to come in the remainder of the agrarian era.

One Consequence of the Growth of Empire Was an Increase in the Economic Surplus Extracted from Conquered Peoples in the form of Tribute: Egyptian Carving Showing Tribute Bearers (about 2000 B.C.).

ADVANCED AGRARIAN SOCIETIES
Technology

During the period in which simple agrarian societies dominated the Middle East, the most important technological advance was the discovery of the technique of smelting iron. Prior to this, bronze had been the most important metal. But since the supply was limited** and the demands of the governing class always took precedence over the needs of peasants, bronze was used primarily for military, ornamental, and ceremonial purposes. It never substantially replaced stone and wood in ordinary tools, certainly not in agricultural tools, and so its impact on the economy was limited.

People knew of iron at least as early as the first half of the third millennium B.C., but apparently only in its meteoric form, which is very scarce.[38] Sometime during the second millennium, however, the Hittites of Asia Minor developed a method for extracting (smelting) iron from iron ore, which was much more abundant. For centuries they kept this a closely guarded secret, which gave them a virtual monopoly on this highly valued commodity. Then, about 1200 B.C., their nation was destroyed. This led to the rapid dispersal of both the Hittite people and the technology of smelting iron.

As one would expect, in view of the class structure of simple agrarian societies, the initial use of iron was limited largely to the governing class. Some of the earliest iron objects recovered from Egypt were a dagger, a bracelet, and a headrest found in the tomb of the pharaoh Tutankhamen. Prior to the military collapse of the Hittite empire, iron was five times more expensive than gold, forty times more than silver. It was not until about 800 B.C. that iron came into general use for *ordinary tools*. Thus, it is not until this period that we can speak of true advanced agrarian societies, although many Middle Eastern societies of the previous three or four centuries were certainly transitional types.

During this transitional period two further discoveries greatly enhanced the value of iron. First it was found that if the outer layers of the iron absorbed some carbon from the fire during the forging process, the metal became somewhat harder. Later it was discovered that this carburized iron could be hardened still further by quenching the hot metal in water, thus producing steel. With these developments, iron became not only more common than bronze but also more useful for both military and economic purposes. As one writer has said, "After the discovery of quench-hardening, iron gradually passed into the position from which it has never subsequently been ousted; it became the supremely useful material for making all the tools and weapons that are intended for cutting, chopping, piercing, or slashing."[39]

From its point of origin in the Middle East, iron making spread until eventually it was practiced in nearly all of the Old World, even in many horticultural societies. By the time of Christ, advanced agrarian societies were firmly established in the Middle East, throughout most of the Mediterranean world, and in much of India and China. Within the next thousand years, the advanced agrarian pattern spread over most of Europe and much of Southeast Asia, and expanded further in India and China. Still later it was transplanted to the European colonies in the New World.

Compared with simpler societies, advanced agrarian societies enjoyed a very productive technology. Unfortunately, the same conditions that slowed the rate of

---

**This was because of the scarcity of tin, an essential component of bronze.

Throughout the Agrarian Era Societies Depended on Humans and Animals as Their Chief Sources of Energy: Indian Peasants Raising Water from Ditch to Irrigate Field. The Man on the Post Moves Back and Forth on the Crossbeam to Raise the Water and to Lower the Bucket Again to the Ditch Below, Where the Other Man Refills It.

technological advance in simple agrarian societies continued to prevail. As a result, their progress was not nearly what one would expect on the basis of their size, the degree of contact among them, and, above all, their store of accumulated information.[40]

Nevertheless, over the centuries quite a number of important innovations were made. A partial list would include the catapult, the crossbow, gunpowder, horseshoes, a workable harness for horses, stirrups, the wood-turning lathe, the auger, the screw, the wheelbarrow, the rotary fan for ventilation, the clock, the spinning wheel, porcelain, printing, iron casting, the magnet, water-powered mills, windmills, and, in the period just preceding the emergence of the first industrial societies, the workable steam engine, the fly shuttle, the spinning jenny, the spinning machine, and various other power-driven tools. Because of these and other innovations, the most advanced agrarian societies of the eighteenth century A.D. were far superior, from a technological standpoint, to their predecessors of 2,500 years earlier.

The level of technological development was not uniform throughout the agrarian world, despite diffusion. Information spread slowly in most cases, and some areas were considerably ahead of others. During much of the advanced agrarian era, especially from A.D. 500 to 1500, the Middle East, China, and parts of India were technologically superior to Europe.[41] In part, this was simply a continuation of older patterns: the Middle East had been the center of innovation for more than 5,000 years following its shift to horticulture. An even more important factor in Europe's relative backwardness, however, was the collapse of the Roman Empire. For centuries afterward, Europe was divided into scores of petty kingdoms and principalities that had only enough resources to maintain the smallest urban settlements and the most limited occupational specialization. Therefore, Europeans were inactive in many of the most promising and challenging technological frontiers of the time. Though they made relative gains during the later Middle Ages—due largely to the diffusion of knowledge from the East—they did not really catch up until the sixteenth century and did not take the lead until even later.

Population: Continuing Trends

Size of Societies and Communities

The populations of advanced agrarian societies were substantially larger than those of any societies that preceded them. This was due partly to advances in agricultural technology that permitted greater population densities and partly to advances in military technology and social organization that aided the process of empire building. The largest simple agrarian society, Egypt, probably had fewer than fifteen million members.[42] In contrast, the largest advanced agrarian society, mid-nineteenth-century China, had approximately 400 million.[††43] While that was exceptional, India reached 175 million in the middle of the nineteenth century, and the Roman and the Russian Empires each had at least seventy million people.[44]

Similar differences are found in communities. The largest cities in simple agrarian societies had populations of about 100,000. By comparison, the upper limit for cities in advanced agrarian societies was about a million.[45] Only the capitals of major empires ever attained this size, however, and they maintained it but briefly. Cities of 100,000, while much more numerous than in simple agrarian societies, were still quite rare by modern standards.

Fertility and Mortality

Birthrates in both simple and advanced agrarian societies have averaged forty or more births per 1,000 population per year, or quadruple that of modern industrial societies.[46] In general, there seems to have been little interest in limiting the size of families, since large families, particularly ones with many sons, were valued for both economic and religious reasons. From the economic standpoint, children were viewed by peasants as an important asset, a valuable source of cheap labor.[47] Children were also important as the only form of "old-age insurance" available to peasants. Religion

---

[††]Growth in China's population *after* the middle of the nineteenth century was due increasingly to the beginnings of industrialization. The same was true in India.

added yet another incentive for large families, either by encouraging ancestor worship, for which perpetuation of the family line was essential, or simply by declaring large families to be a sign of God's favor.[48]

One of the few constraints on the growth of families was the threat of severe deprivation. When crops failed and famine was imminent, families often resorted to infanticide, abandoning their newborn by the roadside or leaving them at the door of a church or monastery in the hope that someone who was able to provide for the baby might take pity and raise the baby.[49] If conditions became bad enough, even older children would be abandoned by their parents (see "Mother Goose Revisited," page 178).

There is also evidence that many women would have liked to avoid the burdens and risks of repeated pregnancies. Unfortunately for them, in societies in which men were dominant and in which an effective contraceptive technology did not yet exist, their wishes had little effect.

Despite their high birthrates, advanced agrarian societies generally grew slowly. Sometimes they failed to grow at all or even declined in size. The reason was that death rates were almost as high as birthrates, and sometimes higher. Wars, disease, accidents, and famine all took their toll. Infant mortality was especially high before the development of modern sanitation and medicine. Studies show that children born in Rome 2,000 years ago lived only twenty years on average.[50] Even as recently as the seventeenth century, the children of British queens and duchesses had a life expectancy of only thirty years, and nearly a third died before their fifth birthday.[51] For the common people, conditions were even worse. With death rates averaging nearly forty per 1,000 per year, life expectancy at birth was barely twenty-five years, and even those who reached adulthood usually died young. (See Table 7.1.)

Large cities were notoriously unhealthy places, especially for the common people. The citizens of Rome, for example, had a shorter life expectancy than those in the provinces.[52] England in the early eighteenth century presented a similar situation. During the first half of that century, there were an estimated 500,000 more deaths

Table 7.1 Average Age at Death of Those Who Reached Adulthood During Agrarian Era

	Males	Females
Early Bronze Age, 3000 B.C.	33.7	29.5
Middle Bronze Age, 2000 B.C.		
Commoners	36.3	30.8
Royalty	35.9	36.1
Late Bronze Age, 1500 B.C.	39.5	32.1
Early Iron Age, 1150 B.C.	38.6	31.3
Imperial Rome, A.D. 120	40.2	34.6
Medieval Byzantium, A.D. 1400	37.7	31.1

Sources: J. L. Angel, "Ecology and Population in the Eastern Mediterranean," *World Archaeology*, 4 (1972), pp. 88–105; and J. L. Angel, "Paleoecology, Paleodemography, and Health," in Steven Polgar, *Population, Ecology, and Social Evolution* (The Hague: Mouton, 1975), pp. 167–190.

than births in London.[53] The reasons for this become clear when we read descriptions of sanitary conditions in medieval cities:

> The streets of medieval towns were generally little more than narrow alleys, the overhanging upper stories of the houses nearly meeting, and thus effectually excluding all but a minimum of light and air. . . . In most continental towns and some English ones, a high city wall further impeded the free circulation of air. . . . Rich citizens might possess a courtyard in which garbage was collected and occasionally removed to the suburbs, but the usual practice was to throw everything into the streets including the garbage of slaughter houses and other offensive trades. . . . Filth of every imaginable description accumulated indefinitely in the unpaved streets and in all available space and was trodden into the ground. The water supply would be obtained either from wells or springs, polluted by the gradual percolation through the soil of the accumulated filth, or else from an equally polluted river. In some towns, notably London, small streams running down a central gutter served at once as sewers and as water supply. . . . In seventeenth century London, which before the Fire largely remained a medieval city, the poorer class house had only a covering of weatherboards, a little black pitch forming the only waterproofing, and these houses were generally built back to back. Thousands of Londoners dwelt in cellars or horribly overcrowded tenements. A small house in Dowgate accommodated 11 married couples and 15 single persons. . . . Another source of unhealthiness were the church vaults and graveyards, so filled with corpses that the level of the latter was generally raised above that of the surrounding ground. In years of pestilence, recourse had to be made to plague pits in order to dispose of the harvest of death.[54]

This account calls attention to one of the striking demographic characteristics of advanced agrarian societies: the disasters that periodically overtook them and produced sharp increases in the death rate.[55] The most devastating of all, the black plague that hit Europe in the middle of the fourteenth century, is said to have killed between a quarter and a half of the population in a four-year period.[56]

Crop failures and famines seldom affected such large areas, but they were more frequent and could be just as deadly. One Finnish province lost a third of its population during the famine of 1696–1697, and many parts of France suffered comparable losses a few years earlier.[57] Even allowing for a considerable margin of error in the reports of such disasters, it is clear from other kinds of evidence—for example, the severe labor shortages and the abandonment of farms that followed plagues and famines—that the number of deaths was huge. For these reasons, the growth of advanced agrarian populations was anything but continuous.

The Economy: Increasing Differentiation

Division of Labor

The growth in both territorial and population size that came with the shift from the simple to the advanced agrarian level brought with it an increase in the division of labor. For the first time, there was significant economic specialization both by regions and by communities, and this was accompanied by increased occupational specialization.

Sanitary Standards Were Low in Most Agrarian Societies: Open-Air Butcher Shop in the Middle East.

The Roman Empire provides a good illustration of both regional and local special-ization. North Africa and Spain were noted as suppliers of dried figs and olive oil; Gaul, Dalmatia, Asia Minor, and Syria for their wine; Spain and Egypt for salted meats; Egypt, North Africa, Sicily, and the Black Sea region for grain; and the latter for salted fish as well.[58] The tendency toward specialization at the community level is illustrated by a passage from a manual for wealthy farmers, written in the second century B.C., which advised:

> Tunics, togas, blankets, smocks and shoes should be bought at Rome; caps, iron tools, scythes, spades, mattocks, axes, harnesses, ornaments and small chains at Cales and Minturnae; spades at Venafrum, carts and sledges at Suessa and in Lucania, jars and pots at Alba and at Rome; tiles at Venafrum, oil mills at Pompeii and at Rufrius's yard at Nola, nails and bars at Rome; pails, oil urns, water pitchers, wine urns, other copper vessels at Capua and at Nola; Campanian baskets, pulley-ropes and all sorts of cordage at Capua; Roman baskets at Suessa and Casium.[59]

Similar patterns are reported in other agrarian societies.[60] Even at the village level a measure of specialization was not uncommon. In the agricultural off-season, peasants

Table 7.2 Occupations of Householders in Two Sections of Barcelona in A.D. 1385

Sailors	227	Longshoremen	50	Silversmiths	29
Merchants	151	Innkeepers	49	Curriers	29
Shoemakers	108	Brokers	45	Notaries	28
Tailors	96	Carpenters	43	Tavern-keepers	27
Fishermen	94	Bakers	40	Spicers	26
Seamen	73	Janitors	39	Bargemen	25
Wooldressers	70	Hucksters	36	76 other occupations	525
Weavers	63	Butchers	34		
Tanners	61	Scriveners	32	Total	2000

Source: Adapted from Josiah Cox Russell, *Medieval Regions and Their Cities* (Bloomington: Indiana University Press, 1972), p. 170.

often turned to handicrafts to make ends meet, and villages often developed a reputation for a particular commodity.

In the larger urban centers occupational specialization reached a level that surpassed anything achieved in simpler societies. For example, a tax roll for Paris from the year 1313 lists 157 different trades, and tax records from two sections of Barcelona in 1385 indicate a hundred occupations (see Table 7.2).[61] The clothing industry alone contained such specialized occupations as wool comber, wool spinner, silk spinner (two kinds), girdle maker, and headdress maker (seven kinds, including specialists in felt, fur, wool and cotton, flowers, peacock feathers, gold embroidery and pearls, and silk). Though such specialization was found only in the largest cities, smaller cities often had forty or fifty different kinds of craftsmen, and even small towns had ten or twenty.[62] In addition to craft specialists, urban centers also had specialists in government, commerce, religion, education, the armed forces, and domestic service. There were also specialists in illegal occupations (e.g., thieves, prostitutes), which were a normal part of urban life in advanced agrarian societies.

Command Economies

Because politics and economics were always highly interdependent in advanced agrarian societies, the people who dominated the political system also dominated the economic system. The leading officeholders in government were usually the chief landholders as well, and in these societies land and control of those who worked it was the most important economic resource. As one economic historian has written, this was a time in which "true wealth consisted in being master."[63]

In these societies, the answers to basic economic questions—how resources should be used, what should be produced and in what quantities, and how those products should be distributed—were determined less by the forces of supply and demand than by arbitrary decisions of the political elite. Thus, these were command, not market economies.[64]

The economy of an advanced agrarian society consisted of two distinct parts: a rural agricultural sector and an urban manufacturing and commercial sector. These were not of equal economic importance, however. One historian has estimated that the Roman state derived approximately twenty times more tax revenue from agriculture than from trade and handicrafts. He went on to say that "this apportionment of the burden of taxation probably corresponded roughly to the economic structure of the empire. All the evidence goes to show that its wealth was derived almost entirely from agriculture, and to a very small extent from industry and trade."[65] The same could be said of every agrarian society. This does not mean, however, that the urban economy was of little interest to members of the governing class. On the contrary, it was of great interest because it provided the luxury goods they valued so highly. The urban economy, however, depended on the ability of the rural economy to produce a surplus that could support the urban population.

In many respects the economy of the typical agrarian society resembled a tree with roots spreading in every direction, constantly drawing in new resources. The pattern was similar to that shown in Figure 7.4. At the economic center of the society was the national capital, controlled by the king or emperor and the leading members of the governing class. Surrounding it were various provincial or regional capitals controlled by royal governors and other members of the governing class. Each of these in turn was surrounded by smaller county seats and market towns controlled by lesser members of the governing class. Finally, each of these towns was surrounded by scores of small villages.

In this system, there was a steady flow of goods from smaller units to larger, or from villages to county seats, and then on to regional and national capitals. Basically this flow was achieved by means of taxation, but it was supplemented by rents, interest on debts, tithes and other religious offerings, and profits, all of which helped transfer the economic surplus from the peasant producers to the urban-based governing class, its allies, and their dependents.

Figure 7.4. As the Arrows Indicate, Goods and Resources Extracted from Villages Flowed to Regional Centers and Then on to the National Capital, with Each Level Lower Keeping What It Could.

With what they retained of their surplus after paying taxes, rents, interest, and other obligations, peasants could go to the urban centers and trade for commodities that were not available in their villages (e.g., metal tools, salt, etc.). Many towns and cities were also religious centers, and the peasants often used these facilities. Finally, the peasants did benefit to some degree from the maintenance of law and order provided by urban-based governments, even though the law was used disproportionately to protect the rights of the governing class and keep the peasants in a subordinate position. The maintenance of order was extremely important in an agrarian society because so much depended on the success of each harvest, and each harvest depended on months of prior effort. Disruption at any point in the agricultural cycle could be disastrous for everyone.

The Rural Economy

In most advanced agrarian societies, the governing elite (which included religious leaders) owned a grossly disproportionate share of the land. Although there are no precise figures for earlier times, the traditional pattern could still be seen recently in many parts of Latin America, the Middle East, and Southeast Asia. Typically, a minority of 1 to 3 percent of the population has owned from one-third to two-thirds of the arable land in these societies.[66]

Not only did the governing class usually own most of the land, but it often owned most of the peasants who worked it. Slavery and serfdom were common in agrarian societies, with large landholdings and large numbers of slaves or serfs normally going hand in hand. Thus, one nineteenth-century Russian nobleman who owned two million acres of land also owned nearly 300,000 serfs. Rulers always had the largest holdings. Prior to the emancipation of the serfs in Russia, the czar owned 27.4 million of them.[67]

Even when the peasant owned his own land and was legally free, he usually found it difficult to make ends meet. A bad crop one year and he had to borrow money at rates as high as 120 percent a year.[68] In any event, there were always taxes, and these usually fell more heavily on the peasant landowner than on his wealthier neighbor, either because of special exemptions granted the latter or simply because of his greater ability to evade such obligations.[69] If a peasant did not own his land, he had to pay rent, which was always high. In addition, he was often subject to compulsory labor service, tithes, fines, and obligatory "gifts" to the governing class.[70]

Because the number and variety of obligations were so great, it is difficult to determine just how large the total was, but in most societies it appears to have been at least half the total value of the goods the peasants produced.[71] The basic philosophy of the governing class seems to have been to tax peasants to the limit of their ability to pay.[72] A story is told of a leading Japanese official of the seventeenth century who, returning to one of his estates after an absence of ten years and finding the villagers in well-built houses instead of the hovels he remembered, exclaimed, "These people are too comfortable. They must be more heavily taxed."[73]

Living conditions for most peasants were primitive, and many were worse off than most hunters and gatherers had been thousands of years earlier. For example, the diet of the average peasant in medieval England consisted of little more than a hunk of bread and a mug of ale in the morning; a lump of cheese and bread with perhaps an onion or two to flavor it and more ale at noon; and a thick soup or pottage with bread and cheese in the evening. Meat was rare and the beer thin. Household furniture consisted

Mother Goose Revisited

Most of us think of Mother Goose rhymes and stories as charming survivals from a simpler, happier world of the past. Yet if we look at them closely, and at other older folk tales, a very different picture emerges. It is a picture of widespread poverty and despair, except for the fortunate few who lived in palaces.

Recall for a moment old Mother Hubbard who went to the cupboard to fetch her poor dog a bone, or the old woman who lived in a shoe and had so many children she didn't know what to do. We also learn something of life in agrarian societies from the story of Tom Thumb. In a late-seventeenth-century French version, the story begins, "Once upon a time there was a woodsman and his wife, who had seven children, all boys. . . . They were very poor, and their seven children were a great inconvenience, because none was old enough to support himself. . . . A very difficult year came, and the famine was so great that these poor folk resolved to get rid of their children."

Shades of Hansel and Gretel! And in the French version of "The Sorcerer's Apprentice," a poor father sells his son to the devil in exchange for an ample supply of food for twelve years.

Though fairy tales often had happy endings, these endings usually depended on magic, trickery, or uncommon luck—not ordinary hard work. Cinderella had her fairy godmother; Jack (of beanstalk fame) combined a generous mix of magic, trickery, daring, and luck to win his fortune; and the miller's son in Puss 'n Boots, who inherited only a cat, but a most remarkable cat indeed.

If Mother Goose has powers to charm, it is because we today overlook the poverty and despair that are portrayed, or we imagine that they are just part of the world of make-believe, like the fairy godmothers who provided the happy endings. But if we look closely at the conditions of life of ordinary people in agrarian societies, we find that there is at least as much truth as fiction in these old rhymes and tales.

---

of a few stools, a table, and a chest to hold the best clothes and any other treasured possessions.[74] Beds were uncommon; most peasants simply slept on earthen floors covered with straw.

Even later in France, toward the end of the agrarian era:

> Great masses of the people lived in a state of chronic malnutrition, subsisting mainly on porridge made of bread and water with some occasional, home-grown vegetables thrown in. They ate meat only a few times a year, on feast days or after autumn slaughtering if they did not have enough silage to feed the livestock over the winter. . . . For most peasants village life was a struggle for survival, and survival meant keeping above the line that divided the poor from the indigent.[75]

But many did not survive and lost their farms. "Then they took to the road for good, drifting about with the flotsam and jetsam of France's *population flottante* (floating population), which included several million desperate souls by the 1780s." The same author concludes by saying, "The human condition has changed so much since then that we can hardly imagine the way it appeared to people whose lives really were nasty, brutish, and short."[76]

In China, conditions were so wretched that female infanticide was widely practiced. One nineteenth-century scholar indicated that in some districts as many as a quarter of the female infants were killed at birth.[77] Sometimes signs were posted near ponds, reading, "Girls may not be drowned here." In rural areas, the traditional greeting when peasants met was "Have you eaten today?" (the equivalent of "How are you today?").

Peasant Using Traditional Plow, Iran.

To compound the misery created by their economic situation, peasants were often subjected to further cruelties. Families were sometimes split up if it served their master's economic interests.[78] Peasants often found it difficult to defend their wives and daughters from the amorous attentions of the governing class, and in some areas the lord of the manor maintained the notorious *jus primae noctis* (i.e., literally, the right of the first night, meaning the right to initial sexual relations with all brides on their wedding nights).[79] Finally, peasants were subject at all times to the whims and tempers of their superiors, who could invoke severe punishments even for minor offenses. Even petty thievery could be punished by death, often by cruel and frightful means.[80]

To the governing class, all this seemed only fitting and proper, since most of them, like their predecessors in simple agrarian societies, viewed peasants as subhuman. In legal documents in medieval England, a peasant's children were listed not as his *familia* but as his *sequela,* meaning "brood" or "litter."[81] Estate records in Europe, Asia, and the Americas often listed peasants with the livestock.[82] Even so civilized a Roman as Cato the Elder argued that slaves, like livestock, should be disposed of when no longer productive.[83]

As shocking as these views seem today, they were clearly rooted in the experiences and interests of agrarian elites. In fact, the lives and experiences of the governing class and the peasantry were so divergent, and their contacts were so limited (normally a class of supervisory officials and retainers stood between them)[84] that it may be more surprising that some members of the privileged class recognized their common humanity than that the majority did not.

Despite the heavy burdens laid on them, not all peasants were reduced to the subsistence level. By various means, many contrived to hide part of their harvest and otherwise evade their obligations.[85] A small minority even managed, by rendering special services to the governing class or by other means, to rise a bit above their fellows, operating larger farms and generally living a bit more comfortably.[86]

For the majority, however, the one real hope for a substantial improvement in their lot lay, ironically, in the devastation wrought by plagues, famines, and wars. Only when death reduced their numbers to the point where good workers were scarce was the governing class forced to bid competitively for their services, thus raising incomes above the subsistence level.[87] Usually, however, high birthrates kept this from occurring, or, when it did, soon brought about a return to the former situation.

The Urban Economy

When we think of famous agrarian societies of the past, most of us conjure up images of cities: Rome, Constantinople, Alexandria, Jerusalem, Baghdad, Babylon, and others that loom large in the historical record. Thus it is with a sense of shock that we discover that rarely, if ever, did all the urban communities of an advanced agrarian society contain as much as 10 percent of its total population, and, in most cases, they held even less.[88]

How can this be? Why are our impressions of these ancient societies wrong? The reason is that their histories were recorded by a small literate minority—people who themselves usually lived in cities and towns and who regarded the life of the rural villages as unimportant and unworthy of their attention. Thus, the historical record is largely a record of city life, particularly the life of the governing class.

The most striking feature of the cities and towns of these societies was the great diversity of people who lived in them. City residents ranged from the most illustrious members of the governing class to beggars and other destitute people who barely managed to stay alive. Unlike many of the cities and towns in industrial societies, these were not primarily centers of economic production. Though some manufacturing was carried on in them, their political and commercial functions, and frequently their religious ones as well, were much more important.

Since cities and towns were the centers of government, and social and cultural centers as well, most members of the governing class preferred to live in them.[89] As a result, urban populations included not only civil and military officials, but the extensive households of the governing class as well. Servants were far more numerous in these societies than in ours, both because of the absence of labor-saving devices and because the governing class viewed manual work of any kind as degrading. Furthermore, one of their chief forms of status competition was to see who could maintain the most luxurious household. The household staff of the head of one small kingdom, Edward IV of England, numbered 400.[90] A more important ruler, such as the Roman emperor at the height of empire, had thousands. As one historian put it, one "is dumbfounded by the extraordinary degree of specialization [and] the insensate luxury" of the imperial household.[91] One group of servants was responsible for the emperor's palace clothes, another for his city clothes, another for those he wore to the theater, yet another for his military uniforms. Other servants attended to eating vessels, a different group to those used for drinking, another to silver vessels, and still others to gold vessels and those set with jewels. For entertainment, the emperor had his own choristers, an orchestra, dancing women, clowns, and dwarfs. Lesser members of the Roman governing class obviously could not maintain household staffs as elaborate as this, but many had staffs of hundreds, and some had a thousand or more. *All this was made possible by the labors of the peasantry.*

Part of the peasants' surplus also went to support two important groups that were allied with the governing class yet separate from it. The first of these was the clergy, of whom more will be said shortly. The second was the merchant class. Merchants were a peculiar group in the structure of agrarian societies. Although some of them were extremely wealthy, they were rarely accepted as equals by members of the governing class—even by those who were much less wealthy. For merchants worked to obtain their wealth, and this, by the values of the governing class, was demeaning.[92] Nevertheless, the latter avidly sought the goods that merchants sold and coveted their wealth, acquiring it whenever they could by taxes, marriage, or outright confiscation.[93] The attitude of the merchants toward the governing class was equally ambivalent: they both feared and envied them, but, given the chance, they emulated their way of life and sought to be accepted by them.

Like modern merchants, the merchants of agrarian societies often created the demand for their goods, thereby spurring productivity. And like modern advertisers, they were primarily interested in creating a demand for luxuries. One reason for this was the high cost of moving goods from town to town. With the primitive transportation available,[94] only lightweight luxury items such as silks, spices, and fine swords could be moved far without costs becoming prohibitive.

A report on China shortly after World War II indicates what an enormous difference modern methods of transportation have made in the cost of moving goods. To ship a ton of goods one mile at that time, the costs were as follows (measured in United States cents at that time).[95]

Steamboat	2.4	Pack mule	17.0
Railroad	2.7	Wheelbarrow	20.0
Junk	12.0	Pack donkey	24.0
Animal-drawn cart	13.0	Carrying by pole	48.0

Figures from Europe are strikingly similar: in 1900, for example, it cost ten times more to move goods by horse-drawn wagon than by rail.[96] In short, modern methods of transportation have slashed this cost by 80 to 95 percent.

The prosperity of the merchant class was due in no small measure to the labors of another humbler class with which merchants were closely affiliated—the artisans, who numbered approximately 3 to 5 percent of the total population.[97] Except for the peasantry, this class was the most productive element in the economy. Most artisans lived in urban centers and, like the rest of the urban population, were ultimately dependent on the surplus produced by the peasants. Craft specialization was rather highly developed in the larger urban centers, as we have seen.

The shops where artisans worked were small by modern standards and bore little resemblance to modern factories. In Rome in the first century B.C., a shop employing fifty men was considered very large.[98] A pewter business employing eighteen men was the largest mentioned in any of London's medieval craft records, and even this modest size was not attained until the middle of the fifteenth century.[99] Typically, the shop was also the residence of both the master craftsman and his workmen, and work was carried on either in the living quarters or in an adjoining room.[100]

The economic situation of the artisans, like that of the merchants, was variable. In Beijing at the time of World War I, wages ranged from $2.50 a month for members of the Incense and Cosmetic Workers Guild to $36 a month for members of the Gold Foil Beaters Guild.[101] Those in highly skilled trades and some of the self-employed fared moderately well by agrarian standards. Apprentices and journeymen in less skilled trades, however, worked long hours for bare subsistence wages. In Beijing, for example, a seven-day workweek and ten-hour workday were typical, and many artisans remained too poor ever to marry.

Merchants and artisans in the same trade were commonly organized into guilds. These organizations were an attempt to create, in an urban setting, a functional approximation of the extended kin groups of horticultural societies. Many guilds spoke of their members as brothers, for example, and functioned as mutual aid associations, restricting entry into the field, forbidding price cutting, and otherwise trying to protect the interests of their members.[102] But a guild included merchant employers as well as artisan employees, and the employers were naturally dominant, controlling key offices and formulating policies that benefited themselves more than the artisans.[103]

Beneath the artisans in the class structure of the cities were a variety of other kinds of people, including unskilled laborers who supplied much of the animal energy required by the system. The working conditions of these men were usually terrible, and accidents and injuries were common. As a result, their work life was short. For example, early in the present century, the average Beijing rickshaw man was able to work only five years, after which he was good for little except begging.[104]

The class of unskilled laborers shaded off into still more deprived groups—the unemployed, the beggars, and the criminals. The high birthrates of agrarian societies ensured a perennial oversupply of unskilled labor, and such people usually migrated to the cities, hoping to find some kind of employment. As long as men were young and healthy, they could usually get work as day laborers. But after they were injured or lost their youth and strength, they were quickly replaced by fresh labor and left to fend for themselves, usually as beggars or thieves. No agrarian society ever found a solution to this problem.‡‡ But then, the leading classes were not especially interested in finding one. The system served their needs quite well just as it was.

Many of the sisters of the men who made up the urban lower classes earned their livelihood as prostitutes. Moralists have often condemned these women as though they elected this career in preference to a more honorable one. The record indicates, however, that most of them had little choice: their only alternative was a life of unrelieved drudgery and poverty as servants or unskilled laborers, and many could not even hope for that.[105] The men they might have married were too poor to afford wives, and the system of prostitution was often, in effect, a substitute for marriage that was forced on these people by society. To be sure, the poor were not the only ones to avail themselves of the services of prostitutes, nor were all women in that "profession" because of poverty. But economic factors were clearly the chief cause of its high incidence in agrarian societies.

---

‡‡Indeed, although the magnitude of this problem was much greater in many agrarian societies, the existence of a sizable homeless population in cities today indicates that it has not been solved by industrial societies either.

Like Modern Advertisers, Merchants Sought to Create a Demand for Their Goods, Especially Luxuries: Market Scene in Morocco.

The number of profitable working years for prostitutes was hardly longer than that for the rickshaw boys, porters, and others who sold their physical assets for a meager livelihood. As a result, the cities and towns in agrarian societies often swarmed with beggars of both sexes. *Estimates by observers suggest that beggars comprised from a tenth to as high as a third of the total population of urban communities.*[106] The proportion was not nearly so high for society as a whole, of course, since many of the rural poor migrated to the cities and towns in the hope of finding greater opportunities.

The Polity: Continuing Development of the State

In nearly all advanced agrarian societies, government was the basic integrating force. In any society created by conquest and run for the benefit of a tiny elite, coercion was necessary to hold things together. Not only did the natural antagonisms of the peasant masses have to be kept in check, but diverse groups of conquered people often had to be welded together politically. The scope of this problem is suggested by the size of some of these societies. Whereas the largest simple agrarian society, Egypt, controlled roughly 800,000 square miles (much of it desert and uninhabited), several advanced agrarian societies covered between two and eight million square miles.

Nearly every advanced agrarian society was a monarchy headed by a king or emperor whose position was usually hereditary. Republican government, in which power was divided among a small ruling elite, was an infrequent exception limited almost entirely to the least powerful and least developed agrarian societies.[107] The prevalence of monarchical government seems to have been the result of the militaristic and exploitative character of societies at this level. Governments were constantly threatening, or being threatened by, their neighbors. At the same time, they were in danger from internal enemies—dissatisfied and ambitious members of the governing class, eager to seize control for themselves, and restless, hostile members of the far larger lower classes. Under such conditions republican government was nearly impossible.[108]

Because of the tendency to romanticize the past, many today are unaware of the frequency of both internal and external conflict in the great agrarian empires. In Rome, for example, thirty-one of the seventy-nine emperors were murdered, six were driven to suicide, four were forcibly deposed, and several more met unknown fates at the hands of internal enemies.[109] Although Rome's record may have been worse than most, struggles for control were common in all advanced agrarian societies.[110]

Because of the absence of significant commercialization, most of the intrasocietal conflict in simple agrarian societies was *intra* class.[111] Members of the governing elite competed and fought one another for social position and control of territory, and, at the village level, individual peasants and peasant families competed for access to the best farmland. What did not happen was conflict *between* these classes. Even wars of conquest were conflicts among elites, not between elites and peasants, and replacement of one elite by another often had little effect on the lives of peasants. In many ways the classes lived in different worlds, and under these conditions the control and taxation by elites may have seemed as natural and inevitable to peasants as the seasons themselves.

Commercialization had the power to change this dramatically. Not only did a wealthy commercial class itself constitute a potential threat to the power of an aristocratic governing elite, but also the introduction of commercial elements into the rural economy could trigger violence. If elites, in order to better meet their financial obligations, demanded higher rents, greater shares of harvests, and more burdensome services from the peasants, they undermined the traditional order on which their control rested, and this could spark peasant rebellions.[§§] For instance, one authority on Russia reports that in the short period from 1801 to 1861, there were no less than 1,467 peasant uprisings in various parts of that country.[112] Most of these disturbances were confined to a limited area only because authorities acted swiftly and ruthlessly. Had they not, many would have spread as widely as the famous English revolt of 1381 or the German Peasants' War of 1524–1525.

External threats were no less frequent or serious, and warfare was a chronic condition. A survey of eleven European countries of the agrarian era found that, on average, these countries were involved in some kind of conflict with neighboring societies nearly every second year.[113] Such conditions encouraged the rise of authoritarian governments.

Most members of the governing class considered political power a prize to be sought for the rewards it offered rather than an opportunity for public service, and the office of king or emperor was the *supreme prize*. Efforts to raise the living standards of the common people were rare, efforts at self-aggrandizement commonplace.[114]

---

§§It is important to note that these peasant uprisings were not revolutions. In fact, in most instances what the peasants wanted was a *return to the old order,* not its replacement with a new one.

Working Equipment for a Member of the Governing Class in Sixteenth-Century Europe.

In many societies, government offices were bought and sold like pieces of property, which the purchasers then used to obtain the greatest possible profit. Officeholders demanded payment before they would act, and justice was typically sold to the highest bidder. No wonder the common people of China developed the saying: "To enter a court of justice is to enter a tiger's mouth."[115]

These practices reflected what is known as the *proprietary theory of the state*, which defines the state as a piece of property that its owners may use, within broad and ill-defined limits, for their personal advantage.[116] Guided by this theory, agrarian rulers and governing classes saw nothing immoral in the use of what we (not they) would call "public office" for private gain. To them, it was simply the legitimate use of

One Use of the Economic Surplus in an Agrarian Society: The Taj Mahal, a Tomb Erected by the Mogul Emperor Shah Jahan in Memory of his Favorite Wife.

what they regarded as their "patrimony." It is said of the Ptolemies of Egypt, for example, that they showed the first emperors of Rome "how a country might be run on the lines of a profitable estate."[117] In the case of medieval Europe, we read:

> The proprietary conception of rulership created an inextricable confusion of public and private affairs. Rights of government were a form of private ownership. "Crown lands" and "the king's estate" were synonymous. There was no differentiation between the king in his private and public capacities. A kingdom, like any estate endowed with elements of governmental authority, was the private concern of its owner. Since *"state"* and *"estate"* were identical, "the State" was indistinguishable from the prince and his personal "patrimony."[118]

The proprietary theory of the state can be traced back to horticultural societies and, in a sense, even to hunting and gathering bands. In those simpler societies, no distinction was made between the private and public aspects of the lives and activities of leaders. When a surplus first began to be produced, at least part of it was turned over to the leader, who held it as trustee for the group. As long as the surplus was small and consisted of perishable commodities, there was little the leader could do with it except redistribute it, thereby winning respect for his generosity. Eventually, however, as we saw in Chapter 6, it grew large enough to permit him to create a staff of dependent retainers who could be used to enforce his wishes. At this point, the proprietary theory of the state was born. Later rulers merely applied it on an ever expanding scale, as productivity and the economic surplus steadily increased.

Recent research provides a good picture of the extremes to which rulers and governing classes have carried the proprietary principle. In late-nineteenth-century China, for example, the average income for families not in the governing class was approximately 20 to 25 taels per year. By contrast, the governing class averaged 450 taels per year, with some receiving as much as 200,000.[119] The emperor's income, of course, was considerably larger even than this. To cite another example, the English nobility at the end of the twelfth century and early in the thirteenth had an average income roughly 200 times that of ordinary field hands, and the king's equaled that of 24,000 field hands.[120] Putting together the evidence from many sources, it appears that the combined income of the ruler and the governing class in most advanced agrarian societies equaled *not less than half of the total national income,* even though they numbered 2 percent or less of the population.[121]

Despite their many similarities, the polities of advanced agrarian societies varied in a number of ways, the most important being the *degree of political centralization.* In some societies the central government was very strong; in others its powers were severely limited. In the main, these differences reflected the current state of the perennial struggle between the ruler and the other members of the governing class. The king or emperor naturally wanted the greatest possible control over his subordinates, and the subordinates just as naturally wanted to minimize his control. Since land (including the peasants who worked it) and political office were the most valuable resources in agrarian systems of stratification, most of the struggles between rulers and the governing class were over them. In a few instances, very powerful rulers gained such great power that both land and political offices were held solely at their pleasure and were subject to instant confiscation if an individual's services were judged unsatisfactory.[122] A Dutch traveler of the early seventeenth century left a vivid picture of the situation in the Mogul empire in India:

> Immediately on the death of a lord who has enjoyed the King's [favor], be he great or small, without any exception—sometimes even before the breath is out of the body—the King's officers are ready on the spot and make an inventory of the entire estate, recording everything down to the value of a single piece, even to the dresses and jewels of the ladies, provided they have not concealed them. The King takes back the whole estate absolutely for himself, except in a case where the deceased has done good service in his lifetime, when the women and children are given enough to live on, but no more.[123]

In Turkey, specially trained slaves became high-ranking officials over whom the sultan held life-and-death power.[124]

At the other extreme, during much of the medieval period in Europe, the governing classes were very independent. Though their lands were typically royal grants given in exchange for pledges of service, their monarchs usually lacked the power to enforce these pledges.[125] Although examples of both extremes can be found, the usual pattern was something in between, and in most cases the powers of the ruler and the governing class were fairly evenly balanced.

Religion: The Emergence of Universal Faiths

During the era in which advanced agrarian societies were dominant, there were a number of important developments in the religious sphere. The most important by far was the emergence and spread of three new religions, Buddhism, Christianity, and

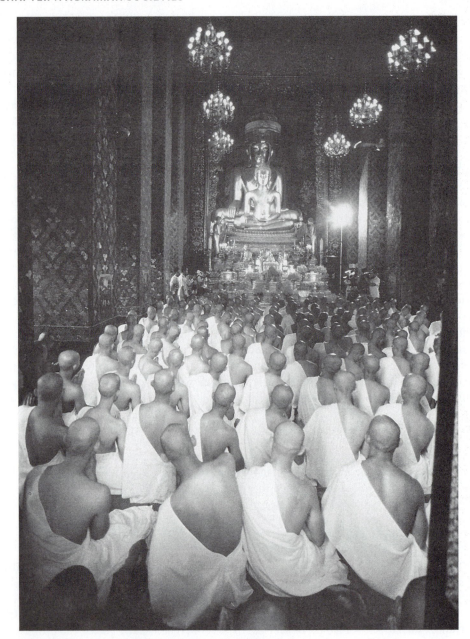

Buddhist Monks at Wat Bevornivet Temple in Thailand.

Islam. Each proclaimed a *universal faith,* and each succeeded in creating a community of believers that transcended societal boundaries. In contrast, in older religions, people's beliefs and loyalties were thought of as local affairs. Where one lived determined the god or gods one worshiped, for the prevailing view was that there were many gods and that, like kings, each had his or her own people and territory.

The ancient Israelites were some of the first to reject this view and move toward a more universalistic outlook. Centuries before the birth of Christ, the prophets proclaimed that there was only one God and that He ruled over the entire world. For a time, Judaism was a missionary religion and won converts in many parts of the Roman world.[126] This ended, however, when early Christian missionaries won most of these Gentile converts to the new faith. From then on, implementation of the universalistic vision became the mission of Christians and Muslims, who eventually converted, at least nominally, most of the population of Europe, North Africa, and the Middle East, and some of the people of India, Central Asia, China, and Southeast Asia.

Buddhism, the other major universal faith, began in India as an offshoot of Hinduism and spread through most of Southeast Asia, China, Korea, and Japan, though it later died out in the land of its origin. Older ethnic faiths, such as Hinduism, Confucianism, and Shintoism, still survived in much of Asia, but even they eventually incorporated some elements of universalism in their thought.

The emergence and spread of universal faiths reflected the broader social and intellectual horizons that resulted from advances in transportation technology and the spreading web of trade relations. Empire building, by bringing diverse populations under a single government, also helped to weaken parochial or "tribal" views. As people's knowledge of other societies increased, and with it their awareness of the essential unity of all humanity, the basic postulate of the older ethnic faiths (i.e., the belief in tribal deities) was gradually undermined.

Another important development was the growing separation of religious and political institutions.[127] Compared with the situation in advanced horticultural and simple agrarian societies, the governments of advanced agrarian societies were much more secular. Kings and emperors were, it is true, still said to rule "by the grace of God"; the divine right of kings was still generally accepted; and occasionally a ruler even claimed to be a god. But few rulers functioned as high priests, and theocracies (i.e., states in which a priesthood rules in the name of a god) were almost unknown. This separation of church and state was part of the more general trend toward institutional specialization that has been so basic in the evolutionary process since the start of the horticultural era.

Despite the growing separation of politics and religion, leaders in the two spheres continued to work closely together. This was especially evident in struggles between the governing class and the common people. When rebellious voices challenged the right of the governing class to control the economic surplus, the clergy usually defended the elite, asserting that their power had been given them by God and any challenge to it was a challenge to His authority.[128] By legitimizing the actions of the governing class in this way, the clergy reduced the need for costly coercive measures against the lower classes.

In appreciation for this, and also because of their own religious beliefs, agrarian rulers were often extremely generous with religious groups, giving them large grants of land and special tax exemptions. In effect, a symbiotic relationship was established, with a religious organization legitimizing the actions of the governing class in return for generous financial support. Modern research indicates that religious groups frequently owned as much as a quarter or a third of a nation's land.[129]

Despite such profitable alliances, most religions of the agrarian era fostered some concern for distributive justice. This is especially evident in Judaism and

Christianity.[130] One historian captured the contradictory nature of medieval Christianity in this discerning characterization: "Democratic, yet aristocratic; charitable, yet exploitative; generous, yet mercenary; humanitarian, yet cruel; indulgent, yet severely repressive of some things; progressive, yet reactionary; radical, yet conservative—all these are qualities of the Church in the Middle Ages."[131]

Magic and Fatalism

Two other aspects of the beliefs of agrarian societies deserve comment: (1) the widespread belief in magic and (2) the equally widespread attitude of fatalism.[132] Logically, these are contradictory. If magic really works, people do not need to be fatalistic, and if they are true fatalists, they should have no confidence in magic. But people are not always logical: they often hope for things they know are impossible. Considering the tremendous pressures operating on the common people in agrarian societies, and their limited sources of information, it is hardly surprising that many of them held these mutually contradictory views.

Fatalism and belief in magic both contributed to the slowdown in the rate of technological advance in agrarian societies. Magic encouraged people to depend on supernatural forces for the answers to their problems. Fatalism convinced them that control was out of their hands. Neither attitude motivated people to try to improve conditions themselves by building better tools or devising better techniques for satisfying their needs.

Kinship: Changing Significance in Society

For individuals, kinship ties remained of great importance throughout the agrarian era. For societies, however, they ceased to be the chief integrating force. In most horticultural societies, the largest and most powerful clan in a society, aided perhaps by dependent retainers, could still provide enough people to staff important political offices. But in advanced agrarian societies, this was no longer possible. Civil and military offices were so numerous that not even the largest of extended families could fill them all.

The fact that kinship ties were no longer the chief integrating force in societies did not mean, however, that they were no longer politically important. The royal office itself was inherited in most societies, as were numerous other political offices. Many of these, civil and military offices alike, were a family's patrimony, handed down like any other family possession from father to son (or, sometimes, daughter). Offices that were not actually owned might still be closed to anyone who was not a member of the nobility or who did not qualify as coming from one of the "right families."

Even in the allocation of offices to which such restrictions did not apply, families continued to play an important role. Family funds might be used to purchase an office, for example. And those who had it in their power to assign an office were naturally influenced by their own family's interests. Although nepotism still occurs in modern industrial societies, it is usually a violation of the law and lacks public approval. In advanced agrarian societies, however, it was an accepted part of life, and there was little criticism, and still less punishment, of those who practiced it.

During the agrarian era, the family remained very important in the economic sphere as well. In fact, it was usually *the basic unit of economic organization*. Businesses

Women's Secret Language

For years, many of the women of Hunan province in China communicated with one another by means of a secret language known as Nushu, which means "female writing." Nushu had a vocabulary of more than 20,000 words and was written with a script that had at least 1,800 characters, each representing a spoken symbol (not a concept, as in most of Chinese calligraphy). In an earlier time, men had also used this script but abandoned it after they became educated in Mandarin.

Girls learned the language from older women, who called themselves "sworn sisters." Often the teacher would sing as she wrote the symbols and the student used the songs as a mnenomic device to remember the lesson. Men, who could understand spoken Nushu, derided the written language as "mosquito scrawls" and believed that "anything to do with women was inferior, insignificant."

Zhao Liming, a Nushu scholar in Beijing, says, "What started as a simple way for women to express themselves became a chronicle of their private anguish."

Many of the surviving writings view marriage as a tragic event and little booklets conveying anxieties about marriage were common wedding gifts in the region.

Source: Douglas Martin, "Yang Huanyi, the Last User of a Secret Women's Code," *New York Times*, Oct. 7, 2004.

were almost always family enterprises; the corporate form of enterprise, owned jointly by unrelated persons, was virtually unheard of, even in the largest cities. And in rural areas the peasant family was the basic work unit.

The family's economic significance is evident in many ways. For instance, because of its economic implications, marriage was considered much too important to be decided by young people; even among the peasantry, marriages were usually arranged by parents, often with the aid of marriage brokers.[133] Sometimes the young couple did not even meet until the ceremony itself. In selecting spouses for their children, parents were primarily concerned with the economic and status implications of the match and only secondarily with other matters. Marriage arrangements often involved an outright economic transaction. The husband might make a payment for the bride, or her parents would provide her with a dowry.[134]

As one would suppose, marriages contracted in this way did not necessarily produce sexual or psychological compatibility between the spouses, but this was not seen as the primary purpose of marriage.

The Role of Women in Agrarian Societies

Viewed from the perspective of a modern industrial society, one of the more striking features of agrarian societies is the subservient role of women. Opportunities outside the family were minimal. Some found employment as servants in the households of the wealthy and powerful; some entered convents or religious orders, with a tiny number becoming priestesses in a few societies (e.g., the Vestal Virgins in Rome). Some became entertainers (actresses, geishas), a fortunate few became concubines or mistresses of wealthy and powerful men, while many more were forced into prostitution. Most, however, married and lived their lives largely within the confines of the family circle. The old German saying, "Kaiser, Kirche, Kinder, Kueche," (i.e., "patriotism, religion, children, and kitchen") nicely summarized what was regarded as the proper sphere of a woman's concerns in most agrarian societies.

Within families, male dominance was the rule and unquestioning obedience to the wishes of father or husband was generally held to be the prime virtue in a woman.[135] Husbands were "generally regarded as quasi-guardians" of their wives; in English Common Law, a woman's husband "acquired extensive rights to the administration and ownership of her property, including full ownership (with no obligation even to give an accounting) of any moneys she received," while in India, under Hindu law, the only property of which a woman was absolute owner consisted mainly of wedding gifts and gifts from relatives.[136]

The subordination of women manifested itself in many other ways as well. For example, under Islamic law, or sharia law, females inherited only half of what a male of the same degree of consanguinity inherited (e.g., daughters inherited only half of what their brothers inherited). Also under Islamic law, a husband could divorce his wife for any reason at all simply by repudiating her three times, and such action was not subject to any kind of review or challenge. In contrast, a wife could divorce her husband only on the grounds of desertion, cruelty, or failure to provide support.[137]

Countless other examples of the inferior status of women in agrarian societies could be cited, but one is too extreme to be ignored. In traditional Hindu society (where cremation of the dead was the usual practice), women when widowed were strongly encouraged or, in some cases, physically forced to throw themselves on their husband's funeral pyre. This practice, known as *suttee,* is based on the ancient Sanskrit word, "sati," meaning a virtuous woman or faithful wife.

Leisure and the Arts

Although the life of the peasant was hard, even harsh, there were occasional opportunities for leisure and recreation.[138] Weddings and religious festivals, for example, were important occasions for people to get together for a good time. Singing and dancing were the chief forms of entertainment at such festivities, and, in most societies, alcoholic beverages added to the merriment. People also amused themselves with games and contests, courtship and lovemaking, gossiping and storytelling, and a host of other activities.

Class distinctions were as evident in leisure activity as in any other, with falconry, jousting, and chess among the activities favored by the governing class. But some forms of entertainment, such as archery and dice, had a universal appeal. Gambling in particular was popular with every class.

The rise of professional entertainers was part of the general trend toward occupational specialization. Actors, minstrels, jesters, clowns, acrobats, jugglers, and geishas are some of the more familiar. In general, the status of such people was extremely low, probably because of their economic insecurity and their excessive dependence on the favor of others. Yet entertainers who had a powerful patron often found their work quite lucrative.

Recreation was frequently raucous and crude. It could also be brutal and violent, and in this the Romans were probably unsurpassed. In their so-called games, first in the Circus Maximus, later in the Colosseum, tens of thousands came to watch wild animals devour helpless victims and armed gladiators maim and kill one another. When the Colosseum was first opened in 80 A.D., the emperor Titus promised the people of Rome 100 consecutive days of such games, with fights to the death between

Recreation Was Frequently Brutal and Violent in Agrarian Societies, and the Romans Were Probably Unsurpassed. Artist's Depiction of One of Their So-Called Games: Gladiators Battling Wildcats.

more than 10,000 prisoners and 5,000 wild animals (including lions, tigers, and elephants), and a naval battle between 3,000 men in an arena especially flooded for the occasion.[139]

In agrarian Europe, cockfights and dogfights were very popular, and public hangings often drew large and exuberant crowds. Wedding parties and other festivities frequently ended in drunken brawls. In fact, violence typically followed drinking. From what we know of life in agrarian societies, it would appear that alcohol simply removed a fragile overlay of inhibitions, revealing people's frustrations and bitterness.

But if the agrarian world at play was often unattractive, its artistic accomplishments were quite the opposite. In their sculpture, their painting, and their architecture, these societies left monuments of lasting beauty. Thousands of cathedrals, churches, mosques, pagodas, temples, and palaces, and the treasures within them, testify to an impressive development of the arts during that era. Achievements in literature were probably no less impressive, though language barriers make it difficult for us to appreciate them as fully.*** Developments in music during most of the agrarian era seem to

---

***Robert Frost once said that "poetry is what gets lost in translation," and anyone who has ever seriously tried to translate a poem understands the complexity of the language problem.

have been less spectacular than in the other arts. Toward the end of the era, however, the invention of new instruments and the genius of composers like Bach, Handel, Mozart, and Beethoven combined to produce an outburst of magnificent music that has transcended societal boundaries in unprecedented fashion.

Most artists were subsidized by the governing class or by the religious elite, drawing on the economic surplus extracted from the peasant masses. Thus, the remarkable artistic achievements of agrarian societies were a product of their harshly exploitative social system. Yet, if the peasants had been allowed to keep the surplus, the result would simply have been more children and thus more poor people. Again, as with horticultural societies, this link between an exploitative class system and impressive cultural achievements reminds us of the difficulty we face in passing ethical judgments on complex sociocultural systems.

Stratification: Increasing Complexity

The basic cleavages in advanced agrarian societies were much the same as they had been in simple agrarian societies and, as a consequence, so were the basic patterns of inequality. The principal division in society was still the one between the governing class and the great mass of peasants and others over whom it exercised control both politically and economically. But the system of stratification had altered in one respect from that of simpler societal types: it had become more complex.

This growing complexity can be seen in two areas. First, in advanced agrarian societies there were more people in occupations whose status fell somewhere between the extremes. These people were either directly employed by the governing class (e.g., household servants, stewards, men-at-arms) or served them indirectly (e.g., merchants, artisans).

Second, advanced agrarian societies experienced a growing overlap in the rankings of different classes of people, especially in terms of wealth and property. Some merchants, for example, now had more wealth than some members of the governing class, and a tiny minority of peasants, by luck and hard work, actually amassed greater wealth than some impoverished members of the nobility. Although members of the governing class still had greater wealth, *on average,* than merchants or any other group, this was no longer true of every member of the class. Similarly, although merchants were, *on average,* wealthier than peasants, there were exceptions.

Figure 7.5 depicts the stratification system of advanced agrarian societies. The ruler was invariably the most powerful, prestigious, and wealthy individual in society: he was, in fact, literally in a class by himself. For example, the English kings Richard I and John, who ruled in the last decade of the twelfth century and the first decade of the thirteenth, had incomes thirty times that of the wealthiest nobleman of the day.[140] By the reign of Richard II, at the end of the fourteenth century, the king's income had risen to forty times that of the wealthiest member of the governing class. In late-fifteenth- and early-sixteenth-century Spain, the king was reputed to enjoy one-third of all the revenues of the land (meaning, apparently, one-third of the economic surplus). Similar patterns are reported in virtually every advanced agrarian society.

At the opposite extreme in the system of stratification was a wretched class of individuals for whose labor the society had no need. These were mostly peasant sons and daughters who were unable to inherit land or to marry someone who did and thus were forced out on their own in a society that suffered a chronic labor surplus. As we have

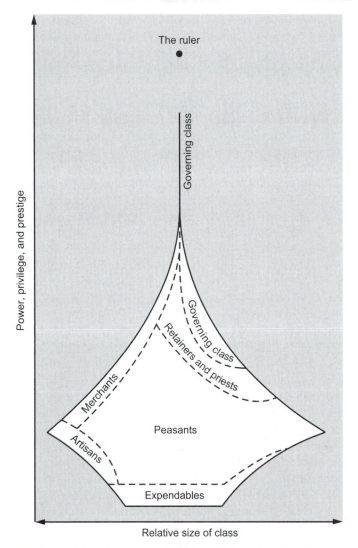

Figure 7.5. Model of the Class Structure of Advanced Agrarian Societies.

seen, these individuals could usually eke out a living while they were young and healthy, but most of them soon drifted into the ranks of the expendables (see Figure 7.5) and died at an early age.[141]

On the whole, the class divisions within advanced agrarian societies were greater than those in simple agrarian societies. And, as we noted earlier, pressures of commercialization were conducive to interclass violence. Though most were local incidents involving small numbers of people, some spread to become large-scale insurrections. Furthermore, despite the fact that peasants generally revolted in order to *restore* traditional class relationships or to *defend* traditional religious beliefs from perceived corruption, their rebellions would later play a role in advancing the interests of the commercial classes.[142] Artisans and merchants also revolted on a number of occasions,[143] and these groups, unlike the peasants, sometimes emerged victorious. In Europe, the merchants were so successful in their challenges to the governing class that eventually *they* became the governing class in many cities and towns. From an evolutionary perspective, this proved to be a very important development indeed, as we will see.

VARIATIONS ON AGRARIAN THEMES

In surveying societies at the same level of development, it is natural to emphasize those characteristics which are found in all or most of them, and to slight the differences. This may give an impression of greater uniformity than really exists. Obviously there were variations in every area of life in advanced agrarian societies, and we have noted many of them, or at least hinted at them in qualifying phrases, saying that a particular pattern was found in "most" or "many" of these societies.

To begin with, advanced agrarian societies varied technologically. The first to emerge resembled their simple agrarian predecessors more than they resembled the advanced agrarian societies of northwest Europe on the eve of the Industrial Revolution. Furthermore, the size of advanced agrarian societies ranged all the way from tiny principalities and city-states to giant empires. Most were monarchies, but a few were republics. Some were governed by enormously powerful autocratic rulers; in others, power was diffused more widely among members of the governing class. Similar variations occurred in almost every area of life.

Clearly, then, there has been variation among societies at the advanced agrarian level—indeed, at every level of societal development. There is, however, one important difference. In the less advanced societal types (i.e., hunting and gathering, fishing, and simple horticultural), intratype variation is due primarily to differences in the *biophysical environment*. We see this clearly when we compare the Eskimo with the Australian aborigines, for example, or the !Kung San of the Kalahari Desert with the Pygmies of the rain forest. In advanced agrarian societies, on the other hand, with few exceptions (e.g., see "Women's Power in a Man's World," or "frontier societies," discussed below) differences in the biophysical environment have not been as important a cause of intratype variation. This is exactly what ecological-evolutionary theory would lead us to expect, since the further a society advances on the evolutionary scale, the greater is its ability to overcome the limitations imposed by the biotic and physical world and the more likely it is, because of geographical expansion, to include within its borders a variety of environments, thus making its overall environment less distinctive.

In studying advanced agrarian societies, historians have often focused attention on religion as the chief source of the differences among them. Thus, they have contrasted Christian societies with Islamic societies, for example, or Buddhist societies with Hindu societies.

There is, of course, no doubt that each of these religions was responsible for social and cultural variations among advanced agrarian societies. Christianity and Islam, like Judaism, had a special day of worship and rest each week, while the Eastern religions did not. Most of the religions encouraged monasticism, but Protestantism and Islam did not. Islam sanctioned the practice of polygyny, which Christianity forbade; Confucianism encouraged ancestor worship; Buddhism encouraged families to send their sons to live in monasteries for a year or two before assuming adult responsibilities; and Hinduism had a hereditary priestly caste. Theologically, there were tremendous

Women's Power in a Man's World

Rae Lesser Blumberg has identified an extremely interesting subset of societies where women have substantially more economic power and higher status than is typical of agrarian societies. Found in southeast Asia, these are agrarian societies that rely on "wet" (irrigated rice) rather than "rain-fed" cultivation *and* practice bilateral or matri-oriented kinship. (Most other irrigated rice societies are in east or south Asia and are marked by a strongly patri-oriented kinship and property system and high levels of patriarchy.) Men usually predominate in land preparation and plowing in all irrigated rice societies. But it is such a labor-intensive crop that women usually are heavily involved in tasks that do not require as much upper-body strength, such as transplanting and harvesting the rice. In fact, all family members can be economically productive. In southeast Asia, however, the fact that the kinship system allows daughters as well as sons to inherit land, and most women earn and manage income (for example, by trading in the market), results in women gaining much more *control* over what they produce, and this translates into greater *economic power*.

As a result, although women are not politically dominant in these southeast Asian irrigated rice societies—matriarchal societies appear to be a myth—their greater role in production *and* their economic power

increase their clout and self-confidence. They have a greater voice in their households and have greater control of their "life options," most importantly with regard to marriage and childbearing; and a more equal position overall.

The existence of these unusual societies has gone largely unnoticed because of the facts that (1) almost all of today's advanced industrial societies emerged from the more male-dominated "rain-fed" agricultural variants (Japan is the big exception; although patriarchal, its background involved irrigated rice cultivation), and (2) the much more numerous patriarchal agrarian societies swamp them statistically (just two of them, China and India, have over 40 percent of world population). But the population in these southeast Asian countries is about the same as the European Union.

Sources: Rae Lesser Blumberg, "Mothers of Invention? The Myth-Breaking History and Planetary Promise of Women's Key Roles in Subsistence Technology," in Yair Amichai-Hamburger (ed.), *Technology and Well-Being* (Cambridge: Cambridge University Press, 2009), pp. 227–240; and "Extending Lenski's Schema to Hold up Both Halves of the Sky—A Theory-Guided Way of Conceptualizing Agrarian Societies that Illuminates a Puzzle about Gender Stratification," *Sociological Theory*, 22 (June 2004), pp. 278–291.

differences among the various religions, and members of advanced agrarian societies often fought and died in order to extend or defend their faith.

Without denying the importance of these and other religious influences, we cannot fail to note that no faith was able to break the "agrarian mold" that shaped the basic patterns of life in these societies.[†††] For regardless of its dominant religion, every advanced agrarian society was much like the rest with respect to its fundamental characteristics. Class structure, social inequality, the division of labor, the distinctive role of urban populations in the larger society, the cleavage between urban and rural subcultures, the disdain of the governing class for both work and workers, the widespread belief in magic and fatalism, the use of the economic surplus for the benefit of the governing class and for the construction of monumental edifices, high birth and death rates—all these and more were present in all advanced agrarian societies.

[†††]For a discussion of religion's role in the rise of industrial societies, see Chapter 9.

Rae Lesser Blumberg Has Identified an Extremely Interesting Subset of Societies Where Women Have Substantially More Economic Power and Higher Status than Is Typical of Agrarian Societies. Burmese Women Plant Rice at the Beginning of the Monsoon Season.

The greatest variations among advanced agrarian societies stemmed not from ideological differences but from differences in their *social environments*. These differences were of two kinds. One involved proximity to trade routes and the other the influence of frontier territories.

From the standpoint of trade, the most advantageous location for a society was at the point where several important trade routes intersected.[144] Having such a location ensured continuing contact with a large number of other societies and increased opportunities for acquiring useful information through diffusion. It also provided a valuable source of income and fostered economic growth and development. Societies that were not so well situated were handicapped and tended to be less developed, unless some compensating factor offset this handicap. Because of the importance of trade routes, societies in the Middle East, where routes from Europe, Asia, and Africa converged, remained at the forefront of social and cultural development for most of the agrarian era. Toward the end, however, as trade with the New World became important, the advantage shifted to western European societies.

A very different kind of environmental influence made itself felt when agrarian populations expanded into territories that previously were uninhabited or were inhabited by smaller, less advanced societies. Under the radically altered conditions that were encountered, traditional patterns of life often broke down and a new and different kind of society—*a frontier society*—emerged briefly.

The first known instance of this was the establishment of the new nation of Israel in the largely uninhabited hill country in the eastern part of Palestine in the thirteenth century B.C.[145] More recently, the process was repeated in the Norwegian-Irish settlement of Iceland; in the settlement of North America by migrants from Britain, France, and other parts of northwestern Europe; in the British settlement of Australia and New Zealand; in the Boer settlement of South Africa; and in the Cossack settlement of the Russian steppes.[146] In each instance the frontier region escaped for a time from the control of traditional authorities and land became available for settlement by lower status members of agrarian societies who were willing to assume the risks and hardships of frontier life.

Frontier societies are of special interest from the standpoint of ecological-evolutionary theory because they show the extent to which the agrarian way of life was shaped by an oversupply of labor and an undersupply of land. When these conditions were eliminated even temporarily, as happened in frontier regions, striking deviations from the usual patterns of agrarian life developed.

To begin with, the settlers tended to be the poor, the dispossessed, the noninheriting sons and daughters, troublemakers, misfits, and even criminals deported by the parent society. Frontier regions held little attraction for the rich and powerful, who preferred to remain close to the traditional centers of power and influence. Thus, in frontier regions established authority was usually weak or absent, and because societal life was not under the control of the governing class, traditional agrarian patterns tended to break down and new patterns emerged.[147]

One of the most significant changes that occurred was the breakdown of the traditional class system. Except when elites created a plantation system and the native population was enslaved or enserfed (as in much of Latin America) or when slaves were imported (as in the Caribbean and the southern United States), a highly egalitarian system of family farms and ranches was likely to develop.[148] This is what happened in Canada, the United States (except in the South), Australia, New Zealand, and South Africa. In these areas there was a chronic shortage of labor; workers were more highly valued than in the older, settled areas, where there was usually a surplus of labor. On the frontier, there were neither enough farmers to cultivate the newly opened land nor enough fighters to defend it. It is not surprising, then, that frontier life generated a striking independence of spirit and a stubborn resistance to authority. Having risked their lives to establish themselves in a new land, frontier settlers were not prepared to hand over their surplus to anyone. Thus, frontier conditions usually broke down the sharp inequalities and exploitative patterns that characterized traditional agrarian societies.

This condition was usually temporary, however. As resistance from the native population came to an end and the population of settlers grew in number and density, as roads were built and governmental authority was established, there was a waning of the spirit of independence and individualism and the traditional system began to reassert itself. To be sure, this did not happen overnight. On the contrary, it usually took a century or more. But in the end, the typical agrarian pattern usually prevailed.

Only one thing ever prevented this from happening—the onset of industrialization. In a number of instances during the last century and a half, the Industrial Revolution generated a new demand for labor before the frontier was fully absorbed into the old system. This happened in the United States, Canada, Australia, and New Zealand. These societies were thus spared the agony of slowly sliding back into the classic agrarian pattern in which a massive, impoverished peasantry is dominated and exploited by a small, hereditary aristocracy.

In the United States, this process had actually gotten well under way in much of the South with its system of slavery. But the Confederacy's defeat in the Civil War and the South's eventual industrialization halted the restoration of the old agrarian system. In other parts of the country, the process had barely begun before the forces of industrialization intervened.

Looking back, it seems clear that the frontier experience was excellent preparation for the Industrial Revolution. Above all, it established a tradition of individual initiative, innovation, and receptivity to change that was lacking in other agrarian societies. Also, by creating a more egalitarian class system, the frontier prepared the way for the more open and fluid class systems of modern industrial societies. These developments help explain the relative ease with which the overseas English-speaking democracies (e.g., the United States, Australia, and Canada) made the transition to the industrial era, and why they have so long been in the forefront with respect to productivity, standard of living, and political stability. It is interesting to speculate on what the situation in these societies might be today if they had been settled a thousand years earlier and a more typical agrarian social system had had time to take root.

AGRARIAN SOCIETIES IN THEORETICAL PERSPECTIVE

The initial effect of the shift from horticulture to agriculture, as we saw at the beginning of this chapter, was an increase in food production. Societies that adopted the plow were able to produce substantially more food in a given territory than those that relied on the hoe and digging stick.

This increase in productivity could be used, as Figure 7.6 indicates, either to expand the economic surplus of the society or to expand its population. Actually, the historical record shows that in most agrarian societies *both* of these things happened to some degree. The expansion of the economic surplus was more significant than population growth, however, since it was a necessary precondition for so many social and cultural changes. Figure 7.6 makes no attempt to portray all of them or all of their interrelationships, since that would require an impossibly complex diagram. Instead, the figure focuses only on the most critical developments.

The single most important consequence of the greater economic surplus was *further growth of the state and of the power of the governing class* that controlled it. This contributed, directly or indirectly, to most of the other important social and cultural changes of the agrarian era. It lay behind the shift from militias to professional armies; the increase in inequality, and the development of ideologies justifying inequality and the power of elites; the rise of the merchant class and the increase in trade and commerce; the growth of urban populations; the increase in the division of labor; and the slowing of the rate of innovation.

Many of the changes in agrarian societies were a continuation of trends that began in horticultural societies. But the shift to agriculture magnified those trends dramatically. To cite a single example, the largest society ever constructed on a horticultural foundation appears to have been the Aztec Empire in the years immediately preceding the Spanish conquest of Mexico. At the peak of its power it is estimated to have controlled a population of fifteen million people.[149] In contrast, mid-nineteenth-century China, before it began to industrialize, had a population of approximately 400 million, and the Roman and Russian Empires each had at least seventy million.[150]

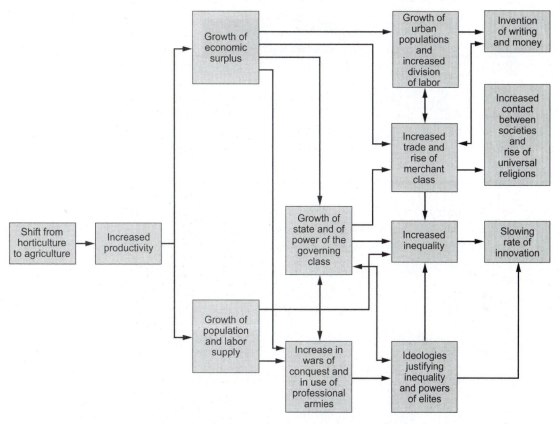

Figure 7.6. Model of the Effects of the Shift from Horticulture to Agriculture.

As great as they are, these differences in population size are probably no greater in degree than differences in many other basic features of these two types of societies. Their numbers, in other words, are but a reflection of the vastly different potentials inherent in the subsistence technologies on which horticultural societies and agrarian societies were built.

CHAPTER 8

Some Evolutionary Bypaths and a Brief Review

Outline
Environmentally Specialized Societal Types
A Brief Review: Sociocultural Evolution to the Eve of the Industrial
   Revolution

ENVIRONMENTALLY SPECIALIZED SOCIETAL TYPES

Up to this point in our survey of human societies, we have concentrated on those types which have been in the mainstream of evolutionary history, the ones that developed their technologies around the resources of fields and forests. The types of societies to which we now turn have adapted to *less common environments*—two to aquatic environments, and one to grasslands and arid environments. Though these specialized kinds of societies have contributed to sociocultural evolution in many important ways, their contributions have been more limited than those of the mainstream societies. This is because of the specialized nature of the problems with which they have dealt in their subsistence activities. For these reasons, we will not examine them in the same detail as the others.

Fishing Societies

To call any group a "fishing" society is something of a misnomer, for no society ever depended exclusively on fishing for its food supply.[1] Except in the Arctic, nearly all fishing peoples obtain fruits and vegetables by foraging or cultivation. Many of them also supplement their diet by hunting and occasionally by raising livestock. To call a society a fishing society, then, merely indicates that fishing is its most important subsistence activity.

In recent centuries fishing societies have been found in many parts of the world, but the majority have been in the northwestern part of North America—Oregon, Washington, British Columbia, and before Alaska. There have also been some in northeastern Asia, among the islands of the Pacific (though most of the Pacific peoples have been simple horticulturalists), in scattered parts of Africa and South America, and elsewhere.

Historically, fishing societies are probably the second-oldest type, emerging a few thousand years before the first horticultural societies. The practice of fishing is, of

African Fishing Village, Benin.

course, even older and more widespread and has provided a supplementary source of subsistence in many societies for thousands of years.

In some ways fishing societies might be regarded as hunting and gathering societies that have adapted to aquatic rather than terrestrial environments. One might argue that the chief difference is simply that fish rather than land animals are the object of the hunt and that the technology of the group is modified accordingly. But there is a reason why fishing societies should be considered a separate societal type: *a fishing economy has the potential for supporting a larger, more sedentary population than a hunting and gathering economy.*

This is because fishing peoples are much less likely to deplete the food resources of their environment than are hunters and gatherers. Fish have much higher reproductive rates than most land animals. In addition, fishing peoples usually work only a small part of their food-producing territory. Even if they catch all the fish in their immediate area, the supply is quickly replenished by the great surplus spawned in adjacent areas. This could not happen with land animals, at least not after hunting and gathering bands occupied most of the habitable territory.

Thus, although fishing societies are only a bit more advanced technologically than hunting and gathering societies, we would expect them to be somewhat larger, more sedentary, and more complex.[2] This is, in fact, precisely what we find. With respect to size, they are more than twice as large. Murdock's data set shows that the average size of modern fishing communities is approximately 90, the average size of hunting and gathering groups only forty (see Table 4.2).[3] With respect to settlement patterns, only 10 percent of the hunting and gathering societies live in permanent settlements, compared to 55 percent of the fishing societies.

The Shui-Jen, or Water People, of Southern China Are Descended from Fishing Peoples of an Earlier Time. They Still Depend on Fishing for Their Livelihood and Remain Largely Separate from the Mainland Population.

Social inequality, too, is both more common and more pronounced. A system of hereditary nobility is found in 28 percent of fishing societies but in only 2 percent of hunting and gathering societies, while slavery occurs in slightly over 50 percent of fishing societies but in only 11 percent of hunting and gathering societies.

Unlike hunting and gathering societies, fishing societies seldom evolved into a more advanced type.* There are several reasons for this. To begin with, territories suited to a predominantly fishing economy are strung out along thin coastal strips, so that it has been virtually impossible to create large, defensible political entities.[4] Instead, when neighboring horticultural societies became powerful enough, fishing societies have usually been conquered and absorbed by them. Even though fishing continued in the area, it became only a minor part of the economy of the larger society, and the leaders of the fishing groups were reduced to the status of minor officials, too weak to defend the local surplus. As a result, fishing communities in *agrarian* societies have often been socially and culturally less advanced (except in subsistence technology) than the fishing communities of more primitive *fishing* societies. Typically, their

---

*It is possible that some evolved directly into maritime societies, but there is no real evidence of this. Maritime societies seem, instead, usually to have evolved out of advanced horticultural or agrarian societies.

Livestock Is the Basic Resource in Herding Societies, and the Size of His Herd Is the Measure of a Man. Large Herds Signify Not Only Wealth But Also Power, for Only a Strong Man or the Head of a Strong Family Can Defend Such Vulnerable Property: Roundup Time in Mongolia.

situation was no better than that of peasant villages, and for the same reason—their surplus was confiscated by more powerful elements in the society.[5]

Herding Societies

Herding societies, like fishing societies, represent an adaptation to specialized environmental conditions. Other than that, the two have little in common. Their environments are radically different, and the technology of herding societies is usually more advanced.

Herding societies cover approximately the same range of technological development as horticultural and agrarian societies. Animals were first domesticated about the same time plants were first cultivated, and the two practices typically went hand in hand in the horticultural and agrarian societies of the Old World.[†] In some areas, however, crop cultivation was severely limited because of insufficient rainfall, too short a growing season (in northern latitudes), or mountainous terrain. This was true of much of central Asia, the Arabian Peninsula, and North Africa, and also parts of Europe and sub-Saharan Africa. Because it was possible to raise livestock in many of these areas, however, a new and different type of society emerged.[‡]

A pastoral economy usually necessitates a nomadic or seminomadic way of life.[6] In fact, "nomad" comes from an early Greek word meaning a "herder of cattle."[7] In the

---

[†]This was not true in most of the New World, where there were almost no large animals suitable for domestication by the time plants were domesticated.

[‡]Most of these societies have also had some secondary means of subsistence, usually horticulture or agriculture on a small scale.

sample of herding societies in Murdock's data set, nearly 90 percent are wholly or partially nomadic. In this respect they closely resemble hunters and gatherers.

Herders are also like hunters and gatherers in the size of their communities. On average, their communities are a bit smaller than fishing communities and much smaller than simple horticultural communities, as the following figures show:

Hunting and gathering communities	40
Herding communities	72
Fishing communities	90
Simple horticultural communities	138

The explanation for this is primarily environmental. Given the sparse resources of their territories, large and dense settlements are impossible.[8]

Despite the small size of their communities, herding societies are usually fairly large. Whereas the typical hunting and gathering or fishing society contains only a single community, and the typical simple horticultural society fewer than a dozen, the average herding society contains several dozen. Thus, the median population of herding societies far surpasses that of the other three types:

Hunting and gathering societies	40
Fishing societies	90
Simple horticultural societies	1,500
Herding societies	5,750

The greater size of herding societies reflects the combined influence of environment and technology. Open grasslands, where the majority of herders live, present few natural barriers to movement and, therefore, to political expansion. Furthermore, since about 2000 B.C., many herding peoples have ridden horses or camels, which made them a potent military force and greatly facilitated their political expansion.

The basic resource in these societies is livestock, and the size of the herd is the measure of a man. Large herds signify not only wealth but also power, for only a strong man or the head of a strong family can defend such vulnerable property against rivals and enemies. Thus, in most of these societies, and especially in the more advanced (i.e., those with horses or camels and herds of larger animals such as cattle), marked social inequality is the rule. Hereditary slavery, for example, is far more common in herding societies than in any other type.[9]

With respect to kinship, herding societies are noteworthy on at least two counts. First, they are more likely than any other type of society to require the payment of a bride price or bride service.[10] Second, they are the most likely to require newly married couples to live with the husband's kinsmen.[11]

These strong patriarchal tendencies have several sources. Above all, they reflect the often militant nature of pastoral life. Raiding and warfare are frequent activities, and as we have noted before, these activities stimulate the growth of political authority. In addition, the basic economic activity in these societies is men's work. In this respect they stand in sharp contrast to horticultural societies, where women often play the dominant role in subsistence activities.

One of the most important technological advances made by herding peoples was the utilization of horses, and later camels, for transportation. This practice originated about 1800 B.C., when certain herding groups in the Middle East began harnessing horses to chariots.[12] By creating a mobile shooting platform for an archer, this gave them an important military advantage over their less mobile agrarian neighbors and enabled them to win control of much of the Middle East—at least until the new technology was adopted by the more numerous agrarian peoples. Herders later learned to *ride* their horses, which led to a new wave of conquests, beginning about 900 B.C.[13]

During the next 2,500 years, a succession of herding groups attacked agrarian societies from China to Europe, frequently conquering them. The empires and dynasties they established include some of the largest and most famous in history—the great Mongol Empire, for example, founded by Genghis Khan early in the thirteenth century A.D. and expanded by his successors. At the peak of its power, the Mongol Empire stretched from eastern Europe to the shores of the Pacific and launched attacks in places as distant as Austria and Japan. Other famous empires and dynasties founded by herding peoples include the Mogul Empire, established in India by a branch of the Mongols; the Manchu dynasty in China; the Ottoman Empire in the Middle East; and the early Islamic states established by followers of the prophet Muhammad.

Despite their many military victories, herding peoples were never able to destroy the agrarian social order. In the end, it was always they, not agrarian peoples, who changed their mode of life. There were a number of reasons for this, but it was primarily because the economic surplus that could be produced by agricultural activities was so much greater than what could be produced by converting the land to herding activities. After a few early conquerors tried to turn fields into pastures, they realized they were, in effect, killing the goose that laid the golden eggs and abandoned their preferred way of life for economic reasons.[14] Thus, despite impressive military victories, the limits of the herding world were never extended.

Although animal husbandry was, and continues to be, an important secondary source of subsistence in the agrarian world, it was the primary source only in areas unsuited to plant cultivation. In recent centuries, even these areas have, in most cases, been brought under the control of agrarian or industrial societies, and herding societies, like other preindustrial types, are vanishing.

Maritime Societies

Maritime societies have been the rarest of all the major societal types. Never have there been more than a few at any one time. Yet, at one time, they played a very important role in the civilized world.

Technologically, maritime societies were much like agrarian societies. What set them apart was the way they used this technology to take advantage of the special opportunities afforded by their environmental situation. Located on large bodies of water in an era when it was cheaper to move goods by water than by land (see page 181), these peoples found trade and commerce far more profitable than either fishing or the cultivation of their limited land resources and gradually created societies in which overseas trade was the chief economic activity.

The first maritime society in history may have been that developed by the Minoans on the island of Crete, around 2000 B.C. We are told that the wealth and power of the Minoan rulers "depended more upon foreign trade and religious prerogative than upon the land rents and forced services."[15] The island location of Minoan society was important, not only because it afforded ready access to the sea, but also because it provided protection against more powerful agrarian societies. In fact, most maritime societies developed on islands or peninsulas that were difficult to attack by land (see photo below). Their only military advantage was in naval warfare.

During the next 1,500 years a number of other maritime societies were established in the Mediterranean world. These included the Mycenaeans, or pre-Hellenic Greeks, about 2000 B.C.; the Phoenicians, the Athenians, and the Carthaginians; and possibly some of the later Greek city-states. The spread of the maritime pattern in this period was largely, perhaps wholly, the result of diffusion and the migration of maritime peoples. Eventually all of these societies were conquered by agrarian societies and either destroyed or absorbed as subunits. This was not the end of overseas trade and commerce, of course, since these were important activities in most advanced agrarian societies. It was, however, a temporary end to societies in which this was the dominant form of economic activity.

Then, more than a thousand years later, there was a revival of maritime societies during the Middle Ages. Venice and Genoa are the best known, but there were others (e.g., Danzig and Lübeck in northern Europe). Later, the Netherlands became an important maritime society and during the seventeenth and eighteenth centuries apparently derived the major part of its income from overseas trade.[16] Britain moved far in this direction in the seventeenth, eighteenth, nineteenth, and early twentieth centuries but probably never quite reached the point where it depended more on overseas commerce than on, first, agriculture and, later, industry. Nevertheless,

Maritime Societies Usually Developed on Islands or Peninsulas That Were Difficult to Attach by Land: Aerial View of the Lebanese City of Sur (formerly Tyre), Once a Maritime Society. In Ancient Times, When Tyre Was in Important Phoenician City-State, It Was an Island. The Land-Bridge That Now Connects the City to the Mainland Was Formed When Alexander the Great Laid Siege to the City in 332 B.C. His Soldiers Built a Causeway from the Mainland That Transformed the Island into the Peninsula That Still Exists Today.

because of the great growth of overseas commerce, Britain acquired a number of the characteristics of maritime societies. Finally, in the twentieth century, Danzig for a time and, more recently, Singapore, emerged as maritime societies.

In many ways maritime societies resembled advanced agrarian societies, particularly their urban centers. But there were also important differences. To begin with, most maritime societies were much smaller, often containing only a single city and the area immediately around it. Only two maritime societies, Carthage and the Netherlands, ever developed empires worthy of the name and, significantly, both of these were *overseas* empires.[17] In each case the empire was created more as an adjunct to commercial activity than as a political venture.

This curious feature is linked with another, more basic peculiarity of maritime societies. In a largely agrarian world in which monarchy was the normal—almost universal—form of government, maritime societies were usually republics. There were some monarchies among them, but this pattern was most likely to occur early in a maritime society's history, suggesting a carryover from a premaritime past.[18]

The explanation for the republican tendency in maritime societies seems to be that commerce, rather than warfare and the exploitation of peasant masses, was the chief interest of the governing class. Being less concerned than the typical agrarian state with conquest and the control of large peasant populations, these nations had less need

A Venetian Merchant's Bedroom Reveals the Wealth That Commercial Activities Brought to Leading Citizens of Most Maritime Societies.

for a strong, centralized, hierarchical government. An oligarchy of wealthy merchants could do the job, since their primary responsibilities would be to regulate commercial competition and to provide naval forces to defend their access to foreign ports.

Another peculiarity of maritime societies was their unusual system of values and incentives. As we saw in the last chapter, the governing class in agrarian societies typically viewed work of any kind as degrading. Since this was the class that all others looked up to and emulated, its view of economic activity rubbed off on the rest. This was especially evident in the case of merchants, who, when they became wealthy, usually gave up their commercial activities. As we noted, this antiwork ethic undoubtedly contributed to the slowdown in the rate of technological innovation and progress.

In maritime societies, in contrast, merchants were the dominant class, and a very different view of economic activity prevailed. Though more research is needed on the subject, there is reason to believe that maritime societies made disproportionate technological and economic contributions to the emergence of modern industrial societies. It is also significant that the rate of technological advance in *agrarian* societies appears to have been correlated with the social and political strength of their merchant class.[19] In other words, *the greater the social status and political influence of its merchants, the higher the rate of technological and economic innovation in preindustrial societies tended to be.* This suggests one possible explanation of the striking differences in levels of development of societies in our own era.

A BRIEF REVIEW: SOCIOCULTURAL EVOLUTION TO THE EVE OF THE INDUSTRIAL REVOLUTION

Now that we have completed our survey of the various types of preindustrial societies, we need to pause and briefly review the ground we have covered. In particular, we should consider how well the evidence we have examined conforms to ecological-evolutionary theory.

As we saw in Chapter 3, the central thesis of this theory is that subsistence technology is the key to societal growth and development, both for individual societies and for the world system of societies. Technological advance expands the limits of what is possible for a society and thereby improves its chances in the process of intersocietal selection. As a consequence, technological advance has also been the basic determinant of the patterns of sociocultural evolution in the world system.

Figure 3.4 suggests that this evolutionary process has generated a number of fundamental trends in the world system. These trends provide us with an excellent test of the validity of ecological-evolutionary theory as it applies to the experience of human societies through the first 99.9 percent of human history.

What exactly *had* happened with respect to each of those trends by the time the agrarian era was coming to a close?

Growth of Human Population

In the opinion of the experts, there were between three and ten *million* people at the end of the hunting and gathering era (8000 B.C.). By the end of the agrarian era (A.D. 1800), there was nearly a *billion* (Figure 8.1 shows the acceleration of population growth at the end of this period).

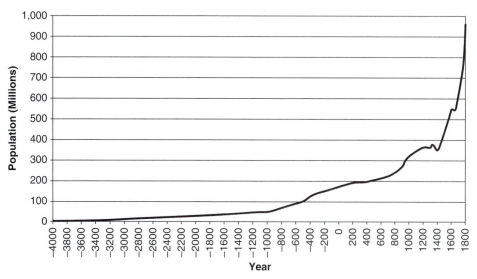

Figure 8.1. World Population 4000 B.C. to A.D. 1800.

Growth in Average Size of Societies and Communities

At the end of the hunting and gathering era, the average size of both societies and communities appears to have been somewhere between twenty-five and fifty. Although it is impossible to obtain reliable estimates of the average size of communities and societies for the entire world system at the end of the agrarian era, there is no doubt that both were substantially larger because by then there were so many horticultural, herding, maritime, and agrarian societies. We also know that, whereas the largest society prior to the horticultural era had no more than a few hundred members at most, by the end of the agrarian era there was one with 400 million, and a number with more than ten million.

Increased Permanence of Communities

Before the first fishing and horticultural societies appeared, nearly all human communities were nomadic. By the end of the agrarian era, only a small minority were nomadic.

Expansion of Societies into New Environments

Most of this trend occurred either before the end of the hunting and gathering era or during the industrial era. The horticultural and agrarian eras, however, did see greatly heightened activity in marine environments. By the end of the agrarian era, oceans, lakes, and rivers had become important both as sources of food and as trade routes.

Increasing Impact of Societies on the Biophysical Environment

Prior to the horticultural era, the most notable impact of human societies on the biophysical environment seems to have been their apparent extermination by human hunters of numerous species of large mammals. Societies of the horticultural and agrarian eras had a far more profound effect on the physical landscape, clearing vast forests, damming rivers, irrigating arid areas, and mining an increasing variety of minerals.

Invention of New Symbol Systems

During the horticultural era, the first primitive record-keeping systems were invented. These were followed, during the agrarian era, by prealphabetic and eventually alphabetic systems of writing, numeral systems, measurement systems, systems of musical notation, and monetary systems.

Increasing Store of Technological Information

During the horticultural and agrarian eras, the store of technological information increased enormously, a fact amply attested to by the great growth of human population. Striking technological advances occurred in plant cultivation, animal domestication, metallurgy, construction, transportation, and communication. By the end of the agrarian era, societies knew how to produce enormous quantities of foods, fibers, and other things; move people and products over great distances; build monumental edifices of great durability; and inflict tremendous damage on one another, to cite but four of the more significant consequences of the expanded store of technological information.

Increasing Store of Other Kinds of Information

During the horticultural and agrarian eras, the store of nontechnological information increased dramatically. By the close of the agrarian era, many societies had amassed great amounts of political, economic, philosophical, ideological, historical, aesthetic, scientific, and other kinds of information. Much of this new information emerged as a by-product of the growing size and complexity of societies, a process that created new problems requiring new solutions and new information and that led to the emergence of new norms, beliefs, and values.

Growth in the Quantity, Diversity, and Complexity of Material Products

No brief summary can do justice to this trend, though there are many comparisons that provide dramatic illustrations. Compare, for example, the greatest structures created by advanced agrarian societies—cathedrals, temples, palaces—with the greatest created by the members of hunting and gathering societies—shelters made from rocks and branches as temporary protection for one or more families. More important, by the end of the agrarian era, human societies were providing the material necessities required to sustain *100 times* more people than they had provided for at the end of the hunting and gathering era.

Increasing Complexity of Social Organization

In hunting and gathering societies, full-time occupational specialization was extremely rare, possibly nonexistent. The usual pattern was a division of labor by age and sex, with part-time specialization by a headman and/or a shaman. In agrarian and maritime societies, in contrast, occupational specialties numbered in the hundreds, and there was a complex division of labor that often involved specialization by communities and even regions. In hunting and gathering societies, the only organized groups were families; whereas in agrarian societies, there were separate communities, often organized into provinces, plus numerous specialized associations, especially religious, political, economic, and educational. Political and religious associations, in particular, were often extremely complex.

Increasing Inequality Within and Among Societies

In hunting and gathering societies, there were only minor status distinctions among individuals. The members of agrarian and maritime societies, however, were usually born into classes, which profoundly influenced their opportunities in life. Similarly, prior to the horticultural era, differences among societies were minimal; but by the end of the agrarian era, advanced agrarian and maritime societies were far wealthier and far more powerful than other societies in the world system.

Accelerating Rate of Social and Cultural Change

During the last 10,000 years of the hunting and gathering era, the rate of social and cultural change was greater than it had been prior to that time. But that could not compare with the increase in the rate of change in the next 10,000 years. Although there was a temporary slowing of the rate of technological innovation during the first part of the agrarian era, it accelerated again well before the end of the agrarian era, as shown in Figure 3.1.

By A.D. 1800, near the close of the agrarian era, the patterns of human life had been dramatically altered for all but the few who still lived in hunting and gathering societies in remote areas. The vast majority of people were now living in either agrarian or advanced horticultural societies, with smaller numbers in simple horticultural, herding, maritime, and fishing societies. This was not, of course, a stable world system. The deadly process of intersocietal selection that had begun thousands of years earlier was still working to the disadvantage of the technologically less advanced. And every time advanced agrarian societies took another step forward, they tilted the balance a bit more in their favor and against the rest.

This was the human condition on the eve of the Industrial Revolution.

PART

III

Industrial Societies and Industrializing Societies

The Industrial Revolution

Outline

Throughout much of the agrarian era, the rate of technological innovation was less than one would expect in view of the size of agrarian societies, the amount of information available to them, and the extent of contact among them. As we have seen, the cause of this lay in their highly exploitative social systems and in the ideologies that shaped their members' economic attitudes and activities. Not surprisingly, these had *negative feedback effects* on both technological innovation and economic development.

Late in the agrarian era, however, the rate of innovation in western Europe increased substantially within a relatively short period of time, and by the latter part of the eighteenth century the Industrial Revolution was well under way. Not long thereafter, England became the first truly industrial society—that is, the first society to derive more than half of its income from productive activities involving machines powered by inanimate energy sources. With this, a new era of far more rapid and pervasive social and cultural change was launched.

What was responsible for this important development? What happened to break the agrarian mold and produce this burst of technological innovation in societies that had been so resistant to change? What happened, in other words, to turn the system of negative feedback into a system of *positive* feedback?

CAUSES OF THE INDUSTRIAL REVOLUTION
The Accumulation of Information in the Agrarian Era

Probably the least heralded of the major causes of the Industrial Revolution was the gradual accumulation of technological information throughout the agrarian era. For despite the slowdown in the *rate* of innovation, discoveries and inventions did not stop. Evidence of significant advances can be found in agriculture, mining, metallurgy, transportation, construction, and various other fields.[1] Advances in construction and engineering, for example, can still be traced if one compares the churches and cathedrals built in western Europe in successive centuries. As a result of many such advances, the store of technological information available in the eighteenth century was far greater than in the thirteenth, just as it had been far greater in the thirteenth century than in the eighth. This enormous store of information held obvious potential for an increase in the rate of technological innovation when other conditions within societies became favorable (e.g., see Table 3.1 and Figure 3.1).

Late in the sixteenth century, during the reign of Queen Elizabeth I, the noted English philosopher and statesman Francis Bacon wrote that three inventions "had changed the whole face and state of things throughout the world"—the mariner's compass, the printing press, and gunpowder.[2] He was right: the world, especially his part of it, had already changed significantly because of these inventions, and the pace of change in western Europe was quickening. Bacon was more insightful than most of his contemporaries in recognizing the importance of technological innovation. But even someone as observant as he could not conceive of the vastly greater changes yet to come, since the first modest stirrings of the Industrial Revolution still lay more than a century in the future.

Advances in Water Transportation and the Conquest of the New World

As Bacon perceived, some innovations of the late agrarian era were more important for societal change than others. Those with a potential for altering agrarian social structure and ideology were most important of all, and, in this respect, improvements in ships and navigation proved to be some of the most critical.

Prior to the introduction of the compass in Europe, late in the twelfth century, navigation beyond the sight of land was so hazardous that it was undertaken only for short distances or in familiar areas, as in crossing the English Channel or the Mediterranean Sea. Acquisition of the compass was followed over the next several centuries by a series of important advances in the technology of shipbuilding. These included the invention of the stern rudder (which replaced steering oars attached to the sides of ships), the construction of larger ships with multiple masts, the substitution of several smaller sails for a single large sail on each mast, and a reduction in the width of ships relative to their length.[3] All of these innovations made ships more responsive and more manageable, and therefore safer on stormy seas.

With such ships at their command, and with the compass to guide them, western European sailors increasingly ventured out into open seas for extended periods. During the fifteenth century, they began a series of voyages intended to find new trade routes to India and China that would enable Europeans to bypass the merchants of the Middle East. Instead, of course, they "discovered" the New World and quickly subdued it. Less than fifty years after Columbus first set foot in America, Spain had conquered the two most powerful societies in the New World, the Incan Empire in Peru and the Aztec Empire in Mexico.*

---

*Despite the undeniable impact of gunpowder on world history, that invention, unlike the compass and printing press, was not a significant cause of the Industrial Revolution. In fact, in the conquest of the New World, the decimation of native populations by diseases brought from Europe (e.g., smallpox, measles), and to which these populations had never developed immunity, appears to have been of much greater importance than European arms.

A Sea-Going Reconstruction of the Nina, One of Christopher Columbus's Fleet on the First Voyage to the New World, Illustrates Advances in Shipbuilding in the Late Medieval Period That Made the Voyage Possible. Note the Multiple Masts and Sails, the Stern Rudder, and the Relatively Narrow Beam.

Almost immediately the conquerors began to ship vast quantities of gold and silver back to Europe. This had a number of consequences, one of which was a tremendous growth in the money economy and a decline in the older barter system.[4] Although money had been used for more than 2,000 years, the supply of precious metals remained so limited that many payments were still made in goods rather than in cash—especially in rural areas, but by no means only there. This situation seriously hindered economic and technological advances because an economy that operates on the basis of barter is not flexible, and the flow of resources from areas of oversupply to areas of short supply is sluggish. Furthermore, it is difficult to determine what is economically most advantageous in a barter system. When money is used, it is much easier for people to calculate their costs and incomes and thus determine which of the alternatives open to them is likely to yield the greatest profit.[5]

Money is extremely important in breaking down barriers to technological innovation. In societies where technological progress has been halting and uncertain for centuries and where there is no efficient accounting system, people with money are reluctant to invest in new and unproven enterprises. Also, where money is scarce, people tend to state obligations (e.g., wages, rents, debts) in relatively inflexible and traditional terms, which makes the economy unresponsive to changing conditions and new opportunities. But all of this began to change in western Europe during the sixteenth and seventeenth centuries in response to the flow of precious metals from the New World.

This influx of gold and silver had a second important effect: it produced inflation.[6] This was a natural consequence of the greatly increased supply of money combined with a much more limited increase in the supply of goods. Prices doubled, tripled, even quadrupled within a century. As is always the case when this happens, some people prospered and some were hurt. In general, those with fixed incomes, especially the landed aristocracy, were hurt, while merchants and entrepreneurs tended to benefit. This meant a marked improvement in the position of merchants relative to the governing class. More of the economic resources of European societies wound up in the hands of people who were interested in, and knew something about, both economics and technology. More than that, *these were people oriented to rational profit making (not a typical orientation in agrarian societies) and therefore motivated to provide financial support for technological innovations that would increase the efficiency of people and machines.* The rise in prices in the sixteenth century was simultaneously a stimulant to feverish enterprise and an acid dissolving traditional relationships.[7]

The benefits to Europe from the discovery of the New World were even greater in the eighteenth and nineteenth centuries than they had been earlier. As the population of European colonists increased, so did opportunities for trade. The colonists provided a growing market for Europe's manufactured goods and paid for them with a swelling flood of cheap and abundant raw materials.[8] Between 1698 and 1775, Britain's trade with its colonies increased more than fivefold,[9] and that was only the beginning. As a result, *the center of world trade shifted for the first time in more than 5,000 years, as western Europe replaced the Middle East in the favored position.*

Looking backward, it is difficult to exaggerate the importance of the discovery and conquest of the New World, with respect both to the rise of European power in the world system of societies and to the subsequent occurrence of the Industrial Revolution. Suddenly, a handful of relatively small societies had access to an enormous treasure house of resources. In addition to the gold and silver, western European societies quickly gained control over vast territories whose forests were a source of great quantities of cheap lumber and, when cleared, provided seemingly endless acres of rich farmland. Contact with the native peoples of the Americas also provided Europeans with information about new plants—especially corn and potatoes—that became valuable new food resources. Never before in history had technologically advanced societies enjoyed such a favorable ratio of resources to population. It was almost as though a new Garden of Eden had been created, but for the benefit of a favored few.

The Printing Press and the Spread of Information

The printing press was another technological innovation that played an important role in helping western European societies break the traditional agrarian mold. Printing sped the dissemination of both new technological and new ideological information, and thus was a major factor in overcoming resistance to innovation and change.[10]

Printing apparently originated in China about the fifth century A.D.[11] This early method of printing was extremely expensive, however, because it required a highly skilled craftsman to engrave the contents of every page on a separate block of wood. As a result, printed materials remained a luxury until Johann Gutenberg, a goldsmith and engraver, invented a system of movable type in the middle of the fifteenth century.[†12] Thus, the expense of skilled engraving was eliminated from printing, except in the manufacture of the type (i.e., letters and other symbols), which could be combined in various ways and used over and over again.

Gutenberg's invention resulted in a tremendous increase in the quantity of printed materials in western Europe. In medieval monasteries, it took ten to fifteen years to produce a single copy of the Bible using traditional methods. It is not surprising, therefore, that before Gutenberg, books in Europe numbered in the *thousands*. In fact it is quite likely that more books were printed in the first fifty years after the invention of the printing press than all the scribes of Europe had produced in the previous thousand years, and by A.D. 1500 there were more than ten *million* printed books.[14] Among the materials that achieved wider circulation were treatises on the new scientific theories of men like Copernicus and Galileo in the sixteenth and seventeenth centuries and books on farming that revolutionized English agriculture in the eighteenth. One of the most significant applications of the printing press, however, occurred less than a century after its invention, when it was used to spread the teachings of the Protestant reformers. Historians today regard the printing press as a major factor in the success of the Protestant movement.[15]

As many scholars have observed, a number of the new Protestant doctrines substantially altered the thinking of many members of agrarian societies in ways that were conducive to economic and other kinds of change.[16] In the first place, the reformers taught that work is an important form of service to God. Martin Luther, for example, insisted that all honest forms of work are as truly Christian callings as the ministry or priesthood. This challenged both the medieval Catholic view of work as a punishment for sin and the traditional aristocratic view of work as degrading and beneath the dignity of a gentleman. At the same time, it supported the efforts of merchants and craftsmen to upgrade their status. Second, the new Protestant faiths undermined fatalism and trust in magic and, in the long run, stimulated the spread of rationalism. Though the reformers dealt with these things only in the area of religion—and even there imperfectly—they strengthened a trend that ultimately had far-reaching consequences.[17] Some branches of Protestantism, for example, encouraged their adherents to plan their lives rather than merely live from day to day, as the name "Methodism" reminds us. Third, many of the newer Protestant faiths emphasized the value of denying the pleasures of this world and living frugally, a practice that enabled those who became economically successful to accumulate capital.

To the extent that people followed these teachings, they developed a new outlook on life: they worked harder, acted more rationally, and lived more thriftily. In short, the

---

[†]Gutenberg's key achievement was the development of a system for manufacturing, and printing with, interchangeable *letters*. Centuries earlier the Chinese had developed and used movable type, but it did not have the impact of Gutenberg's invention because written Chinese is based on ideograms rather than letters. Thus, it requires tens and even hundreds of thousands of unique characters to communicate what European languages, based on the Roman alphabet, can convey with various arrangements of twenty-six letters.[13]

Reformation remolded the attitudes, beliefs, and values of countless people in ways that undermined the traditional agrarian economy and stimulated economic and technological innovation. Related to this, certain branches of Protestantism, notably Calvinism, elevated the activities of merchants and businessmen to a status they had not previously enjoyed in any agrarian society. As one scholar has noted, this was not surprising in a faith which had its headquarters in Geneva and its most influential adherents in other leading business centers, such as London, Antwerp, and Amsterdam.[18]

Protestantism was also important to economic development because of the insistence of the reformers that people should be able to read the Bible for themselves and thus have direct access to God's word. This meant that literacy assumed a new significance in societies that became Protestant: it became a religious obligation for the masses rather than an option for elites. But while the initial motivation for the spread of literacy among the masses was religious, its most important long-term effects were broader. More literate populations proved to be more innovative and creative than their less literate competitors, and societies that encouraged literacy at an early date gained an important advantage over other societies in the developmental process.[19]

In summary, it seems more than coincidence that the Industrial Revolution had its beginnings in predominantly Protestant nations. The new Protestant ideology, like the conquest of the New World, undermined belief systems and social structures that had been formidable barriers to innovation and change. Above all, it encouraged a new respect for work and rational planning and discouraged both fatalism and reliance on magic. But it is important to recognize that the success of the Reformation movement and its influence on the subsequent course of European history were due in no small measure to prior changes in technology and economics and to the discovery and conquest of the New World with its vast treasure of natural resources. The latter development was especially important because it enabled many of those who adopted the Protestant work ethic to prosper to a degree that otherwise would not have been possible, thereby confirming the validity of the new ethic and reinforcing it. In short, the Protestant Reformation was an important link in the chain of causation that led to the Industrial Revolution, even if it was not the critical link that some have suggested.[20]

Advances in Agriculture

Throughout the agrarian era, the chief restraint on societal growth and development was the state of agricultural technology. The rural elite, so long as it managed to extract a surplus sufficient to maintain its customary lifestyle, was content to preserve the status quo. And the peasants, so long as they managed simply to survive, were content to follow the practices inherited from their forebears—or if not content, at least not motivated to change them. Thus agriculture, which was the basis of the economic surplus, remained largely the same from one century to the next.

In the sixteenth century, however, the situation began to change in much of western Europe.[21] The growth of trade, the increased use of money, and, above all, inflation began to undermine the traditional agrarian system. On the one hand, a growing number of large landowners found that as transportation costs declined in the wake of advances in shipping, markets for certain farm commodities (e.g., wool, grain) expanded. On the other hand, the effects of inflation were threatening the profitability of their farms, which depended on rents and other obligations that had been established long before the rise in prices. Many landowners realized that if they hoped to maintain their traditional standard of living under the new economic conditions, they had to try something new. Some of them therefore brought new land under cultivation by draining swamps, or by enclosing for their own private use what had previously been "common land," pastures available to both peasants and elites. Other landowners turned to raising sheep in an effort to benefit from the growing trade in wool. Still others eliminated traditional modes of payment by which tenants paid their landlords through customary services or with goods or produce, and began to require instead payments of money, which had become more important in economic relationships and which could more easily be adjusted to take account of inflation. Thus, during the sixteenth and seventeenth centuries, agriculture in Europe, and particularly in England, gradually became more profit oriented and capitalistic and less governed by tradition and custom.

Then, in the eighteenth century, a new wave of inflation hit western Europe, and landowners were again faced with a choice between innovation and a declining standard of living.[22] In England, where the traditional system of agriculture had already been seriously weakened, a number of other important innovations were adopted. Early in the century, for example, one landowner devised a system of crop rotation that enabled farmers to keep all of their land continuously under cultivation; previously, farmers had to leave land fallow, or uncultivated, one year in four in order to restore its fertility. A little later another landowner discovered the principle of selective breeding, simultaneously making a fortune for himself from his stud farm and greatly improving the quality of British livestock. Other members of the rural elite invented a variety of simple machines that increased the efficiency of farm labor, while still others published books expounding the new techniques. The practice of enclosing common lands, meanwhile, continued.

By the end of the eighteenth century, the traditional system of agriculture had been replaced in most of England by a new system of larger, more efficient farms operated on rational and capitalistic principles. But the adoption of this new system meant the massive displacement of many poor rural families whose labor was no longer needed and whose right to common lands was no longer protected by tradition. Some of these people migrated to the new frontier societies overseas. Many others, however, migrated to the cities and towns, where they became a source of cheap labor in the mills and factories that were beginning to appear.

A Model of the Causes of the Industrial Revolution

Figure 9.1 summarizes the principal causes of the Industrial Revolution. As the model indicates, *the basic cause was the growing store of technological information in the latter part of the agrarian era.* Advances in navigation and shipbuilding were especially important because, without them, the societies of western Europe could not have won control of the resources of two vast continents. This revolutionary development, abetted by the success of the Protestant Reformation, led to changes in economics, social organization, and ideology, which made it possible for these societies to break the historic agrarian mold. Because of this, the longtime agrarian pattern of negative feedback from social organization and ideology to technology was transformed into a positive one, thereby freeing creative forces that had been curbed for centuries.

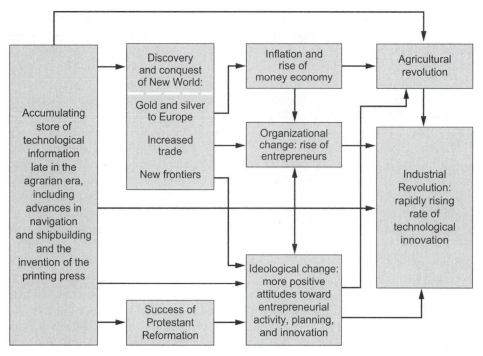

Figure 9.1. Model of the Causes of the Industrial Revolution in Western Europe.

It is interesting to note that England, the first society to become industrialized, experienced significant change in several of the factors that are primarily responsible for shaping a society's development. Its environment was drastically altered through the discovery and conquest of the New World, and its store of both technological and ideological information underwent substantial change in the sixteenth, seventeenth, and eighteenth centuries. These developments combined to produce major changes in the processes of innovation and selection. These developments will also provide us with useful clues when, in a later chapter, we ponder the question of why societies trying to industrialize today find it so much more difficult than did the societies that industrialized a hundred years or more earlier.

A BRIEF HISTORY OF THE INDUSTRIAL REVOLUTION

Before the end of the nineteenth century, economic historians were already beginning to use the term "Industrial Revolution" to refer to the series of dramatic technological and economic innovations that occurred in England during the period from about 1760 to 1830. In their view, the mechanization of the textile industry; the technical advances in, and expansion of, the iron industry; the harnessing of steam power; the establishment of the factory system; and other, related developments of that period had transformed English society. What was still essentially an agrarian society in the middle of the eighteenth century had become an industrial society by the middle of the nineteenth.

The time limits that early writers assigned to the Industrial Revolution are now widely questioned. Most scholars today believe it is a mistake to put a terminal date on a revolution that is still continuing.[23] Others argue that 1760 is too late a starting date, since the acceleration in industrial activity began not in the middle of the eighteenth century but in the middle of the sixteenth or earlier.[24]

There is some merit in both criticisms. The rate of technological advance did, in fact, begin to accelerate long before 1760, as we have seen. But it does not follow that we should treat those earlier developments as part of the Industrial Revolution. To be meaningful, this term should be limited to *the period during which the productive activities of societies were rapidly transformed by the invention of a succession of machines powered by newer, inanimate sources of energy, such as coal, electricity, petroleum, and natural gas.* Using this criterion, we cannot put the start of the Industrial Revolution much, if any, before the middle of the eighteenth century when steam power was applied to the practical problem of pumping water out of the coal mines.

The other criticism of the dates is sounder: the Industrial Revolution definitely was not over by 1830. Only its first phase ended at that time. Subsequently, there have been three other phases, and each has contributed substantially to the importance of industrial activity in the societies involved and to their transformation.

We cannot assign precise dates to these phases, since they are all rather arbitrary divisions in what has been essentially a continuous process of development. However, by organizing our review in terms of phases, we can see more clearly the progression of events. In the first phase, which began in mid-eighteenth-century England, the revolution was concentrated in the textile, iron, and coal industries; and the invention of the first true steam engine was the most important innovation. The second phase got its start in the middle of the nineteenth century and involved rapid growth in the railroad industry, the mass production of steel, the replacement of sailing ships by steamships, and use of the new technology in agriculture. Around the turn of the century, the Industrial Revolution entered a third phase, with rapid growth in the automobile, electrical, telephone, and petroleum industries. World War II marked the beginning of a fourth phase, distinguished by remarkable developments in aviation, aluminum, electronics, plastics, nuclear power, computers, and automation.

These four phases should not be thought of as stages that each society must pass through to become industrialized. On the contrary, many societies in recent decades have skipped over certain phases, or at least parts of them, and combined elements from different phases. For example, a third world nation today often develops its railway, highway, and air transportation systems simultaneously. But a review of the way things happened *initially* enables us to see how one innovation often made further innovations possible, even imperative.

First Phase: Steam Engines, Iron, Coal, Textile Machines, Factories (Circa 1760–1850)

The first phase of the Industrial Revolution, as we noted, began in the middle of the eighteenth century and lasted about a hundred years. Geographically, it was centered in England. Many of the best-known innovations occurred in the textile industry and were of two kinds: machines that increased the efficiency of human labor, and machines that harnessed new sources of energy. The flying shuttle is a good example of the first—and a good example, too, of the way one invention stimulated others. Because it enabled one weaver to do the work formerly done by two, spinners could no longer keep up with the demand for yarn. This disruption of the traditional balance between spinning and weaving triggered a succession of further inventions. First, the traditional spinning wheel was replaced by the spinning jenny, which enabled a worker to spin four threads simultaneously and, after a number of modifications, 120 threads. But although the spinning jenny was a tremendous improvement from the standpoint of speed, its yarn was so coarse and loose that flax had to be mixed in with the cotton to produce a satisfactory fiber. This was remedied with the water frame, a machine that could satisfactorily spin pure cotton; and later with the spinning mule, whose cotton threads were stronger and finer. All of these advances in spinning reversed the earlier situation: Now weaving was the bottleneck in the industry—until a new series of innovations in weaving machines helped restore the balance once again. This was to become a pattern of development that was to be repeated often in industrial societies.

By the end of the eighteenth century, the new looms had become so large and heavy that they were almost impossible to operate. To work the treadle even at a slow speed required two powerful men—and they had to be relieved after a short time.[25] This led to a search for alternative sources of power. One possibility was waterpower, which had already been used for a variety of purposes for centuries.[26] But England was poorly supplied with suitable streams and rivers, and the wheels and troughs used in water systems were extremely inefficient.[27] Eventually, James Watt developed the first true steam engine,[28] a source of power that could be employed anywhere, and by the end of the century it had been adapted for use in the textile industry.

The net effect of these innovations was such a rapid expansion of the British textile industry that between 1770 and 1845 its contribution to the national income increased more than fivefold.[29] This was an extraordinary rate of growth by the standards of

James Hargreaves's Spinning Jenny.

traditional agrarian societies. The actual increase in production was even larger, since per unit costs of production dropped considerably during this period.

One of the immediate consequences of advances in textile production was *the creation of the factory system*. Prior to the Industrial Revolution, and even during its early years, spinning and weaving were cottage industries. Entrepreneurs provided the raw materials, and poor families, working in their own homes and using their own spinning wheels and looms, provided the labor. But after heavier and more expensive machines came to be used, this arrangement was impossible: Families could neither afford the new equipment nor power it. Businessmen were forced to buy their own machines, construct buildings to house them, and provide engines to run them, thereby creating the factory system that has become such a prominent feature of modern industrial societies.

Iron was another industry that expanded greatly during the first phase of the Industrial Revolution. Despite increasing demand for iron by both the textile industry and the military, technical difficulties greatly restricted its manufacture until late in the eighteenth century. One problem was England's growing shortage of wood, which was used to make charcoal for smelting and refining. This problem had been partially solved earlier in the century, when it was found that coke (derived from coal) could be substituted for charcoal, at least in the smelting process. But a serious bottleneck remained. Because it is hard and brittle, pig iron must be converted into wrought, or malleable, iron before it can be used for most purposes. This process required charcoal and was very time-consuming until the traditional forge was replaced by the newly invented coal-fired blast furnace. These innovations opened the way for rapid expansion: In 1788, England produced only 68,000 tons of iron; by 1845, it produced twenty-four times that.[30] The new blast furnaces also made it possible to perform all the processes of iron making in a single establishment. Thus, the factory system spread from the textile industry to the iron industry.

Between them, the iron industry and the steam engine substantially increased the demand for coal. At the same time, the steam engine helped alleviate the ancient problem of flooding in coal mines by providing a source of power to pump out the water that constantly seeped into shafts and tunnels. The growth of the coal industry, though not quite so dramatic as that of the iron industry, was still impressive: In 1760, Britain produced barely five million tons; by 1845, the figure had risen over ninefold.[31]

No discussion of developments in this period would be complete without mention of the machine-tool industry. Although never as large or financially important as the textile, iron, and coal industries, it was crucial for technological progress because it produced the increasingly complex industrial machinery. This industry, which began undramatically with the invention of the first practical lathe, was soon producing machines capable of precision work to the thousandth of an inch.[32] For many years a single tool was used for drilling, boring, grinding, and milling; but special tools were gradually designed for each operation.

Another striking advance in the eighteenth century was the production of machines with interchangeable parts. This greatly facilitated industrial growth, since damage to one part of a complex machine no longer meant that the entire machine had to be discarded or a new part specially made. Spare parts could now be kept on hand and replacements made on the spot by mechanics with limited skills and equipment.

During this initial phase of the Industrial Revolution, shortly after 1800, Britain became the first nation in which machine-based industry replaced agriculture as the most important economic activity, and thus the first industrial society.[33] The United States would not reach this point until about 1870.[34]

Second Phase: Railroads, Steamships, Steel, Rubber, Farm Machines (Circa 1850–1900)

The second phase of the Industrial Revolution began in the middle decades of the nineteenth century. Expansion continued at a rapid pace in the textile, iron, and coal industries, but now there were breakthroughs in a number of others as well. By the end of the century, industrialization had occurred in most segments of the British economy. Meanwhile, the Industrial Revolution began to make significant headway in several other countries of northwestern Europe and in the United States.

One of the most important developments during this phase was the application of the steam engine to transportation, something inventors had been trying to accomplish for decades. By 1850 most of England was linked together by a network of railroads.[35] The results were tremendous: The greatly reduced cost of moving goods by rail led to a significant reduction in the price of most heavy bulk commodities, and this in turn led to greater demand. In addition, railroads helped break down local monopolies and oligopolies (i.e., markets with only a few sellers), and this increased competition and further lowered prices. Thus, England gradually became a single giant market for a growing number of commodities, a development destined to have far-reaching consequences.

Even before the steam engine was adapted to land transportation, it had been used on water. For many years, however, steamships were limited to coastal and river shipping, both because inefficient engines made it impossible to bunker enough wood or coal for long voyages and because paddle wheels worked poorly in high seas. Then, in only a few decades, several things happened. More efficient compound engines substantially reduced the amount of fuel required; iron and steel began to replace wood in ship construction, permitting longer and larger vessels with greater carrying capacity (the upper limit in length for wooden ships was only about 300 feet); and the screw propeller replaced the cumbersome and easily damaged paddle wheel.[36] After this, steamships increased so rapidly that by 1893 steam tonnage exceeded sailing tonnage worldwide.

In the iron industry, meanwhile, a way was finally found to produce steel cheaply and in large quantities, making it available for many new purposes.[37] Between 1845 and the early 1880s, Britain's production of iron and steel increased more than fivefold.[38] This meant that in less than a century, from 1788 to the early 1880s, the increase was a hundredfold, and the quality of the product was vastly improved.

The tremendous growth in railroads and steamships and the expansion of the iron industry all combined to increase the demand for coal. Though there were no spectacular breakthroughs in mining techniques, improvements in engines and in the quality of steel tools pushed production up fivefold.[39]

A number of new industries emerged in addition to the railroads, none as important at the time, but some destined to surpass them later on. The rubber industry developed after Charles Goodyear discovered the technique of vulcanization, which prevented rubber goods from becoming sticky in hot weather, stiff and brittle in cold. About the same time, Samuel Morse and several others invented the telegraph, and this quickly became the basis of another new industry. Then, in the 1860s, the electric dynamo was invented, and the door was opened to the use of electricity in industry. A second critical development in this field, the invention of the transformer, helped alleviate one of the greatest impediments to the use of electricity: the loss of energy during long-distance transmission. The petroleum industry also got its start in these years, chiefly by providing a substitute for whale oil in lighting homes.

The Industrial Revolution began to have an impact even on agriculture, through improved equipment (e.g., sturdier steel plows), new kinds of machines (e.g., threshing machines, mowers, reapers, steam plows), and synthetic fertilizers from the growing chemical industry. The result was a substantial increase in productivity. In Germany, for example, production per acre rose 50 percent in only twenty-five years. In the United States, the number of hours required to produce a given amount of corn and wheat was cut in half between 1840 and 1900.[40]

An important organizational innovation in this second phase of the Industrial Revolution was the *multidivisional enterprise with a hierarchy of salaried managers*.[41] This occurred first in the new railroad, steamship, and telegraph industries, all of which required workers in widely scattered locations. No longer was it possible for a single family to fill all or even most of the managerial positions needed to supervise employees and coordinate their activities: hired personnel had to assume this responsibility. This was an important step in the development of the modern corporation.

Another spur in this direction was the great quantity of new material products that had become available to the members of society. As further advances in production and transportation continued to lower the cost of goods and increase the demand for them, the sheer volume of sales made it impossible for the owners of some businesses to oversee all the transactions. For example, around the turn of the century, Sears, Roebuck was processing 100,000 orders a day, more than any merchant of an earlier generation would have handled in a lifetime.[42] As sales increased, so did the number of retail outlets in a wide variety of businesses, each requiring a local manager at first, and eventually intermediate layers of management.

Throughout this period, industrialization was spreading rapidly in northwest Europe and North America. Before the century closed, Britain had lost its position of economic and technological dominance. The iron and steel industry illustrates the trend: although Britain nearly doubled its production of pig iron between 1865 and 1900, its share of the world market dropped from 54 to 23 percent.[43] Its chief rivals were the United States and Germany, whose respective shares rose from 9 to 35 percent and from 10 to 19 percent.

As these figures indicate, though industrialization was spreading, it was still largely limited to a few countries. The United States, Britain, Germany, and France, for example, produced 84 percent of the world's iron in 1900. A similar picture emerges when we look at national shares of world manufacturing activity in 1888 (see Table 9.1). The fact that "all other countries" contributed more to all types of manufacturing than to iron production indicates that the new technology spread faster in light industries, such as textiles, than in heavy industries. This was because light industries required

Table 9.1 Percentage Distribution of World Industrial Output (Excluding Handicrafts), in 1888 and 1937, by Society

Society	1888	1937
United States	32	34
United Kingdom	18	10
Germany	13	11
France	11	5
Russia	8	10
Japan	No data	4
All others	17	26

Source: Calculated from W. S. Woytinsky and E. S. Woytinsky, *World Population and Production: Trends and Outlook* (New York: Twentieth Century Fund, 1953), pp. 1003–1004.

less capital and because the rate of innovation in them had slowed considerably, thus reducing the need for highly skilled and innovative personnel.

The last factor points to a final characteristic of this phase of the Industrial Revolution: a growing dependence on science and engineering. Before 1850 most of the major advances were made by simple craftsmen or gentlemen amateurs. After that date, key inventions came primarily from people with formal technical or scientific training. This was especially true in the chemical industry, but it was evident in others as well.

Finally, near the end of the nineteenth century, the innovative process began to be institutionalized, and laboratories were built to enable teams of trained people to work together to solve technical problems.[44] The laboratories established by Thomas Edison exemplified the new trend, and the successes he and others achieved led many to emulate them, especially in Germany and the United States. These developments also contributed to the growth of scientific study in universities, to the training of engineers, and to increasing cooperation between innovative industries and institutions of higher education. Most of these developments did not come to full flower, however, until the third and fourth phases of the Industrial Revolution.

Third Phase: Automobiles, Airplanes, Telephones, Electricity, Petroleum, Radios, Movies (Circa 1900–1950)

Early in the twentieth century, the Industrial Revolution entered a new phase that involved the rapid spread of important new technologies in the fields of transportation and communication as well as new technologies for harnessing energy and creating synthetic materials. These developments largely resulted from various inventions and discoveries of the late nineteenth century, especially the internal combustion engine, the telephone, the radio, moving pictures, the electrical generator, and plastics; each of which subsequently transformed the lives of hundreds of millions of people.

One of the most important developments was the enormous expansion of the automobile industry. In 1900, barely 20,000 cars were produced worldwide, but by midcentury, production totaled eight million.[45]

The auto industry's rapid growth had a profound impact on a number of other industries as well. On the eve of World War II, for example, the manufacture of cars in

Early Assembly Line: Dropping the Engine into the Ford Model T Chassis, Highland Park, Michigan.

the United States was consuming 20 percent of the nation's steel, 54 percent of its malleable iron, 73 percent of its plate glass, and 80 percent of its rubber.[46] More striking yet, 90 percent of the nation's gasoline was being consumed by automobiles, a development that was largely responsible for the thirteenfold increase in petroleum production between 1900 and 1940.[47]

In the field of communications, technological change transformed the economy and daily life in other ways. By midcentury, telephones and radios had become standard items in tens of millions of households in industrial societies, and movies had become a commonplace experience in the lives of most individuals. Once again, it is hard to exaggerate the impact of these technologies on industrial societies and, in the case of radio and movies, their impact on the beliefs and values of vast numbers of people.

These and other important developments were made possible by the rapid expansion of the electrical industry. Between 1900 and 1950, world capacity to produce electricity increased a hundredfold.[48] With the availability of inexpensive electric power, electric lights replaced gaslights and candles in the vast majority of households, and electricity was increasingly used to power household appliances, ranging from refrigerators and vacuum cleaners to radios and toasters. Industrial uses of electrical power also grew enormously.

During the third phase of the Industrial Revolution, technology came to play an increasingly important role in warfare. Tanks and other motorized vehicles replaced the cavalry, while aircraft added a radically new component to military operations. Meanwhile, newly developed weapons systems—such as poison gas, germ warfare, and nuclear weapons—although never employed to their full potential, added fearsome and deadly new elements to the arsenals of many nations.

No previous war depended as heavily on industrial production as World War II, and all the nations involved extended themselves to increase their output of military supplies. Because of the importance of aircraft, the aviation industry received a tremendous stimulus. In the United States, for example, the production of planes rose from 3,600 in 1938 to more than 96,000 in 1944.[49] Although the manufacture of aircraft dropped off substantially after the war ended, the air transport industry (both passenger and cargo) began an explosive growth that continues to the present day.

During the third phase of the Industrial Revolution, as during the second, industrial technology spread to new parts of the world, leading to changes in the relative ranking of nations in economic terms. While the United States continued to be the leader, producing a third of the world's industrial output, Britain, Germany, and France lost ground relatively (see Table 9.1) despite substantial growth in absolute terms. In contrast, important gains were registered by Japan and a number of other nations.

Fourth Phase: Television, Computers, Transistors, the Internet, Plastics, Globalization (Circa 1950–Present)

The current phase of the Industrial Revolution is commonly referred to as "the information age" because it has revolutionized access to information in many forms. Earlier inventions, from the printing press to radios and the movies, had, of course, done much to democratize access to information, but television, computers, and the Internet speeded and extended the process enormously.

Commercial television got its start only in the midcentury, but by 1960, 87 percent of American homes had a television set, and some even had multiple sets.[50] Today, TV sets are standard equipment in nearly every household in industrial societies and in ever-increasing numbers of industrializing societies.

Television revolutionized human experience to a degree that few other innovations have equaled. It has enabled hundreds of millions of ordinary people to see and vicariously experience in their homes all manner of things far outside the range of normal everyday experience. They can, for example, "travel" to remote parts of the globe and observe at close range and in complete safety and comfort the lives of jungle animals and undersea creatures, erupting volcanoes and other natural disasters, and close-up views of the surface of the moon and Mars. They can also watch their political leaders debate alternative policies or witness the ravages of wars in distant areas.

Unfortunately, television, like the movies, often provides a grossly distorted view of society by focusing on deviant and unrepresentative lifestyles and behavior. Violence in all its manifestations is portrayed with extraordinary frequency. For example, in one four-year period, in which the homicide rate in American society dropped 20 percent, coverage of murders on the major TV network evening news shows increased 721 percent.[51] It is not surprising, therefore, that more recently, when the firearm homicide rate dropped 49 percent from its peak in 1993, a majority of the population believed it had actually increased.[52]

Although broadband technology is dispersing control of media content, television and the movies still put enormous power in the hands of the tiny and mostly invisible elite who largely control the content of what the public sees. It gives them the power to manipulate and transform the values, beliefs, and ultimately the actions of vast numbers of people.[‡] In recent years, television has increasingly set the agenda for politicians in the United States and elsewhere. By supplying dramatic and heartrending visual images of suffering in remote regions, television newscasters have on several occasions successfully pressured Western political leaders to intervene in military conflicts where their own nations' interests were minimally involved (e.g., Somalia, Bosnia, Liberia).

The second major invention of the information age has been the computer. The first computers were huge, bulky machines with limited capabilities. It was not until tiny transistors loaded on silicon chips were substituted for vacuum tubes that computers began to be the extraordinarily useful machines we know today.

Not only are transistors far smaller than vacuum tubes, but they have paved the way for a fantastic continuing process of miniaturization and power saving. As recently as 1971, the best silicon chip contained only 2,300 transistors, whereas today they have more than a *billion*.[54] This amazing process of miniaturization began in large measure because of the American space program of the 1960s. New rocket engines had made it possible for the first time for engineers to build spacecraft capable of escaping Earth's gravitational pull, but even these powerful engines could carry only a small payload. Weight reduction was imperative, and the miniaturization of equipment of every kind, including computers, was one of the obvious solutions.

Today, transistors are essential parts of everyday life. In addition to computers, they are the electronic brains in tens of millions of cars, jets, television sets, toys, cameras, wristwatches, faxes, smart phones, iPods, musical instruments, and countless other devices.

Computers have transformed the world of work, creating and storing the countless files and records on which businesses and governments depend. Even farming, that most traditional of occupations, is increasingly computerized and automated. For some time, dairy farmers have used electronic sensors linked to computers that enable them to record and analyze data on the health, food intake, weight, and other vital

---

[‡]Advertising provides the most obvious example of this, but more subtle instances can be found in the programs themselves and in movies where potentially dangerous or harmful activities are portrayed in a positive light and without any indication of the risks involved (e.g., smoking/lung cancer and emphysema, casual sex/sexually transmitted diseases and unwanted pregnancies, drug use/drug addiction and its consequences).

The potential for media manipulation has increased greatly as computer generated images (CGI) have made it possible to create video of people saying and doing things they never said or did, and the images are so realistic that it is impossible for viewers to tell that they are merely creations of some unseen image-meister. In the movie *Contact*, for example, this new technology was used to create the appearance of President Bill Clinton holding a press conference to discuss contact with aliens from outer space. The political dangers of misuse of this new technology are hard to exaggerate.

signs of each and every cow; now they are able to use robots that basically allow cows to milk themselves, and apparently the cows are happier and more productive![55]

Recently, the Internet has vastly expanded the reach of the information age. By means of a single computer in one's home or smartphone, one can gain direct and almost instant access to an incredible variety of information, ranging from the entire contents of encyclopedias to the latest quotations from stock markets around the world, and one can communicate with people worldwide.

These new technologies of the information age are not the only developments of importance in recent decades. New materials technologies have made a wide range of useful and inexpensive new fabrics available (e.g., rayon, nylon, polyester) and an even wider range of materials made of polymers, especially plastics. The latter are especially important, since plastics have become one of the most versatile of modern materials: they can now be manufactured to almost any set of specifications and are used in everything from toys to heavy construction projects. The drug industry—both legal and illegal—is another area that has expanded enormously in recent decades as a result of major technological breakthroughs.

One of the most important developments of the current phase of the Industrial Revolution has been the rapid spread of industrial technology to societies outside

The First General-Purpose Digital Computer, ENIAC (Electronic Numerical Integrator and Computer), Occupied 1,500 Square Feet, Weighed Thirty Tons, Had No Storage Memory, and Did Not Have the Processing Power of a Modern Smart Phone.[53]

Table 9.2 Percentage Distribution of Gross World Product (GWP), by Society in 2012

Society	GDP*	Percentage Share of GWP
United States	15,684,800	22.9
China	8,227,103	12.0
Japan	5,959,718	8.7
Germany	3,399,589	5.0
France	2,612,878	3.8
Great Britain	2,435,174	3.6
Brazil	2,252,664	3.3
Russian Federation	2,014,775	2.9
Italy	2,013,263	2.9
Total of the above	$44,599,964	65.1
All others	$23,891,293	34.9

Source: Calculated from World Bank, *World Development Indicators* online database, http://databank.worldbank.org/data/views/reports/tableview.aspx.
*In millions of 2012 U.S. dollars.

northwestern Europe and North America. In 1888, 83 percent of the world's industrial output occurred in just five societies: the United States, Britain, Germany, France, and Russia (see Table 9.1). Even as recently as 1937, these five societies were responsible for 78 percent of the world's industrial output. Today, by comparison, these five are responsible for only about 38 percent, and China now ranks second (see Table 9.2).

As Table 9.2 suggests, the fourth phase of the Industrial Revolution has been a period of extraordinary economic growth in most societies. Gross domestic product (GDP) is a measure of the value of all the goods and services produced in a society. In the second half of the twentieth century, the combined GDPs of the industrialized societies of Europe, North America, Japan, and Australia rose more than 600 percent, while the combined GDPs of the industrializing societies of the developing world increased nearly 800 percent![56] Such growth on a global scale is unprecedented.[§]

Key Innovations: New Energy, New Machines, New Materials

When studying the Industrial Revolution, it is easy to become so immersed in the details of individual inventions and discoveries that we fail to see the larger picture. When we look for basic patterns, however, we find that the revolution in technology has involved three kinds of critical innovations.

First, the Industrial Revolution has greatly increased the amount of *energy* available to societies. New technologies have made accessible for the first time vast quantities of

---

[§]Although some argue that the gains in GDP have not benefited the majority of people in third world societies, this view is challenged by data on trends in infant mortality, life expectancy, literacy, school enrollments, and other basic indicators of quality of life. While millions in the third world are still mired in poverty, millions of others have experienced significant improvements in living standards. To appreciate the magnitude of the change, one need only compare current conditions in those societies with those of the agrarian era.

energy stored in coal, petroleum, natural gas, and certain radioactive materials. The importance of this development is difficult to exaggerate.

Second, the Industrial Revolution has produced thousands of *new machines* that use this energy to perform an enormous variety of tasks. These machines provide billions of people with countless goods and services—many of which were previously unavailable to even the most powerful kings and emperors.

Third, the Industrial Revolution has made available many *new materials* to use in the construction of new machines and new products. Plastic has probably been the most useful new material to date, for it is easily the most versatile material that humans have ever worked with.

Collectively, these three sets of innovations—the vast new stores of energy, the new machines, and the new materials—have transformed the world. As we will see in the next several chapters, these advances in our species' ability to take resources from the biophysical environment and convert them into things we need or want have given rise to a social and cultural revolution unequaled in history, not only in its scope and speed but also in the enormity of its impact on human life.

A Caution: The Dark Side of the Industrial Revolution

Although it is clear that the Industrial Revolution has been an extraordinary achievement, it has not come without tremendous cost to millions and now poses a potential threat to the entire human race. Millions of factory workers, miners, and others were compelled to work under physically exhausting and dangerous conditions, and while these conditions have been greatly improved in industrial societies, it is largely because much of this kind of work has been exported to less developed societies (e.g., China).

Thanks to advances in military technology, warfare has become deadlier than ever. No war, to date, has ever compared with World War II in numbers of casualties, civilian as well as military.** Today, nuclear weapons have the potential of making human life impossible over vast territories. More recently, *cyber warfare* has created the possibility of seriously disrupting the complex network of relationships that undergirds the daily life of every society. As industrial societies and their citizens have become more dependent on computers and the Internet for storing and transmitting information of every kind, from operating nuclear power plants to recording billions of financial transactions daily, these societies have become ever more vulnerable to attacks on their computers and the Internet. In 2007, the Russian government appears to have carried out an extremely disruptive attack on the tiny nation of Estonia in retaliation for Estonia's removal of a statue that the Soviet government had installed when Estonia was still under Soviet rule.[57] More recently, the U.S. Army has begun training cadets at West Point in the skills required for defense against cyber attacks, and since 2006 there has been over a hundred cyber attacks on U.S. businesses and government agencies believed to be the work of a single foreign military.[58] Another unattractive aspect of technological advance is that it provides the means for

---

**In fairness, however, it should be noted that earlier conflicts often took a heavier toll proportionately. In other words, though the numbers killed or injured were fewer, the percentage of the populations that became casualties was greater.

governments to acquire greater control over citizens. All kinds of information about members of industrial societies today is overtly or covertly collected and stored by private companies and governments. Private companies use it to more effectively predict our behavior and market their products, and government has been accessing and using that information to identify potential terrorists and predict terrorist acts. In both cases the temptation and potential for abuse is enormous.

Finally, the new industrial technologies are having an unprecedented impact on the biophysical environment on which human life depends. How serious this is remains to be seen, but if any of the more ominous predictions concerning climate change prove to be correct (and these are still far from certain, see page ooo), the costs of the Industrial Revolution could more than offset its benefits.

These are matters to which we will return in the final chapter. In the meantime, however, we need to keep in mind that the Industrial Revolution's chief effect has been to increase the power of human beings—both for good and for ill.

CAUSES OF THE CONTINUING INDUSTRIAL REVOLUTION

As the twenty-first century progresses, the technological revolution that began in the eighteenth century shows no signs of abating. On the contrary, the rate of innovation continues to accelerate. Thus, to understand the Industrial Revolution it is not enough merely to understand the forces that gave it its start several centuries ago. We also need to understand the forces that are responsible for its continuation today.

Greater Informational Resources and a Larger Population

Several of these forces are ones that we first identified in Chapter 3. For example, the existing store of useful information about the material world is far greater today than ever before, as is its accessibility, and our means of processing it. This means that the informational resources available to would-be innovators today are vastly greater than in the past (see Table 3.1 and the related discussion, pages 57–58). In addition, the human population is substantially larger today than it was over two centuries ago, and this means more minds at work on the problems confronting human societies. And, as its complexity and reach grow, the problems that follow and the adjustments they require, themselves become a further spur to innovation. As we have seen so far, much of the history of technological advance is a result of coping with the consequences of earlier technological advances.

Changing Attitudes toward Innovation

In preindustrial societies, traditions have always been held in high esteem, and change has generally been viewed as undesirable, even dangerous. Innovators, far from being praised or admired for their efforts, have commonly been accused of abandoning the hallowed ways of the past and of their forebears. Because of this strong attachment to the past, social scientists often refer to preindustrial societies as "traditional" societies.

In contemporary industrial societies, in contrast, the attitude toward innovation and change is largely positive. Members of these societies are not just tolerant of innovation: *they expect, actively promote, and encourage it.* Many, in fact, are *neophiles,* people who love novelty for its own sake. In the arts, for example, innovation is often praised merely because of its novelty and without regard to aesthetic criteria (see "Neophilic Art"), with the result that on a number of occasions entries submitted to art exhibits as hoaxes have won prizes.

In the educational world, a strongly positive attitude toward innovation is also much in evidence. In preindustrial societies, the basic function of education was simply to transmit the cultural heritage of the past to successive generations, and great emphasis was placed on rote learning of materials. Today, most educators scorn memorization and argue that the chief aim of schools should be to train young people to think creatively. Universities, in turn, have increasingly become centers of research and innovation. Faculty members are often expected to devote considerably more time and energy to developing new knowledge (research) than to teaching.

The institutionalization of innovation is also evident in industry and government. Industrial enterprises and governmental agencies have created countless research centers within their own organizations, and they often subsidize research in universities as well. As a result, expenditures for research and development have risen enormously. In the United States, for example, even after adjustments for inflation, these expenditures have increased more than tenfold since 1953.[59] Industrial societies are the first in history to search systematically and continuously for new technological answers to human problems.

The reasons for the modern attitude toward innovation and change are not hard to find. For the most part, the changes that have already occurred have meant improvements in the quality of life for the vast majority of people in industrial societies—greatly improved standards of living, improved health, and greater longevity. Under the circumstances, it would be much more surprising if people's attitudes toward change had *not* changed.

The Rise of Modern Science

The emergence of *science* as a major new institutional system is another development that has contributed greatly to the continuing revolution in technology. Although science is sometimes confused with technology, the two are not the same. Science is the search for general and abstract principles that explain the workings of the world we

---

Neophilic Art

Some time ago, the Associated Press reported that two valuable pieces of modern sculpture stored in the yard outside an important art gallery—tangles of rusting metal—had been mistaken for junk and carted away by trash collectors.

More recently, a custodian at the Boulder Public Library inadvertently disposed of an exhibit made up of foul-smelling trash collected in a local park and carefully assembled by University of Colorado art students because he failed to recognize its artistic merit.

And experts are still debating whether a painting that a California woman purchased from a thrift shop for five dollars is actually a very valuable work by abstract expressionist Jackson Pollack and, therefore, worth millions of dollars, or simply an "ugly splattering of paint" by some rank amateur.

As these examples suggest, even in innovative societies, not quite everyone is able to appreciate the artistic value of neophilic art, just as in the old fairy tale not quite everyone was able to appreciate the beauty of the emperor's "new clothes."

live in. Technology, in contrast, is information about specific ways in which the material world can be manipulated to satisfy human needs and desires. It is a much more practical and down-to-earth body of information.

Science and technology today are obviously interdependent. Almost all modern science presupposes an advanced technology. Modern science is possible only because of technological advances that have enhanced the powers of our senses and of our brains, thus enabling us to learn things which would otherwise remain forever unknown. For example, modern molecular biology and modern medical science are possible only because of the invention of the microscope and the electron microscope, which revealed for the first time the previously invisible and unknowable world of cells and molecules, bacteria, and viruses. Similarly, modern astronomy is possible only because of the invention of the telescope, the radio telescope, and space probes, which extend the range of our vision far beyond what was previously possible.

But if modern science is a product of the Industrial Revolution, it is also an important cause of its continuation. Today, technological advance depends increasingly upon the kind of abstract, theoretical knowledge that is the special concern of the sciences. More and more, fundamental discoveries and major inventions are the work of men and women with advanced scientific training, and less and less the work of untrained mechanics. Without the contributions of modern science, it is highly unlikely that the rate of technological innovation would still be accelerating.

War

Prior to the Industrial Revolution, military technology changed slowly. As a result, military success among societies at the same level of development depended largely on the size of armies and the organizational and tactical skills of their commanders.

Today, in contrast, military technology becomes obsolete in a very short time, and the size of armies and their commanders' skills are often less important than the productive capacity of a nation's economy and the skills of its engineers and scientists. To maintain its relative military preeminence, the United States has invested enormous sums in technological research of many kinds.[60] Although the aim of this research is to create new and improved weapons systems, the new technologies that result often have significant nonmilitary applications. A classic example of this is the silicon chip, which was developed in response to the need to reduce the size and weight of materials used in the space program, a program whose funding has depended greatly on its military relevance.

Environmental Feedback

For the first time in history, the most significant changes in the biophysical environments of most societies may not be the result of spontaneous natural forces but, rather, of human actions (see Chapter 15). The global ecosystem now has to support a much larger human population than ever before, and the standards of living for much of this population are steadily rising. As a result, natural resources of every kind are being consumed far more rapidly than in the past, and supplies of many of them are threatened with depletion. In addition, many new technologies have had unanticipated side effects, such as acid rain. The need to solve such problems leads to further research and the development of still newer technologies. Thus, technological advance has itself become one of the most important causes of the need for continued technological advance.

The Desire for Ever Higher Standards of Living

Finally, it is clear that one of the most important factors responsible for the continuing Industrial Revolution is the desire of most people for ever higher standards of living. One might suppose that the tremendous improvements in living standards in industrial societies during the last two hundred years would satisfy their members, but this has not been the case. The desire for goods and services seems insatiable: the more people have, the more they want.

This appears to be part of our genetic heritage—an element of human nature that results from our enormous capacity for learning and especially from our powers of imagination. No matter what we have, or what we are able to do, we can always dream of more. And having dreamed, some are driven to make the dream a reality. Where this process will end—or if it will end—no one can say. For the present, however, it is a powerful force contributing to the continuing revolution in technology.

VARYING LEVELS OF INDUSTRIALIZATION IN THE WORLD SYSTEM OF SOCIETIES

Societies today differ enormously in the degree to which they have industrialized. Some rely almost entirely on the newer energy sources, such as coal, oil, natural gas, and nuclear energy, while others still depend primarily on human and animal power; that is, wind, water, and wood. Some have become almost totally dependent on machine technology while others still rely primarily on hand tools. And some are now heavily dependent on new kinds of materials, while others still depend largely on traditional ones.

Unfortunately, there is no single measure of industrialization that enables us to gauge perfectly the degree to which contemporary societies have adopted the new industrial technology. Different measures reflect different aspects of industrialization and thus yield somewhat different rankings of societies. Whatever measure is used, however, it must be a *per capita* (i.e., per person) measure, to take account of differences in the population size of societies. For example, if we simply took the total production of societies as a measure (see Table 9.2, which *uses gross world product*, or GWP), China would appear to be one of the most industrialized societies in the world system. But this is a distortion caused by China's huge size: its level of industrialization is still actually rather low by contemporary standards (as Table 9.3 shows).

One of the better measures currently available is the GDP, or gross domestic product, per capita. It is the per capita value of all the goods and services produced in a society in a specified period of time. It is, thus, a measure of the productivity of an economy. According to this measure, Luxembourg currently is the most industrialized society in the world.

Table 9.3 reveals several important patterns. First, there are enormous differences in the levels of industrialization of contemporary societies. Second, only a small minority of them can be considered full-fledged industrial societies. Third, with the exception of Japan, Singapore, and South Korea, all of these are either in Europe or were settled primarily by European peoples. Fourth, most of the least industrialized societies are in Africa and Asia, while most of the intermediate cases are found in Latin America, the Middle East, and eastern Europe.

Table 9.3 GDP Per Capita for Selected Contemporary Societies, 2012 in U.S. Dollars

Luxembourg	$107,476	Brazil	$11,340	Congo-Kinshasa	$3,154
Norway	$99,558	Turkey	$10,666	Morocco	$2,925
Switzerland	$79,052	Malaysia	$10,381	Sri Lanka	$2,923
Australia	$67,036	Mexico	$9,742	Philippines	$2,588
Denmark	$56,210	Lebanon	$9,705	Bolivia	$2,576
Sweden	$55,245	Panama	$9,534	Honduras	$2,264
Canada	$52,219	Costa Rica	$9,391	Papua New Guinea	$2,184
Singapore	$51,709	Suriname	$8,864	Nicaragua	$1,754
United States	$49,965	Romania	$7,943	Ghana	$1,605
Austria	$47,226	Colombia	$7,752	Vietnam	$1,596
Japan	$46,720	South Africa	$7,508	Sudan	$1,580
Finland	$46,179	Azerbaijan	$7,228	Nigeria	$1,555
Netherlands	$46,054	Botswana	$7,191	Yemen	$1,494
Ireland	$45,836	Bulgaria	$6,986	India	$1,489
Belgium	$43,413	Peru	$6,573	Zambia	$1,469
Iceland	$42,658	Iraq	$6,455	Pakistan	$1,290
Germany	$41,514	China	$6,091	Ivory Coast	$1,244
France	$39,772	Dominican Republic	$5,736	Cameroon	$1,151
United Kingdom	$38,514	Angola	$5,485	Senegal	$1,032
New Zealand	$37,749	Thailand	$5,474	Cambodia	$946
Italy	$33,049	Jamaica	$5,472	Chad	$885
Israel*	$31,281	Ecuador	$5,456	Kenya	$862
Spain	$29,195	Algeria	$5,404	Zimbabwe	$788
South Korea	$22,590	Serbia	$5,190	Haiti	$771
Slovenia	$22,092	Jordan	$4,945	Benin	$752
Greece	$22,083	Tonga	$4,494	Bangladesh	$747
Portugal	$20,182	Bosnia and Herzegovina	$4,447	Nepal	$707
Czech Republic	$18,608	Tunisia	$4,237	Mali	$694
Trinidad and Tobago	$17,934	Albania	$4,149	Sierra Leone	$635
Slovak Republic	$16,934	Ukraine	$3,867	Rwanda	$620
Chile	$15,363	Paraguay	$3,813	Tanzania	$609
Uruguay	$14,449	El Salvador	$3,777	Guinea	$591
Lithuania	$14,150	Mongolia	$3,673	Mozambique	$579
Russian Federation	$14,037	Guyana	$3,584	Uganda	$547
Latvia	$14,009	Indonesia	$3,557	Central African Rep.	$473
Croatia	$13,227	Georgia	$3,508	Ethiopia	$470
Venezuela	$12,767	Kosovo	$3,453	Madagascar	$447
Poland	$12,708	Guatemala	$3,368	Liberia	$422
Hungary	$12,622	Armenia	$3,338	Niger	$383
Argentina	$11,558	Syria	$3,289	Congo-Brazzaville	$272
Gabon	$11,430	Egypt	$3,187	Malawi	$268

Source: World Bank Indicators, 2012, http://data.worldbank.org/indicator/NY.GDP.PCAP.CD.
*2011 Data.

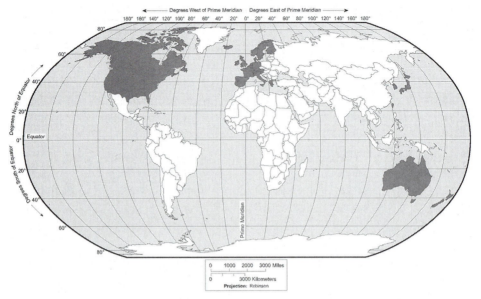

Figure 9.2. Industrial Societies in the Early Twenty-First Century Are Darkened.
Source: Adapted from the Arizona Geographic Alliance. Used with permission.

When we consider the distribution of these societies on a map of the world (see Figure 9.2), it becomes clear that nearly all of the technologically most advanced societies are in temperate regions, while nearly all of the least advanced are located in tropical or semitropical regions. This is no coincidence. Rather, it is an indication of the tremendous importance of the *biophysical environment.* As we have noted before, environmental variables, such as climate, the quality of soils, and the prevalence of disease have had an enormous impact on societal development, not only in the distant past but also in the modern era. Although little attention has been paid to these variables by even the most eminent of scholars,[61] they have been a kind of "hidden" factor in the developmental process, greatly favoring some societies and badly handicapping others.[62]

In the remainder of this chapter and in those that immediately follow, we will be concerned with the small minority of societies that are highly industrialized. Our goal is to see how the new technology they have created has transformed the conditions of life for the hundreds of millions of people living in them. Then, in Chapter 14, we will turn to developing societies, which retain far more of the elements of their preindustrial past.

CONSEQUENCES OF THE INDUSTRIAL REVOLUTION

From an early date it was clear that the Industrial Revolution involved more than just a change in the techniques of production: it was also producing far-reaching changes in virtually every aspect of human life. Though our chief concern in this volume is with the long-run consequences of the revolution, we cannot ignore its impact on the lives of those who were first exposed to it and the new social order to which it gave rise.

During the Early Stages of the Industrial Revolution, Numbers of Children Were Employed in Factories Both in the United States and Britain: Textile Mill Employees in North Carolina, 1908.

Initial Consequences

The first indication of serious change came with the invention of the new spinning and weaving machines in the late eighteenth century. Because of their greatly increased size and weight, they required specially constructed buildings and either steam engines or waterfalls to power them. In short, the new technology necessitated the creation of factories.

Factories, however, required a concentrated supply of dependable labor. A few of the early ones were built in the open countryside, but their owners quickly found they could not hire enough workers unless they built adjoining tenements and thus, in effect, created new urban settlements. Most factories were built in or near existing towns, and the cry that went out from them for workers coincided with the declining need for labor on the farms.

Although the ensuing migration to urban areas was not new, its *magnitude* was, and most communities were unable to cope with the sudden influx. The migrants were badly prepared for their new way of life. Sanitary practices that had been tolerable in sparsely settled rural areas, for example, became a threat to health, even to life itself, in crowded urban communities.

Equally serious problems resulted from the abrupt disruption of social relationships. Long-standing ties of kinship and friendship were severed and could not easily be replaced, while local customs and institutions that had provided rural villagers with some measure of protection and support were lost for good. Thus, it was an uprooted, vulnerable mass of people who streamed into towns and cities and were thrown into

Children and the Factory System

The following testimony was given by Peter Smart to a parliamentary committee in Britain investigating working conditions in 1832. Similar testimony was provided by numerous others.

Q. Where do you reside?

A. At Dundee.

Q. Have you worked in a mill from your youth?

A. Yes, since I was 5 years of age.

Q. Had you a father and mother in the country at the time?

A. My mother stopped in Perth, about eleven miles from the mill, and my father was in the army.

Q. Were you hired for any length of time when you went?

A. Yes, my mother got 15 shillings for six years, I having my meat and clothes.

Q. What were your hours of labor, as you recollect, in the mill?

A. We began at 4 o'clock in the morning and worked till 10 or 11 at night; as long as we could stand on our feet.

Q. Were you kept on the premises constantly?

A. Constantly.

Q. Locked up?

A. Yes, locked up.

Q. Night and day?

A. Night and day; I never went home while I was at the mill.

Q. Do the children ever attempt to run away?

A. Very often.

Q. Were they pursued and brought back again?

A. Yes, the overseer pursued them and brought them back.

Q. Did you ever attempt to run away?

A. Yes, I ran away twice.

Q. And you were brought back?

A. Yes; and I was sent up to the master's loft, and thrashed with a whip for running away.

Q. Do you know whether the children were, in point of fact, compelled to stop during the whole time for which they were engaged?

A. Yes, they were.

Q. By law?

A. I cannot say by law; but they were compelled by the master; I never saw any law used there but the law of their own hands.

Source: Parliamentary Papers, 1831–1832, vol. XV.

---

situations utterly foreign to them, and into a way of life that often culminated in injury, illness, or unemployment. A multitude of social ills—poverty, alcoholism, crime, vice, mental and physical illness, personal demoralization—were endemic.

Local officials had neither the means nor the will to cope with rampant problems in housing, health, education, and crime. Cities and towns became more crowded, open space disappeared, and people accustomed to fields and woodlands found themselves trapped in a deteriorating environment of filthy, crowded streets and tenements; polluted air; and long workdays rarely relieved by experiences of either beauty or hope.[63]

The misery of the new urban dwellers was compounded by the harshness of the factory system, which often operated along quasi-penal lines.[60] Regardless of how hard life had been before, country folk had at least had some control over their own hour-to-hour movements; but now work was, if anything, longer, more arduous, and more restrictive. Women and children, though they had always worked extremely hard in homes and fields, now worked in factories with dangerous, noisy machinery and in dark and dangerous mines. Minor infractions of complex rules, such as whistling on the job or leaving a lamp lit a few minutes too long after sunrise, led to fines, and more serious infractions to floggings. One observer of the period wrote poignantly of hearing children, whose families could not afford clocks, running through the streets in the dark, long before the mills opened, so fearful were they of being late.[64]

The immediate effects of industrialization have been traumatic for vast numbers of people in virtually every society that has made the transition from agrarianism. The details have varied, but the suffering has been no less acute in socialist societies than in capitalist. Whether life for the new urban working class was better or worse than it had been for the peasants and the urban lower classes of the old agrarian societies is still a matter of debate.[62] But one point is not debatable: the transition to an industrial economy has exacted a cruel price in terms of human suffering and demoralization for countless millions of people.

Long-Run Consequences: An Overview

In subsequent chapters we will examine in detail the new societies and the distinctive life patterns that have resulted from two centuries of industrialization. For the moment, however, we will note just a few of the most important and most striking consequences. Collectively, these changes in population, social organization, ideology, and language add up to a revolution without parallel in human history, from the standpoint of scope as well as speed.

1. World population has multiplied tenfold (from 725 million to more than seven billion) just since 1750, a rate of growth more than fifteen times higher than the rate between the time of Jesus and 1750.
2. The rural-urban balance within societies has been reversed: agrarian societies were approximately 90 percent rural, whereas several advanced industrial societies are more than 80 percent urban.
3. The largest urban communities of the industrial era are more than thirty times the size of the largest of the agrarian era.
4. Women in industrial societies give birth to only a small fraction (e.g., one-quarter or one-fifth) of the number of children borne by women in preindustrial societies.
5. Life expectancy at birth is nearly three times greater in advanced industrial societies than it was in agrarian.
6. The family, for the first time in history, is no longer a significant *productive* unit in the economy.
7. The role and status of women in the economy and in society at large have changed substantially.
8. The role and status of youth have also changed, and youth cultures have become a significant factor in the life of industrial societies.
9. The average per capita production and consumption of goods and services in advanced industrial societies is nearly fifteen times that of advanced agrarian societies.
10. The division of labor is vastly more complex.
11. Hereditary monarchical government has disappeared in industrial societies, except occasionally as a ceremonial and symbolic survival, and the proprietary theory of the state has vanished entirely.
12. The functions and powers of government have been vastly enlarged.

13. Free, public education systems have been established, and illiteracy has been largely eliminated in industrial societies.

14. New ideologies have spread widely (notably republicanism, socialism, capitalism, nationalism, hedonism, environmentalism, and pragmatism), while older ones inherited from the agrarian era have been substantially altered or have declined in influence in industrial societies.

15. To the degree they can meaningfully be compared to agrarian societies, it is estimated that the speed of travel has increased a hundred times and the speed of communication ten million times, rendering the entire planet, in effect, smaller than England in the agrarian era.

16. A global culture has emerged,evidenced in styles of dress, music, language, technology, and organizational patterns (e.g., factories, public schools).

17. Global political institutions (e.g., the United Nations, the World Court) have been established for the first time.

18. Several societies have acquired the capacity to obliterate much of the human population.

All this in only a little more than 250 years!

CHAPTER 10

Industrial Societies

Technologies and Economies

Outline
The Technological Foundation of Industrial Societies
The Economies of Industrial Societies
Globalization: Increasing Integration of the World Economy

There is no sharp line of demarcation that separates industrial societies from what we will refer to later as industrializing societies (see Chapter 14). Levels of industrialization vary by degree, with societies ranging from those, like Luxembourg, Norway, and Switzerland (see Table 9.3), that are highly industrialized to others, like Niger, the Congo, and Malawi, where modern industrial technology has had a very limited impact. If we base our classification of societies primarily on data provided by the World Bank on gross domestic product (GDP) per capita, it appears that there are currently almost thirty societies that are consistently in the top echelon that should be considered industrial societies. These are:

Australia	Germany	Luxembourg	South Korea
Austria	Greece	Netherlands	Spain
Belgium	Iceland	New Zealand	Sweden
Canada	Ireland	Norway	Switzerland
Denmark	Israel	Portugal	United Kingdom
Finland	Italy	Singapore	United States
France	Japan	Slovenia	

It is important to recognize that there are substantial differences even among these societies with respect to their degree of industrialization. Luxembourg, for example, has five times more GDP per capita than does Portugal, and Canada and the United States have more than two times as much. Because of these differences, our focus when discussing industrial societies, in this and following chapters, will be primarily on those societies that have been at the forefront of industrialization.

It should also be noted that the majority of the societies with the highest GDPs per capita are located in western Europe (or are offshoots of them). Ecological-evolutionary theory suggests that this is no mere coincidence.

THE TECHNOLOGICAL FOUNDATION OF INDUSTRIAL SOCIETIES

The best way to appreciate the dramatic difference between an agrarian society and an industrial one is to look at the measurable changes that have occurred as a result of the shift from the older technology to the new, and agricultural productivity is a good place to begin. As Table 10.1 shows, the application of industrial technology to agriculture has had a revolutionary impact on production, making it possible to produce a given quantity of grain, fiber, milk, or meat with only a tiny fraction of the human labor required in the older agrarian technology.* The labor used to produce a given quantity of wheat, corn, cotton, and chicken has been cut 99 percent. In the case of milk and beef, the reductions have been somewhat less but are still dramatic. Because of these advances in agricultural technology, tens of millions of people who would otherwise be working on farms are able to be employed in other ways. As a result, the percentage of farmers and farmworkers in the American labor force dropped from 69 percent in 1840 to less than 2 percent today.[1]

The basic cause of this remarkable trend has been the harnessing of new energy sources. In agrarian societies, people and animals were the chief sources of the energy used in most work activity, such as pushing, pulling, digging, lifting, and cutting. Their efforts were supplemented to some extent by wind power and waterpower. As recently as 1850 these four sources still supplied over 87 percent of the energy used in work activities in the United States. Today, they account for less than 1 percent.[†2] In their stead, industrial societies use coal, petroleum, natural gas, hydroelectric power, and nuclear power. Except for coal, these sources were still untapped in 1850, and even coal had not been used as a substitute for human and animal energy until the invention of the steam engine in the eighteenth century.

Table 10.1   Productivity of American Agriculture, 1800–2009

Production of	Number of Worker Hours Required			
	1800	1910–1917	2009	Percent Reduction
100 bushels of wheat	373	106	4	99
100 bushels of corn	344	135	3	99
1 bale of cotton	601	276	3	99
1,000 pounds of milk	n.a.*	38	2	95
1,000 pounds of beef	n.a.*	46	8	83
1,000 pounds of chicken	n.a.*	95	1	99

Sources: U.S. Department of Commerce, Bureau of the Census, *Historical Statistics of the United States: Colonial Times to 1970*, Series K 445–485; and U.S. Department of Agriculture, National Agricultural Statistics Service, *Agricultural Statistics 2012*, Table 9–20.
*Not ascertained.

---

*In this discussion, we draw heavily on data from the United States because excellent statistical materials make it possible to trace trends back to the nineteenth century.
†Wind and falling water continue to be used to generate *electricity*, which is then harnessed to do work. Because of growing concern about pollution, they have been attracting greater attention in recent years (see Chapter 15).[3]

The Application of Industrial Technology in Farming Has Had a Revolutionary Impact on Production, Making It Possible to Reduce the Labor Required for Many Tasks. The Tree-Canopy Shaker Shown Here Can Harvest 36,000 Pounds of Oranges from One Hundred Trees in Less than Fifteen Minutes—a Task that Would Take Four Pickers an Entire Day.

Not only have energy sources changed, but the quantities used have multiplied enormously. In 1850, all the prime movers in the United States (human bodies, work animals, steam engines in factories, sailing ships, etc.) generated less than nine million horsepower; today, it is a staggering 30 trillion.[4] According to recent figures, when all energy sources are totaled, the United States consumed, in a single year, the equivalent more than *seven tons of oil for every man, woman, and child in the population!*[5]

This remarkable increase in the production and consumption of energy has been closely linked to enormous increases in the production and consumption of a wide variety of other things. In the case of iron and steel, for example, British production multiplied nearly 7,000-fold between 1750 and 1970,[6] while production in the United States increased 12,000-fold from 1820 to 1974.[7] And, although the amount and world share of steel produced in the United States has been declining for several decades,[‡] world production grew more than 60 percent in the first decade of this century.[8]

[‡]Iron and steel production has declined in a number of industrial societies in recent years largely because newer materials, such as aluminum and plastics, have come to replace iron and steel in the manufacture of many things.

The production and consumption of raw materials in modern industrial societies are tremendous. In the most recent year for which figures are available, the United States consumed, on a per capita basis, nearly 5 tons of crushed stone; 715 pounds of cement; 145 pounds of lime; 93 pounds of sulfur, 377 pounds of iron ore; 204 pounds of clay; 203 pounds of gypsum; and 400 pounds of salt, to cite but a few items.[9]

Change in a society's gross national product (GNP), corrected for the effects of inflation, is one of the best ways to measure the magnitude of the technological advance brought about by industrialization.[§] It tells us the extent to which the changes in technology have enhanced a society's ability to produce goods and services. When we compare British society's GNP in 1830 with current figures, we find that there has been a more than *thirtyfold* increase.[10] As striking as this figure is, it is less than one-fourth of the American figure, which shows a more than *140-fold* increase since 1870.[11] As these figures indicate, the technologies of industrial societies are much more powerful and productive than the technologies of even the most advanced agrarian societies of the past. Small wonder that advances in technology have been accompanied by revolutionary changes throughout society.

THE ECONOMIES OF INDUSTRIAL SOCIETIES

In modern industrial societies, the impact of technological innovation is usually registered first in their economies. The economy of a society is, in effect, an institutionalized set of answers to the basic questions of production and distribution: What kinds of goods and services will be produced? By whom and where? In what quantities? At what prices? And by what means will they be allocated to the various members of society?

The way in which these questions are answered reflects, to a large degree, constraints imposed by the environment, by the technology on which a society depends, and by the necessity of keeping the productive system functioning. But it also reflects the beliefs and values—the ideology—of those who control the society. Thus, historically, there were fundamental differences between the economies of the Communist societies of eastern Europe and the Western industrial democracies (see the excursus to Chapter 14). Still today, there are differences among industrial societies, though these differences are not nearly as great as those that existed just twenty years ago.

Before we consider these differences, however, we need to consider the characteristics that are common to the economies of all industrial societies. These shared characteristics are a response to the new technology on which each of these societies depends.

The Urbanization of Production

Prior to the Industrial Revolution, agriculture was the chief form of economic activity, production was centered in rural areas, and farmers were a substantial majority of the labor force. In addition to farming, the rural population often engaged in a variety of crafts during the winter months, using this less demanding period as a time to earn

---

[§]Although it is important to use per capita measures when comparing two or more societies of different sizes (as in Table 9.3), when we compare the same society at two different times, *total* GNP or *total* GDP is the preferred measure, since our goal is to identify the magnitude of the change that has occurred in a society's productive capacity.

additional income. Urban populations were small, and many urban residents were members of the governing class and not actively involved in the labor force. Moreover, many of the urban dwellers who were employed produced nonessential goods and services for the enjoyment of the upper class.

The Industrial Revolution changed all this. As we saw in Chapter 9, new machines required the development of factories and large concentrations of industrial workers. At the same time that new urban industries were generating a growing demand for workers in cities and towns, technological advances in agriculture were reducing the need for workers on farms. As a result, industrialization led to a massive migration of people from rural areas to urban—a migration that only now seems to be nearing its end in the most advanced industrial societies.

The effect of these changes has been to shift the locus of production in societies from rural areas to urban. In most advanced industrial societies today, 3 percent or less of GDP comes from agricultural activity.[12] Equally important, the rural economy of industrial societies has been completely transformed. Many of the people who live in rural areas today commute to work in urban communities, and if they farm at all they do so only on weekends. Similar patterns have also developed in Western societies: by 1970 the majority of American "farmers" were already earning more from nonfarm activities (e.g., work in factories) than from the sale of farm products.[13]

Rise in Productivity and in the Standard of Living

The most striking characteristic of the economies of industrial societies is their remarkable productivity. As we noted earlier, Britain's gross national product has grown more than *thirtyfold* since 1830, and that of the United States more than a *hundredfold* just since 1870. Most other industrialized societies have experienced comparable growth. Because most of this increase in productivity has not been consumed by population growth, there has been an enormous increase in the size of the economic surplus in every industrial society.

In agrarian societies, the modest economic surplus was appropriated by a small minority of the population, and if the rich got richer, the poor generally got poorer. But because today per capita income in Britain is more than *twelve times* what it was in 1830, and in the United States it is *fifteen times* what is was in 1870, it has been possible for the incomes of both elites and nonelites to increase.[14] Precisely how industrialization has affected the *relative shares* of income going to elites and nonelites is an issue we will return to in Chapter 12, but for now it should be noted that the growth in the economic surplus has greatly improved the standard of living for the vast majority of people in industrial societies.

The magnitude of the gains in the living standards of the masses is evident when we compare the lifestyle of the average member of most industrial societies today to that of the typical peasant in agrarian societies of the past, or to that of workers during the early phases of the Industrial Revolution. Most members of industrial societies today enjoy a food supply that is larger, more dependable (i.e., less subject to acute shortages), and of higher quality and greater variety than was available in any agrarian society of the past. Most live in superior housing, with an indoor water supply, plumbing, electricity, usually central heating, and sometimes even air conditioning in warmer climates. The majority of their homes and apartments are equipped with furnishings and appliances that are more than adequate for health and comfort, and some of them would have aroused envy in the elites of agrarian societies of the past. Widespread educational opportunities are available and so is vastly improved health care. Modern transportation and communication systems broaden and enrich their lives and provide them with varied forms of entertainment. And countless other goods and services, unheard of in agrarian societies, are also available to the majority of people in most industrial societies and to a large minority in the rest.

This is not to suggest that life in industrial societies is free of problems: obviously, it is not. But it is clear that industrialization has meant a remarkable improvement in the standard of living for the average individual compared with that of the average individual in preindustrial or early industrial societies. Relative to the peasant masses of the agrarian era, most members of industrial societies live lives of unbelievable affluence and abundance. And there are very few people in these societies whose standard of living approaches the degradation of the expendables of agrarian societies. Even those dependent on public welfare are much better off than that.

The Shift from Labor-Intensive to Capital-Intensive Industries

The basis of the enormous productivity and affluence of modern industrial societies is their fantastic store of technological information. But most of this information would be useless unless it were *converted into capital goods*. Without the complex machines, factories, transportation facilities, power plants, and other capital goods essential to production in an industrial society, the output of its workers would not be much greater than that of workers in agrarian societies.

We can see the importance of capital goods when we compare two contemporary industries, one capital-intensive and the other labor-intensive. The petroleum industry is a good example of the former: it has expensive, highly automated machinery and a small labor force. The retail sales fast-food industry, utilizing simpler and less expensive machines, is far more labor-intensive. Exxon-Mobil, for example, recently reported annual sales of $5,461,638 *per employee,* while the sales of Wal-Mart were about $16,176 per employee per year.[15]

One of the chief reasons for the tremendous growth in per capita GNP in industrial societies has been the massive movement of workers away from small, capital-poor family farms and into capital-intensive industries during the last 150 years. As these farmers joined the urban labor force, their economic contribution increased substantially. Since about 80 percent of the population of the typical agrarian society were food producers, in contrast to a tiny minority—in most cases less than 3 percent—in industrial societies, the impact of that shift has been tremendous.

Today, however, that flow has largely ended, and with it a major boost to economic growth. The small, traditional family farm has been largely replaced by huge agribusinesses that are as capital-intensive as some urban-based industries. To appreciate the changes that have occurred in agriculture, one need only consider vertically integrated Smithfield Foods, recently purchased by the Chinese firm, Shuanghui International Holdings Ltd.[16] Employing a "birth to bacon" approach to pork production that encompasses genetics, artificial insemination, automated feeding, and computer-regulated temperature and ventilation, it generates thirteen billion dollars in revenue a year, and its 973,000–square-foot meatpacking plant in Tar Heel, North Carolina, the world's largest, can process 32,000 hogs a day.[17]

Although agricultural operations on this scale are still unusual, small-scale farming with minimal capitalization is becoming a thing of the past in a growing number of industrial societies. According to the most recent figures available, the average farm in the United States has assets of $934,575 and the largest 8.5 percent of farms account for 63 percent of agricultural sales.[18]

Changes in the Labor Force

The Shift from Primary Industries

From the onset of industrialization there has been a movement of workers out of primary industries, the ones that produce raw materials (i.e., farming, fishing, mining, and forestry). In traditional agrarian societies, these industries provided a livelihood for 80 percent or more of the labor force. With industrialization, most of these people, or their children, gradually moved either into secondary industries, the mills and factories that process the raw materials and turn them into finished products, or into tertiary industries, which provide the great variety of services found in industrial societies—education, health care, police and fire protection, social services, government, retail trade, and so on. As industrialization proceeds, the initial rapid growth in secondary industries slows down considerably, and tertiary industries become the chief area of growth in the economy.

Table 10.2 shows how striking this process has been in the United States, completely transforming the labor force in the last 150 years. From a nearly 70 percent concentration of workers in primary industries, more than 80 percent are now in tertiary industries, and growth in these industries continues at the expense of the other two. Similar trends are found in every industrial society, although growth in the tertiary industries, historically, has been much less pronounced in the societies of eastern Europe.

Table 10.2 Changing Patterns of Employment in the U.S. Labor Force, 1840 to 2010; Percentages Employed in Primary, Secondary, and Tertiary Industries

Year	Primary Industries	Secondary Industries	Tertiary Industries	Total
1840	69	15	16	100
1870	55	21	24	100
1900	40	28	32	100
1930	23	29	48	100
1960	8	30	62	100
1990	3	25	72	100
2000	2	21	77	100
2010	2	16	82	100

Sources: Calculations based on U.S. Dept. of Commerce, Bureau of the Census, *Historical Statistics of the United States: Colonial Times to 1970*, Series D 152–166; U.S. Bureau of the Census, *Statistical Abstract of the United States 2002*, Table 591; and Bureau of Labor Statistics, Table 2.1, Employment by Major Industry Sector, 2012.

Growth of White-Collar Jobs

Another striking change in the labor force has been the rapid expansion of white-collar, or nonmanual, jobs. This trend is especially evident in the United States. At the beginning of the twentieth century, only 17 percent of American workers were employed in white-collar jobs; today, more than 70 percent are in such jobs (see Table 12.4, p. 309).[19]

The rapid growth of white-collar jobs has been associated with the growth of the tertiary, or service, industries. As opportunities for farm employment have declined, opportunities for employment in clerical and sales work, the professions, and management have increased. More recently, jobs in the secondary industries (i.e., manufacturing, construction) have also begun to decline, both in absolute and in relative terms, and this has meant a decline in blue-collar jobs. In 1960, for example, 30 percent of American workers were employed in secondary industries. Today, that figure is only about 16 percent (see Table 10.2).

Increased Employment of Women Outside of Households

Until the twentieth century, most women worked only within households—as wives, mothers, sisters, or daughters in their own family's household, or as servants in someone else's. The Industrial Revolution and the new technology changed this. Today, the majority of women in industrial societies are also employed outside households, working for corporations, state enterprises, and other kinds of work organizations.

In many work organizations, especially in the service sector, a majority of the workers are women. This is particularly true of a number of white-collar jobs that have come to be identified as women's jobs (e.g., nursing, social work, elementary school teaching, secretarial work, clerical work, retail sales work of most kinds). Despite efforts by feminists to discourage the sexual division of labor, it is remarkably persistent, at least partly because of the preference of many women, but also because of the demands of marriage and family life.

Growth in the Size of Work Organizations

Workers today find themselves increasingly in the employ of organizations of enormous size. Governments have become the largest employers of all. The federal government of the United States, for example, currently employs 2.8 million people,** and state and local governments employ an additional 19.8 million.[21] The city of New York alone employs more than 400,000 people.[22] And despite recent downsizing, many private corporations still employ large numbers of workers: Walmart has 2,100,000; IBM 426,751, McDonald's 400,000; United Parcel Service 400,600; and Target 355,000; to name some of the largest.[23]

Increase in Occupational Specialization

Growth in the size of work organizations along with advances in technology have been responsible for yet another important trend: the substantial increase in the level of occupational specialization. Contemporary industrial societies have an astonishing

---

**The increasing practice of outsourcing to contractors renders this a serious underestimate of "actual" employment.[20]

number of highly specialized occupations. The U.S. Department of Labor lists more than 28,000 different kinds of jobs that are found in American society today.[24] The meat-packing industry illustrates the extremes to which occupational specialization is often carried. Forty-hour-a-week jobs in that industry include:

belly opener	gut sorter	rump sawyer
bladder trimmer	head boner	side splitter
brain picker	jowl trimmer	skull grinder
foot cutter	leg skinner	snout puller
gut puller	lung splitter	toe puller

Further increases in specialization seem unlikely in most blue-collar occupations, since extreme specialization appears to be counterproductive: Workers quickly become bored and this often leads to carelessness, hostility, and even sabotage. In many industries, management has responded by diversifying work activities, thus reversing the historic trend toward greater specialization. Indiana Bell Telephone, for example, used to assemble its telephone books in twenty-one steps, each performed by a different clerk. Now, each clerk has responsibility for assembling an entire book, with the result that labor turnover (a sensitive measure of worker morale) was reduced as much as 50 percent.[25] Some years ago, Volvo, the Swedish automobile manufacturer, conducted two experiments to reduce boredom and improve morale. One was a system of job rotation involving work at a variety of highly specialized tasks; the other was a system of teamwork involving groups of three to nine workers who share a common set of responsibilities, choose their own leader, and are paid on the basis of group output.[26] These changes reduced Volvo's annual worker turnover from 40 to 10 percent. Other industries are responding to the problem of boredom by replacing workers with robots and other automated machines.

While the trend toward greater occupational specialization is apparently waning in blue-collar occupations, it is still growing in many kinds of white-collar jobs. This is especially evident in professional and managerial occupations, where many people seem to derive greater satisfaction from their work when their areas of responsibility and expertise are more narrowly defined. This is because professional and managerial occupations usually involve such complex bodies of information that no one can master them entirely; as a result, frustration is more likely to come from too little specialization than from too much. Thus, general practitioners in medicine have been largely replaced by a variety of medical specialists, just as general historians in the academic world have been replaced by specialists in such fields as medieval English history and nineteenth-century German history. In addition, some of the traditional components of professional and managerial jobs are now being performed by machines, and more efficiently. This is true, for example, of some kinds of teaching (e.g., foreign-language instruction, elementary math) and medical diagnosis (e.g., MRI, PET, and CAT scans, computerized laboratory tests).

Formation of Labor Unions

Since the beginnings of the Industrial Revolution, large numbers of workers have found themselves confronted with similar problems and grievances, including long working hours (70-hour workweeks were not uncommon in the past), inadequate pay, dangerous working conditions, abusive supervisors, and lack of job security.

These conditions have led to the formation of labor unions designed to protect and promote the common interests of workers.

In some instances, unions have been organized along craft or trade lines, such as bricklayers and carpenters unions. Others have been organized on an industry-wide basis, as in steelworkers and autoworkers unions. In several instances, unions have been organized on a national basis, with every worker in the entire nation eligible to join.

Prior to the twentieth century, the membership of labor unions consisted almost entirely of blue-collar workers. Now, however, a substantial minority are employed in white-collar jobs. In the United States, for example, a growing proportion of labor union members are white-collar workers, and many of them are public school teachers or other government employees.

The degree to which the current labor forces of industrial societies are unionized varies greatly (see Table 10.3). More than 60 percent of eligible workers in Sweden, Denmark, and Finland are currently members of unions, whereas less than 10 percent are in France.

The change in union membership has also varied greatly across advanced industrial societies. As Table 10.3 shows, in the most recent years for which we have reliable data, union membership declined substantially in the majority of industrial societies. In the United States, although 35 percent of workers were members of unions in 1945, fewer than 12 percent of workers, and fewer than 7 percent of those employed in the *private sector,* are union members today.[27] And, although membership in unions grew substantially in Finland, Belgium, Sweden, and Denmark between 1970 and 2003, in recent years it has declined.

Command and Market Economies

In the prehistoric past, before societies were able to produce a sustained economic surplus, all economies were essentially *subsistence* economies in which each community provided for its own members' needs, and trade and exchange were limited to nonessentials (e.g., feathers, amber, and other objects valued for ceremonial and aesthetic reasons). With the shift from hunting and gathering to farming, conditions changed in a number of important ways. No longer was it necessary for all adults to be food producers. New and more specialized kinds of occupations began to emerge, trade and commerce increased, and political systems developed that were able to impose the will of small political elites on the other members of society.

With these developments, subsistence economies began to be supplemented either by command economies or by market economies. A *command economy* is elitist: basic choices among economic alternatives are made by a tiny political elite. Sometimes these decision makers claim to act on behalf of the population as a whole, but they are not willing to transfer their enormous decision-making power to the larger population on whose behalf they claim to act.

In a *market economy,* in contrast, producers freely exchange what they produce for goods and services produced by others. Prices are set by the forces of supply and demand, that is, by the relative quantity and quality of the various things that are available and by the relative eagerness of would-be consumers. As this suggests, decision making in a market system is considerably more dispersed than in a command economy.

Table 10.3 Percentage of Workers in Labor Unions in Industrial Societies, 2008, and Change in Union Membership, 1970–2003, and 2003–2008

Society	Percentage in Unions, 2008	Percent Change 1970–2003	Percent Change 2003–2008
Sweden	68.3	10.3	−12.4
Denmark	67.6	10.0	−4.0
Finland	67.5	22.8	−8.9
Norway	53.3	−3.5	0.1
Belgium	51.9	13.3	−6.4
Italy	33.4	−3.3	−0.8
Ireland	31.9	−17.9	−9.6
Austria	29.1	−27.3	−17.9
Canada	27.2	−6.5	−4.3
United Kingdom	27.1	−15.5	−7.6
New Zealand	20.6	−33.1	−6.7
Germany	19.1	−9.5	−15.4
Netherlands	18.8	−14.2	−15.6
Australia	18.2	−27.3	−20.4
Japan	18.1	−15.4	−7.9
Switzerland	17.5	−11.2	−1.4
Spain	14.6	3.4	−10.3
United States	11.9	−11.1	−3.9
Korea	10.3	−1.5	−8.2
France	7.6	−13.5	−8.9
Median	23.9	−10.3	−8.1

Sources: The Organisation for Economic Co-operation and Development iLibrary, Trade Union Density, http://www .oecd-ilibrary.org/employment/data/trade-unions/trade-union-density_data-00371-en;jsessionid=2di8s6uo0tj6o .delta?isPartOf=/content/datacollection/lfs-tu-data-en; union membership change from 1970 to 2003 from Jelle Visser, "Union Membership in 24 Countries," *Monthly Labor Review* (January 2006), pp. 38–49, Table 2.

Outsourcing

Perhaps the most important development in the economies of industrial societies in recent years has been the transfer of the production of many goods and services from these societies to others that are much less industrialized and where labor costs are much lower. This process has been going on for a number of years, but has accelerated as advances in the technologies of transportation and communication have driven down the costs of moving goods and services and made them ever cheaper.

An early version of outsourcing developed in the years following World War II when many American textile manufacturers found it profitable to move their production facilities from New England to southern states, such as the Carolinas and Georgia. Fifty years later, these same businesses and others as well began to find it profitable to move their production facilities to Mexico, China, Thailand, and even Mongolia. In Europe, German automobile manufacturers and other western European manufacturers have begun to transfer production facilities to Poland and other parts of formerly Communist eastern Europe.

One of the newest developments in outsourcing has been the transfer of service sector jobs to countries such as India and China. Thanks to inexpensive satellite phone service, this practice has become highly popular with catalogue sales companies and other businesses that employ large numbers of people to handle relatively simple and routine business transactions with the aid of computers. India has been especially attractive in this regard because of the number of people there who speak English (a by-product of British colonial rule). China and India have also both been attractive as places to find skilled programmers who can be hired at a fraction of the cost of programmers in Europe and America.

The chief beneficiaries of outsourcing and the new technologies on which it is based are the high-level managers of multinational corporations and investors in these companies. Although there is considerable criticism of outsourcing because of the loss of large numbers of well-paying jobs in industrial societies, little has been done about it because of the political influence of multinational corporations and their leaders. By contributing heavily to political campaigns, they have been able to ensure, thus far, that politicians do little to interfere. When challenged, politicians

One of the Striking Developments of the Last Century Has Been the Transformation of an Ever-Growing Number of Small, Local Businesses into Multinational Corporations: Walmart Supermarket in Nanjing, China. Walmart, Now a Global Corporation, Began as a Single, Local Retail Store in a Small Town in Arkansas in 1962.

who support outsourcing point to the lower costs to consumers that result from the practice. And it is true that those who are fortunate enough to continue to hold well-paying jobs in industrial societies benefit from outsourcing. Unfortunately, it is quite another story for those who lose their jobs and become unemployed or are forced to take much lower paying ones.

The Rise of Market Economies

The origins of modern market systems can be traced back to the simple barter systems of prehistoric societies. But a full-fledged market economy (i.e., one in which market forces shape the majority of major economic decisions) was not possible until the use of money became widespread and most of the goods and services people valued had acquired a monetary value. In addition, the basic economic resources of land, labor, and capital had to be freed from traditional constraints on their use and transfer. People had to be free to sell ancestral lands when that was profitable; workers had to be free to leave their jobs and take new ones when they could get higher wages or better working conditions; and owners of businesses had to be free to use their capital however they wished. Restraints on economic activity based on family sentiments, religious taboos, social customs, or organizational restrictions (guild restrictions on output, for example, or legal restrictions on the movement of serfs and slaves) had to be substantially reduced or eliminated. In short, individual economic advantage, as measured in monetary terms, had to become the decisive determinant of economic action.

The High Temple of Capitalism: The New York Stock Exchange in Lower Manhattan.

As we saw in Chapter 9, the discovery of the New World gave a powerful impetus to the first requirement: The great flow of gold and silver led to the emergence of a money economy in western Europe. At the same time, a series of ideological changes weakened traditional social bonds that had previously immobilized both people and property. These same factors also sparked the Industrial Revolution, and once that was under way and the economy had changed further, the effects became cumulative. Each change stimulated further change; the more resources that came under the control of western Europe's entrepreneurial class, the better able they were to promote other changes.

By the end of the nineteenth century it looked as if every industrial society would soon have a market economy. Industrial societies were coming increasingly under the control of political parties that were dominated by businessmen committed to the philosophy of laissez-faire capitalism, or free enterprise. Following the teachings of Adam Smith, this new governing class argued that the most productive economy, and the most beneficial, was one in which governmental restrictions were held to a minimum.

Moves Toward Mixed Economies

It was not long, however, before it became evident that the new market economy was not the unmixed blessing its enthusiasts made it out to be. In their pursuit of profits, businessmen often adopted practices that were harmful to others. In an attempt to cut labor costs, many employers fired adult workers and replaced them with children, simultaneously creating adult unemployment and endangering the health and welfare of children. Efforts to reduce costs also led to dangerous working conditions and the production of shoddy, even unsafe, merchandise.

Protests were soon raised, sometimes by social reformers like Robert Owen, sometimes by poets and novelists like Thomas Hood and Upton Sinclair. Even before the middle of the nineteenth century, the British Parliament began enacting legislation to protect society against the extremes of free enterprise. The Factory Acts of 1833 and 1844, the Mines Act of 1842, and the Ten Hour Law of 1847 prohibited the employment of children under the age of nine in textile factories, restricted children under thirteen to six and a half hours of work per day in factories, forbade the employment of boys under ten and women in the mines, limited women and young people aged thirteen to eighteen to ten working hours per day, and provided for inspectors to enforce these laws.[28] By 1901 the minimum age for child labor in England was raised to twelve, and in 1908 limitations were finally imposed on the working hours of men. Other legislation forced employers to provide for the safety of their employees in dangerous industries and established the first minimum wage.

None of these reforms would have come about, however, without the efforts of workers themselves. By the latter part of the eighteenth century, small groups of workers had already begun banding together to negotiate with their employers on wages, hours, and working conditions. During the nineteenth century, the labor movement had many ups and downs, but by 1900 there were two million members of labor unions in Britain and nearly a million each in the United States and Germany.[29]

Before that date, however, another major defect in the market system had become evident. There was a tendency for it to lose its competitive character and evolve in the direction of monopolies. This danger was greatest in older, established industries in

Children Often Performed Hard Labor in Early Industrial Societies: Boys Working in a U.S. Coal Mine Circa 1903.

which there was little technological innovation and in which *fixed costs* were a significant part of total costs.

Fixed costs are costs of production that do not increase in proportion to the quantity of goods produced. The costs of designing, tooling, and advertising a new-model car, for example, are all fixed costs: they remain essentially the same whether five million cars of that model are produced or only one million. As a result, the company that sells five million cars can usually either price its cars less than its competitors or offer a better car for the same money. Either way, the larger company tends, over time, to win an ever larger share of the market, which increases its advantage even more.[‡‡]

[‡‡]General Motors enjoyed this kind of advantage in the American automobile market until the 1970s when sharp increases in the price of gasoline made fuel efficiency of prime importance to consumers and to the American government, which began to mandate more fuel-efficient vehicles. This created a unique opportunity for Japanese automakers, who had long been producing small, fuel-efficient cars. In addition, Japanese labor costs were substantially lower than those in the United States, and by the 1970s the cost of transporting cars overseas had declined dramatically. The final straws that broke the camel's back and destroyed General Motors' longtime market advantage were (1) the enormous and increasingly inefficient managerial bureaucracy that had been allowed to develop over the years, which left the company without the leadership it needed to adjust to rapidly and drastically changing conditions; and (2) a union that was equally slow to recognize the threat posed by Japanese automakers and that refused to make concessions when this became imperative. As a result, General Motors' share of the American market has steadily declined for thirty years despite the enormous advantage it once enjoyed simply by virtue of its once huge market share.

Table 10.4 Illustration of How Fixed Costs Contribute to the Growth of Monopolies in a Free Enterprise System

Time Period and Firm	Number of Units Sold	Variable Costs*	Fixed Costs*	Total Costs	Cost per Unit**
Time I:					
Company A	10,000	$10,000	$5,000	$15,000	$1.50
Company B	9,000	9,000	5,000	14,000	1.56
Company C	8,000	8,000	5,000	13,000	1.63
Time II:					
Company A	11,500	11,500	5,000	16,500	1.43
Company B	8,500	8,500	5,000	13,500	1.59
Company C	7,000	7,000	5,000	12,000	1.71
Time III:					
Company A	13,000	13,000	5,000	18,000	1.38
Company B	8,000	8,000	5,000	13,000	1.63
Company C	6,000	6,000	5,000	11,000	1.83

*Variable costs need not be exactly proportional to sales volume, and fixed costs need not be exactly identical for all firms, but they are shown this way to make the essential principles clearer.

** Cost per unit equals total cost divided by number of units sold.

Table 10.4 illustrates how, in an industry in which fixed costs are relatively great compared to variable costs, the company that has the highest volume of sales has a *growing competitive advantage*. Note that the amount that the three companies in the example spend on variable costs varies directly with the number of units each produces—$1 per unit. But fixed costs are the same for each company—$5,000—regardless of how many units it produces. Thus, the differences in "cost per unit" are due entirely to the influence of fixed costs. Note also that the initial pricing advantage enjoyed by Company A because of its initial high volume of sales enables that company to gain a growing share of the market, and, with it, an increasing ability to undersell its competitors. As this example illustrates, if pure market forces were allowed to operate with no restrictions, smaller competitors would eventually be forced out of business in any industry in which fixed costs are a significant part of total costs.

In an effort to prevent the growth of monopolies, the United States passed the Sherman Antitrust Act in 1890. Although it has not been vigorously enforced, this act has served as a deterrent. A number of industries might now be dominated by a single company had not the managers of the leading firms been fearful of the legal consequences. For example, economists and even industry leaders have testified before Congress that economies of scale made it possible for General Motors (GM) to undersell its American competitors by a substantial margin for many years. But rather than face antitrust action, GM's managers chose to price their cars competitively, thereby increasing their profits while perhaps offering their customers a bit more car for the money.[30]

The situation in which an industry is dominated not by a single firm but by a very few of them is known as *oligopoly*. This has become common in capitalist societies. Table 10.5 gives some idea of the range of corporate concentration across industries in

Table 10.5 Percentage of Production by the Four Largest Companies in Selected Industries in the United States

Industry	Percentage	Industry	Percentage
Cigarettes	98	Battery manufacturing	58
Breweries	89	Tortillas	57
Light trucks	84	Explosives	52
Breakfast cereals	80	Iron and steel mills	51
Small arms ammunition	79	Petroleum refining	47
Tires	73	Fluid milk	46
Bottled water	72	Coffee and tea	43
Dog and cat food	71	Small arms	35
Distillers	69	Pharmaceuticals	29
Turbines	68	Newspapers*	20
Soap and detergent	67	Computers	17

Source: U.S. Department of Commerce, Bureau of the Census, *American Factfinder*, (ECO731SR) Manufacturing, Subject Series: Concentration Ratios 2007 Economic Census.
*Share of circulation among top 100 newspapers computed from data reported by Infoplease, http://www.infoplease .com/ipea/A0004420.html.

the United States today. As a rough rule of thumb, economists consider an industry oligopolistic when as few as four companies control 50 percent or more of production.[31] This standard can be deceptive, however, because the degree of national concentration means different things in different industries, depending chiefly on whether the market is local, regional, or national. The newspaper industry in the United States, for example, might appear highly competitive since, according to recent data, the four largest companies produce only about 20 percent of the papers. But a moment's reflection reminds us that most newspapers produce for a local market, and in most communities the paper or papers are owned by a single person or firm.[32] Since the same is true of a number of other industries as well, Table 10.5 may actually *understate* the extent of oligopoly in some industries.

Where oligopoly prevails, the law of supply and demand often stops functioning, primarily because collusion between firms is so easy. Collusion can take various forms. A fairly common practice in the construction industry is *bid rigging,* whereby firms get together and decide among themselves who will take which job and then bid accordingly, with the "low" bid set as high as they dare. *Price leading,* a perfectly legal practice, appears to be standard procedure in several major industries: one firm, usually the largest, sets its prices at a level that ensures profits for all and maximizes profits for itself. In this situation, competition is largely restricted to secondary matters, such as design and advertising.

Another development that has weakened the role of market forces has been the increase in what is known as *vertical integration,* the process by which a company gains control of companies in other industries that either supply it with materials or buy its products.[33] A furniture manufacturer, for example, buys up a number of lumber companies and sawmills to provide its raw materials and then buys into retail establishments that sell the furniture it produces. In this way, it eliminates many of the uncertainties of the market situation. Another device with a similar purpose is the establishment of interlocking directorates, which bring the top officials or directors of a company on which one depends for some essential commodity onto the controlling board of one's own company. This device is widely used to bring officers of major banks onto the boards of firms that require ready access to large amounts of capital.[34]

Finally, the market system has been weakened by the nature of military technology. Modern warfare requires the mobilization of all of a nation's economic resources. Obviously this effort must be planned and implemented far in advance of the outbreak of hostilities. In societies that wish to maintain a strong military position, this inevitably leads to the development of a military-industrial complex from which most elements of the market system are eliminated. For one thing, there is only one buyer for the product, the government. In addition, there is frequently only one producer, and seldom more than a handful, for a particular weapons system. The situation is prejudicial to an open market in yet another way: the military is not inclined to shop around for bargains, because this increases security risks, and truly competitive bidding encourages companies to cut corners and turn out defective products. So long as the military has the taxing power of the government behind it, it has little motivation to economize. Thus, there is a natural tendency for market forces to be replaced by the principles of command in the vast and important area of military procurement, even in societies whose leaders are committed to the principles of free enterprise.

We can summarize most of the foregoing by saying that the experience of the last two hundred years has revealed *three basic flaws in market systems.* First, not only do they fail to protect the weaker and more vulnerable members of society, such as workers and consumers, but they also compel the strong to act ruthlessly if they wish to remain strong. Second, the market system has what might be called a built-in tendency to self-destruct, which causes most free competitive markets to evolve into oligopolistic or monopolistic markets unless checked by governmental intervention. Finally, the market system cannot respond adequately to many or most of the needs of society as a whole, as contrasted with the needs and desires of individuals.

This final flaw is particularly evident during societal crises, such as wars, depressions, or environmental crises. As long as individuals and organizations are free to act according to what they perceive as their own best interests, the more selfish ones tend to win out. A corporation that responds voluntarily to environmental problems by installing expensive antipollution devices, for example, may well find itself at a competitive disadvantage with firms that do not.

For a variety of reasons, then, even those societies that have remained ideologically most committed to the market system and to the principle of free enterprise now have what can only be described as *mixed market–command economies.* The nature of the economic mix varies considerably from society to society, with governmental intervention in, and control of, the economy being greater in Scandinavia and western Europe and less in Japan, the United States, and Canada. But even where market elements are predominant, the role of government in the economic life of societies is enormous. Businesses are obliged to operate within limits set by an increasingly complex system of governmental regulations. Minimum wage laws must be observed, government-prescribed safety standards maintained, and compulsory social insurance payments for workers made, to name but three of the many controls that the governments of industrial societies now exercise.

A good measure of the greatly increased power of government in the economic life of all Western industrial societies is the growth in the percentage of GDP that governments control through taxes and use to support various activities. As Table 10.6 indicates, the governments of industrial societies, on average, spent less than 10 percent of their societies' GDPs in 1870, and now spend more than 45 percent. Even more striking is the fact that the United States, which still ranks fairly low among industrial societies in government spending, experienced a more than tenfold increase in this period.

Finally, it should be noted that in most of the societies of Europe, major industries, such as steel, telecommunications, auto manufacturing, airlines, and utilities, have, until recently, been operated as state enterprises. In a survey conducted some years ago, it was found that the majority of the most basic industries in all but one of those societies were state owned.[35] More recently, however, several of these societies have decided that a number of these industries could be operated more efficiently as private enterprises subject to governmental regulation rather than as purely state enterprises.

Viewed from a sociological perspective, the mixed economies that have evolved in industrial societies during the last hundred years reflect an effort by the members of these societies to achieve two goals that seem, to some degree at least, mutually contradictory. On the one hand, they want the economic growth and higher standard of living that market systems seem better able to provide. On the other hand, they also

Table 10.6 Government Spending as a Percentage of GDP, 1870–2013

Society	1870	1920	1960	2013
France	12.6	27.6	34.6	56.6
Belgium	*	*	30.3	53.6
Austria	*	14.7	35.7	51.2
Italy	11.9	22.5	30.1	50.8
Sweden	5.7	8.1	31.0	50.7
Netherlands	9.1	13.5	33.7	50.3
United Kingdom	9.4	26.2	32.2	45.6
Germany	10.0	25.0	32.4	44.7
Norway	3.7	13.7	29.9	44.1
Japan	8.8	14.8	17.5	41.4
Canada	*	13.3	28.6	40.8
United States	3.9	7.0	27.0	39.5
Australia	*	*	21.2	36.6
Switzerland	*	4.6	17.2	32.9
Average	8.3	15.9	28.7	45.6

Sources: *The Economist*, Sept. 20, 1997; The Organisation for Economic Co-operation and Development, *General Government Accounts* http://www.oecd-ilibrary.org/economics/data/general-government-accounts_na-gga-data-en;jsessionid=i9kjn6hae3bi.delta; and DataMarket http://datamarket.com/.
*No data available.

want the economic security and attention to the needs of society that command econ-omies seem better equipped to provide.

Small groups of ideologues continue to argue for a purer type of economic system, but the majority of citizens in industrial societies seem to prefer the more pragmatic ap-proach represented by a mixed market-command economy. While people argue end-lessly over details of the mix, there seems to be limited popular support for abandoning or substantially reducing either of the two basic components of the mixed economy.

Evolution of the Modern Corporation

In the preindustrial past, most economic activity was carried on as a family enterprise. Today, this is no longer true; the corporation has become the dominant form of busi-ness organization, especially in industrial societies.

The corporate form of organization first appeared in Europe in the early Middle Ages when governments began to grant charters to towns, universities, religious orders, and guilds. These charters established them as legal entities with rights and responsi-bilities separate and distinct from those of the individuals who were their members.

The concept of a governmentally chartered corporation with legal rights and re-sponsibilities was first extended to a profit-making enterprise in the year 1600 under Queen Elizabeth I with the incorporation of the newly formed East India Company; not long thereafter charters were also granted to the Hudson's Bay Company and the Royal African Company.[36] Later in the seventeenth century, the Dutch and French gov-ernments followed suit. These new entities were all semipublic institutions, serving si-multaneously as agents of their governments as well as profit-making enterprises.

From an economic standpoint, corporations offered one very great advantage over the traditional family-owned business. They made it feasible for wealthy families to un-dertake the substantial risks of investing large amounts of capital in a business that re-quired outfitting costly fleets of sailing ships to travel halfway round the world at a time when their safe return was far from assured. In effect, by joining and pooling just a part of the resources of any single family, these families were able to minimize the risk of finan-cial disaster while enjoying the opportunity to share in potentially enormous profits.

Over the years, a variety of changes were made in the nature of corporations, mostly to make them more attractive to those who controlled them, but sometimes to make them more accountable to the public. For example, they gradually ceased to be agents of the governments that chartered them and became increasingly the profit-making organizations we know today.

Another important change came in the nineteenth century when the concept of *limited liability* was adopted. Prior to the nineteenth century, stockholders in most corporations had unlimited liability: in case of bankruptcy they could lose not only their investment in the company but all their personal property as well. This naturally made investors extremely cautious; unless they had intimate knowledge of a business and those running it, they were taking an enormous risk. The passage of laws limiting the liability of stockholders to the investment itself greatly stimulated the flow of capi-tal into this new form of enterprise.

In industrial societies today, nearly all the largest and most powerful private en-terprises are corporations. In the United States in recent years, for example, more than 70 percent of businesses with annual receipts of one million dollars or more have been corporations, and the net profit of corporations was twice that of partnerships and nearly four times that of (nonfarm) proprietorships.[37] Moreover, for some time now, the very largest concerns, those with annual profits in the hundreds of millions or billions of dollars, have all been corporations.[38]

As corporations have grown, there has been a tremendous change in their character, especially with respect to their control. The largest ones are rarely controlled by the people who own them (i.e., the stockholders); they are controlled by employees who have been hired to manage them, especially their CEOs.[39] This shift is a consequence of the fragmentation of stock ownership that has accompanied the enormous growth in size of these organizations. In some corporations, no one owns even as much as 1 percent of the stock, and most stockholders own only a minute fraction of 1 percent. Furthermore, the stockholders are scattered around the world. Mobilizing a majority of the owners of voting stock to wrest control from the managers is extraordinarily difficult and expensive.

The character of the corporation was also altered during the twentieth century by increasing government control. As we have seen, this intervention of government into the economy was a response to the inherent defects of an unregulated market system. Over the years, the scope of government involvement in corporations has steadily increased, creating some problems while alleviating others. Many economic questions that were once resolved by the forces of supply and demand came to be decided by governmental action. For example, the governments of virtually all industrial societies have introduced and enforce rules governing conditions of employment (e.g., minimum wages, maximum hours, maternity and paternity leave, treatment of the handicapped, worker safety, etc.) as well as regulations governing the quality of products, such as food and drugs, and the truthfulness of marketing practices.

Corporate leaders have not been content, however, merely to sit back and let government extend its influence over the operation of their businesses. On the contrary, they have fought back vigorously and with considerable success. More than a hundred years ago, in 1884, American President Rutherford B. Hayes declared, "This is a government of the people, by the people, and for the people no longer. It is a government of the corporations, by the corporations, and for the corporations."[40]

Through the use of huge campaign contributions and skillful lobbying of politicians, many highly profitable corporations have managed to have laws written in such a way that they are able to avoid paying any tax at all on their profits. Many businesses have even managed to obtain substantial governmental subsidies. Thus, the relationship between corporations and the governments of industrial societies is constantly in flux as corporate leaders seek to minimize the influence of governmental regulations and restraints and as public pressures exercised through the political process seek to set limits on the actions of these leaders and their organizations.

GLOBALIZATION: INCREASING INTEGRATION OF THE WORLD ECONOMY

One of the most striking developments of the industrial era has been the rapidly expanding web of economic relations among and between societies worldwide. Human societies have exchanged goods with one another since prehistoric times, but the volume of trade was always small because of the limitations of technology. Since the cost of transporting goods was often greater than the cost of producing them, intersocietal trade was largely restricted, for thousands of years, to small items of substantial value, especially luxury goods produced for elites.

With advances in ship construction and navigational technology in the thirteenth, fourteenth, and fifteenth centuries, the volume of international trade began to increase. By 1850, the volume of goods exchanged was six times what it had been in 1750, and in 1950, it was twenty times what it was in 1850.[41] At the end of the last century, the dollar value of international trade (corrected for inflation) was growing at a rate that would be equivalent to a 400-fold increase if it lasted a century.[42]

Table 10.7 Trade as a Percentage of GDP, 2011

Society	Trade as a Percentage of GDP
Singapore	386.8
Luxembourg	321.8
Ireland	187.9
Belgium	167.4
Netherlands	157.1
Slovenia	144.5
Austria	111.3
South Korea	110.1
Iceland	109.7
Denmark	101.6
Germany	95.3
Sweden	93.7
Switzerland	91.6
Finland	82.3
Portugal	75.8
Israel	71.5
Norway	69.7
United Kingdom	66.6
Canada	62.1
Spain	61.3
Italy	59.1
New Zealand	59.0
Greece	58.2
France	56.8
Australia	40.8
United States	31.7
Japan	31.2
Median	**82.3**

Source: World Bank, *World Development Indicators*, online database, http://databank.worldbank.org/data.

Note: A percentage greater than 100 indicates that the sum of imports and exports combined was greater than all the goods and services produced within the society that year.

The result of this trend has been a substantial increase in the division of labor among societies and a growing economic integration of the world system. The other side of the coin, of course, is that societies are steadily declining in economic self-sufficiency. As Table 10.7 shows, the value of trade is now 60 percent or more of GDP in most advanced industrial societies.

The societies of western Europe have moved further in this direction than other industrial societies and have formed the European Union, whose goal is the integration of the economies of the member societies. This development could be the prelude to political unification and the formation of a new multinational society embracing much of Europe.

In the world system as a whole, movement toward economic and political unification is far less advanced, but a number of international organizations—economic and political—have emerged, most of them in the last half-century. These include the International Monetary Fund, the Food and Agriculture Organization, the World Bank, the International Labor Organization, the World Health Organization, the International Court of Justice, and the United Nations.

One of the striking developments of the last century has been the transformation of an ever-growing number of businesses into multinational corporations. Some now have a greater volume of sales outside their home countries than within them. Sixty percent of Coca-Cola's revenues, for example, are outside the United States, and McDonald's now operates in one hundred countries.[43] Sony, a leading Japanese corporation, makes

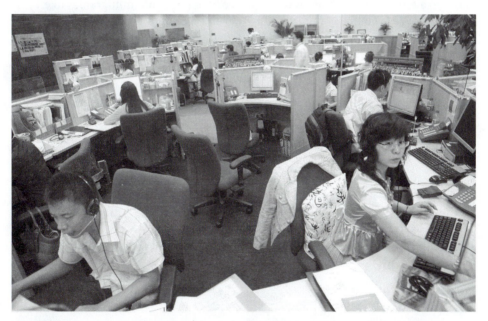

With Globalization, Both Workers and Jobs Often Move Overseas: Chinese Employees Working in Cubicles at the Hewlett-Packard Call Center in Dalian, China. In the Last Decade, Hewlett-Packard Co., IBM Corp., Britain's BT Group PLC and Some 230 Foreign Companies Have Flocked to Dalian to Set Up Business Software and Outsourcing Facilities, Creating a New Center for a Multibillion-Dollar Global Industry.

three-quarters of its sales abroad, and more than three-quarters of the sales of GlaxoSmithKline, a British-owned drug manufacturer, are outside of Europe.[44] Multinational corporations not only increasingly sell their products or services abroad but, as we have noted (see Outsourcing, pp. 257–259), increasingly produce abroad as well. In many cases, corporations based in industrial societies manufacture products in third world societies to take advantage of cheaper labor.

Economic integration is further heightened through foreign-aid programs and foreign loans, the latter provided by private corporations as well as by governments and intergovernmental bodies like the World Bank. Banks in Europe, Japan, and North America have extended tens of billions of dollars of loans to third world societies. Nor is borrowing limited to the third world: the United States has become the world's largest debtor nation.

Finally, integration of the world economy is taking the form of massive movements of workers among societies. Some of this movement involves managers, technical specialists, and other highly skilled workers in multinational corporations who accept assignments in foreign countries for months or years at a time. Far more often, however, it is poorly educated, unskilled workers migrating—legally or illegally—from less developed societies in Asia, Africa, and Latin America to advanced industrial societies in Europe and North America where they often displace less skilled native-born workers who are unwilling or unable to work for substandard wages. Sweatshop employers and others who profit from hiring these immigrants use their substantial political clout to protect and encourage both legal and illegal immigration, since it enables them to hold wages to a minimum for millions of workers, native-born and immigrants alike.

The future is not likely to see any significant reversal of the trend toward greater economic integration within the world system of societies. The technologies of communication and transportation have advanced to the point where economic ties between societies are almost as easy to create and sustain as ties within societies. Today, no nation—and few large corporations—can afford to be isolated from the expanding economic network of the world system.

CHAPTER 11

Industrial Societies
Ideologies and Polities

Outline

As we saw in the last chapter, industrialization has increased the size of economic surpluses and fundamentally altered the nature of the labor forces and economies of industrial societies. In the process, it has greatly expanded the range of what people are able to do and, thereby, has greatly increased the potential impact of ideologies and collective decision making on social life. Knowledge of the key tenets of modern ideologies and of their relationship with political institutions is essential to an understanding of industrial societies and more especially the differences among them. Therefore, before we trace the development of modern industrial politics and consider the impact of the mass media on politics and life, we will first explore the origins and key elements of the dominant ideologies of the industrial era.

IDEOLOGIES IN INDUSTRIAL SOCIETIES

During the last five centuries the bounds of human knowledge have expanded enormously. The voyages of exploration that began in the fifteenth century gave humans their first accurate view of the earth as a whole. Astronomers of the sixteenth and seventeenth centuries did the same for the solar system. More recently, the natural sciences have given us a vision of a universe of incredible complexity, whose age is measured in billions of years and whose size must be expressed in billions of light-years. And, finally, in the last hundred years, the social sciences have begun the task of demythologizing the social order, challenging ancient beliefs about the nature of man, and subjecting virtually every aspect of human life to systematic scrutiny.

Theistic Religions

This flood of new information about ourselves and the world we live in has shaken and unsettled many traditional beliefs, and the institutional systems based on them.

This is especially evident in the case of theistic religions. The thought forms of the great historic faiths—Judaism, Christianity, Islam, Hinduism, and Buddhism—bear the imprint of the agrarian era during which they developed. But beliefs about the natural world and the social order that were "self-evident" during the agrarian era often appear alien and antiquated to members of industrial societies. This has created an acute crisis for theistic faiths in industrial societies. Religious leaders have tried, in many cases, to translate the most important elements of their traditions into modern terms, while steering a course between irrelevant orthodoxy and heretical innovation. The turmoil and controversy within the Roman Catholic Church created by Vatican Council II was but one in a series of intellectual crises that began at the time of Copernicus and Galileo.

Not surprisingly, given its origins and history, the United States is more religious than most other industrial societies. For example, although surveys have shown that many people in industrial societies call themselves believers, a *strong* belief in god is widespread only in the United States and Israel (see Table 11.1).[1] And, while the percentage of people claiming to have attended religious services in the previous week

Table 11.1 Percent in Industrial Societies Certain God Exists, by Age

	Under 28	Over 68	Difference
Israel	69.1	52.7	+16.4
United States	53.8	66.0	−12.2
Portugal	41.4	75.4	−34.0
Italy	35.9	66.7	−30.8
Ireland	29.5	70.1	−40.6
Spain	21.8	65.4	−43.6
Netherlands	20.8	34.3	−13.5
New Zealand	18.8	30.2	−11.4
Germany (Old West)	17.8	36.4	−18.6
Slovenia	17.6	39.1	−21.5
Switzerland	15.6	42.2	−26.6
Australia	14.7	36.7	−22.0
Great Britain	9.2	22.3	−13.1
Norway	8.5	18.3	−9.8
Sweden	8.4	14.9	−6.5
Denmark	8.1	22.3	−14.2
France	7.9	25.7	−17.8
Austria	7.7	31.9	−24.2
Japan	2.0	7.8	−5.8
Germany (Old East)	0.0	12.7	−12.7
Median	16.6	35.4	−16.0

Source: Adapted from NORC/University of Chicago, Tom Smith, "Beliefs about God Across Time and Countries," April 18, 2012, Table 8, http://www.norc.org/PDFs/Beliefs_about_God_Report.pdf.

has remained basically unchanged at about 40 percent for more than sixty years in the United States, Canadians reporting attendance in the previous week dropped from 60 percent in 1945 to about 20 percent in recent years.[2] In Ireland, the decline has been even more striking. Weekly attendance at Mass dropped from 91 percent in 1973 to 34 percent in 2005.[3]

There is also evidence that substantial numbers of "believers" in western Europe doubt fundamental tenets of their religions, such as life after death and the existence of hell or the devil.[4] Moreover, when asked to choose from a list of possibilities those things that are especially important to encourage in children, less than 8 percent, on average, chose religion.[5] In virtually all industrial societies people are placing increasing faith in new *secular* ideologies in their efforts to solve their own and their societies' problems.

Finally, what is especially striking about religious belief in industrial societies is its strong correlation with age. In all but Israel, younger people are much less likely to be strong believers than older ones. In Ireland, for example, 70 percent of men and women aged sixty-eight or older reported that they were certain God exists, but slightly less than 30 percent of those less than twenty-eight years of age shared this

---

Changing Catholic Belief and Practice in France and the United States

Shortly after the death of Pope John Paul II, *La Vie,* a Catholic publication in France, reported the results of a poll of French Catholics regarding their views on matters of religious belief and practice. The most striking finding was the high percentage who rejected their church's teachings and who hoped for change under the then new pope, Benedict XVI. For example, 87 percent hoped that Benedict would give church approval to modern methods of contraception, 82 percent hoped that he would allow priests to marry, 81 percent believed that he should approve of abortion under some circumstances, and 72 percent expressed the wish that he would allow the ordination of women—all beliefs that had been strongly condemned and rejected by Benedict's predecessor, John Paul II.

A recent survey of Catholics in the United States found that roughly 70 percent dissented from their church's teachings on a series of issues including whether priests should be allowed to marry, whether women should be allowed to become priests, and whether artificial methods of birth control (e.g., the pill, condoms) could be used. Moreover, while only a third of Catholics believed abortion to be acceptable under any circumstances,

three-quarters believed abortion was acceptable under some circumstances.

In another recent survey, only 48 percent of Catholics believed the papacy was essential to the Catholic faith, and only 46 percent accepted their church's claim to be the only true church—dramatic changes from the recent past in Catholic belief. Reflecting the rapidity of change, Catholics under the age of forty were found to be five times more likely than older Catholics to believe that they themselves had the moral authority to make decisions regarding abortions and were not obliged to accept the clergy's view.

Ironically, most of the striking changes in Catholic beliefs and practice revealed by these and other surveys occurred during papal reigns of John Paul II and Benedict XVI who both sternly rejected all efforts to relax church rules and doctrines.

Sources: Laurie Goodstein and Megan Thee-Brenan, "U.S. Catholics in Poll See a Church Out of Touch," *New York Times,* March 6, 2013; Elaine Sciolino, "Young Europeans Seek a Papal Dialogue," *New York Times,* April 23, 2005; and William V. D'Antonio, James Davidson, Dean Hoge, and Katherine Meyer, *American Catholics: Gender, Generation, and Commitment* (Walnut Creek, Calif.: Altamira Press, 2001), pp. 49 and 161.

confidence. In Italy, the comparable figures were 67 and 36 percent, while in Spain the difference was even greater than in Ireland. Relatively, the trend is not as pronounced in the United States as in most industrial societies, but even there the basic pattern is evident. Overall, the prospects for the future of theistic religions in industrial societies do not look promising. As the older generation dies off, it is being replaced by a generation that is much less supportive of traditional faiths.

New Secular Ideologies

Beginning in seventeenth- and eighteenth-century Europe, a number of new ideologies appeared in which the role of supernatural beliefs was substantially reduced or totally eliminated. While some of these new ideologies quickly died out, a number of

Luther Nailing His Famous 95 Theses to the Door of the Castle Church, Wittenberg, Germany, 1517. Luther's Doctrine of the Priesthood of All Believers Had Revolutionary Social Implications: Though Luther Was Slow to See This, Others Soon Did.

them not only survived but also prospered in the industrial era. The most important of these new faiths have been democratic republicanism, capitalism, democratic socialism, revolutionary socialism (or communism), environmentalism, nationalism, pragmatism, and hedonism. It is these ideologies that guide the members of industrial societies in shaping their economies, polities, and their lives in general.

Democratic republicanism, as its name suggests, is a special form of the more general ideology known as *republicanism.* The basic doctrine of republicanism is its repudiation of hereditary monarchy—the type of government that prevailed in most agrarian societies of the past—and the proprietary theory of the state (see pp. 185–186).

Although republicanism has existed as an ideology for thousands of years, republican governments were rare in the agrarian era, except in maritime societies. Prior to the nineteenth century, most republicans rejected democratic republicanism, preferring instead *oligarchical republicanism.* In other words, they advocated a form of government in which power was concentrated in the hands of a few wealthy individuals, as it was in maritime societies. Oligarchical republicans have generally been distrustful of the masses of common people, afraid that they would misuse the powers of government if they ever gained political control.

The government of the United States in the first fifty years following the American Revolution provides a good example of oligarchical republicanism. Most members of the new political elite thought it wise to limit political power to a small minority of the population—men of property who, in their view, had the greatest stake in the welfare of society and also the greatest capacity to govern. In the new constitution adopted by the state of North Carolina in 1776, for example, the right to vote was limited to

The Founding Fathers of the United States Created an Oligarchical Republic, Not a Democratic Republic: The Constitutional Convention, Philadelphia, 1787.

landowners, and the right to sit in the state senate was limited even more—to those who owned 300 acres. To be eligible to be governor of the state, a man had to have a net worth of £1,000, eight times the net worth of the average white adult male in the South at the time.[6] Similar provisions were present in the constitutions of virtually all the other states in post revolutionary America.

Not everyone in early America was satisfied with oligarchical republicanism, and even in the eighteenth century there were some who advocated *democratic* republicanism, or what Abraham Lincoln would later describe as "government of the people, by the people, and for the people." Not surprisingly, many of the most ardent advocates of democratic republicanism were people who lived on what was then the western frontier. As we saw in Chapter 7 (pp. 198–199), frontier regions have long been noted for their egalitarianism and their resistance to established systems of authority. With strong support from this increasingly important part of the population, democratic republicanism won growing support in the early decades of the nineteenth century. With the election of Andrew Jackson in 1828, the fate of oligarchical republicanism in the United States was sealed. Property requirements for voting were gradually reduced and soon eliminated altogether. By the late 1850s, nearly all white males were eligible to vote.*

Since that time, democratic republicanism has been the dominant political ideology in American society and has won the support of hundreds of millions of other people throughout the world. Nevertheless, only a small minority of societies are as yet governed by democratic principles, and these are largely confined to the industrial societies of Europe, North America, Australia, South Korea, and Japan. There are, however, a number of exceptions in Latin America, Asia, and Africa.

Capitalism is another important new ideology of the industrial era. Its intellectual father was Adam Smith, a Scottish professor of moral philosophy who combined an analytical mind with a crusading nature.[7] In his most influential work, *An Inquiry into the Nature and Causes of the Wealth of Nations,* published in 1776, Smith made a powerful case for the thesis that the intervention of government into the economic life of a society retards growth and development. The only legitimate function government can perform in the economic sphere, according to Smith, is to enforce contracts that individuals enter into freely. To do more than this is harmful. Smith backed up his argument with an impressive analysis designed to show that the law of supply and demand, operating in a truly free market,† would ensure that "the private interests and passions of men" are led in the direction "most agreeable to the interest of the whole society."[8] It would be a self-regulating system, but it would function, said Smith, as though an "invisible hand" were at work, ensuring the best possible outcome.

Smith's work laid the foundation for the emerging academic discipline of modern economics. More important, his basic beliefs about the harm done by governmental intervention in the economy became the basis of a powerful new ideology that for

---

* Later, the Fifteenth Amendment to the Constitution, adopted in 1870, extended the franchise to blacks, and the Nineteenth, adopted in 1920, extended it to women. The 1964 civil rights bill and 1965 voter's rights act were subsequently passed by Congress to enforce the Fifteenth Amendment.
†As we saw in the last chapter, no society has ever had a "truly free market" system overall. That is an abstract, theoretical construct—but some have had more free market elements than others.

more than 200 years has exercised a profound influence on societies around the globe. This ideology has provided moral justification for policies that minimize governmental control of those in business and business enterprises. In societies where capitalism is the dominant ideology, the term "free enterprise" has become a symbol that is often invoked with considerable success to influence public opinion. As we will see shortly, the realities of contemporary capitalism are substantially different from its ideals, as has been true, of course, of every ideology from Christianity to socialism.

Another important new ideology of the industrial era is *socialism*. While its underlying principle has been applied in hunting and gathering societies for thousands of years, the modern concept dates from the nineteenth century and was an explicit response to, and reaction against, the realities of early capitalism. Socialists argued that the basic economic resources of a society should be the common property of all its members and used for the benefit of all. Where proponents of capitalism praised free enterprise for the growth in productivity it generated, socialists attacked it for its harsh working conditions, its low wages and economic inequality, its unemployment, its child labor, its boom-and-bust cycles, and its alienating and exploitative character. Where capitalists advocated the private ownership of the means of production (i.e., mines, factories, railroads, utilities), socialists favored public ownership. Where capitalists argued that economic inequality is necessary to provide incentives for people to work productively, socialists insisted that a more egalitarian distribution would achieve a better result.

Since early in its history, the socialist movement has been split into a variety of warring sects that have often fought more with one another than with the advocates of capitalism and other ideologies.[9] The most important of the struggles has been between *democratic* socialism and *revolutionary* socialism.

Democratic socialism assumes that socialist principles have an inherent appeal to most people. Its proponents therefore maintain that, in democratic societies, socialists should seek power by electoral means and that, after coming to power, they should let other political parties compete freely for the support of the electorate and return to power anytime they can win a majority of the vote. Democratic socialists believe that any other policy defeats one of socialism's basic aims: to maximize the freedom of individuals. They argue that political democracy is as essential to socialism as public ownership of the means of production, and that failure to practice political democracy subverts the very nature of socialism.

During the twentieth century, parties adhering to these principles (e.g., the New Democratic Party in Canada, the Labour Party in Britain, the Social Democratic Party in Germany, and the Socialist Party in France) developed large followings and won many elections. Because of the continuing appeal of capitalist principles in these societies, however, none of these parties has tried to entirely abolish private ownership of the means of production. Although they have taken some steps in that direction (i.e., they have nationalized some industries), the major thrust of their policies has been the creation of a *welfare state*. In other words, they have used the powers of government to tax the profits of privately owned enterprises to fund health, educational, and social service programs that benefit ordinary citizens who do not own any significant amount of property. This allows everyone to share in the benefits of the productive system without totally abolishing private ownership and control.

Karl Marx

In contrast, the other major faction within the socialist movement doubted the possibility of achieving socialism through peaceful, democratic means. *Revolutionary socialists* maintained that this can be achieved only by force and by the expropriation of private property. Karl Marx was the spiritual father of revolutionary socialism, and his writings and political activities in the nineteenth century laid the foundation for the Communist parties of the twentieth century. In societies controlled by his followers, he occupied an honored status not unlike that accorded great religious figures of the past. His doctrines were taught to children in all the schools, his writings were cited by the party elite to justify their policies, and pictures and statues of him were placed in prominent locations.

Marx believed that the evils found in societies can be traced to the influence of the institution of private property. This institution stimulates greed and selfishness, exploitation, injustice, and oppression. By destroying it, humans can free themselves forever from these evils and set human societies on a new course that will lead in time to the development of a world in which freedom, justice, and equality prevail and in which everyone's material and spiritual needs are met.

Marx based these beliefs on a complex and interesting theory of history in which he argued that capitalism, as did all previous systems of production, contains the seeds of its own destruction and that socialist revolutions, led by members of the then new and growing army of industrial workers, are not only inevitable but will also ultimately prevail. In short, after a brief but bloody period of revolution, human societies will advance to a stage of societal development in which everyone's legitimate needs and desires will be fulfilled. In an initial phase of this new stage of development, people will be rewarded according to the socialist principle "to each according to his *work*." In a later, higher phase of development, people will be rewarded according to the communist principle "to each according to his *need*."

Marxist socialism has been a far more comprehensive ideology than either capitalism or democratic socialism. Where these other ideologies allow people to make their own choices in most aspects of their lives, Marxism has traditionally imposed its own standards on everything from politics and economics to art and religion. In this respect, Marxism resembles traditional religions more than it does other modern secular ideologies.[10]

For much of the twentieth century, it seemed that revolutionary socialism was destined to become the most successful and the most powerful of the new secular ideologies. For several decades following World War II, Communist parties seized power in more than twenty societies ranging from China to Cuba and from Mozambique to the former Czechoslovakia. In France and Italy, Communist parties were able to enlist the support of millions of voters, while in other countries, such as Britain and the United States, growing numbers of intellectuals, journalists, university professors, media celebrities, and students were sympathetic to the ideals of revolutionary socialism and to the revolutionary movements around the world that endorsed those ideals.

This period of growth and expansion came to an end in the late 1980s with the collapse of the Soviet empire in eastern Europe and with the termination of its financial and other support of expansionist revolutionary socialist parties in Cuba, Vietnam, and elsewhere, and with China's increasingly rapid movement toward a mixed economy. During the 1970s and 1980s, the flaws and failures of the revolutionary socialist regimes in the Soviet Union, China, Cuba, and elsewhere gradually became more and more evident, first to the citizens of the countries involved, and later even to outsiders. Today, Marxism survives chiefly in scattered parts of the third world, and, perhaps, in intellectual circles and universities in the West.[‡]

As faith in the moral compasses provided by traditional theistic religions and secular Marxism has eroded in recent decades, *environmentalism* has offered an attractive new alternative. Going beyond more conventional concerns with reducing toxic pollution and preserving natural resources for the enjoyment of future generations, it offers a new moral code and ascetic purpose for humans—to forgo the exploitation of habitat and consumption of natural resources for human purposes and benefit, and, instead, preserve nature for nature itself.

Some of its more extreme forms have clear parallels with, and may be viewed as, substitutes for elements of Judeo-Christian beliefs—an initial Eden or paradise prior to modern exploitation and despoiling, a fall from grace, and a coming judgment or doomsday if humans don't repent and atone for their environmental transgressions.[11] There is even an eerie echo of medieval Christianity's "indulgences" in the buying of "carbon credits" to offset (the sins of) emitting carbon dioxide into the atmosphere.

And, whereas imputing religious or supernatural causes to natural disasters and calamities, such as hurricanes and tornadoes, produces widespread ridicule in a secular society, invocation, without evidence, of global warming or global climate change as their cause by politicians and commentators produces only occasional protest by very few in the scientific community. When virtually any weather or climatic event, such as an increase or decrease in rainfall or storms, can be seen as evidence of human-caused climate change, it becomes more of a (nonfalsifiable) belief than a scientific explanation.

[‡]For a detailed discussion of the reasons for the collapse of Marxist socialism in the Soviet Union, China, and elsewhere, see Chapter 15 of the 7th, 8th, 9th, or 10th editions of *Human Societies*.

In fact, that is probably the most fearsome potential consequence of the growth of this ideology. When one deals with a complex system of variables, such as that which constitutes our global climate, where the flap of a butterfly's wing can theoretically trigger a hurricane, it is important to get the science right. Without doing so, well-intentioned actions may produce unanticipated and unwanted negative consequences.[§]

Unfortunately, if environmentalism makes potential explanations of climate change matters of faith rather than science, it may, despite its good intentions, actually hinder our ability to understand the causes of, and to mitigate, human impact on global climate. We look back with contempt and a degree of puzzlement on the effect that subordination of science and learning to theistic religion had in Europe in the "Dark Ages" or to Soviet Marxism in the Stalin era, but we may not see or appreciate the potential danger of subordinating them to environmentalism today.[12]

The sixth of the major new secular ideologies is *nationalism*.[13] As with other ideologies, some of its elements have existed for thousands of years: group loyalty and tribalism, for example, are hardly new. During the agrarian era, however, the peasant masses, who made up 80 percent or more of the population, had little interest in politics beyond the village level.[14] The rise and fall of empires were of no concern to them—unless, of course, they were drawn into these struggles against their will. This lack of interest in politics at the national level was only natural in societies in which the dominant ideology defined the state as the private property of the ruler.

Nationalism has been a potent ideology in colonial territories ever since the American Revolution, and it is important today in many societies of the third world that became free of colonial control only in the last century. More importantly, it is also a potent—even a virulent—force among the various ethnic and religious minorities within both industrial and industrializing societies, as the history of the former Soviet Union and Yugoslavia in the second half of the twentieth century and, more recently, Syria and Iraq demonstrate.

In many societies in recent decades, nationalism has been combined with other ideologies. The Nazi (literally National Socialist in German) regime in Germany prior to, and during, World War II is one example. In American society, nationalism of a far milder variety is sometimes linked to Christianity and capitalism to form what some have called the nation's "civil religion."[15]

The next of the major new ideologies, *pragmatism,* differs from all the others in one essential respect: it offers no preconceived ideas as to how societies should be organized. Rather, it asserts that social institutions should be judged by their *consequences* and those that prove beneficial should be strengthened and preserved while those that are not should be eliminated.

Two American philosophers, Charles Peirce and William James, were the spiritual fathers of modern pragmatism. Like Adam Smith and Karl Marx, they developed, expanded, and systematized certain ideas that had existed for centuries. Although the

---

[§]For example, programs mandating the production and use of ethanol have produced a number of unanticipated environmental, social, and economic problems (e.g., see "Natural Resources and the Biophysical Environment" in Chapter 15).

teachings of Peirce and James have not given rise to any organized group of disciples, the basic principles of pragmatism have been adopted widely in the modern world. In fact, it is no exaggeration to say that many contemporary world leaders who profess to believe in other ideologies are also, to a greater or lesser degree, pragmatists. For example, Deng Xiaoping, China's former Communist leader, once said, regarding his un-Marxist economic innovations, that he did not care if a cat was black or white as long as it caught mice. Such leaders have discovered that no ideology can provide a completely satisfactory blueprint for organizing and governing society. If they hope to be successful, or merely retain power, they have to improvise, and this means they have to adopt the pragmatic principle of judging policies and programs by their consequences.

The last of the new ideologies is *hedonism,* or the pursuit of pleasure. Hedonism has not given rise to organized political movements. Rather, it has become a pervasive influence in the lives of hundreds of millions of individuals. Its more obvious manifestations can be seen in the enormous expansion in the last hundred years of industries that seek to satisfy hedonistic desires—movies, television, sports, tourism, vacationing, popular music and concerts, gambling, drugs, and all the rest that cater to the desires of individuals (see "Leisure and the Arts" in Chapter 13).

This desire for pleasure is nothing new, but the productivity and affluence of industrial societies have produced vastly greater opportunities for its satisfaction. The economic impact of this on industrial societies is obvious in the rapid expansion of the entertainment and leisure industries noted above.[16] Its political impact, in contrast, is far more subtle but no less important: Politicians are increasingly judged by their ability to "entertain," and when politics appears boring, as it often does, people lose interest, and small groups with special interests (economic, religious, and so on) find it easier to advance those interests.

Surprising as it may seem, despite their many differences, the new secular ideologies all have one thing in common: *they are all based on the belief that human destiny is largely subject to human control.* This is in sharp contrast to ideologies that originated in the preindustrial past. Those ideologies asserted that events depended on forces beyond human control—fate, God, the gods—and taught that the way to appease those forces was through magic, ritual, and adherence to tradition.

Members of modern societies are not nearly so passive. New information in areas ranging from science to history has improved their understanding of human nature and of the world they inhabit, while new technological information has increased their capacity to alter and adapt to that world. The result has been a growing awareness of humanity's potential for shaping its own future. This awareness underlies all the new secular ideologies of the industrial era, and the members of contemporary societies have come to rely increasingly on these ideologies, and less and less on traditional ones, in their efforts to control their lives and shape the life of society as a whole.

DIFFERENCES AMONG INDUSTRIAL SOCIETIES

Because of their similar technologies and their increasingly pragmatic ideologies, industrial societies are similar to one another in many ways, as is apparent to anyone who has traveled among them. There are also, of course, important differences, and these reflect differences in their biophysical environments, in their social environments, and in numerous features of the cultures they have inherited from the past (see Figure 1.2, p. 20). The effects of such differences can be clearly seen when we compare traditionally Protestant Sweden in northern Europe with traditionally Catholic Italy in southern Europe, for example, or former frontier societies, such as Australia and the United States, with their motherland, England.

The most significant differences among industrial societies in the past hundred years, however, have been consequences of the new secular ideologies. As technology has expanded the limits of the possible for these societies and increased the range of their alternatives, *the ideologies that guide them in choosing among the alternatives and in using their enormous economic surpluses have become an important source of societal variation.* Industrial societies have many potentially significant options available to them that were not available to any society in the past, and they are guided in making their choices among these options by the beliefs and values contained in their ideologies.

The importance of ideology was never more evident than in the former revolutionary socialist societies of eastern Europe—the Soviet Union, East Germany, Czechoslovakia, Poland, and Hungary—and in comparisons of these societies with the much more pragmatic democracies of western Europe, North America (Canada and the United States), Australia, and Japan. Prior to the 1990s, differences between these two sets of societies were strikingly evident in their politics, economics, education, mass media, stratification, religion, and even art. As we discuss in the excursus to Chapter 14 ("Marxist Societies as Natural Experiments"), the rulers of those societies, guided by Marxist ideology, conducted some of the most important, albeit horrifying, social experiments in human history, testing the "limits of the possible" in new ways. Students of human societies need to study these experiments and learn why they failed, since it is often possible to learn as much or more from experiments that fail than from those that succeed.

Among the western democracies, the United States has enjoyed political, military, and economic preeminence since World War II. In matters of ideology, the democracies differ considerably in the degree to which they have adopted and institutionalized the principles of socialism or, conversely, of capitalism. Since the primary difference between socialists and capitalists concerns the issue of *how and by whom* basic economic decisions are made, the relative strength of the two ideologies in a society is reflected in *the extent to which its economy is regulated or controlled by government.*

One measure of this control is how much of a society's GDP is consumed by its government. As Table 10.6 (p. 265) made clear, governments consume far more in most western European and Scandinavian democracies than in Canada, Australia, Japan, and the United States. This reflects the popularity of democratic socialism in western and northern Europe and the success of its Social Democratic parties in creating and expanding what has come to be called "the welfare state" or "welfare capitalism." In contrast, the much lower levels of governmental expenditure in Japan, Canada, the United States, and Australia reflect traditions that emphasize private or individual, as opposed to governmental, decision making in economic matters.

THE POLITIES OF INDUSTRIAL SOCIETIES

A society's polity is an institutionalized set of answers to questions about how it should be governed, who will have power to make what decisions, and under what conditions?

How will those decision makers be chosen, and when and how will they be replaced? Above all, what limits or checks, if any, will there be on their powers?

The answers to these questions obviously reflect a society's dominant ideology, whether it involves belief in the divine right of kings, belief in democracy, belief in the doctrines of Karl Marx or Adam Smith, or those of environmentalists. The answers also say something about a society's level of technological development. For it is no coincidence that multiparty democracy is a product of the industrial era and is found most often in industrial societies. In fact, we cannot understand the polities of industrial societies unless we recognize the remarkable political transformation that has occurred in them as a by-product of industrialization.

The Democratic Trend

Prior to the Industrial Revolution, nearly all large and powerful nations were monarchies governed by hereditary kings and emperors. The power to govern was believed to be a God-given right, and the state was viewed as the private property of the ruling family. The state and the ruler's estate were one and the same—and the heads of states were "rulers," not merely "leaders." In 1750, the republican idea that the powers of government are derived from the consent of the governed was still only a thesis for philosophers to debate, not a political reality.

Today, the older view of government has all but disappeared, especially in industrial societies. While a few of them still retain some of the trappings of monarchy, as in Britain, Sweden, Spain, and Japan, the Western industrial societies are all democratic republics. Even in eastern Europe, where oligarchical republicanism recently held sway, the democratic form of republicanism has been taking hold.

People who are sensitive to the undemocratic elements that still exist in Western industrial societies sometimes have difficulty appreciating the enormity of the changes that have occurred in almost all industrial societies. These include not just the introduction of contested elections and the formation of political parties that mobilize the masses of people in support of particular leaders and policies, but also—most important of all—*the exercise of the powers of government to benefit the masses of ordinary people in countless ways.* This was unheard of in agrarian societies of the past, where the powers of government were used almost entirely for the benefit of the governing class.

The nature of the change may best be symbolized by the way ordinary people are referred to in legal codes. In agrarian societies of the recent past, they were called "subjects," in industrial societies today, they are "citizens."

Democracy as a Variable

In discussing political systems, we should resist the temptation to think in categorical, either-or terms. To divide governments into those that are democratic and those that are not is to oversimplify. In the real world, governments differ by degree in their practice of democracy, and the degree of democracy in a given society often changes over time. Thus, we need to think of democracy as a variable like other societal characteristics, such as population size or economic productivity. Thinking of democracy in this way helps us recognize why large and complex societies can never be completely democratic. Full and equal participation by everyone in every political decision in

284 CHAPTER 11: INDUSTRIAL SOCIETIES: IDEOLOGIES AND POLITIES

societies with millions of people facing a multitude of issues is *impossible*.[17] Thus, not surprisingly, even the most democratic industrial society has never achieved more than a *representative* form of democracy.

Once we recognize the variable nature of democracy, we can better appreciate the magnitude of the change that has occurred in the polities of Western industrial societies during the last 150 years or so. As recently as 1865, 76 percent of the members of the British Parliament were members of the aristocracy and gentry (i.e., the old governing class of preindustrial Britain), and nearly half the seats were filled in uncontested elections.[18] One-quarter of the members of Parliament belonged to just thirty-one families, a fact that led one writer of the period to refer to Parliament as "one vast cousinhood."[19]

In the United States, as we noted in our discussion of ideologies, the government was originally an *oligarchical republic*. The right to vote was limited to men of property, as in Britain, and the great majority of people were denied this right. This was still true even half a century after the republic was established. In the presidential election of 1824, only 350,000 votes were cast, indicating that less than 10 percent of the adult population was entitled to vote.[20] Since then, the elimination of property requirements for the right to vote and to hold office; the abolition of slavery; the extension of the franchise (i.e., the right to vote) to blacks, women, and eighteen-year-olds; the passage of the civil rights and voters rights acts; the direct election of senators; and the "one person, one vote" decision of the Supreme Court have greatly increased not only the percentage of Americans who are eligible to vote but, equally important, also the effectiveness and importance of their votes. As a result, more than 60 percent of all governmental expenditures in the United States today are for social programs that largely benefit the masses of ordinary people.[21] This is a tremendous change from the practices of governments during the agrarian era.

Similar trends can be observed in the recent history of the other Western democratic societies, although nearly all of them lagged behind the United States in removing property requirements for the right to vote (see Figure 11.1). In Sweden and Britain, for example, these requirements were not finally removed until after World War I.[22] On the other hand, as we saw in Table 10.6, the democracies of western Europe now spend a much higher percentage of their total income on social programs than the United States does.

In thinking about the democratic trend in industrial societies in the last two hundred years, it is tempting for those of us who live in these societies to become self-congratulatory. We need to remind ourselves, however, that despite all that has been achieved, we are still, in most societies, a very long way from the ideal of *equal* political influence for all.

Elections today cost increasingly huge sums of money. The Federal Election Commission estimates that seven *billion* dollars was spent in the 2012 presidential election, and staggering amounts are spent in Senate and House elections.[23] More that eighty-five *million* dollars was spent in the most expensive 2012 Senate election—Scott Brown versus Elizabeth Warren in Massachusetts—and 67 *million* dollars was spent in the most expensive House election—Christopher Murphy versus Linda McMahon in Connecticut (see also, the boxed insert, "Money and Politics," on p. 286).[24]

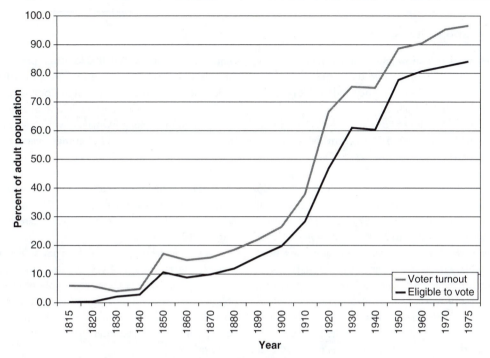

Figure 11.1. Extension of the Franchise in Western Europe: 1830 to 1975.
Source: Percentage of population age twenty and older eligible to vote, and turnout at elections, calculated from data on Austria, Belgium, Denmark, Finland, Germany, Italy, the Netherlands, Norway, and Sweden presented in Peter Flora (et al.) *State Economy and Society in Western Europe 1815–1975*, vol. 1, *The Growth of Mass Democracies and Welfare States* (Chicago: St. James Press, 1983).

To become a serious candidate even for an important local office in a town of any size, one usually has to be able to raise or possess substantial sums. The same is true, but on a vastly larger scale, for candidates for major state or national offices. Without financial backing, most candidates have little chance. As a result, those individuals and groups that are wealthy enough to be able to make the kind of large contributions required have disproportionate influence on the outcome of elections and thus on the policies that winning parties and candidates adopt. Moreover, once in office, politicians find that by supporting the policies of those who can and do contribute to campaigns, they can ensure their own repeated reelection. Thus, one might say that the governments of industrial societies have become, in varying degrees, *plutocratic democracies.*

Fortunately, however, there are some limits on the power of wealth. If conditions become intolerable, the most skillful use of political advertising and other resources that money can buy will probably not prevent the electorate from removing from office those it believes are responsible. In short, despite the great power of wealth in modern democracies, the electorate possesses a veto power over the actions of officeholders that it can use if those actions become too obviously harmful to the interests of the majority.

Money and Politics

Mark Hanna, a well-known Republican leader a century ago, once said, "There are two things that are important in politics. The first is money, and I can't remember what the second one is."

Things have changed little in the American political system since Hanna's day, as recent news reports make clear. For example, the *Seattle Times* reported that Senator Patty Murray (D-WA) and two representatives in Congress from Washington received $46,000 in campaign contributions from executives of a small boat company, and then secretly inserted a provision (a so-called earmark) into a defense spending bill that compelled the Navy to spend $4.6 million for a boat that the Navy did not want and never used. The boat was subsequently given away. To make matters worse, because there was a cap, or limit, on total Navy appropriations at the time, this expenditure prevented the Navy from using $4.6 million for its real needs.

In another case, the *New York Times* reported that a representative from Alaska, Donald Young, secretly inserted a provision in an appropriations bill that called for the expenditure of $10 million to build a road in southwest Florida, thousands of miles from the district he represented. Not surprisingly, he was the recent recipient of a $40,000 contribution from a wealthy real estate developer who owned 1,000 acres in the area and stood to benefit enormously from the appropriation.

In one of the most egregious instances of money's influence on politics, court records show that former representative Duke Cunningham (R-CA) published what the press called a "bribe menu" in which he blatantly listed his price for various services. The menu showed an escalating scale for bribes starting at $140,000 for a $16 million Defense Department contract. Each additional $1 million in contract value

required an additional $50,000 for the representative. All this was carefully spelled out on a card framed under the seal of the United States Congress.

Representative Cunningham is one of a small minority of twenty sitting lawmakers who have had the misfortune to be convicted of crimes over a twenty-five year period. Although all of them were expelled from Congress, none lost their extremely generous congressional pensions. With normal life expectancy, Cunningham can expect to receive $1.8 million for his services while another in the group can look forward to $2.9 million.

As some might say, "Crime does pay, at least if you commit the right kind of crime." Unfortunately, despite countless efforts to limit the role of money in politics, even today only a tiny minority of American political leaders are ever indicted and convicted for selling out to moneyed interests. Most find ways to avoid prison.

It is not surprising, therefore, to learn that in the elections of 2012, candidates for Congress and the presidency raised and spent more than seven billion dollars. Clearly, Mark Hanna knew whereof he spoke, and his words are as true today as when he spoke them!

Sources: Wolf Blitzer, "The Situation Room," *CNN*, February 1, 2013; Paul Krugman, "Death of the Machine," *New York Times*, October 19, 2007; Eric Lichtblau and Scott Shane, "Phone Companies Seeking Immunity Gave to Senator," *New York Times*, October 23, 2007; David Heath and Hal Bernton, "$4.5 Million for a Boat that Nobody Wanted," *Seattle Times*, October 14, 2007; David Kirkpatrick, "Alaska Gets Campaign Cash; Florida Road Gets U.S. Funds," *New York Times*, June 7, 2007; CNN.com, transcripts, November 16, 2007; "From Cash to Yachts: Congressman's Bribe Menu," *ABC News*, November 16, 2007; and Opensecrets.org, November, 17, 2007.

Causes of the Democratic Trend

The tremendous strength and appeal of democratic ideology have been among the more remarkable characteristics of the industrial era. In the history of industrial societies, there has been only a single instance in which members of a democratic nation abandoned democracy in favor of another form of government, and that happened in a society (Germany in the 1930s) that was confronted by an exceptional set of circumstances, both economic and political. Thus, the record suggests that the democratic trend has been no accident, but rather a response to a powerful set of social forces.

For the most part, these seem to be the same forces that gave rise to *all* the major new ideologies of the industrial era—the Protestant Reformation, the conquest of the New World, and, most important of all, the Industrial Revolution. Protestantism appears to have been especially significant in the early rise and spread of democratic beliefs and values.[25] If it did nothing else, the Protestant Reformation proved that established authority *could* be challenged and overthrown. But even more important, the Protestant doctrine of the priesthood of all believers—the doctrine that all believers are equal in God's sight and can relate directly to Him without the mediation of the clergy—had *political implications of a revolutionary nature.* Though the reformers, Luther and Calvin, did not recognize this, others soon did, and the bitter German Peasants' Revolt of 1524–1525 and the Leveler movement a century later in England were both stimulated by it.

This new doctrine also led to the adoption of democratic or semidemocratic forms of church government by the more radical Protestant groups, such as the Anabaptists, Mennonites, Baptists, Quakers, Puritans, and Presbyterians. *It is no coincidence that democratization began in church governments some generations before it began in civil governments.* Nor is it coincidence that when it did begin in civil government, its early successes were chiefly in countries where the democratization of church governments had already made considerable headway. The first major and enduring victory of the democratic movement was in the United States, a country that since colonial days had been a refuge for the more radical and more democratic Protestant groups.

The conquest of the New World was another important factor in the spread of democratic government. Conditions in the frontier regions of the United States, Canada, and Australia were far more favorable to democracy than conditions in the older, heavily settled societies of Europe. In fact, the Jacksonian movement, which did so much to broaden the base of political participation in American society, had its greatest strength in what was then the western frontier. The conquest of the New World was also important because, as we noted in Chapter 9 (see pp. 218–220), it weakened the power of the traditional governing classes in European societies and strengthened the influence of the merchant class, which had long been noted for its republican tendencies.

As important as these influences were, however, the democratic movement would not have succeeded without the Industrial Revolution. Industrialization eliminated the need for large numbers of unskilled and uneducated workers living at or near the subsistence level, and as new sources of energy were tapped and new machines invented, societies had to produce more skilled and educated workers. But people with skills and education are much less likely to be politically apathetic and servile. On the contrary, they tend to be self-assertive, jealous of their rights, and politically demanding.[26] Such characteristics are essential in a democracy, for they hold in check the powerful oligarchical tendencies that are present in any large and complex social system.

Industrialization also made possible the remarkable development of the *mass media.* To a great extent this has been a response to the spread of literacy and to the increased demand for information generated by the rising level of education. Through newspapers, magazines, radio, and television, the average citizen of a modern industrial society is vastly more aware of political events than his or her counterpart in agrarian societies. Although much of the information received is superficial and distorted, it nevertheless generates interest and concern. Thus the media not only satisfy a need, they also help create it.[27]

Finally, industrialization, by stimulating the growth of urban communities, further strengthened democratic tendencies. Isolated rural communities have long been noted for their lack of political sophistication and for their paternalistic political patterns. Urban populations, in contrast, have always been better informed and more apt to challenge established authority without waiting for conditions to become desperate. Thus, merely by increasing the size of urban populations, industrialization contributed to the democratic trend.

Mass Political Parties

The growth of democracy and the rise of industrial societies have produced a totally new kind of political organization, the mass political party, which serves to mobilize public opinion in support of political programs and candidates. Wherever there are more candidates than offices, there is a process of selection, and the candidates who are supported by parties usually win.

Party organizations differ in several respects. Some, such as the Republican and Democratic parties in the United States, are largely pragmatic, *brokerage-type parties.* They have few strong ideological commitments or well-defined political programs. Their chief goal is to gain control of public offices in order to trade favors with special interest groups, offering preferential legislative treatment in exchange for electoral and financial support. In this type of party, discipline is weak, since each elected official is free to work out his or her own "deals." Some degree of party unity is maintained, however, because once an interest group establishes close ties with the officials of a certain party, it usually continues working with them. This is reinforced by the tendency of the more ideologically inclined to separate into opposing camps, progressives gravitating toward one party, conservatives toward the other. Sometimes the more ideologically inclined win control of the party machinery, but usually this is short-lived.

In contrast to brokerage-type parties, many of which were formed in the nineteenth century, political parties formed in the twentieth century have often had strong ideological commitments. Such parties, including both fascist parties of the right and socialist parties of the left, traditionally had well-developed programs designed to transform society, and their leaders were willing to be defeated again and again rather than compromise principles they held sacred. Since World War II, however, many of these parties have become less ideological and more pragmatic.

Nationalist ideologies have been linked with political parties in several industrial societies. The most famous was the German National Socialist Workers (Nazi) Party organized by Adolf Hitler following Germany's defeat in World War I. Usually, however, nationalist ideologies are simply one element in the overall program of the major conservative parties in democratic societies. Thus, the Republicans in the United States, the Conservatives in Britain and Canada, and the conservatives in France usually place more emphasis on national defense and other policies relevant to nationalist ideals than their opponents do.

In ethnically divided societies, minorities sometimes form nationalist parties to protect or promote their own group's special interests. This has happened among the French in Canada, the Scottish and Welsh in Britain, and the Basques in Spain.

Finally, religious groups in western Europe and Japan have formed a number of political parties. The most successful of these have been the Christian-Democratic parties formed by Catholics in Italy, Germany, Austria, and several other countries. While the original aim of these parties was to defend the Catholic Church's position on such issues as birth control, abortion, divorce, and tax support for church schools, they have often become the chief conservative opposition to Social Democratic parties.

A more recent development in party organization in industrial societies has been the formation of so-called Green parties by environmentally concerned groups. Concerns with environmental issues have grown considerably in much of Europe in recent decades in response to the Chernobyl nuclear accident in the former Soviet Union, and Europe's dying forests and polluted air and bodies of water. Although the size of the Green parties' presence has risen and fallen over the years, they continue to hold seats in the European Parliament.[28]

Aerial View of the Chernobyl Nuclear Power Plant, Site of the World's Worst Nuclear Accident, Which Gave Powerful Impetus to Green Parties in Western Europe, Is Seen in April 1986, Two or Three Days After the Explosion in What Was Then the Soviet Union but Is Now Ukraine.

The future of these parties is uncertain because they are still small, and there are increasing signs that the established parties are adopting stronger policies on environmental issues to regain the support of voters who shifted to the Green parties.[29] But modern technology could change things overnight: another Chernobyl explosion, Fukushima accident, or comparable environmental disaster, especially one in western Europe itself, and the Green parties could become a major force.

Special Interest Groups

The industrial democracies are made up of a great variety of groups, each with its own special interests. Labor and management are two of the more familiar, but there are many others. In American society, for example, blacks, Hispanics, religious groups, the elderly, single mothers, veterans, professional groups, women, men, pro-choice groups, pro-life groups, environmentalists, pro-gun advocates, anti-gun advocates, gay-lesbian-bisexual-transgender, groups representing individual industries, and dozens more are organized to promote their own interests. Each has interests that conflict, to a greater or lesser degree, with the interests of other groups, and often with the interests of society as a whole.

One of the more difficult problems facing democratic societies today is that of protecting the interests of society as a whole against the claims and demands of these special interests.** Paradoxically, it is far easier for politicians to rally support for programs that offer special favors to limited interest groups than for programs designed to promote the common good.‡‡ The reason is simple: since political success in a democratic society depends on voter support, politicians tend to respond most readily to the appeals of groups that are able to mobilize large numbers of voters. Some rationalize their actions by arguing that the interests of society are simply the sum of the interests of its parts, but that argument ignores the systemic nature of human societies.

Interest groups vary greatly in their ability to influence public policy, and their influence is largely a function of three factors: (1) their ability to mobilize large numbers of people in support of candidates or parties, (2) their ability and willingness to make substantial financial contributions to politicians and their campaigns, and (3) their ability to garner mass media attention.

The first of these factors is essentially consistent with democratic values: policies that have the greatest amount of support should prevail within constitutionally defined limits. Financial power, however, is quite another matter. The ability of one married couple to spend nearly thirty-seven million dollars in support of their preferred candidates and party (as Sheldon and Miriam Adelson did in the 2012 elections in the United States) totally contradicts the democratic principle of "one person, one vote,"

**An overwhelming majority of Americans—80 percent—believe that the Congress is more interested in pandering to special interest groups than in serving the needs of people who elected them.[30]

‡‡The construction of the interstate highway system in the United States, for example, was primarily a response to a massive lobbying effort by the trucking industry, the highway construction industry, the cement industry, and the automobile industry, and only secondarily a response to the public's desire for safer and faster highways.

Democracy in Germany

On the sixtieth anniversary of the defeat of Germany in World War II, the noted German author and Nobel Prize winner, Guenther Grass, asked the question whether Germany's postwar democratic government is successfully addressing his country's most basic problems, such as widespread and persistent unemployment. His conclusion was that it is not.

The reason, he argued, was "the ring of lobbyists" representing the multinational corporations and Germany's banks. Their sole concern has been the maximization of profits, without regard to the cost of this for the majority of ordinary citizens. As he put it at one point, "The mere announcement of corporate

takeovers and mergers and the resultant dismissal of [large numbers of] workers and employees makes share prices rise, and this is regarded unthinkingly as the price to be paid for 'living in freedom,'" and the inevitable price Germans must pay for the benefits of globalization. In short, Grass asks, "Whose interests is Germany's democratic government serving?"

Without prejudging the answer, this is a question that needs to be asked about a growing number of other modern democratic governments.

Source: Guenter Grass, "The Gravest Generation," *New York Times,* May 7, 2005.

---

or equal influence for all.[31] The same is true when unions, businesses (such as General Electric), or professional organizations (such as trial lawyers or doctors) obtain lucrative legislative benefits by generous contributions. In fact, as many groups have found, there is seldom any other investment that pays such handsome dividends as investments in politics and politicians.

Politicians often claim that contributions cannot buy their votes; they only buy access. Skeptics, however, incline to the view that buying access and buying votes—or outright bribery—are often impossible to differentiate. As a result, many believe that the influence of money in the political process in a number of industrial societies (e.g., the United States, Japan, Germany, and Italy) threatens to transform these societies to plutocracies, or government by the rich (see "Democracy in Germany").

The Mass Media

One of the most important developments of the industrial era has been the emergence of the mass media as a major political force, not only in industrial societies, but in other societies as well. The rise of the media to their present position of influence and power is the result of a succession of technological breakthroughs.

The story of the mass media is generally thought to begin with the penny newspapers of New York in the 1830s. Because the price of these papers brought them within the reach of a substantial portion of the population, a tiny group of individuals—publishers and journalists—were able to transmit their views and opinions to large numbers of readers, most of whom had no opportunity to check the accuracy of most of what they read. Thus, publishers and journalists quickly found themselves in a position of considerable power in societies where public opinion was becoming increasingly important, thanks to the rise and spread of democratic institutions. The popularity, and hence the success and influence, of newspapers was greatly enhanced during this same period by the invention of the telegraph in 1837, which enabled them to provide information about important events in distant places much more quickly than was possible by any other means then available.

During the next hundred years or so, other inventions enhanced the power of the mass media still more by adding the enormously powerful elements of sound and visual imagery. The new technologies—especially radio and television—created an even greater concentration of power in the hands of a few since these media were able to reach national and even international audiences. Thus, in modern industrial societies the media elite—a few hundred individuals, or a few thousand at most—were able to shape the flow of information and could manipulate public opinion in ways that elected officials could not afford to ignore.

Although the media elite lacked the power themselves to enact legislation, they were able, in large measure, to set the agenda for elected officials. In other words, they were able to make it all but impossible for elected officials to ignore those issues that they deemed to be of primary concern, or contrariwise were able to keep an issue from gaining traction by ignoring it. This was because journalists were "gatekeepers" who controlled the flow of information within a society. No television newscast could possibly report all of the day's political news that was of importance in the brief twenty-three minutes that were available (after time out for commercials) on the major networks' evening newscasts. Even the *New York Times,* whose motto is "All the News That's Fit to Print," provides no more than a highly abridged summary of the day's events. Editors and reporters were constantly forced to pick and choose which among them they would report and, equally important, which they would feature and which they would "bury" on an inside page, or, in the case of television news, mention only briefly, if at all, and without visual imagery.

Because of this power, the media elite had considerable influence over the public's perception of what the problems confronting society, and requiring political action, actually were. When these elite "gatekeepers" acted in concert in selecting the political stories they feature and the slant they gave them, as they commonly did, elected officials could ignore them only at their own peril.

The visual imagery television provides has proved an especially potent force, since visual images stir the emotions far more powerfully than the written or spoken word. The power to choose among competing visual images, and to select the tiny handful that would be shown to tens of millions of people, was an awesome power in a democratic society, especially when it was in the hands of such a small group of individuals who were all but invisible and subject to only the most limited of controls by the public as a whole.

A study of the presidential election of 1976 in the United States provides a dramatic illustration of the power the media elite had to influence the political life of a democratic society.[32] That year Jimmy Carter won a very modest plurality in the first Democratic primary in the small state of New Hampshire. He received just 28 percent of the vote compared to 23 percent for the candidate who ran second and 49 percent for other candidates. Although Carter's victory at the polls was extremely modest, since he received only a little more than 10 percent of the total vote cast (counting the vote in the Republican primary), his victory in the media was overwhelming. Both *Time* and *Newsweek* featured him on their covers and devoted 90 percent of their reports on the primary to him! In the week that followed, both television and the daily press gave Carter four times the coverage of all his Democratic Party rivals combined.

This proved to be decisive, because, as researchers found, 95 percent of the voters in subsequent primaries voted for the candidate they felt they knew best—and that, thanks to the media, was Jimmy Carter.

Media journalists strive to project an image of impartiality and objectivity, but in recent years a growing number of them have acknowledged the presence of intentional bias. Thus, a former president of CBS News said at one point that "our job is to give the people not what they want but what we decide they ought to have," and a president of ABC News asserted that while media journalists "can't decide *everything* that people should be allowed to see [emphasis in the original], they have the right and responsibility to impose their own judgments in presenting the news."[33] Regardless of how one judges the uses to which the media elite put their power, one can only agree that the power they enjoyed in modern democratic societies was impressive.

Recently, however, the ability of the media elite to control the flow of political information has begun to be challenged by bloggers, new cable channels, smartphones, and YouTube videos that bypass or take special delight in attacking biases in the mainstream media and in catching their errors and omissions.[34] And while recent polls show that the majority of people still turn to television for their news, 30 percent now rely on Facebook and 8 percent on Twitter.[35] Twitter is an especially popular and growing source of news among younger, more mobile, and better educated consumers.[36] Confidence in newspapers and television news are at, or near, all-time lows.[37] As a result, the mainstream media have increasingly been following up on stories developed by these nontraditional sources. If these trends continue, which seems highly likely, then the ability of the traditional media elite to control the flow of information in industrial societies could be drawing to a close.

Political Conflict and Stability

Every social system generates internal conflict, and industrial societies are no exception. Nevertheless, their success in channeling such conflict into nonviolent forms is

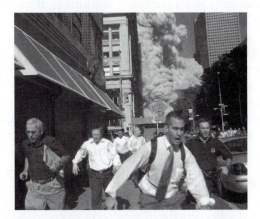

The Visual Imagery That Television Provides Has Proven an Especially Potent Force, since Visual Images Stir Emotions Far More Powerfully than the Written or Spoken Word. People Run from the Collapse of the World Trade Center in This September 11, 2001, Photo.

remarkable. Compared with agrarian societies in particular, they are much less prone to revolutions, coups, and other serious political upheavals. This is especially true of the democracies and other societies that are past the transitional or early phase of industrialization. Some time ago, a study of sixty-two societies found an extremely strong statistical correlation between their levels of political stability and their levels of economic development.[38]

There are a number of reasons for the political stability of the Western industrial democracies. First, their greater productivity and their higher standards of living give the majority of the population a vested interest in political stability. Revolution and anarchy would be very costly for most members of advanced industrial societies. Second, a democratic ideology strengthens the allegiance of most segments of the population to their government and weakens support for revolutionary movements. Especially noteworthy in this connection is the loyalty shown by the military and the absence of military coups in advanced industrial societies. Finally, the very complexity of the structure of industrial societies seems to generate a readiness to compromise on most controversial issues. This is partly *because there are so many people in intermediate positions between the contending groups.* Most of the population, for example, has modest property holdings. Such people are likely to benefit from peaceful compromise and therefore reject extreme or violent proposals. Contrary to Marx's expectations, this is true of the great majority of blue-collar workers. Moreover, since the complexity of industrial societies means that each individual simultaneously fills a number of different roles and often belongs to a variety of groups, people who are opponents in one controversy are often allies in another. For example, middle-class whites and blacks who may be divided over racial issues often find themselves allied on economic issues. This, too, has a moderating effect.

Although political conflicts are restrained in industrial societies, they are still present in various forms and involve a wide range of issues. The most common type of conflict is between economic classes, and, in most democratic nations, this has become the basic framework for partisan politics. Typically, some parties appeal primarily to the working class and other less advantaged elements in the population, promising improved conditions if they are elected. Opposing parties rely for support on the more privileged elements in the population and campaign for office on a platform promising economic growth.

Historically, Sweden has provided a good example of a strong relationship between economic class and party preference. Support for the Socialist and Communist parties has been more than twice as strong in the working class as in the middle and upper classes.[39] The strength of the relationship between party preference and economic class varies greatly in industrial societies, being strongest in Scandinavian societies and weakest in North American.[40] The limited relation between class and party preference in the United States and Canada is due in part to the absence of major working-class parties with strong ideological commitments. In both countries, the major parties are pragmatic, brokerage types that tend to downplay class-related issues.

Another factor that influences the relation between economic class and party preference is the presence of serious ethnic and religious divisions within a population. It is probably no coincidence that the countries with the strongest relation between class and party preference are generally the most homogeneous both ethnically and religiously.

In contrast, Canada has been divided for years by struggles between an English-speaking majority and a large, French-speaking minority. In both Canada and the United States, religion, ethnicity, and race have been important determinants of party preference.

Modern industrial democracies differ dramatically from traditional agrarian societies by virtue of their inclusion of ethnic and religious minorities, and the economically disadvantaged in the political process. In agrarian societies, such groups had little or no political power. In industrial societies, in contrast, these groups have sometimes won control of the machinery of government, or at least a share in it, as the working class has done in Scandinavia, the French in Canada, and the Catholics in the Netherlands.

The Growth of Government

Apart from the rise of democracy, the most important political change associated with industrialization has been the growth of government. The range of activities and the diversity of functions performed by government are far greater in modern industrial societies than in any other type of society. In a traditional agrarian society, the government's chief functions were defense, taxation, the maintenance of law and order, and the support of religion. In modern industrial societies, the last of these has usually been dropped, but dozens of new functions have been added.

Many of the new functions of government arise because they are required by an industrial system. For example, with industrialization, machines increasingly do the work that was once done by illiterate, unskilled workers, but the economy requires more educated workers. To ensure continuing economic growth, public educational systems must be created, first at the elementary level, then at the secondary, and finally at the university level. Only governments have the power to raise the money needed to finance such expensive systems.

A better-educated populace quickly becomes a more demanding populace. Educated people want or require things that uneducated peasants in agrarian societies of the past never dreamed of: health care, pensions for their later years, dependable systems of transportation and communication, adequate housing, and much more.[41] While private businesses can supply many of these things, there are some they cannot supply and others they cannot supply profitably for the entire population.

Highways are an example of the former, housing of the latter. A modern highway system is both too complex (requiring land-condemnation powers, for example) and too unprofitable to be constructed with private resources. Housing, on the other hand, can be profitably supplied by private businesses for most of the population in most industrial societies, but governments must step in to provide housing for those who cannot afford what is offered by private enterprise.

In the Western industrial democracies, much of the growth of government reflects the influence of two important developments we noted earlier: (1) the rise of democracy, and (2) the movement away from pure free market capitalism toward a mixed economy. In the first instance, a democratic system of government provides the masses of ordinary citizens with a powerful instrument for pressuring elites to satisfy their needs and desires. In the second, a mixed economy is, by definition, one in which government plays a greatly expanded role.

In the former revolutionary socialist societies of Soviet Russia and eastern Europe, despite their claims of representing the people's will, the absence of a democratic system of government made it far more difficult for ordinary citizens to express their wishes and to pressure political elites into using the society's resources for things they wanted. Despite this, a vast expansion of the scope of governmental activity occurred, simply because socialism led to the virtual abolition of private enterprise. Thus, while the mechanisms involved in eastern Europe and in the Western democracies were different, the end result in both cases has been a vast expansion in the scope and power of government.

Governmental Bureaucracies: Their Expansion and Transformation

One of the best measures of the growth of government is the size of the governmental bureaucracy. In the United States, as Figure 11.2 shows, the number of civilian employees in the federal government rose steadily for more than a century and a half.

The number of federal employees per 100,000 population increased an astonishing 2,500 percent between 1816 and 1970. Although the number of federal employees has declined since 1970 (due, in part to outsourcing of governmental responsibilities), this was more than offset by the rapid growth of state and local governments. In fact, taken together, federal, state, and local governments now employ nearly twenty-three million people, or more than 16 percent of the civilian labor force.[42]

The great growth in the powers of governments and in the size of their bureaucracies has made top administrative officials extremely powerful and relatively wealthy figures in industrial societies. Although this might be interpreted as simply a perpetuation of the old agrarian pattern with its dominance by a hereditary governing class, it is not. Government offices are no longer private property to be bought and sold and inherited by one's children. Rather, they tend to be assigned competitively on the basis of education and experience. Furthermore, in the exercise of office, officials are expected to act on the basis of the public interest rather

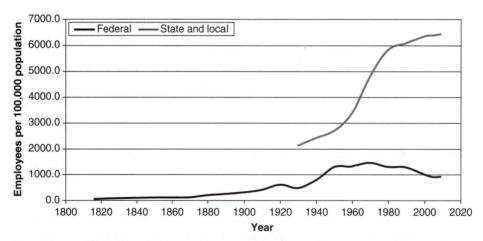

Figure 11.2. United States Federal and Local Government Employment: 1816 to 2009.
Sources: U.S. Bureau of the Census, *Historical Statistics of the United States: Colonial Times to 1970*, series A 1-5, Y 318–334; *Statistical Abstract of the U.S. 2008*, Tables 7 and 447, *Statistical Abstract of the U.S. 2007*, Tables 2 and 482; *Statistical Abstract of the U.S. 2003–4*, Table 453; *Statistical Abstract of the U.S. 2012*, Table 2 and Tables 461.

than of private advantage. Although reality falls far short of these ideals, there is a marked contrast between the practices of officials in most modern industrial societies and the practices of those in traditional agrarian societies. Members of industrial societies have discovered this repeatedly in their dealings with officials of many of the governments of less industrialized societies of the third world, where bureaucratic corruption is often a customary way of life.

In large measure, the explanation for the change lies in the newer ideologies, which assert that the powers of government are derived from the people and should therefore be used for their benefit. This is in sharp contrast to the traditional ideology of agrarian societies, which defined the state as the property of the ruler. When modern officials use public office for private advantage, they are subject to a variety of official sanctions, including criminal prosecution. Such constraints were rare in agrarian societies of the past.

Despite the less venal behavior of public officials in industrial societies, the growing size and power of government bureaucracies have become matters of concern. A series of Gallup polls taken since 1967 shows that far more Americans fear big government than fear big business or big labor. Even before September 11, 2001, and the ensuing legislation that expanded the investigative powers of government agencies, 64 percent saw big government as a threat to the nation compared with 24 percent who saw big business, and 9 percent who saw big labor as threats; and, despite some fluctuations, those figures remain largely unchanged today.[43] More ominously, 87 percent said that the federal government violated their constitutional rights at least occasionally, and 70 percent expected it would do so in the future.[44] No surprise, then, that trust in government is near an all-time low, and, in a recent poll, "dysfunctional government" was identified as the most important problem facing the country.[45]

One of the chief problems of bureaucracies everywhere is to maintain a sense of public responsibility in their personnel. Officials in welfare agencies, for example, often become more concerned with enlarging their staffs and raising their own rank and salary than with delivering services to those whom the agency was created to serve. In most governmental bureaucracies, it is also difficult to get individuals to accept responsibility for decisions. Buck passing, paper shuffling, and endless delays become standard operating procedures. Because of the tremendous division of labor, and hence of responsibility, within these organizations, it is frequently impossible to establish accountability; and; as a result; these patterns persist year after year, and generation after generation. These problems were especially serious in the former Communist governments of eastern Europe, where command economies put enormous power in the hands of a greatly expanded and extremely complex set of bureaucracies, but they are increasingly evident in all industrial societies today.[46]

So far, critics of bureaucratic power have not come up with any workable alternative. The sheer size and complexity of government in a modern industrial society make mass participation in decision making impossible. A substantial delegation of power, therefore, is inevitable, and those to whom the power is delegated generally do what they deem appropriate. This is one of the most serious limitations to the application of democratic principles in any large-scale organization.

POLITICAL GLOBALIZATION AND THE CHALLENGE
TO THE NEW WORLD ORDER

One of the most striking features of the modern era has been the growing interdependence of people and societies around the globe brought about by rapid advances in the technologies of communication and transportation. As we have seen (pp. 267–270), international trade has expanded enormously since 1750, and multinational corporations have become commonplace. Not only goods and organizations, but people, too, are moving from society to society, sometimes as tourists, sometimes as employees in multinational corporations, and increasingly as migrants, both legal and illegal.

Paralleling these economic developments, ties between societies at the political level have steadily increased. One manifestation of this in the twentieth century was the creation of international governmental agencies, ranging from regional bodies, such as the European Union, the Organization of African States, and the Organization of American States, to global entities, such as the United Nations, the World Court, and the World Trade Organization.

Political globalization is also evident in the emergence and spread of less structured political movements across national boundaries. Republicanism (i.e., opposition to monarchical government) and later the democratic movement were two of the earliest, with origins in the eighteenth and nineteenth centuries. Later, in the nineteenth and early twentieth centuries, the socialist and communist movements spread widely. More recently, the human rights movement, the women's movement, and Islamic fundamentalism have become worldwide in scope. Thanks to the modern technologies of communication and transportation, it is all but impossible for the more powerful members of societies to prevent the infiltration from abroad of movements such as these and their ideologies.

Another very different kind of development in the realm of global politics has been the progressive reduction in the number of nations with major military establishments. Prior to World War II, many nations could be said to be roughly equal militarily: Britain, France, Germany, Japan, the Soviet Union, and possibly even the United States. By the end of the war, only the United States and the Soviet Union remained major military powers. This situation continued for nearly half a century until the Soviet Union collapsed in response to fatal internal flaws in its economy and polity. As a result, the United States became the only remaining military superpower, and a dominant force in global politics, able to ignore or even defy the wishes of much of the rest of the world community.

Despite its enormous military power, American supremacy has not gone unchallenged. Surprisingly, the challenge has not taken the traditional form of a military buildup by some competing nation. Rather, the challenge has taken a radically different form: the utilization by a loosely organized, grassroots multinational movement (Islamic fundamentalism) of selected elements of modern technology capable of terrorizing vast civilian populations and disrupting the functioning of highly interdependent social networks with the intent of undermining a population's will to resist.

How this new kind of struggle will end or what its long-run consequences will be are impossible to foresee at this point. It seems safe to say, however, that the outcome and consequences will be powerfully influenced by the technologies that both sides are able to bring to bear and also by the ability of Islamic fundamentalism to continue to recruit followers willing to kill and die for the cause.

CHAPTER 12

Industrial Societies

Social Stratification

Outline
Stratification in Industrial Societies
Vertical Mobility
Social Inequality: Two Basic Trends

STRATIFICATION IN INDUSTRIAL SOCIETIES

As the technologies of societies have advanced, their systems of stratification have grown more complex. Wealth, income, and other differences were minimal in hunting and gathering societies, but they grew ever larger with the emergence of horticulture and then agriculture. Following the Industrial Revolution, the complexity of stratification systems has increased at an accelerating rate, but in some aspects, the trend toward ever increasing inequality appears to have slowed or actually reversed itself.

The increased productivity of industrial technology and the declining rate of population growth have greatly expanded the range of possibilities for inequality, and refinements in the division of labor have created numerous occupational positions between the highest paid and most respected, and the lowest paid and least respected. There has also been an increase in the degree to which different dimensions of inequality are independent of one another—people high or low on one dimension are not necessarily high or low on all, or even most, others. Furthermore, as we noted in Chapter 10, increasing productivity has also raised the standard of living of the average person in industrial societies.

As a result, it is no longer possible to characterize stratification as a simple matter of a few "haves" and a huge majority of "have nots," as was the case in the typical advanced agrarian society. Also, because the size of the economic "pie" in industrial societies has grown so much over time, it is not possible to make statements about whether the wealth or income of different segments of the population has gone up or down simply on the basis of whether their proportionate "slice of the pie" is growing or declining. For, if the pie is growing, the competition for wealth and income is not a zero-sum "game." In fact, the *wealth* or *income* of the rich or the poor may actually be growing in periods when their wealth or income *share* is shrinking.

All of this means that we must examine different dimensions of stratification separately, and that we must distinguish between the degree of inequality on a given dimension and the amounts of that social good held by different segments of the population. We will also want to look at long-term trends in inequality in industrial societies and to compare the extent of inequality in industrial societies to that found in contemporary and past preindustrial societies.

Political Stratification

Despite the differences in the political systems of industrial societies, one thing is true of them all: Their political elites have the greatest influence in choosing among the wide range of options available to industrial societies and in influencing the way their huge economic surpluses will be apportioned. Therefore, in examining the patterns of inequality in industrial societies, we begin with these elites and with the system of political stratification.

In agrarian societies, the governing elite was generally a small, homogeneous, and well-defined group, and top positions were often hereditary. In industrial societies, there is a greater openness of the political system that allows a somewhat more diverse set of people to enter the ranks of the political elite through multiple channels, and multiparty electoral systems produce and sustain competing groups of elites. To complicate matters further, constitutional principles in democratic republics often provide a variety of checks on executive authority, while federal systems divide political power between national officials and regional officials.

In the United States, for example, political power is divided among officials at federal, state, and local levels, and among executive, legislative, and judicial branches of government. Moreover, these people have achieved office in a variety of ways. Some have been appointed, others elected. Of the latter, some have been elected as Republicans, others as Democrats, and still others have run as third-party candidates or in nonpartisan elections. Political power also lies in the hands of many people who hold no governmental office and exercise no governmental responsibilities. These are people who command substantial economic resources (e.g., heads of large corporations, heads of large private foundations, wealthy individuals) or who are able to deliver large blocs of votes (e.g., heads of labor unions, leaders of some ethnic and religious groups). Last, but hardly least, those who influence and shape the flow of information in American society—newspaper editors, television newscasters, and others—help define the nation's political agenda and influence the decision-making process (see "The Mass Media," pp. 291–293).

The composition of the political elites of other industrial societies varies somewhat from society to society, depending on the relative strength of the various ideologies and interest groups within them. Also, it tends to change over time in response to technological advances, international developments, and other events. But most of the groups mentioned above are influential in most of the Western democracies and compete with one another for control of the economic surplus and for a voice in shaping the policies of their societies on issues.

In a number of industrial societies, there is a strong symbiotic relation between politicians and economic elites. This is especially evident in societies with brokerage-type political parties, such as the United States. In these societies, politicians constantly

Nine of the Most Powerful Individuals in U.S. Society, Members of the Supreme Court of the United States (in 2014). Seated Left to Right: Justice Clarence Thomas, Justice Antonin Scalia, Chief Justice John G. Roberts, Justice Anthony M. Kennedy, Justice Ruth Bader Ginsburg. Standing Left to Right: Justice Sonia Sotomayor, Justice Stephen G. Breyer, Justice Samuel Anthony Alito, Justice Elena Kagan.

need money to finance expensive election campaigns (e.g., see Chapter 11, p. 284–286), while economic elites seek legislative favors (e.g., lower taxes, larger governmental subsidies, less restrictive regulation) that only politicians can provide. Although this kind of symbiotic relationship is strongest where brokerage-type parties are dominant, leaders of some of the more ideologically oriented parties (e.g., the German Social Democrats) have discovered that electoral success can depend on economic conditions, and this often forces them to work more closely with economic elites than they might otherwise choose to do.

Control of the economic surplus in industrial societies is not simply a matter of elites versus the masses, as it is sometimes made to appear. Different sets of elites often come into conflict with one another. For example, President Ronald Reagan's tax proposals in 1985 led to conflicts between the heads of older "rust-belt" industries of the Midwest and executives in the newer high-tech industries in other parts of the United States. President George W. Bush's proposals regarding use of national forests and other wilderness areas led to sharp conflicts between the timber industry and its employees on the one hand and environmentalists on the other, and President Obama's "green energy" policies have adversely affected coal and petroleum producers.

Another significant feature of the relation between elites and the masses in Western industrial societies is the amount of power that has been acquired by organizations representing large blocs of ordinary citizens. The growth in power of labor organizations in the twentieth century is a good example of this. By organizing politically and economically, union members were able to share significantly in the benefits of the rapidly expanding economy. Traditional elites resisted less vigorously than they might have been expected to, because the rapid expansion of the surplus made it possible for them to avoid costly conflicts while still obtaining greater benefits for themselves. In other words, the great expansion of the economic surplus changed the nature of the conflict from the near *zero-sum game* (see Glossary) it had been throughout most of the agrarian era to a strongly *positive-sum game* from which almost everyone could benefit.

More recently, organizations have been formed to promote a variety of different viewpoints (e.g., on birth control and abortion, gun control, and same-sex marriage) and the interests of a variety of nonelite groups (e.g., racial minorities, women, retired people, the handicapped). While such groups have never gotten all they wanted, they have often won important concessions, including a larger share of the economic surplus.

Today, because of the enormous productivity of industrial societies and because of their democratic polities, almost all parts of the population share to some degree both in the control of the economic surplus and in its benefits. To be sure, they do not share equally in either, but they do share in them. As a result, the vast majority of the members of these societies enjoy a standard of living far above the subsistence level. Even people who are classified as living in poverty in these societies usually live considerably above the subsistence level—which is why so many people in industrializing societies are eager to migrate to the Western democracies.

Because so many different groups have a voice in modern democratic societies, no year passes without efforts to redistribute wealth and income or effect other changes. Although elected officials make most of the final decisions, they know that they can be replaced if a majority of the electorate becomes dissatisfied with their actions—or inaction. This makes it impossible for them to ignore the more pressing concerns of the masses of ordinary citizens.

The Distribution of Income

In industrial societies, incomes vary enormously. In the United States, for example, there are many families whose annual incomes total less than $15,000 per year, even when the value of welfare payments, food stamps, housing subsidies, medical aid, unemployment compensation, social security, and other benefits is included. At the other end of the income scale, there are numerous athletes, entertainers, and business executives with incomes of $10 million or more per year. The average CEO makes more than 200 times that of the average worker in their firm, and beyond them, there is a tiny group of entrepreneurs and CEOs who make $100 million or more in a single year, and there are several families with enormous fortunes that should, at normal interest rates, provide them with incomes of roughly one billion dollars per year

Table 12.1 The Fifteen Wealthiest Individuals in the World

Name	Net Worth in Billions	Location
William Gates III	$76.0	United States
Carlos Slim Helu	$72.0	Mexico
Amancio Ortega	$64.0	Spain
Warren Buffett	$58.2	United States
Lawrence Ellison	$48.0	United States
Charles Koch	$40.0	United States
David Koch	$40.0	United States
Sheldon Adelson	$38.0	United States
Christy Walton & family	$36.7	United States
Jim Walton	$34.7	United States
Liliane Bettencourt	$34.5	France
Stefan Persson	$34.4	Sweden
Alice Walton	$34.3	United States
S. Robson Walton	$34.2	United States
Bernard Arnault & family	$33.5	France

Source: *Forbes*, The World's Billionaires, http://www.forbes.com/billionaires/list/.
Note: Rankings and net worth subject to change.

(see Table 12.1).[1] Thus, the ratio of the highest to the lowest family incomes in the United States may be as much as 100,000 to 1.

In fact, the United States has one of the most unequal distributions of income of any of the advanced industrial societies (see Table 12.2). The highest-earning 20 percent of households receive nearly three times the share of the lowest-earning 40 percent. Canada's income distribution is substantially more equal—the ratio is about 2 to 1—falling at the average for advanced industrial societies.

Nonetheless, incomes in industrial societies, including the United States, are much more *equally* distributed than they are in most contemporary nonindustrial societies. As the bottom two rows of Table 12.2 show, in industrial societies the shares of income going to the lowest-earning 40 percent are generally higher (19.9 versus 16.7), and the shares going to the highest-earning 20 percent are generally lower (40.2 versus 46.8) than in nonindustrial societies. Furthermore, the median ratio of the highest to lowest income shares is only 2.0 to 1.0 for industrial societies compared to 2.8 to 1.0 for nonindustrial societies. Also, because the economies of industrial societies are so much more productive than those of other societies (see Tables 9.2 and 9.3), the incomes of even the lowest-earning industrial households are actually relatively high. By our estimate, the lowest-earning households in industrial societies have more than nine times the income of their counterparts in industrializing agrarian societies, and more than forty times that of their counterparts in industrializing horticultural societies (see Table 14.5).[2]

Moreover, despite fairly steady increases in income inequality in recent decades, there is no evidence that over the longer term income inequality has been increasing in the United States. In fact, over the past seventy years or so, income inequality has

Table 12.2 Percentage Shares of Income Received by Highest-Earning 20 Percent and Lowest-Earning 40 Percent of Households in Industrial Societies

Society	Highest-Earning 20 Percent	Lowest-Earning 40 Percent	Ratio of Highest 20 to Lowest 40
Japan	35.7	24.8	1.4
Finland	36.7	23.7	1.5
Denmark	35.8	23.4	1.6
Norway	37.2	23.6	1.6
Sweden	36.6	23.1	1.6
Germany	36.9	22.2	1.7
Austria	37.8	21.9	1.7
South Korea	37.5	21.5	1.7
Luxembourg	38.9	21.4	1.8
Netherlands	38.7	20.8	1.9
Slovenia	39.4	21.0	1.9
Belgium	41.4	21.5	1.9
Canada	39.9	19.9	2.0
France	40.2	19.8	2.0
Switzerland	41.3	19.8	2.1
Ireland	42.1	19.7	2.1
Spain	42.0	19.1	2.2
Greece	41.5	18.6	2.2
Italy	42.0	18.5	2.3
Australia	41.3	17.9	2.3
New Zealand	43.8	17.8	2.5
United Kingdom	44.0	17.6	2.5
Portugal	45.9	16.8	2.7
Israel	44.9	16.2	2.8
United States	45.8	16.1	2.8
Singapore	49.0	14.5	3.4
Industrial median*	**40.2**	**19.9**	**2.0**
Nonindustrial median**	**46.8**	**16.7**	**2.8**

Source: World Bank, *World Development Indicators,* online database, www.worldbank.org.
Note: Latest figures reported, but years vary.
*The ratio medians were computed from the data for each society, not from the median shares for the different *types* of societies.
**Median for 126 other societies.

decreased somewhat (see Figure 12.1). Income inequality dropped dramatically after the stock market crash of 1929 and it continued to fall into the 1960s. Then, it started to increase in the late 1970s. Despite its steady climb since, it has not yet reached its pre-Depression levels. It is important to note that the fact that the *relative* share of income going to a segment of households declined does not necessarily mean that their *incomes* declined. For example, it would be a mistake to conclude that as the

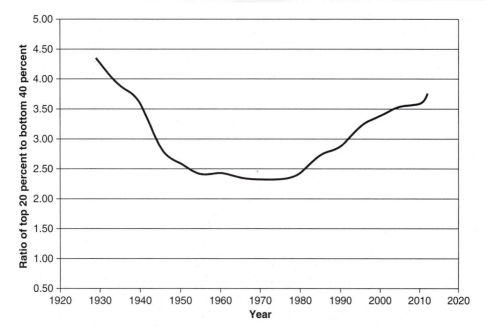

Figure 12.1. United States Family Income Inequality from 1929 to 2012, Ratio of Top 20 Percent to Bottom 40 Percent.

Sources: U.S. Bureau of the Census, *Historical Statistics of the United States: Colonial Times to 1970*, series G319–336 (1929 through 1945), Historical Income Tables, and Families (1950 through 2012), Table F-2.

share of the top-earning 20 percent in the United States declined from 1929 through 1950 their income declined. In fact, over this period the incomes of *all* groups increased, but since the income of the lowest-earning 40 percent grew faster than that of the top 20 percent, the income gap between them shrank somewhat in this period.[3]

Table 12.3 clearly shows the positive-sum nature of income in the United States over the past four decades. Although the *income shares* of all but the highest-earning 20 and 5 percent of households and families declined, *not a single income segment experienced a decline in income.* And, this accounts for inflation. Thus, although the income gap between the highest earning and the other segments grew substantially in this time period, none of them suffered a net loss of income. Unlike the commonly heard zero-sum cliché that the "rich got richer, and the poor got poorer," the truth is that the "rich indeed got much richer, but the poor got a little richer too!"

In 2012 dollars, household income went from $48,019 in 1967 to $71,274, and, since, as we shall see in the next Chapter (Table 13.3, p. 327) households are substantially smaller today, this increasing income was spread over a smaller number of people.[4] These increases in household income, however, have largely been a result of the fact that more household members, especially married women with children, have entered the paid labor force (see Figure 13.1).

Individuals show a similar trend of increase net of inflation. Per capita income doubled, and, using the longest periods reported in the U.S. Census Historical Statistics, we can see that from 1947 to 2012, the median of men's incomes increased 69 percent and

Table 12.3 Share and Mean Income of Quintiles in the U.S., 1967 to 2012

Quintile	Bottom 20	2nd 20	3rd 20	4th 20	Top 20	Top 5
	Households Share (%)					
2012	3.2	8.3	14.4	23.0	51.0	22.3
1967	4.0	10.8	17.3	24.2	43.6	17.2
% Change	−19.3	−22.9	−17.0	−4.8	+17.1	+29.7
	Mean Income $2012					
2012	11,490	29,696	51,179	82,098	181,905	318,052
1967	9,617	26,645	42,538	59,518	107,111	168,961
% Change	+19.5	+11.4	+20.3	+37.9	+69.8	+88.2
	Families Share (%)					
2012	3.8	9.2	15.1	23.0	48.9	21.3
1967	5.4	12.2	17.5	23.5	41.4	16.4
% Change	−30.5	−24.4	−13.8	−1.9	+18.1	+29.7
	Mean Income $2012					
2012	15,534	38,184	62,464	95,474	202,559	352,338
1967	14,762	33,011	47,448	63,635	112,364	177,778
% Change	+5.2	+15.7	+31.6	+50.0	+80.3	+98.2

Source: U.S. Census, Historical Tables H2, H3, http://www.census.gov/hhes/www/income/data/historical/household/index.html; F2, F3, http://www.census.gov/hhes/www/income/data/historical/families/index.html.

women's 135 percent. And, from 1953 to 2012, African-American men's incomes rose 77 percent and women's 251 percent.[5] The striking rise in women's incomes is, in part, a reflection of both how low and how far behind men they were at the start of the period, but it is also clear evidence that the income gap between men and women has closed substantially. We will see further evidence of this in the next chapter. Thus, while it is important to recognize that incomes have declined from their peak at the start of the Great Recession in 2007, the long-term positive-sum trend is undeniable and is indicative of the rising productivity and growing earnings in industrial societies.[6]

Finally, as large as the income ratio of the highest to lowest earning households is in industrial societies today, income inequality in industrial societies is not nearly as great as it was in agrarian societies of the not-so-distant past. As we saw in Chapter 7, the top 1 or 2 percent of families in those societies generally received not less than *half* the total income. In contrast, the top 5 percent of American households currently receive only about 22 percent of the nation's total income.[7] And, unlike the situation in the typical agrarian or early industrial society, relatively few individuals remain persistently in the lowest income categories year after year. According to two ten-year Treasury Department studies, spanning the years 1979 to 2005, more than 60 percent of the individuals who were in the very lowest income category at the start of each study had moved to a higher income quintile ten years later. In fact, in both time periods more than 7 percent ended up in the *very highest income category*.[8] Similarly, an earlier study found that only about 30 percent of the individuals living in poverty in the United States in one year were still living in poverty a year later, and only about 2 percent remained in poverty eight years or longer.[9]

The Distribution of Wealth

Wealth has long been more unequally distributed than income in industrial societies. For instance, although, as we just saw in the last section, figures for the United States show that 22 percent of total income is earned by the top 5 percent of households, 21 percent of the wealth is owned by the richest 1 percent of individuals.[10]

These figures exaggerate the difference, however, because inequalities in wealth are much more closely linked to age than are inequalities in income. As individuals grow older, most accumulate household furnishings and other possessions, pay off mortgages on their homes, and build up equity in pension funds. For example, the most recent study (2012) of asset ownership in the United States showed that the youngest families (under age 35) had a median net worth, in 2010 dollars, of $65,300; middle-aged families (ages 55 to 64) had a net worth of $880,500 (the highest of all age categories); and the oldest families (over 75) had a net worth of about $677,800.[11]

Turning to *trends,* there is no clear evidence that ownership of wealth has consistently grown more concentrated. In fact, as Figure 12.2 shows, data gleaned from estate tax records indicate that the percentage of wealth owned by the richest 1 percent of individuals, after reaching a peak of more than 40 percent in 1930, dropped dramatically during the Great Depression and has remained in the low 20s in the years following World War II.* Although the share of wealth of the *very* richest has increased substantially in recent years—according to *Forbes,* the 400 richest Americans constitute about 0.0002 percent of the adult population—the share accruing to the top 1 percent has remained relatively constant.[13] This may be partly explained by the relative "democratization" of stock ownership that has occurred in recent years. The percentage of corporate stock held by people *indirectly* through mutual funds and pension plans increased from 17 to 33 between 1986 and 2000, and since 1986 the fraction of American families that own stock, directly or indirectly, increased from less than one-third to about one-half.[14]

It is certainly possible, however, that the growing inequality in income could begin to produce increasing wealth inequality in coming years.

Occupational Stratification

For most members of industrial societies, their occupations are the chief determinant of their income and wealth. About 62 percent of the national income of the United States today, for example, is distributed in the form of wages, salaries, and fringe benefits of employment, such as health insurance and employers' contributions to pensions and social security.[15]

As we noted earlier, the range of benefits received by people in different kinds of occupations varies greatly in the United States, with the top 10 percent enjoying incomes that are ten, fifteen or more times larger on average than the incomes of those in the bottom 10 percent—the unemployed, part-time workers, and the unskilled. A handful

---

*Alternative measures of wealth concentration show a "U" shape. Thus, despite the overall higher levels they show, there is not an increase in inequality over the time period.[12]

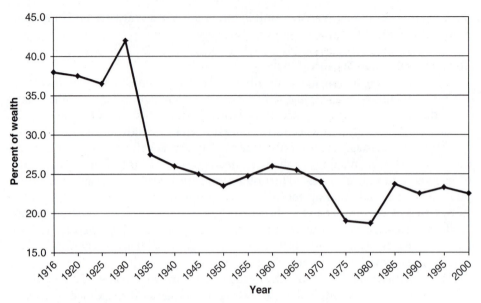

Figure 12.2. Wealth Owned by Top 1 Percent of Individuals in the United States from 1916 to 2000.
Source: Wojciech Kopczuk and Emmanuel Saez, "Top Wealth in the United States, 1916–2000: Evidence from Estate Tax Returns," National Bureau of Economic Research, working paper, March, 2004.

of people at the very top of the occupational ladder in the Western democracies—business leaders, entertainers, and athletes—are paid about 1,000 times more than full-time workers who receive the minimum wage.

Prior to World War II, lower white-collar workers enjoyed, on average, higher incomes than skilled blue-collar workers in the United States.[16] Since then, however, the relative rankings of these two classes have gradually been reversed, creating the present pattern, which favors skilled manual workers in many countries. An even more important change in the occupational system in industrial societies has been the substantial growth in the relative number of high- and middle-status occupations. As Table 12.4 indicates, the percentage of white-collar jobs in the American labor force has quadrupled since the beginning of the last century; the percentage of blue-collar workers has declined somewhat, and, as we saw in Chapter 10, farm employment has plummeted. These developments have brought about an important change in the class structure of American society and, to a lesser extent, other industrial societies. No longer are the majority of people concentrated in the lower class, as in agrarian societies of the past (see Figure 7.5, p. 195). Today, most of the people in most industrial societies are members of the middle class. This is yet another consequence of the technological innovations that have so transformed the conditions of life for members of these societies since the beginnings of industrialization.

Educational Stratification
One of the great achievements of industrial societies has been the tremendous expansion of educational opportunities. Formal education is no longer a privilege limited to

Table 12.4 Distribution of Adult Population among Occupational Classes in the U.S., 1900 and 2010 (in Percentages)

Occupational Class	1900	2010
White-collar	17	73
Blue-collar	45	25
Farmer and farm laborer	38	2
Total	100	100

Sources: Figures based on data in U.S. Dept. of Commerce, Bureau of the Census, *Historical Statistics of the United States: Colonial Times to 1970,* series D182–232, and U.S. Bureau of the Census, *Statistical Abstract of the U.S., 2012,* Table 620.

children of a small affluent minority. Today, all children are allowed to attend school for ten years or more at public expense.[†]

Despite the great increase in educational opportunities, inequalities in their utilization persist. Some young people drop out of school as soon as possible, while others go on to receive advanced degrees. The amount of education an individual receives is a function of many things—intelligence, motivation, health, peer influence, family tradition, family resources, and so forth.[17]

Differences in educational achievement, whatever the cause, have substantial consequences for subsequent achievement in the occupational system of stratification. Most jobs in modern industrial societies have educational prerequisites, and insufficient years of education or lack of an appropriate diploma can bar otherwise qualified individuals from careers in many fields. In effect, modern personnel practices have created a civilian counterpart to the traditional military caste system, with its sharp distinction between officers and enlisted personnel. Just as the ceiling on promotion for enlisted troops is normally the rank of sergeant, so the ceiling on promotion for less educated workers in industry tends to be the rank of foreman or, possibly, plant superintendent. Higher positions in industry and government are usually reserved for people with a college or university degree who are recruited directly from outside the organization. Figure 12.3 illustrates the pattern.

The importance of educational stratification today is clearly evident in data on the relationship between education and income. The most highly educated Americans, for example, receive more than three times more income than their least educated counterparts and have only one-fifth the risk of unemployment.[18] Because of the great economic value of education in modern industrial societies, many economists and sociologists have begun to refer to it as "human" capital. Like the more traditional forms of capital, it has the power to produce income.

Racial and Ethnic Stratification

Many industrial societies have racial or ethnic divisions within them. Canada, for example, has a serious cleavage between its French- and English-speaking populations, Belgium between Flemings and Walloons, and the United States between

---

[†]As noted in Chapter 9, this is largely a legacy of the Protestant Reformation and its encouragement of mass literacy.

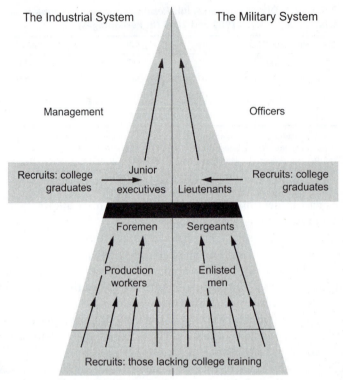

Figure 12.3. Model of Recruitment and Promotion in Modern Industry Compared with Recruitment and Promotion in the Military.

African-Americans and European-Americans—to cite but three of the more prominent instances. When membership in an ethnic or racial group has an appreciable influence on an individual's access to the benefits a society offers, the group has become, in effect, a class.

Classes of this kind, however, are different from most others in several respects. For one thing, the resource that is involved in ethnic and racial systems of stratification is an *ascribed* characteristic: Racial or ethnic background, unlike occupation and education, cannot be altered by individual effort. In addition, racial and ethnic classes usually have a greater degree of class consciousness than most others; more, say, than people with high school diplomas, more even than manual workers. Finally, because physical traits (i.e., appearance) and primary relationships (i.e., ties with family and close friends) are often involved, it is more difficult for an individual to move into or out of an ethnic or racial class.

The most striking example of this type of stratification in the United States involves the two major racial groups. Since colonial times, African-Americans have been a subordinate group. Before the Civil War, the majority of African-Americans were slaves and the property of members of the white group. Even before the Emancipation Proclamation in 1862, however, a few African-Americans had established businesses and become wealthy (some even became slave owners themselves); but despite African-Americans' achievements, they continued to suffer from handicaps imposed because of race.

Today, most of the more obvious of these limitations have been removed. Civil rights legislation ensures African-Americans equal treatment in stores, hotels, restaurants, and other business establishments, and affirmative action programs even provide preferential treatment in college admissions, hiring, and promotions, though more subtle forms of discrimination sometimes continue in housing, club membership, mortgage lending, and some other areas.

In some respects, however, it would appear that little or no progress has been made in recent decades. For example, in 2012 African-American families earned about 62 percent of what white families earned, virtually the same as they did forty years earlier.[19] In other respects it would appear that conditions may actually have deteriorated. More than half of African-American families with children are headed by women, and nearly 68 percent of African-American births today are to unmarried women (up from 38 percent in 1970).[‡][21] Children in these families are deprived not only of a father's contribution to socialization but of an important source of income as well. Black female-headed households earn less than half of what black married-couple households earn, and black female-headed households contain the vast majority of the black children who live in poverty.[22] Many of these youngsters enter school lacking a strong foundation for learning and later leave school poorly equipped to compete in the demanding occupational system of a modern industrial society. Whatever the underlying causes of the high proportion of female-headed families among African-Americans (a subject of controversy), its impact on children is undeniable.[§]

However, this is only part of the picture. There is also evidence of substantial economic progress. The percentage of African-American children in poverty has dropped from 46.3 in 1992 to about 35 in 2009.[24] Moreover, as we saw earlier, the incomes of African-Americans has been growing faster than that of their white counterparts. Whereas in 1940 black men made only about 41 percent of what white men earned, today they earn more than 75 percent, and, whereas black women earned only 36 percent of what white women earned in 1940, today they earn 84 percent of what white women earn.[25]

Perhaps even more significant, the percentage of African-Americans in middle-class occupations has grown from less than 10 percent in 1940 to about 50 percent today (see Figure 12.4). Black homeownership is now 46 percent, double what it was in 1940, and just off its recent record of 48 percent.[26]

These figures reveal a basic division within the African-American population. The removal of legal and social barriers opened a wide range of opportunities for those with the family and educational resources to pursue them, but it also led to a growing rift between them and others lacking such resources. Furthermore, since the effects of these social, economic, and educational deprivations persist and are passed

---

[‡]The comparable figures for whites are: percentage of white female-headed families, 16.8; percentage of white births to unmarried women, 26.[20]

[§]For example, by some estimates, children from a fatherless home are nine times more likely to drop out of high school, five times more likely to commit suicide, and twenty times more likely to end up in prison.[23]

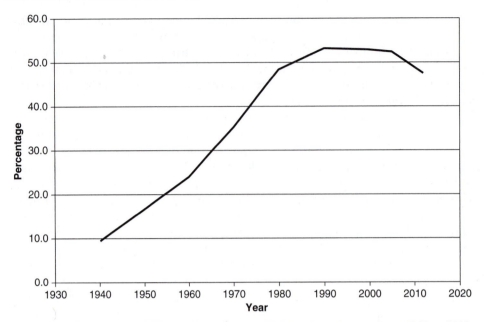

Figure 12.4. Percentage of African-Americans in Middle-Class Occupations 1940 to 2012.
Sources: William Julius Wilson, *The Declining Significance of Race: Blacks and Changing American Institutions*, 2d. ed.
(Chicago: University of Chicago Press, 1980), chap. 6; and U.S. Bureau of the Census, *Statistical Abstract of the
U.S.*, 2007, Table 602; Current Population Survey 2013, Table 11.

on across generations, movement out of this disadvantaged class may be becoming
more difficult. For example, while the median income of the highest-earning 5 percent
of African-American households rose more than $92,000, net of inflation, between
1975 and 2012, the income of the lowest-earning 20 percent actually *declined* by more
than $800.[27]

In Canada, the most serious cleavage is along ethnic lines and divides French-
speaking Canadians from English-speaking ones. Although the French settled the
country first, they were later conquered by the British, who dominated the political
system from the eighteenth century on. The problem was further aggravated because
the English industrialized the country while the French clung to an agrarian way of
life. As a result, the English also dominated the economy, even in Quebec, the home
province of the French.[28] In recent years the French have succeeded in eliminating
most discriminatory practices through political action, but a substantial minority desires political independence.[29]

Age and Sex Stratification

Inequalities based on age and sex have been a part of every human society, past as
well as present. To some extent, these inequalities reflect genetic differences among
the members. On average, men have been stronger than women, and they have not
been burdened biologically by the responsibility for bearing and nursing children.
Adults have been larger, stronger, and more knowledgeable than children, though

aged adults have become disadvantaged whenever their health, vitality, and mental abilities have declined.**

These biologically based differences have been reinforced and extended in most societies by cultural norms. Thus, the fact that the average woman is not as strong as the average man has often led to norms that exclude *all* women from activities for which *some* women would be physically qualified.

With respect to age and sex stratification, modern industrial societies resemble preindustrial societies in many ways. Continuity can be seen most clearly in the frequency with which older men still control the more powerful organizations. Most members of Congress and state legislatures in the United States, for example, are men, and in the 113th Congress the average age of representatives was fifty-seven and of senators sixty-two.[30] Most business leaders are also men, and although the CEOs of top corporations are three years younger than their counterparts twenty years ago, their average age is still fifty-five.[31] Finally, an earlier study of American military leaders, all of whom were male, found that their average age was fifty-four.[32]

In all industrial societies, women's wages are lower than men's (see Table 12.5). According to the most recent data, in industrial societies women, on average, earn about 67 percent of what men earn, but the figure varies from a low of 43 percent in

Table 12.5 Ratio of Women's to Men's Wages in Industrial Societies

Society	Ratio	Society	Ratio
Singapore	0.82	Australia	0.65
Ireland	0.77	Greece	0.65
New Zealand	0.76	Switzerland	0.64
Norway	0.75	Slovenia	0.64
Denmark	0.73	Germany	0.62
Canada	0.73	Japan	0.60
Finland	0.71	Austria	0.59
Iceland	0.70	Portugal	0.57
Sweden	0.69	Israel	0.55
Netherlands	0.69	Spain	0.55
Luxembourg	0.69	South Korea	0.54
United Kingdom	0.68	Italy	0.49
Belgium	0.68	France	0.43
United States	0.67	**Median**	**0.67**

Source: *World Economic Forum*, "The Global Gender Gap Report 2012," Wage Equality Survey, Appendix, Table D2. Note this estimate for the United States is different than that in Figure 12.5.

**The social status of older people is also affected by the prevailing rate of social change. In societies where social change is slow or imperceptible, the value of their experience is high, because their knowledge continues to be relevant. On the other hand, where the rate of social change is high, especially technological and economic change, the value of their experience is low because much of their knowledge is often obsolete.

France to 82 percent in Singapore. Canada is above the average, and the United States is right at the average.[††]

There are a variety of reasons for this income disparity, but the most important appears to be the persistence of the division of labor between the sexes. In all industrial societies there are certain occupations that are filled primarily by men and others that are filled primarily by women (in addition, there are some in which there is a more balanced representation of the sexes), and women, despite their occupation, generally have greater household and child care responsibilities than men. The occupations filled primarily by women usually have lower wages or salaries than those filled primarily by men. They also tend to be occupations that offer fewer opportunities for promotion to more responsible positions.

The concentration of women in these lower-paying jobs is partly a heritage of the past when women seldom worked for long outside the home (see Figure 13.1, p. 335) and

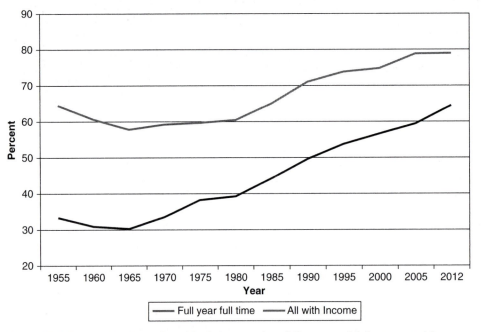

Figure 12.5. Ratios of Women's to Men's Income for all Persons with Income and for Full-Time, Full-Year Employees, 1955 to 2012.
Source: U.S. Bureau of the Census, Historical Income Tables, Tables P-8 and P-36 (http://www.census.gov/hhes/www/income/data/historical/people/).

[††]Although these estimates allow comparisons across industrial societies, the figure for the United States is slightly different than that in the lower part of Figure 12.5. It is also worth noting that, according to one study, the ratio of women's to men's incomes in the United States is relatively low, not because of greater discrimination against women, but because of the greater disparity between the incomes of high- and low-paying jobs in the United States (e.g., see Table 12.2). The concentration of women in lower-paying jobs thus depresses women's incomes more relative to men's than it does in societies where the occupational income disparity is lower.[33]

Angela Merkel, Germany's First Female Prime Minister, with Former Russian President Dmitry Medvedev at the Chancellery in Berlin.

when those who did were assumed (often incorrectly) to be supplementing their husband's or father's income and, therefore, were less in need of high wages than men, who were expected to be the primary providers for families.[‡‡] Once established, this pattern has persisted because it tends to shape the expectations and aspirations of men and women. Thus, the pattern of women's employment has become, in part, a matter of choice, with some women viewing marriage as a more attractive alternative than the job market and a commitment to family as more rewarding and more important than a commitment to career.

But it is also rooted in the present. Married women in the paid labor force find that they must constantly balance the demands of their jobs and careers against those of their families and children. And, although there is some evidence that husbands with working wives are today performing more household and child care functions than they did in the past, the majority of these responsibilities still accrue to wives.[35]

Nevertheless, the wage gap between men and women has generally closed with advancing industrialization. In the United States, for example, employed women's wages as a percentage of men's rose from less than 50 in 1890 to nearly 65 in 1950, but then dropped a bit and hovered around 60 between 1950 and 1980.[36] Women's wages began to rise steeply in the 1980s and today, for women who work full time, all year, their wages are around 81 percent of men's.[37] In fact, between 1995 and 2012, after adjusting for inflation, while white men's incomes rose by only 1.7 percent, white women's

---

[‡‡]According to one study, there was a clear "marriage penalty" in the United States in 1900. It estimates that married women, on average, were paid 30 percent less than their unmarried cohorts.[34]

incomes rose by 19.5 percent, black women's by 22.1 percent, and black men's by 4.1 percent.[38] The weekly wages of women aged twenty-five to thirty-four are now 90 percent of, and never married women make 96 percent of, their male cohorts.[39] There is every reason to expect this gap will continue to shrink, as women's skills and labor experience continue to grow, and as larger numbers of women move into high-paid "traditionally male" occupations and move up the corporate ladder (e.g., see The Changing Role of Women, in Chapter 13, pp. 332–339).[40]

The legal and political standing of women has also greatly improved as a result of industrialization. Laws that once restricted their right to own property have been eliminated, and women now own much of the wealth in all Western societies. For instance, an analysis of estate tax returns in the United States indicated that, today, nearly half of the top wealth holders are women.[41] Barriers to higher education have also been largely eliminated. In fact, in the United States, women now earn the *majority* of bachelor's degrees and doctorates (see Table 13.4, p. 336). Even in the political arena, women have made substantial gains. In 1900, women were permitted to vote only in New Zealand and in four American states.[42] Today, they enjoy this right in every industrial society. Women are also a growing presence in the parliaments of industrial societies, holding an average of 28 percent of the seats in industrial society parliaments, an increase of more than 50 percent in just the last two decades, and women have served as prime ministers of a growing number of societies including Australia, Britain, Canada, Denmark, Finland, France, Germany, Israel, New Zealand, Norway, Slovenia, and South Korea.[43]

VERTICAL MOBILITY

Compared with agrarian societies, industrial societies offer many more opportunities for individuals to improve their status. In agrarian societies, high birthrates ensured an oversupply of labor in almost every generation. At every level in society, a substantial percentage of the children were obliged to work in occupations of lower status than their parents or to join the ranks of beggars, outlaws, prostitutes, and vagabonds. Although a few improved their situation, far more were downwardly mobile.[44]

In industrial societies, conditions are strikingly different. Falling birthrates have reduced the oversupply of labor, while technological advances have greatly increased the proportion of high-status, high-income jobs. Furthermore, because the upper classes have smaller families than the lower classes, opportunities are created for many children of the latter to become upwardly mobile. Finally, flawed though they are, the systems of free public education in industrial societies give talented and disciplined children from the lower classes an opportunity to acquire skills that can help them move up the social ladder.

As a result of these developments, there is no industrial society in which the rate of downward mobility greatly exceeds the rate of upward mobility. At worst, downward mobility may be slightly greater in a few of them.[45] In most industrial societies, however, there appears to be more upward mobility than downward, a remarkable change from the recent preindustrial past.

This development has undoubtedly been a factor in reducing the threat of working-class revolution predicted by Marx and his followers. If, in every generation, a quarter or more of the children of workers are able to rise into the ranks of the middle class, resentment against the system is almost certain to be less than if only a few move up the ladder, the pattern Marx expected. Furthermore, since those who rise tend to be the more talented and ambitious members of the working class, much of its potential leadership for protest movements is lost.

SOCIAL INEQUALITY: TWO BASIC TRENDS

In agrarian societies of the past, systems of inequality were often built into the legal codes. There was no pretense that people were equal. Some were legally classified as members of a privileged nobility, some as commoners, others as slaves or serfs, and their legal rights and privileges varied accordingly. Democracy as we understand it was unknown in these societies. Political decisions were the God-given prerogative of a tiny elite; the rest of the population had no voice in decision making. The only thing that limited the power of the governing elite was the knowledge that if conditions became too oppressive the masses might revolt. Because of their enormous power, the ruler and the rest of the governing class together usually enjoyed not less than half of the national income and sometimes as much as two-thirds.[46]

In advanced industrial societies, legally based hereditary status has been virtually eliminated. In Britain and a few other societies, titles of nobility remain, but nearly all the special rights and privileges that were once attached to them no longer exist. Equally important, the disadvantaged legal statuses of serf and slave have been completely abolished. Although social inequalities remain, they are no longer based solely on the accident of birth.

In addition, opportunities for participation in political decision making have substantially broadened in industrial societies. The franchise has been extended ever more widely until virtually the entire adult population is now able to vote in all of them (see Figure 11.1). Although the system falls far short of equal influence for all, it is, by democratic standards, a tremendous advance over the situation that prevailed in agrarian societies not long ago.

Finally, income inequality has been greatly reduced in industrial societies. Though substantial inequalities still exist, the change has been tremendous. As we have seen (e.g., Table 12.2), the top 20 percent of the population in industrial societies appears to receive only about 40 percent of the national income, compared to the 50 percent or more received by the top 1 or 2 percent of the population in historical agrarian societies, and the nearly 50 percent received by the top 20 percent of current industrializing societies.

Thus, *the overall level of inequality in industrial societies is considerably less than that in agrarian societies of the past or in most nonindustrial societies in the world today.* The best explanation for this egalitarian trend seems to be the enormous growth in productivity unleashed by the Industrial Revolution, together with the demographic transition.[47] With per capita national incomes increasing rapidly, the dominant classes found it was no longer in their interest to fight all the claims of other classes to a larger share of the economic surplus.

Periodic concessions to the lower and middle classes could help elites preserve much of their power and privilege. By giving ground in relative terms (i.e., by conceding

Table 12.6 Quality of Life in Industrial Societies

Society	HDI*
Norway	0.96
Australia	0.94
United States	0.94
Netherlands	0.92
Germany	0.92
New Zealand	0.92
Ireland	0.92
Sweden	0.92
Switzerland	0.91
Japan	0.91
Canada	0.91
South Korea	0.91
Iceland	0.91
Denmark	0.90
Israel	0.90
Belgium	0.90
Austria	0.90
Singapore	0.90
France	0.89
Finland	0.89
Slovenia	0.89
Spain	0.89
Italy	0.88
Luxembourg	0.88
United Kingdom	0.88
Greece	0.86
Portugal	0.82
Industrial median	**0.90**
Nonindustrial median**	**0.55**

Source: United Nations, Human Development Indicators, accessed: 11/21/2013, from: http://hdr.undp.org.
*Human Development Index, an index of well-being based on measures of life expectancy, literacy, education, and income.
**Median for sixty-six industrializing nonindustrial societies (see Table 14.6).

a larger share of total income to nonelites), they could even improve their economic position in absolute terms (i.e., their total income and wealth actually increased). This was possible because technological advances had transformed the old zero-sum game that prevailed in most preindustrial societies into a positive-sum game. Elites apparently concluded that it was better to settle for a smaller share of a much larger pie than to fight to preserve their historic share and, in the process, risk an end to economic growth and the loss of all the benefits it afforded.

An important consequence of this is the rising standard of living and the improved life chances of the average member of industrial societies. For the past few years, the United Nations has tried to develop an objective measure of the quality of life afforded by different societies in the world system today. Table 12.6 shows the results of their most recent effort. Industrial societies are all clustered near the top of this scale with an average score of 0.90 out of a possible 1. In contrast, industrializing societies lagged far behind this achievement with an average score of only 0.55.

This gap between the rich and poor nations of the world reveals the other side of the development coin: While on the one hand, the advancing technology of industrialization has helped reduce the level of inequality *within* industrial societies, on the other, it has increased inequality *among* societies in the world system. The gap has been widening ever since the start of the industrial era. For instance, in 1860, the wealthiest quarter of the world's population controlled 58 percent of world income, but by 2012 the seven largest and most advanced industrial societies (see Table 9.2, less China), which comprise 12 percent of the world's population, controlled about 50 percent, and the share of the bottom quarter fell from 12.5 to less than 2 percent.[48] With new technology gradually eroding the barriers between societies, the social impact of this trend is bound to increase. We will return to this subject in Chapter 14, when we examine the complex problems of the third world as it struggles to develop economically in the shadow of far wealthier and more powerful societies.

CHAPTER 13

Industrial Societies

Population, the Family, and Leisure

Outline
Population
The Family
Leisure and the Arts
Problems and Progress
Industrial Societies in Theoretical Perspective

Industrialization has dramatically altered the size, rates of growth, and spatial distribution of the populations of industrial societies. These changes, in turn, have had a major impact on the size, composition, and functioning of households and families in these societies and how people spend their time. In this chapter, we will first examine the long-term trends in population and then trace some of their most important effects on families, age and sex roles, and leisure in industrial societies.

POPULATION

Growth in Size of Societies

The populations of industrial societies have grown substantially over the past two centuries, though not nearly as much as their technological advances and gains in productivity would lead one to expect. For example, England and Wales had a population of approximately nine million at the start of the nineteenth century, and their current population is about 57 million.[1] While this five- to sixfold increase is impressive when compared to rates of population growth in the preindustrial past, it falls far short of the more than thirtyfold increase in Britain's gross national product during that same period (see Chapter 10). The same thing is true of other societies that have industrialized, with the exception of the United States, Canada, Australia, and other former frontier societies that entered the industrial era with populations that were abnormally small for their geographical size.

To better understand the reasons for this pattern of growth in population, we must consider the three factors that together determine the rate of population change: fertility, mortality, and migration.

Trends in Health and Longevity

Throughout the agrarian era, sickness and disease were a pervasive features of human life. Prior to the invention of the microscope, it was impossible for anyone even to know of the existence of bacteria or viruses, much less to devise effective means of combating them. Medical knowledge was not advanced much beyond what had existed at the end of the hunting and gathering era and, for most illnesses, people were forced to rely on faith healing, magic, or medical practices of dubious value (e.g., the use of leeches and bloodletting) when they became ill.* As we have seen (see p. 172), average life expectancy at birth in even the most advanced agrarian societies was as low as twenty to twenty-five years, and even the children of royalty and the upper classes did not have a much greater life expectancy.[2]

During the industrial era, however, there has been an explosive growth in the store of information concerning the prevention and cure of disease—especially most communicable diseases, such as influenza, tuberculosis, diphtheria, and smallpox, which once killed large numbers of people and afflicted many more.[†] As a result, the death rate from communicable diseases has dropped tremendously (see Table 13.1). Life expectancy in the United States was less the fifty at the start of the twentieth century and is now nearly eighty; more than three times that found in advanced agrarian societies.

Table 13.1 Death Rates for Communicable Diseases in the U.S., 1860–2010

	Deaths per 100,000 Population per Year**		
Cause of Death	**Mass., 1860***	**U.S., 1900**	**U.S., 2010**
Influenza and pneumonia	***	202	15.1
Tuberculosis	365	194	0.2
Gastritis, enteritis, etc.	***	143	0
Typhoid fever	76	31	0
Diphtheria	68	40	0
Smallpox	27	***	0
Measles	18	13	0
Scarlet fever	***	10	0

Sources: U.S. Dept. of Commerce, Bureau of the Census, *Historical Statistics of the United States: Colonial Times to 1970,* pp. 58 and 63; and Bureau of the Census, *Statistical Abstract of the United States, 2002,* Tables 100 and 101; National Center for Health Statistics, "Health United States 2012," May 30, 2013.
*Massachusetts was the first state to keep reliable statewide records on the causes of death; reliable national data are not available before 1900.
**A zero indicates that the rate is less than 0.1 per 100,000 population.
***Not reported.

---

*Some recent research has found leeches very helpful in preventing blood-clotting when reattaching severed fingers and other parts. This, of course, was not the use to which leeches were put in the preindustrial era.
†Diseases, such as AIDS still kill far too many people, but they too are being increasingly mitigated and controlled.

Before Industrial Advances in Sanitation, Vaccination, and Medicine This Was a Common Sight: Early Photo of a Hospital Crowded with Children.

Moreover, whereas half or more of the babies born in hunting and gathering and horticultural societies, and a quarter or more of those born into relatively prosperous agrarian villages *died before they reached their fifteenth birthday*, in industrial societies, *99 percent survive*.[3] Equally important, they will live far healthier lives than was possible for most in preindustrial societies.

Declining Birthrates and Increasing Immigration

As health conditions improved and death rates declined, industrial societies experienced a period of rapid population growth. This was because birthrates remained at traditional levels, which created a widening gap between birthrates and death rates.

Within a few decades, however, birthrates also began to decline. During the last 150 years or so, technological advances on various fronts (e.g., the vulcanization of rubber, the development of the contraceptive pill, safe methods of abortion and sterilization) have made it possible for members of industrial societies to control the number of their offspring by safe and effective means. At the same time, technological advances in other areas, together with various social changes (e.g., the creation of social security programs, prohibitions against child labor), have virtually eliminated the historic economic incentive for having children. In addition, the increasing employment of women outside the home has made child rearing more difficult and more expensive. As a result, birthrates have dropped greatly in all industrial societies.

In most industrial societies, in fact, birthrates have dropped substantially below the level required to keep populations at their present size. To maintain stable populations, women in industrial societies today must have, on average,

Table 13.2 Total Fertility Rate in Industrial Societies

Society	Total Fertility Rate*
South Korea	1.2
Singapore	1.2
Japan	1.4
Greece	1.4
Italy	1.4
Spain	1.4
Germany	1.4
Portugal	1.4
Austria	1.4
Switzerland	1.5
Luxembourg	1.5
Slovenia	1.6
Canada	1.6
Belgium	1.8
Netherlands	1.8
Denmark	1.8
Finland	1.8
Sweden	1.9
Australia	1.9
Norway	1.9
United States	1.9
United Kingdom	2.0
France	2.0
Iceland	2.0
Ireland	2.1
New Zealand	2.1
Israel	3.0
Industrial median	**1.8**
Nonindustrial median	**2.4**

Source: World Bank, World Development Indicators, www.worldbank
.org/.
*The total fertility rate is an estimate of the number of children the
average woman will have in her lifetime.

about 2.11 children each.[‡] As Table 13.2 makes clear, the fertility rate in nearly every industrial society is well below this figure. If these rates were to continue, industrial societies as a group would experience a nearly 15 percent decline in population over the next seventy-five years, and South Korea, Slovenia, and Singapore, which have the

---

[‡]Because some girls die before reaching the age of reproduction, and because some couples are infertile, those women capable of bearing children have to have slightly more than two apiece.

lowest fertility rates, would experience a 50 percent decline. And while the United States and Iceland would maintain their populations, only Israel and New Zealand would experience an increase.

Declines of any substantial magnitude are unlikely, however, because of the great influx of immigrants from the developing world. The economic opportunities and high standards of living in the industrial democracies, together with the growth of the welfare state and its many benefits, are a powerful magnet for people whose own societies are suffering in the throes of the early stages of industrialization.

Although the overwhelming majority of emigrants from developing societies remain within the developing world, there is a substantial flow of people out of these societies and into the advanced societies. For example, from 2000 to 2010, there was a net migration out of less developed and into advanced industrial societies of nearly thirty-five million.[4] The United States received more than ten million; Italy nearly four million; Canada more than two million; and Great Britain, France, and Australia considerably more than a million migrants each.[5] As a result, about 28 percent of Australia's population is now foreign-born, as is 21 percent of Canada's, 14 percent of the United States', and 9 percent of Italy's.[6] Immigration of this magnitude would create problems in any society, but it is especially serious when substantial cultural differences are introduced into populations that have been culturally homogeneous for centuries. It is difficult to exaggerate, for example, the cultural gulf that separates devout Muslims from Pakistan, Turkey, and Algeria from the nominally Christian but largely secularist native populations of England, Germany, and France.[§] Even when the migrants are Christians from southern Europe, as with Slavic immigrants in Germany or the Portuguese in Luxembourg, the effect can be unsettling.

But when high levels of immigration are combined with global economic recession and high rates of unemployment, the situation can become explosive. The rising rates of ethnic violence and the resurgence of xenophobia in western Europe are obviously a result of this volatile mixture of ethnicity and economics.[7] But even if their economies recover and their unemployment rates drop substantially, industrial societies will still confront serious ethnic, racial, and religious strains. As the continuing conflict in India, the Philippines, South Africa, Northern Ireland, and the recent explosions of violence in Iraq, and parts of the former Soviet Union and Yugoslavia attest, ethnic, racial, and religious conflicts are some of the most enduring and intractable problems faced by societies.

Population Distribution: The Growth of Urban Populations
Another revolutionary demographic change has been the massive shift of population from rural areas to cities and towns. Even in the most advanced agrarian societies of

---

[§]One indication of the magnitude of this gulf emerged in the late 1980s when Muslim immigrants in England—a nation that prides itself on freedom of expression—threatened to assassinate the author of a book they found offensive, while burning his book in public rallies and threatening stores that sold it. More recently, problems have emerged in France, where Muslim immigrants have challenged traditional dress codes in the schools and engaged in anti-Semitic activities of various kinds, and in Germany and England where young Muslim men have been recruited by al Qaeda to engage in terrorist activities in the United States and elsewhere.

Berliners Shocked by Murders of Muslim Women

In recent decades, millions of Muslims from the Middle East and Africa have migrated to Europe, bringing with them many of their traditional beliefs and practices. One such practice that has shocked most Germans is the practice whereby male family members feel obliged to kill any female member of the family who brings shame or dishonor on the family by violating traditional standards of conduct.

In a period of only a few months in late 2004 and early 2005, six young Muslim women were killed by close relatives for staining their family's honor. In a recent case, a twenty-three-year-old single mother was gunned down on the street by three of her brothers. Seven years earlier, her father, a strict Muslim, sent her back to Turkey to marry a cousin whom she had never seen. When the marriage failed, she returned to Berlin with her young son. Back in

Berlin, she distanced herself from her family and sought to assimilate into German society. She abandoned the traditional head covering and sometimes even drank alcohol. All of this so shamed her father and brothers that they apparently felt justified in killing her.

Such crimes are rarely mentioned in the German press for fear of drawing charges of racism, but this case was so open and flagrant that it could not be hushed up, and Germans, like members of other industrial societies, are being forced to rethink the question of the costs and benefits of mass immigration from societies that have radically different cultural traditions.

Source: Jeffrey Fleishman, "'Honor' Suspected in 6 Berlin Killings," *Los Angeles Times*, March 20, 2005.

the past, the limitations of agricultural technology required that 90 to 95 percent of the population live in rural areas where the basic raw materials were produced. Since urban communities were dependent on the surplus that could be extracted from the peasantry, they could never grow beyond 5 to 10 percent of the population.

Advances in agriculture in the last 200 years removed this constraint on urban growth. Thanks to the new technology, farms required far fewer workers (see Table 10.2). Simultaneously, the new system of factory production, with its need for large concentrations of workers, stimulated the growth of cities and towns. As a result, nearly 80 percent of the populations of industrial societies now live in urban areas.

Nowhere are the consequences of the Industrial Revolution more clearly evident than in the major cities of the industrial world. Vast concentrations of people live and work in organizational systems of extraordinary complexity. Most of the time these systems function so smoothly that we forget the complex infrastructure of water and sewer systems, power systems, communications systems, and transportation systems on which they depend. It is only when we experience such disasters as earthquakes, hurricanes, or war, and these systems break down for a time, that we are reminded of the technological foundation on which industrial societies are built and on which they depend.

THE FAMILY

The impact of industrialization on kinship has been no less dramatic than its impact on population, the economy, the polity, and stratification. The consequences for kinship, the oldest institutional system in human societies, can be seen in its changing

Emigration from the Third World to Advanced Industrial Societies Has Become So Great That Immigrants Often Outnumber the Native Population in Large Sections of Major Cities: Produce Shop in Chinese Section of Vancouver, British Columbia.

functions, in the smaller size and altered composition of households and families, and in the changing roles of women and young people.

Changing Structure of Households and Families

Even a glance at Table 13.3, reveals cumulative changes in household and family composition over the past half century that can only be described as *seismic*. Although it shows that a majority of families fifty years ago were not the "Leave it to Beaver" or "Father Knows Best" image of 1950s TV—a married couple with one or two children—today they constitute only a fifth of U.S. households. In fact, more people live alone than in such arrangements. Even more dramatic is the rise in the labor force participation of married women with young children, from less than 20 percent in 1960 to more than 60 percent today (see also Figure 13.1). Serial divorce and marriage have created increasingly diverse "blended families," and a dramatically growing number of households are headed by women.[8] Clearly there has been a revolution in the living arrangements of people in advanced industrial societies.

But even these striking structural changes understate the change in attitudes and values that they embody. Recently, Australia became the eighteenth country to perform same-sex marriages, and sixteen states in the U.S. now recognize gay marriage, something unimaginable only a decade ago.**[9] Cohabitation and interethnic and interracial

---

**Given the dynamism of this movement, these numbers undoubtedly will be larger when you read this.

Table 13.3 Quantitative Features of U.S. Households and Families 1960 to 2010

	1960	1970	1980	1990	2000	2010
			Households			
Number in Millions	52.8	63.4	80.8	93.3	104.7	117.5
Average Size	3.3	3.1	2.8	2.6	2.6	2.6
Percent Families	85.0	81.2	73.7	70.8	68.8	67.1
Percent Married Couples	74.3	70.5	60.8	56.0	52.8	49.7
Percent Married w/Children <18	48.4	40.3	30.9	26.3	24.1	20.9
Percent One Person	13.1	17.1	22.7	24.6	25.5	26.7
			Families			
Average Size	3.67	3.58	3.29	3.17	3.17	3.16
			Percentage of Women in the Paid labor Force			
All	37.7	43.3	51.5	57.5	60.2	58.6
Single	58.6	56.8	64.4	66.9	68.9	63.3
Married	31.9	40.5	49.9	58.4	61.1	61.0
Married W/Children <6	18.6	30.3	45.1	58.9	62.8	61.6*
Marriages per 100,000	8.5	10.6	10.6	9.8	8.2	6.8*
Divorces per 100,000	2.2	3.5	5.2	4.7	4.1	3.4*
Ratio Divorce/Marriage	0.26	0.33	0.49	0.48	0.50	0.50*

Source: U.S. Bureau of Census, *Statistical Abstract of the United States 2006, 2009, 2012*.
*2009 figure.

marriages are at all time highs, and while out-of-wedlock births have dropped dramatically since 1991 among teenagers, they have steadily increased for other ages.[10] In fact, today, unmarried couples now account for more than 40 percent of live births in the United States. And this phenomenon is not limited to the United States, 65 percent of births are to cohabiting couples in Iceland, and more than half in Belgium, France, Slovenia, Norway, and Sweden.[11]

Changing Functions of the Family

In the simplest human societies, the basic integrative force in societal life was the kin group, an all-purpose organization that provided for the physical, political, economic, educational, religious, and psychic needs of all its members. As societies grew in size and complexity, this had to change. No longer could an individual's relationships with other people always be defined in terms of kinship. New roles and organizations began to emerge and, as a result, the functions of the kin group were gradually eroded.

Although this process began thousands of years ago, kin groups remained of great importance throughout the agrarian era. Above all, the nuclear family (i.e., mother, father, and children) was still the basic productive unit in the economy. The peasant family was almost invariably a work unit, and this was also true of many other families. Place of work and place of residence were normally the same, and all the members of a family, including the children, shared in the work.

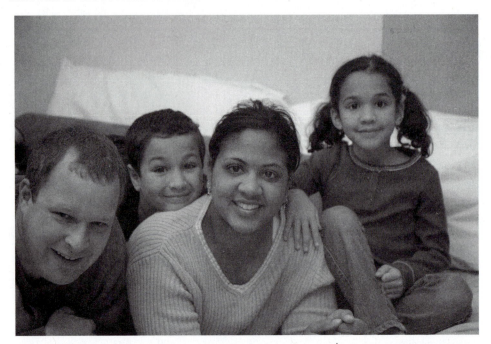

In Industrial Societies, Marriage Has Become an Arrangement That Is Undertaken Primarily to Enhance Personal Happiness and to Permit Individuals to Fulfill Personal Goals, Such as Establishing a Home or Having Children.

Government, too, was still a family affair. Members of the political elite usually inherited their status, while the royal family considered the state its personal property. Education remained primarily a family responsibility: boys usually learned the male role and productive skills from their fathers; girls learned theirs from mothers and aunts. With the growth of urban communities, the kinship system was not always as strong or pervasive as it had been in simpler societies. But family ties remained central in the lives of most people and provided the basic framework for societal life.

In industrial societies, many of the family's traditional functions have been eliminated or greatly altered. The family is now an economic unit only in terms of consumption, not of production. Families no longer control the political system; nepotism (preferential treatment of relatives in the workplace) may still occur, but it is not accepted as normal or legitimate. Schools, religious groups, and other organizations have assumed much of the responsibility for the education, socialization, and supervision of children, and a wide variety of organizations, from youth groups to summer camps and from vocational schools to universities, have taken over the task of providing young people with the skills they will need in their adult lives.

But the family has not been stripped of all its historic functions. Some of the most critical functions, including reproduction and the early socialization of children, still fall, at least in some measure, to the family. And as the larger kin system, or extended family, has diminished in importance, and as societal life has become increasingly complex and depersonalized, the family's responsibilities have in some ways become more important. For example, it usually bears the primary responsibility for fulfilling the psychic and emotional needs of its members. With respect to children, the family is still expected to be the major factor in personality development, instilling basic values, providing affection, offering guidance and encouragement in school and career decisions, training in the use of money, and much more. And all of this must be accomplished in a social environment that is culturally far less homogeneous, and therefore far more difficult, than the one in which most agrarian families raised their children.

Marriage today is undertaken for more personal reasons than in the past. Because most horticultural and agrarian societies viewed marriage largely in economic terms, marriages were usually arranged by parents with economic considerations in mind. The individuals most intimately involved were often denied even veto power. Sexual attraction and affection were not considered of primary importance: everyone knew that these might grow or wane, but the family's need for a firm economic base would persist.

In industrial societies, in contrast, marriage has become an arrangement that is undertaken primarily to enhance personal happiness and to permit individuals to fulfill personal goals, such as establishing a home or having children. Most people today view marriage as the union of two people who are attracted to one another both physically and emotionally and who hope to find pleasure, comfort, convenience, and companionship by sharing their lives.

In short, marriage and the family are becoming more a matter of choice than of necessity. One indication of this is the growing number of people who live apart from any family group. One reason for this is the decision of many young adults to postpone or forgo marriage. Since 1960, the average age of women at marriage has risen from twenty to twenty-seven and of men from twenty-three to twenty-nine in the United States, and in Canada it is twenty-nine for women and thirty-one for men.[12] And today about a quarter of the adult population has chosen not to marry.[13] Unlike previous generations, however, many unmarried or divorced people today share living accommodations with another person. Recent data indicate that there are more than four million cohabiting couples in the United States of which more than 600,000 are same-sex.[14]

Causes of Change in the Family

Change in the family is essentially the result of technological advance and the organizational and ideological changes that have followed in its wake. One of the most important of these has been the enormous increase in specialization. Specialized organizations of various kinds have steadily removed from home and family much of the responsibility for a wide range of services. These include not only educating and caring for the young, but also caring for the ill and the aged, processing food and preparing meals, making and caring for wearing apparel, and much more. As a result, the nuclear family itself has become a much more specialized institution.

Specific elements of the new technology have also had a great impact on the nuclear family, especially those that have given people control over fertility. Because of advances in methods of limiting family size, couples today have a much wider range of options available to them in almost every area of their lives than couples had in societies of the past. Nothing better illustrates how technological advance expands the

During the Nineteenth and Early Twentieth Centuries, Large Families Were the Rule: The Dudleys of Richmond, Virginia, 1903.

"limits of the possible," for individuals and families as well as for societies, than these advances.

Industrialization has also served to undermine the traditional authority structure of the family. The father is no longer the head of the family in the way he was in agrarian societies, and parents do not have nearly as much control over their children's conduct as they had in agrarian societies or earlier in the industrial era. Peer group influence and the mass media have become much more powerful than family influences for many teenagers, and serious family conflict often results.

In large measure, the drastic decline in parental authority is an inevitable result of the technological and other changes that have destroyed the family's role as a productive unit that had to work together for the mutual benefit, even the survival, of its members. Related to this, industrialization has had the effect of drawing families apart both physically and psychologically. Most fathers and many mothers are away from home all day because of work, while schools and other organizations draw children out of the family for other purposes. Today, children in the lower grades may spend more time with their teachers than with their mothers, and teenagers often spend more time with friends than with parents or siblings. Similarly, husbands and wives see less of one another or of their children than of their coworkers.

Another important cause of the decline of authority within the home has been the new democratic ideology which has permeated industrial societies, which carries with it an individualistic bias that puts more emphasis on the rights of individuals than on their responsibilities to the groups to which they belong. Just as the democratic trend has altered roles within political, economic, and educational institutions, so, too, has it altered roles within the family.

A final factor contributing to the weakening of family ties is the greater number of options available to individuals who wish to sever those ties. Divorce is easier, and so is economic independence for women, even women with children (see The Changing Role of Women, pp. 332–339). As a result of all of these factors—increased specialization, new ideologies, and new technologies—the family today is far less cohesive than its agrarian predecessor.

Finally, the extended family has been substantially weakened by technological advances that make the populations of industrial societies highly mobile. Although the lower cost and greater ease of transportation and communication make it possible for individuals to stay in contact with relatives across greater distances, the relationships are not as intimate as when relatives live within the same community.

The Family in Industrial Societies

One of the most drastic changes in the nuclear family is in the number of children. British marriages contracted around 1860 produced a median of six children. Barely two generations later, the median had dropped to two.[15] Families with eight or more children declined from 33 percent of the total to only 2 percent. Although the decline was more rapid in Britain than in most industrial societies, the general pattern has been quite similar.[16]

Comparisons like this are somewhat misleading if we assume that they also reflect the degree of change in the number of children actually living within a family at the same time. In the earlier period, the death rate among children was so much higher than it is today that there were often considerably fewer children living in an agrarian family than were born into it. Another factor that reduced the number of children living with their parents at any given time was the long duration of the childbearing period. Women who had eight, ten, or more children often bore them over a period of twenty years or more. Typically, by the time the youngest children were five or ten, many of their older siblings had left home or died. Thus, although the nuclear family was larger in agrarian societies, the number of its members who actually lived together at any one time was not as different as the change in birthrates suggests.

Perhaps more significant than the shrinking size of the nuclear family is the change that occurred in its composition due to increases in divorce and in the number of people raising children outside of marriage. During the last hundred years, the divorce rate in virtually every industrial society has risen substantially. In the United States in 1890 it was only 0.5 per 1,000 population per year; today it is 3.4.[††][18] In large measure, this trend is a result of the altered functions of the family, the changed perception of marriage which accompanied it, the new options available to women, and the newer attitudes of society toward divorce. Remarriage rates have also dropped substantially in recent years. While about half of divorced people remarried in 1990, today less than a third do.[19]

[††]It has declined rather steadily, however, from its peak of 5.3 reached in 1979 and 1981.[17]

Despite the great increase in divorce, its impact on the family has not been as dramatic as one might suppose. This is because marriages during the agrarian era, and early in the industrial era, were disrupted about as often as they are today, though for a different reason: the death of one or both parents. In eighteenth-century Sweden, approximately 50 percent of nuclear families were broken by parental death before all the children had reached adulthood; in late-eighteenth-century France, the figure was 60 percent; and in early-twentieth-century India it was 70 percent.[20] Thus, despite the high divorce rate, the percentage of ever-married women between the ages of forty-five and sixty-four who were still living with their first husband remained virtually unchanged in the United States during most of the twentieth century.

More recently, however, there has been a rapid increase in one-parent families. This trend has been particularly pronounced in the United States, where 33 percent of all children under the age of eighteen live in single-parent homes.[21] Three-quarters of these are headed by women.[22] In fact, the proportion of families with children that are single parent has nearly tripled since 1970.[23]

This kind of family arrangement has not worked out well for large numbers of the people involved. Thirty-one percent of all female-headed families in the United States have incomes below the poverty level, compared with 6 percent of families with both parents present.[24] In addition, many of the children in these families do poorly in school and become involved in crime or with drugs. In short, these families contribute disproportionately to several of the major problems confronting modern industrial societies.

The family today also has fewer extended kin living with it. Its household less frequently accommodates aged grandparents or unmarried aunts and uncles. This is no longer necessary in most cases because modern urban communities provide so many alternative facilities for single individuals—apartments, retirement homes, restaurants, laundries, and so on. Moreover, as these facilities have developed, changes have occurred in societal values: most members of industrial societies are jealous of their privacy and value it more highly than the benefits they might enjoy as members of larger and more inclusive households.

The Changing Role of Women

Nowhere are the effects of industrialization on society's norms, values, and sanctions seen more clearly than in the changing role of women.[25] Throughout history most women spent their prime years bearing children, nursing them, caring for them when they were sick or dying, and rearing them when they survived; doing domestic chores; tending gardens; and often helping in the fields. It is hardly surprising, therefore, that women seldom played significant roles outside the home or made outstanding contributions to the arts or public life.

The first signs of change came in the nineteenth century when the economic benefits of large families began to be outweighed by their costs. Efforts to limit fertility were soon aided by innovations in the area of birth control. During the nineteenth and early twentieth centuries, however, the average woman still produced a large family, still had babies for whom there was no alternative but prolonged breastfeeding, still carried the full burden of child care and housework, and sometimes was also obliged to work outside the home.

"I Never Meant to Leave Ambition at the Altar"

The following poem was written around 1920 by Hettie Barlow Dudley, who is shown seventeen years earlier in the photograph on p. 330 with the other members of her family. In addition to the nine children shown, two others died in infancy of whooping cough. Soon after the picture was taken, her husband fell seriously ill and for more than a year she was the sole support of her large family. To provide for them, she made candy on a commercial scale, and the older boys in the family sold and delivered it to families and stores throughout Richmond. When her husband recovered, he announced that he would now take over the management, but she was unwilling to accept this and opted instead to terminate the business, thus bringing a promising entrepreneurial career to an abrupt end.

This poem, which she titled "The Living Poem," captures in a wry and moving manner the ways in which family responsibilities constrained and frustrated most ambitious and talented women in the era before modern technology provided effective means of birth control and laborsaving devices for the home. But the poem also reflects an indomitable spirit that enabled this woman to take pride and find happiness in what she was able to achieve within the constraints imposed on her.

Weary of my ceaseless tasks
    Of baking and of broiling,
I sought to cultivate my soul
    And end my labored toiling.
I set the mop and broom aside,
    Determined not to falter.
I surely never meant to leave
    Ambition at the altar.
I planned to write some poems rare
    To reach the Hall of Fame.
I yearned to win great honors
    To decorate my name.
And so I sought my pad and pen
    And sat me down to think.
Then, just as I began to write
    The baby spilled the ink.
So then I found a pencil
    And sharpened it quite fine.
But, goodness me! my muse had fled!
    I could not write a line.
I thought of birds and flowers,
    Of meadows and of brooks.
But ere I could arrange my thoughts
    I heard, "Ma, where'r my books?"
I waited till the kids were off
    At school another day,

I put the baby in the yard,
    And there I bade her stay.
Then, just as I had shaped my wits,
    And a fine rhyme was turning,
A neighbor rushed in calling loud,
    "Hettie, your pies are burning."
I am afraid I ne'er will rank
    With Hemans nor with Browning.*
I am afraid that laurel wreath
    Will ne'er my brow be crowning.
No matter when or where I try
    To put my thoughts on paper,
That Imp called "Interruption"
    Starts cutting up some caper.
So now I've laid them all aside,
    My glowing aspirations.
But as I cook and sweep and sew
    I have my compensations.
The world may watch—my friends may wait:
    My home is what I show 'em.
My happiness, my laurel wreath.
    I live, not write, my poems.

*The poets referred to are Felicia Hemans, whose work was much admired by William Wordsworth, and Elizabeth Barrett Browning.

Because women were usually supplementary wage earners for their families, they were not trained for skilled jobs and were relegated to those that paid the least. Their availability for work at low wages posed a threat to the emerging labor movement, and, as a consequence, women were virtually excluded from it. It was, in effect, a working-*men's* movement, and its goal was to wrest a greater share of the growing economic surplus from the upper classes.

In contrast, the early women's movements in Western societies were dominated by the better educated, more leisured, and economically secure women of the upper classes, and their goals were primarily to obtain for women some of the legal and civil rights already enjoyed by men: the right to vote, to hold public office, to own property, and to attend universities. Late in the nineteenth century, they also became concerned with the situation of working mothers and sought to have their hours of employment shortened and night work eliminated entirely.

By the 1920s, the original goals of the women's movements in some Western industrial societies had been largely achieved and these movements declined.[‡‡] Changes continued to occur in the roles of women, but chiefly as a result of technological innovations—not because of organized political efforts. These innovations included many laborsaving devices for the home, such as refrigerators, freezers, automatic washing machines and dryers, vacuum cleaners, electric irons, and frozen foods, all of which, taken together, greatly reduced the time and energy consumed by housekeeping. The development of a safe alternative to breastfeeding and more effective methods of birth control were especially important in freeing married women from historic constraints on their lives and in enabling substantial numbers of them to seek employment and engage in other activities outside the home for the first time.

During the twentieth century, there was a rapid increase in women's participation in the labor force in most industrial societies. Figure 13.1 shows the percentage of women in various age categories who were in the paid labor force in 1890, 1960, and 2012. As the plotted percentages clearly show, in each succeeding period a larger percentage of women at every age have been employed. Today 58 percent of all American women are employed outside the home, including nearly 74 percent of those between the ages of twenty and fifty-four.[27] Increasing numbers of married women, and married women with children, have entered and remained in the labor force. Figure 13.2 shows one of the important reasons why. Although the incomes of married-couple families have increased substantially in recent decades, this is primarily because more married women are now working for pay. The incomes of families where the wife is not in the paid labor force have remained virtually unchanged for over forty years.

The tremendous increase in women's participation in the labor force in recent decades has been the foundation for the new women's movement that began in the 1960s. This newer movement has had a diversity of goals, but one underlying objective: to break the restrictive molds in which societies have cast women. This is based on the premise that with a single exception—women's capacity for childbearing—the differences

---

[‡‡]In France, by contrast, women could still not open bank accounts or apply for passports until the late 1930s and could not vote until 1945. In Spain, they could not serve as a witness in court or as a judge or even open a bank account until the 1970s.[26]

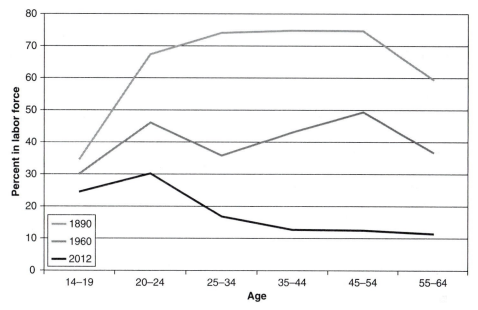

Figure 13.1. Female Labor Force Participation by Age, 1890, 1960, 2012.
Sources: James P. Smith and Michael P. Ward, *Women's Wages and Work in the Twentieth Century* (Santa Monica: Rand, 1984), Table 1; U.S. Bureau of the Census, *Statistical Abstract of the U.S.,* 1965, Table 298; *Statistical Abstract of the U.S.,* 2007, Table 574; Bureau of Labor Force Statistics, Household Data Annual Averages, Table 3, Employment Status of Civilian Non-Institutional Population By Age, Sex, Race.

between the sexes no longer provide a valid basis for the division of labor. Modern technology is able to compensate to a large degree for differences that are purely physical (e.g., strength, lactation), while differences with psychological components (e.g., emotional responses, competitiveness) are, to some, as yet an undetermined degree the result of socialization rather than genetics and therefore modifiable.

The changes that have occurred in the labor force in recent decades are striking. While women constitute 47 percent of the labor force today, they comprise 51 percent of persons employed as managers and professionals.[28] These changes have been matched by equally striking changes in women's access to higher education, especially postgraduate education, in recent decades (see Table 13.4).

The patterns of change vary somewhat among industrial societies. Thus, despite the progress noted above, the proportion of women who hold *senior* managerial positions is lower in the United States than in many other industrial societies.[29] And, as Table 13.5 shows, the United States is far behind most other industrial societies in the proportion of women in national legislatures.

The women's movement also emphasizes that power and prestige in modern societies derive from activities outside the family and that if women are to have equal access to these rewards and share equally in shaping society's institutions, they must participate fully in both the economy and the polity. But women cannot have equal access to the more interesting and demanding jobs and to promotions, higher pay, political offices, and other opportunities outside the home as long as the burden of

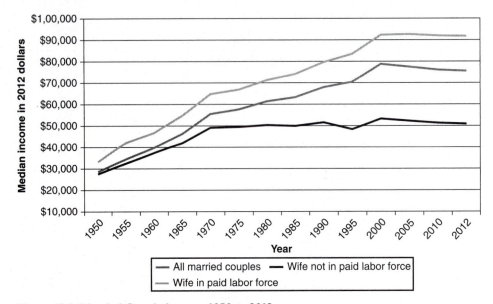

Figure 13.2. Married Couple Income 1950 to 2012.
Source: U.S. Census Bureau, Historical Income Tables—Families, Table F-7 (http://www.census.gov/hhes/www/income/data/historical/families/).

Table 13.4 Percentage of Degrees Awarded to Women in the U.S., 1960 and 2011

Type of Degree	1960	2011
Bachelor's degree	38.5	57.2
Doctor of Philosophy	10.5	51.4
Master of Business Administration	3.6	45.8
Law	2.5	47.1
Medicine	5.5	48.4
Engineering	0.3	22.3

Source: National Center for Educational Statistics, *Digest of Educational Statistics,* 2012, http://nces.ed.gov/index.asp.

responsibilities within the home is divided so unequally.[§§] Thus, the women's movement seeks both to increase men's participation in household responsibilities and child care and to spread the burden of child care by tax rebates for working parents and by the creation of tax-supported child care centers.

Studies have shown that although men are now spending more time doing housework and childcare, men spend more time working for pay, while women spend considerably more time on family responsibilities, even if they are employed outside the home.[31] The greater burden of household and child care responsibilities is, of course,

---

[§§]For example, for some time now, the wage gap between men and women virtually disappeared when you compared the incomes of single childless women to those of their male peers.[30]

Table 13.5 Percentage of Seats in National Parliaments Held by Women in Industrial Societies, 2012

Society	Percent
Sweden	44.7
Finland	42.5
Iceland	39.7
Norway	39.6
Denmark	39.1
Netherlands	38.7
Belgium	38.0
Spain	36.0
Germany	32.9
New Zealand	32.2
Slovenia	32.2
Switzerland	29.0
Portugal	28.7
Austria	27.9
France	26.9
Australia	24.7
Canada	24.7
Singapore	24.2
United Kingdom	22.5
Luxembourg	21.7
Italy	21.4
Greece	21.0
Israel	20.0
United States	18.0
South Korea	15.7
Ireland	15.1
Japan	7.9
Mean	**28.3**
Median	**27.9**

Source: World Bank, *World Development Indicators*, online database http://databank.worldbank.org/data.

one reason for both the differences in earnings between the sexes and the lower proportion of women who rise to *senior* supervisory and managerial positions (see the box Organizational Discrimination or Individual Preference?). The Family and Medical Leave Act in the United States—requiring employers to allow unpaid leave for those caring for children or sick parents—may help families to cope better with births and the medical needs of other family members, but it is unlikely to alter the imbalance in family responsibilities between the sexes. Industrial societies in Europe, especially the Scandinavian societies, have tried to do more in this regard. For instance, in Sweden

Organizational Discrimination or Individual Preference?

Some time ago, a large American corporation was sued by several of its female employees for discriminating against women in promotions. In support of their claim they showed that while 82 percent of the entry-level clerical jobs in the company were filled by women, only 74 percent of the promotions had gone to women. This, they charged, was clear evidence of discrimination.

Management in this company had long prided itself on its policy of promoting on the basis of merit and was greatly distressed by the suit and by the allegation that it had failed in this regard. To find out whether it had, in fact, failed and, if so, how, the company hired sociologists to study the matter.

Interviews with 850 employees of the firm demonstrated that women in entry-level clerical positions were much less likely than their male counterparts to seek, or even to desire, promotions (e.g., 39 percent of the women reported that they had no desire for a higher level position compared to 21 percent of the men). Also, male employees in these positions were twice as likely as female employees to have requested promotion during the previous year (28 percent versus 14 percent). Females, however, were more likely to report that they had received encouragement from management when they sought promotion (70 percent versus 55 percent). These and other findings indicated that the lower rate of promotion for women in this company was the result of choices made by the women themselves rather than sex discrimination by the company. These findings raised the obvious question of why women were less inclined to seek promotion than men. Further research indicated that both men and women saw promotions as

requiring longer working hours and a greater burden of responsibility. This was a price that fewer women were willing or able to pay, especially married women. Whether by choice or necessity, they and their spouses had apparently developed a division of labor within the family that assigned primary responsibility for providing income to the husband and primary responsibility for child care and care of the home to the wife. Thus, the job was a secondary responsibility for the majority of married women in these entry-level positions and this led, not surprisingly, to lower rates of promotion.

This study also found, however, that among individuals already in supervisory positions, the rates of promotion were the same for both sexes. The authors of this study concluded that this was because the selective process operating in the entry-level positions weeded out those individuals of both sexes who were unwilling or unable to make the sacrifices required by supervisory responsibilities. This further supported the conclusion that it was a mistake to infer from the simple statistics on rates of promotion that the company was guilty of sex discrimination.

One cannot infer from this one study that all differences in rank and income between the sexes in industrial societies are the result of women's preferences, but it serves as a caution against the common assumption that sex discrimination is the sole explanation, or even the chief explanation, for the underrepresentation of women in managerial positions.

Source: Adapted from Carl Hoffman and John Shelton Reed, "Sex Discrimination?—The XYZ Affair," *The Public Interest,* no. 62 (1981), pp. 21–39.

the parents of a newborn child are given 480 days of leave per child at 80 percent of pay, and they decide how to divide the time between them.[32]

Despite efforts such as these to deal with the changing role of women, numerous problems remain. Many individuals find it difficult to combine the role of employee with the roles of parent and spouse and to meet all of their responsibilities. More often than not, the demands of the job take precedence, and marital and parental obligations are sacrificed (e.g., many children are left alone and unsupervised).

Efforts to expand nursery schools and other child care facilities have only partly met the need, even in eastern Europe, where women's involvement in the labor force was greatest. The former Communist East Germany, for example, was reputed to have had the most extensive and the best child care system of any industrial society, but even it provided for only 60 percent of children under three years of age.[33]

For women themselves, the consequences of changes in their role are becoming increasingly evident. Not surprisingly, there has been considerable erosion of many traditional differences between the sexes in areas beyond employment and family life. It is evident in everything from clothing to mental and physical health, and from to-bacco and alcohol consumption to frequency of crime, automobile accidents, suicide, and, perhaps, even in facial structure.[34] Years ago, Betty Friedan argued that middle-aged women suffered less from depression and insomnia than they did previously, and others reported a decline in the use of tranquilizers by women. On the other hand, the once-large difference between the sexes in smoking habits has all but vanished, and among teenagers, more girls than boys now smoke. Similarly, differences in the incidence of heart disease between men and women are declining, and one study found that heart disease among middle-aged mothers employed in clerical and sales jobs was twice as common as among housewives.[35] And, finally, in the last half century, the percentage of arrests involving women has more than doubled.[36]

The Changing Role of Youth

In preindustrial societies, children were typically given chores to do while they were still quite young, and their responsibilities increased with every year. By their middle teens, sometimes earlier, they were doing much the same work as their parents and other adults. Reminders of this older pattern still survive in the rites of passage of some religious groups (e.g., confirmation rites and bar and bat mitzvahs), which occur around the age of thirteen. In an earlier era, these signaled the end of childhood and the beginning of adulthood, a period in which the individual was obliged to earn his or her own way and contribute to the support of others.

With the rise of industrialization, the need for human labor was reduced to such an extent that children came to be viewed as a threat to adults in the job market, and labor unions fought to make child labor illegal. Their efforts were reinforced by the passage of legislation to make school attendance compulsory. Young people were thus gradually edged out of the labor force or into marginal, part-time jobs. In the home, there were fewer siblings for older children to care for and fewer chores to perform. As opportunities for participation in the adult world were curtailed, a new age role gradu-ally emerged. Whereas most people in their teens, and certainly those in their early twenties, had previously been viewed as young adults, they came increasingly to be seen as occupying an intermediate role, a role of neither adult nor child.

Most individuals in this new age role are students. In 1890 only about 6 percent of Americans aged fourteen to seventeen attended high school; today about 98 percent do.[37] Moreover, 40 percent of those aged twenty to twenty-four are enrolled in school.[38] Such high levels of enrollment suggest that industrial societies may have expanded their educational institutions well beyond what is actually needed to equip people for their roles in the economy or even for their roles as citizens in a democratic society.[39] In addition, these societies have failed to take account of the fact that some individuals are not disposed to be students for such a long period. Many young people have little interest in the intellectual aspect of education, or even in its vocational relevance, but would rather move quickly into adult roles. They frequently discover, however, that there are no viable alternatives. Many who drop out of the educational system have trouble finding employment and getting established in the world of work.

As always happens when one segment of a population is cut off for an extended period from full participation in the life of the larger society, young people in industrial societies have developed their own subculture. Many of its more distinctive features (e.g., music, sports, experimentation with sex and drugs) are a natural consequence of the distinctive attributes of youth, such as vitality, curiosity, the desire for fun and excitement, and resistance to adult authority. The innovative nature of youth culture in areas such as music, language, and dance is at least partly the result of deliberate efforts to establish a barrier between youth and adults. The faster youth culture changes, the harder it is for adults to keep up with it, thereby keeping them at a distance and preventing them from moving in and dominating the youth scene.

At a more fundamental level, however, youth culture simply reflects many of the distinctive characteristics of industrial societies themselves: their high rate of innovation, their affluence, their leisure, their emphasis on hedonism, their emphasis on individuality, and their tendency to specialize. The preoccupation of young people with changing fads and fashions, for example, can be viewed as simply another expression of their society's enormous economic surplus and its love of novelty.

The differences between the norms and values of the youth culture and those of the larger society can cause serious problems, however, especially when they involve decisions with long-term implications. Teenage pregnancy is a compelling example of this. Despite the fact that rates have been falling in recent years, every year in the United States, more than 600,000 girls in their teens become pregnant, usually because they begin sexual activity while they are still emotionally immature and have inadequate information on reproduction and contraception.[40] These individuals are thus forced to make decisions that neither their own experience nor the norms and values of the youth culture have equipped them to make. Should the girl have an abortion or have the child? Marry the father or remain single? Put the child up for adoption or struggle to raise it alone?

Even when the decision to marry is made without the complications of an unplanned pregnancy, teenage marriages are high-risk ventures, largely because the qualities that the youth culture values most highly in the opposite sex have little to do with the qualities that adults value in a marriage partner. Similarly, because their peer group values success in sports more highly than success in academics, many boys make a heavy investment in athletics at the expense of their studies, only to find their skills no longer in demand once they are through high school or college. The NCAA calculates that the odds of a high school athlete making it all the way to the professional ranks are nearly infinitesimal: 0.03 percent for basketball, 0.08 for football, and 0.50 for baseball.[41]

In most industrial societies, great numbers of specialized youth groups have developed, each with its own distinct subculture. In the democracies these have included religious cults, counterculture groups, street gangs, motorcycle gangs, communes, and political groups of various persuasions.

Crimes of violence are associated with youth in all industrial societies. In the United States, for example, 60 percent of those arrested for robbery, the legal definition of which involves the threat or use of violence, are under twenty-five, as are 50 percent of those arrested for weapons offenses, and 46 percent for murder.[42] Political violence is also largely the work of younger people, though older adults often guide such activity.

Many attempts have been made to explain the tendency toward violence among younger people, especially younger males, in industrial societies. In American society, scholarly explanations often place the blame on society (e.g., widespread unemployment among youth, income inequality, racism).[43] But in trying to understand this phenomenon, it is important to keep in mind what many experts seem not to realize: Young men were often involved in crimes of violence in agrarian societies, and most hunting and gathering and horticultural societies provided frequent, socially approved opportunities for violence in hunting or warfare. While there is yet no definitive explanation of violence in younger men, it is certain that the causes are complex and most certainly include the biological influences of age and sex as well as distinctive characteristics of the individual, his family and friends, and the larger society. Without waiting for more precise explanations, however, industrial societies would do well to provide more socially acceptable (even socially useful) activities and programs that offer the kind of emotional and physical outlets most young men clearly require.

The Generation Gap

One of the striking developments of recent decades has been the substantial widening of the cultural gulf between the generations. To be sure, there have always been tensions in the relations between the generations simply because of differences in experience, energy, power and authority, and the varied problems that are central at different stages in the life cycle (e.g., school, marriage, job, declining health). These have always created some degree of tension between parents and their offspring and between older and younger people.

Today, however, these tensions and the cultural gulf between the generations appear to be greater than ever before. Basically, this is because of the increasing rapidity of social and cultural change brought about by the rising rate of technological innovation.

Nowhere is this more evident than in the world of popular culture. It is not merely that songs that were once popular in the youth of the older generations have been replaced by newer songs. Even musical styles and the content of songs are radically altered.

Most people become wedded emotionally to music and other elements of popular culture in their early years and are unwilling or unable to change. Thus, as new musical styles and other elements of culture displace older forms, a cultural gulf is opened up between the generations. In addition, as we grow older, learning becomes more difficult with the result that the older generation is slower to adopt new technologies, such as the computer and all of its seemingly endless spin-offs, such as burners and scanners.

This has given rise to a serious new conflict. Until recently, the older generation was always the more experienced and knowledgeable and, on that basis alone, could claim a right to exercise authority. Now, however, in areas of rapid cultural change, this is no longer the case. On the contrary, in certain respects the younger generation is better informed. This is especially likely in the case of new technological gadgetry and of popular culture in its various manifestations.

The ramifications of this cultural divide extend far beyond such obvious matters as musical or artistic taste and technological skills. They can be seen clearly in the varying attitudes of different age groups to issues pertaining to marriage and the family and sexual behavior. Younger people are much more accepting of premarital sex, varieties of sexuality, sexual identity, and same-sex marriage. Older people who were socialized in an earlier era when these behaviors were considered sinful or even criminal are less likely to be accepting.

In extreme cases, the generational gap leads to almost total incomprehension of even the basic needs of those who are older or younger. A dramatic instance of this was reported not long ago when a twenty-four-year-old student, who heads the youth organization of Germany's largest conservative party, was quoted as complaining about older people getting costly hip replacements at public expense. "Why," he said, "couldn't they just make do with crutches, as in the old days." As one observer noted, this student's views were "nothing less than an invitation to generational warfare."[44]

LEISURE AND THE ARTS

No preindustrial society ever offered such rich and varied opportunities for recreation as modern industrial societies provide. With the aid of electronic devices, one can now "command" performances by the world's greatest symphony orchestras, artists, and actors (even many now dead), all in the comfort of one's own home. With other elements of modern technology, individuals can travel quickly and comfortably to distant lands or, alternatively, bring the sights and sounds of those places into their own living rooms via television or digitally. For those who prefer physical activity, there are scores of opportunities, from zip-lines to paintball.

Industrial societies are also unique in the extent to which they have commercialized recreation. Entertainment and the manufacture of equipment for leisure activities are important industries. Ironically, even when members of industrial societies go camping to get "back to nature," they usually take numerous products of modern technology with them (e.g., GPS, polymer tents, clothing and blankets; and solar-powered chargers for their camping equipment, electronic devices, and smartphones).

One of the attractive features of leisure in industrial societies is its relative democracy. Many members of these societies enjoy substantial amounts of leisure and most can afford a wide variety of recreational activities. Members of agrarian societies of the recent past would find the opportunities available to the average member of modern industrial societies unbelievable.

Although technology's influence on the growth of leisure and on the creation of new recreational activities is obvious, its impact on the fine arts may not be. Yet the modern symphony orchestra is a triumph of modern technology, while recent trends in sculpture and painting reflect, at least in part, the influence of new materials and new processes that were not available to artists of an earlier era. It is also significant to note that modern art, with its movement away from realism and toward impressionism, expressionism, and abstractionism, began in the latter half of the nineteenth century as the new technology of photography was coming into its own. One cannot help but wonder if the new approach to painting and sculpture would have evolved if technology had not provided the camera as a substitute means of depicting reality and capturing images of people, places, and events for posterity. In any event, one of the many important consequences of the new technology for the arts has been an indirect one: traditional standards have given way to the belief that "newer is better" (see Neophilic Art, p. 238). This could not occur except in societies that have benefited greatly from change in other areas.

But it is television that has most altered modern life and leisure. The average household has more than two televisions, and recent data indicate that an average American youth today annually spends more time watching television (1,200 hours) than in school (900 hours), where by age eighteen they will have witnessed 150,000 violent acts.[45] And, although in recent years there has been a decline in *traditional* television viewing, when television content viewed on computers, smartphones, and tablets is added, total viewing time has actually increased. Every week in the United States, children watch an average of 24.6 hours, will see more than 300 commercials, and 54 percent of four to six year olds said they would rather watch TV than spend time with their fathers.[46] Over a lifetime, the average American will have spent nine years watching television.[47]

There are a number of reasons for television's great appeal. It combines the most attractive features of the other media: like printed matter and the radio, it can be enjoyed in the comfort of one's home, and, like movies, it presents things vividly. In addition, it informs and entertains while requiring almost no mental or physical effort on the viewer's part. This makes it especially attractive for people who are tired at the end of a day's work or who are simply unwilling or unable to engage in more demanding activities.

Because the images created by television are so vivid, they impress themselves on our consciousness in ways not unlike personal experience. Celebrities seen repeatedly on the screen become to many people a very real part of their lives; countless viewers have written expressions of love, even proposals of marriage, to actors and actresses whom they have never met. More important, events witnessed on television have the power to affect millions of people emotionally. Images of events such as the assassination of President Kennedy, the first moon landing, the collapse of the twin towers of the World Trade Center in New York on 9/11, and a variety of natural disasters have been indelibly etched in the memories of millions because their images were captured and broadcast on television.

Despite their seeming objectivity, television images have the potential to greatly distort and bias perceptions of social reality. Visually stunning events captured on film or digitally are likely to be seen over and over again by large audiences while unrecorded events, however significant, are not. The heart-rending images of starving children in the Darfur region of Sudan (see p. 353) made relief efforts there all but inevitable, but millions starve and die elsewhere every year in relative oblivion because their plight is not captured digitally. Thus, rather than being the product of objective analysis and reasoned judgment, public opinion, public policies, and collective social action may lurch and career haphazardly in response to such erratic contingencies as the availability of recorded images of an event or problem, the time constraints of network news broadcasts, and the viewing habits of television audiences.

Soap operas and network prime time shows also create unrealistic and biased images. For example, some time ago, a month-long analysis of network prime time shows found a grossly distorted image of the American labor force: there were twelve prostitutes shown for every machinist, two butlers for every government worker, and twelve times more detectives than production workers.[48] More recent studies have found that television dramas also provided a grossly distorted view of hospital emergency rooms and crime. On television, efforts to resuscitate patients with CPR were successful two-thirds of the time, whereas in the real world such efforts are successful only 15 percent of the time, and murders and assaults are much more frequent and more likely to be solved than in reality.[49]

It is not surprising, therefore, that, despite its popularity, people have mixed feelings about television.[50] Although more than half of those once polled named television as "the most enjoyable way to spend an evening," an almost equal number complained that "they spent too much time watching television," and 79 percent said "most Americans watch too much TV!"[51] A number of social critics also contend that television has exacerbated many of the most serious problems confronting modern industrial societies— crime, violence, teenage pregnancy.

Television has begun to encounter increased competition from computer games and the Internet for the time and attention of younger male viewers. One survey of TV audiences found a significant decline in viewing among teenage and young adult males, because they were spending more time on smartphones, the Internet, and video games. But as we noted above, some of that time is spent watching streaming video and other television content.[52] Nonetheless, this may be yet another instance in which a newer technology begins to displace an older rival and competitor. And, as it was with the advent of earlier inventions and discoveries, it is yet to be determined whether, on balance, these new technologies enhance and extend human contact and interaction or become a barrier to, or substitute for, authentic interaction and social engagement.

PROBLEMS AND PROGRESS

The members of contemporary industrial societies are in a paradoxical situation. They are, on average, far healthier, wealthier, and freer to choose among alternative lifestyles than were the vast majority of people during the last 5,000 years, and they are probably happier as well (see pp. 378–380). *Yet they are far more vocal concerning the shortcomings and problems of their societies.*

Like so many other changes, this is basically a consequence of industrialization. The media and multiparty political systems combine to keep social problems before the attention of the general public. Better education and new ideologies, meanwhile, provide people with an enhanced capacity for envisioning and anticipating improvements in their living conditions and in other areas, and if improvements do not occur, they often become critical of both their leaders and the social system. Finally, affluence gives people the means and leisure to voice their opinions, and democratic polities give them the opportunity. As a result, social problems receive far more attention and are far more salient in democratic industrial societies than in any other kind of society.

There are, of course, good grounds for the concerns expressed by members of industrial societies. Their new high-information, high-energy technologies have a potential for creating problems more serious than those that confronted societies of the past. The threat of nuclear war and the pollution of the environment are the most obvious, but they are not the only ones. Others include the rapid consumption of nonrenewable resources, the weakening of family ties, drug and alcohol abuse, urban decay, and the use of terrorist tactics as a means of achieving political goals. In addition, many older problems persist, even though progress has been made in dealing with some of them.

Although there is considerable controversy concerning the amount of progress industrial societies have actually achieved in dealing with humanity's problems, there is general agreement on several points. First, despite the presence of many continuing problems from the past, the most serious problems facing industrial societies today are either new problems or old problems with major new dimensions. Second, these problems are largely by-products, or consequences, of technological advance. Third, although many of these problems are distressingly complex, most could be alleviated by rational human effort—though in many cases not without great cost to many people. Finally, a completely problem-free society is not likely ever to be achieved, partly because of our species' genetic heritage, partly because of the constraints of the environment, partly because of the extraordinary complexity of modern social systems, and partly because the very process of problem solving itself so often creates new needs and new problems.

Because the problems that remain unsolved by one generation define the agenda for the next generation, we will postpone our analysis of social problems until the final chapter. In that chapter we will be concerned primarily with the future and what can, and cannot, be said about it.

INDUSTRIAL SOCIETIES IN THEORETICAL PERSPECTIVE

When we compare modern industrial societies with societies of the past, it is clear that they are a radically new type of sociocultural system. This is evident in everything from the family to the polity, and from ideology to technology. The foundation for these societies is, of course, their rich store of information, especially the technological information that enables them to harness vast amounts of energy to drive enormously productive machines.

If human societies had never created this technology, we would all still be in the agrarian era. The vast majority of people would still be illiterate peasant farmers eking out a marginal existence, women's lives would still be dominated by the cycle of reproduction and child care, and authoritarian elites who knew little and cared less about the lives of the masses would still regard the economic surplus as their rightful property. If we imagine a different sequence of events—one in which industrial societies had evolved but were subsequently forced to return to the technology of the agrarian era— *75 percent or more of the world's current population would die.* For an agrarian technology could not sustain more than a fourth or a fifth of the world's present population.

We will not try to trace here all the consequences of the shift from an agrarian to an industrial technology or detail all the causal linkages, as we did at the end of earlier chapters. These consequences are so numerous, and the linkages so complex, that a single diagram could not do justice to them. Instead, we will simply restate some of the basic points that have emerged from our analysis.

First, in industrial societies as in their predecessors, *technological innovation continues to be the most basic underlying force responsible for societal change and development.* Although other kinds of innovations also influence the course of social and cultural change, they tend to be dependent on prior technological change. We have seen numerous examples of this, especially in the new beliefs and values that shape these societies' institutions—beliefs and values which had little or no impact prior to industrialization.

Second, *many of the trends of the industrial era are continuations of trends that began in earlier eras.* Although industrialization intensified them, each of the following was initiated by technological advance in the more distant past:

> The growing store of, and enhanced ability to access and process, information
> The increasing ability to produce and harness energy
> The growing productivity of societies
> The expanding economic surplus
> The growth of world population
> The growth in size of societies and communities
> The increasing diversity of material products
> The growth of capital goods
> The increasing division of labor *within* societies
> The increasing division of labor *among* societies
> The increasing economic interdependence of societies
> The growing complexity of associations and communities
> The relative decline in importance of kinship systems
> The increasing number and variety of symbol systems
> The increasing impact of human activities on the biophysical environment
> The increasingly destructive potential of military technology

Third, *some of the trends in industrial societies are new and represent a break with trends of the past.* The most significant of these involves inequality. During the long period between the close of the hunting and gathering era and the early stages of the industrial era, technological advance was accompanied by a steady decline in both political and economic equality. As a result, either advanced agrarian or early industrial societies achieved the dubious distinction of having the greatest degree of inequality of any type of society in history. Advanced industrial societies have appreciably reversed this trend. Other new trends include democratization; greatly improved opportunities for education; more upward mobility; declining birth and death rates; the institutionalization of science, research, and innovation; and changes in the family and related roles, especially in those of women and youth.

Fourth, *industrial societies are the first in human history in which the greatest threats posed by the biophysical environment are products of prior human activity.* Before the Industrial Revolution, famine and disease were two of the greatest threats to societies. Technology and science have succeeded in eliminating the first of these scourges in industrial societies, and they have brought the second largely under control: the members of industrial societies now die primarily from degenerative diseases that reflect the natural limits of our species' life span. Now, however, societies are threatened by feedback effects of their own technology on the biophysical environment.

Industrializing

Hybrid Societies

Outline

Despite the rapid growth and spread of industrial technology in the recent past, most people in the world today still live in what are best described as "industrializing hybrid societies." These are societies in which many elements of traditional, pre-industrial cultures still flourish but coexist to greater or lesser degree with various elements of modern industrial technology and the kind of culture and social institutions that have developed in response to it.

One of the most striking features of these hybrid societies is the variation that exists in the degree to which they have managed to adapt to, and benefit from, the new technology. Some, such as China and a number of societies in eastern Europe, have been quite successful and are now experiencing rapid economic growth and rising standards of living. In contrast, others, such as Haiti and many of the sub-Saharan African societies have lagged badly economically and have experienced serious social unrest and political instability. Still others fall somewhere between the two extremes.

TWO TYPES OF INDUSTRIALIZING SOCIETIES

There is, of course, no single explanation for all the differences that exist. Many factors have been involved. Success or failure has sometimes depended on the biophysical environment as ecological-evolutionary theory would lead us to expect (see Fig. 1.2, p. 20).

The Old and the New: Indian Farmer Plowing with Oxen under High-Power Electrical Transmission Lines.

Some societies have been blessed with valuable natural resources, such as oil, gas, and other important minerals; some are able to grow crops that command good prices in world markets. In contrast, many industrializing hybrid societies lack these advantages.

But that is only part of the story. As ecological-evolutionary theory reminds us, societies must also adapt to their sociocultural environment, and their social and cultural heritages are extremely important. Thus, we should expect societies with an agrarian heritage—or industrializing agrarian societies* as we will call them—to

---

*Thirty-nine societies are classified as industrializing agrarian in the analyses that follow. They are (in alphabetical order): Afghanistan, Argentina, Bolivia, Brazil, Cambodia, Chile, China, Colombia, Costa Rica, Dominican Republic, Ecuador, Egypt, El Salvador, Guatemala, Guyana, Honduras, India, Jamaica, North Korea, Laos, Lebanon, Malaysia, Mexico, Morocco, Myanmar (Burma), Nepal, Nicaragua, Pakistan, Panama, Paraguay, Peru, Philippines, Sri Lanka, Syria, Thailand, Tunisia, Turkey, Uruguay, and Vietnam Because data are not available on many social characteristics for a number of these societies, however, the number of industrializing agrarian societies in the tables below will sometimes be smaller.[1]

adapt to the challenges and stresses of industrialization and globalization much more successfully than industrializing horticultural societies,[†] or those with a horticultural heritage.

As we saw in Chapters 6 and 7, agrarian societies have been significantly more advanced technologically than horticultural societies. Plow agriculture enabled societies to be far more productive than societies that depended on the hoe and digging stick. Greater productivity meant a larger economic surplus, and this, in turn, meant the growth of urban populations; a more complex division of labor; more extensive trade and commerce; written records; a monetary system; and a more powerful, stable, and complex government.

All of these things that industrializing agrarian societies have brought to the industrial era have given them an important advantage with respect to economic development in the new sociocultural environment. Thus, for example, when multinational corporations decide to "outsource" certain aspects of production in order to reduce labor costs, they are far more likely to turn to societies with an agrarian heritage than to ones with a horticultural heritage. The former are much more likely to have a labor force with relevant experience and skills. These same societies are also much more likely to have individuals with human capital in the form of the knowledge, skills, and motivation needed to create modern businesses of their own and thus contribute further to their society's development.

In seeking to understand the reasons for the sharp differences among industrializing societies today with respect to economic development, one should never forget that, without exception, all the highly industrialized societies that we examined in Chapters 9–13 have developed from an agrarian foundation. Not one of them evolved directly from a horticultural past.

ECONOMIES AND POPULATION GROWTH

The economies of industrializing societies consist of two very different sectors that reflect their hybrid nature. One is a sector in which traditional modes of economic activity persist and flourish. This is found chiefly in rural areas and smaller towns, though elements are often found even in the largest and most modern cities. In this sector, technology and other elements of the economy are much as they have always been, and so, too, is the level of productivity.

The other, or modern, sector of the economies of these societies is centered in urban areas, though elements are sometimes found in rural areas where modern agribusinesses (e.g., coffee and tea plantations) or mining have been introduced. This sector of the economy is often dominated by powerful foreign interests in the form of multinational corporations.

[†]Thirty societies are classified as industrializing horticultural in the analyses that follow. They are (in alphabetical order): Benin, Burkina Faso, Burundi, Central African Republic, Chad, Congo (Brazzaville), Congo (Kinshasa), Côte d'Ivoire, Ghana, Guinea, Haiti, Kenya, Liberia, Madagascar, Malawi, Mali, Mauritania, Mozambique, Niger, Papua New Guinea, Rwanda, Senegal, Sierra Leone, Somalia, Tanzania, Togo, Uganda, Zambia, and Zimbabwe. Because data are not available on many social characteristics for a number of these societies, however, the number of industrializing horticultural societies in the tables below will sometimes be smaller.[2]

These corporations sometimes control more resources and have greater power than the governments of the societies in which they operate. Moreover, they are usually able easily to transfer their operations and the jobs and income they provide to some other country if that is advantageous. For example, if cheaper labor or more favorable governmental policies can be found elsewhere, these corporations have no hesitation moving.

Industrializing societies are especially vulnerable when, as is usually the case, their own population does not provide a significant market for the product or products produced. Only a handful of industrializing societies—most notably China and India—have domestic markets large enough and profitable enough to compel the heads of multinational corporations to think twice before moving elsewhere.

Many hybrid societies, especially industrializing horticultural societies, suffer from another serious problem. Many are highly dependent on income from a single commodity or a small set of commodities (see Table 14.1). This leaves them vulnerable to any shift in the world economy that affects their special commodities. Technological innovations, such as the invention of fiber optics that replace copper wiring or synthetic fibers that replace cotton, or shifts in consumer preferences, such as changing food tastes, may permanently reduce, or even wipe out, demand for the product. Overproduction of a key commodity, such as coffee, can produce temporary "gluts" in the world market and drive the price of the commodity down, and if lower prices spur producers to increase production to compensate for lost income, prices can spiral even lower. This volatility creates an unstable "boom-or-bust" atmosphere that is not conducive to rational economic planning and development by either businesses or governments. Instead, it encourages a speculative approach that has as its goal making a quick profit and then transferring capital to safer investments elsewhere.

Overly rapid population growth has been an even more serious source of economic woes for industrializing horticultural societies. Despite the fact that these societies have enjoyed rates of economic growth comparable to those of industrial societies for several decades now, this has not led to much improvement in the standards of living of their people. In fact, in some of these societies, such as Congo (Kinshasa) and Niger, poverty has increased greatly and overall standards of living, as reflected in per capita income, have actually declined.

As Table 14.2 makes clear, most of the economic gains that industrializing horticultural societies have enjoyed in recent decades have been consumed by population growth and the need to feed more people. In the fifty-two years from 1961 to 2012, 82 percent of the gains in gross domestic product of these societies, on average, was consumed by the need to support population growth, thus leaving only 18 percent of the benefits of economic growth available for improvements in living standards. In contrast, in industrial societies, 73 percent of the benefits of economic growth were available to support improvements in living conditions, and in industrializing agrarian societies, 55 percent.[‡]

[‡]That understates the problem for industrializing societies since not all the difference between a society's rate of increase in GDP and in GDP/capita results in higher living standards, especially in the short run. Some is invested in capital goods with the benefits accruing later.

Table 14.1 Dependence on Leading Exports for Industrializing Societies (in Percentages)

Society	Top Commodity	Dependence on Top Commodity	Dependence on Top Three Commodities
		Industrializing Agrarian	
Costa Rica	Fruits	52	64
Ecuador	Petroleum	52	78
Mexico	Petroleum	47	62
Tunisia	Petroleum	46	69
Sri Lanka	Tea	45	65
Afghanistan	Fruit	42	61
Bolivia	Natural Gas	42	71
Pakistan	Rice	42	67
Chile	Copper	41	68
Syria	Petroleum	41	61
Myannmar (Burma)	Natural Gas	40	74
Colombia	Petroleum	39	68
Paraguay	Oil Seeds	37	69
North Korea	Coal	33	57
India	Petroleum	32	63
Laos	Copper	30	71
Vietnam	Petroleum	28	56
Honduras	Coffee	27	51
Panama	Fish	27	64
Peru	Gold	26	54
Nepal	Vegetables	25	44
Uruguay	Beef, Dairy, & Leather	25	44
Lebanon	Gold	22	43
Morocco	Fish	22	49
Argentina	Cereals	21	41
Cambodia	Rubber	21	55
Malaysia	Fats & Oils	21	55
Nicaragua	Coffee	21	48
El Salvador	Coffee	20	43
Brazil	Iron	19	41
China	Petroleum	18	35
Dominican Republic	Tobacco	18	42
Philippines	Copper	18	38
Egypt	Petroleum	17	42
Guatemala	Fruits	16	47
Turkey	Petroleum	16	44
Thailand	Petroleum	14	39
Median		**27**	**55**

(Continued)

Table 14.1 Dependence on Leading Exports for Industrializing Societies (in Percentages)
(Continued)

Society	Top Commodity	Dependence on Top Commodity	Dependence on Top Three Commodities
		Industrializing Horticultural	
Chad	Petroleum	89	99
Zambia	Copper	80	87
Congo (Brazzaville)	Petroleum	79	88
Malawi	Tobacco	65	80
Burundi	Coffee	61	83
Mali	Gold	59	93
Liberia	Rubber	54	77
Guinea	Aluminum	51	91
Ghana	Cocoa	49	73
Mozambique	Aluminum	46	63
Mauritania	Iron	45	84
Burkina Faso	Cotton	44	88
Central African Rep.	Forestry	41	83
Ivory Coast	Cocoa	39	71
Paua New Guinea	Gold	39	71
Benin	Cotton	38	63
Senegal	Petroleum	37	65
Sierra Leone	Pearls & Gems	35	66
Somalia	Live Animals	35	85
Rwanda	Coffee & Tea	30	83
Uganda	Coffee & Tea	30	50
Congo (Kinshasa)	Copper	28	63
Niger	Uranium Ore	28	88
Kenya	Tea	27	57
Madagascar	Fish	26	57
Tanzania	Gold	22	43
Togo	Cocoa	19	55
Haiti	Coffee	18	49
Zimbabwe	Nickel Ores	17	41
Median		**38.5**	**72**

Source: UNCTAD, *The State of Commodity Dependence 2012*, http://vi.unctad.org/digital-library//////?task=dl_doc&doc_name=731state.

Population growth rates of 2.0 and 2.6 percent per year may not sound very high, but they are twenty to twenty-five times the average rate of growth of world population during the whole of the agrarian era. A society growing at a rate of 2.0 percent per year will double in size in just thirty-five years, and a society growing at a rate of 2.6 percent will double in only twenty-seven years.

Table 14.2 Average Annual Percentage Rates of Economic and Population Growth 1961 to 2012, by Societal Type

	Industrial	Industrializing Agrarian	Industrializing Horticultural
GDP growth rate	3.3	4.7	3.4
Population growth rate	0.8	2.0	2.6
GDP per capita growth rate	2.4	2.6	0.6
Number of societies*	27	38	29

Source: *World Bank*, World Data Bank, World Development Indicators, http://databank.worldbank.org/data/views/variableSelection/selectvariables.aspx?source=world-development-indicators.
*Data not available for all societies in all years.

   When societies grow this fast, it is extraordinarily difficult to satisfy even the most basic needs of their members. Thus, famines have become a recurring feature of life in many industrializing horticultural societies, and the destruction of forests has made firewood (an essential of life for much of the population of these societies) increasingly difficult to obtain.

Kevin Carter's Pulitzer Prize-Winning "Picture of an Emaciated Girl Collapsing on the Way to a Feeding Center, as a Plump Vulture Lurked in the Background, Was Published First in The New York Times and The Mail & Guardian, a Johannesburg Weekly. Later It Was Displayed in Many Other Publications as a Metaphor for Africa's Despair. The Reaction to the Picture Was So Strong That The Times Published an Unusual Editors' Note on the Fate of the Girl. Mr. Carter said She Resumed Her Trek to the Feeding Center. He Chased Away the Vulture . . . Afterward, He told an Interviewer in April, He Sat under a Tree for a Long Time, 'Smoking Cigarettes and Crying.'" Bill Keller, *New York Times*, July 29, 1994.

Rapid population growth also increases greatly the number of school-age children. Thus, high birthrates make universal free public education prohibitively expensive, yet, without this, societies lack the human capital (i.e., a literate and educated labor force) needed to compete in the new global economy.

On top of all this, widespread poverty limits severely the demand for anything more than the basic necessities of life. As a result, there is little demand for the kinds of goods and services that have become essential components of the economies of industrial societies, thus precluding many opportunities for small-scale entrepreneurial innovation and activity.

Fortunately, despite substantial resistance to efforts to limit population growth by many Catholic, Muslim, and nationalist leaders, there are a few signs of change. Several Catholic bishops in sub-Saharan Africa have broken with the Vatican's insistence that any use of condoms is sinful. Meanwhile, in Rwanda, where the population has been growing at a rate of 3 percent per year, and women on average gave birth to six children, lawmakers passed legislation to offer economic incentives to couples who limit themselves to no more than three children and to promote vasectomy as a means of birth control.[3] As one government official stated, "Three percent annual population growth literally means 93 percent poverty increase."[4]

IDEOLOGIES

Throughout much of the industrializing world today, advocates of competing ideologies are locked in bitter struggles for power and dominance. In China and Cuba, for example, there is an ongoing struggle between advocates of democracy and members of the Communist Party who fight to preserve the party's monopoly of political power. In Muslim societies, the struggle is between fundamentalist Islamists, moderate Muslims, and secularists. In Nigeria, the struggle is between Christians who tend to be oriented toward Western values and modernization and Muslims who seek to impose traditional Islamic standards on the whole of society.

During most of the twentieth century, Marxism appeared to be the ideological wave of the future in most poorer societies. The promises of Marxists held tremendous appeal, not only for the poor and downtrodden but also for intellectuals and many of the better educated.

Now in the twenty-first century, however, Marxism has lost much of that appeal. Its failure to deliver on the many promises Marxists made has largely destroyed its credibility (see excursus Marxist Societies as Natural Experiments at end of this chapter). Today, a harsh and intolerant version of Islam has largely taken its place in the hearts and minds of growing numbers of younger Muslims around the world.

This development is extremely important because this version of Islam rejects most of the values on which economic growth and development depend. Education for the masses is largely limited to memorization of the Koran and other religious materials. In Iran, billboards inform Iranians that if they memorize the Koran in its entirety they will be awarded a formal university degree.[5] People are trained to believe that improvement of conditions in this world is far less important than the attainment of paradise in the next. Governments should be controlled by religious leaders, as in Iran, and their decrees are believed to have the authority of Allah (God) behind them. Modern methods of birth control are considered sinful and large families are

A Farmer Rides by a Billboard That Promotes China's One-Child Policy on the Outskirts of a Village Near Dongying in Shandong Province. The Sign Urges People to "Improve the Quality of the Population" and "Control the Population Increase." Though the One-Child Policy Is Strictly Enforced in Cities, in Rural Areas Many People Ignore the Rules or Willingly Pay Fines in Order to Have More Children.

encouraged. And last, but not least, advocates of this fundamentalist version of Islam view with great hostility all who do not share their beliefs. This includes even fellow Muslims who adhere to more tolerant interpretations of the faith.

In an era of globalization, when the newer technologies of transportation and communication have facilitated greatly increased contacts between peoples and nations, these contacts have both promoted the spread of Islamic fundamentalism and made it more of a threat than in earlier times. As the events of 9/11 demonstrated, developments in one part of the world today can easily lead to serious repercussions thousands of miles away.

POLITIES AND CONFLICTS

The polities of hybrid industrializing societies of the world today are as varied as their economies. They range from ones in which civil war and armed conflict are chronic conditions to those in which stability is achieved by harshly authoritarian governments and still others in which reasonably representative democratic governments exist.

The least stable governments are found somewhat more often in societies with a horticultural heritage. The list is long and familiar: Haiti, Uganda, Rwanda, Burundi, Sierra Leone, Ivory Coast, Liberia, and the Congo, all of which have been in the news in recent years. Earlier, others, such as Angola and Mozambique, were on the list and may yet appear again.

*Intra*societal conflict has also been a problem in many industrializing agrarian and horticultural societies. Bitter civil or revolutionary wars have raged or are raging in Syria, Ivory Coast, Somalia, Congo, Myanmar, Iraq, Afghanistan, Nigeria, Sri Lanka, Laos, Colombia, Peru, and others.[6]

As a number of observers have noted, political instability tends to be associated with high birth rates and stagnant or deteriorating economies. When societies produce large numbers of children—especially boys—who have few opportunities for an education or stable employment, joining a rebel militia or other private army becomes an attractive option. One study found that 80 percent of the civil conflicts that broke out in the 1970s, '80s, and '90s occurred in countries where at least 60 percent of the population was under thirty years of age.[7]

High birth rates and low rates of economic growth, as we have seen, are especially common in industrializing horticultural societies. They are also found in a number of industrializing agrarian societies, especially those with predominantly Muslim

Many Industrializing Societies Have Been Forced into a Specialized Ecological Niche as Producers of Raw Materials for Industrial Societies. For Years, Much of Ghana's Foreign Exchange Has Come from the Sale of Cocoa, Which Is Shown Being Collected at a Marketing Cooperative.

populations, but also in some with largely Roman Catholic populations. Both Muslim and Catholic religious leaders have vigorously opposed efforts to control population growth with unfortunate political and economic consequences for the societies involved.

The chief alternative to political instability and civil war in most industrializing societies has been repressive and authoritarian government. This is especially likely to emerge in the aftermath of civil war: The victors in these struggles know that they owe their success and their control of government to the use of force and that their defeated enemies are watching for any signs of weakness on their part. Thus, ruthless suppression of critics and opponents becomes the order of the day. Robert Mugabe's regime in Zimbabwe and Saddam Hussein's former regime in Iraq have been classic examples of this. As Table 14.3 indicates, the members of industrial societies enjoy a much greater degree of freedom in their daily lives than do the members of industrializing societies, and industrializing agrarian societies enjoy a higher degree of freedom on average than do the members of industrializing horticultural societies.

The more serious conflicts in industrializing societies tend to reflect major social cleavages in these societies. Sometimes these are ethnic in nature, sometimes religious, sometimes economic, and sometimes a combination of two or more of these elements.[§]

Such conflicts are especially difficult to resolve when they have an ideological component, since ideologies fire up the irrational and emotional elements in human nature. Marxism, with its utopian ideals, was notable in this regard in the last century, but fundamentalist religions have replaced it as the more powerful force in industrializing societies today. Fundamentalist Islam has been especially successful, and a fundamentalist version of Hinduism has attracted millions of followers in India.[8]

Table 14.3 Average Level of Freedom, by Societal Type

	Industrial	Industrializing Agrarian	Industrializing Horticultural
Mean level of freedom*	6.8	4.3	3.7
Median level of freedom*	7.0	4.5	3.5
Number of societies	27	39	29

Source: Calculations derived from 2013 data reported by Freedom House, "Country Ratings and Status, 1973–2013," http://www.freedomhouse.org/report-types/freedom-world.
*The freedom score is the average for political rights and civil liberties; we reversed the original coding so 1.0 is not free, and 7.0 is most free.

[§]One of the striking features of most industrializing horticultural societies is how new they are. With only a few exceptions, these societies were created in the late nineteenth or early twentieth centuries. Most are products of European colonialism, and their boundaries are largely the result of rivalries among the former colonial powers and have had little to do with the boundaries of the older societies they replaced. Actually, the process by which these societies were created was not too different from that by which many industrial societies were formed; although, in the latter the process occurred so long ago that its effects are usually minimal today. However, as the long-time struggle in Northern Ireland and the continuing struggle of the Basques in Spain remind us, in some of these societies conflict continues.

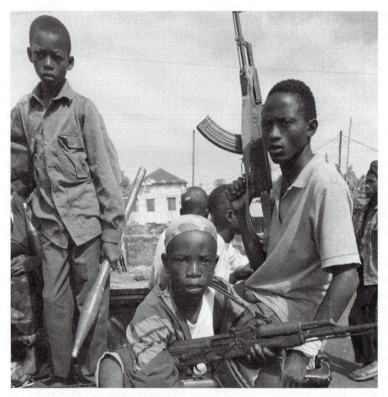

Boy Soldiers Ready for Action in Liberia.

Leaders, and would-be leaders, in industrializing societies have been quick to recognize that these militant versions of traditional faiths have great appeal to young men. By joining with others in what they have been taught to think of as a noble cause, they gain not only honor in their community and enhanced self-respect but also the hope for a better life either in this world or the next.

Even when there is no religious basis for conflict, ethnic or tribal differences can ignite it. This can be seen in societies as different from one another as Afghanistan and Rwanda. Although virtually all Afghans are Muslim, the different ethnic groups have been engaged in a long-standing struggle for power that has destabilized a succession of governments for decades. In Rwanda, the two major ethnic groups, the Hutu and the Tutsi, are both nominally Christian, but that did not prevent the Hutus from practicing genocide against the Tutsis or the Tutsis from retaliating.

Fortunately, the picture is not entirely bleak. There have been some successes. A few industrializing societies have representative democratic governments that have survived for decades, while a number of others have managed to replace authoritarian regimes with democratic governments. India and Costa Rica are notable examples of the former; Chile, Brazil, and most of the previously Communist nations of eastern Europe are examples of the latter.

Political corruption is a problem to some degree in virtually all societies, but it tends to be much worse in industrializing societies. The temptation provided by vast sums of public money is too great for many politicians to resist, even in economically advanced democratic societies; and in less developed societies, where opportunities for achieving wealth are limited and the risk of punishment is minimal, it is overwhelming. In the Congo, for example, an international grant of $1.8 million to repair the capital city's broken-down buses was reportedly "swindled down" to just $200,000 by the time it reached the Transportation Ministry, while in Gabon the president used misappropriated public funds to build himself a $650 million marble palace with revolving rooms and walls that disappeared at the touch of a button. More recently, government officials in Malawi siphoned off $5.3 million from public funds, crippling the public health sector, which lead Norway, the European Union, and the International Monetary Fund to withhold future aid and loans until the corruption is addressed.[9]

For a number of years, the oil-rich Arab nations were generous providers of foreign aid to sub-Saharan African societies, but eventually they cut back because of bad experiences. A leading Arab publication reported, "In some cases now coming to light, for every $1 million of aid, less than $100,000 finds effective applications in African countries like Zambia and [the Congo]."[10]

More recently, the World Bank estimated that Africa annually loses $148 *billion* a year to corruption, an amount equivalent to one-quarter of Africa's total GDP![11] Every year, corrupt officials swindle 20 to 40 percent of official development assistance; in nonmonetary terms, this means the loss of "hospitals, schools, clean water, roads and bridges . . . that would have certainly changed the fortunes of families and communities."[12]

Transparency International, an organization that monitors governmental corruption around the world, today ranks New Zealand, Finland, Denmark, and Sweden as the least corrupt, and Burundi, Chad, Haiti, Myanmar, Afghanistan and North Korea as the most corrupt. Overall, corruption is far less of a problem in industrial societies than in either type of industrializing society (see Table 14.4).** The pervasive corrosive impact of corruption on economic development is hard to exaggerate.

One encouraging sign in the often unlovely world of industrializing societies that has to be noted is the gradual movement of China in a more democratic direction in

Table 14.4 Average Level of Perceived Corruption, by Societal Type

	Industrial	Industrializing Agrarian	Industrializing Horticultural
Median level of corruption*	25	66	67
Number of societies	27	39	29

Source: Calculations derived from data on the *Corruption Perceptions Index 2012*, reported by Transparency International, http://www. http://cpi.transparency.org/cpi2012/.
*The corruption score is the degree of corruption as perceived by business people, academics, and risk analysts. We have reversed the original coding so 0 is highly clean and 100 is highly corrupt.

**It should be noted that in agrarian and horticultural societies of the past there was seldom any distinction made between public funds and the private wealth of rulers, and lesser officials customarily depended on bribes as their primary source of income.[13] Thus, what we today call corruption is essentially just one more way in which the cultural heritage of the past continues to influence the life of industrializing societies.

recent decades. For example, by official count the number of independent nongovernmental organizations (NGOs) in China has risen from virtually zero two decades ago to nearly 500,000 today, and that excludes tens of thousands of groups that are not officially registered.[14] If they were counted, some calculate that the total would be as high as two million. Many of these organizations challenge the authoritarian structure of the Chinese polity on matters ranging from environmental issues to official corruption, and they are slowly moving the government in the direction of more openness and accountability. Public protests have grown steadily in China since the 1990s from less than 10,000 to an estimated 180,000 in 2010, and they have been surprisingly effective in recent years.[15] Since roughly one-fifth of the world's population lives in China, and since China promises to become an increasing power in world affairs in the years ahead, these developments are no small matter.[16]

SOCIAL STRATIFICATION

Social inequality tends to be substantially more pronounced in industrializing societies than in economically more developed industrial societies. As Table 14.5 indicates, the top 20 percent of the population in both industrializing agrarian and industrializing horticultural societies receives a larger share on average of their societies' total income than does the top 20 percent in industrial societies, and the bottom 20 percent in industrializing societies receives a smaller share than the bottom 20 percent in industrial societies. In industrial societies, the top 20 percent receives roughly five times as much as the bottom 20 percent. In contrast, the top 20 percent in industrializing agrarian and industrializing horticultural societies receives about eleven and eight times as much, respectively. Moreover, because the economies of the industrial societies are so much more productive, the smaller *shares* of income received by the highest 20 percent represent much larger *dollar incomes*. Thus, the industrial societies have *both* the richest rich, *and* the richest poor!

One explanation for these differences seems to be that as societies grow more productive and populations grow more slowly, elites become more willing to accept a

Table 14.5 Mean Income Share and Standardized Income, by Societal Type

Income Measure	Industrial	Industrializing Agrarian	Industrializing Horticultural
	Highest-Earning 20 Percent		
Median Percentage Share	40.8	50.1	47.3
Median Standardized Income*	$77,253	$16,005	$2,892
	Lowest-Earning 20 Percent		
Median Percentage Share	7.5	4.7	6.1
Median Standardized Income	$15,433	$1,587	$350
Number of Cases	26	34	26

Source: World Bank, World Development Indicators, http://databank.worldbank.org/data/views/variableSelection/selectvariables.aspx?source=world-development-indicators.

*Standardized incomes are calculated as the proportionate share of income by the population quintiles (percentage/20) multiplied by the per capita GDP of the society (at purchasing power parity in current (2012) U.S. dollars. They are, thus, indicators of the per capita incomes of these population segments that can be compared across societies. Due to data availability on shares, their years vary. For the use of a similar measure and its general rationale, see Patrick D. Nolan, "A Standardized Cross-National Comparison of Incomes," *The Sociological Quarterly* 34, no. 4 (Winter 1992).

somewhat smaller share of a much larger economic pie in order to create and maintain political stability and thus protect their positions of privilege.[17] Thus, while they lose something in *relative* terms, they gain far more in *absolute* terms, and they simultaneously become politically more secure. Most elites in industrial societies seem to believe this trade-off is well worth the price. In contrast, in industrializing societies, where the economic pie is much smaller and political systems less stable, elites are more inclined to grab as much as they can whenever they can.

Those at the bottom of the social ladder in most industrializing societies experience living conditions that are far worse than their counterparts in industrial societies. Famine and starvation are not uncommon, especially in industrializing horticultural societies, and elites and the governments they control seldom care enough to help. Aid, if it comes, is usually the result of efforts by humanitarian groups based in industrial societies, and, as we saw above, even this is often diverted before it reaches those for whom it is intended. Uncontrolled, or poorly controlled, diseases such as HIV/AIDS are widespread, and local elites do little to help. When jobs can be found, working conditions are often appalling—brutally long hours, dangerous working conditions, and low wages. Child labor is widespread. Even slavery still exists in a number of societies. In fact, The Global Slavery Index estimates there are nearly thirty *million* people living in slavery *today*, and thirty-eight of the fifty worst-offending nations are on the continent of Africa.[18] Mauritania, with 150,000 captives in a population of 3.8 million, is the worst offender; but a high prevalence is found in Benin, the Ivory Coast, Gambia, Gabon, and Senegal.[††20]

But it is not only those at the bottom of the social ladder in industrializing societies for whom life is hard. Except for the elites, the quality of life for most people is not all that good, and this is especially true in industrializing horticultural societies, as Table 14.6 makes clear. Given the conditions that exist, the migrations of millions of people from industrializing societies to industrial societies, reported in Chapter 12, are hardly surprising.

EDUCATION

It is hard to exaggerate the importance of education and what it means for the economic development and social well-being of industrializing societies. All the most prosperous societies in the world today have invested heavily in education. In the United States and Japan—two of the more striking examples of economic growth during the twentieth century—high levels of national expenditures on education preceded and accompanied industrialization.[21] In Japan, half the male population was literate by the 1870s, while in the United States almost 90 percent of white males were literate by this time.

The relation between education and economic growth is borne out by studies that indicate that expansion of primary and secondary school enrollments, especially the latter, has been linked to increases in per capita GNP.[22] These same studies found, however, that expanded enrollments in higher education did not have the same effect.

[††]According to the Index, India, with fourteen million, has the largest *number*, but it is ranked fourth in *incidence*, and more than 16 percent of the total are in sub-Saharan Africa.[19]

Table 14.6 Quality of Life Index in Industrializing Societies, 2012

Society	HDI*	Society	HDI
Industrializing Agrarian Societies		Pakistan	0.52
Chile	0.82	Myanmar	0.50
Argentina	0.81	Nepal	0.46
Uruguay	0.79	Afghanistan	0.37
Panama	0.78	**Median**	**0.69**
Mexico	0.78	**Industrializing Horticultural Societies**	
Costa Rica	0.77	Ghana	0.56
Malaysia	0.77	Congo (Kinshasa)	0.53
Lebanon	0.75	Kenya	0.52
Peru	0.74	Madagascar	0.48
Brazil	0.73	Tanzania	0.48
Jamaica	0.73	Senegal	0.47
Ecuador	0.72	Mauritania	0.47
Turkey	0.72	Papua New Guinea	0.47
Colombia	0.72	Togo	0.46
Sri Lanka	0.72	Haiti	0.46
Tunisia	0.71	Uganda	0.46
Dominican Republic	0.70	Zambia	0.45
China	0.70	Benin	0.44
Thailand	0.69	Rwanda	0.43
El Salvador	0.68	Ivory Coast	0.43
Bolivia	0.68	Malawi	0.42
Paraguay	0.67	Zimbabwe	0.40
Egypt	0.66	Liberia	0.39
Philippines	0.65	Sierra Leone	0.36
Syria	0.65	Burundi	0.36
Guyana	0.64	Guinea	0.36
Honduras	0.63	Central African Republic	0.35
Vietnam	0.62	Mali	0.34
Nicaragua	0.60	Burkina Faso	0.34
Morocco	0.59	Chad	0.34
Guatemala	0.58	Mozambique	0.33
India	0.55	Congo (Zaire)	0.34
Cambodia	0.54	Niger	0.30
Laos	0.54	**Median**	**0.43**

Source: United Nations, International Human Development Indicators, accessed: 11/21/2013, from: http://hdr.undp.org.
*Human Development Index, an index of well-being based on measures of life expectancy, literacy, education, and income.

The reasons for this are not clear, but it may be that in the earlier stages of industrialization in a society the growth of basic education—the so-called three Rs, reading, writing, and arithmetic—is more important than the much more limited growth of university-level education.

As Table 14.7 indicates, industrializing horticultural societies have once again been at a disadvantage when compared with industrializing agrarian societies. Far fewer young people in these societies are getting the kind of basic education on which economic growth and development depend. Thus, once again these societies find themselves badly handicapped in the increasingly competitive world of economic globalization.

Finally, it should be noted that the education of girls, which has traditionally been neglected in most of the less developed societies, has proven extremely effective in

Table 14.7 Median Secondary School Enrollment as a Percentage of Population, Ages 14 to 17, by Societal Type

	Industrial	Industrializing Agrarian	Industrializing Horticultural
Females	94.2	68.6	17.0
Males	93.6	67.5	22.7
Number of societies	21	21	24

Source: World Bank, *World Development Indicators*, online database, http://www.worldbank.org/.

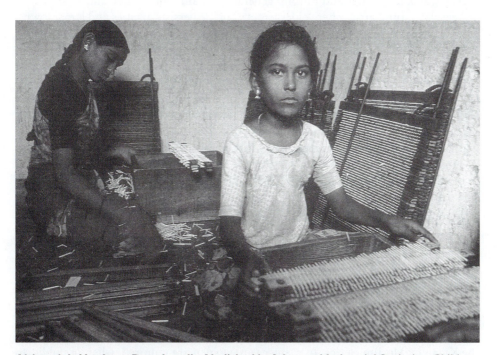

Although It Has Long Been Legally Abolished in Advanced Industrial Societies, Child Labor Continues to Be Quite Common in Many Industrializing Societies: A Young Girl at Work in a Match Factory in Southern India.

reducing birthrates of these societies whenever it has been introduced. This has had obvious political and economic benefits for those societies that have supported this. Unfortunately, however, the education of girls and women continues to be resisted or even opposed by religious leaders in most Muslim societies, thus contributing to the persistence of the political and economic problems of those societies.

KINSHIP

Ties of kinship have been a basic element in every human society from the Stone Age to the present. This has been true of both the nuclear family made up of parents and their children and the extended family that includes aunts, uncles, cousins, and grandparents.

As we have seen, in preindustrial societies, families were important economically, not merely as consumers but even more as producers. They were also important politically, since political offices and the power they afforded were typically regarded as the "property" of certain families.

In industrial societies today, the economic importance of the family and kinship are greatly reduced for most of the population, though some families are able to pass on control of businesses, other forms of wealth, and other benefits (e.g., education) from one generation to the next; and a small but growing number of families, such as the Rockefellers, Kennedys, Clintons, and Bushes, are able to provide their children and grandchildren with important political advantages as well.[23] In industrializing hybrid societies, too, family ties and kinship generally remain quite important, especially in more isolated rural areas where older patterns of life persist. In cities and larger towns, where many people are employed by modern businesses, kinship ties tend to be less important. Even here, however, such ties can be crucial, as when workers are hired on the basis of recommendations from relatives, a not uncommon practice.

Politically, kinship remains extremely important in most industrializing societies. The Gandhi family in India is a classic example, with three generations of family members serving as prime ministers for most of the years since India won its independence. Even in a Communist country, such as North Korea, a family dynasty has maintained control since independence. Although there are no systematic studies to document the proposition, it appears that at lower levels in the political systems of industrializing societies (i.e., in provinces and in local communities), the transmission of political power within families is even more common.

THE STATUS OF WOMEN

For people accustomed to the status of women in advanced industrial societies today, the status of women in most industrializing societies is both surprising and shocking. In the developed world, as we have seen, industrialization has been a powerful force that has greatly reduced the impact of gender differences on people's lives.

The same cannot be said for most industrializing societies. This is especially true of Muslim societies, where women's lives are greatly restricted by interpretations of the Koran by Muslim clerics. In many cases, women are required, when in public, to wear clothing that covers their bodies from head to toe except for their hands, feet, and all or part of their face. In some cases (as in Saudi Arabia) women are forbidden to

The Worst Place to Be a Woman

As Helen Cooper, a reporter, stepped from the tiny single-engine plane that brought her to the city of Bukavu in the Congo, she felt that it was like returning home to her native Liberia, another land "ravaged by years of pointless civil wars." She saw fetid, trash-filled streets; abandoned buildings damaged by rockets and other projectiles "common to all of the continent's numerous civil wars"; and a few decrepit cars filled with ten, fifteen, even twenty people.

What struck her most, however, were the women. As she drove into the city, she passed countless women, young and old, though "old in Africa means 35 or so." "These were the women I grew up with in Liberia, the women all across Africa—the worst place there is to be a woman—who somehow manage to carry the entire continent on their backs."

Cooper tells of one image from Bukavu that she cannot get out of her mind. "It is of an old woman in her 30s." She was walking up a hill, carrying so many logs that her chest was parallel to the ground. "Her husband was walking just in front of her. He carried nothing. Nothing in his hand, nothing on his shoulder, nothing on his back. He kept looking back at her, telling her to hurry up."

"In Liberia, when their sons were kidnapped to fight in wars, and when their husbands came home from brothels and infected them with H.I.V., and when government soldiers invaded their houses and raped them in front of their teenage sons, these were the women who kept selling fish and cassava and kola nuts to feed their families and who ignored the threats of young men who vowed more war if their chosen presidential candidate, a former soccer player, didn't win. And, finally, these were the women who, in Liberia, recently elected one of their own, Ellen Johnson-Sirleaf, to become the first female president of an African nation."

Source: Helen Cooper, "Waiting for Their Moment in the Worst Place on Earth to Be a Woman," *New York Times*, November 16, 2005.

---

drive cars, and in other places (as in Afghanistan a few years ago) they are forbidden to attend school. In most of these societies, most occupations are closed to women, and within marriages, husbands have far more power, both legal and informal, than their wives (e.g., see Table 14.8).[24] For example, under traditional Islamic practice, husbands can divorce their wives simply by stating on several successive days, "I divorce you," but wives have no comparable right.

In non-Muslim industrializing societies the status of women is generally better, although rarely as good as in the more industrialized societies of Europe and North America. A good marriage is the best that most women can hope for, even if their lives are dominated by the wishes of their husbands and severely restricted by the demands of childbirth and child rearing. Even worse, in many industrializing horticultural societies of sub-Saharan Africa, the notorious practice of female genital mutilation persists, especially in rural areas.[25]

Slowly, however, changes are beginning to occur. In Morocco, for example, the king recently decreed that a minority of seats in the parliament would be reserved for women. A woman has even served as prime minister in a growing list of industrializing societies including Burundi, the Central African Republic, Guyana, Haiti, India, Jamaica, Mali, Mozambique, Pakistan, Peru, the Philippines, Rwanda, Senegal, Sri Lanka, Thailand, and Turkey.[26] This, however, has not greatly improved the lives of the vast majority of women in those societies.[27]

Table 14.8 When Jobs Are Scarce, Men Should Have More Right to a Job Than Women

Society	Percent Agreeing
India	84
Pakistan	82
Egypt	75
China	73
Turkey	67
South Korea	60
Lebanon	51
Kenya	46
Argentina	43
Japan	41
Brazil	37
France	20
Germany	19
United States	14
Spain	12
United Kingdom	12

Source: "Gender Equality Universally Embraced, but Inequalities Acknowledged," Pew Research Center, Global Attitudes Project, p. 9, http://pewglobal.org/files/pdf/Pew-Global-Attitudes-2010-Gender-Report.pdf.

INDUSTRIALIZING SOCIETIES IN THEORETICAL PERSPECTIVE

Not many years ago, the prospects for industrializing societies looked bright. All they had to do, it appeared, was follow the path blazed by the societies that had already industrialized. In fact, some believed that because developing societies had the earlier experience of industrial societies to draw on, they would be able to avoid many of the pitfalls of modernization and speed up the process.

Today, that prediction seems hopelessly naive. In many of the less developed societies, economic growth has been distressingly slow. Improvements in the standard of living for the masses of their citizens have been especially disappointing. Hundreds of millions of people continue to live in poverty, with little prospect of any significant improvement in their situation.

Why were earlier predictions so wrong? Why have so many societies been unable to take greater advantage of the vastly expanded store of technological information that is now available?

One answer, originally developed by a group of Latin American scholars in the 1960s and known as *dependency theory,* is that the difficulties of the less developed societies are due to their social environment or, more specifically, to the actions of industrial societies.[28] The backwardness and problems of the less developed societies, they argue, are the result of exploitation and oppression by the more developed societies. Dependency theory is, in effect, an extension to the global level of Marx's (zero-sum) theory that the impoverishment of some is an inevitable consequence of the growing wealth of others.

There have been a number of versions of dependency theory, each providing a somewhat different explanation of the problems confronting industrializing societies, but all of them locate the source outside the industrializing societies themselves.[29] Some blame multinational corporations, some blame the governments of industrial societies, and others blame the capitalist world economy that has caused so many developing nations to concentrate on the production of raw materials and on low-technology industries. Whatever the explanation, dependency theorists blame the difficulties of the industrializing societies on Western industrial societies.

Another group of scholars, employing *modernization theory*, developed a very different explanation of the problems confronting industrializing societies. They found the source of these problems within the industrializing societies themselves.[30] As with dependency theory, there have been a number of versions of modernization theory, but most of them focused on the attitudes and values of the members of industrializing societies as the chief deterrent to industrialization. The difficulties of these societies, in their view, are due to the persistence of ideologies and institutional systems that were inherited from the preindustrial past and are incompatible with the needs and requirements of industrialization. They point out, for example, the persistence of fatalism, trust in magic, resistance to innovation and change, and the conflict between traditional, more casual patterns of work and the requirements of modern industrial enterprises (see p. 368, Traditional Values and Norms Regarding Work). They emphasize the consequences of illiteracy and the lack of the information, training, and skills that are essential in the modern world. In short, modernization theory locates the causes of lagging development within the less developed societies themselves, rather than in their social environments.

In any attempt to evaluate the relative merits of dependency theory and modernization theory, it is important to keep two things in mind. First, there is little evidence to support the claim of many dependency theorists that life was better in most industrializing societies before the industrial era. Such a view cannot be supported by the historical record of the last 5,000 years. It is a mistake, therefore, to ask, "What has caused these societies to *regress*?" Rather, the question must be, "Why have the conditions in so many of them improved so slowly?" The second point to remember is that there is no reason to assume that the source of problems in industrializing societies is primarily internal or primarily external. On the contrary, ecological-evolutionary theory asserts that the characteristics of human societies—including the degree of their development—are the product of both internal and external forces (see Figure 1.2, p. 20). To ignore or neglect either aspect is to misunderstand and misinterpret the complex process of societal development.

One indication of the danger of neglecting either set of forces is provided by the results of the foreign aid programs created by Western industrial societies in recent decades. Because of the tremendous success of the Marshall Plan in rebuilding Germany following the massive destruction of World War II, many Western leaders assumed that large transfers of capital to the less developed societies of Asia, Africa, and Latin America would produce similar results. Unfortunately, however, the results of such aid to most of these societies have been extremely disappointing. As noted earlier, much of the money was wasted on ill-conceived projects or simply vanished into the pockets of corrupt officials. It has gradually become clear that the success of foreign

Traditional Values and Norms Regarding Work

Industrializing horticultural societies face formidable barriers to industrialization that are largely a result of their centuries of reliance on horticulture. Among them are their distinctive values and norms regarding work. Some years ago, the Inter-African Labour Institute characterized the work traditions of horticultural Africa this way:

1. Work is viewed in its relation to the basic institution of family or clan; within the family, it is divided on the basis of age and sex.
2. Work is linked with religious rites.
3. Work activities are evaluated in the light of a subsistence economy rather than a profit economy (i.e., they are oriented more to the production of the necessities of life than to the production of an economic surplus).
4. Work requires neither foresight nor planning.
5. Time is largely irrelevant in work activities; no time limits are set for most tasks.
6. There is little specialization.
7. For men, work is episodic; when a task has to be done, men often do it without a break, but intervals of inactivity are long and frequent.
8. Men hardly ever work alone; work activities (e.g., hunting parties and work parties) often resemble a collective leisure activity in modern industrial society.

These traditions did little to prepare the members of these societies, especially the men, for work in a modern industrial economy. A parallel list of the characteristics of work in industrial societies would, in fact, be almost the opposite.

One of the biggest problems is suggested by item 7. As we saw in Chapter 6, cultivation is often primarily women's work. Men's responsibilities tend to be limited to the occasional clearing of new gardens. While women do the sustained, tedious chores—planting, cultivating, and harvesting crops—men are free to do more interesting and exciting things—hunting, fighting, politicking, socializing, and participating in ceremonial activities. The disciplined, routinized, often boring patterns of work that are typical of an industrial economy are seldom experienced by men in these societies. In this respect, the peasant farmers of agrarian societies are far better prepared for industrialization. Yet even they have found the transition difficult.

Sources: This list is based on a report from the Inter-African Labour Institute, *The Human Factors of Productivity in Africa,* as summarized in William H. Lewis, ed., *French-Speaking Africa: The Search for Identity* (New York: Walker, 1965), p. 168. Many of these propositions were also supported in papers presented to a subsequent conference on competing demands for labor in traditional African societies, cosponsored by the Joint Committee on African Studies of the Social Science Research Council, the American Council of Learned Societies, and the Agricultural Development Council. See William O. Jones, "Labor and Leisure in Traditional African Societies," *Social Science Research Council Items,* 22 (March 1968), pp. 1–6.

---

aid programs depends as much on the characteristics of the recipient society as on the generosity of the donors. Effective use of large amounts of capital presupposes supportive institutions and ideologies in the recipient society, plus large numbers of people with administrative and technical skills and honest elites capable of organizing vast and complex programs.

The greatest deficiency of both modernization theory and dependency theory, however, is their failure to focus more closely on the distinctive demographic situation of industrializing societies. For the fact is that no society, except for newly settled frontier societies (e.g., the United States and Canada), has ever successfully industrialized while burdened with anything approaching the rate of population growth existing in many of these societies today. As we have seen, even impressive economic gains can be completely consumed by rapid population growth. It is no coincidence that the most striking instance of economic growth and development in recent decades has occurred in China in the wake of that society's adoption of its extremely strict "one-child" policy.

From the perspective of ecological-evolutionary theory, it is clear that the demographic peculiarities of industrializing societies, as well as those characteristics of ideology and social structure that work against the resolution of their problems, all stem from a more basic underlying source. In most societies throughout human history, all the basic components of their sociocultural systems—population, technology, ideology, social structure, and material products—evolved more or less in concert with one another. In contrast, in societies industrializing today, selected elements of an enormously powerful industrial technology have been introduced into social and cultural systems that are still geared to much less potent agrarian or advanced horticultural technologies.

Not surprisingly, these societies have had enormous difficulty in coordinating technological advance with changes in other areas of life. Even the Western industrial democracies, in which new technology evolved largely in concert with changes in population, ideology, social structure, and material products, have encountered difficulties in adjusting to the new and rapidly changing industrial technology. In fact, most of their major problems reflect the failure of political ideologies, religious beliefs and values, legal norms, organizational principles, and other cultural and structural elements to respond quickly enough to the new conditions created by ongoing changes in technology.

Considering the problems it created even in those societies in which it evolved, it is hardly surprising that an industrial technology creates far greater ones when it is introduced as an alien force in societies still geared to simpler technologies. And when only selected elements of the new technology are introduced (e.g., television, explosives, the Internet), the results can be disastrous.

Pakistan provides a good example of this. Over the last hundred years, improvements in transportation (especially railroads) and food production reduced the number of deaths from famine, and programs of mass immunization and other health measures reduced deaths from disease. While this drastic reduction in the death rate was occurring, the vast majority of Pakistanis, unlike the members of earlier industrializing societies, were not really involved in the industrialization process as a whole. Most of them continued to live as peasant farmers, eking out a marginal existence on tiny farms, using traditional tools and techniques. As a result, their religious beliefs, values, and customs remained much as they had been for centuries, with large families highly valued and change viewed with profound skepticism. Not surprisingly, poverty, terrorism, and internal and external conflict have been ongoing, and only a repressive authoritarian government has been able to prevent even worse.

In the past, such imbalances in a sociocultural system would have been corrected through the play of natural forces. We saw earlier in Chapter 6 how population pressures during the late hunting and gathering era led to the over-killing of large game animals and, eventually, to the emergence of a more advanced technology and a new way of life. And we have seen how plagues and famines of the past periodically decimated the populations of agrarian societies, restoring their demographic equilibrium. In the case of India and numerous other societies industrializing today, however, more advanced societies have repeatedly prevented this from occurring by shipping in large amounts of food. In doing so, however, they have created the likelihood of more serious crises and greater problems in the future.

As Malthus warned more than two centuries ago, if fertility is not curbed by the forgoing of children, forces such as war, civil strife, famine, drought, and disease will halt population growth. The longer it takes for industrializing societies to adopt technological and other cultural solutions to high rates of fertility, the greater the chance that these negative forces will play a major role in checking population growth. They are, in fact, already playing a significant role in parts of the developing world, especially in sub-Saharan Africa.[31]

Of one thing we can be sure: the problems of industrializing societies are not going to be solved quickly. Because of the failure of most of these societies to control population growth in the past, they have large numbers of young people who are only now entering the reproductive years. Of every hundred sub-Saharan Africans alive today, forty-two are under fifteen years of age; in contrast, of every hundred Europeans, only sixteen are that young.[32] Because of the disproportionately large number of children and teenagers in industrializing societies, most of their populations will increase substantially in the next several decades *even if every couple from now on were to limit itself to only two children.*

In summary, industrializing societies provide a fascinating test of ecological-evolutionary theory, and other theories as well. Their problems are so complex that they compel us to consider all the components of sociocultural systems—population, culture, material products, social organization, and social institutions—as well as the relations among them. They also compel us to consider the relation of these sociocultural systems to the larger world system—which is good preparation for an analysis of the future, our primary concern in the final chapter.

EXCURSUS: MARXIST SOCIETIES AS NATURAL EXPERIMENTS

In a laboratory experiment, a researcher introduces a new factor in an experimental group. Then, to determine if the new factor caused a change or made a difference, the researcher compares what happened in the experimental group to what occurred in a control group. Since every effort is made to assure that the two groups are exactly the same except for the one new factor, it is reasonable to assume that it, and it alone, was the cause of any difference between the groups.

"Natural experiments" are similar to laboratory experiments in many ways, but they lack the strong controls that make everything else exactly the same. First, in a natural experiment the change or difference is not introduced by the researcher. Instead, it is something that happens naturally in a natural setting (e.g., an earthquake, technological innovation, political revolution). Second, because it does not occur within a controlled laboratory setting, where other things are held constant, it is much harder to determine the precise cause of any differences observed. Nonetheless, if a number of such natural experiments occur and the results are similar, one can start to make fairly firm inferences about causes.

This is the case with political revolutions that have attempted to put Marxist ideals into practice in a number of societies (e.g., the former Soviet Union, China, Cuba, and North Korea). Since very similar results have been obtained at different times, in societies at different levels of technological development, with different cultural backgrounds, and in different regions of the world, it is much more likely that implementation of the ideology, rather than some other factor, is the cause.

Where they have gained power and influence, the efforts of revolutionary socialists to institute social and political change constitute massive (natural) social experiments. And, in our judgment, these efforts to transform societies into communist utopias must be judged massive failures, and we ask: What lesson(s) can be learned from these efforts?

Because Marx's theory of revolutionary socialism put so much emphasis on the role of private ownership of the means of production (what he called private property) as a cause of human misery and despair, it was easy to believe that outlawing private property would set in motion a series of forces that would ameliorate most, if not all, social ills (e.g., see Chapter 11, pages 278–279).

Unfortunately, as Weber, Mosca, and Michels had predicted, this was not to be the case. It appears that it is *control* of the forces of production, not legal title to them, that is the crucial factor. Ironically, therefore, rather than eliminating political inequality and exploitation, abolishing private property actually made political and economic inequality worse. It centralized social control in the hands of a new even more powerful ruling class—the *nomenklatura*. Rather than decentralizing control and increasing human liberty and happiness as Marx had predicted, it centralized control of virtually all aspects of the life of citizens in the hands of the state and the elite who ran it.

A Small Part of Communism's Cambodian Harvest of Death—An Estimated Two Million in Total—in What Came to Be Called the Killing Fields: Skulls Seen in Phnom Penh in This 1981 Photo. The Authorities Say These Victims Were Tied Together by Rope Before Being Executed by Followers of Premier Pol Pot, Who Was Ousted from Power in Early 1979.

As a result, these societies became, within the limits imposed by their technologies, totalitarian. And, as a growing body of previously suppressed information about crime, alcoholism, worker absenteeism, suicide and mortality rates in these societies comes to light, it is clear that worker alienation and human despair increased, not decreased, in these societies. The "new class" that ran these societies appropriated for itself numerous privileges and rights that it denied to the general population.

Furthermore, the full magnitude of the environmental damage produced by revolutionary-socialist was effectively concealed for decades by these regimes. In the absence of a free press and legal political opposition, elites in them were completely unaccountable for the environmental damage and human costs of their policies.

No discussion of the polities of revolutionary-socialist societies would be complete without some discussion of the enormous growth of their political bureaucracies. It is especially ironic that Marx should have supposed that the abolition of private property would lead to the withering of the state. What happened instead, as Mosca and Weber more accurately forecast, is that the state and state bureaucracies flourished as never before.

In the state bureaucracies of these command economies, power and privilege are a function of the number of people and the size of the budget one controls. Thus, there is always a built-in incentive for every administrator to expand his or her own operation. Moreover, in contrast to the private sector of market-oriented societies, there are no measures of profitability that act to keep these tendencies in check. Western Marxists often criticized the Soviets for the bureaucratization of Soviet society, without recognizing the degree to which the elimination of private property and markets has been responsible for this trend.

Even more stark and alarming, though, has been the extraordinarily high human cost of such centralized power. The human toll of Stalin's forced collectivization of peasants, Mao's "cultural revolution" and "great leap forward," and Pol Pot's revolutionary reforms stagger the imagination. In their attempts to radically restructure the polities and economies of these societies, tens of millions were imprisoned, allowed to starve, or were brutally executed.

Rudolph Rummel, professor emeritus at the University of Hawaii, who has studied various forms of organized violence for decades, coined the term "democide" (genocide and mass murder) to denote the deliberate killing of populations by their governments. By his estimate, revolutionary-socialist (communist) governments were responsible for the murder of 148 *million* people in the twentieth century. It is important to emphasize that this figure *excludes combatants killed in war.* Of these, Communist China was responsible for seventy-seven *million,* and the Soviet Union for sixty-two *million,* both surpassing Hitler's much better-known murder toll of twenty-one *million.* Although Pol Pot killed far fewer people, an estimated two million, given the much smaller size of Cambodia, (seven million), he may have *caused the deaths of more than one-quarter of the population!*

Thus, unfortunately, despite the lofty rhetoric and utopian goals, the most important lesson that can be drawn from the comparison of the relatively successful, limited, pragmatic reforms of the Western "democracies" in the twentieth century with the abject failure and human misery caused by the massive reforms of revolutionary-socialist societies, may be that *people should be distrustful of social theorists, politicians, revolutionaries, and activists who promise too much.*[33]

CHAPTER 15

Retrospect and Prospect

Outline
Looking Back
Looking Ahead

When studying something as complex as the evolution of human societies, it is easy to become so immersed in details that one loses sight of the larger picture. For this reason, we begin this final chapter with a brief look back over the long sweep of human history. Then we go on to consider an important question that we could not address until this point: What has sociocultural evolution really meant for humanity? More specifically, how has technological advance affected the quality of human life? Has it brought greater freedom, justice, and happiness? Or has the quality of life declined?

After considering these questions, we will turn our attention to *the future*. What lies ahead for human societies? Can ecological-evolutionary theory help us anticipate the problems and prospects of the next few decades? This is an important question and a practical one as well. For most of us will live in that world, and it could be very different from the world we live in today.

LOOKING BACK

When we look back over the long course of hominid history, we see that we and our societies are an integral part of the global ecosystem and that our species' development has always been part of the same grand process of biological evolution that shapes all life on this planet. Yet it is equally clear that our species' development has been different from that of the rest of the biological world in some fundamental ways. If we understand where and how our path diverged, we can better understand our problems and those of our societies, and perhaps be able to create a better, happier future.

The Divergent Path

For millions of years there was little to suggest that our early ancestors were destined to become anything more than just another variety of primate. But genetic changes eventually provided them with the ability to create *symbol systems*, a trait that is as much a product of natural selection as wings, gills, social instincts, and other adaptive mechanisms in the biotic world.

With the aid of symbol systems, hominids were able to use their primate capacity for learning to far greater advantage. They could now create and share vast amounts of information that had been gleaned from individual experience. Eventually, hominid societies came to depend far more on new cultural information than on new genetic information in their adaptive efforts, and *human evolution came to be shaped primarily by the processes of cultural innovation and selection, rather than by the processes of biological evolution.*

The explanation of the tremendous adaptive capacity of cultural information is its potential for creating diversity. In this respect, it is like genetic information, which is responsible for the striking diversity in the biotic world. In the case of cultural information, however, *all the diversity is concentrated within a single species.* As a result, despite a common genetic heritage, human individuals become, with culture, far more varied than the members of any other species. Human societies are also extremely varied—again, unlike the situation in other social species. Though such diversity enhances our species' survival potential, it is a major source of problems, both within and among societies.

Another manifestation of culture's capacity for creating diversity is the great variety of needs and desires that humans have developed, *needs and desires not even remotely related to our survival as individuals or as a species.* To satisfy these culturally generated or intensified needs, societies have depended primarily on the kind of information—technological—that helps people utilize environmental resources in new ways and for new purposes. As technology advanced, however, it altered the conditions of life, and as that happened, further needs emerged. Efforts to satisfy these needs created further change, which led in turn to new needs, a process of positive feedback that has continued at an accelerating pace for over 10,000 years.

Through this process, *humans established a new and unique relationship with the biophysical environment.* Since every other species of plant or animal uses the resources of its environment to satisfy only a limited set of genetically programmed needs, this characteristic is perhaps the most fundamental divergence of all.

The Question of Progress

Despite the problems that have attended our species' reliance on culture, one thing is clear: *culture has been a highly successful adaptive mechanism.* Humanity has not only survived, it has flourished by biological standards: There are far more of us alive today than at any time in the past, and our numbers are growing rapidly. Moreover, humans have spread into an enormous variety of environments—another important measure of biological success.

But numbers and dispersion are not enough on which to base an assessment of *human* evolution. We must also ask whether the process of sociocultural evolution has meant progress in terms of more uniquely human criteria and goals, such as freedom, justice, and happiness.

It is not easy to assess progress in terms such as these. For one thing, these concepts are so broad that they apply to countless aspects of human life. For another, the way we define them is the product of past experience, and this, as we have seen, varies greatly among individuals, groups, and societies. Nevertheless, because the subject is too important to ignore, we must at least make the effort to evaluate human progress in terms of these goals and try to determine whether our species' growing store of cultural information has had the effect of advancing or hindering them.

Freedom

The high value that the members of modern industrial societies attach to freedom is revealed in the growing challenge to all forms of authority, not only in the liberal democracies of the West but in the formerly authoritarian nations of eastern Europe and Asia as well. Even those who are not in the forefront of the libertarian movement are likely to consider the degree of freedom accorded individuals one of the basic measures of the attractiveness, and hence the progress, of a society, and they would deny that a technologically advanced, politically repressive society is truly progressive.

But human freedom is more than the absence of repressive social controls; it is also freedom from restraints imposed by nature. People who must spend most of their waking hours in an exhausting struggle to produce the necessities of life are not truly "free"—even if there are few social restraints on their actions.* A woman whose life is a long succession of unwanted pregnancies is not "free"—regardless of the kind of society she lives in. Disease, physical and mental handicaps, geographical barriers, and all the laws of nature restrict people and deny them freedom. For freedom does not exist where there are no alternatives, and freedom can be measured only by the range of choices that are available. The fewer the viable choices, the less freedom there is—and it matters little whether the constraints are imposed by nature, by other people, or by government.

Once we recognize this, it becomes clear that humanity's long struggle to advance technologically is not irrelevant to the desire for freedom. Every technological innovation reflects the desire to overcome natural limitations on human action. Thanks to this struggle, some of us are now free to talk across oceans, free to travel faster than sound, free to live longer lives in better health while enjoying a range of experiences that far surpass in richness and variety what was available to the greatest kings and emperors of the past.

There has been a price to pay, of course: technological progress has necessitated larger and more complex social systems. If we want the option of flying to another part of the country instead of walking there, or of watching the day's events on a screen in our hand or home instead of hearing about them weeks later, we have to accept certain social controls. The goods and services essential for those options can be produced only where there are organizations with rules and with sanctions to enforce the rules, and individuals with authority to exercise the sanctions. And these organizations can function efficiently only within a society that has rules to govern the relationships among them, and an authority system to enforce those rules. The only alternative is anarchy—and the loss of all the freedoms that modern technology affords.

Critics of modern society often say that the price has been too high, that the increased social restrictions outweigh the gains in freedom we derive from modern technology.[1] This is a matter all of us must decide for ourselves. In doing so, however, we need to beware of romanticizing the past. Before deciding that people are less free

---

*Thus, we might say they have "liberty" but not "freedom."

than they used to be, we must read accounts of peasant life in agrarian societies and of the life of horticultural and hunting and gathering peoples. In doing this, we must resist the temptation to abstract the attractive features and ignore the unattractive ones. We must remember that slavery and serfdom were not accidental characteristics of agrarian societies, but reflections of basic, inescapable conditions of that way of life, as were the high mortality rate and short life span of most hunting and gathering peoples.

Once we recognize the danger of comparing some rosy version of life in less advanced societies with the negative side of life in industrial societies, we are in a better position to consider whether freedom is a correlate of technological advance. We can say, first of all, that technological progress has clearly raised the *upper* limit of freedom in human societies. Individuals with the greatest measure of freedom in contemporary societies—that is, the richest or most powerful members—enjoy a far wider range of choice than individuals with the greatest measure of freedom in agrarian societies, and the elites of agrarian societies had far more freedom than the elites of less advanced societies. This has been true with respect to everything from the use of a leisure hour to the use of a lifetime. In this sense, then, there is a high positive correlation between technological advance and gains in human freedom.

The relation between technological advance and freedom for the *average* member of society is more complicated. If we compare the typical peasant in an agrarian society with a typical hunter and gatherer, it is not at all clear that there were gains. In fact, the peasant had to live with a lot of new social controls while gaining very little freedom from natural controls. Thus, during much of the course of history—especially after the formation of the state—the average individual probably experienced a *decline* in freedom. With industrialization, however, the pattern changes.[2] Once the difficult period of transition is past, technological progress and freedom for the average person are positively related, as Figure 15.1 illustrates. Whether people in industrial societies have more freedom than hunters and gatherers is less certain. Clearly they may have fewer physical and biological restraints, but it is not clear whether they have more or fewer social ones. For, although hunting and gathering societies were smaller and less complex than industrial, there was little, if any, privacy in them. "Privacy" is a fragile and modern invention.

Before leaving the subject of freedom, we should take note of the popular misconception that governmental activity necessarily results in a loss of freedom for the members of society. This is at best a half-truth. Laws do, of course, place restrictions on people, but in democratic societies this is often done in order to increase freedom, not reduce it. The Pure Food and Drug Act in the United States, for example, was designed to restrict the freedom of businesspeople who were willing to sell spoiled food and dangerous drugs for profit, but it increased the freedom of the millions of people who used their products. Sometimes, of course, laws restrict everyone's freedom in one area—the freedom to proceed at will through a busy intersection, for example—in order to preserve it in others. In short, most legal norms *redistribute* freedom.

Justice

Justice has to do with the *fairness* of a society in its treatment of its members. Although no one would quarrel with the idea that a society should be "fair," we run into serious

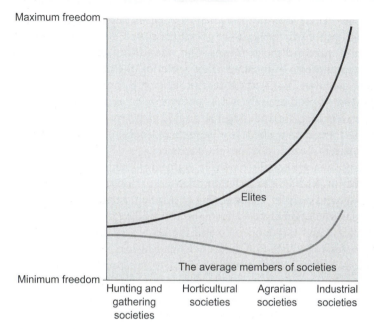

Figure 15.1. Trends in Freedom for Elites and for Other Members of Societies.

difficulties when we try to define what this means. Is a society fair when it rewards people on the basis of their contributions to the common good, or is it more equitable to allocate rewards on the basis of individual needs? Should handicapped individuals, for example, be paid the same as those who are able to outproduce them with less effort? And how does one arrive at a fair evaluation of the relative contributions of people in dissimilar activities—a symphony conductor, a bricklayer, a housewife, a garbage collector, a student?

And what about punishments? Does a "fair" society punish its members strictly in accordance with the letter of the law, or is it fairer to take circumstances and intent into account? What of a parent's theft to feed a hungry child, for example, or a mercy killing? And should a society deal more severely with those in positions of power than with other members of society when they commit crimes, or should everyone be treated equally? Questions like these point to the difficulty of measuring progress with respect to justice. Since an adequate treatment of the subject would require volumes, all we can do here is call attention to basic trends and offer tentative conclusions.

To begin with, as we observed in earlier chapters, social inequality became more pronounced as societies advanced technologically and status became increasingly dependent on the family into which one was born. The result was a weakening of the link between a person's *efforts* and a person's rewards. Whereas every normal, healthy boy in a hunting and gathering group had a chance of becoming the best hunter (and hence the most important man) in his society, a peasant's son had little hope of advancing even a notch above his father's social level, no matter how hard he tried. Increasingly rigid stratification systems locked people into roles and situations where they could neither develop nor use their talents, while those with little talent might occupy positions for which they were grossly unsuited.

The trend in punishment, meanwhile, was toward increasingly harsh and discriminatory treatment. In most agrarian societies, the privileged were free to abuse members of the lower class without fear of reproof; if the latter retaliated, they would be punished swiftly and severely. A master involved in a conflict with his slaves or serfs was often both prosecutor and judge; he could beat them with impunity and, in many societies, kill them if he wished. Nor were there legal sanctions against the beating of children by parents, employers, or schoolmasters.

Courts of law were equally harsh. In eighteenth-century England, the death penalty could be invoked for 222 different offenses, including such minor infractions as the theft of a handkerchief, the shooting of a rabbit, or the forgery of a birth certificate.[3] Nor was execution always a humane process: we are told that the hangman in Elizabethan England was "an artist, and the knife was his chief instrument; the art consisting in tossing his man off the ladder, hanging him, but cutting him down before he breaks his neck, so that he may be dismembered and disemboweled while still alive."[4]

In general, societies seem to have become less fair and less just as they advanced technologically. With industrialization, however, there are clear signs of a reversal. With respect to material rewards, industrialization has resulted in a decline in some aspects of social inequality among the members of a society. Public education now provides at least *some* chance for most children to develop their abilities, and women and minorities have gained numerous legal and economic opportunities long denied them. Industrial societies are also more solicitous of their poor and their handicapped, and provide a far broader range of legal rights and protections for their members, whatever their social status. Criminal justice is far less harsh. Industrial societies today rarely execute their members, and never for minor offenses, nor do they maim them, as was common in the agrarian era. In short, after a long period of declining justice with respect to both rewards and punishments, there is finally movement in the other direction.

Happiness

Of all the possible measures of progress, happiness is the most elusive, for it depends so much—perhaps primarily—on the quality of interpersonal relations—whether there is love, mutual respect, cooperation, and so forth. And these things do not depend on the level of technological development. Studies of modern hunting and gathering groups indicate that the most primitive peoples develop these qualities as surely as members of modern industrial societies do.[5]

There are several ways, however, in which technological progress is relevant to this kind of happiness. To begin with, some of life's greatest tragedies involve the premature death of a loved one—a cherished child, a parent, or a partner in a happy marriage. We saw how common this was in most societies prior to the Industrial Revolution and can therefore appreciate how the recently increased life span has contributed to human happiness. Even today, technological advance has a powerful impact on life expectancy: according to one recent study, more than 67 percent of the variation in life expectancy among societies can be explained by differences in commercial energy use.[6]

Increasing Longevity: Blessing or Curse?

The average life expectancy of members of industrial societies today are rising rapidly and already appear to be far higher than anything in the known past. As recently as 1930 average life expectancy in American society was only 59.7 years; today it is nearly eighty. In 1930 only three individuals in a thousand could expect to live to age ninety. Now, less than a century later, the number has increased more than sevenfold. Even more astounding, the proportion surviving to one hundred has increased twenty-seven-fold in this same period. In short, there has been a revolution in life expectancy and a virtual explosion in the numbers of elderly people.

On first thought, this seems to be a marvelous achievement and wonderful blessing. Long life has been one of the major goals of most humans throughout history.

There is a downside, however, to this revolution. As people grow older, health tends to decline and physical and mental problems increase. The older the population grows, the smaller the proportion of people who are able to work full-time, or even part-time, and the larger the proportion that becomes dependent on others both financially and physically.

From being producers, most people gradually become net consumers, increasingly dependent on others. From the societal standpoint, year by year the needs of the elderly consume more and more of the national budget leaving less and less for other needs and requirements. Collectively, this silent revolution has already produced major change in industrial societies and is certain to produce further change in the years ahead, especially if life expectancy rises to 120 years as many experts now predict.

As with so many other major transformations in the life of societies, this revolution is largely the result of technological innovations and the subsequent adjustments and changes in social institutions as people attempt to take advantage of innovations such as the development of new drugs and vaccines; replacements of more and more body parts (e.g., hearing aids, hip replacements, artificial hearts); and regenerative medicine (e.g., cell therapy, gene therapy, tissue engineering), which its advocates say will enable the body to slow, halt, or even reverse the aging process. In short, we seem to be creating the brave new world!

But will it ultimately prove a blessing or a curse? The results on this question are still out.

Sources: *National Vital Statistics Reports*, 61, no. 3 (Sept. 24, 2012); and Roger Cohen, "When I'm Sixty-Four," *New York Times*, Dec. 25, 2012.

Health, too, contributes to happiness. When we are seriously ill, life may not seem worth living. Disease was very poorly understood through most of human history, and technological advance prior to the Industrial Revolution had minimal impact in this area. More recently, however, advances in sanitation and medicine have dramatically improved the physical well-being of the members of many societies. Unfortunately, modern medical technology has also had a negative effect: it has been used to keep alive individuals who, in simpler societies, would, mercifully, be allowed to die. On balance, however, the result has undeniably been positive.

Hunger, another cause of enormous human misery over the centuries, has been drastically reduced in many societies as a result of industrialization. As recently as the eighteenth century, local crop failures in much of Europe could result in starvation because of an inadequate transportation network. Today, thanks to advances in technology, food supplies can be safely stored for long periods and moved to areas of scarcity in every industrial society and in an increasing number of industrializing ones.

The industrialization of agriculture has also meant a substantially improved food supply, with respect to quality, quantity, and diversity, for most members of industrial societies. During the winter, for example, people can now enjoy fresh fruits and vegetables shipped in from areas with different growing seasons. Nor do the members of industrial societies have to subsist on short rations in the months prior to harvest, as most members of traditional agrarian societies had to do. As with improvements in health, it is easy to take such benefits for granted and to lose sight of the numerous links between technological advance and human happiness.

The increased production of other kinds of goods and services, especially nonessential ones, has probably had much less effect on happiness. The absolute quantity of luxuries we enjoy is often not as important to us in this regard as how they compare with what other people have. Thus the headman in a simple horticultural society may be quite content with his few special possessions, because they are more than his neighbors own and as good as anything he knows about, while middle-class Americans and Canadians, surrounded with goods and services the headman never dreamed of, may feel terribly deprived when they compare themselves with more prosperous neighbors. In other words, insofar as happiness depends on nonessential material possessions, the *relative* degree of inequality may be more important than anything else.

When we take into account the advances in health, the greater abundance and improved quality of food, and the drastic reduction in premature deaths, to say nothing of the improvements in freedom and justice, it is clear that industrialization has eliminated the source of much of the misery of earlier eras. Putting it all together, we are again led to the tentative conclusion that the long-term trend for the average individual has been curvilinear, as shown in Figure 15.1. Conditions seem to have been more conducive to human happiness for the average individual in hunting and gathering societies than in horticultural societies, and better in horticultural than in agrarian or even early industrial. But with further advances in industrialization, the situation of the average individual seems to have improved considerably, reversing the long-term trend.

For some time now, the Gallup Poll and other researchers have found a striking relation between the level of happiness expressed by the people they interviewed and the level of technological advance of the societies in which they lived.[7] The same relation was found between societal development and people's satisfaction with specific aspects of their lives (e.g., family life, health, housing, work). The results of the original survey led George Gallup to comment: "For centuries, romantics and philosophers have beguiled us with tales of societies that were 'poor but happy.' If any such exist, the survey failed to discover them."

According to the most recent poll of 156 countries, all ten of the happiest, and fifteen out of the twenty happiest societies are industrial. Household income appears to be the strongest predictor, and the highest scores are found in North America (7.1) and Western Europe (6.7), while the lowest scores are found in South Asia (4.8) and sub-Saharan Africa (4.6).[8] In fact, the long-term relationship between societal development and human happiness closely resembles the lower line in Figure 15.1; the average level of happiness appears to have declined from the hunting and gathering era through the agrarian era and then improved more recently with industrialization.[9]

Concluding Thoughts

It should be clear by now that there is no simple one-to-one correspondence between technological advance and progress in terms of freedom, justice, and happiness. In fact, one may well ask whether technological advance has not lured societies into evolutionary paths where the costs often outweigh the benefits.

Had human history come to an end several hundred years ago, before the Industrial Revolution transformed societies, one would have been forced to answer affirmatively. During the last hundred years, however, technological advance has begun to make a strong positive contribution to the attainment of humanity's higher goals. Whether this will continue in the future is another question. We can say this, however: Technology has at last brought into the realm of *the possible* a social order with greater freedom, justice, and happiness than any society has yet known.

Whatever our judgment about the wisdom of our species' pursuit of technological advance, one thing is clear: *For the evolution of human societies as a whole, technological advance can be equated with sustained progress only in the limited sense of growth in the store of cultural information.*

LOOKING AHEAD

A noted scholar once wrote, "The past is not dead history; it is living material out of which man makes the present and builds the future."[10] Humanity has indeed created the present world from materials of the past and, just as surely, is now laying the foundation for the future. But what kind of future will it be? And what kinds of changes are we likely to encounter in the next several decades?

Trying to foresee the future has always been a risky business. A hundred years ago, for example, some very knowledgeable people proclaimed that warfare had developed to the point where no further advances in weaponry could be expected![11] Despite the difficulties, it is important to try to anticipate what lies ahead, because the sooner we recognize problems and begin to address them, the better our chances of finding solutions.

There are several things to keep in mind as we try to see across the years. First, we need to be aware that there are some potential developments that cannot be anticipated but which could alter the picture substantially—the emergence of some new and virulent pestilence or plague, for example, or a shift in climate that is unrelated to human activity. Second, the subject we can speak about with the greatest confidence when discussing the future, especially the next quarter of a century or so, concerns the *problems* societies will face. For the serious, unresolved problems of societies today will almost surely continue to be problems in the years ahead.

Third, and finally, the more thoroughly a prediction is *grounded in a tested analysis of the past and present,* the better its chances of success. Our predictions will thus be based on our analysis of societal evolution up to the present, with special attention to anticipated changes in population, the biophysical environment, technology, ideology, political and economic institutions, the world system of societies, and the higher human goals.

We will not attempt to make flat, unqualified predictions but rather frame statements which say that certain outcomes seem likely under given circumstances. This puts

The Dramatic Growth of World Population Inspired This Classic "Farnk & Earnest" Cartoon by Bob Thaves.

the assumptions on which our predictions are based out in the open where others can examine them and challenge or modify them as new information or insights become available. In time, this should lead to more useful and more accurate predictions.

Population

One of the greatest challenges human societies face in the years ahead is that of slowing the rapid growth of population that has occurred in the last 250 years. In 1750, on the eve of the Industrial Revolution, the human population was less than 800 million. Since then, it has increased *ninefold* and is now growing at a rate of about eighty million every year.

Few today realize how unprecedented this pattern of growth is. During the 10,000 years between the end of the hunting and gathering era and the beginning of the Industrial Revolution, it took from 1,400 to 3,000 years for world population just to double.[†12]

Were numbers to continue to grow at the present rate, world population would more than double by the end of this century. Obviously this will not happen; the resources of this planet—food, water, energy, minerals—cannot support anything like this number, and it is doubtful that people could tolerate the psychological stresses of the crowding such numbers imply. Long before the population reached thirteen or fourteen billion, food and water shortages, water and air pollution, disease and epidemics, and wars waged for control of increasingly scarce resources would all drive up the death rate.

The question, therefore, is not whether the rate of growth of the human population will decline—that is inevitable. The real question is how this decline will come about. Will brutal natural forces, such as famine and plague, take control and do the job, or will people have the wisdom and foresight to take the steps that are necessary before those forces take over?

At present, there are grounds for both optimism and pessimism. On the darker side, there is the inescapable fact that the present rate of growth—a net increase of nearly eighty million people per year, or the addition of more than two Canadas

---

[†]Had the population grown at its present rate of 1.1 percent per year, and had there been just a single man and woman at the end of the last Ice Age 12,000 years ago, world population today would number 2.1×10^{57} (i.e., the number 21 followed by 56 zeros).[13]

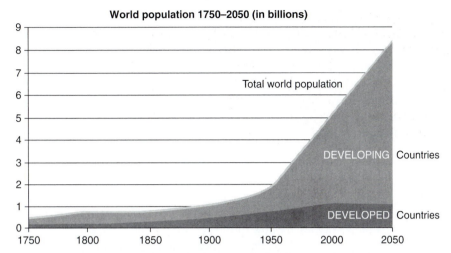

Figure 15.2. Past Trends and Future Estimates of World Population.
http://gcevoices.com/ep/files/2012/02/HUMAN_population-490.gif

crowded onto an already crowded planet—is far beyond our planet's capacity to sustain for long. In addition, because of the extraordinary rate of growth in recent decades, a disproportionate share of the world's population has yet to enter the child-bearing years. And finally, there are a number of powerful and well-organized groups that strongly oppose the practice of birth control. Muslims and the Catholic Church have been at the forefront of the fight in the United Nations to withhold funding for family planning efforts, and they enjoy the support of many Orthodox Jews and evangelical Protestants.

Fortunately, there is also a brighter side to the picture. Birthrates have been dropping in many of the industrializing societies of the third world, where nearly all the population growth has been concentrated in recent decades (see Figure 15.2).[‡] In South Korea, for example, women now have only 1.2 children on average, and in Thailand and China, 1.4 and 1.7, respectively.[14] Even when you exclude China, women in the world's developing countries now average fewer than three children apiece, down substantially from six a generation ago.[15] Although this is still more than replacement level, the trend is encouraging.

Another encouraging fact is the growth in the number of people who have come to understand that the success of a society is measured by the *quality of life* of its members, not by their numbers. Twice as many people crowding streets and highways does nothing to improve the quality of life; on the contrary, it lowers it. And creating babies faster than jobs are created, as in many of the poorest third world societies today, only enlarges the pool of desperate people who are ready recruits for warlords and revolutionaries, and it invites crime and violence.

[‡]As we noted earlier, birthrates in industrial societies are now well below the level needed to sustain these societies at their present size. Were it not for immigration from third world societies, these societies, as a group, would now have declining populations.

On balance, prospects for continuing decline in the rate of population growth are encouraging, but it is equally clear that world population will not be stabilized before it becomes substantially larger than it already is. The most recent estimate by the United Nations predicts that the world will add another one billion people in the next twelve years, and population will reach 9.6 billion by 2050, slightly more than thought a few years ago; fertility rates have risen in some industrializing horticultural societies because of the large number of young people in them.[16]

In the decades ahead, an ever-growing proportion of the world's population will be crowded into cities. The percentage of the world's population that lives in cities has increased from 29 percent in 1950 to 53 percent today.[17] Much of this urbanization has been concentrated in developing societies; in fact, the number of people living in cities in developing societies surpassed that of advanced industrial societies around 1970, and the gap has been widening at an accelerating rate ever since. Some of the largest, most densely populated cities are now in the developing societies, and they continue to grow. For example, the city of São Paulo in Brazil has grown from 2.5 million in 1950 to nearly twenty-one million today. Lagos, Nigeria, and Karachi, Pakistan, have reached densities of 34,500 and 67,000 people per square mile respectively—both continue to grow in size and are becoming more crowded.[§18]

One other demographic trend that we can anticipate is continuing, and probably increasing—is migration from third world societies to industrial societies. This trend, as we have seen (Chapter 13), is already well under way. It is possible to envision the day when the indigenous populations of some industrial societies will become minorities in their own homelands, a development that would almost certainly have explosive political consequences. In fact, this has already happened in the small Baltic republic of Latvia, where Russian immigrants now outnumber native Latvians.

Natural Resources and the Biophysical Environment
As the human population grows in size, the demand for natural resources of every kind—food, water, forest products, minerals—is bound to increase. While increasing demand for these resources is nothing new—and has often been the impetus for technological advances in the past—*the rate of this increase in the years ahead will be unprecedented.* This is unavoidable given the impact of the rate of population growth acting in concert with the growing demand throughout the world for better standards of living—a demand that has been stimulated by the new technologies of transportation and communication that have brought awareness of Western standards to peoples throughout the world and greatly raised their expectations.

Efforts to predict the future of energy sources and supplies are fraught with perils. In large part this is because, as we've mentioned before, technological innovations and breakthroughs are almost impossible to foresee with any clarity. Nowhere has this been more evident than in predictions of the future of fossil fuels, especially petroleum and natural gas.

Several times since 1919, noteworthy scientists and government officials have announced that the "end of oil" was imminent. During the 1970s, for example, there were

§By comparison, New York City overall has a density of about 27,000 per square mile.

claims that the supply of petroleum was finite and as rates of consumption continued or increased there would soon be a decline in supply. While some experts were more optimistic, Kenneth Deffeyes of Princeton University, was "99% certain" that oil production would "peak" in 2004 or 2005.[19]

The importance of such a possibility is hard to exaggerate. Modern industrial economies and the quality of life they have made possible are dependent on the availability of vast quantities of cheap energy, and this is what petroleum and natural gas have provided for more than a century. To make matters worse, if the supply of petroleum declines in the near future, it will be at a time when the demand for it is rapidly increasing in both industrial and industrializing societies. The growth in demand in China would be especially important because China combines a huge population with an extremely rapid rate of industrialization.

But as the price of oil rose, extraction of petroleum from shale became economically profitable, and production of it has boomed in Canada and the United State.[20] This, together with improved extraction techniques and other technological innovations have boosted production worldwide. Thus, production of oil is now not expected to decline but to continue to grow; and, with the development of "fracking," the production of natural gas is expected to grow even more dramatically.[21] This development is especially noteworthy, because natural gas is perhaps the most likely and most attractive "bridge" to future alternative sources of energy.[22]

There are, of course, alternative energy sources available, but none seem capable of providing a cheap and problem-free alternative to oil and natural gas. At one time, coal was thought to be an alternative, since it exists in vast quantities and is not costly to mine or transport. Unfortunately, most coal deposits contain large amounts of sulfur and when burned produce pollution and acid rain.

Other alternative energy sources also present daunting problems. For example, hydrogen, which some tout as the solution to the impending energy crisis, actually has more potential as a delivery system than a new source of energy, because its production requires more than twice as much energy as it yields![23] Nuclear power is not only potentially dangerous but also may be more costly than once thought when one factors in the costs of safely disposing of its radioactive waste materials and shutting down nuclear plants when their relatively short life-span ends. Solar power, too, is expensive when used to generate electricity and is likely to remain so; it also poses serious problems in areas where hours of sunlight are limited.

Finally, many today argue that biofuels derived from vegetation of various kinds are the solution to the energy crisis. In Europe, for example, politicians and environmentalists have believed until recently that palm oil obtained from the forests of southeast Asia could provide a new and renewable source of clean energy. Unfortunately, research indicates that clearing the land to create palm oil plantations not only destroys forests but also puts huge amounts of carbon into the atmosphere. Moreover, the new plantations require large amounts of chemical fertilizer (that itself consumes fuel in its production) to sustain. As one Dutch environmentalist stated, the results of the research were "shocking and totally smashed all the good reasons we initially went into palm oil."[24]

In the United States, politicians representing agribusiness interests promote the production of ethanol, a biofuel made from corn. While very attractive politically, it, too, is far from a satisfactory solution to the energy crisis. For one thing, the *net* energy produced per unit of energy consumed is far less than that produced by petroleum. In fact, Cornell University Professor David Pimental, argues that its production from corn actually produces a *net energy loss!*[25] Even more serious, the production of ethanol is driving up the cost of food around the world. A study by economists projects that the number of hungry people in the world could increase by more than 50 percent by 2020 as a result of increased production of ethanol.[26] In short, there seems to be no viable substitute for fossil fuels on the immediate horizon.

Food is another critical resource whose supply is threatened by population growth. Despite the fact that world agriculture produces 17 percent more calories per person than it did thirty years ago, the United Nations estimates that nearly 870 million people suffer from "chronic undernourishment" today.[27] More than 850 million of them live in developing societies, and they lack the access to cultivatable land or the income to obtain a sufficient supply food.[28] It is estimated that "undernutrition" may have been responsible for half of the 7.6 million childhood deaths in developing societies in 2010.[29] In addition, a number of researchers have argued that overexploitation from advancing technology (e.g., trawl nets, drift nets, GPS, sonar) threatens to cause "the end of fish" in the world's oceans.[30] While there is considerable disagreement about the more alarmist predictions, there is general agreement that the world's marine fisheries reached a peak in the 1990s and have declined since.[31] But while the wild catch has stagnated, the harvest from fish farms has continued to grow; as a result, fish raised on farms now constitute more than 40 percent of the global harvest.[32]

As the Chinese have discovered, it is impossible to halt population growth in less than a quarter of a century, even when unusually rigorous population control policies are adopted and enforced—and no other third world nation has even dared to undertake anything comparable to the Chinese population control program. Thus, many societies—especially those in sub-Saharan Africa, which have already grown to a point where they are no longer able to feed themselves—will continue to face the possibility of widespread hunger and starvation in the years ahead.**

Arable land may well be the most critical of all the resources on which humans depend. Unfortunately, a number of developments are combining to cause a reduction in the supply available, especially in the poorest parts of the world. Currently, it is estimated that *every year* the world loses forty-five square meters of cultivatable land *per person*, and the situation is even worse in sub-Saharan Africa where the loss is seventy-five square meters.[33] As a result, about 24 percent of the world's arable land has been degraded or made unusable by this and other practices, such as overgrazing, inappropriate land use (e.g., cultivation on steep hillsides, causing erosion), and salinization of irrigated land.[34] In the years ahead, technological fixes may not be enough to offset the combined impact of population growth and loss of arable land.

Water is another resource whose supply is threatened in many areas by population growth. This is especially acute in arid regions, such as the Middle East, where

---

**While donations of food from abroad may provide a solution in the short run, it is not likely to prove an effective solution to overpopulation in the long run, especially if the societies involved are unwilling to address the cause of the problem.

water shortages sometimes even threaten to lead to war.[35] The threat of water shortage is not limited to less industrialized societies, however. Industrial societies, too, are finding that as their populations increase, and as industrial and agricultural demands for water rise, resources that once seemed ample are now stretched to the limit and conflicts over their control are becoming increasingly common (see, for example, the continuing conflict in California).[36] The United Nations has predicted that by 2030, water demand will be 40 percent above sustainable supply and nearly half the world could face shortages of fresh water. Moreover, since irrigation consumes over 70 percent of the water supply, this may also mean less food.[37]

Finally, *biological diversity* is a resource that is increasingly threatened by the growth of human populations. Unlike food, water, and energy, the importance of this resource was unappreciated until quite recently. Now, however, we are beginning to recognize that the diversity of plants and animals on this planet may well prove vital to human health and well-being in the long-term future. We are only now beginning to recognize the enormous value of the information stored in the genes of obscure species of plants and animals, information that can be used by medical science in a variety of ways. In addition, modern developments in agriculture have made us dependent on a dangerously small number of varieties of crops, all of which are vulnerable to a variety of threats including new, mutant species of insect pests and plant diseases.[38] Last, but not least, some are even beginning to appreciate that biological diversity is an essential aspect of the physical beauty of this planet.

As societies have sought to meet the demands of their growing populations and their rising expectations, they have been compelled to adopt increasingly powerful technologies of various kinds, many of which introduce new and hazardous materials into the environment. The problem of pollution now affects both the air we breathe and the rivers, streams, and other bodies of water on which we depend. Factories and automobiles generate enormous quantities of pollutants of many kinds. Farms, too, have become a serious source of pollution as efforts to increase production have led to a growing dependence on toxic pesticides and powerful chemical fertilizers that enter the food chain and contaminate water supplies. Even families and individuals contribute to the problem as they make increasing use of plastics, chemicals of various kinds, and other man-made materials that are difficult and expensive to dispose of and that accumulate as mountains of waste in landfills.

Some of the most dangerous pollutants are the radioactive materials that accumulate as by-products of the activities of military organizations, nuclear power plants, and medical centers. These materials pollute the environment for hundreds, and sometimes even thousands, of years, and no completely safe and economical method of disposing of them has yet been found. As these materials continue to accumulate in the environment, the impact on human health and welfare can only increase.

For many, the most alarming threat to the environment has come from predictions of imminent change in climate as a result of the buildup in the atmosphere of heat-trapping "greenhouse gases" produced by fossil-fuel burning. Studies by NASA indicate that the average temperature on the earth's surface has risen by about 1.4 degrees Fahrenheit since 1880.[39] Other studies indicate that the sea level rose about nine inches in the same time period.[40] This climate-change theory, and computer-modeling based on it, led to a number of dire predictions, including the submerging of islands and coastal cities, ever more frequent and more intense storms, draughts, floods, crop failures, and continued melting of glaciers and polar ice.[41] Many predicted that a number of these trends would even accelerate, with devastating results.[42]

Not all scientists, however, are convinced by claims that the changes of the past century were entirely, or even largely, the result of increasing greenhouse gasses and human activity.[43] Skeptics pointed out that the geological record indicated that change-ability had been the rule, not the exception, throughout our planet's history, and that the computer simulations on which predictions of future change were based were seri-ously flawed. In addition, they noted that the evidence of continuing global warming was not altogether unambiguous. For example, satellite-derived measures of tempera-ture in the lower atmosphere during the last decades of the twentieth century failed to reveal any increase, suggesting to some that land-based measures of temperature were flawed by proximity to heat sources (e.g., cities), and NASA issued a correction that made 1934, not 1998, the hottest year on record in the United States.[44]

Subsequent events and measurements have strengthened the arguments of the skeptics. Many of the dire predictions failed to be confirmed, and perhaps most dev-astating to their arguments was the failure of the computer models to predict actual temperature change (e.g., see Figure 15.3).[45] Despite the continued rise in CO_2 in the atmosphere following a very hot 1998, there has been virtually no rise in global tem-perature in the decade and a half since.[46] The after-the-fact explanations of *why* the models did not fit the data, at best, indicate that important measurements or variables were left out, or, at worst, that the theory is incomplete or flawed.[47]

The inability of the experts to agree on the nature and causes of recent changes, or the seriousness of the problem (predictions of temperature change in the present cen-tury vary all the way from zero to eleven degrees), creates a dilemma for policy makers, as even the experts themselves acknowledge: Precipitate action would be extremely costly and might prove unnecessary, thus diverting resources from other serious problems, but inaction could also be extremely costly if the threat is real. As a result, one climatologist concluded that it would be crazy to do nothing, but "we shouldn't do everything either; we don't want to squander resources on something that might turn out to be a nonproblem."[48]

Technology

Technological advance has been the most important factor in shaping the evolution of the world system in the past, and there is little reason to doubt that it will continue to be of major, perhaps paramount, importance in coming decades. Many of the most pressing problems of societies today are stimulating searches for technological solu-tions, and the new technologies that result will almost certainly give rise to social and cultural changes of many kinds.

Rate of Change

Benjamin Franklin once said that nothing is certain in this world but death and taxes. Were he alive today, he might add technological advance. A prediction of continuing advance at an accelerating rate does not depend simply on an extrapolation of the current trend. The basic factors responsible for the trend—the magnitude of the exist-ing store of information, the great size of societal populations, and the amount of

Figure 15.3. Perhaps the Most Serious Challenge to the Arguments of Human-Caused Climate Change Advocates Is the Failure of Their Computer Models to Predict Actual Temperature Changes. As the Figure Shows, All the Models Predicted Increases in Global Temperatures, Many Quite Dramatic, Following a Very Hot 1998, but There Has Been Virtually No Rise in Global Temperature in the Decade and a Half Since.

communication among societies (see pp. 57–62)—are still operative and give every indication of providing even stronger impetus to innovation in the future than they do today. Furthermore, for the first time in history advanced industrial societies are engaging in a systematic, large-scale pursuit of new information. Investments in scientific and technological research and development have grown tremendously, while computers and other devices that increase our ability to acquire, analyze, and process information add their own impetus to the rate of change.

The only things that are likely to slow the rate of technological innovation in the next several decades are a major nuclear war, collapse of the world economy, or an environmental catastrophe.

Content of Change

Up to this point, industrial societies have relied on fossil fuels (coal, petroleum, and natural gas) as the principal sources of the vast quantities of energy on which their way of life has come to depend. Now, however, coal, as we have seen, while still cheap and abundant, poses serious problems of air pollution, acid rain, and all fossil fuels generate greenhouse house gasses which many suspect may contribute to climate change.

The Myth of Primitive Environmentalism

In recent years, many well-intentioned environmentalists and others have popularized the view that technologically less-advanced peoples have been far more respectful of the environment than ourselves. Their goal has been to stimulate feelings of guilt among members of industrial societies and thus promote support for environmental causes.

But the question has to be asked, "Is their thesis supported by the evidence?"

Unfortunately, the answer to this question appears to be "No." It is true, of course, that technologically less-advanced societies have been much less destructive of the environment than highly developed industrial societies. But that is because their technologies have been so much less powerful than those of modern industrial societies, not because they have been more respectful of the environment or more protective of it.

There are today many examples of insensitivity to the environment by preliterate peoples. One of the most striking of these, and one of the most instructive, is the case of the inhabitants of Easter Island in the southeast Pacific.

Easter Island was first settled around 900 A.D. by Polynesians who practiced horticulture and fishing. In the early years, the island was like a Garden of Eden, rich in resources. It was heavily forested with giant palm trees that could be made into ocean-going canoes and provided fronds that were ideal for making sails and ropes, thatching houses, and weaving baskets and mats. For an extended period, as the population increased to about 15,000, the inhabitants enjoyed a rich and varied diet that included seabirds that nested in abundance on the island as well as fish and sea mammals caught offshore.

Within a century or two following settlement of the island, affluence had increased to the point where local chieftains began to compete with one another building the huge and mysterious statues for which the island is famous today (see photo)—a task that required an enormous expenditure of manpower. All this was possible because of the abundance of resources and the relative ease of obtaining them. In the process of erecting these statues, and as population increased, the inhabitants gradually cleared the forest until eventually there were literally no trees left on the island.

This proved to be an ecological disaster, since the trees were the islanders most precious resource. Fishing became unproductive without ocean-going canoes, and, to make matters worse, all the once-abundant seabirds that nested on the island were killed off. As a result, by the time the first Europeans arrived in 1722 A.D., living conditions had deteriorated badly and population had declined sharply.

Europeans who visited the island in the years that followed were baffled to explain how the small number of impoverished inhabitants they found on this almost barren island had been able to create, move great distances, and raise on pedestals hundreds of these giant statutes that weighed from 10 to 270 tons. Only in very recent years, thanks to careful research, have archaeologists been able to reconstruct the remarkable history of the rise and fall of human life on Easter Island.

If the history of Easter Island tells us anything at all, it tells us that the argument for environmentalism does not depend on dubious myths about the wisdom and insights of preliterate peoples. Rather, the history of Easter Island serves as a stark reminder that those who neglect or abuse precious ecological resources are doomed to pay a heavy price. In fact, if we reflect on the matter, we can begin to see in the history of this one little island a possible precursor of what could yet develop on the much larger island we know as Planet Earth if we, too, misuse and abuse its critical resources.

Source: Jared Diamond, "Twilight at Easter," *New York Review*, March 25, 2004, pp. 6–10.

Is the History of Easter Island a Precursor of What May Develop in the Years Ahead on the Much Larger Island We Call Planet Earth? One of the Giant Stone Figures of Ancestors Erected by Easter Islanders, in a More Prosperous Time, Before the Destruction of the Local Environment.

As a result, governments and corporations are increasingly exploring the feasibility of alternative sources of energy. Advances have been made and research is increasing in a number of fields ranging from nuclear energy to wind and solar power. Unfortunately, as we have noted, none of these alternative technologies is without serious limitations or drawbacks, and it remains to be seen if the limitations can be overcome and solutions can be found in time to prevent a serious decline in living standards in advanced industrial societies.

For now, these alternatives are able to serve only as supplements to the fossil fuels. It is predicted that, at their present rates of growth, all the alternatives combined (nuclear, wind, solar, tidal, biomass, hydroelectric, and geothermal), will only provide about a fifth of the world's energy needs by 2040.[49]

Of more immediate concern, successful efforts are under way on many fronts to improve the *end-use efficiency* of the various machines now in use in societies. In 1980, the average end-use efficiency of the machines in the most advanced industrial societies was estimated to be only 10 percent.[50] In other words, 90 percent of the energy consumed by them was wasted (e.g., by the generation of heat by equipment intended to provide light) or consumed in the production and transmission of energy to the ultimate consumer. While anything approaching 100 percent efficiency is impossible,

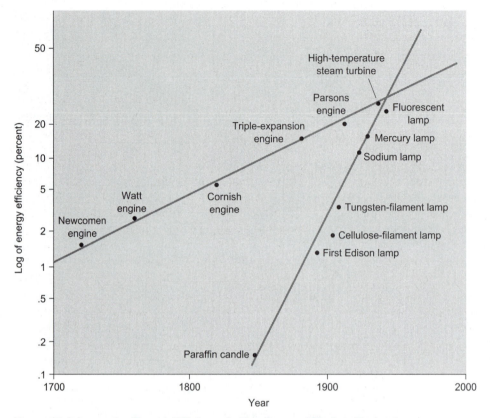

Figure 15.4. Increasing Energy Efficiency in Two Areas of Modern Technology— Steam Engines and Illumination. Note the Logarithmic Scale That Is Used to Plot Energy Efficiency. If an Ordinary Linear Scale Had Been Used, the Trend Lines Would Be Even Steeper.

there is some evidence of improvement in this regard. For example, one measure of energy efficiency, the amount of energy it takes to produce a dollar of GDP in the United States, dropped by 50 percent from 1950 to 2008.[51] But energy use in developing societies is increasing quite rapidly, and these are the least efficient utilizers of energy resources.[52] The history of modern technology provides ample grounds for optimism about the prospect for further increasing the energy efficiency of many existing technologies. Figure 15.4 shows the steady improvement that has been achieved in the efficiency of both steam engines and forms of lighting, and the same could be demonstrated for other technologies as well.

On another front, numerous organizations are trying to develop more economical ways of recycling the refuse of societies. Industrial societies in particular produce enormous quantities of solid waste. Municipal governments in the United States dispose of more than 250 million tons of it a year, nearly three times the amount they handled just fifty years ago.[53] Disposal of these mountains of refuse has become an increasingly expensive problem, and recycling is a potential solution, since it converts some of the waste into useful materials. Unfortunately, there is still no simple technology for converting most of it; and, even where appropriate technology exists, the direct costs of conversion are often greater than the market value of the recycled materials.[54] But, with the seriousness of the waste disposal problem becoming increasingly obvious, investment in research is growing and prospects are good for advances in recycling technology in the decades just ahead.[55]

Safer disposal of toxic substances will be another focus of research. Untold amounts of radioactive water, nerve gas, industrial waste, and other lethal materials are currently buried or stored in perishable containers. Scientists have made a number of breakthroughs with respect to some of these problems. For instance, some time ago, they found bacteria, weeds, and clay that can be used to extract plutonium—an extremely hazardous waste product of nuclear reactors that remains radioactive for thousands of years—from the wastewater in which it is stored, rendering it far more compact and thus much easier to dispose of. Similar techniques are now being developed to clean contaminated water and to render other toxic wastes harmless.[56] As the costs and dangers of toxic contaminants mount, there will undoubtedly be further advances in the development and application of these technologies.

Population control is another area in which there will probably be technological innovations in the next quarter century. Although technologies for limiting population growth already exist, many third world societies have been slow to accept them, as we have seen. Ideological and economic changes will have to occur before this problem is fully overcome, but the development of cheaper, safer, simpler, and more reliable methods of contraception, sterilization, and abortion will speed the process. For example, one new technique currently being tested is the administration of ovulation-controlling hormones by injection. Some women in third world nations appear to be much more receptive to shots administered by medical personnel than to pills or devices they use at home, and vasectomy has proven to be attractive to men in some sub-Saharan African societies.

The current effort to find technological solutions for hunger, which is so widespread in the third world, will certainly continue in the years ahead. Although this problem is primarily the result of rapid population growth in these societies, it is aggravated by certain dietary patterns, such as the eating of meat. Since the meat of a grain-fed animal delivers only about one-eleventh to one-seventeenth of the calories of the grain consumed by the animal eaten, it dramatically increases the amount of grain consumed by human populations.[57] Therefore, primarily as a result of rising demand in advanced industrial societies, less than half the grain produced in the world is now directly consumed by people, more than a third of it is fed to livestock, and the balance is used to produce fuel.[58]

Thus, the fact that meat consumption has been declining in the more advanced industrial societies in recent years, because of health concerns, bodes well for future world grain supplies. The consumption of red meat in the United States fell from a high of 150 pounds per person in 1971 to (an estimated) 101 pounds in 2014.[59] But the future is clouded by the fact that meat consumption has been increasing in a number of societies with rapidly growing economies and rising standards of living (e.g., South Korea, Taiwan, China). Because of its enormous population, improvements in the Chinese economy are having substantial impact on world meat production and consumption.[60]

At present there are a number of new technologies at various stages of development that promise to increase the world's food supply, though not without problems or risks. One of these, fish farming, is already in operation in a number of societies and promises to provide an increased supply of high-quality protein at relatively low cost. World production has more than doubled since the mid 1990s, reaching sixty-seven million tons in 2012; in fact, world production of farmed fish recently surpassed beef production, and about half of the fish consumed in the world today were raised on a farm.[61] Fish farming, or aquaculture as it is also known, is not without its problems. When huge numbers of fish are raised in a small, confined area, disease often takes a heavy toll. In addition, as fish farms grow in number and size, they consume ever-increasing quantities of small fish, such as herring and menhaden, that become feedstock for the larger fish being farmed, thus depleting the supply of these fish that are so important in the food chain that sustains populations of larger fish in the wild.

Another promising innovation is soilless cultivation, which involves a recycled mixture of water and nutrients that is sprayed on the roots of plants suspended in frames. Developed in Israel, this technique should greatly increase food production in arid and semiarid areas. In addition, the new technology of recombinant DNA, a discussion of which follows, is providing new and modified strains of plants and animals. Once again, however, this new technology is not without problems and potential risks.

Electronics is another area in which significant advances can be expected in the years ahead. Despite the enormous progress already achieved in miniaturizing transistors, one expert estimated that the process had gone only "a little past half way" toward the point where shrinking would have to end because of the laws of physics. Others, however, suggest that when that point is reached, scientists and engineers will find ways to circumvent those limits with new materials and methods.[62]

The most exciting new area in electronics in recent years—one whose impact is expected to rival that of transistors—is the development of micro-electro-mechanical systems, popularly known as MEMS. MEMS sensors, built on silicon chips, translate physical actions into computational data. Tiny motors, called actuators, then translate computational commands back into physical responses. Air bags used in automobiles to protect riders in the event of a crash provide a familiar example of the application of these devices. The sensor, which consists of a whisker of silicon, can detect a car's sudden deceleration when it hits an object and instantly instructs the air bag to inflate. This device costs less than half the price of the mechanical sensors it replaced, and it has proved much more reliable.[63] MEMS have a wide variety of possible uses, and engineers are already at work on MEMS that do everything from protecting buildings and bridges against earthquakes to ones that conduct medical tests and enhance medical procedures of various kinds.

Yet another fundamental innovation with revolutionary potential for human societies in this century is the advancing technology of recombinant DNA. In recent years geneticists have learned how to remove a bit of genetic material from the cell of one kind of organism and implant it in the cell of another species. This technology is particularly fascinating from the perspective of ecological-evolutionary theory, for it marks a new stage in our species' capacity for handling information. Until recently, the only information we could manipulate and recombine was cultural information. Now we can use the genetic alphabet in the same way (but only to a very limited extent so far) to create combinations of genetic information which do not exist in nature and which can serve as tools for accomplishing human purposes.

So far, most applications of recombinant DNA technology involve the transplantation of genes that govern the production of rare proteins from the cells of slower-breeding animals, including humans, into the cells of plants and bacteria. Bacteria grow and divide so rapidly that a single one can produce one hundred trillion identical cells in twenty-four hours, each one containing at least one hundred molecules of the desired protein.[64] In this way, large quantities of rare and valuable chemicals (e.g., insulin) can be produced at minimal cost.

By engineering the genes in plants and bacteria, scientists have created tobacco plants that produce antibodies, potatoes that produce serum albumin, yeast that produces insulin and malaria drugs, and rape plants that produce enkephalin, a pain-killer normally produced in the human brain.[65] These are just the beginning of what promises to become a flood of important innovations employing recombinant DNA.

Many other kinds of technological innovations can also be expected during the next few decades. Substantial resources are being invested in medical research of various kinds, including research on organ transplants and genetic diseases. Striking advances have recently been made in communications, data processing, and office automation, and further advances in these areas should be only a matter of time. In addition, it is very possible that some unanticipated breakthrough or breakthroughs, comparable to the silicon chip or recombinant DNA, will lay the foundation, as all fundamental innovations do, for a host of new applications.

Ideology
The most striking changes in ideology in the last several decades have been the virtual collapse of Marxism and the rise of a militant fundamentalist version of Islam. Both developments have had far-reaching consequences.

Marxist governments still remain in control in North Korea, China, Vietnam, and Cuba; but in China, especially, Communist Party leaders have abandoned nearly all the basic principles for which the party once stood and now seem to cling to power simply for its own sake and for the benefits it provides them personally. Apart from North Korea, Vietnam, and Cuba, Marxism's ideological appeal today seems limited to a few small groups of revolutionaries in remote areas, as in Columbia, Nepal, and parts of Peru.

In contrast, militant Islam has been gaining strength throughout the Muslim world and even in some industrial societies to which Muslims have migrated. Though it has been present in many societies for centuries, its recent emergence as a force on the world stage began only in the late 1970s with the overthrow of the Shah's regime in Iran by the Ayatollah Khomeini and his followers. More recently, the movement has spread widely, partly under the former leadership of Osama bin Laden and partly under the influence of Muslim teachers and clergy in schools and mosques funded by the Saudi Arabian government. This militant version of Islam teaches hatred of all

Islamic Jihadists Exploded Ten Bombs on Four Crowded Commuter Trains in Madrid, Spain, on the Morning of March 11, 2004, Killing 191 People and Injuring 1,400.

nonbelievers and even of Muslims who do not follow its harsh and puritanical teachings.[††]

In this respect, militant Islamists deviate from traditional Islamic teaching, which has stressed the need for respect for Christians and Jews. In Sura 29, the Koran instructs Muslims to "dispute not with the People of the Book [i.e., the Bible, hence Christians and Jews] save in the most courteous manner . . . and say, 'We believe in what has been sent down to us and what has been sent down to you; our God and your God is one, and to Him have we surrendered.'"[67]

To the degree that the militant or fundamentalist version of Islam becomes dominant in societies in North Africa, the Middle East, and southern Asia, it becomes a powerful force retarding economic development and cultural modernization. Fundamentalist Muslims believe that the sole or primary purpose of education is to teach the Koran and the principles of Islam as interpreted by their leaders; they have little interest in children learning secular subjects such as science, history, or literature. Religious leaders and political leaders tend to be one and the same, as has been the case in Iran since the Ayatollah Khomeini came to power back in the late 1970s. Women's role

---

[††]In a widely publicized case in 2006, Muslim religious leaders and judges in Afghanistan condemned to death a man who became a Christian convert. Only pressure from the U.S. government saved his life, though he was forced into exile in Italy. According to one expert on Islamic law, executions of Muslims who reject Islam have occurred in a number of cases in recent years in Iran and Saudi Arabia.[66]

in society is severely limited; basically, women are to be wives and mothers, and their primary responsibilities are to serve the men in their families and to bear children. Education for girls is believed to be unimportant, or even harmful, and birth control in any form is considered sinful. The ultimate goal of fundamentalist Muslims is to re-create an Islamic society of the kind that they imagine existed fourteen hundred years ago in the early days of the faith and to spread their version of Islam to the non-Muslim world.

Fundamentalist Muslims have little tolerance for nonbelievers, whom they label "infidels," or for fellow Muslims who do not share their stern and backward-looking faith. Thus, conflicts become all but inevitable, even with Muslim leaders and governments judged to be insufficiently orthodox. Conflicts with non-Muslim peoples and governments have become increasingly common in this era of globalization when Western businesses and governments have become active in Muslim societies and when Muslims themselves migrate, as millions have done, to non-Muslim societies, especially in Europe. This is a subject to which we will return shortly in our discussion of terrorism (see p. 405).

Outside the Muslim world, and even within parts of that world, pragmatism seems to have become the dominant ideology. As the late Chinese leader, Deng Xiaoping, famously declared in abandoning Marxism, it does not matter whether a cat is black or white as long as it catches mice. In other words, Marxist principles should be subordinated to the practical test of whether they work, and if capitalist principles work better, China should adopt them—as it has.

In advanced industrial societies, as we have seen, capitalist principles themselves have been modified by the emergence of the welfare state and governmental regulations that limit the harsher effects of laissez-faire capitalist competition. Here, too, pragmatism seems to have become the order of the day.

At the individual level in most advanced industrial societies, and in many industrializing societies as well, as affluence has increased, hedonism, or the pursuit of pleasure for its own sake, has become ever more popular. It has become especially popular among young people, even in some Islamic societies, such as Iran, where it competes successfully with the sterner, more puritanical vision of fundamentalism, particularly among more affluent young people.

Polity

During the twentieth century, the most striking political trend was the spread of democracy. This involved both the increasing democratization of societies in western Europe and North America, where the process was already under way, and the beginnings of democracy in many societies in other parts of the world.

The year 1989 saw the beginning of a remarkable series of political changes in eastern Europe, when the Communist Party was forced to renounce its monopoly of power and compete with other parties in relatively free elections. Though the process has been flawed in many respects in a number of these societies, a return to the totalitarian, one-party system of the past seems unlikely.

In the less developed countries (LDCs) of the world, the prospects for increasing democracy are mixed. They appear to be good in those societies that are industrializing most rapidly and whose better-educated populations insist on a greater voice in

The General Assembly of the United Nations: Every Nation, Regardless of Size, Has an Equal Vote.

the formulation of governmental policies that affect their daily lives. In many LDCs, however, especially in those with a horticultural background and those with large Muslim populations, the prospects for democracy are not nearly as promising. Faced with the staggering problems created by runaway population growth, and with a social and cultural heritage that equips them poorly for competition in the modern world economy, most of these societies will find democracy difficult if not impossible to achieve in the near future.

Looking further ahead, the prospects for Muslim societies appear somewhat more promising. If the experience of Iran is any guide, enthusiasm for fundamentalist Islam appears to wane after a few decades. Many young people, when exposed to alternative ways of life via satellite TV, social media, or foreign travel, begin to resist the efforts of their elders to impose rigid Islamic codes. This is not true of all of them by any means, however, as the cases of Osama bin Laden and other jihadists demonstrated. For them, the goal is the creation of a strict Muslim theocratic state. At this point it is difficult to predict which set of influences will ultimately prevail, though one suspects that the struggle to create a strict Islamic state will prove much more satisfying than the reality of such a government once it has been established.

Finally, we must not overlook the possibility of increasing use of terrorism as a political weapon in the years ahead. Osama bin Laden and his fellow jihadists have demonstrated that, thanks to modern technology, terrorists today are able to command the attention of even the most powerful governments and to influence their actions. Although we have come in recent years to associate the use of terror with fundamentalist Islam, terrorism is a weapon that is available to any political movement that is able to stir the passions of its followers, especially ethnic and religious movements that are able to persuade their followers that they have been victimized by others. Thus, we are not likely to see the end of terrorist activities any time soon.

Economy

Barring a major collapse of the world economy, there will probably be continuing economic growth for the world system as a whole during the next quarter century. The wider application of techniques that are already known should so improve energy efficiency that increased productivity will be ensured, even as energy costs increase. In addition, there will almost certainly be advances in energy technology that boost world production higher still.

Whether living standards also rise will depend on the number of people who must share the fruits of the increased productivity. Population growth could well offset the effects of the rise in the gross world product (GWP) and thus prevent significant improvement in living standards for the world as a whole. And even if per capita GWP rises, it does not necessarily follow that per capita GDP will rise in every society. Improvements are unlikely in many African societies, where, because of runaway population growth, economic disaster and starvation pose serious threats. Although the situation may be alleviated temporarily by international aid programs, the basic problems in these societies will persist until their leaders face up to the problems confronting them. Unfortunately, there are few signs of this so far.

In contrast, a number of industrializing agrarian societies will probably join the ranks of industrial societies in the next quarter century. Based on current levels of development and current rates of economic growth, Argentina and several of the eastern European societies, especially Hungary and the Czech Republic, seem likely candidates in the near future.

China is an especially interesting and important case, since after decades of economic stagnation under Communism, and despite continuing Communist Party control, for several decades the country has had the fastest-growing economy in the world and is already the second largest with a GDP of $8.2 trillion (see Table 9.2).[68] The key to this remarkable turnaround has been the virtual abandonment of Marxist ideology by the new leadership of the party. One knowledgeable American journalist wrote a few years ago that he didn't know of a single Chinese Communist Party member who still believed in Marxism, and that one high-ranking Party official told him that his favorite economist was Milton Friedman, a leading American advocate of laissez-faire capitalism.[69]

With its population of more than 1.3 billion, China has a huge domestic market that enables Chinese businesses to spread their fixed costs widely (see p. 262), an important competitive advantage in world markets. In addition, Chinese labor costs are very low and the skill level is rising rapidly. For example, Chinese universities are currently producing several times as many engineers as the United States and Great Britain.[70] As Bill Gates said recently, "When I compare our high schools to what I see when I travel abroad, I am terrified for our work force of tomorrow. . . . In the international competition to have the biggest and best supply of knowledgeable workers, America is falling behind."[71] As a result, a growing number of people believe that

China Now Has the Fastest-Growing Economy in the World: Nanpu Bridge and Massive Highway Cloverleaf in Shanghai.

China is on its way to supplanting the United States as the dominant economy in the world system and that this will become "the Chinese century."[72]

The Chinese abandonment of Marxism, it should be noted, is part of a larger trend in recent years, namely the decline of support for socialist solutions to economic problems and the spread of capitalism. This has occurred not only in previously Communist societies, such as China and Russia, but also in India and western Europe, where a process of privatization of previously state-owned enterprises has occurred. Although this trend may have largely run its course by now, a return to widespread governmental ownership of economic enterprises seems unlikely unless a major economic disaster comparable to the Great Depression of the 1930s occurs.

Many of the economic problems of American society have been worsened by unwise political leadership. In recent years, American political elites have allowed the national debt to pile up to record levels in order to fight costly wars abroad while neglecting vital needs at home, especially the needs of the educational system on which so much in the future depends. As Bill Gates noted, and as numerous studies have shown, the graduates of American schools do not compare favorably with graduates of most other industrial societies, especially in the important areas of mathematics and science, and they perform even less well than graduates of some less developed societies (see Table 15.1).

The problems facing the United States and other current industrial societies are aggravated by the increasing power of multinational corporations whose executives are far more concerned with their own personal interests than with the well-being of

Table 15.1 Average Mathematical Literacy Scores, by Society, for Fifteen-Year-Old Students, 2012

Society	Score	Society	Score
Shanghai-China	613	Russian Federation	482
Singapore	573	Slovak Republic	482
Hong Kong-China	561	United States	481
Chinese Taipei	560	Lithuania	479
South Korea	554	Sweden	478
Macao-China	538	Hungary	477
Japan	536	Croatia	471
Switzerland	531	Israel	466
Netherlands	523	Greece	453
Finland	519	Serbia	449
Canada	518	Turkey	448
Belgium	515	Romania	445
Germany	514	Cyprus	440
Vietnam	511	Bulgaria	439
Austria	506	Un. Arab Emirates	434
Australia	504	Thailand	427
Ireland	501	Chile	423
Slovenia	501	Malaysia	421
Denmark	500	Mexico	413
New Zealand	500	Uruguay	409
Czech Republic	499	Costa Rica	407
France	495	Albania	394
Great Britain	494	Brazil	391
Iceland	493	Argentina	388
Latvia	491	Tunisia	388
Luxembourg	490	Jordan	386
Norway	489	Colombia	376
Portugal	487	Qatar	376
Italy	485	Indonesia	375
Spain	484	Peru	368

Source: Program for International Student Assessment (PISA) and Organization for Economic Cooperation and Development, Table M-4, National Center for Education website, http://nces.ed.gov/surveys/pisa/pisa2012/pisa2012highlights_3a.asp.

their employees or their own society. Thus, if it is more profitable to outsource production to China and other low-wage countries, they seldom hesitate.

Another economic trend that is almost certain to continue is the increasing division of labor in the world system. Since 1750, the volume of international trade has increased well over 2,000-fold, which is, in part, a reflection of the growth of societal economic specialization during that time. This trend is a consequence of technological advances that have drastically reduced the cost of moving goods. Societies now export things that they can produce more cheaply than other societies and import what they find more costly to produce. As we have seen, however, the practice of outsourcing (see pp. 257–259) has created serious hardships for many workers in industrial societies whose jobs have been moved abroad.

The world economy, which is essentially a capitalist economy, has not been without its disadvantages, especially for societies that specialize in products whose value on the world market is low or fluctuates sharply. Yet even these societies have found this system more rewarding than trying to produce for themselves everything they need. For a few societies, the oil producers in particular, the system has worked enormously to their advantage, greatly enhancing their position in the world system of societies. In the long run, however, they will not be able to rely exclusively on this once highly profitable product, and their future in the world economy will come to depend on the extent to which they use their oil profits to build more diversified modern economies.

In the years ahead, economic ties among societies are likely to grow even stronger than they are today. As this happens, societies will gradually lose more and more of their economic independence. At some point many societies, perhaps most, will find that these economic ties have become so vital that they cannot afford to remain vulnerable to disruption by international disputes or war. When that point is reached, it may provide an enormous impetus to develop greater international cooperation, and, perhaps, some form of world government (see the next section The World System).

Finally, there is one glaring defect in the economies of virtually every contemporary society that will almost surely become more apparent during coming decades. This is the failure to attach realistic "price tags" to things. The costs of *disposing of* waste materials, for example, are not currently included in the price of most commodities. The seriousness of this problem first became evident as aging nuclear power plants had to be shut down. In pricing the electrical power produced by these plants, no one had factored in the extremely high hidden costs of disposing of dangerous radioactive materials and of finally sealing off the power plants themselves. More recently, we have also become aware of the failure of producers to factor in the cost of disposing of countless other kinds of materials that are being produced in ever-increasing quantities, especially plastics and other products that are not biodegradable. Fortunately, some parts of the enormous quantities of waste materials generated by modern industrial technology (e.g., paper and various metals) lend themselves to recycling. Overall, however, no society has yet fully adjusted to the real costs of the waste products of modern technology, and when societies do adjust, they may well experience some decline in living standards.

The World System
As the world system of societies becomes increasingly integrated economically and in other ways, societies will become more dependent on one another. The growing interdependence of societies in the European Union is one of the most important developments in this respect but almost certainly not the last. As the volume and importance

of international trade increases, societies in other parts of the world may well initiate similar programs.

With increasing economic integration, individual societies will be ever more vulnerable to anything that threatens the functioning of the system as a whole. Above all, they will be vulnerable to war, regardless of where it occurs or which nations are involved.

There is no need to recount here estimates of the number of deaths and the magnitude of destruction that a nuclear war would produce. Suffice it to say that virtually all who have studied the matter carefully, including people of very different ideological persuasions, agree that such a war would be a catastrophe. Not only would the combatants be damaged beyond imagination, but neutral societies and noncombatants would also suffer enormously from radioactive fallout and from the disruption of the world economy that would inevitably follow.

As noted earlier (see pp. 236–237) cyber warfare is becoming an increasing threat, especially for highly industrialized societies. As more and more aspects of daily life (from medical records to electrical power grids) become dependent on computer networks, disruption of those networks for any extended period would be disastrous and could easily lead to widespread death and destruction.

In the decades ahead, the threat of nuclear war will no longer lie exclusively with the NATO powers and Russia, as it did in the recent past. The technology of nuclear weapons is now more widespread, and several industrializing societies already have small nuclear arsenals. The greatest danger, therefore, is likely to come from the use of these weapon systems by irrational or fanatical leaders or from a process in which some limited conflict escalates out of control (e.g., between India and Pakistan). Another threat is the possibility that nuclear weapons may fall into the hands of a terrorist organization, such as al Qaeda.

The potential for such conflicts in the next several decades is not inconsiderable. Even if relations among the major powers continue to improve, resource shortages and population pressures could lead to deteriorating relations among many other societies. For example, in an era of growing water shortages, it is worth noting that 200 of the world's major river basins are shared by at least two different societies.

Another cause for concern at present is the possibility of spreading ethnic conflicts within present or former multiethnic states, such as the former Soviet Union and Yugoslavia. Struggles among their constituent groups (e.g., between Azerbaijanis and Armenians, or Georgians, Ukrainians and Russians, or tribal groups in various African nations) could easily involve other societies in an escalating process similar to that in which the struggles within the multiethnic Austro-Hungarian Empire in the early twentieth century contributed to the outbreak of World War I.

Faced with such threats, one solution would seem to be the formation of a world government that would not interfere with the internal affairs of societies but which would have the authority, the mechanisms, and the power necessary to monitor the production of weapons and control their use. One of the most difficult problems in such an endeavor stems from the great discrepancies in economic development and in standards of living between industrial and industrializing societies. The twenty-seven most advanced industrial societies, for example, currently have a median per capita GDP of $39,752, more than *thirty times* that of the 31 poorest countries in the world, $1,210.[73]

In this 1945 File Photo, an Allied War Correspondent Stands in the Ruins of Hiroshima, Japan, Just Weeks After the City Was Leveled by an Atomic Bomb. The Bomb Killed Some 140,000 People—Some Instantly, Others Within Months. Three Days Later, the United States Dropped a Second Bomb on Nagasaki, Killing an Estimated 70,000 People Shortly Before the End of World War II. Advances in Weapons Technology Since Have Led to Bombs That Have Thousands of Times the Explosive Force.

Inclusion of industrializing societies in a world polity would almost certainly lead to demands for a substantial redistribution of world wealth and income. In exchange for permission to monitor their military installations, industrializing societies would probably insist upon major economic concessions. But this could easily kill enthusiasm for world government by members of industrial societies. For if world income were distributed equally among the world's societies, per capita income and standards of living would decline dramatically in industrial societies.

Although this is hardly an attractive prospect, some less extreme version of income redistribution (e.g., very gradual) may eventually occur. Even if it still seemed harsh to advanced societies, they might consider it preferable to the continuing threat of war and disruption of the world economy. If there were to be a viable compromise, however, governments should begin to narrow the economic gap between societies. Strong incentives should be provided to industrializing societies to drastically reduce population growth so that their standards of living can be improved, and industrial societies should be prepared to sacrifice some of their own potential growth to provide these incentives and to reduce the gap between haves and have-nots.

Somewhat more likely in the next few decades is a gradual strengthening of the United Nations, the closest thing to a world polity that now exists. The greatest obstacle to the effectiveness of that organization is probably the system of representation in the General Assembly, which provides an equal vote for the People's Republic of China, with its population of more than 1.3 *billion,* and for Tuvalu with its population of 12 *thousand.* The special powers vested in the Security Council—the veto power in particular—partly compensate for this, but the present organizational structure of the United Nations as a whole does not generate much confidence on the part of the larger and more powerful nations whose support is crucial.

As events of recent years have demonstrated, wars between nations are not the only source of disruption: There are also the actions of terrorists. Islamic *jihadists,* especially, have demonstrated an ability to disrupt daily life for those they consider infidels, including other Muslims who do not share their understanding of Islam. The rise of Islamic fundamentalism has been fueled by the aggressive actions of Israel and the United States in the Middle East and by the inability of Muslim societies to meet the needs of large numbers of their citizens. Since no solution to either problem seems likely any time soon, terrorism may well continue as a disruptive force for years to come.

Thus far, the actions of jihadists have been limited in scope; the 9/11 felling of the twin towers of the World Trade Center in New York (see photo on p. 293) has been their most destructive act. There is no assurance, however, that far worse may not be in store. For example, if jihadists were able to explode a nuclear device in some major city, such as London or New York, the death toll would be far greater and the disruptive ramifications on the larger society, and even on the global economy, are hard to imagine, given the complex interlinkages within and among modern industrial societies.

The Higher Goals

Early in this chapter we reached the conclusion that sociocultural evolution has, more often than not, been accompanied by declining levels of freedom, justice, and happiness for the majority of people, but that technological advances in the past 200 years have reversed this trend, at least for the vast majority of members of industrial societies. It would be gratifying to be able to predict that the increasing industrialization of the world system during the next century will have a similar impact on the world as a whole. As our examination of population trends, the environment, and other matters has made clear, however, the prospects for greater attainment of humanity's higher goals in the decades immediately ahead are uncertain.

In many industrializing societies, we may well see a decline in individual freedom accompanied by an increase in the number of authoritarian regimes. This could have the effect of alleviating some human misery, however, since such regimes would be better able to control birthrates and thus perhaps lower the number of severely malnourished individuals in these societies. But even if this happens, there is not likely to be any great gain in either happiness or justice, since many will still be doomed to lives of abject poverty in crowded slums and shantytowns. What is more, population growth and shortages of vital resources will probably retard the pace of industrialization in many societies during the next few decades, greatly delaying the day when advances in productivity begin to provide appreciable benefits for the majority of their members.

Whatever difficulties human societies experience during the next few decades, however, they may suffer even more later in the present century. Levels of freedom, justice, and happiness are almost certain to decline seriously for the world system as a whole during that period—unless humanity begins *soon* to address its most basic problems. Our potential for shaping a better world is still, at this point, good—nearly as good, in fact, as it has ever been. But this situation will not last: *the range of attractive options will decline with every year we fail to act*. Thus, the larger the human population becomes before growth is halted, the more likely it is that future political regimes will be harshly authoritarian and individual freedoms severely limited. The more the biophysical environment is damaged before that trend is reversed, the less likely it is that the human population *as a whole* will ever enjoy the enormous potential benefits of an industrial economy. And the longer sociocultural evolution continues to be shaped primarily by the blind forces of conflict and intersocietal selection, the more likely it is that our future will be shaped by convulsive changes that are forced upon us by developments beyond our control.

The latter, in fact, is precisely the outcome predicted for human societies by some who have considered the problem. For example, the late Robert Heilbroner, an economic historian long noted for his insightful analyses, wrote a book entitled *An Inquiry into the Human Prospect* in which he forecast developments such as nuclear wars among societies that are experiencing severe population and environmental crises.[74] He predicted, in effect, a future in which the forces of nature—including the irrational forces that are part of our genetic heritage—determine the effects of problems that *humanity failed to resolve*.

Heilbroner was not unaware of our species' remarkable adaptive capabilities. In fact, he believed that, in principle, we are capable of solving our problems through social and cultural mechanisms. What he doubted is our ability to do it *in time to avoid catastrophe*. He felt that it will require too long to alter certain dangerous behavior patterns—patterns that reflect our genetically based tendencies toward individualism, self-centeredness, and expansiveness of needs, and which are reflected in our lack of cooperation, our lack of concern for future generations and for members of other societies, and our disinclination to deny ourselves. Heilbroner pointed out the futility of pinning our hopes on what we believe possible for humanity eventually to *become*. Rather, he said, we must consider what people are likely *to be* during the period in question, and he noted that the socialization process tends to produce individuals who are a generation or more behind the times, people who, tomorrow, will finally be prepared to respond to yesterday's problems.[75]

More recently, Bill Joy, one of the major innovators in the computer field and one of the founders of Sun Microsystems, echoed Heilbroner's warnings. In an article in *Wired* magazine, he declared that the rapid pace of technological innovation today could prove catastrophic.[76] Joy is especially concerned with the potential dangers of genetic engineering, robotics, and nanotechnology. He points out that a lethal virus created in a laboratory or a genetic experiment that goes awry could prove unstoppable and irreversible because of its self-replicating nature. Joy notes that the genomic sequence for the plague is already on the web for anyone to see and use. He believes it is time that we begin to question our traditional assumption that good science and good technology are the same as beneficial science and beneficial technology. Joy quotes with approval Bertrand Russell's assertion that if there is one element in human nature that is stronger than self-preservation, "it is the desire to get the better of the other fellow."

Even if one does not agree with Heilbroner and Joy, it is impossible to deny that certain aspects of our genetic heritage seriously handicap us in our efforts to solve our most urgent problems or that the socialization process and other social and cultural mechanisms are often inadequate in helping societies adapt to the conditions created by rapidly changing technology. But while there is nothing we can (or should) do to alter our genetic mechanisms, at least in the near future, *we can alter our social and cultural mechanisms.*

Of all the species on this planet, ours is the only one not doomed to have its evolutionary course shaped entirely by forces beyond its control. Thanks to symbol systems and culture, we can not only comprehend the evolutionary process, but we also may be able to chart for ourselves an evolutionary course within the limits set by our genetic heritage on the one hand and the constraints of the biophysical environment on the other—a course that can provide for most people a reasonable degree of freedom, justice, and happiness.[77]

But we also have the option to ignore this possibility until it is too late.

A.D. A system of dating (chronology) that locates events in terms of years since the estimated birth of Christ. The initials are from the Latin, *anno Domini,* "year of the Lord." (See B.C. and B.P.)

Adaptation The process of adjusting to, or changing, environmental conditions; hence, broadly, problem solving.

Adaptive Something that helps a system or organism survive in its environment.

Agrarian era The period in world or regional history when agrarian societies were the technologically most advanced (about 3000 B.C. to A.D. 1800).

Agrarian society A society that depends primarily on plow agriculture for subsistence. Advanced agrarian societies have iron tools and weapons; simple agrarian societies do not.

Agriculture The cultivation of fields using the plow.

Anthropoids An order of primates that includes monkeys, apes, and humans.

Archaeology The study of societies and cultures of the past, based on analysis of their physical remains.

Arithmetic mean An "average" or measure of central tendency that is computed by dividing the sum of a set of items by the number of items in the set.

Artisan A craftsperson. The term is usually applied to a worker who, unlike a modern factory worker, uses hand tools and produces a complete product.

Autocracy Rule by one person (compare with *Democracy, Oligarchy, Plutocracy,* and *Theocracy*).

Autonomous Self-directing; free from outside political control.

Band A nomadic community at the hunting and gathering level; most bands are also societies.

B.C. A system of dating (chronology) that locates events in terms of years "before (the birth of) Christ." (See A.D. and B.P.)

Biological drive A genetically programmed predisposition to respond in a general way to a stimulus (compare with *Instinct*).

Biological evolution The process of genetic change by which existing species of plants and animals have developed out of preexisting species.

Biophysical environment The biological and physical aspects of the environment.

Body language Communication system involving physical movements and gestures.

B.P. A system of dating (chronology) that locates events in terms of years "before the present." (Compare with A.D. and B.C.)

Bureaucracy (1) The administrative component of a government or formal organization; (2) an administrative system that is characterized by a highly formalized division of labor, a hierarchical system of authority, and action guided by a complex and formalized system of rules.

Capital goods Things that are necessary for the production of other things (e.g., plows, land, and draft animals for grain cultivation, or investment assets for making money in a capitalist society).

Capital-intensive industry An industry which depends on expensive machinery to produce its products (compare with *Labor-intensive industry*).

Capitalism An economic system in which the means of production are privately owned and the basic problems of production and distribution are settled within a market system, with minimal governmental regulation or control (see *Market economy,* and contrast with *Socialism*).

Carnivore A meat-eating animal.

Civilization An advanced sociocultural system. The term is usually reserved for the cultures of societies with urban communities and writing.

Clan A kin group whose members claim descent from a common ancestor.

Class (1) An aggregation or group of people whose overall status is similar; (2) an aggregation or group of people who share some important resource that affects their access to power, privilege, or prestige.

Command economy An economy in which the basic questions of production and distribution are decided by political elites (contrast with *Market economy*).

Communication The exchange of information by means of signals or symbols.

Communism A state of society envisioned by Marx and others in which the distribution of goods and services would be based on individual need; a society in which there is no inequality.

Community An informally organized group whose members are united by a common place of residence or by a common subculture.

Comparative A method of study that develops knowledge through systematic comparisons (see *Science*).

Constant Something that is the same everywhere or cannot change (compare with *Variable*).

Continuity The persistence of cultural elements in a society.

Cooperation Interaction by two or more individuals for their mutual benefit.

Culture Symbol systems and the information they convey.

Customs Informal norms that define acceptable behavior in a society or in a subgroup within a society.

Cyber Warfare The use of computers by societies to attack and cripple or destroy other societies' computer-based social systems, especially their economic and military systems.

Democracy A political system in which sovereignty is vested in the people (contrast with *Autocracy, Oligarchy,* and *Theocracy*).

Demography The study of populations, especially their size, composition, and change.

Determinism The belief that a specific set of identifiable factors is sufficient to explain completely a given phenomenon.

Development, societal A process of change in which technological advance causes greater organizational complexity within a society or set of societies (compare with *Growth*).

Diffusion Transmission of cultural elements from one society to another, or from one group to another within a society.

Discovery New cultural information acquired by means other than diffusion (compare with *Invention*).

Distributive justice Ideas about what is a fair or just distribution of valued items in a society.

DNA Deoxyribonucleic acid; the chemical molecule that embodies genetic information.

Drive See *Biological drive*.

Ecological-evolutionary theory Theory concerning (1) the relationships within and among human societies, (2) the relationships between societies and their biophysical environments, and (3) the processes of sociocultural change and development.

Ecology The science of the relationships of living things to one another and to their environments.

Economic surplus Production that exceeds what is needed to keep the producers of essential goods and services alive and productive.

Economy The economic system of a group, especially a society; in effect, an institutionalized set of answers to basic questions concerning the production and distribution of goods and services.

Egalitarian Characterized by relative equality among members of a group.

Elites The most powerful and privileged members of a society or institutional system.

Empirical Derived from the senses, observable.

Energy The capacity for performing work.

Environment Everything external to an entity (organism, population, society, etc.) that affects it, or is affected by it, in any way.

Era A period of time during which a particular type of society is the most advanced in existence (e.g., the agrarian era).

Ethnography The description of sociocultural systems based on direct observation.

Evolution Long-term directional patterns of change that result from the interplay of three forces: (1) forces of continuity, (2) forces of innovation and change, and (3) forces of selection (see *Biological evolution* and *Sociocultural evolution*).

Extended family A group of related individuals that is more inclusive than the nuclear family and less inclusive than the clan.

Falsifiable A proposition, theory, or hypothesis that can be shown to be false, and which therefore can be tested.

Family A group organized around ties of kinship (see also *Nuclear family* and *Extended family*).

Feedback A special type of causal relationship in which part of the effect produced by an initial cause or event reverts back to its source, modifying or reinforcing it (i.e., the influence that B exerts on A as a result of A's earlier influence on B).

Feudalism A system in which elites pledge loyalty and military service to a sovereign in return for power over local political and economic affairs.

Fishing society A society dependent primarily on fishing, or fishing and gathering, for subsistence.

Fixed costs Costs of production that remain more or less constant regardless of the number of units produced (contrast with *Variable costs*).

Frontier society An agrarian society that is expanding into territories which are uninhabited, or inhabited by much less advanced societies.

Function (1) A characteristic activity of a person, thing, or institution; or (2) a consequence of, or purpose served by, that activity.

Fundamental innovation An invention or discovery that either (1) opens the way for many other innovations or (2) alters the conditions of human life so that many other changes become either possible or necessary.

Gathering Foraging for wild fruits and vegetables.

Gene The basic unit of heredity; a conveyer of genetic information.

Genetic constants Genetic attributes that are the same in every population of a species.

Genetic variables Genetic attributes that vary among the populations within a species.

Governing class A class, often hereditary, from which the political leaders of a society are recruited.

Gross domestic product (GDP) The monetary value of the goods and services produced within a society during a specified period (usually a year).

Gross national product (GNP) Gross domestic product plus net income from other nations.

Gross world product (GWP) The total value of goods and services produced in all societies.

Group Generally an aggregation whose members (1) cooperate to satisfy common, or complementary, needs; (2) have shared norms; and (3) have a sense of common identity. The term is applicable to a society and also to intersocietal and intrasocietal aggregations.

Growth An increase in size. For societies, the term may refer either to population size or to territorial size (compare with *Development, societal*).

Guild A mutual aid association of merchants and artisans in the same trade (found in agrarian and maritime societies).

Headman The leader of a local community in a preliterate society.

Herbivore A plant eater.

Herding society A society dependent primarily on herding for subsistence.

Hominid A member of the genus *Homo*, which includes our own species as well as an undetermined number of humanlike species that preceded us but are now extinct.

Homo sapiens Our species. Some would include Neanderthals (*Homo sapiens neaderthalensis*) with *Homo sapiens sapiens*.

Homo sapiens sapiens Our subspecies; biologically modern humans.

Horticultural era The period in history when there were no societies technologically more advanced than horticultural societies (about 8000 to 3000 B.C.).

Horticultural society A society that depends primarily on gardening for subsistence. Advanced horticultural societies are differentiated from simple by the manufacture of metal tools and weapons.

Horticulture The cultivation of small gardens using a hoe or digging stick as the chief tool. Horticulture is differentiated from agriculture by the absence of the plow.

Hunting and gathering era The period in history when there were no societies more advanced than hunting and gathering (to about 8000 B.C.).

Hunting and gathering society A society that depends primarily on hunting and gathering for subsistence.

Hybrid society A society that relies about equally on two or more of the basic modes of subsistence.

Hypothesis A tentative explanation, often derived from a theory, that is tested with evidence.

Ideology Cultural information used to interpret human experience and order societal life. An ideology consists of a system of beliefs and related norms and values.

Industrial era The period in history when industrial societies have been dominant (from about A.D. 1800 to the present).

Industrialization A process of increasing reliance on inanimate sources of energy and the machines powered by them (compare with *Modernization*).

Industrial Revolution The revolution in technology that began in England in the eighteenth century and has since spread through most of the world system.

Industrial society A society that derives most of its wealth and income from productive activities dependent on machines powered by inanimate energy sources (e.g., coal, petroleum, natural gas, hydroelectric power, nuclear power).

Information A record of experience that is stored in the memory system of a plant, animal, or machine.

Innovation The process of introducing new cultural elements into a society (e.g., inventions, discoveries); the new cultural element itself (see *Variations*).

Instinct A genetically programmed predisposition to react with a specific sequence of behaviors to a stimulus (compare with *Biological drive*).

Institution A system of social relationships and cultural elements that develops in a society in response to some set of basic and persistent needs (e.g., raising children).

Institutional system A system of interrelated institutions.

Intersocietal selection The process of selection whereby some societies survive while others become extinct.

Invention An innovation that results from a useful new combination of information already possessed by a society (compare with *Discovery*).

Labor-intensive industry An industry which depends on large numbers of workers to produce its products (compare with *Capital-intensive industry*).

Language A system of symbols.

Laws Written norms enforced by a government.

Learning The process by which an organism acquires, through experience, information with the potential for changing its behavior.

Legitimate That which is morally or legally justified by the norms or laws of a group.

Legitimize To make legitimate; to provide an ideological or moral justification for a practice that might otherwise be regarded as objectionable.

Macrosociology The branch of sociology that studies large social systems, especially human societies and the world system of societies.

Maritime society A society in which overseas commercial activity is the primary source of wealth and income.

Market economy An economy in which the basic problems of production and distribution are resolved by the forces of supply and demand (see *Capitalism,* and contrast with *Command economy*).

Mass media Communications media that influence the masses (e.g., television, radio, newspapers, magazines, and movies).

Mean, arithmetic See *Arithmetic mean.*

Median An "average" or measure of central tendency that is the middle number in a series of numbers arranged in order from lowest to highest.

Millennium A period of 1,000 years.

Mixed economy An economy that combines two or more basic principles of economic decision making, especially one that combines market and command principles.

Mobility, vertical See *Vertical mobility.*

Modernization All the long-term social and cultural changes associated with industrialization (compare with *Industrialization*).

Monogamy Marriage with but one person at a time (compare with *Polygamy*).

Monopoly A commodity market with only a single seller.

Nationalism An ideology that emphasizes the importance of a nation or an ethnic group.

Neophilia The love of novelty or change for its own sake.

Nomad A member of a group that has no fixed settlement and moves about periodically (usually in a well-defined territory) to obtain food and other necessities.

Norms Rules of behavior to which sanctions—rewards and punishments—are attached. Norms may be formal and sanctions specific (e.g., laws) or informal and diffuse (e.g., customs).

Nuclear family A married couple and their unmarried children living with them.

Oligarchy The rule of the few (contrast with *Autocracy, Democracy,* and *Theocracy*).

Oligopoly A commodity market dominated by a few sellers.

Omnivore An animal that eats both plants and other animals.

Organism A living entity; a plant or animal.

Outsourcing The transfer of jobs and machines from one society to another in order to reduce the costs of production and to make a corporation more profitable or competitive.

Peasant An agricultural worker in an agrarian society.

Per capita income National income divided by population size.

Plutocracy Government by the wealthy.

Polity The political system of a group, especially of a society; in effect, an institutionalized set of answers to basic questions concerning the governance of a society.

Polyandry A very rare form of marriage in which a woman may have two or more husbands at the same time (compare with *Polygyny*).

Polygamy The general term for any form of marriage which permits multiple spouses (see *Polyandry* and *Polygyny*).

Polygyny A form of marriage in which a man may have two or more wives at the same time (compare with *Polyandry*).

Population (1) Organisms of the same species that tend to interbreed because of geographical proximity; (2) the members of a society, or a subgroup within a society, considered collectively.

Positive-sum game A contest in which the sum of gains and losses is a positive number; the gains of one participant are not necessarily at the expense of others (contrast with *Zero-sum game*).

Pragmatism The belief that social arrangements should be judged on the basis of their consequences rather than on the basis of preconceived ideas.

Prejudice A preconceived opinion or feeling regarding a group.

Primary group A small group in which face-to-face relations of at least a fairly intimate and personal nature are maintained; a family or clique.

Primary industries Industries that produce or extract raw materials (especially farming, mining, forestry, and fishing).

Primates An order of mammals that includes the anthropoids and prosimians.

Process A series of related events with a definable outcome.

Race A breeding population in which certain traits occur with a frequency that is appreciably different from that of other breeding populations within the same species; among humans, races have been differentiated on the basis of skin, hair, and eye color, hair type, body build, and shape of face and head.

Rate of natural increase The difference between annual births and deaths in a society; the rate at which a population would grow if there were no migration into or out of it.

Religion The basic beliefs of a group of people concerning the forces ultimately shaping human life and the world and the practices associated with those beliefs. The term can refer to nontheistic ideologies, such as communism and humanism, but is more often applied to ideologies that involve theistic beliefs.

Republic Representative government.

Revolution Change that is unusually sudden, rapid, violent, or far-reaching.

Revolutionary socialism A socialist ideology developed by Marx and Engels and extended by Lenin that advocates the seizure of power by adherents and denial of power to others, sometimes called "Marxism" or "Marxism-Leninism"; a totalitarian or semitotalitarian system of government.

Role Behavioral expectations and obligations of the occupant of a social position. The term may also be used to refer to the part a group, institution, or other social unit plays in the life of a society.

Sanction A reward or punishment; also, the act of rewarding or punishing.

Science A method of developing a cumulative body of empirically verified knowledge through systematic comparisons and the testing of hypotheses and theories.

Secondary group Any group that is larger and more impersonal than a primary group.

Secondary industries Industries that process raw materials and turn out finished products.

Selection The process that determines the fate of the variations (1) in a gene pool, (2) in a sociocultural system, or (3) in the world system of societies (see *Intersocietal selection, Intrasocietal selection,* and *Variations*).

Serf A peasant farmer who is bound to the land and subject to the owner of the land.

Shaman A person believed to enjoy special powers because of a relationship he or she has established with the spirit world; a medicine man.

Signal An information conveyer whose form and related meaning are both determined genetically (contrast with *Symbol*).

Slavery A system in which some people are the legal property of others.

Social Having to do with relationships among the members of societies.

Social controls Mechanisms that order societal life by regulating people's actions and relationships; norms and their related sanctions.

Social environment The other social systems with which a given social system has contact.

Social institution See *Institution*.

Socialism An economic system in which there is little or no private ownership of the means of production (compare with *Capitalism*).

Socialization The lifelong process through which individuals learn to become functional members of their society.

Social movement A loose-knit group that seeks to change society.

Social organization The network of relationships among the members of a society or group.

Social structure See *Social organization* and *Structure*.

Social system A generic term that may be applied to all kinds of human groups, from primary groups to the world system of societies.

Societal Of or pertaining to a society or societies.

Society, human A human population is considered a society to the degree that it is politically autonomous and its members engage in a broad range of cooperative activities.

Sociocultural A combination of social and cultural elements.

Sociocultural evolution Long-term trends in the world system of societies that result from the interplay of the forces of continuity, innovation, and selection.

Sociocultural system A system composed of a human population and its social organization, culture, material products, and social institutions; a human society.

Sociology The branch of science that specializes in the study of human societies.

Species A distinct population of organisms that is reproductively isolated (i.e., cannot reproduce with populations of other organisms).

State The government of a society by full-time officials.

Status The relative rank of a person, role, or group, according to culturally defined standards.

Stratification Class or status differentiation within a population; hence, inequality.

Structure The organization of the parts of a system.

Subculture The distinctive culture of a group within a society.

Subsistence The material necessities of life; also, the process by which they are obtained.

Subsistence technology The technology that is used by the members of a society to obtain the basic necessities of life.

Surplus See *Economic surplus*.

Symbol An information conveyer whose form and meaning are determined by those who use it (contrast with *Signal*).

System An entity made up of interrelated parts.

Systemic A feature inherent in a particular system, or having the qualities of a system.

Tabula rasa Literally "blank slate"; the belief that children were infinitely malleable through education and socialization.

Technology Cultural information about the ways in which the material resources of the environment may be used to satisfy human needs and desires.

Tertiary industries Industries that perform services (e.g., retail trade, government, the professions).

Theocracy A society ruled by a priesthood in the name of some deity, or by a ruler believed to be divine.

Theory A logically connected set of propositions that provide an empirically confirmed explanation of some aspect of the natural world, or a coherent set of principles that form the basic frame of reference for a field of inquiry.

Third world Industrializing societies or less developed societies in the world today.

Tribe A general term for a people whose members speak a common language or dialect, possess a common culture that distinguishes them from other peoples, and know themselves, or are known, by a distinctive name.

Urban community A community whose inhabitants are wholly or largely freed from the necessity of producing their own food, fibers, and other raw materials.

Values Cultural judgments about what is good (valuable) and what is not; moral beliefs to which the members of a group subscribe.

Variable Any characteristic that can differ across observations; something that can vary or change (compare with *Constant*).

Variable costs Costs of production that tend to vary in proportion to the number of units produced (contrast with *Fixed costs*).

Variations Products of the process of innovation; new or alternative elements in a sociocultural system (see *Innovation* and *Selection*).

Vertebrates Animals with backbones.

Vertical mobility Change of status, either upward or downward.

Working class Members of modern industrial societies belonging to families headed by manual workers.

World system The totality of human societies and their interrelationships.

Zero-sum game A contest in which gains and losses must sum to zero; the gains of any participant are necessarily at the expense of other participants (compare with *Positive-sum game*).

Many of the figures and tables for preindustrial societies are based on data from a machine-readable version of George Peter Murdock's *Ethnographic Atlas* (1,267 cases), which originally appeared in installments of *Ethnology* (1962–1971), and a number of original data sets for a standard sample of societies (186 cases) made available by their authors in machine-readable form through the electronic journal *World Cultures.*

In most of the tables and figures we report results from analyses of the *Ethnographic Atlas* data because they depict the experience and characteristics of the largest, most extensive "sample" of human societies. To guard against the possibility that the total data set gives a distorted or lopsided picture of human societies, however, all the analyses were recomputed for a subset (734 cases) of the *Ethnographic Atlas* argued to be more "representative" of human societies. In all instances results for this "world sample" were substantially the same as those for the complete *Atlas.*

In those cases where the standard sample data sets contain information not available in the *Atlas,* we report results using them. The "standard sample" was carefully constructed to "represent" the regional, cultural, and developmental diversity of human societies, and as new variables are added, the volume and diversity of data on it continue to grow. This growing body of data greatly extends cross-cultural research possibilities and strongly complements the *Atlas.* The original sources of data and the variables we used are identified below.

Dominant mode of subsistence was coded according to information on the society's percent dependence on each of five basic modes of subsistence (V1–V5 in the *Atlas,* V203–V207 in the standard sample): (1) hunting, (2) gathering, (3) fishing, (4) animal husbandry, and (5) agriculture; together with information on the presence or absence of metals (V44, V55 in the *Atlas,* V248, V249 in the standard sample), and the presence or absence of the plow (V39 in the *Atlas,* V243 in the standard sample).

After summing the scores for hunting and gathering to produce a composite measure of societal dependence on these two modes of subsistence, we classified societies on the basis of the following criteria:

1. If dependence on hunting and gathering, fishing, or animal husbandry totaled 6 or greater (more than 56% reliance), that mode was coded as dominant (i.e., the society was coded "hunting and gathering," "fishing," or "herding," respectively).

2. If agriculture was 6 or greater, the plow ABSENT, and metals ABSENT, the society was coded "simple horticultural."

3. If agriculture was 6 or greater, the plow ABSENT, and metals PRESENT, the society was coded "advanced horticultural."

4. If agriculture was 6 or greater, and the plow PRESENT, the society was coded "agrarian."

5. If a dependence score was 4 (36–45%), or 5 (46–55%), and NO OTHER MODE WAS SCORED AS HIGH OR HIGHER, that mode was classified dominant.

6. If no score was 4 or greater, two modes were scored equally high, or if relevant data were missing, the society was coded "other."

7. Also, because of their anomalous and hybrid nature, "mounted hunters" (those in which hunting and gathering was dominant, and in which V40 in the *Atlas*

or V244 in the standard sample indicated horses were present) were coded "other." These coding rules produced the following distributions of societal types:

Distribution of Societal Types in Different Data Sets

	Ethnographic Atlas		World Sample		Standard Sample	
Societal Type	N	%	N	%	N	%
Hunting and gathering	174	21	84	16	27	17
Simple horticultural	155	19	146	27	35	22
Advanced horticultural	246	30	140	26	38	24
Agrarian	103	13	90	17	32	20
Fishing	60	7	38	7	11	7
Herding	78	10	37	7	16	10
Totals	816	100	535	100	159	100

Note: 451 cases from the *Ethnographic Atlas,* 199 from the world sample, and 27 from the standard sample were missing relevant data, or were otherwise not classifiable according to the criteria. It should also be noted that the numerical base for particular tables and figures in the text varies because of missing data on the traits in question.

Data Sources for Tables and Figures

Table 4.2 Median Size: *Ethnographic Atlas,* Political Integration [*World Cultures,* V89].

Table 4.3 Craft Specialization: *Ethnographic Atlas,* Craft Specialization [*World Cultures,* V55–V60].

Figure 4.3 Complex Status Systems: *Ethnographic Atlas,* Class Stratification [*World Cultures,* V65].

Figure 4.4 Belief in a Supreme Creator: *Ethnographic Atlas,* High Gods [*World Cultures,* V34].

Figure 5.2 Leaders' Exercise of Authority, Marc H. Ross, "Political Decision Making and Conflict: Additional Cross-Cultural Codes," *Ethnology* 22 (1983), pp. 169–192 [*World Cultures,* STDS30: V763].

Table 5.3 Community Size: *Ethnographic Atlas,* Mean Size of Local Communities [*World Cultures,* V31].

Table 5.4 Private Ownership of Land: *Ethnographic Atlas,* Inheritance Rule for Real Property [*World Cultures,* V73].

Table 5.5 Emphases in Child-Rearing: Herbert Barry III, Lili Josephson, Edith Lauer, and Catherine Marshall, "Traits Inculcated in Childhood: Cross Cultural Codes 5," *Ethnology* 15 (1976), pp. 83–114 [*World Cultures,* STDS13: V306–V309, V322–V325].

Table 5.6 Types of Games: *Ethnographic Atlas,* Games [*World Cultures,* V35].

Table 6.1 Population Density: George Peter Murdock and Caterina Provost, "Measurement of Cultural Complexity," *Ethnology* 12 (1971), pp. 379–392 [*World Cultures:* STDS06: V156].

Table 6.2 Division of Labor: *Ethnographic Atlas,* Sex Differences in Agriculture [*World Cultures,* V54].

Table 6.3 Matrilineality: *Ethnographic Atlas,* Descent [*World Cultures,* V43].

Figure 6.5 Slavery: *Ethnographic Atlas,* Type of Slavery [*World Cultures,* V69].

Further information on tables and analyses is available from the authors.

Chapter 1

1. World Bank 2013, *World Energy Outlook 2011*, International Energy Agency, http://www.world bank.org/en/topic/energy/overview.

2. For the importance of an "ecosystem" approach for sociology, see William R. Catton Jr., "Foundations of Human Ecology," *Sociological Perspectives*, 37 (1994), pp. 75–95, and William R. Catton Jr., *From Animistic to Naturalistic Sociology* (New York: McGraw-Hill, 1966).

3. Kingsley Davis, *Human Society* (New York: Macmillan, 1949), p. 27. See also Alfred E. Emerson, "Human Cultural Evolution and Its Relation to Organic Evolution of Insect Societies," in Herbert Barringer et al. (eds.), *Social Change in Developing Areas: A Reinterpretation of Evolutionary Theory* (Cambridge, Mass.: Schenkman, 1965), pp. 50–51.

4. Edward O. Wilson, *Sociobiology: The New Synthesis* (Cambridge, Mass.: Belknap, 1975), part III.

5. See, for example, Elizabeth Cashdan, "Hunters and Gatherers: Economic Behavior in Bands," in Stuart Plattner (ed.), *Economic Anthropology* (Stanford, Calif.: Stanford University Press, 1989), pp. 21–48, and *World Almanac and Book of Facts 2002* (New York: World Almanac Books, 2002), pp. 780–781.

6. Wilson, chap. 27; Ian Tattersall, *The Human Odyssey: Four Million Years of Human Evolution* (New York: Prentice-Hall, 1993), chap. 4; Monroe Strickberger, *Evolution* (Boston: Jones and Bartlett, 1990), chap. 19; Donald Johanson and James Shreeve, *Lucy's Child: The Discovery of a Human Ancestor* (New York: Morrow, 1989), chap. 9; Alexandra Maryanski and Jonathan H. Turner, *The Social Cage: Human Nature and the Evolution of Society* (Stanford, Calif.: Stanford University Press, 1992).

7. This definition is a slightly modified version of that provided by W. H. Thorpe, *Learning and Instinct in Animals,* 2d ed. (Cambridge, Mass.: Harvard University Press, 1963), p. 55. See also Zick Rubin, Letitia Anne Peplau, and Peter Salovey, *Psychology* (Boston: Houghton-Mifflin, 1993), pp. 109–110.

8. Wilson, pp. 151–152.

9. Sherwood L. Washburn and David A. Hamburg, "The Implications of Primate Research," in Irven DeVore (ed.), *Primate Behavior: Field Studies of Monkeys and Apes* (New York: Holt, 1965), p. 613.

10. Nicholas Wade, "Insight into Human-Chimp Differences," *New York Times,* Apr. 12, 2002; Nicholas Wade, "Researchers Say Gene Is Linked to Language," *New York Times,* Oct. 5, 2001; Tattersall, chap. 4; Sherwood Washburn, "The Evolution of Man," *Scientific American,* 239 (Sept. 1978), p. 204; Dorothy Miller, "Evolution of the Primate Chromosomes," *Science,* 198 (Dec. 16, 1977), pp. 1116–1124. See also Mary-Claire King and A. C. Wilson, "Evolution at Two Levels in Humans and Chimpanzees," *Science,* 188 (Apr. 11, 1975), pp. 107–116.

11. See Jonathan Turner and Alexandra Maryanski, *Incest: Origins of the Taboo* (Boulder, Colo: Paradigm, 2005), pp. 144–147, for an excellent summary of the evolutionary changes that have occurred in the human brain and made human cultures possible.

12. For important differences between what we call "behavioral" and "symbolic" culture, see Christophe Boesch and Michael Tomasello, "Chimpanzee and Human Cultures," *Current Anthropology,* 39 (Dec. 1998), pp. 591–614; and Carel P. van Schaik, Marc Ancrenaz, Gwendolyn Borgen, Birute Galdikas, Cheryl D. Knotts, Ian Singleton, Akira Suzuki, Sri Suci Utami, and Michelle Merrill, "Orangutan Cultures and the Evolution of Material Culture," *Science,* 299 (Jan. 3, 2003), pp. 102–105. For further information on widely cited examples of "behavioral" culture see

"Wildlife Adaptations and Behaviours: Culture," BBC, http://www.bbc.co.uk/nature/adaptations/Animal_culture; Michael Balter, "Strongest Evidence of Animal Culture Seen in Monkeys and Whales," *Science Now*, Apr. 16, 2013; Frans B. M. deWaal, "Cultural Primatology Comes of Age," *Nature*, 399 (June 17, 1999), pp. 35–36; and Luke Rendell and Hal Whitehead, "Culture in Whales and Dolphins," *Behavioral and Brain Sciences*, 24 (2001), pp. 309–382.

13. This paragraph is based on Wilson, pp. 176–185. See also Steven Pinker, *The Language Instinct: How the Mind Creates Language* (New York: William Morrow, 1994), chap. 11.

14. Karl von Frisch, "Dialect in the Language of the Bees," *Scientific American*, 167 (Aug. 1962), pp. 3–7.

15. Masukazu Konishi, "The Role of Auditory Feedback in the Control of Vocalization in the White-Crowned Sparrow," *Journal of Comparative Ethology*, 22 (1965), pp. 770–783.

16. See, for example, Francine Patterson, "Conversations with a Gorilla," *National Geographic*, 154 (Oct. 1978), pp. 438–466; or Steven Roger Fischer, *A History of Language* (London: Reaktion Books, 1999). But also see a transcript of a "live chat" with Koko that raises serious questions concerning Patterson's translations and interpretations of Koko's symbol use at http://pubpages.unh.edu/~jel/kokotranscript.html. For other, more skeptical views of the ability of apes to use symbols, see Roger Brown, "Why Are Signal Languages Easier to Learn Than Spoken Languages? Part Two," *Bulletin of the American Academy of Arts and Sciences*, 32 (Dec. 1978), pp. 38–39; Martin Gardner, *Science: Good, Bad, and Bogus* (Buffalo, N.Y.: Prometheus, 1981), pp. 391–408; Joel Wallman, *Aping Language* (Cambridge: Cambridge University Press, 1992). Pinker, op. cit., and James Trefil, *Are We Unique? A Scientist Explores the Unparalleled Intelligence of the Human Mind* (New York: Wiley, 1997), chaps. 3 and 4.

17. Ian Tattersall, *The Monkey in the Mirror: Essays in the Science of What Makes Us Human* (New York: Harcourt, 2002); John E. Pfeiffer, *The Emergence of Man*, 2d ed. (New York: Harper & Row, 1972), p. 381, citing Jane van Lawick-Goodall as authority; see also Robbins Burling,

"Primate Calls, Human Language, and Nonverbal Communication," *Current Anthropology*, 34 (Feb. 1993), pp. 25–33; and Marc Hauaer, Noam Chomsky, and W. Tecumseth Fitch, "The Faculty of Language: What Is It, Who Has It, and How Did It Evolve?" *Science*, 298 (Nov. 22, 2002), pp. 1569–1579.

18. Jon Lackman, "Dugon, Haus You Dinikin, Du-Ah: The Secrets of Twin Speak," *Slate*, Aug. 24, 2011, http://www.slate.com/articles/life/twins/2011/08/dugon_haus_you_dinikin_duah.2.html; Hilton Als, "We Two Made One" *The New Yorker*, Dec. 4, 2000.

19. C. M. Matthews, *Words Words Words* (London: Lutterford, 1979), p. 138.

20. Helen Keller, *The Story of My Life* (New York: Doubleday, 1903; and Norton, 2003).

21. Robert Lord, *Comparative Linguistics*, 2d ed. (London: English Universities Press, 1974), pp. 288–289.

22. See for example Simon E. Fisher and Matt Ridley, "Culture, Genes, and the Human Revolution," *Science*, 340 (May 24, 2013), pp. 929–930.

23. For a good summary of these developments, see Marvin Harris, *The Rise of Anthropological Theory* (New York: Crowell, 1968), chap. 2.

24. For a good review of the early history of social research, see Bernard Lecuyer and Anthony Oberschall, "Sociology: The Early History of Social Research," in *International Encyclopedia of the Social Sciences* (New York: Macmillan and Free Press, 1968), vol. 15, pp. 36–53.

25. For several influential statements of an ecological-evolutionary approach see O. D. Duncan, "Social Organization and the Ecosystem," in R. E. L. Faris (ed.), *Handbook of Modern Sociology* (Chicago: Rand McNally, 1964), pp. 39–45; and Walter Goldschmidt, *Man's Way: A Preface to the Understanding of Human Society* (New York: Holt, 1959). See also Marvin Harris, *Cultural Materialism: The Struggle for a Science of Culture* (New York: Random House, 1979), and Steven K. Sanderson, *Evolutionism and Its Critics* (Boulder, Colo: Paradigm, 2007).

Chapter 2

1. Anatol Rapaport, "Systems Analysis: General Systems Theory," *International Encyclopedia of*

the *Social Sciences* (New York: Macmillan and Free Press, 1968), vol. 15, p. 454.

2. Francis Thompson, "The Mistress of Vision," *Selected Poems of Francis Thompson* (London: Burns Oates & Washbourne and Jonathan Cape, 1908).

3. Chandler Burr, "Homosexuality and Biology," *The Atlantic Monthly,* Mar. 1993, pp. 47–65; Bruce Bower, "The Birth of Schizophrenia: A Debilitating Mental Disorder May Take Root in the Fetal Brain," *Science News,* 143 (May 29, 1993), pp. 346–347; and for a critique of some oversimplifications and errors, see John Horgan, "Eugenics Revisited," *Scientific American,* 268 (June 1993), pp. 122–131.

4. John Locke, *An Essay Concerning Human Understanding* (New York: Dover, 1959, first published 1690).

5. Richard Machalek, and Michael W. Martin, "Sociology and the Second Darwinian Revolution: A Metatheoretical Analysis," *Sociological Theory,* 22 (2004), pp. 445–476; Steven Pinker, *The Blank Slate: The Modern Denial of Human Nature* (New York: Viking, 2002); Reinhold Niebuhr, *The Nature and Destiny of Man* (New York: Scribner, 1943), vol. 1; Robert Heilbroner, *An Inquiry into the Human Prospect* (New York: Norton, 1991), chap. 4; and Jan Szczepański, *Polish Society* (New York: Random House, 1970), p. 100 and chap. 9.

6. Stephen Jay Gould, "Human Babies as Embryos," *Natural History,* 85 (Feb. 1976), p. 22ff.

7. Stephen Jay Gould, *Ever Since Darwin* (New York: Norton, 1977), pp. 63–69.

8. Theodosius Dobzhansky, *Mankind Evolving* (New York: Bantam, 1962), pp. 224–225; and John E. Pfeiffer, *The Emergence of Man,* 2d ed. (New York: Harper & Row, 1972), chap. 18.

9. Kingsley Davis, "Final Note on a Case of Extreme Isolation," *American Journal of Sociology,* 52 (Mar. 1947), pp. 432–437; Rene A. Spitz, "Hospitalism," *The Psychoanalytic Study of the Child,* 1 (1945), pp. 53–72, and "Hospitalism: A Follow-up Report," *The Psychoanalytic Study of the Child,* 2 (1946), pp. 113–117; and Boris Cyrulnik, *The Dawn of Meaning* (New York: McGraw-Hill, 1993), pp. 82–86 and pp. 95–96.

10. Pfeiffer, pp. 429–430, and Carl Sagan, *The Dragons of Eden* (New York: Ballantine Books, 1977), pp. 47–48.

11. George Kingsley Zipf, *Human Behavior and the Principle of Least Effort: An Introduction to Human Ecology* (New York: Hafner, 1965, first published 1949).

12. Helena Curtis, *Biology,* 2d ed. (New York: Worth, 1975), pp. 717–720; and Pinker, *The Language Instinct.*

13. Noam Chomsky, *Syntactic Structures* (The Hague: Mouton, 1957); *Aspects of the Theory of Syntax* (Cambridge, Mass.: MIT Press, 1965); and *Cartesian Linguistics* (New York: Harper & Row, 1966); Pinker, *The Language Instinct*; and Nicholas Wade, "Researchers Say Gene Is Linked to Language," *New York Times,* Oct. 5, 2001.

14. Melvin Konner, *The Tangled Wing: Biological Constraints on the Human Spirit* (New York: Holt, Rinehart and Winston, 1982), pp. 147–151.

15. For a more detailed discussion of this subject, see Gerhard Lenski, *Power and Privilege* (New York: McGraw-Hill, 1966), pp. 25–32.

16. William Graham Sumner, *Folkways* (New York: Mentor, 1960, first published 1906), p. 32.

17. J. S. Weiner, *The Natural History of Man* (Garden City, N.Y.: Doubleday Anchor, 1973), p. 170.

18. Theodosius Dobzhansky, Francisco Ayala, G. Ledyard Stebbins, and James Valentine, *Evolution* (San Francisco: Freeman, 1977), chap. 5.

19. For discussions of the relation between human physique and climate, see Theodosius Dobzhansky, *Mankind Evolving* (New York: Bantam, 1962), p. 287ff; Weiner, p. 160ff.; E. Adamson Hoebel, *Anthropology: The Study of Man,* 3d ed. (New York: McGraw-Hill, 1966), p. 214ff; and B. J. Williams, *Evolution and Human Origins: An Introduction to Physical Anthropology* (New York: Harper & Row, 1973), chap. 13.

20. Weiner, pp. 153 and 167; and L. Luca Cavalli-Sforza, Paolo Menozzi, and Alberto Piazza, *The History and Geography of Human Genes* (Princeton, N.J.: Princeton University Press, 1994).

21. Dobzhansky, et al., p. 148. Randolph Nesse, "When Bad Genes Happen to Good People," *Technology Review* (May/June 1995), pp. 30–40.

22. Dobzhansky, et al., p. 158ff.

23. Paul R. Ehrlich and Richard W. Holm, *The Process of Evolution* (New York: McGraw-Hill, 1963), fig. 11.1, p. 253.

24. Cavalli-Sforza et al.

25. Fred Blumenthal, "The Man in the Middle of the Peace Talks," *Washington Post,* July 14, 1968.

26. Richard Lederer, *Anguished English: An Anthology of Accidental Assaults upon Our Language* (New York: Dell, 1987), p. 138.

27. Curtis, p. 159.

28. Hoebel, p. 35.

29. Laura Martin, "'Eskimo Words for Snow': A Case Study in the Genesis and Decay of an Anthropological Example," *American Anthropologist,* 88 (1986), pp. 418–423.

30. Karl G. Heider, *The Dugum Dani: A Papuan Culture in the Highlands of West New Guinea* (New York: Wenner-Gren Foundation, 1970), pp. 32–33.

31. Hoebel, p. 35.

32. Robert Lord, *Comparative Linguistics,* 2d ed. (London: English Universities Press, 1974), p. 316. For other interesting examples of changes in the meanings of words, see Charlton Laird, *The Miracle of Language* (Greenwich, Conn.: Premier Books, 1953), p. 54ff.

33. Personal communications, Siobhan Williams, Jan. 13 and 19, 2005.

34. For an excellent discussion of the differences between human communication with signals and symbols, see Robbins Burling, "Primate Calls, Human Language, and Nonverbal Communication," *Current Anthropology,* 34 (Feb. 1993), pp. 25–53; and Terrence W. Deacon, *The Symbolic Species: The Co-Evolution of Language and the Brain* (New York: Norton, 1997).

35. V. Gordon Childe, *Man Makes Himself* (New York: Mentor, 1951), p. 144ff; Joannie M. Schrof, "From Tax Audits to Poetry," *U.S. News & World Report,* Nov. 5, 1990, p. 70; and Denise Schmandt-Besserat, *Before Writing: From Counting to Cuneiform* (Austin, Tex.: University of Texas Press, 1992), p. 1.

36. This view of ideology borrows from Talcott Parsons's thesis that the prime function of religion is making sense out of the totality of human experience. If the term "religion" is defined to include nontheistic faiths (as we do in this volume), religion in the historic Western sense becomes one form of ideology. See Parsons, *The Structure of Social Action* (New York: Free Press, 1968), vol. 2, pp. 566–567, 667–668, and 717.

37. See, for example, Robert S. Merrill, "Technology: The Study of Technology," *International Encyclopedia of the Social Sciences,* vol. 15, p. 576.

38. Ralph H. Turner, "Role: Sociological Analysis," *International Encyclopedia of the Social Sciences,* vol. 13, pp. 552–557.

39. For example, see Donald J. Treiman, *Occupational Prestige in Comparative Perspective* (New York: Academic Press, 1977).

40. For a more extended discussion of strata and classes, see Lenski, pp. 73–82.

41. James K. Feibleman, *The Institutions of Society* (London: G. Allen, 1956), p. 52.

Chapter 3

1. For an early statement of this distinction, see F. Stuart Chapin, *Cultural Change* (New York: Century, 1928), p. 345.

2. A. L. Kroeber, *Anthropology* (New York: Harcourt, Brace, 1948), pp. 353–355. For other examples, see Howard A. Rush, "Right Time and Place: Many Medical Discoveries Found to Result from Series of Accidents," *New York Times,* June 8, 1969; Irving Page, "A Sense of the History of Discovery," *Science,* Dec. 27, 1974, p. 1161; and Vern Riportella, "Fifty Years of Radio Astronomy," *Science News,* 123 (Apr. 30, 1983), p. 283.

3. Glynn Isaac, "The Food-Sharing Behavior of Protohuman Hominids," *Scientific American,* 238 (Apr. 1978), pp. 90–108.

4. For an early statement of this principle, see William F. Ogburn, *Social Change* (New York: Viking, 1922), chap. 6.

5. William F. Ogburn and Dorothy S. Thomas, "Are Inventions Inevitable? A Note on Social Evolution," *Political Science Quarterly,* 37 (Mar. 1922), pp. 83–98.

6. Ogburn mentioned this factor briefly, but did not stress it. (1950 edition, p. 110).

7. Basil Davidson with F. K. Buah, *A History of West Africa* (Garden City, N.Y.: Doubleday Anchor, 1966), pp. 8–9; William H. McNeill, *Plagues and Peoples* (Garden City, N.Y.: Doubleday Anchor, 1976).

8. Ralph Linton, *The Study of Man* (New York: Appleton-Century, 1936), pp. 326–327. Reprinted by permission of Prentice-Hall, Inc.

9. For example, see Richard Wilkinson, *Poverty and Progress: An Ecological Perspective on Economic Development* (New York: Praeger, 1973); and Marvin Harris, *Cannibals and Kings: The Origins of Cultures* (New York: Vintage Books, 1977).

10. Ogburn, 1950 edition, p. 107.

11. Rudolf Braun, "Zur Einwirkung soziokulturelle Umweltbedingungen auf das Unternehmverhalten," in Wolfram Fischer (ed.), *Wirtschafts und sozialgeschichtliche Probleme der frühen Industrialisierung* (Berlin: Colloquium, 1968), p. 257.

12. Hans Zinsser, *Rats, Lice and History* (New York: Little Brown, 1934).

13. Robert Carneiro, "Political Expansion as an Expression of the Principle of Competitive Exclusion," in Ronald Cohen and Elman Service (eds.), *Origins of the State* (Philadelphia: Institute for the Study of Human Issues, 1978), pp. 205–223.

14. F. G. Bailey, *Tribe, Caste, and Nation* (Manchester: Manchester University Press, 1960).

15. O. D. Duncan, "Social Organization and the Ecosystem," in R. E. L. Faris (ed.), *Handbook of Modern Sociology* (Chicago: Rand McNally, 1964), pp. 37–39. See also Leslie White, *The Science of Culture* (New York: Grove, 1949), pp. 363–393.

16. See William F. Cottrell, *Energy and Society* (New York: McGraw-Hill, 1955), p. 2, for a somewhat similar assertion concerning energy's impact on human life.

17. Robert Carneiro, "On the Relationship between Size of Population and Complexity of Social Organization," *Southwestern Journal of Anthropology,* 23 (1967), pp. 234–243.

18. Ernest Gellner, *Plow, Sword and Book: The Structure of Human History* (Chicago: University of Chicago Press, 1989).

19. Robert S. Gottfried, *The Black Death: Natural and Human Disaster in Medieval Europe* (New York: Free Press, 1983), chap. 7.

20. Donald T. Campbell, "On the Conflicts between Biological and Social Evolution and between Psychology and Moral Tradition," *American Psychologist,* 30 (Dec. 1975), pp. 1103–1126.

21. See, for example, Ernst Mayr, *The Growth of Biological Thought: Diversity, Evolution, and Inheritance* (Cambridge, Mass.: Belknap, 1982), chap. 8.

22. Thorstein Veblen, *Imperial Germany and the Industrial Revolution* (New York: Macmillan, 1915); Elman Service, "The Law of Evolutionary Potential," in Marshall Sahlins and Elman Service (eds.), *Evolution and Culture* (Ann Arbor: University of Michigan Press, 1960), pp. 93–122; see also Patrick D. Nolan, and Gerhard Lenski, "Techno-Economic Heritage, Patterns of Development, and the Advantage of Backwardness," *Social Forces,* 64 (1985), pp. 341–358.

23. "By Installation of New Equipment Communication Expands Throughout the Country: MCIT," Bakhtar News, Sept. 3, 2012, http://www.bakhtarnews.com.af/eng/business/item/3844-by-installation-of-new-equipment-communication-expands-throughout-the-country-mcit.html.

Chapter 4

1. See Marvin Harris, *The Rise of Anthropological Theory* (New York: Thomas Y. Crowell, 1968), chap. 2; and Robert Nisbet, *Social Change and History* (New York: Oxford, 1969), chap. 4.

2. This method of classification is an expansion and modification of one developed earlier by Walter Goldschmidt in *Man's Way: A Preface to the Understanding of Human Society* (New York: Holt, 1959), chap. 6, and also reflects the influence of V. Gordon Childe, *Man Makes Himself* (New York: Mentor Books, 1951).

3. See, for example, R. F. Watters, "The Nature of Shifting Cultivation: A Review of Recent Research," *Pacific Viewpoint,* 1 (1960), pp. 59–99.

4. See Jacquetta Hawkes, *Prehistory: UNESCO History of Mankind* (New York: Mentor Books, 1965), chap. 6, for a good summary of archaeological finds relating to fishing. See also Grahame Clark and Stuart Piggott, *Prehistoric Societies* (New York: Knopf, 1965), chap. 7.

5. Bernadette Arnaud, "First Farmers," *Archaeology,* Nov./Dec. 2000, pp. 56–59; Robert J. Wenke, *Patterns in Prehistory: Humankind's First Three Million Years* (New York: Oxford University Press, 1990), chap. 6; Robert Braidwood, "The Earliest Village Communities of Southwest Asia Reconsidered," and Karl Butzer, "Agricultural Origins in the Near East as a Geographical Problem," in Stuart

Struever (ed.), *Prehistoric Agriculture* (Garden City, N.Y.: Natural History Press, 1971), pp. 222 and 249.

6. James Mellaart, *Earliest Civilizations in the Near East* (London: Thames and Hudson, 1965), p. 105; and R. J. Forbes, *Studies in Ancient Technology* (Leiden: Brill, 1971–1972), vols. 8 and 9.

7. See, for example, Leslie Aitchison, *A History of Metals* (London: MacDonald, 1960), vol. 1, p. 41; and Forbes.

8. E. Cecil Curwen and Gudmund Hatt, *Plough and Pasture: The Early History of Farming* (New York: Collier Books, 1961), p. 64.

9. Aitchison, pp. 102 and 111–113; and Forbes, vol. 9, chap. 3.

10. Mellaart, p. 20; and Wenke, chap. 6.

11. Wenke, p. 240.

12. William H. McNeill, *The Rise of the West: A History of the Human Community* (New York: Mentor Books, 1965), p. 150.

13. See Appendix, pp. 417–418, for details concerning our use of these data.

14. Goldschmidt, p. 115.

15. This method of classifying religious beliefs is based on work by G. E. Swanson in *The Birth of the Gods: The Origin of Primitive Beliefs* (Ann Arbor: University of Michigan Press, 1960), chap. 3. For some proposed explanations of why such beliefs would vary across societies, see Emile Durkheim, *The Elementary Forms of the Religious Life* (New York: Free Press, 1965); Swanson; and John Simpson, "Sovereign Groups, Subsistence Technology, and the Presence of a High God in Primitive Societies," in R. Wuthnow (ed.), *The Religious Dimension in Quantitative Research* (New York: Academic Press, 1979), pp. 299–310.

16. Leslie White was the leading proponent of this point of view for many years. See, for example, his stimulating but extreme essay, "Energy and the Evolution of Culture," in *The Science of Culture* (New York: Grove Press, 1949), pp. 363–393.

17. Talcott Parsons is one of many who have consistently minimized the role of technology in the process of social change. Though not as extreme as some in his views, he was very influential. See *Societies: Evolutionary and Comparative Perspectives* (Englewood Cliffs, N.J.: Prentice-Hall, 1966), especially pp. 113–114, for his views.

Chapter 5

1. See, for example, Jonathan Turner and Alexandra Maryanski, *Incest: Origins of the Taboo* (Boulder, Colo.: Paradigm, 2005), p. 124ff.

2. Roger Lewin, "Man the Scavenger," *Science,* 224 (May 25, 1984), pp. 861–862; and Bruce Bower, "Hunting Ancient Scavengers," *Science News,* 127 (Mar. 9, 1985), pp. 155–157.

3. J. S. Weiner, *The Natural History of Man* (Garden City, N.Y.: Doubleday Anchor, 1973), p. 50ff.; and C. Owen Lovejoy, "The Natural Detective," *Natural History* (Oct. 1984), pp. 24–28.

4. Glynn Isaac, "The Food-Sharing Behavior of Protohuman Hominids," *Scientific American,* 238 (Apr. 1978), pp. 90–108.

5. Turner and Maryanski, ch. 4.

6. Geza Teleki, *The Predatory Behavior of Wild Chimpanzees* (Lewisburg, Pa.: Bucknell University Press, 1973).

7. Jacquetta Hawkes, *Prehistory: UNESCO History of Mankind,* vol. 1, part 1 (New York: Mentor Books, 1965), p. 172. See also Grahame Clark and Stuart Piggott, *Prehistoric Societies* (New York: Knopf, 1965), p. 45; or Grahame Clark, *The Stone Age Hunters* (London: Thames and Hudson, 1967), p. 25.

8. William Laughlin, "Hunting: An Integrating Behavior System and Its Evolutionary Importance," in Richard Lee and Irven DeVore (eds.), *Man the Hunter* (Chicago: Aldine, 1968).

9. Turner and Maryanski, ch. 5.

10. Jonathan Turner, *On the Origins of Human Emotions: A Sociological Inquiry into the Evolution of Human Affect* (Stanford, Calif.: Stanford University Press, 2000).

11. Turner and Maryanski, p. 126.

12. H. V. Vallois, "The Social Life of Early Man: The Evidence of Skeletons," in Sherwood Washburn (ed.), *Social Life of Early Man* (Chicago: Aldine, 1961), pp. 214–235.

13. S. A. Semenov, *Prehistoric Technology,* trans. M. W. Thompson (New York: Barnes and Noble, 1964), pp. 202–203.

14. E. Adamson Hoebel, *Anthropology,* 3d ed. (New York: McGraw-Hill, 1966), pp. 176–177; and Hawkes, pp. 212–213.

15. This and the following statements about the bow and arrow are based on Semenov, pp. 202–204.

16. Hawkes, p. 212.

17. J. G. D. Clark, *Prehistoric Europe: The Economic Basis* (London: Methuen, 1952), pp. 132–133.

18. Hawkes, pp. 184–188.

19. Clark and Piggott, pp. 93–95.

20. A. Martin Byers, "Symboling and the Middle-Upper Palaeolithic Transition: A Theoretical and Methodological Critique," *Current Anthropology*, 35 (Aug. 1994), pp. 369–399; William Noble and Iain Davidson, "The Evolutionary Emergence of Modern Human Behaviour: Language and Its Archaeology," *Man*, June 1991, pp. 223–253; and, for a critical view see Michael Chazan, "The Language Hypothesis for the Middle-to-Upper Paleolithic Transition: An Examination Based on a Multiregional Lithic Analysis," *Current Anthropology*, 36 (Dec. 1995), pp. 749–768.

21. L. J. Angel, "Paleoecology, Paleodemography and Health," in Steven Polgar (ed.), *Population, Ecology and Social Evolution* (The Hague: Mouton, 1975), table 1, pp. 182–183.

22. Fekri Hassan, *Demographic Archaeology* (New York: Academic Press, 1981), chap. 12.

23. For summaries of work on hunters and gatherers, see Richard Lee and Irven DeVore (eds.), *Man the Hunter* (Chicago: Aldine, 1968); Carleton S. Coon, *The Hunting Peoples* (Boston: Little, Brown, 1971); and Elman Service, *The Hunters* (Englewood Cliffs, N.J.: Prentice-Hall, 1966).

24. This figure is based on Elkin's estimate that there were approximately 300,000 aborigines in Australia at the time of the first white settlement. This estimate was divided by sixty, a very generous estimate for the average size of these societies. See A. P. Elkin, *The Australian Aborigines*, 3d ed. (Sydney: Angus and Robertson, 1954), p. 10.

25. Our calculations are based on twenty-seven societies in Murdock's data set.

26. See Table 4.2 of this volume.

27. Gertrude E. Dole, "The Development of Patterns of Kinship Nomenclature" (Ph.D. dissertation, University of Michigan, 1957), p. 26, found an average life expectancy at birth in very primitive societies of only twenty-two years and also found that individuals who live to age fifty are rare. Allan Holmberg, *Nomads of the Long Bow: The Siriono of*
Eastern Bolivia, Smithsonian Institution, Institute of Social Anthropology, 10 (Washington, D.C., 1950), p. 85, reported that the average life span among the Siriono was only thirty-five to forty years even among those who survived infancy.

28. Gina Bara Kolata, "!Kung Hunter-Gatherers: Feminism, Diet, and Birth Control," *Science*, 185 (Sept. 13, 1974), p. 934.

29. Nancy Howell, "Feedback and Buffers in Relation to Scarcity and Abundance: Studies of Hunter-Gatherer Populations," in David Coleman and Roger Schofield (eds.), *The State of Population* (New York: Basil Blackwell, 1986), pp. 156–187.

30. William Divale, "Systemic Population Control in the Middle and Upper Paleolithic: Inferences Based on Contemporary Hunters and Gatherers," *World Archaeology*, 4 (1972), fig. 11, p. 230; and John Whiting, "Effects of Climate on Certain Cultural Practices," in Ward Goodenough (ed.), *Explorations in Cultural Anthropology: Essays in Honor of George Peter Murdock* (New York: McGraw-Hill, 1964), table 9, pp. 528–533.

31. Don Dumond, "The Limitations of Human Population: A Natural History," *Science*, 187 (Feb. 28, 1975), p. 715.

32. Kolata, op. cit.

33. See, for example, John Garvan, *The Negritos of the Philippines* (Vienna: Ferdinand Berger, 1964), p. 27; or Edwin Loeb, *Sumatra: Its History and People* (Vienna: Institut für Volkerkunde, 1935), p. 283, on the Kubu.

34. Only one of the seventeen nonnomadic hunting and gathering societies in Murdock's data set depended on hunting and gathering for more than three-quarters of its subsistence, whereas three-quarters of the 150 nomadic hunting and gathering societies were in this category. The one exception among the nonnomadic societies (the Nomlaki) was located in the Sacramento Valley of northern California, a territory as favorable for a hunting and gathering people as any in the world (see Baumhoff, pp. 205–231).

35. Colin Turnbull, "The Mbuti Pygmies of the Congo," in James Gibbs (ed.), *Peoples of Africa* (New York: Holt, 1965), pp. 286–287.

36. James Woodburn, "Ecology, Nomadic Movement and the Composition of the Local

Group among Hunters and Gatherers: An East African Example and Its Implications," in Peter J. Ucko, Ruth Tringham, and G. W. Dimbleby (eds.), *Man, Settlement and Urbanism* (London: Duckworth, 1972), p. 201ff.

37. Lorna Marshall, "The !Kung Bushmen of the Kalahari Desert," in James Gibbs (ed.), *Peoples of Africa* (New York: Holt, 1965), pp. 243–278.

38. Richard B. Lee, "Work Effort, Group Structure and Land-Use in Contemporary Hunter-Gatherers," in Ucko et al., pp. 181–184.

39. A. R. Radcliffe-Brown, "The Social Organization of Australian Tribes," *Oceania,* 1 (1930), pp. 44–46.

40. Elkin, p. 56 (Doubleday Anchor edition).

41. Service, *The Hunters,* p. 32ff. For some exceptions, see Colin Turnbull, *Wayward Servants, The Two Worlds of the African Pygmies* (Garden City, N.Y.: Natural History Press, 1965), pp. 109–112.

42. George Peter Murdock, *Social Structure* (New York: Free Press, 1949), chap. 1.

43. See, for example, Elkin, p. 50; Ivor Evans, *The Negritos of Malaya* (London: Cambridge, 1937), p. 254; and Garvan, p. 82.

44. Service, *The Hunters,* p. 42.

45. David Aberle, "Matrilineal Descent in Cross-Cultural Perspective," in D. Schneider and K. Gough (eds.), *Matrilineal Kinship* (Berkeley: University of California Press, 1961), p. 677; or Burton Pasternak, *Introduction to Kinship and Social Organization* (Englewood Cliffs, N.J.: Prentice-Hall, 1976), pp. 111–112.

46. Elman Service, *Primitive Social Organization: An Evolutionary Perspective* (New York: Random House, 1962), chap. 3, especially p. 61.

47. See, for example, Elkin, pp. 134–137.

48. Lorna Marshall, in Gibbs, pp. 257–258. Quoted by permission of Holt, Rinehart and Winston, Inc. See also Charles Hose and William McDougall, *The Pagan Tribes of Borneo* (London: Macmillan, 1912), pp. 190–191; Holmberg, p. 11; or Loeb, p. 300.

49. See, for example, Walter Goldschmidt, *Nomlaki Ethnography, University of California Publications in American Archaeology and Ethnology,* 42 (Berkeley, 1951), pp. 333–335 and 417–428.

50. See, for example, Loeb, p. 294, or Holmberg, pp. 30 and 91.

51. Colin Turnbull, pp. 287 and 297; Frederick McCarthy and Margaret McArthur, "The Food Quest and the Time Factor in Aboriginal Economic Life," in Charles Mountford (ed.), *Records of the American-Australian Expedition to Arnhem Land* (Melbourne: Melbourne University Press, 1960), pp. 190–191; Kenneth MacLeish, "The Tasadays: Stone Age Cavemen of Mindanao," *National Geographic,* 142 (Aug. 1972), pp. 243–245; Richard B. Lee, "What Hunters Do for a Living, or How to Make Out on Scarce Resources," in Lee and DeVore, pp. 36–37.

52. See Marshall Sahlins, "Notes on the Original Affluent Society," in Lee and DeVore, pp. 85–89.

53. Goldschmidt, p. 417. See also Asen Balicki, "The Netsilik Eskimos: Adaptive Responses," and the comments of Lorna Marshall and Colin Turnbull, in Lee and DeVore, pp. 78–82, 94, and 341, for challenges to the effort to portray life in hunting and gathering societies as idyllic and trouble-free.

54. Lee and DeVore, op. cit.

55. See, for example, Lee, p. 40.

56. Coon, *The Hunting Peoples,* p. 176.

57. In the hunting and gathering societies in Murdock's data set, hunting was entirely a male activity in 96 percent of the cases and predominantly a male activity in the rest. On the other hand, gathering was wholly or largely a female activity in 87 percent of the societies and predominantly a male activity in only 4 percent (in the remainder the activity was shared by both sexes).

58. Of the hunting and gathering societies in Murdock's data set, 53 percent defined this as a male responsibility, 26 percent as a female responsibility, and 21 percent as appropriate to both sexes.

59. I. Schapera, *Government and Politics in Tribal Societies* (London: Watts, 1956), p. 93. See also Holmberg's description of the Siriono headman quoted on p. 107 of this volume, and Hose and McDougall, p. 190, on the Punan shaman. Other specialists, much less common, may include part-time workers in certain arts and crafts and occasionally an assistant to the headman. Such individuals are most likely to be found in settled communities that depend less than totally on hunting and gathering or in those with especially favorable environments.

See, for example, Goldschmidt, pp. 331–332, and Elkin, p. 254ff.

60. See, for example, Colin Turnbull, pp. 287–288; Evans, pp. 57 and 112–113; Garvan, p. 66; or Hose and McDougall, p. 191. Turnbull warns, however, that many scholars exaggerate the dependence of the Pygmies on the neighboring horticultural villagers. He maintains that they turn to the villagers only for luxuries and diversion. See *Wayward Servants,* pp. 33–37.

61. Gerhard Lenski, *Power and Privilege* (New York: McGraw-Hill, 1966), pp. 95–96.

62. Occasionally there might be a second official. See, for example, Kaj Birket-Smith, *The Eskimos,* rev. ed. (London: Methuen, 1959), p. 145; Goldschmidt, pp. 324–325; and Frank Speck, *Penobscot Man* (Philadelphia: University of Pennsylvania Press, 1940), pp. 239–240.

63. Holmberg, pp. 59–60. Quoted by permission of the Smithsonian Institution Press. Following an older usage, Holmberg referred to the leaders of Siriono bands as "chiefs." In current usage, such persons are usually referred to as "headmen," and the term "chief" is reserved for the leaders of multicommunity societies. For this reason, the term "headman" has been substituted.

64. See, for example, John Cooper, "The Ona," in Julian Steward (ed.), *Handbook of South American Indians,* Smithsonian Institution, Bureau of American Ethnology, Bulletin 143 (Washington, D.C., 1946), vol. 1, p. 117; A. R. Radcliffe-Brown, *The Andaman Islanders* (Glencoe, Ill.: Free Press, 1948), p. 47; Hose and McDougall, p. 182, on the Punan of Borneo; Speck, p. 239, on the Penobscot of Maine; I. Schapera, *The Khoisan Peoples of South Africa* (London: Routledge, 1930), p. 151; and Roland Dixon, "The Northern Maidu," in Carleton S. Coon (ed.), *A Reader in General Anthropology* (New York: Holt, 1948), p. 272.

65. I. Schapera, *Government and Politics,* p. 117. Quoted by permission of C. A. Watts & Co., Ltd. See also A. H. Gayton, *Yokuts-Mono Chiefs and Shamans,* University of California Publications in American Archaeology and Ethnology, 24 (Berkeley, 1930), pp. 374–376.

66. See, for example, Colin Turnbull, *Wayward Servants,* chaps. 11 and 12; or *The Forest People* (New York: Simon & Schuster, 1961), on the Mbuti Pygmies. As he indicates, the office of headman is sometimes found among these people, but it has been more or less forced on them by the Bantu villagers and is of little significance except in their contacts with these villagers.

67. See, for example, Schapera, *Government and Politics,* p. 193, or Turnbull, *Wayward Servants,* pp. 100–109.

68. See John Honigmann, *The Kaska Indians: An Ethnographic Reconstruction,* Yale University Publications in Anthropology, 51 (1954), pp. 90–92 and 96–97; Radcliffe-Brown, *The Andaman Islanders,* pp. 48–52; and Schapera, *The Khoisan Peoples,* pp. 151–155.

69. Schapera, *The Khoisan Peoples,* p. 152.

70. Radcliffe-Brown, *The Andaman Islanders,* p. 50.

71. Schapera, *The Khoisan Peoples,* p. 152.

72. See, for example, Evans, p. 21; Marshall, "!Kung Bushmen," p. 248; or Radcliffe-Brown, *The Andaman Islanders,* p. 29. For an exception, see Birket-Smith, pp. 145–146. For intermediate cases, see Honigmann, pp. 84, 88, and 96; Elkin, p. 45; and H. Ling Roth, *The Aborigines of Tasmania* (London: Kegan Paul, Trench, Trubner, 1890), p. 71.

73. Sometimes certain trees become the private property of an individual who stakes a special claim to them, but this is uncommon and the number of trees involved is generally small. See, for example, Radcliffe-Brown, *The Andaman Islanders,* p. 41, or Goldschmidt, p. 333.

74. See, for example, McCarthy and McArthur, "The Food Quest and the Time Factor in Aboriginal Economic Life," pp. 179–180; Schapera, *The Khoisan Peoples,* pp. 100–101; Radcliffe-Brown, *The Andaman Islanders,* p. 43; Hose and McDougall, p. 187; or Speck, p. 47.

75. Radcliffe-Brown, *The Andaman Islanders,* pp. 44–48.

76. See, for example, Goldschmidt, pp. 324–326.

77. Among the sample of hunting and gathering societies in Murdock's data set, 53 percent had provision for the hereditary transmission of the office, usually to a son of the previous headman.

78. William D. Davis, *Societal Complexity and the Sources of Primitive Man's Conception of the Supernatural* (Ph.D. dissertation, University of

North Carolina, Chapel Hill, 1971), chap. 5. Davis reports such beliefs in all but one of the eleven hunting and gathering societies he studied. See also Service, *The Hunters,* pp. 68–70.

79. For descriptions of shamans and their practices, see Evans, chaps. 19–20; Coon, *The Hunting Peoples,* chap. 16; Honigmann, pp. 104–108; Schapera, *The Khoisan Peoples,* pp. 195–201; Radcliffe-Brown, *The Andaman Islanders,* pp. 175–179; Elkin, chap. 11; or Gayton, pp. 392–398.

80. See, for example, Dixon, p. 282.

81. Ibid., p. 272.

82. Jacob Baegert, S. J., "Account of the Aboriginal Inhabitants of the California Peninsula," in Coon (ed.), *A Reader in General Anthropology,* p. 79. See also Radcliffe-Brown, *The Andaman Islanders,* p. 177.

83. See, for example, Elkin, chap. 7; Marshall, "!Kung Bushmen," pp. 264–267; Turnbull, "The Mbuti Pygmies," pp. 306–307; or Coon, *The Hunting Peoples,* chap. 14.

84. Herbert Barry III, Irving L. Child, and Margaret K. Bacon, "Relation of Child Training to Subsistence Economy," *American Anthropologist,* 61 (1959), p. 263. See also Michael R. Welch, "Subsistence Economy and Sociological Patterns: An Examination of Selected Aspects of Child Training Processes in Preindustrial Societies" (Ph.D. dissertation, University of North Carolina, Chapel Hill, 1980).

85. Some of the best evidence of religious motivation comes from Australia (see Elkin, pp. 191–192, or 232–234). For an example of art employed as an instrument of sympathetic magic, see Evans, p. 130ff.

86. For example see Keith A. Roberts, *Religion in Sociological Perspective* (Homewood, Ill.: Dorsey Press, 1984), pp. 67–72.

87. Turnbull, "The Mbuti Pygmies," pp. 308–312, *The Forest People,* chap. 4, and *Wayward Servants,* pp. 259–267.

88. See, for example, Hose and McDougall, p. 192, and Speck, p. 270ff.

89. Turnbull, *The Forest People,* p. 135.

90. This definition is based on Hoebel, *Anthropology,* p. 572; and Elkin, *The Australian Aborigines,* p. 25.

91. Examples are provided by the Punan of Borneo (Hose and McDougall, p. 183) and the Mbuti Pygmies of Africa (Turnbull, *Wayward Servants,* pp. 100–109).

92. Schapera, *The Khoisan Peoples,* p. 76. Quoted by permission of Routledge & Kegan Paul, Ltd.

93. See, for example, Goldschmidt, p. 324.

94. For similar comparisons, see Grahame Clark, *The Stone Age Hunters,* chap. 4; and Pfeiffer, *The Emergence of Man.*

95. See, for example, Clark and Piggott, *Prehistoric Societies,* p. 130ff; or Hole and Heizer, *An Introduction to Prehistoric Archeology* (New York: Holt, 1965), pp. 225–226.

96. See "Kalahari Conservatives," *Science News,* 140 (Dec. 14, 1991), p. 398.

97. Orlando Lizama, "Death of Woman Marked Tribe's End: First Seen by Magellan," *Washington Post,* Aug. 17, 1975.

98. Marshall, p. 273.

99. Kolata, p. 932.

Chapter 6

1. Robert J. Wenke, *Patterns in Prehistory: Humankind's First Three Million Years* (New York: Oxford University Press, 1990), chap. 6.

2. Ibid., pp. 261–269; for example, see Marvin Harris, *Cannibals and Kings: The Origins of Cultures* (New York: Vintage Books, 1978); Brian Hayden, "Research and Development in the Stone Age: Technological Transitions among Hunters-Gatherers," *Current Anthropology,* 22 (1981), pp. 519–548; Mark Cohen, *The Food Crisis in Prehistory* (New Haven: Yale University Press, 1977).

3. H. E. Wright, "The Environmental Setting for Plant Domestication in the Near East," *Science,* 194 (1976), pp. 385–389; cited in Wenke, p. 235.

4. Wenke, chap. 6; John Wilford, "The Seeds of History: A Find in Mexico," *New York Times,* May 9, 1997, "Squash Seeds Show Andean Cultivation is 10,000 Years Old, Twice as Old as Thought," *New York Times,* June 29, 2007; and Tom D. Dillehay, Jack Rossen, Thomas C. Andres, and David E. Williams, "Preceramic Adoption of Peanut, Squash, and Cotton in Northern Peru," *Science,* 316 (June 29, 2007), pp. 1890–1893.

5. Kent Flannery, "The Origins of Agriculture," *Annual Review of Anthropology,* 2 (1973), pp. 271–310, p. 307; cited in Wenke, p. 234; Jared Diamond, *Guns, Germs, and Steel* (New York: Norton, 1997), chap. 7.

6. Wenke, chap. 6.

7. Johan Goudsblom, *Fire and Civilization* (New York: Penguin, 1992), pp. 28–33.

8. See Bernadette Arnaud, "First Farmers," *Archaeology,* Nov./Dec. 2000, pp. 56–59, on recent discoveries in northern Syria dating back to 9600 B.C. For earlier work, see Robert Braidwood and Bruce Howe, "Southwestern Asia beyond the Lands of the Mediterranean Littoral," in Robert Braidwood and Gordon Willey (eds.), *Courses toward Urban Life: Archeological Considerations of Some Cultural Alternatives* (Chicago: Aldine, 1962), pp. 137, 152–153, and 346; James Mellaart, *Earliest Civilizations of the Near East* (London: Thames and Hudson, 1965), pp. 12, 32–38, 47–50, and 81; or Barbara Bender, *Farming in Prehistory* (London: John Baker, 1975), chap. 6; Wenke, pp. 246–249.

9. Braidwood and Howe, p. 140; Mellaart, chap. 3ff.; V. Gordon Childe, "The New Stone Age," in Harry Shapiro (ed.), *Man, Culture, and Society* (New York: Oxford Galaxy, 1960), p. 103; E. Cecil Curwen and Gudmund Hatt, *Plough and Pasture: The Early History of Farming* (New York: Collier Books, 1961), p. 33.

10. Current thinking is that plant cultivation emerged independently in five clusters of sites forming an arc from the South Levant (Israel), through Syria and Iraq, to the Zagros Mountains in Iran around 12,000 years ago, see George Wilcox, "The Roots of Cultivation in Southwestern Asia," *Science,* 341 (July 5, 2013), pp. 39–40, and Simone Riehl, Mohsen Zeidi, and Nicholas J. Conard, "Emergence of Agriculture in the Foothills of the Zagros Mountains of Iran," *Science,* 341 (July 5, 2013), pp. 65–67. See also, Jacquetta Hawkes, *Prehistory: UNESCO History of Mankind,* vol. 1, part 1 (New York: Mentor Books, 1965), pp. 442–452; Mellaart, p. 42; Childe, "The New Stone Age," p. 107.

11. Childe, "The New Stone Age," pp. 100–101.

12. See, for example, Farmer, pp. 204–205; or Curwen and Hatt, p. 68 and chap. 16.

13. V. Gordon Childe, *What Happened in History,* rev. ed. (Baltimore: Penguin, 1964), pp. 64–65.

14. Mellaart, pp. 50–51, or Jean Perrot, "Palestine-Syria-Cilicia," in Braidwood and Willey, pp. 156–157.

15. Hawkes, pp. 384–395; Childe, "The New Stone Age," pp. 104–105; or Perrot, pp. 154–155.

16. Hawkes, pp. 395–401; and Mellaart, pp. 40–42.

17. Arnaud, p. 56.

18. Childe, "The New Stone Age," p. 105. Elsewhere Childe speaks of twenty-five to thirty-five households as "a not uncommon number" in central Europe and southern Russia. See *What Happened in History,* p. 66.

19. Mellaart, p. 36; or Hawkes, p. 310.

20. Wenke, p. 326.

21. Mellaart, pp. 81–101; W. K. Stevens, "Prehistoric Society: A New Picture Emerges," *New York Times,* Dec. 16, 1986; Wenke, p. 326.

22. See, for example, Childe, "The New Stone Age," p. 106, or *What Happened in History,* pp. 67–68. See also Braidwood and Howe, p. 138.

23. Mellaart, p. 36. See also p. 84 for his views on Çatal Hüyük.

24. Childe, "The New Stone Age," p. 106; Wenke, p. 327.

25. Denise Schmandt-Bessert, "The Earliest Precursor of Writing," *Scientific American,* 238 (Jan. 1978), pp. 50–59.

26. Mellaart, pp. 43–44.

27. See Childe, *What Happened in History,* p. 67.

28. Childe, "The New Stone Age," p. 106, *What Happened in History,* p. 67; and Wenke, chap. 6.

29. For a good review of these developments, see Hawkes, pp. 401–410 and 414–417; or V. Gordon Childe, *Man Makes Himself* (New York: Mentor, 1953), pp. 76–80.

30. Childe, "The New Stone Age," p. 107, or *What Happened in History,* p. 74; and Wenke, pp. 360–361.

31. Karl Heider, *The Dugum Dani: A Papuan Culture in the Highlands of West New Guinea* (New York: Wenner-Gren Foundation, 1970). See also the film *Dead Birds,* based on the same society.

32. Childe, "The New Stone Age," p. 107.

33. For the ethnographic evidence, see table 4.2, p. 87.

34. A careful comparison of societies in the two eras suggests that modern simple horticulturalists may be a bit less advanced than their prehistoric predecessors. For example, 40 percent of those in Murdock's sample did not make pottery and 60 percent did not engage in weaving, both common practices in simple horticultural societies of prehistoric times.

35. See Kwang-chih Chang, *The Archaeology of Ancient China* (New Haven: Yale University Press, 1963), pp. 130–131. See also Curwen and Hatt, pp. 16–18, on truths contained in ancient traditions.

36. The quotations in this paragraph are all from Chang, pp. 131–133, and are used by permission of Yale University Press.

37. Our calculation is based on Murdock's data set.

38. See, for example, Rae Lesser Blumberg, "Mothers of Invention? The Myth-Breaking History and Planetary Promise of Women's Key Roles in Subsistence Technology," in Yair Amicai-Hamburger (ed.), *Technology and Psychological Well-Being*, (Cambridge: Cambridge University Press, 2009), pp. 227–259.

39. See, for example, Julian Steward and Louis Faron, *Native Peoples of South America* (New York: McGraw-Hill, 1959), p. 300, with reference to villagers who occupied most of the northern half of South America, that "kinship was the basis of society throughout most of this area." Many similar statements could be cited.

40. See E. Adamson Hoebel, *Anthropology*, 3d ed. (New York: McGraw-Hill, 1966), pp. 374–376, for a good, brief summary of these functions.

41. For similar findings based on Murdock's earlier sample of 565 societies, see David Aberle, "Matrilineal Descent in Cross-cultural Perspective," in David Schneider and Kathleen Gough (eds.), *Matrilineal Kinship* (Berkeley: University of California Press, 1961), table 17.4, p. 677.

42. The first interpretation is suggested by Aberle, p. 725; he states that "in general, matriliny is associated with horticulture, in the absence of major activities carried on and coordinated by males." See also Janet Saltzman Chafetz, *Sex and Advantage* (Totowa, N.J.: Rowman & Allenheld, 1984), pp. 42–43, and Rae Lesser Blumberg, "Extending Lenski's Schema to Hold Up Both Halves of the Sky—A Theory-Guided Way of Conceptualizing Agrarian Societies that Illuminates a Puzzle about Gender Stratification," *Sociological Theory* 22 (June 2004) pp. 278–291. Blumberg argues that kinship variables can often serve as "proxies for female economic power" (p. 285). The latter interpretation is suggested by Harris, *Cannibals and Kings*, chap. 6; and Charles S. Green, personal communication.

43. This dual role seems to have been quite common in South America. See Julian Steward and Louis Faron, *Native Peoples of South America* (New York: McGraw-Hill, 1959), p. 301, on the Indians of eastern Brazil and the Amazon Basin; or Julian Steward, "The Tribes of the Montaña and Bolivian East Andes," in Julian Steward (ed.), *Handbook of South American Indians*, Smithsonian Institution, Bureau of American Ethnology, Bulletin 143 (Washington, 1948), vol. III, p. 528. For a slightly different pattern in North America, see Irving Goldman, "The Zuni Indians of New Mexico," in Margaret Mead (ed.), *Cooperation and Competition among Primitive Peoples*, rev. ed. (Boston: Beacon Press, 1961), p. 313.

44. Robert Lowie, "Social and Political Organization," in Steward, *Handbook*, vol. V, p. 345. For examples of this, see Steward, *Handbook*, vol. III, pp. 85, 355, 419, and 478. See also Steward and Faron, p. 244.

45. See, for example, Alfred Métraux, *Native Tribes of Eastern Bolivia and Western Matto Grosso*, Smithsonian Institution, Bureau of American Ethnology, Bulletin 134 (Washington, 1942), p. 39, on the Araona; or Leopold Pospisil, "Kaupauku Papuan Political Structure," in Vern F. Ray (ed.), *Systems of Political Control and Bureaucracy in Human Societies*, Proceedings of the 1958 Meetings of the American Ethnological Society (Seattle), p. 18.

46. For a more detailed discussion of these bases of status, see Gerhard Lenski, *Power and Privilege* (Chapel Hill: University of North Carolina Press, 1984, first published 1966), pp. 126–131.

47. See Steward and Faron, pp. 302–303, on the former, and pp. 213–214, 243, and 248–249, on the latter.

48. Marvin Harris, *Cows, Pigs, Wars, and Witches: The Riddles of Culture* (New York: Random House, 1974), pp. 75–80, and Blumberg, "Extending Lenski's Schema," pp. 282–284.

49. William Divale, "Systemic Population Control in the Middle and Upper Paleolithic," *World Archaeology,* 4 (1972), fig. 9, p. 228.

50. Data provided by Leo Simmons, *The Role of the Aged in Primitive Society* (New Haven: Yale University Press, 1945), show that scalp taking or headhunting was a frequent practice in only one of five hunting and gathering societies but in thirteen of fourteen horticultural societies.

51. Alfred Métraux, "Warfare-Cannibalism-Trophies," in Steward, *Handbook,* vol. V, pp. 400–401. Quoted by permission of the Bureau of American Ethnology.

52. Colin Renfrew, *Before Civilization* (Cambridge: Cambridge University Press, 1979), p. 167; and Renfrew and Bahn, p. 296.

53. R. J. Forbes, *Studies in Ancient Technology,* 2d ed. (Leiden, Netherlands: Brill, 1972), vol. 9, p. 30; or Leslie Aitchison, *A History of Metals* (London: MacDonald, 1960), vol. 1, p. 21.

54. Forbes, vol. 9, pp. 32–34; or Aitchison, p. 40.

55. Aitchison, p. 40; Forbes, vol. 8, p. 26; or Ronald Wallace, *Those Who Vanished* (Homewood, Ill.: Dorsey, 1983), pp. 294–295.

56. Childe, *Man Makes Himself,* p. 99.

57. V. Gordon Childe, *The Bronze Age* (London: Cambridge, 1930), p. 11.

58. See, for example, Childe, *New Light,* p. 116. There is still some uncertainty about this point.

59. William Watson, *The Chinese Exhibition* (a guide to the exhibition of archaeological finds of the People's Republic of China, exhibited in Toronto, 1974), p. 14.

60. Renfrew and Bahn, p. 296.

61. Some bronze seems to have been manufactured accidentally a few centuries earlier as a result of using copper derived from ores containing tin, but the deliberate and conscious alloying of metals did not begin in the Middle East until after 3000 B.C. See Forbes, vol. 9, pp. 151–152. Recent research by scholars at the University of Pennsylvania suggests that the invention of bronze may have occurred in Thailand prior to 3600 B.C., which would explain why bronze was an integral part of advanced horticultural societies in China, but not in the Middle East.

62. William Watson, *China: Before the Han Dynasty* (New York: Praeger, 1961), p. 57.

63. Te-k'un Cheng, *Archaeology in China: Shang China* (Cambridge, England: Heffer, 1960), pp. 206–207.

64. Shang kings, for example, mounted "many military expeditions with an army of between 3,000 and 5,000 men." Cheng, p. 210; and Cho-yun Hsu, *Ancient China in Transition* (Stanford, Calif.: Stanford University Press, 1965), p. 67.

65. See note 58 above.

66. Cheng, pp. 200–206.

67. Cheng, pp. 200–215 and 248. For a more detailed picture of the system of stratification in the Chou era, see Hsu, *Ancient China in Transition.* In reading this book one must keep in mind that the Chan Kuo period, the "period of the warring states," is included, and by then, north-central China seems to have reached the agrarian level of development.

68. Watson, *China: Before the Han Dynasty,* p. 141, and Chang, p. 195ff.

69. Aitchison, p. 97.

70. Hsu, pp. 3–7 and chap. 4.

71. Chang, p. 150.

72. Watson, *China: Before the Han Dynasty,* p. 106. See also Hsu, p. 15ff., on the interrelations between religion and politics in Chou China.

73. Chang, pp. 150 and 159.

74. Ibid., p. 171.

75. Sonia Cole, *The Prehistory of East Africa* (New York: Mentor, 1965), pp. 46 and 299–301.

76. Meyer Fortes, in Meyer Fortes and E. E. Pritchard (eds.), *African Political Systems* (London: Oxford, 1940) p. 5.

77. In one study of twenty-two African horticultural societies, a correlation of 0.67 (Kendall's tau) was found between level of political development and level of social inequality (see Lenski, p. 163). See also Basil Davidson with F. K. Buah, *A History of West Africa: To the Nineteenth Century* (Garden City, N.Y.: Doubleday Anchor, 1966), p. 174.

78. See Lucy Mair, *Primitive Government* (Baltimore: Penguin, 1962), especially chap. 4.

The discussion that follows is based largely on her work. See also Lenski, chaps. 6 and 7; Morton Fried, *The Evolution of Political Society* (New York: Random House, 1967); and Elman Service, *Origins of the State and Civilizations: The Process of Cultural Evolution* (New York: Norton, 1975).

79. Estimated from the map in Davidson, p. 68.

80. I. Schapera, *Government and Politics in Tribal Societies* (London: Watts, 1956), p. 169. See also the Swazi proverb that "nobles are the chief's murderers."

81. See, for example, Davidson, chap. 14.

82. See, for example, George Peter Murdock, *Africa: Its Peoples and Their Culture History* (New York: McGraw-Hill, 1959), p. 37.

83. See, for example, P. C. Lloyd, "The Yoruba of Nigeria," in James Gibbs (ed.), *Peoples of Africa* (New York: Holt, 1965), pp. 554–556.

84. For an example of a multicommunity society, see P. R. T. Gurdon, *The Khasis* (London: Macmillan, 1914). This author reports that these people were divided into fifteen small states averaging 15,000 in population and controlling about 400 square miles apiece (pp. 1 and 66).

85. Lenski, pp. 160–162. See also Davidson, pp. 76–77.

86. Remy Chauvin, *The World of Ants: A Science Fiction Universe* (New York: Hill and Wang, 1970); Erich Hoyt, *The Earth Dwellers: Advenures in the Land of Ants* (New York: Simon and Schuster, 1996); Caryl P. Haskins, *Of Ants and Men* (London: Allen and Unwin, 1943); Edward O. Wilson, *Sociobiology: The New Synthesis* (Cambridge, Mass.: Harvard University Press, 1975); and George Oster and Edward O. Wilson, *Caste and Ecology in the Social Insects* (Princeton, N.J.: Princeton University Press, 1978).

87. Paul Ricon, "Date Limit Set on First Americans," *BBC Science,* Aug. 5, 2003; John Noble Wilford, "New Answers to an Old Question: Who Got Here First?" *New York Times,* Nov. 9, 1999; Brian Fagan, *The Journey from Eden: The Peopling of Our World* (New York: Thames and Hudson, 1990), chap. 15.

88. This view is reinforced by archaeological finds revealing the progressive evolution of maize, beans, and other crops from wild, uncultivated forms to the cultivated forms found today. See Marvin Harris, *People, Culture, Nature,* 3d ed. (New York: Harper & Row, 1980), p. 165; Wallace, p. 218ff; or Wenke, pp. 251–259.

89. For a valuable survey of these developments, see Harris, chap. 10; for an extended survey of the three most highly developed cultures of the New World, the Aztecs, Mayas, and Incas, see Victor von Hagen, *The Ancient Sun Kingdoms of the Americas* (Cleveland: World, 1961). See also William Sanders and David Webster, "The Mesoamerican Urban Tradition," *American Anthropologist,* 90 (1988), pp. 521–546; and Norman Hammond, *Ancient Maya Civilization* (New Brunswick, N.J.: Rutgers University Press, 1982).

90. Renfrew and Bahn, pp. 300–301.

91. See Stephen Williams, *Fantastic Archaeology: The Wild Side of North American Prehistory* (Philadelphia: University of Pennsylvania Press, 1991), but for an alternative view, see Stephen C. Jett, "Precolumbian Transoceanic Contact," in Jesse D. Jennings (ed.), *Ancient North Americans* (San Francisco: W. H. Freeman, 1983), pp. 593–650.

92. Marvin Harris, *The Rise of Anthropological Theory* (New York: Crowell, 1968), p. 4.

93. Wenke, pp. 279, 477, 519–520.

94. Harris, p. 4. Emphasis added.

95. See, for example, the writings of Count Joseph A. deGobineau or Houston Stewart Chamberlain.

96. See, for example, Charles Singer, "Epilogue: East and West," in Charles Singer (ed.), *A History of Technology* (Oxford: Clarendon Press, 1956), vol. II, pp. 754–772; or William H. McNeill, *The Rise of the West* (Chicago: University of Chicago Press, 1963), parts I and II.

97. Renfrew and Bahn, p. 305.

98. Robert W. Steel, "Africa: Natural Resources," in *Encyclopaedia Britannica,* vol. 1, p. 258; Philip L. Wagner, "Tropical Agriculture," *Encylopaedia Britannica,* vol. 22, p. 255; Andrew Kamark, "The Resources of Tropical Africa," *Daedalus,* III (Spring 1982), p. 159; Andrew Kamark, *The Tropics and Economic Development* (Baltimore: Johns Hopkins University Press, 1976); and Frederic Pryor, "The Invention of the

Plow," *Comparative Studies in Society and History,* 27 (1985), pp. 727–743.

99. William H. McNeill, *Plagues and Peoples* (Garden City, N.Y.: Doubleday Anchor, 1976); Kamark, "Resources," pp. 159–160; Matt Clark, "Blight of the Tropics," *Newsweek,* June 26, 1978, pp. 83–84; Paul Harrison, *Inside the Third World* (Harmondsworth, England: Penguin, 1982), chap. 16; and Erik Eckholm, "River Blindness," *New York Times Magazine,* Jan. 8, 1989, p. 20ff.

Chapter 7

1. V. Gordon Childe, *What Happened in History* (Baltimore: Penguin, 1964), p. 77.
2. Ibid., chap. 4.
3. This paragraph and the one that follows are based on B. H. Farmer, "Agriculture: Comparative Technology," in *International Encyclopedia of the Social Sciences* (New York: Macmillan and Free Press, 1968), vol. 1, pp. 204–205.
4. Robert J. Wenke, *Patterns in Prehistory: Humankind's First Three Million Years* (New York: Oxford University Press, 1990), p. 373.
5. See Gudmund Hatt, "Farming of Non-European Peoples," in E. Cecil Curwen and Gudmund Hatt, *Plough and Pasture: The Early History of Farming* (New York: Collier Books, 1961), pp. 217–218.
6. Childe, *What Happened in History,* p. 89.
7. V. Gordon Childe, *Man Makes Himself* (New York: Mentor Books, 1951), p. 100.
8. Farmer, p. 205.
9. E. Cecil Curwen, "Prehistoric Farming of Europe and the Near East," in Curwen and Hatt, pp. 64–65; or C. W. Bishop, "The Origin and Early Diffusion of the Traction Plow," *Antiquity,* 10 (1936), p. 261.
10. Denise Schmandt-Besserat, *Before Writing: From Counting to Cuneiform* (Austin, Tex.: University of Texas Press, 1992), especially pp. 1–34, and pp. 195–199.
11. Wenke, chaps. 13 and 14.
12. Samuel Noah Kramer, *The Sumerians* (Chicago: University of Chicago Press, 1963), p. 123.
13. Childe, *Man Makes Himself,* pp. 143–144.
14. See, for example, Sir Leonard Woolley, *The Beginnings of Civilization, UNESCO History of Mankind,* vol. 1, part 2 (New York: Mentor Books, 1965), pp. 116, 119, 198, and 449ff.
15. Sir Leonard Woolley, *Prehistory* (New York: Harper & Row, 1963), vol. 1, part 2, p. 127.
16. Margaret Murray, *The Splendour That Was Egypt* (London: Sidgwick & Jackson, 1949), p. 174.
17. On Mesopotamia, see Woolley, *Beginnings,* p. 356; or A. Leo Oppenheim, *Ancient Mesopotamia: Portrait of a Dead Civilization* (Chicago: University of Chicago Press, 1964), pp. 84–85. On Egypt, see Ralph Turner, *The Great Cultural Traditions: The Foundations of Civilization* (New York: McGraw-Hill, 1941), vol. 1, p. 187; or George Steindorff and Keith Seele, *When Egypt Ruled the East,* rev. ed. (Chicago: Phoenix Books, 1963), p. 83.
18. Robert Adams, "Factors Influencing the Rise of Civilization in the Alluvium: Illustrated by Mesopotamia," in Carl Kraeling and Robert Adams (eds.), *City Invincible: A Symposium on Urbanization and Cultural Development in the Ancient Near East* (Chicago: University of Chicago Press, 1960), p. 33.
19. Wenke, pp. 338–345.
20. See, for example, Kramer, pp. 88–89; Woolley, p. 125; or Kingsley Davis, "The Origin and Growth of World Urbanism," *American Journal of Sociology,* 60 (1955), p. 431. See also Oppenheim, p. 140, who, though declining to estimate size, reports Nineveh to have been larger than Ur (generally thought to have been over 100,000) and Uruk nearly as large; or Mason Hammond, *The City in the Ancient World* (Cambridge, Mass.: Harvard, 1972).
21. Woolley, *Beginnings,* p. 185ff; or Steindorff and Seele, pp. 89–90.
22. Woolley, *Beginnings,* p. 188. Later armies were even larger.
23. Turner, p. 312.
24. McNeill, p. 68; Turner, pp. 310–311; Steindorff and Seele, chap. 9; Pierre Montet, *Everyday Life in Egypt: In the Days of Ramesses the Great,* trans. A. R. Maxwell-Hyslop and Margaret Drower (London: E. Arnold, 1958), chap. 10; Oppenheim, pp. 70ff., 230ff., and 276–277.
25. Oppenheim, p. 276. As one writer reports, "Sumerian bureaucracy has left us a staggering

number of texts; we are unable to venture a guess as to how many tablets beyond the far more than 100,000 now in museums may be buried in southern Mesopotamia."

26. Childe, *Man Makes Himself,* pp. 148–149, or Childe, *What Happened in History,* p. 144.

27. See especially Kramer, p. 231, or Samuel Noah Kramer, *It Happened at Sumer* (Garden City, N.Y.: Doubleday, 1959), p. 3.

28. See Turner, p. 263, or Childe, *What Happened in History,* p. 118.

29. Childe, *What Happened in History,* pp. 118–119.

30. Classic statements on this can be found in Georg Simmel, *The Philosophy of Money* (New York: Routledge, 2011, first published in 1907); and Max Weber, Gunter Roth, and Claus Wittich (eds.), *Economy and Society: An Outline of Interpretive Sociology* (Berkeley: University of California Press, 1978), chap. II, vol. 1.

31. See Turner's excellent treatment of this topic, pp. 317–323.

32. Adolf Erman, *Life in Ancient Egypt,* trans. H. M. Tirard (London: Macmillan, 1894), p. 128.

33. Childe, *Man Makes Himself,* p. 180, quoted by permission of C. A. Watts & Co. See also McNeill, p. 53, or Childe, *What Happened in History,* p. 183ff.

34. Childe, *Man Makes Himself,* p. 181. Elsewhere, Childe adds a third innovation (or a fifth to the total list), the invention of glass in Egypt. See *What Happened in History,* p. 183.

35. See Childe, *Man Makes Himself,* chap. 9, for a classic discussion of this subject. The analysis that follows is heavily indebted to Childe's provocative discussion but varies in some details and emphasis.

36. See Childe, *What Happened in History,* p. 184.

37. For a classic statement of this principle, see Gaetano Mosca, *The Ruling Class,* translated by Hannah Kahn (New York: McGraw-Hill, 1939), p. 53.

38. For a good summary of the early history of iron, see Leslie Aitchison, *A History of Metals* (London: MacDonald, 1960), vol. 1, pp. 97–110. The discussion that follows is based largely on Aitchison.

39. Ibid., p. 113.

40. See, for example, Charles Singer's comparison of the level of technology in the ancient empires of Egypt and Mesopotamia prior to 1000 B.C. and later in Greece and Rome, in "Epilogue: East and West in Retrospect," in Charles Singer (ed.), *A History of Technology* (Oxford: Clarendon Press, 1956), vol. II, pp. 754–755.

41. Ibid., pp. 754–772.

42. This estimate was based on the known boundaries of these societies and on the fact that the Roman Empire, which was much larger and contained a much smaller percentage of uninhabitable land, had a maximum population of only about seventy million. See *The Cambridge Ancient History* (London: Cambridge, 1939), vol. XII, pp. 267–268. It is also noteworthy that in Roman times Egypt had a population of only six to seven million. Even if allowance is made for the greater size of the Egyptian empire in the days of Egypt's independence, it is difficult to imagine a total population much in excess of fifteen million. See Charles Issawi, *Egypt in Revolution: An Economic Analysis* (New York: Oxford, 1963), p. 20.

43. Chung-li Chang, *The Chinese Gentry: Studies on Their Role in Nineteenth-Century Chinese Society* (Seattle: University of Washington Press, 1955), p. 102.

44. On India, see Kingsley Davis, *The Population of India and Pakistan* (Princeton, N.J.: Princeton University Press, 1951), pp. 24–25; on Rome, see *Cambridge Ancient History,* pp. 267–268, or *UNESCO, History of World Population Growth,* p. 15; on Russia, see Blum, p. 278.

45. See, for example, Tertius Chandler and Gerald Fox, *3000 Years of Urban Growth* (New York: Academic Press, 1974).

46. Warren Thompson and David Lewis, *Population Problems,* 5th ed. (New York: McGraw-Hill, 1965), p. 386; O. Andrew Collver, *Birth Rates in Latin America: New Estimates of Historical Trends and Fluctuations* (Berkeley, Calif.: Institute of International Studies, 1965), pp. 26–30; D. V. Glass and D. E. C. Eversley, *Population in History* (Chicago: Aldine, 1965), pp. 467, 532, 555, and 614. One of the lowest rates for an agrarian society prior to the twentieth century was for eighteenth-century Sweden, and it was nearly 36 per 1,000 (Glass and Eversley, p. 532).

47. See, for example, Horace Miner, *St. Denis: A French-Canadian Parish* (Chicago: Phoenix Books, University of Chicago Press, 1963), p. 65; G. G. Coulton, *The Medieval Village* (Cambridge: Cambridge University Press, 1926), p. 322; Manning Nash, *The Golden Road to Modernity: Village Life in Contemporary Burma* (New York: Wiley, 1965), pp. 265–266.

48. See, for example, John Noss, *Man's Religions*, rev. ed. (New York: Macmillan, 1956), pp. 227, 304ff., and 420–421; and *Miner*, pp. 65–66.

49. John Boswell, *The Kindness of Strangers: The Abandonment of Children in Western Europe from Late Antiquity to the Renaissance* (New York: Pantheon, 1989).

50. Harrison Brown, *The Challenge of Man's Future* (New York: Viking Compass, 1956), p. 75.

51. H. Hollingsworth, "A Demographic Study of the British Ducal Families," in Glass and Eversley, tables 2 and 5, pp. 358 and 360.

52. Brown, p. 75.

53. Warren Thompson, *Population Problems*, 3d ed. (New York: McGraw-Hill, 1942), p. 73.

54. M. C. Buer, *Health, Wealth, and Population in the Early Days of the Industrial Revolution, 1760–1815* (London: Routledge, 1926), pp. 77–78. Quoted by permission of Routledge & Kegan Paul, Ltd.

55. D. E. C. Eversley, "Population, Economy, and Society," in Glass and Eversley, p. 52; and William H. McNeill, *Plagues and Peoples* (Garden City, N.Y.: Doubleday Anchor, 1976).

56. Robert S. Gottfried, *The Black Death* (New York: Free Press, 1983), p. xiii.

57. K. F. Helleiner, "The Vital Revolution Reconsidered," in Glass and Eversley, p. 79.

58. Turner, p. 911.

59. F. R. Cowell, *Cicero and the Roman Republic* (London: Penguin, 1956), p. 79. Quoted by permission of Penguin Books.

60. See, for example, Jerome Blum, *Lord and Peasant in Russia from the Ninth to the Nineteenth Century* (Princeton, N.J.: Princeton University Press, 1961), pp. 126 and 394–395, on Russia; or Ralph Linton, *The Tree of Culture* (New York: Vintage Books, 1959), p. 231, on China.

61. S. B. Clough and C. W. Cole, *Economic History of Europe* (Boston: Heath, 1941), p. 25.

62. Ibid. See also Blum, pp. 16 and 126.

63. Marc Bloch, *Feudal Society*, trans. L. A. Manyon (Chicago: University of Chicago Press, 1962), p. 192. See also Robert Heilbroner, *The Making of Economic Society* (Englewood Cliffs, N.J.: Prentice-Hall, 1962), p. 27; H. R. Trevor-Roper, "The Gentry 1540–1640," *The Economic History Review Supplements*, no. 1 (n.d.).

64. Heilbroner, pp. 9–44.

65. A. H. M. Jones, *The Later Roman Empire 284–602: A Social, Economic and Administrative Survey* (Oxford: Blackwell, 1964), vol. 1, p. 465.

66. Gerhard Lenski and Jean Lenski, *Human Societies*, 4th ed. (New York: McGraw-Hill, 1982), table 7.2, p. 190.

67. Blum, pp. 356–357.

68. Gideon Sjoberg, *The Preindustrial City* (New York: Free Press, 1960), p. 215.

69. See, for example, Chung-li Chang, *Income of the Chinese Gentry* (Seattle: University of Washington Press, 1962), pp. 37–51.

70. For a survey of these obligations, see Gerhard Lenski, *Power and Privilege* (New York: McGraw-Hill, 1966), pp. 267–270.

71. Ibid., p. 228.

72. See, for example, Blum, p. 232, or W. H. Moreland, *The Agrarian System of Moslem India* (Allahabad, India: Central Book Depot, n.d.), p. 207.

73. George Sansom, *A History of Japan* (Stanford, Calif.: Stanford Press, 1963), vol. III, p. 29.

74. H. S. Bennett, *Life on the English Manor: A Study of Peasant Conditions, 1150–1400* (London: Cambridge, 1960), pp. 232–236.

75. Robert Darnton, *The Great Cat Massacre and Other Episodes in French Cultural History* (New York: Basic Books, 1984), p. 24. Quoted by permission of the publisher.

76. Ibid., p. 29.

77. Robert K. Douglas, *Society in China* (London: Innes, 1894), p. 354.

78. Blum, pp. 424 and 428, on Russia; and Gunnar Myrdal, *An American Dilemma* (New York: McGraw-Hill, 1964), p. 931, on the American South.

79. See Coulton, pp. 80 and 464–469; Blum, pp. 426–427; G. M. Carstairs, "A Village in

Rajasthan," in M. N. Srnivas (ed.), *India's Villages* (Calcutta: West Bengal Government Press, 1955), pp. 37–38.

80. Bennett, p. 196; Coulton, pp. 190–191, 248–250, and 437–440.

81. G. G. Coulton, *Medieval Panorama* (New York: Meridian Books, 1955), p. 77, or Thompson, p. 708.

82. William Stubbs, *The Constitutional History of England* (Oxford: Clarendon Press, 1891), vol. 1, p. 454n.; Wolfram Eberhard, *A History of China*, 2d ed. (Berkeley: University of California Press, 1960), p. 32; and Yosoburo Takekoshi, *The Economic Aspects of the History of the Civilization of Japan* (New York: Macmillan, 1930), vol. 1, pp. 60–63.

83. See A. E. R. Boak, *A History of Rome to 565 A.D.*, 3d ed. (New York: MacMillan, 1943), p. 127; or Cowell, *Cicero and the Roman Republic,* p. 64. For an example of the application of Cato's principle in medieval Europe, see Bennett, p. 283.

84. See, for example, Bloch, p. 337; or George Homans, *English Villagers of the Thirteenth Century* (Cambridge, Mass.: Harvard, 1942), p. 229.

85. See, for example, Morton Fried, *The Fabric of Chinese Society: Study of the Social Life of a Chinese County Seat* (New York: Praeger, 1953), pp. 104–105; Moreland, pp. 168 and 207; and Bennett, pp. 100–101, 112–113, and 131ff.

86. See, for example, "The Franklins in Thirteenth-Century England" in Homans, pp. 248–250.

87. May McKisack, *The Fourteenth Century* (Oxford: Clarendon Press, 1959), pp. 331–340; Philip Lindsay and Reg Groves, *The Peasants' Revolt, 1381* (London: Hutchinson, n.d.), pp. 30, 34, and 63; Charles Langlois, "History," in Arthur Tilley (ed.), *Medieval France* (London: Cambridge, 1922), pp. 150–151; and Paul Murray Kendall, *The Yorkist Age* (Garden City, N.Y.: Doubleday, 1962), p. 171ff.

88. Sjoberg, p. 83; Lynn White, *Medieval Technology and Social Change* (Oxford: Clarendon Press, 1962), p. 39; Henri Pirenne, *Economic and Social History of Medieval Europe* (New York: Harvest Books, n.d., first published 1933), p. 58; J. C. Russell, *British Medieval Population* (Albuquerque: University of New Mexico Press, 1948), p. 305; Blum, pp. 268 and 281.

89. See Sjoberg, pp. 108–116; or Samuel G. Stoney, *Plantations of the Carolina Low Country* (Charleston: Carolina Art Association, 1938), p. 36.

90. Kendall, p. 157.

91. Jerome Carcopino, *Daily Life in Ancient Rome* (New Haven: Yale University Press, 1940, p. 70).

92. See, for example, Sjoberg, p. 183ff. For an interesting example of the persistence of this pattern into the latter part of the nineteenth century in England, see W. Somerset Maugham, *Cakes and Ale* (New York: Pocket Books, 1944), p. 29.

93. On acquisition by marriage, see Elinor Barber, *The Bourgeoisie in Eighteenth Century France* (Princeton, N.J.: Princeton University Press, 1955), p. 89; or Sansom, vol. III, pp. 128–129. On confiscation, see B. B. Misra, *The Indian Middle Classes* (London: Oxford, 1961), pp. 25–27; Takekoshi, vol. II, p. 251ff.; Kendall, p. 181; or Sir James Ramsay, *A History of the Revenues of the Kings of England: 1066–1399* (Oxford: Clarendon Press, 1925), vol. I. p. 58.

94. Clough and Cole, p. 442.

95. John Lossing Buck, *Secretariat Paper, No. 1, Tenth Conference of the Institute of Pacific Relations* (Stratford on Avon, 1947), reprinted in Irwin T. Sanders et al., *Societies around the World* (New York: Dryden Press, 1953), p. 65. "Cost," in this case, is a good comparative measure of the energy and effort necessary to move goods by these means.

96. Clough and Cole, p. 445. See also R. J. Unstead, *The Rise of Great Britain: 1688–1837* (London: A. & C. Black, 1978), pp. 97, 81, and 92.

97. See, for example, John Nef, *The Conquest of the Material World* (Chicago: University of Chicago Press, 1964), p. 69.

98. Cowell, p. 80. See also William Woodruff, *Impact of Western Man: A Study of Europe's Role in the World Economy* (New York: St. Martin's, 1966), p. 254.

99. Sylvia Thrupp, *The Merchant Class of Medieval London* (Ann Arbor: Ann Arbor Paperbacks, University of Michigan Press, 1962), p. 9.

100. See, for example, Nef, p. 78.

101. Sidney Gamble, *Peking: A Social Survey* (New York: Doran, 1921), pp. 183–185.

102. Thrupp, pp. 19, 30.

103. Ibid., pp. 23 and 29–31; James Westfall Thompson, *Economic and Social History of Europe in the Later Middle Ages, 1300–1530* (New York: Century, 1931), p. 398.

104. Gamble, p. 283.

105. In Asia many were sold into prostitution by their parents. See Gamble, p. 253. Many more, in every part of the world, were ignorant country girls seeking work in the city who were trapped by hired procurers, while still others were driven into prostitution by unemployment and lack of funds. See M. Dorothy George, *London Life in the Eighteenth Century* (London: Kegan Paul, Trench, Trubner, 1925), pp. 112–113.

106. See, for example, Frederick Nussbaum, A History of the Economic Institutions of Modern Europe (New York: Crofts, 1933); Frank Aydelotte, Elizabethan Rogues and Vagabonds (Oxford: Clarendon Press, 1913), p. 4; or A. L. Beier, Masterless Men: The Vagrancy Problem in England 1560–1640 (London: Methuen, 1985), chap. 2.

107. Lenski, pp. 197–198.

108. For the effect of war on the forms of government, see Herbert Spencer, The Principles of Sociology (New York: Appleton, 1897), vol. II, part 5, chap. 17; Pitirim Sorokin, Social and Cultural Dynamics (New York: Bedminster Press, 1962), vol. III, pp. 196–198; or Stanislaw Andrzejewski, Military Organization a*nd Society* (London: Routledge, 1954), pp. 92–95.

109. These figures were calculated from A. E. R. Boak, A History of Rome, using the list of emperors from Harold Mattingly, Roman Imperial Civilization (New York: Doubleday Anchor, 1959), pp. 351–355.

110. For figures on several other societies, see Lenski, p. 235.

111. The discussion of conflict in agrarian societies and the importance of commercialization is based on Lenski, chaps. 8–9; and John H. Kautsky, *The Politics of Aristocratic Empires* (Chapel Hill, N.C.: University of North Carolina Press, 1982), especially chaps. 12 and 13.

112. Wolfram Eberhard, *Conquerors and Rulers: Social Forces in Medieval China* (Leiden, Netherlands: Brill, 1952), p. 52; and Blum, p. 558.

113. Sorokin, vol. II, chap. 10, especially p. 352. Quincy Wright, *A Study of War* (Chicago: University of Chicago Press, 1965), p. 653, reports wars on average in nearly two-thirds of the years from 1500 to 1699 for five European powers and Turkey.

114. See, among others, Lenski, pp. 210–242 and 266–284, for more detailed documentation.

115. Douglas, p. 104.

116. See Max Weber, *The Theory of Social and Economic Organization,* trans. A. M. Henderson and Talcott Parsons (New York: Free Press, 1947), pp. 341–348; and Max Weber, *Wirtschaft und Gesellschaft,* 2d ed. (Tübingen: Mohr, 1925), vol. II, pp. 679–723.

117. Mattingly, p. 137. See also Turner, vol. II, p. 620, or Michael Rostovtzeff, *The Social and Economic History of the Roman Empire,* rev. ed. (Oxford: Clarendon Press, 1957), p. 54.

118. Hans Rosenberg, *Bureaucracy, Aristocracy, and Autocracy: The Prussian Experience 1660–1815* (Cambridge, Mass.: Harvard University Press, 1958), pp. 5–6. Quoted by permission of Harvard University Press.

119. Chang, *The Income of the Chinese Gentry,* Summary Remarks, supplement 2, and chap. 1.

120. On the king's income, see Ramsay, vol. I, pp. 227 and 261. For the income of the nobility, see Sidney Painter, *Studies in the History of the English Feudal Barony* (Baltimore: Johns Hopkins University Press, 1943), pp. 170–171. For the income of field hands, see Bennett, p. 121.

121. Lenski, pp. 219 and 228.

122. See, for example, Albert Lybyer, *The Government of the Ottoman Empire in the Time of Suleiman the Magnificent* (Cambridge, Mass.: Harvard, 1913); or Moreland, *Agrarian System of Moslem India.*

123. F. Pelsaert, *Jahangir's India,* trans. W. H. Moreland and P. Geyl and quoted by Misra, p. 47. Quoted by permission of W. Heffer & Sons, Ltd.

124. Lybyer, pp. 47–58, and 115–117.

125. See, for example, James Westfall Thompson's statement that "the medieval state was a loose agglomeration of territories with rights of property and sovereignty everywhere shading into one another," in *Economic and Social History of*

the Middle Ages (New York: Appleton-Century-Crofts, 1928), p. 699. See also Bloch, especially chaps. 14–24; Blum, chap. 2; or Sidney Painter, *The Rise of the Feudal Monarchies* (Ithaca, N.Y.: Cornell, 1951), and *Studies in the History of the English Feudal Barony.*

126. See Kenneth Scott Latourette, *A History of Christianity* (New York: Harper, 1953), pp. 15–16.

127. See Robert Bellah, "Religious Evolution," *American Sociological Review,* 29 (1964), pp. 367–368.

128. See, for example, Lenski, pp. 7–9. See also Kendall, p. 232ff.

129. Lenski, pp. 257–258.

130. Ibid., pp. 262–266, gives a more detailed treatment of this aspect of religion.

131. J. W. Thompson, *Economic and Social History of the Middle Ages,* p. 684.

132. See, for example, Carlo Levi, *Christ Stopped at Eboli* (New York: Farrar, Straus, 1947), chap. 11ff., for a good description of the role of magic in one agrarian community. On fatalism, see, for example, Edward Banfield, *The Moral Basis of a Backward Society* (New York: Free Press, 1967), pp. 36–37, 41, and 107ff.

133. Sjoberg, p. 146ff.

134. Ibid., p. 155.

135. Ibid., p. 163ff.; Henry Orenstein, Gaon: Conflict and Cohesion in an Indian Village (Princeton, N.J.: Princeton University Press, 1965), pp. 53–57; Kendall, chaps. 11 and 12; L. F. Salzman, English Life in the Middle Ages (London: Oxford University Press, 1927), pp. 254–256.

136. "Family Law," Encyclopaedia Britannica, 15th ed., vol. 19, p. 80.

137. "The Culture of Islam," ibid., vol. 22, p. 33.

138. Bennett, p. 260. For other descriptions of the uses of leisure in agrarian societies, see Margaret Wade Labarge, *A Baronial Household of the Thirteenth Century* (New York: Barnes & Noble, 1966), chap. 10; Bennett, chap. 10; or G. G. Coulton, *Medieval Panorama* (New York: Meridian Books, 1955), chaps. 8 and 44.

139. F. R. Cowell, Everyday Life in Ancient Rome (New York: Putnam, 1961), p. 173.

140. The data in this paragraph are drawn from Lenski, p. 212.

141. For further details on the expendables, see Lenski, pp. 281–284.

142. For example, see Barrington Moore, Jr., *Social Origins of Dictatorship and Democracy: Lord and Peasant in the Making of the Modern World* (New York: Beacon Press, 1966); Theda Skocpol, *States and Social Revolutions: A Comparative Analysis of France, Russia, and China* (New York: Cambridge University Press, 1979); Jack Goldstone, *Revolution and Rebellion in the Early Modern World* (Berkeley: University of California Press, 1991); and Kautsky.

143. See, for example, H. van Werveke, "The Rise of the Towns," in *The Cambridge Economic History of Europe* (London: Cambridge Press, 1963), vol. 3, pp. 34–37; L. Halphen, "Industry and Commerce," in Tilley, pp. 190–192; or Pirenne, *Economic and Social History of Medieval Europe,* pp. 187–206.

144. Amos H. Hawley, *Human Ecology* (New York: Ronald, 1950), pp. 242 and 387.

145. Gerhard Lenski, *Ecological-Evolutionary Theory: Principles and Applications* (Boulder, Colo.: Paradigm, 2005) chap. 8. See also Marvin Chaney, "Ancient Palestinian Peasant Movements and the Formation of Premonarchic Israel," in David Freedman and David Grof (eds.), *Palestine in Transition: The Emergence of Ancient Israel* (Sheffield: Almond Press, 1983), pp. 39–90; Norman K. Gottwald, "Two Models for the Origin of Ancient Israel: Social Revolution or Frontier Development," in E. B. Huffmon et al. (eds.), *The Quest for the Kingdom of God: Studies in Honor of G. E. Mendenhall* (Winona Lake, Ind.: Eisenbrauns, 1983), pp. 5–24; and Volkmar Fritz, "Conquest or Settlement? The Early Iron Age in Palestine," *Biblical Archaeologist,* 50 (June 1987), pp. 84–100.

146. See, for example, Richard Tomasson, *Iceland: The First New Society* (Minneapolis: University of Minnesota Press, 1980), chaps. 1 and 8; and Philip Longworth, *The Cossacks* (New York: Holt, Rinehart, 1970).

147. For the classic statement of the effect of frontier life, see Frederick Jackson Turner, *The Frontier in American History* (New York: Holt, 1920).

148. See James G. Leyburn, *Frontier Folkways* (New Haven, Conn.: Yale Press, 1936).

149. Holly Peters-Golden, "The Aztec," in *Culture Sketches: Case Studies in Cultural Anthropology*, 3d ed. (Boston: McGraw-Hill, 2002).

150. Chung-li Chang, *The Chinese Gentry* (Seattle: University of Washington Press, 1955), p. 102; *Cambridge Ancient History*, pp. 267–268; and Blum, p. 278.

Chapter 8

1. According to Murdock's data, the Manus of New Guinea come as close to full dependence on fishing as any people in the world. See *Ethnology*, vol. 6, no. 2 (Apr. 1967), pp. 170–230. Yet, as Margaret Mead indicates in her report, these people also depend heavily for their subsistence on garden products that they obtain through trade from neighboring peoples and to a lesser degree on pigs that they raise or obtain through trade. See Margaret Mead, *Growing up in New Guinea* (New York: Mentor Books, 1953, first published 1930), especially pp. 173–174.

2. For an earlier discussion of this point, see Gordon Hewes's excellent paper, "The Rubric 'Fishing and Fisheries,'" *American Anthropologist*, 50 (1948), pp. 241–242.

3. Our calculation from Murdock data, see appendix pages 378–379.

4. See Hewes, pp. 240–241.

5. For an interesting account of one such group, see Wilmond Menard, "The Sea Gypsies of China," *Natural History*, 64 (Jan. 1965), pp. 13–21.

6. See, for example, Lawrence Krader, "Pastoralism," in *International Encyclopedia of the Social Sciences* (New York: Macmillan and Free Press, 1968), vol. II, pp. 456–457; or Carleton Coon, "The Nomads," in Sydney Fisher (ed.), *Social Forces in the Middle East* (Ithaca, N.Y.: Cornell University Press, 1955), pp. 23–42.

7. John L. Myres, "Nomadism," *Journal of the Royal Anthropological Institute*, 71 (1941), p. 20.

8. Krader reports that the average density of population in Mongolia was less than one per square mile, and among the Tuareg of Africa it was even lower ("Pastoralism," pp. 458–459).

9. It is found in 61 percent of these societies compared to 2 to 35 percent of other types.

10. This is found in 88 percent of these societies, compared to 37 to 82 percent of other types.

11. This requirement occurs in 97 percent of herding societies, compared to 72 to 87 percent of other types.

12. See John Keegan, *A History of Warfare* (New York: Vintage, 1994); William McNeill, *The Rise of the West: A History of the Human Community* (New York: Mentor Books, 1965), p. 126ff.; or Ralph Turner, *The Great Cultural Traditions* (New York: McGraw-Hill, 1941), p. 259.

13. For a good discussion of this important subject, see McNeill, p. 256ff.

14. Although François Nielsen presents a well-reasoned argument that herding and agrarian societies should be placed in a single subsistence category—"secondary products societies"—based on their shared reliance on animal traction/animal production technology ("Macrosociology and the Emerging Synthesis," http://www.unc.edu/~nielsen/special/s5/glo402.pdf), our view that these are diametrically opposed modes of production, as we have shown here, makes it difficult for us to agree.

15. McNeill, p. 111.

16. Charles Boxer, *The Dutch Seaborne Empire, 1600–1800* (London: Hutchison, 1965); and Peter Burke, *Venice and Amsterdam: A Study of Seventeenth Century Elites* (London: Temple Smith, 1974).

17. On the less familiar Carthaginian empire, see Donald Harden, *The Phoenicians* (New York: Praeger, 1963), chaps. 5 and 6. The British Empire, it might be noted, was also an overseas empire.

18. The Netherlands changed from a republic to a monarchy in the nineteenth century because of decisions made by foreign powers at the Congress of Vienna, not because of internal Dutch preference (Wout Ultee, personal communication, Dec. 2, 1988).

19. Compare, for example, the status of merchants and the rate of innovation for Europe during the sixteenth, seventeenth, and eighteenth centuries with the situation in India. Both were higher in Europe. Although this could have been coincidence, the evidence suggests a causal link.

Chapter 9

1. Charles Singer et al. (eds.), *A History of Technology* (Oxford: Clarendon Press, 1954–1956), vols. 1 and 2. See also Terry S. Reynolds, "Medieval Roots of the Industrial Revolution," *Scientific American*, 251 (July 1984), pp. 123–130.

2. Michael Mann, *The Sources of Social Power* (Cambridge: Cambridge University Press, 1986), vol. I, p. 445.

3. William H. McNeill, *The Rise of the West* (Chicago: University of Chicago Press, 1963), pp. 570–571.

4. S. B. Clough and C. W. Cole, *Economic History of Europe* (Boston: Heath, 1941), pp. 127–128.

5. Again see classic statements on this by Georg Simmel, *The Philosophy of Money* (New York: Routledge, 2011, first published 1907); and Max Weber, Gunter Roth, and Claus Wittich (eds.), *Economy and Society: An Outline of Interpretive Sociology,* (Berkeley: University of California Press, 1978), chap. II, vol. 1.

6. Ibid.

7. R. H. Tawney, *Religion and the Rise of the West* (New York: Mentor Books, 1947), p. 117.

8. Immanuel Wallerstein, *The Modern World-System* (New York: Academic Press, 1974), especially chap. 2.

9. Tawney, p. 257.

10. Elizabeth Eisenstein, *The Printing Press as an Agent of Change* (Cambridge: Cambridge University Press, 1979), vols. I and II.

11. James M. Wells, "The History of Printing," *Encyclopaedia Britannica*, vol. 18, p. 541.

12. Wells, pp. 541–542; and N. F. Blake, *Caxton: England's First Publisher* (New York: Barnes & Noble, 1976), chap. 1.

13. Daniel J. Boorstin, *The Discoverers* (New York: Random House, 1983), chaps. 62–63.

14. Ann Stanford, "A Link with the Past," *Endeavors*, vol. 2, no. 2 (Spring 1985), p. 8; Michael Clapham, "Printing," in Singer, op. cit., vol. II, p. 27; and Boorstin, pp. 533–534.

15. See, for example, Arthur G. Dickens, *Reformation and Society in Sixteenth Century Europe* (New York: Harcourt, Brace, 1966).

16. See, especially, Max Weber, *The Protestant Ethic and the Spirit of Capitalism,* trans. Talcott Parsons (New York: Scribner, 1958); or Reinhard Bendix, *Max Weber: An Intellectual Portrait* (Garden City, N.Y.: Doubleday, 1960), chaps. 3–8.

17. Ernest Gellner, *Plow, Sword and Book: The Structure of Human History* (Chicago: University of Chicago Press, 1989), chaps. 4 and 5.

18. Tawney, pp. 92–93.

19. Neil Smelser and S. M. Lipset (eds.), *Social Structure and Mobility in Economic Development* (Chicago: University of Chicago Press, 1967), p. 29ff.

20. On the controversy, see, for example, Jacques Delacroix and François Nielsen, "The Beloved Myth: Protestantism and the Rise of Industrial Capitalism in Nineteenth-Century Europe," *Social Forces*, 80 (2001), pp. 509–553.

21. Clough and Cole, pp. 185–194.

22. Ibid., pp. 308–315.

23. See, for example, Robert Heilbroner, *The Making of Economic Society* (Englewood Cliffs, N.J.: Prentice-Hall, 1962), pp. 101–102.

24. See, for example, John Nef, *The Conquest of the Material World* (Chicago: University of Chicago Press, 1965), especially part 2.

25. Paul Mantoux, *The Industrial Revolution in the Eighteenth Century,* rev. ed. (London: Cape, 1961), pp. 243–244.

26. Reynolds, "Medieval Roots."

27. Mantoux, p. 312.

28. Earlier in the century, Thomas Savery and Thomas Newcomen invented the atmospheric engine, which laid the foundation for Watt's work. Its only practical use, however, was to pump water out of mines.

29. Phyllis Deane and W. A. Cole, *British Growth 1688–1959: Trends and Structure* (London: Cambridge, 1962), p. 212.

30. For 1788, see Clive Day, *Economic Development in Europe* (New York: Macmillan, 1942), p. 134; for 1845, see Deane and Cole, p. 225.

31. Deane and Cole, pp. 55 and 216.

32. S. Woytinsky and E. S. Woytinsky, *World Population and Production: Trends and Outlook* (New York: Twentieth Century Fund, 1953), p. 1147.

33. *British Historical Statistics* (Cambridge: Cambridge University Press, 1988), p. 822.

34. U.S. Department of Commerce, Bureau of the Census, *Historical Statistics of the United States, Colonial Times to 1970,* series F238–239.

35. J. H. Clapham, *An Economic History of Modern Britain,* 2d ed. (London: Cambridge, 1930), vol. 1, pp. 391–392.

36. Clough and Cole, pp. 594–595.

37. Ibid., pp. 535–537.

38. Deane and Cole, p. 225.

39. Ibid., p. 216.

40. *Historical Statistics of the U.S., Colonial Times to 1970,* p. 500.

41. Alfred D. Chandler Jr., *The Visible Hand: The Managerial Revolution in America* (Cambridge, Mass.: Belknap Press, 1977), part II.

42. Ibid., p. 232.

43. Clough and Cole, p. 538.

44. Alfred D. Chandler, "Industrial Revolutions and Institutional Arrangements," *Bulletin of the American Academy of Arts and Sciences,* 33 (May 1980), pp. 40–45.

45. The first figure is an estimate based on Clough and Cole's report of French production in 1902 (p. 773) and Woytinsky and Woytinsky's report of American production in 1900 and 1902 (p. 1168). See also James M. Laux, *In First Gear: The French Automobile Industry to 1914* (Liverpool: Liverpool University Press, 1976), fig. 5. The second is from Lester Brown, Nicholas Lenssen, and Hal Kane, *Vital Signs 1995: The Trends that are Shaping our Future* (New York: Norton, 1995), p. 83.

46. Woytinsky and Woytinsky, p. 1164.

47. The 1900 figure is estimated from information provided by Woytinsky and Woytinsky, pp. 897–900; the 1940 figure is from fig. 257, p. 897.

48. Woytinsky and Woytinsky, p. 966.

49. Ibid., p. 1171.

50. Calculated from *Historical Statistics of the U.S.,* Series R 93–105 and Series A 288–319.

51. *The Washington Post,* Aug. 13, 1997.

52. D'Vera Cohn, Paul Taylor, Mark Hugo Lopez, Catherine A. Gallagher, Kim Parker and Kevin T. Maass, "Gun Homicide Rate Down 49% Since 1993 Peak; Public Unaware: Pace of Decline Slows in Past Decade," PEW, May 7, 2013, http://www.pewsocialtrends.org/2013/05/07/gun-homicide-rate-down-49-since-1993-peak-public-unaware/.

53. Mary Bellis, "The History of the ENIAC Computer," About.com Guide, Inventors, n.d., http://inventors.about.com/od/estartinventions/a/Eniac.htm; Dirk Strauss, "Power in Your Palm: The Computing Power in Today's Smartphones," Bit Rebels, n.d., http://www.bitrebels.com/technology/power-in-your-palm-the-computing-power-in-todays-smartphones/.

54. "Transistor Count," Wikipedia, n.d., http://en.wikipedia.org/wiki/Transistor_count; William Broad, "Incredible Shrinking Transistor," *New York Times,* Feb. 4, 1996; "Intel Announces Transistor Breakthrough," Associated Press, June 11, 2001. According to one commentator, Frederic E. Davis, "Electrons or Photons?" *Wired,* Mar./Apr. 1993, two decades ago: "Had automobile technology advanced at a similar pace over the past 20 years, your car would travel 500,000 miles an hour, get a million miles to the gallon, and cost a measly $1,000."

55. *New York Times,* July 21, 1997; David Szondy, "Lely Astronaut A4 Milking Robot Lets Cows Milk Themselves," Gizmag, Sept. 2, 2013, http://www.gizmag.com/lely-astronaut-a4/28901/.

56. Calculations based on data in World Bank, *World Tables,* 3d. ed., vol. I (Baltimore: Johns Hopkins University Press, 1983), table 1; World Bank, *World Development Report, 1982* (New York: Oxford University Press, 1982), table 2.0; *World Development Indicators 1997; and* World Bank, *World Development Indicators,* online database, www.worldbank.org/data/onlinedatabases/onlinedatabases.html.

57. Mark Landler and John Markoff, "After Computer Siege in Estonia, War Fears Turn to Cyberspace," *New York Times,* May 29, 2007.

58. Michael Muskal, "Chinese Army Likely Behind Cyber Attacks, U.S. Security Firm Says," *Los Angeles Times,* Feb. 19, 2013; Cory Kilcannon, "Cadets Trade Trenches for Firewalls," *New York Times,* May 10, 2009; and David Sanger, John Markoff, and Thom Shanker, "U.S. Steps Up Efforts on Digital Defenses," *New York Times,* Apr. 28, 2009.

59. Congressional Budget Office, *Federal Support for Research and Development*, June 2007; Patrick J. Clemins, *Historical Trends in Federal R&D*, 2012, American Association for the Advancement of Science.

60. See the high percentage of all research and development expenditures coming from the U.S. Department of Defense, *Statistical Abstract of the U.S., 1997*, table 967.

61. See, for example, Max Weber and Karl Marx.

62. See, for example, William H. McNeill, *Plagues and Peoples* (Garden City, N.Y.: Double-day Anchor, 1976); Jared Diamond, *Guns, Germs, and Steel: The Fate of Human Societies* (New York: Norton, 1997).

63. J. L. Hammond and Barbara Hammond, *The Town Labourer: 1760–1830* (London: Guild Books, 1949, first published 1917), vol. I, chap. 3.

64. Ibid., chaps. 2 and 6–9; or J. T. Ward (ed.), *The Factory System* (New York: Barnes & Noble, 1970), vols. I and II.

65. Hammond and Hammond, vol. I, pp. 32–33.

66. Compare and contrast the work of Hammond and Hammond, *The Town Labourer*, or Eric Hobsbawm, "The British Standard of Living, 1790–1850," *Economic History Review*, 2d series, 10 (1957), pp. 46–61, with Thomas Ashton, "The Standard of Life of the Workers in England, 1790–1830," *Journal of Economic History*, 9 (1949), supplement, pp. 19–38.

Chapter 10

1. Our calculations from U.S. Department of Commerce, Bureau of the Census, *Historical Statistics of the United States: Colonial Times to 1970*, series D-152–153; and U.S. Department of Commerce, Bureau of the Census, *Statistical Abstract of the United States, 2012*, table 620.

2. J. Frederic Dewhurst and associates, *America's Needs and Resources* (New York: Twentieth Century Fund, 1955), p. 1116; and *Statistical Abstract of the U.S., 1967*, table 752.

3. Lester Brown, Hal Kane, and Ed Ayres, *Vital Signs 1993: The Trends That Are Shaping Our Future* (New York: W. W. Norton, 1993), p. 58; Lester Brown, Christopher Flavin, and Hal Kane, *Vital Signs 1996* (New York: Norton, 1996), pp. 56–57; *Vital Signs 2005* (Washington, DC: Worldwatch Institute, 2005), p. 34, pp. 36–37.

4. Our calculation based on *Historical Statistics of the U.S.*, series S-1; *Annual Energy Review*, U.S. Energy Information (Sept. 2012), table 1.1, http://www.eia.gov/aer. Since the last edition only went to 1995, it greatly understated the magnitude of this increase.

5. World Bank, *World Development Indicators* online database, www.worldbank.org/data/onlinedatabases/onlinedatabases.html.

6. The 1750 figure is from W. S. Woytinsky and E. S. Woytinsky, *World Population and Production: Trends and Outlooks* (New York: Twentieth Century Fund, 1953), p. 1100; the 1970 figure is from United Nations, *Statistical Yearbook, 1971*, tables 121 and 122, and is converted to short tons.

7. The 1820 figure is from Woytinsky and Woytinsky, p. 1101; the 1974 figure is from *Statistical Abstract of the U.S., 1989*, table 1182.

8. World Steel Association, *Steel Statistic Yearbook 2011*.

9. Consumption figures are from the *Statistical Abstract of the U.S., 2010*, table 871; population 2. Per capita calculations are our own.

10. *British Historical Statistics* (Cambridge: Cambridge University Press, 1988), pp. 837–841; *World Development Report 1982*, table 1; *World Development Indicators 1997* CD-ROM (Washington: World Bank, 1997); and World Bank, *World Development Indicators* online database http://data.worldbank.org/indicator?display=default; in recent years, estimates of growth are based on growth in GDP.

11. *Historical Statistics of the U.S.*, Series F-3; *World Development Indicators 1997*; and World Bank, *World Development Indicators* online database http://data.worldbank.org/indicator?display=default; in recent years, estimates of growth are based on growth in GDP.

12. *World Development Indicators* online database.

13. Associated Press, Aug. 7, 1972.

14. See notes 10 and 11, in recent years, estimates of growth are based on growth in GDP per capita.

15. Exxon Mobil calculated from Wikipedia, "List of Largest Companies by Revenue, (June 6, 2014)

http://en.wikipedia.org/wiki/List_of_largest_companies_by_revenue," McDonald's, Wikipedia (June 6, 2014) http://en.wikipedia.org/wiki/Mc-Donald's. See also, Steve Hargreaves, "Exxon Reports Record Profits of Nearly 16 Billion," CNN Money, July 26, 2012 http://money.cnn.com/2012/07/26/news/companies/exxon-profit/.

16. "Smithfield Foods Closes Sale to China's Shuanghui," Associated Press, Sept. 27, 2013.

17. Revenues from Smithfield Foods, *Annual Report*; David Barboza, "Goliath of the Hog World," *New York Times,* Apr. 7, 2000.

18. Average assets, our calculation from the *Statistical Abstract of the U.S. 2012,* tables 839, and 825; sales concentration from U.S. Environmental Protection Agency, "Demographics," Apr. 15, 2013, http://www.epa.gov/agriculture/ag101/demographics.html.

19. *Historical Statistics of the U.S.,* Series D-182–232; and *Statistical Abstract of the U.S., 2012,* table 619.

20. For example, see Mark Drajem and Kathleen Miller, "No Reprieve for Contract Workers' Wages Lost in Shutdown," Bloomberg, Oct. 14, 2013, http://www.bloomberg.com/news/2013-10-14/no-reprieve-for-contract-workers-wages-lost-in-shutdown.html.

21. *Statistical Abstract of the U.S., 2012,* table 451.

22. Ibid.

23. "Top Companies: Biggest Employers," CNN Money, Global 500, http://money.cnn.com/magazines/fortune/global500/2011/performers/companies/biggest/.

24. U.S. Department of Labor, *Dictionary of Occupational Titles* (Washington: GPO, 1977, 1981); and *DOT* online index, http://www.immigration-usa.com/dot_index.html.

25. *Newsweek,* Mar. 26, 1973, p. 79.

26. Pehr Gyllenhammar, "Volvo's Solution to Blue Collar Blues," *Business and Society,* Autumn 1973.

27. *Statistical Abstract of the U.S., 2012,* table 664.

28. S. B. Clough and C. W. Cole, *Economic History of Europe* (Boston: Heath, 1941), pp. 693–698.

29. G. D. H. Cole, *A Short History of the British Working Class Movement* (New York: Macmillan, 1927), vol. II, p. 202; and Carroll P. Daugherty,

Labor Problems in American Industry (Boston: Houghton Mifflin, 1941), p. 405.

30. See, for example, "Chrysler Says GM Sets U.S. Car Prices," *Raleigh News and Observer,* Sept. 13, 1979, a report of testimony at a congressional hearing by the chairman of the Chrysler Corporation.

31. G. Warren Nutter, "Industrial Concentration," *International Encyclopedia of the Social Sciences* (New York: Macmillan and Free Press, 1968), vol. 7, p. 221.

32. Share of circulation computed from data in *World Almanac and Book of Facts 2008,* (New York: World Almanac Books, 2008), p. 237.

33. John Kenneth Galbraith, *The New Industrial State* (New York: Signet, 1968), pp. 38–39.

34. Michael P. Allen, "The Structure of Interorganizational Elite Cooptation: Interlocking Corporate Directorates," *American Sociological Review,* 39 (1974), pp. 393–406.

35. *The Economist,* Dec. 30, 1978.

36. Clough and Cole, p. 148ff.; or Edward S. Mason, "Corporation," in *International Encyclopedia of the Social Sciences,* vol. 3, pp. 396–403.

37. Calculations based on data in the *Statistical Abstract of the U.S., 2012,* tables 744 and 745.

38. *Forbes,* May 12, 1980, pp. 214 and 236.

39. See Robert A. Gordon, *Business Leadership in the Large Corporation* (Berkeley: University of California Press, 1961); or Edward S. Mason (ed.), *The Corporation and Modern Society* (Cambridge: Harvard University Press, 1959), on American corporations; and P. Sargant Florence, *Ownership, Control, and Success of Large Companies* (London: Street and Maxwell, 1961); "The View from the Boardroom," *Wall Street Journal,* Oct. 27, 2003; and David Granick, *The European Executive* (Garden City, N.Y.: Doubleday Anchor, 1964), on European corporations.

40. Erik Assadourian, "When Good Corporations Go Bad," *World Watch,* 18 (May/June 2005), p. 19.

41. Richard Easterlin, "Economic Growth," in *Encyclopedia of the Social Sciences,* vol. 4, p. 405.

42. Calculations based on United Nations, *Statistical Yearbook, 1965,* table 148; and *Statistical Abstract of the U.S., 1979,* table 1539.

43. Atossa Araxia, "Coca-Cola Reports Higher Profit, Sticks by Long-term Plan," Reuters, Oct. 15, 2013; "McDonald's Gets a Toehold in Vietnam," Associated Press, July, 16, 2013.

44. Based on recent company reports.

Chapter 11

1. *BBC News* online, "What the World Thinks of God," Feb. 28, 2004; and Gabrielle Bauer, "God and Other Mysteries: Soul or Spirit, Angel or Afterlife: Here's What Canadians Believe, and Why," *Reader's Digest*, Canadian ed., November 2003, pp. 50–59.

2. *The Gallup Poll: Public Opinion 1991* (Wilmington, Del.: 1992), p. 238; John G. Stackhouse Jr., "The Renaissance of Religion in Canada," *Books & Culture*, Nov./Dec. 2002, www.christianity-today.com/bc/2002/006/5.20.html; Bauer, "God and Other Mysteries"; and "State of the Canadian Church," 2007, Part 1: A Nation of Believers?," http://canadianchristianity.com/state-canadian-church-part-nation-believers-211/.

3. Russell Shorto, "Keeping the Faith," *New York Times Magazine*, Apr. 8, 2007.

4. *Index to International Public Opinion, 1980–81* (Westport, Conn.: Greenwood), pp. 526–537.

5. *Index to International Public Opinion, 1990–91* (Westport, Conn.: Greenwood), p. 594.

6. Hugh Lefler, *North Carolina History* (Chapel Hill: University of North Carolina Press, 1934), pp. 108–109. For the net worth of free Southerners in 1774, see *Historical Statistics of the U.S.*, p. 1175. The median would almost certainly be lower than the average reported here.

7. Robert Heilbroner, *The Worldly Philosophers*, rev. ed. (New York: Time Books, 1961), chap. 3; and Jacob Viner, "Adam Smith," in *International Encyclopedia of the Social Sciences*, vol. 14, pp. 322–329.

8. Heilbroner, p. 47.

9. See, for example, Daniel Bell, "Socialism," in *International Encyclopedia of the Social Sciences*, vol. 14, pp. 506–532.

10. Maurice Duverger, *Political Parties: Their Organization and Activity in the Modern State*, trans. Barbara North and Robert North (London: Methuen, 1959), pp. 118–119; and Gerhard Lenski,

Ecological-Evolutionary Theory: Principles and Applications (Boulder, Colo.: Paradigm, 2005), pp. 227–228.

11. For an elaboration of this view see Michael Crichton, "Environmentalism as a Religion," http://www.pe.tamu.edu/DL_Program/gradu-ate_seminar_series/Documents/MichaelCrich-ton_evironmentalism.pdf.

12. For a discussion of medieval Europe, see David C. Lindberg, *The Beginnings of Western Science: The European Scientific Tradition in Philosophical, Religious, and Institutional Context, 600 B.C. to A.D. 1450* (Chicago: University of Chicago Press, 1992), chap. 9; for an example of Soviet science, see Stephen Jay Gould "A Hearing for Vavilov," in *Hen's Teeth and Horse's Toes* (New York: W.W. Norton, 1994), pp. 134–144.

13. Hans Kohn, "Nationalism," *International Encyclopedia of the Social Sciences*, vol. 2, pp. 63–70.

14. John H. Kautsky, *The Politics of Aristocratic Empires* (Chapel Hill: University of North Carolina Press, 1982), part IV.

15. Robert Bellah, "Civil Religion in America," *Daedalus*, 96 (Winter 1967), pp. 1–21. See also Will Herberg, *Protestant-Catholic-Jew* (Garden City, N.Y.: Doubleday, 1955).

16. Tim Bertoni, and Patrick Nolan, "Dead Men Do Tell Tales: The Apotheosis of Celebrities in 20th Century America," Sociation Today, vol. 10, 1 (Spring/Summer 2012), http://www.ncsociology.org/sociationtoday/v101/dead.htm.

17. For example, see Robert Michels, *Political Parties: A Sociological Study of the Oligarchical Tendencies of Modern Democracies*, (NY: Free Press, 1966, first published 1915); and Robert Dahl and Edward Tufte, *Size and Democracies: The Politics of the Smaller European Democracies*, (Redwood City, Calif.: Stanford University Press, 1976).

18. W. L. Guttsman, *The British Political Elite* (London: Macgibbon & Kee, 1963), pp. 18 and 41.

19. A. Todd, *On Parliamentary Government* (London: Longmans, 1887), p. 622; and W. L. Guttsman (ed.), *The English Ruling Class* (London: Weidenfeld and Nicolson, 1969), p. 154.

20. U.S. Department of Commerce, Bureau of the Census, *Historical Statistics of the U.S.: Colonial Times to 1970,* Series Y–83.

21. Romina Boccia, Alison Acosta Fraser, and Emily Goff, "Federal Spending by the Numbers 2013: Government Spending Trends in Graphics, Tables, and Key Points," The Heritage Foundation, http://www.heritage.org/research/reports/2013/08/federal-spending-by-the-numbers-2013.

22. Judith Ryder and Harold Silver, *Modern English Society* (London: Methuen, 1970), p. 74; Dankwort Rustow, *The Politics of Compromise: A Study of Parties and Cabinet Government in Sweden* (Princeton, N.J.: Princeton University Press, 1955), pp. 84–85.

23. Federal Election Commission, "Statement of Chair Ellen L. Weintraub," Jan. 31, 2013 http://www.fec.gov/members/weintraub/statements/weintraub_statement_20130131.pdf .

24. Kyle Trygstad, "The Most Expensive House and Senate Races of 2012," *Roll Call*, Dec. 23, 2012.

25. Kenneth A. Bollen, "Political Democracy and the Timing of Development," *American Sociological Review,* 44 (Aug. 1979), pp. 572–587.

26. Many studies have documented the relationship between high rates of literacy and education on the one hand and democratic government on the other. See, for example, Daniel Lerner, *The Passing of Traditional Society: Modernizing the Middle East* (New York: Free Press, 1958), especially pp. 63–64 and 86–89; or S. M. Lipset, *Political Man* (Garden City, N.Y.: Doubleday, 1960), pp. 53–58.

27. On the relationship between democracy and the development of the mass media, see Lerner, *Passing of Traditional Society,* and Lipset, pp. 51–52.

28. Wikipedia, Dec. 3, 2013, "European Parliament"; and A. S. Banks, Alan J. Day, and Thomas C. Muller (eds.), *Political Handbook of the World 1997* (Binghamton, N.Y.: CSA, 1997); and http://www.Europarl.europa.eu.

29. James Markham, "Greening of European Politicians Spreads," *New York Times,* Apr. 12, 1989.

30. Dan Farber, "Poll: 70 Percent Angry or Dissatisfied with Washington," *CBS News*, Feb. 11, 2010.

31. Seth Cline, "12 Biggest Donors of the 2012 Election," *U.S. News & World Report,* Oct. 26, 2012.

32. Thomas E. Patterson, *The Mass Media Election: How Americans Choose Their President* (New York: Praeger, 1980).

33. Harry Waters, "Brave New Documentary," *Newsweek,* June 10, 1985, p. 71.

34. See, for example, Barryck Rifki, "The Social Media Revolution and the End of Mass Media," *Mindthis,* Sept. 19, 2011, or Doreen Carvajal, "Europe Teems with Web Dailies that Twit the Mainstream Press," *New York Times,* Feb. 21, 2005.

35. Lydia Saad, "TV American's Main Source of News," Gallup, July 8, 2013.

36. Amy Mitchell, "Twitter News Consumers: Young, Mobile and Educated," Pew Research Journalism Project online, Nov. 4, 2013.

37. Elizabeth Mendes, "Americans' Confidence in Newspapers Continues to Erode: Fewer than One in Four Americans Confident in Newspapers, TV News," Gallup online, June 17, 2013.

38. Ivo Feierabend and Rosalind Feierabend, "Aggressive Behaviors within Polities, 1948–1962: A Cross-National Study," *Journal of Conflict Resolution,* 10 (1966), table 3. Results of this study suggest that rates of political instability are greatest in societies making the transition from agrarian to industrial, though results were not statistically significant. See also Douglas Hibbs, *Mass Political Violence: A Cross-National Causal Analysis* (New York: Wiley, 1973), chap. 3.

39. Walter Korpi, *The Democratic Class Struggle* (London: Routledge & Kegan Paul, 1983), figure 5.3.

40. See *Human Societies,* 11th ed., Table 11.3 based on our calculations using the following sources: Robert Alford, *Party and Society* (Chicago: Rand McNally, 1963), pp. 136, 202–203, 234–235, and 274–275; Richard Rose (ed.), *Electoral Behavior: A Comparative Handbook* (New York: Free Press, 1974), pp. 147, 294, 334, and 398; Hannu Uusitalo, "Class Structure and Party Choice: A Scandinavian Comparison," *Research Report No. 10* (1975), Research Group for Comparative Sociology, University of Helsinki, p. 21; Roy Pierce, *French Politics and Political Institutions* (New

York: Harper & Row, 1968), table 10; Richard Rose, "Class and Party Divisions: Britain as a Test Case," *Sociology,* 2 (1968), pp. 129–162; Erik Allardt and Yrjo Littunen (eds.), *Cleavages, Ideologies and Party Systems: Contributions to Comparative Political Sociology,* in a series entitled Transactions of the Westermarck Society (Helsinki: The Academic Bookstore, 1964), vol. 10, pp. 102 and 212; S. M. Lipset, *Political Man* (Garden City, N.Y.: Doubleday, 1960), pp. 225 and 227; *Gallup Political Index,* Report No. 17 (Oct. 1966), p. 15 and inside back cover; S. M. Lipset, "Industrial Proletariat in Comparative Perspective," in Jan Triska and C. Gati (eds.), *Blue Collar Workers in Eastern Europe* (London: Allen & Unwin, 1981), figure 1.1; Walter Korpi, *The Democratic Class Struggle* (London: Routledge & Kegan Paul, 1983), figure 5.3; and *Index to International Public Opinion 1985–86,* pp. 410, 411, and 4.

41. See, for example, Lipset, *Political Man,* chaps. 2 and 4.

42. *Statistical Abstract of the U.S., 2012,* table 461, and table 2.

43. "Trust in Government," Gallup online, Nov. 12, 2013; *Gallup Poll 1995;* and *Gallup Poll: Public Opinion 1991* (Wilmington, Del.: Greenwood, 1992).

44. Slightly smaller percentages believed that state and local governments had violated their constitutional rights also (i.e., state, 83 percent; local, 75 percent), the *Gallup Poll: Public Opinion 1995* (Wilmington, Del.: Greenwood, 1996), p. 252.

45. "Trust in Government Nears Record Low, But Most Federal Agencies are Viewed Favorably," Pew Research Center for the People & the Press online, Oct. 18, 2013; Frank Newport, "Dysfunctional Gov't Surpasses Economy as Top U.S. Problem: Highest Percentage Citing Dysfunctional Government Dysfunction in Gallup History," Gallup online, Oct. 9, 2013.

46. Urii Davydov, "Technology and Bureaucracy," *Sotsiologicheskie Issledovaniia,* 5 (1988), pp.116–127; and "The Weberian Renaissance," *Sotsiologicheskie Issledovaniia,* 3 (1986), pp. 56–68.

Chapter 12

1. Elliot Blair Smith and Phil Kuntz, "CEO Pay 1,795-to-1 Multiple Wages Skirts U.S. Law," Bloomberg online, Apr. 20, 2013.

2. For more discussion of this issue, see Patrick D. Nolan, "A Standardized Cross-National Comparison of Incomes," *Sociological Quarterly,* 33 (1992), pp. 599–609.

3. The increase was 2.6 percent for the lowest-earning fifth, and 12.2 percent for the next lowest fifth; our calculations from U.S. Census Bureau, Historical Income Tables, table F-3, http://www.census.gov/hhes/www/income/data/historical/families/index.html.

4. U.S. Census Bureau, Historical Income Tables, table H-10, http://www.census.gov/hhes/www/income/data/historical/household/index.html.

5. U.S. Census Bureau, Historical Income Tables, tables P-AR 8 and P-5, http://www.census.gov/hhes/www/income/data/historical/people/.

6. Robert Pear, "Median Income Rises, but Is Still 6% Below Level at Start of Recession in '07," *New York Times,* Aug. 21, 2013.

7. U.S. Census Bureau, Historical Income Tables, table H-3.

8. U.S. Department of the Treasury, "Income Mobility in the U.S. from 1996 to 2005," Report of the Department of the Treasury, Nov. 13, 2007, table 7.

9. Findings of the Panel Study of Income Dynamics conducted by the University of Michigan Institute for Social Research, reported in Claudia Smith Brinson, "Study Debunks Poverty Myths," *The State,* Mar. 29, 1992; and William P. O'Hare, "A New Look at Poverty in America," *Population Bulletin,* 51, no. 8 (Sept. 1996), Population Reference Bureau.

10. Internal Revenue Service, Statistics on Income, http://www.irs.gov/taxstats/index.html; and Wojciech Kopczuk and Emmanuel Saez, "Top Wealth in the United States, 1916–2000: Evidence from Estate Tax Returns," National Bureau of Economic Research, working paper, Mar. 2004.

11. Jesse Bricker, Arthur B. Kennickell, Kevin B. Moore, and John Sabelhaus, of the Board's

Division of Research and Statistics, prepared this article with assistance from Samuel Ackerman, Robert Argento, Gerhard Fries, and Richard A. Windle, "Changes in U.S. Family Finances from 2007 to 2010: Evidence from the Survey of Consumer Finances," *Federal Reserve Bulletin* 98 no. 22 (June 2012), http://www.federalreserve.gov/pubs/bulletin/2012/pdf/scf12.pdf.

12. For example, see G. William Domhoff (reporting Wolff's figures), "Wealth, Income, and Power," Who Rules America?, updated Feb. 2013, http://www2.ucsc.edu/whorulesamerica/power/wealth.html.

13. Kopczuk and Saez, "Top Wealth in the United States, 1916–2000."

14. *Statistical Abstract of the U.S., 2012,* table 1211, and *Federal Reserve Bulletin* 98 no. 22 (June 2012), table 7.

15. Bureau of Economic Analysis, http://www.bea.gov/index.htm.

16. See *Historical Statistics of the U.S.: Colonial Times to 1957* (1960), Series G-169–190.

17. See, for example, Christopher Jencks et al., "The Wisconsin Model of Status Attainment," *Sociology of Education,* 56 (1983), pp. 3–19.

18. Bureau of Labor Statistics, "Earnings and Employment by Educational Attainment," May 22, 2013.

19. U.S. Census Bureau, Historical Income Tables, table F-7.

20. Steven Nelson, "Census Bureau Links Poverty with Out of Wedlock Births," *U.S. News & World Report,* May 6, 2013.

21. Ibid., and *Statistical Abstract of the U.S., 2012,* table 64.

22. Our calculations from U.S. Census Bureau, *Historical Income Tables,* table F-7, and *Income, Poverty, and Health Insurance Coverage in the United States: 2006,* Sept. 2007.

23. Reported by M. Dart from *Principal's Association Report on High Schools,* U.S. Bureau of the Census, D.H.H.S., and *Fulton County Georgia Jail Populations* and Texas Department of Corrections, 1992; see also, Paul R. Amato, "Life-Span Adjustment of Children to Their Parents' Divorce," *Children and Divorce,* 4, no. 1 (1994); and Sara McLanahan and Gary Sandefur, *Growing Up with a Single Parent: What Hurts, What Helps* (Cambridge, Mass.: Harvard University Press, 1994).

24. *Statistical Abstract of the U.S., 2012,* table 712; and our calculations from U.S. Census Bureau, Historical Income Tables, table F-7.

25. Data from a Rand Corporation Study reported in *New York Times,* Mar. 2, 1986; *New York Times,* Nov. 16, 1997; U.S. Census Bureau, Historical Income Tables, table P-2; Stephan Thernstrom and Abigail Thernstrom, *America in Black and White: One Nation Indivisible* (New York: Simon and Schuster, 1997) p. 195; Bureau of Labor Statistics, "Highlights of Women's Earnings in 2012," report 1045, Oct. 2013; and *Statistical Abstract 2012,* table 691.

26. William Julius Wilson, *When Work Disappears* (New York: Knopf, 1996), U.S. Bureau of the Census, *Housing Vacancies and Home Ownership* (Jan. 1998); Robert A. Callis and Linda B. Cavanaugh, U.S Bureau of the Census, "Residential Vacancies and Ownership," July 24, 2003; National Urban League, *The State of Black America 2012;* and *World Almanac and Book of Facts 2008,* p. 367.

27. U.S. Census Bureau, Historical Income Tables, table HO3B, and Wilson, *When Work Disappears,* p. 195.

28. See, for example, Everett C. Hughes, *French Canada in Transition* (Chicago: University of Chicago Press, 1943), especially chap. 7. See also John Porter, *The Vertical Mosaic: An Analysis of Social Class and Power in Canada* (Toronto: University of Toronto Press, 1965), chap. 3.

29. John Burns, "Separatists Vying for Quebec Power," *New York Times,* Sept. 24, 1989.

30. Congressional Research Office, "Membership of the 113th Congress: A Profile," R42964, http://www.CRS.gov.

31. "CEO Statistics," Statistic Brain, Dec. 25, 2013, http://www.statisticbrain.com/ceo-statistics/.

32. Calculated from Morris Janowitz, *The Professional Soldier* (New York: Free Press, 1960), p. 63.

33. Francine D. Blau and Lawrence M. Kahn, "The Gender Earnings Gap: Learning from

International Comparisons," *American Economic Review,* 82 (May 1992), pp. 533–538.

34. James P. Smith and Michael P. Ward, *Women's Wages and Work in the Twentieth Century* (Santa Monica, Calif.: Rand, 1984).

35. Douglas Martin, "For Many Fathers, Roles Are Shifting," *New York Times,* June 20, 1993; Maida Odom, "Women Doing Double Duty, Research Finds," *The State,* Sept. 18, 1993; and Carol Kleiman, "Housework Said to Impede Women's Careers," *Chicago Tribune,* reported in *The State,* Feb. 13, 1992; Martin O'Connell "Where's Papa! Father's Role in Child Care," *Population Trends and Public Policy,* 20 (Sept. 1993).

36. Sylvia Nasar, "Women's Progress Stalled? Just Not So," *New York Times,* Oct. 18, 1992.

37. Bureau of Labor Statistics, "Highlights of Women's Earnings in 2012," report 1045, Oct. 2013, table 2.

38. U.S. Census Bureau, Historical Income Tables, table P-2.

39. Bureau of Labor Statistics, "Highlights of Women's Earnings 2012, table 1.

40. Bryce Covert, "Number of Women CEOs at Major Companies Jumps by 4 Percent," *Think-Progress,* July 8, 2013, http://thinkprogress.org/economy/2013/07/08/2266831/number-of- women-ceos-at-major-companies-jumps-by-4-percent/; U.S. Department of Labor, "An Analysis of the Reasons for the Disparity in Wages Between Men and Women," final report, Jan. 12, 2009.

41. Kopczuk and Saez, "Top Wealth in the United States, 1916–2000."

42. William J. Goode, *World Revolution and Family Patterns* (New York: Free Press, 1963), p. 55.

43. World Bank, *World Development Indicators,* "Proportion of Seats Held by Women in National Parliaments, www.worldbank.org/;, "Women Prime Ministers," Wikipedia; and Population Reference Bureau, "Women of Our World 2005," http:/www.prb.org.

44. Gerhard Lenski, *Power and Privilege: A Theory of Social Stratification* (Chapel Hill: University of North Carolina Press, 1984, first published 1966), p. 289ff; and David Herlihy, "Three Patterns of Social Mobility in Medieval History," *Journal of Interdisciplinary History,* 3 (1973), p. 632.

45. Lenski, p. 412.

46. Ibid., p. 228.

47. Ibid., pp. 313–318, for a more thorough discussion of this subject.

48. L. J. Zimmerman, *Poor Lands, Rich Lands: The Widening Gap* (New York: Random House, 1965), table 2.8, p. 38; and our calculations based on *World Development Indicators,* www.worldbank.org/data/. See also: Banerjee, Abhijit Vinayak, Roland Benebou, and Dilip Mookherjee (eds.) *Understanding Poverty* (New York: Oxford University Press, 2006).

Chapter 13

1. Thomas McKeown, *The Modern Rise of Population* (New York: Academic Press, 1976), p. 2; and Steve Doughty, "Budge up! Population of England and Wales Sells by 400,000 in a Year," Mail online, June 26, 2013.

2. Caleb Finch, "Life Expectancy at Birth in the Greco-Roman World," *Proceedings of the National Academy of Sciences of The U.S.,* 107, supp. 1, Jan. 26, 2010.

3. Monroe Strickberger, *Evolution* (Boston: Jones and Bartlett, 1990), p. 501; Rebecca Storey, "An Estimate of Mortality in a Pre-Columbian Urban Population," *American Anthropologist,* 87 (1985), pp. 519–535; and our calculation from *Statistical Abstract of the U.S., 2012,* table 110.

4. "World Population Prospects: The 2012 Revision," United Nations Department of Economic and Social Affairs: Population Division, Population Estimates, and Projections.

5. Ibid.

6. "Foreign Born," Wikipedia.

7. For example, see "Violence Continues in France over Islamic Veil Ban," *CBS News,* July 21, 2013; "Violence In Europe Leaves People Fearful," NPR, May 28, 2013; Liz Alderman, "Greek Far Right Hangs a Target on Immigrants, *New York Times,* " July 10, 2012 http://www.nytimes.com/2012/07/11/world/europe/as-golden-dawn-rises-in-greece-anti-immigrant-violence-follows.html?pagewanted=all; Luke Baker and Stephen Adler, "'Nationalism and Xenophobia' on Rise Ahead of European Elections," Reuters, Oct. 30, 2013; "Religious Conflict on the Rise

in Sweden: Study," *The Local: Sweden's News in English*, August 10, 2011; Stephen Borthwick, "Immigrant Violence in Sweden Reaches New High," Examiner.com, June 10, 2010; "Conflict Diary," Ethnic Conflict Information Centre, various dates, http://www.notholt.net/fields_of_fire/conflicts_by_region.html#euro; Lori Hinnant and Milos Krivokapic, "France Riots 2012: Amiens Violence Rocks French District In North," Huff Post World, Aug. 16, 2012.

8. Natalie Angier, "The Changing American Family," *New York Times*, Nov. 25, 2013.

9. Ibid.

10. Ibid.

11. Carl Haub, "Rising Trend of Births Outside Marriage," *Population Reference Bureau*, Apr. 2013, http://www.prb.org/Publications/Articles/2013/nonmarital-births.aspx.

12. *World Almanac, 2008*, p. 158, U.S. Bureau of the Census, *American Fact Finder*; and "Indicators of Well-Being in Canada," Employment and Social Development Canada, n.d., http://www4.hrsdc.gc.ca/h.4m.2@-eng.jsp.

13. "Percent Never Married, 1970–2010," Infoplease, n.d., http://www.infoplease.com/ipa/A0763219.html.

14. Jonathan Vespa, Jamie M. Lewis, and Rose M. Kreider, "America's Families and Living Arrangements: 2012," U.S. Department of Commerce, Bureau of the Census, issued Aug. 2013, http://www.census.gov/prod/2013pubs/p20-570.pdf.

15. *Royal Commission on Population Report* (London: H.M. Stationery Office, 1949), p. 26.

16. See, for example, U.S. Department of Commerce, Bureau of the Census, *Historical Statistics of the United States: Colonial Times to 1970*, p. 53.

17. *Statistical Abstract of the U.S., 2002*, table 66.

18. Ibid., table 133.

19. Sharon Jayson, "Remarriage Rates Plunge as Divorced Americans Have Doubts," *USA Today*, Sept. 16, 2013; and Edward L. Kain, *The Myth of Family Decline: Understanding Families in a World of Rapid Social Change* (Lexington, Mass.: Lexington Books, 1990).

20. Calculations based on Warren Thompson and David Lewis, *Population Problems*, 5th ed. (New York: McGraw-Hill, 1965), p. 374;

J. Bourgeois-Pichat, "The General Development of the Population of France Since the Eighteenth Century," in D. V. Glass and D. E. C. Eversley (eds.), *Population in History* (Chicago: Aldine, 1965), p. 498; and W. S. Woytinsky and E. S. Woytinsky, *World Population and Production: Trends and Outlooks* (New York: Twentieth Century Fund, 1953), p. 181.

21. Vespa, Lewis, and Kreider, "America's Families and Living Arrangements: 2012," our calculation.

22. Ibid., our calculation.

23. Ibid., and *Statistical Abstract of the U.S., 1996*, table 74.

24. U.S. Census Bureau, "Income, Poverty, and Health Insurance Coverage in the United States: 2012," *Current Population Reports*, Sept. 2013.

25. In this section we have drawn heavily on suggestions provided by Joan Huber in two of her papers, "Toward a Socio-Technological Theory of the Women's Movement," *Social Problems*, 23 (1976), and "The Future of Parenthood: Implications of Declining Fertility," in Dana Hiller and Robin Sheets (eds.), *Women and Men* (Cincinnati: University of Cincinnati Press, 1976), pp. 333–351.

26. Jane Kramer, "Taking the Veil," *The New Yorker*, Nov. 22, 2004, p. 69.

27. U.S. Bureau of Labor Statistics, "Women in the Labor Force: A Databook," Mar. 26, 2013, http://www.bls.gov.

28. Ibid.

29. Jana Kasperkevic, "These Charts About Women in Leadership Prove How Far the U.S. Is Behind the Rest of the World," *Business Insider*, Mar. 13, 2012, http://www.businessinsider.com/women-worldwide-still-struggle-to-break-into-leadership-roles-2012-3.

30. Jane Waldfogel, "Working Mothers Then and Now: The Effects of Maternity Leave on Women's Pay," in Francine Blau and Ronald Ehrenberg (eds.), *Gender and Family Issues in the Workplace* (New York: Russell Sage, 1997); and "Watch the Wage Gap Disappear," *Kiplinger's Personal Finance Magazine*, July 1996.

31. Danielle Kurtzleben, "Vive La Difference? Gender Divides Remain in Housework, Child

Care," *U.S. News,* June 22, 2012; Bureau of Labor Statistics, "American Time Use Survey—2012 Results," June 20, 2013; and United Nations, *The World's Women 1970–1990: Trends and Statistics* (New York: United Nations, 1991), table 7A.

32. Erin Killian, "Parental Leave: The Swedes Are the Most Generous," NPR, Aug. 8, 2011.

33. Michael Getler, "Emancipation for E. German Women," *Washington Post,* Apr. 24, 1979.

34. Nancy Walsh, "Smoking Deaths Now Equal in Women and Men," Medpage Today, Jan. 23, 2013, http://www.medpagetoday.com/Primary-Care/Smoking/36981; "Number of Women Arrested for DUI Has Doubled Over Past 30 Years," *CBS Los Angeles,* Sept. 12, 2013; Daniel Bates, "Men and Women Look More Alike Than Ever Before, Scientists Claim," Mail Online, Apr. 5, 2011, http://www.dailymail.co.uk/sciencetech/article-1373617/Men-women-look-alike-scientists-claim.html; Joann Lublin, "As Women's Roles Grow More Like Men's, So Do Their Problems," *Wall Street Journal,* Jan. 14, 1980. See also *New York Times* series of articles, "Women's Lives: A Scorecard of Change," Aug. 20–22, 1989; and U.N., *The World's Women 1970–1990,* pp. 56–57.

35. U.N., *World's Women 1970–1990.*

36. *Historical Statistics of the U.S.: Colonial Times to 1970,* Series H-1004 and H-1005; and *Statistical Abstract of the U.S., 2012,* table 320, our calculation.

37. U.S. Department of Education, National Center for Educational Statistics, *Digest of Educational Statistics, 2013,* table 103.20, http://nces.ed.gov/programs/digest/d13/tables/dt13_103.20.asp; and Cynthia Crossen, "In 1860, America Had 40 Public High Schools; Teachers Chopped Wood," *Wall Street Journal,* Sept. 3, 2003; *Statistical Abstract of the U.S., 2007,* table 208.

38. U.S. Department of Education, National Center for Educational Statistics, *Digest of Educational Statistics, 2013,* table 103.20.

39. See, for example, Dale J. Stephens, "Do You Really Have to Go to College?" *New York Times,* Mar. 7, 2013; and Randall Collins, "Functional and Conflict Theories of Educational Stratification," *American Sociological Review,* 36 (1971), pp. 1002–1019.

40. Our calculation from *Statistical Abstract of the U.S., 2012,* tables 84 and 102.

41. NCAA Research, "Estimated Probability of Competing in Athletics Beyond the High School Interscholastic Level," Sept. 24, 2013, http://www.ncaa.org/wps/wcm/connect/public/ncaa/pdfs/2012/estimated+probability+of+competing+in+athletics+beyond+the+high+school+interscholastic+level.

42. Our calculations from FBI, Uniform Crime Reports, *Crimes in the United States 2012,* Arrests, table 38, http://www.fbi.gov/about-us/cjis/ucr/crime-in-the-u.s/2012/crime-in-the-u.s.-2012/tables/38tabledatadecoverviewpdf.

43. See, for example, Nick Cohen, "What Causes Crime? Some Argue Moral Breakdown, Others Social Deprivation," *The Independent,* June 4, 1995; and Richard Quinney, *The Social Reality of Crime* (Boston: Little, Brown, 1970).

44. Mark Landler, "German Youth Leader Urges: Let Them Use Crutches," *New York Times,* Dec. 27, 2003; see also, Nick Gillespie and Veronique de Rugby, "Generational Warfare: Old-age Entitlements vs. the Safety Net," Reason, Aug./Sept. 2012, http://reason.com/archives/2012/07/23/generational-warfare.

45. Eric Savitz, "CES: Survey Finds Traditional TV Viewing Is Collapsing," *Forbes,* Jan. 9, 2012, http://www.forbes.com/sites/ericsavitz/2012/01/09/ces-survey-finds-traditional-tv-viewing-is-collapsing/; "Watching Television," Child Trends Data Bank, Feb. 2013, http://www.childtrends.org/wp-content/uploads/2012/05/55_Watching_TV.pdf; "Television Watching Statistics," Statistics Brain, Dec. 7, 2013, http://www.statisticbrain.com/television-watching-statistics/; and Urie Bronfenbrenner, "The Disturbing Changes in the American Family," *Search* (Fall 1976), pp. 11–14.

46. Bureau of Labor Statistics, "American Time Use Survey—2012 Results," June 20, 2013; "Television Watching Statistics," Statistics Brain.

47. Ibid; and Jane Brody, "TV's Toll on Young Minds and Bodies," *New York Times,* Aug. 3, 2004.

48. Elka Jones, "Reality vs. Fantasy in Occupational Portrayals on the Small Screen" *Occupational Outlook Quarterly,* Fall 2003, http://www.bls.gov/opub/ooq/2003/fall/art01.pdf; and Robert

Kalaski, "TV's Unreal World of Work," *American Federationist,* Dec. 1980, vol. 87, No 12, pp. 16–21. But see also, Stacy Smith, Marc Choueti, Ashley Prescott, and Katherine Pieper, "Gender Roles & Occupations: A Look at Character Attributes and Job-Related Aspirations in Film and Television, An Executive Report," Geena Davis Institute on Gender in Media, n.d., http://www.seejane.org/downloads/key-findings-gender-roles-2013.pdf.

49. Jones, "Reality vs. Fantasy"; Jerome Groopman, "Being There," *The New Yorker,* Apr. 3, 2006, p. 35; Lucy Townsend, "How Unrealistic Is Murder on Television," BBC News Magazine, Jan. 16, 2013.

50. Joseph Carroll, "One in Four Parents Worry That Their Children Watch Too Much TV," Gallup, Nov. 29, 2006, http://www.gallup.com/poll/25588/One-Four-Parents-Worry-Their-Children-Watch-Too-Much.aspx.

51. *Gallup Poll 1991,* p. 49; and "79% Say Americans Watch Too Much TV," *Rasmussen Reports,* Aug. 20, 2013.

52. John Schwartz, "Leisure Pursuits of Today's Young Man," *New York Times,* Mar. 29, 2004; and "Watching Television," Child Trends Data Bank, Feb. 2013, http://www.childtrends.org/wp-content/uploads/2012/05/55_Watching_TV.pdf.

Chapter 14

1. See Gerhard Lenski and Patrick Nolan, "Trajectories of Development: A Test of Ecological-Evolutionary Theory," *Social Forces,* 63 (Sept. 1984), pp. 1–23 for the initial classification; Gerhard Lenski and Patrick Nolan, "Trajectories of Development: A Further Test," *Social Forces,* 64 (Mar. 1986), pp. 794–795; Patrick Nolan, "World System Status, Techno-Economic Heritage, and Fertility," *Sociological Focus,* 21 (Jan. 1988), pp. 9–33; and Gerhard Lenski and Patrick Nolan, "Trajectories of Development Among Societies," pp. 187–201, in Gerhard Lenski, *Ecological-Evolutionary Theory: Principles and Applications* (Boulder, Colo.: Paradigm, 2005) an updated revision of the "Trajectories" paper.

2. Ibid.

3. Dominick Shattuck, "Vasectomy Acceptance in Rwanda: The Intersection of Need, Knowledge and Access," *World Vasectomy Day,* Oct. 15, 2013, http://worldvasectomyday.org/vasectomy-acceptance-in-rwanda-the-intersection-of-need-knowledge-and-access/; Tyjen Tsai, "Vasectomy an Option for African Men in Family Planning," *PRB,* Dec. 2011, http://www.prb.org/Publications/Articles/2011/africa-vasectomy.aspx.

4. "Three-Child Limit Planned," Reuters, Feb. 14, 2007.

5. Azadeh Moaveni, "Letters from Tehran," *New York Times Book Review,* May 27, 2007.

6. For example, see Global Security.org http://www.globalsecurity.org/military/world/war/index.html; or Wars in the World http://www.warsintheworld.com/.

7. Celia Dugger, "Very Young Populations Contribute to Strife, Study Concludes," *New York Times,* Apr. 6, 2007.

8. Kristin Romey, "Flashpoint Ayodhya: Did Hindu Hard-Liners Recruit Archaeologists to Rewrite History?" *Archaeology,* July/Aug., 2004, p. 49ff.; also, William Dalrymple, "India: The War Over History," *New York Review of Books,* Apr. 7, 2005, pp. 62–65.

9. "Government Corruption 'Cripples' Malawi's Health Sector," Oct. 24, 2013, *IRIN,* UN Office for the Coordination of Humanitarian Affairs, http://www.irinnews.org/report/98990/government-corruption-cripples-malawis-health-sector.

10. David Lamb, "Africans Find Independence a Hard Road," *Los Angeles Times,* Feb. 15, 1979; Ray Vicker, "Arab Nations Growing More Cautious about Dispensing Aid to Third World," *Wall Street Journal,* Sept. 4, 1980; see also, Robert Guest, "Africa Earned Its Debt," *New York Times,* Oct. 6, 2004.

11. Mary Mensah, "Corruption Swallows 25% of Africa's GDP according to World Bank Survey," Graphic Online, Mar. 12, 2013, http://graphic.com.gh/archive/General-News/corruption-swallows-25-of-africas-gdp-according-to-world-bank-survey.html.

12. Ibid.

13. Gerhard Lenski, *Power and Privilege* (Chapel Hill, N.C.: University of North Carolina Press, 1987, chs. 7–9.

14. "Number of NGOs in China Grows to nearly 500,000," *ChinaDaily*, Mar. 20, 2012, http://www.chinadaily.com.cn/china/2012-03/20/content_14875389.htm; and Dongwei Liu, "NGOs Emerge in China, but Face More Challenges," Reuters, Oct. 7, 2013, http://www.trust.org/item/20131007121609-glx02/.

15. "Protests and Dissent in the People's Republic of China," Wikipedia; and see "Protest Prompts China to Cancel Jiangmen Uranium Plant," July 13, 2013, BBC New China, http://www.bbc.co.uk/news/world-asia-china-23298663; Barbara Demick, "Protests in China over Local Grievances Surge, and Get a Hearing," Oct. 8, 2011, *Los Angeles Times*, http://articles.latimes.com/2011/oct/08/world/la-fg-china-protests-20111009.

16. Howard French, "Citizen's Groups Take Root Across China," *New York Times,* Feb. 15, 2007.

17. Lenski, pp. 313–318.

18. Robyn Dixon, "Slavery Still Haunts Africa, Where Millions Remain Captive," *Los Angeles Times*, Oct. 17, 2013, http://articles.latimes.com/print/2013/oct/17/world/la-fg-wn-slavery-africa-20131017.

19. Ibid.

20. Ibid.

21. Neil Smelser and S. M. Lipset (eds.), *Social Structure and Mobility in Economic Development* (Chicago: Aldine, 1966), p. 29ff. Other statistics cited in this paragraph are from the same source. See also, Herbert Passin, *Society and Education in Japan* (New York: Columbia University Press, 1965), p. 57.

22. John Meyer et al., "National Economic Development, 1950–70," in John Meyer and Michael Hannan (eds.), *National Development and the World System* (Chicago: University of Chicago Press, 1979), chap. 6.

23. See, for example, Kitty Kelley, *The Family* (New York: Doubleday, 2004), on the Bush family.

24. See also "Afghan Students Protest Women's Rights Decree" Associated Press, May 23, 2013, http://www.nytimes.com/2013/05/23/world/asia/afghan-students-protest-womens-rights-decree.html.

25. "Female Genital Mutilation: 30 million Girls 'At Risk'," BBC News Africa, July 22, 2013, http://www.bbc.co.uk/news/world-africa-23410858.

26. "List of Female Prime Ministers," Wikipedia.

27. For example, see Tasneem Nashrulla, "The Best and Worst Places To Be A Woman," BuzzFeed World, Oct. 25, 2013, http://www.buzzfeed.com/tasneemnashrulla/the-best-and-worst-places-to-be-a-woman; "The Global Gender Gap Report 2013," World Economic Forum, http://www3.weforum.org/docs/WEF_GenderGap_Report_2013.pdf; Jane Perlez, "Elite Kenyan Women Avoid a Rite: Marriage," *New York Times,* Mar. 3, 1991; James Brooke, "A Rape Case Fuels Debate Across Brazil," *New York Times*, July 5, 1992; Jane Perlez, "Uganda's Women: Children, Drudgery and Pain," *New York Times*, Feb. 24, 1991; "In Parts of India, Families Kill Baby Girls Rather Than Raise Them," *Los Angeles Times,* Feb. 27, 1994; Tom Masland, Rod Norland, Melinda Liu, and Joseph Conterras, "Slavery," *Newsweek*, May 4, 1992, pp. 30–39; Charles Wallace, "Slavery, 20th Century Style," *Los Angeles Times,* Aug. 6, 1991; Emily MacFarquar, "The War Against Women: Violence, Poverty, and Abuse," *U.S. News & World Report,* Mar. 28, 1994, pp. 42–48; *U.S. News & World Report,* "The Echoes of Sita: A Lethal Age-Old Contempt for Women Persists," pp. 54–55; Toni Nelson, "Violence Stalks Women Worldwide," pp. 134–135, in Lester R. Brown, Christopher Flavin, and Hal Kane, *Vital Signs 1996* (New York: Norton, 1996); and Kate Chalkey, "Female Genital Mutilation: New Laws, Programs Try to End Practice," *Population Today*, 25, no. 10, (Oct. 1997), pp. 4–5, Population Reference Bureau.

28. See, for example, Andre Gunder Frank, *Capitalism and Underdevelopment in Latin America* (New York: Monthly Review Press, 1969); Theotonio Dos Santos, "The Structure of Dependence," *American Economic Review,* 60 (1970), pp. 231–236; or Celso Furtado, *Economic Development of Latin America* (Cambridge: Cambridge University Press, 1970).

29. Compare, for example, Frank, op. cit., with Johan Galtung, "A Structural Theory of Imperialism," *Journal of Peace Research,* 8 (1971), pp. 81–117.

30. See, for example, W. W. Rostow, *The Process of Economic Growth* (New York: Norton, 1962); Wilbert Moore and David Feldman, *Labor Commitment*

and Social Change in Developing Areas (New York: Social Science Research Council, 1960); S. N. Eisenstadt, *Modernization* (Englewood Cliffs, N.J.: Prentice-Hall, 1966); Talcott Parsons, *The System of Modern Societies* (Englewood Cliffs, N.J.: Prentice-Hall, 1971); or Alex Inkeles and David Smith, *Becoming Modern* (Cambridge, Mass.: Harvard University Press, 1974).

31. For example, see Mark Tran, "David Attenborough: Trying to Tackle Famine with Bags of Flour Is 'Barmy': BBC Presenter Links Famine to Overpopulation and Warns If We Do Not Curb Growth the Natural World Will," *Guardian*, Sept. 18, 2013, http://www.theguardian.com/global-development/2013/sep/18/david-attenborough-famine-population; Jonathon Porritt, "Who Would Have Thought It? Population Growth And Famine Would Appear Linked!" *Population*, Nov. 7, 2011, http://www.jonathonporritt.com/blog/who-would-have-thought-it-population-growth-and-famine-would-appear-be-linked; and Sylvia Nasar, "It's Never Fair to Just Blame the Weather," *New York Times*, Jan. 17, 1993.

32. World Bank, *World Development Indicators*, www.worldbank.org/data/.

33. Rudolph Rummel, http://www.hawaii.edu/powerkills/; Gaetano Mosca, *The Ruling Class* (New York: McGraw-Hill, 1939); Robert Michels, *Political Parties: A Sociological Study of the Oligarchical Tendencies of Modern Democracy* (Glencoe, Ill.: Free Press, 1958); Milovan Djilas, *The New Class: An Analysis of the Communist System* (New York: Praeger, 1957); George Konrád and Ivan Szelényi, *The Intellectuals on the Road to Class Power: A Sociological Study of the Role of the Intelligentsia in Socialism* (New York: Harcourt, Brace, Jovanovich, 1979); Stephane Courtois, et al., *The Black Book of Communism: Crimes, Terror, Repression* (Cambridge, Mass.: Harvard University Press, 1999); Robert Conquest, *Reflections on a Ravaged Century* (New York: Norton, 2001); Jasper Becker, *Hungry Ghosts: Mao's Secret Famine* (New York: Free Press, 1996); Robert Conquest, *The Harvest of Sorrow: Soviet Collectivization and the Terror-Famine* (New York: Oxford University Press, 1986); Lewis Feuer (ed.), *Marx & Engels: Basic Writings* (New York:

Anchor, 1959); and Robert C. Tucker (ed.), *The Marx Engels Reader* (New York: Norton, 1978).

Chapter 15

1. See, for example, Jacques Ellul, *The Technological Society*, translated by John Wilkinson (New York: Vintage Books, 1967).

2. Aexandra Maryanski and Jonathan Turner, *The Social Cage: Human Nature and the Evolution of Society* (Redwood City, Calif.: Stanford University Press, 2003).

3. George R. Scott, *The History of Capital Punishment* (London: Torchstream Books, 1950), pp. 39–40.

4. Dover Wilson, *The Essential Shakespeare*, as quoted by Ivor Brown in *Shakespeare* (New York: Time Books, 1962), p. 112.

5. See, for example, Colin Turnbull, *The Forest People* (New York: Simon & Schuster, 1961); or John Garvan, *The Negritos of the Philippines* (Vienna: Ferdinand Berger, 1964).

6. Bob Blain, *Golden Threads of Sociological Theory* (Bloomington, Ind.: Author House, 2004), pp. 123–124; see also Oskar Burger, John P. DeLong, and Marcus J. Hamilton, "Industrial Energy Use and the Human Life History," *Scientific Reports*, Aug. 5, 2011, http://www.nature.com/srep/2011/110805/srep00056/full/srep00056.html.

7. Ruut Veenhoven, "Is Life Getting Better?: How Long and Happy People Live in Modern Society," *European Psychologist*, special issue on "Human Development and Well-Being," 2005; see also his earlier study, *Happiness in Nations: Subjective Appreciation of Life in 56 Nations, 1946–1992* (Rotterdam: Risbo, 1993).

8. John Helliwell, Richard Layard, and Jeffrey Sachs (eds.), "World Happiness Report 2013," Sept. 9, 2013, http://unsdsn.org/files/2013/09/WorldHappinessReport2013_online.pdf.

9. Veenhoven.

10. Rene Dubos, *So Human an Animal* (New York: Scribner's, 1968), p. 270.

11. See, for example, Friedrich Engels, as cited by D. G. Brennan in Foreign Policy Association (ed.), *Toward the Year 2018* (New York: Cowles, 1958), p. 2.

12. Bill McKibben, "Reaching the Limit," *New York Review of Books*, May 29, 1997, pp. 32–35.

13. Using McKibben's method.
14. World Bank, *World Development Indicators*, www.worldbank.org/.
15. Ibid.
16. "World Population Projected to Reach 9.6 billion by 2050—UN Report," UN News Centre, June 13, 2013, http://www.un.org/apps/news/story.asp?NewsID=45165#. UrxlGdJDtLM.
17. Lester R. Brown, et al., *Vital Signs 1997* (New York: Norton, 1997); and World Bank, *World Development Indicators*: Urbanization, http://wdi.worldbank.org/table/3.12/.
18. Wendell Cox, "Annual Update on World Population: 2013," *NewGeography*, Oct. 30, 2013, http://www.newgeography.com/content/003608-annual-update-world-urbanization-2013; and United Nations, "World Urbanization Prospects: The 2001 Revision," http://www.un.org/esa/population/publications/wup2001/wup2001dh.pdf.
19. Kenneth S. Deffeyes, *Beyond Oil: The View from Hubbert's Peak* (New York: Hill and Wang, 2005), p. 49; and Peter Maass, "The Breaking Point," *New York Times Magazine*, Aug. 21, 2005; but, see too Jad Mouawad, "Oil Innovations Pump New Life into Oil Wells," *New York Times*, Mar. 5, 2007; Jerome R. Corsi, "Beyond the 'Peak-Oil Production' Hoax," World Net Daily, Dec. 8, 2005, http://www.worldnetdaily.com/news/article.asp?ARTICLE_ID=47738; Kevin Kelleher, "How Long Will the Oil Age Last?: Geologists Say the End Is Nigh, New Recovery Tech May Tell a Different Story," *Popular Science*, Aug. 17, 2004; and James Howard Kunstler, *The Long Emergency* (New York: Atlantic Monthly Press, 2005), p. 49.
20. Robert Bryce, "Peak Oil Cut Is Proved Spectacularly Wrong," *Investors Business Daily*, Apr. 1, 2013, http://www.robertbryce.com/articles/487-peak-oil-cult-is-proved-spectacularly-wrong; George Monbiot," We Were Wrong on Peak Oil. There's Enough to Fry Us All," *Guardian*, July 2, 2012, http://www.theguardian.com/commentisfree/2012/jul/02/peak-oil-we-we-wrong; Leonardo Maugeri, "The Shale Oil Boom: A U.S. Phenomenon," Discussion Paper 2013-05, Belfer Center for Science and International Affairs, Harvard Kennedy School, June 2013, http://belfercenter.ksg.harvard.edu/publication/23191/shale_oil_boom.html; "Growing Oil and Natural Gas Production Continues to Reshape the U.S. Energy Economy," *U.S. Energy Information Administration*, Dec. 16, 2013.
21. Ibid.
22. For example, see Robert Bryce, *Power Hungry: The Myths of Green Energy and the Real Fuels of the Future* (New York: Public Affairs, 2010).
23. Deffeyes, chap. 9; but that too could be changing, see "New Water Splitting Technique Efficiently Produces Hydrogen Fuel," *Science Daily*, Aug. 1, 2013, http://www.sciencedaily.com/releases/2013/08/130801142331.htm.
24. Elisabeth Rosenthal, "Once a Dream Fuel, Palm Oil May Be an Ecological Nightmare," *New York Times*, Jan. 31, 2007; and, see Alex Kirby, "Palm Oil: Green Fuel or Rainforest Killer?" *RTTC*, Mar. 5 2013 http://www.rtcc.org/2013/03/05/palm-oil-green-fuel-or-rainforest-killer/.
25. Julia Layton," Is Ethanol Really More Eco-Friendly Than Gas?" *HowStuffWorks*, Jan. 2007, http://auto.howstuffworks.com/fuel-efficiency/alternative-fuels/ethanol-facts.htm.
26. Mike Meyers, "What Must Come First: Fuel or World Hunger?" *Minneapolis-St. Paul Star Tribune*, Feb. 12, 2007; and, see Patrick Michaels, "A Hungry World? Oh Well, Let Them Eat Ethanol," *Forbes*, July 22, 2012, http://www.forbes.com/sites/patrickmichaels/2012/07/22/a-hungry-world-population-oh-well-let-them-eat-ethanol/.
27. "World Hunger and Poverty Facts," *World Hunger Education Service*, n.d., http://www.worldhunger.org/articles/Learn/world%20hunger%20facts%202002.htm.
28. Ibid.
29. "World Child Hunger Facts," *World Hunger Notes*, n.d., http://www.worldhunger.org/articles/Learn/child_hunger_facts.htm.
30. Brad Plumer, "Just How Badly Are We Overfishing the Oceans," *Washington Post*, Oct. 29, 2013, http://www.washingtonpost.com/blogs/wonkblog/wp/2013/10/29/just-how-badly-are-we-overfishing-the-ocean/; and Daniel Pauly, "Aquacalypse Now," *New Republic*, Sept. 28, 2009, http://www.newrepublic.com/article/environment-energy/aquacalypse-now.

31. Plumer; and J. Matthew Roney, "Taking Stock: World Fish Catch Falls to 90 Million Tons in 2012," *Earth Policy Institute*, Nov. 19, 2012, http://www.earth-policy.org/indicators/C55/fish_catch_2012.

32. Roney, Ibid.

33. "Land Degradation: Land Under Pressure," 2011 Global Food Policy Report, International Food Policy Research Institute, http://www.ifpri.org/node/8441.

34. Ibid.

35. "Water Conflict Chronology List," *Pacific Institute*, n.d., http://www.worldwater.org/conflict/list/; "Water Resources," Wikipedia; and Priit J. Vesilind, "Water: The Middle East's Critical Resource," *National Geographic*, 183, no. 5 (May 1993), pp. 38–71.

36. For example, see Adam Nagourney and Felicity Barringer, "Fees and Anger Rise in California Water War," *New York Times*, Apr. 23, 2012, http://www.nytimes.com/2012/04/24/us/san-diego-takes-water-fight-public.html?_r=0; and "Californians Move to 'Toilet-to-Tap' Water Recycling," PBS, Online Newshour, Feb. 11, 2008, http://www.pbs.org/newshour/extra/features/us/jan-june08/water_2-11.html; and the special issue of *National Geographic,* "Water: The Power, Promise, and Turmoil of North America's Fresh Water," Nov. 1993.

37. Edith M. Lederer, "Nearly Half the World Could Face Water Scarcity By 2030, UN Chief Warns," Associated Press, Mar. 22, 2013, http://www.ctvnews.ca/world/nearly-half-the-world-could-face-water-scarcity-by-2030-un-chief-warns-1.1207996; Stewart M. Patrick, "The Coming Global Water Crisis," *Atlantic*, May 9, 2012, http://www.theatlantic.com/international/archive/2012/05/the-coming-global-water-crisis/256896/; and "U.N. Chief Warns of Water Shortages: Secretary-General Says Scarcity of Water Contributes to Armed Conflicts, Poverty," *CBS News,* Jan. 25, 2008, http://www.cbsnews.com/stories/2008/01/25/tech/main3752531.shtml.

38. Tom Oswald, Ned Walker, Leo Zulu, "Can Food Production Increase Without Disease Risk?" *Michigan State University Today*, Nov. 1 2013, http://msutoday.msu.edu/news/2013/can-food-production-increase-without-disease-risk/; Oliver Moore, "Natural Resources Challenges to Future Food Security," *Agroforestry World*, Apr. 17, 2013, http://blog.worldagroforestry.org/index.php/2013/04/17/1950/; Dan Charles, "Wild Bees Are Good For Crops, But Crops Are Bad For Bees," NPR, Mar. 1, 2013, http://www.npr.org/blogs/thesalt/2013/03/01/173167125/wild-bees-are-good-for-crops-but-crops-are-bad-for-bees; "Banking against Doomsday," *The Economist*, Mar. 10, 2012, http://www.economist.com/node/21549931; and "World's Food Supply at Risk," *National Geographic*, 181, no. 4 (Apr. 1991), pp. 74–105.

39. "NASA Finds Sustained Long-Term Climate Warming Trend," NASA, Jan. 15, 2013, http://www.nasa.gov/topics/earth/features/2012-temps.html.

40. "Climate Change Indicators in the United States," U.S. Environmental Protection Agency, 2012, http://www.epa.gov/climatechange/science/indicators/oceans/sea-level.html.

41. For example, see "The Current and Future Consequences of Global Change," NASA, http://climate.nasa.gov/effects; and M. L. Parry, O. F. Canziani, J. P. Palutikof, P. J. van der Linden and C. E. Hanson, (eds.), IPCC, 2007: Summary for Policymakers, *in: Climate Change 2007: Impacts, Adaptation and Vulnerability.* (Cambridge: Cambridge University Press, 2008), 7–22. For example, see Matt McGrath, "Climate Slowdown Means Extreme Rates of Warming 'Not as Likely'," BBC, http://www.bbc.co.uk/news/science-environment-22567023; and James Taylor, "As Its Global Warming Narrative Unravels, The IPCC Is in Damage Control Mode," *Forbes*, Sept. 26, 2013, http://www.forbes.com/sites/jamestaylor/2013/09/26/as-its-global-warming-narrative-unravels-the-ipcc-is-in-damage-control-mode/print/.

42. J. T. Houghton et al., eds., *Climate Change 2001: The Scientific Basis* (Cambridge: Cambridge University Press, 2001); World Meteorological Organization, "WMO Statement on the Status of the Global Climate in 2001."

43. For example, see Stephen McIntyre and Ross McKitrick, "Corrections to the Mann et al. (1998)

Proxy Data Base and Northern Hemispheric Average Temperature Series," *Energy and Environment,* 14 (2003), pp. 751–771; Stephen McIntyre and Ross McKitrick, "Hockey Sticks, Principal Components and Spurious Significance," *Geophysical Research Letters,* 32 (Feb. 12, 2005), see also: http://www.uoguelph.ca/~rmckitri/research/trc.html; Andrew Revkin, "Computers Add Sophistication, But Don't Resolve Climate Debate," *New York Times,* Aug. 31, 2004; Andrew Revkin, "New Research Questions Uniqueness of Recent Warming," *New York Times,* Oct. 5, 2004; Peter Foukal, Gerald North, and Tom Wigley, "A Stellar View on Solar Variations and Climate," *Science,* 306 (Oct. 1, 2004), pp. 68–69; and Jacopo Pasotti, "Daggers Are Drawn over Revived Cosmic Ray–Climate Link, *Science,* 319 (Jan. 11, 2008), p. 144. Richard A. Kerr, "Millennium's Hottest Decade Retains Its Title, for Now," *Science,* 307 (Feb. 11, 2005), pp. 828–829.

44. S. Fred Singer, "Hit and Myth of Global Warming," *Washington Times,* July 7, 2002; "Whoops! NASA Off by Decades on Hottest Year," *Scientific American,* Aug. 17, 2007, http://www.sciam.com/article.cfm?id=news-bytes-of-the-week-warmest-year-revised; and Ross R. Kittrick, and Patrick J. Micahels, "Quantifying the Influence of Anthropogenic Surface Processes and Inhomogeneties on Grided Global Climate Data," *Journal of Geophysical Research,* 2007, vol. 112, issue D24.

45. For example, see Larry Bell, "In Their Own Words: Climate Alarmists Debunk Their 'Science'," *Forbes,* Feb. 5, 2013, http://www.forbes.com/sites/larrybell/2013/02/05/in-their-own-words-climate-alarmists-debunk-their-science/2/.

46. For example, see Ross McKitrick, "IPCC Models Getting Mushy," *Financial Post,* Sept. 16, 2013, http://opinion.financialpost.com/2013/09/16/ipcc-models-getting-mushy/; and Roy W. Spencer, "STILL Epic Fail: 73 Climate Models vs. Measurements, Running 5-Year Means," June 6, 2013, http://www.drroyspencer.com/2013/06/still-epic-fail-73-climate-models-vs-measurements-running-5-year-means/.

47. Stephanie Paige Ogburn and ClimateWire, "Missing Data from Arctic One Cause of Pause in Temperature Rise," *Scientific American,* Nov. 18, 2013, http://www.scientificamerican.com/article.cfm?id=missing-data-from-arctic-one-cause-of-pause-in-temperature-rise; and Richard Harris, "A Cooler Pacific May Be Behind Recent Pause In Global Warming," NPR, Aug. 29, 2013, http://www.npr.org/2013/08/29/216415005/a-cooler-pacific-may-be-behind-recent-pause-in-global-warming.

48. Fred Singer, "Hit and Myth of Global Warming," *Washington Times,* July 7, 2002; and "Climate Caution Is about the Policies, Not the Science," The American Interest, Aug. 2, 2013, http://www.the-american-interest.com/blog/2013/08/02/climate-caution-is-about-the-policies-not-the-science/.

49. "International Energy Outlook 2013," U.S. Energy Information Administration, July 25, 2013, http://www.epa.gov/climatechange/science/future.html.

50. Elias P. Gyftopolous, "Energy: Everybody's Business," *Forbes,* Oct. 27, 1980, p. 86.

51. "US Economic Energy Efficiency 1950–2008," True Cost, Jan. 9, 2010, http://truecostblog.com/2010/01/09/us-economic-energy-efficiency-1950-2008/.

52. Brendan Pastor, "Energy Subsidies in Developing Countries: An Inefficient Policy?" *Media Global News,* Apr. 24, 2013, http://www.mediaglobal.org/2013/04/24/energy-subsidies-in-developing-countries-an-inefficient-policy/; and Nicola Cantore, "Energy Efficiency in Developing Countries for the Manufacturing Sector," working paper 15/2011, United Nations, http://www.unido.org//fileadmin/user_media/Publications/Research_and_statistics/Branch_publications/Research_and_Policy/Files/Working_Papers/2011/WP152011%20Energy%20Efficiency%20in%20Developing%20Countries%20for%20the%20Manufacturing%20Sector.pdf.

53. The figures are 88.1 million tons in 1960, and 250.4 million tons in 2011, from "Municipal Solid Waste Generation, Recycling, and Disposal in the United States: Facts and Figures for 2011," U.S. Environmental Protection Agency, May 2013, http://www.epa.gov/osw/nonhaz/municipal/pubs/MSWcharacterization_508_053113_fs.pdf.

54. Michael C. Munger, "Recycling: Can It Be Wrong, When it Feels So Right?" *CATO Unbound*, June 3, 2013, http://www.cato-unbound.org/2013/06/03/michael-c-munger/recycling-can-it-be-wrong-when-it-feels-so-right.

55. For example, see Freda Ding, "Green Investments: 10 Recycling Stocks Trading on US Exchanges," Kapital Wire. What's Hot http://wire.kapitall.com/investment-idea/investing-in-recycling-stocks/; and J. Michael Kennedy, "Seattle's Recycling Success Is Being Measured in Scraps," *New York Times*, Oct. 10, 2007.

56. Jesse Emspak, "How Bacteria Clean Up Nuclear Waste," *Discovery News*, Sept. 9, 2011, http://news.discovery.com/tech/biotechnology/how-bacteria-clean-up-nuclear-waste-110909.htm; Keith Veronese, "10 Surprising Things That Bacteria Like to Eat," May 24, 2012, http://io9.com/5908318/10-surprising-things-that-bacteria-like-to-eat; and Miranda Wang and Jeanny Yao, "Using Bacteria to Break Down Plastic Waste," Engineering.Com, Aug. 2, 2013, http://www.engineering.com/DesignerEdge/DesignerEdgeArticles/ArticleID/6109/Using-Bacteria-to-Break-Down-Plastic-Waste.aspx.

57. *Vital Signs, 2003*, p. 30.

58. "Grain Harvest Sets Record, But Supplies Still Tight," World Watch Institute, Dec. 30, 2013, http://www.worldwatch.org/node/5539.

59. "Per Capita Consumption of Poultry and Livestock, 1965 to Estimated 2014, in Pounds," National Chicken Council, Nov. 8, 2013, http://www.nationalchickencouncil.org/about-the-industry/statistics/per-capita-consumption-of-poultry-and-livestock-1965-to-estimated-2012-in-pounds/.

60. Ronald Trostle and Ralph Seeley, "Developing Countries Dominate World Demand for Agricultural Products," USDA, Aug. 05, 2013, http://www.ers.usda.gov/amber-waves/2013-august/developing-countries-dominate-world-demand-for-agricultural-products.aspx#.UsHx09JDtLM; Sid Perkins, "A Thirst for Meat: Changes in Diet, Rising Population May Strain China's Water Supply," *Science News*, Jan. 19, 2008; and *Vital Signs,* 2007–2008.

61. Janet Larsen and J. Matthew Roney, "Farmed Fish Production Overtakes Beef," *Earth Policy Institute,* June 12, 2013, http://www.earth-policy.org/plan_b_updates/2013/update114; "Milestone: 50 Percent of Fish Are Now Farmed," LiveScience, Sept. 8, 2009, http://www.livescience.com/5682-milestone-50-percent-fish-farmed.html.

62. William Broad, "The Incredible Shrinking Transistor . . .," *New York Times,* Feb. 4, 1997.

63. John Markoff, "New Wave in High Tech: Tiny Motors and Sensors," *New York Times,* Jan. 27, 1997; "Predicting the Future of MEMS," Conventor, Oct. 12, 2013, http://www.coventor.com/blog/predicting-the-future-of-mems/.

64. Jessica Tuchman Mathews, "Factories Too Tiny to See," *Washington Post,* Jan. 23, 1980.

65. Erika Gebel, "Making Insulin," Diabetes Forecast, July 2013, http://www.diabetesforecast.org/2013/jul/making-insulin.html; Emily Singer, "Microbes Can Mass-Produce Malaria Drug," *MIT Technology Review,* Apr. 10, 2013, http://www.technologyreview.com/news/513441/microbes-can-mass-produce-malaria-drug/; and Sandra Blakeslee, "Human Genes Turn Plants into Factories for Medicines," *New York Times,* Jan. 16, 1990.

66. Barbara Slavin, "Afghan Christian's Plight Draws U.S. Pressure," *USA Today,* Mar. 20, 2006; See also: Jane Perlez, "Once Muslim, Now Christian and Caught in the Courts," *New York Times,* Aug. 24, 2006.

67. William Dalrymple, "The Truth About Muslims," *New York Review of Books,* Nov. 4, 2004, p. 32.

68. For example, see "China's Century:' More and More Economies Will Want to Trade in Yuan'," *RT,* Dec. 4, 2013, http://rt.com/op-edge/chinese-yuan-gain-power-713/; and Ted C. Fishman, "The Chinese Century," *New York Times Magazine,* July 4, 2004, p. 27. But see also "Josef Joffe, "China's Coming Economic Slowdown," *Wall Street Journal,* Oct. 25, 2013, http://online.wsj.com/news/articles/SB10001424052702304402104579151511303083436.

69. Nicholas D. Kristof, "A Little Leap Forward," *New York Review of Books,* June 24, 2004, p. 56.

70. Keith Bradsher, "Next Made-in-China Boom: College Graduates," *New York Times,* Jan. 16, 2013, http://www.nytimes.com/2013/01/17/business/

chinas-ambitious-goal-for-boom-in-college-graduates.html?pagewanted=1&_r=0; Hannah Richardson, "Warning over Shortage of Engineering Graduates," BBC Sept. 30, 2012, http://www.bbc.co.uk/news/education-19760351; and Thomas Friedman, "It's a Flat World After All," *New York Times Magazine,* Apr. 3, 2005, p. 37.

71. Prepared remarks by Bill Gates, co-chair, February 26, 2005, http://www.gatesfoundation.org/media-center/speeches/2005/02/bill-gates-2005-national-education-summit.

72. Fishman, p. 24; but see also Joffe.

73. Our calculation for industrial societies compared to that for "low income" countries; data are for GDP per capita (purchasing power parity) in current international dollars; from *World Development Indicators,* http://www.worldbank.org/.

74. Robert Heilbroner, *An Inquiry into the Human Prospect* (New York: Norton, 1974).

75. Ibid., pp. 121–122.

76. Jon Gertner, "Proceed with Caution," *New York Times Magazine,* June 6, 2004, pp. 32–36.

77. For a cautiously optimistic outlook, see Jared Diamond, *Collapse: How Societies Choose to Fail or Succeed* (New York: Viking, 2005), chap. 16.

Chapter 1

1-1a, Andrea J Smith/Shutterstock
1-1b, Clem Haagner/Photo Researchers
1-1c, James R. Holland/Stock Boston
1-2, Clinton Moffat/Shutterstock
1-3, Canada Transport, Canadian Government
1-4, American Foundation for the Blind

Chapter 2

2-1, Hellen Sergeyeva/Shutterstock
2-2, szefei/Shutterstock
2-3a, American Museum of Natural History
2-3b, right, Lynn McLaren/Photo Researchers
2-4, Courtesy of Department of Antiquities, Ashmolean Museum, Oxford
2-5, Henri Cartier-Bresson/Magnum
2-6, ID1974/Shutterstock

Chapter 3

3-1, Peter Southwick/Stock Boston
3-2, Cartoon, Ed Fisher, by permission of the artist
3-3, © Underwood & Underwood/Corbis

Chapter 4

4-1, Omikron/Photo Researchers
4-2, USAID Photo/Agency for International Development

Chapter 5

5-1, Press Association via AP Images
5-2, Pichugin Dmitry/Shutterstock
5-3, Prehistoric Division, Museum of Natural History, Vienna
5-4, By permission of Peter J. Ucko and Andrea Rojenfeld, Paleolithic Cave Art, 1967, Wiedenfeld Publishers
5-5, By permission of John Marshall, Peabody Museum, Harvard University
5-6, Penny Tweedie/Woodfin Camp & Associates
5-7, American Museum of Natural History
5-8, Colonel Charles W. Furlong

5-9, National Anthropological Archive, Smithsonian Institution.

Chapter 6

6-1, American Museum of Natural History
6-2, American Museum of Natural History
6-3, From Napoleon A. Chagnon, *Yanomano: The Fierce People* © 1968 by Holt, Rinehart, Winston, Inc. Reprinted by permission of CBS College Publishing.
6-4, From W. Watson, *Early Civilization in China,* © 1970, Thames & Hudson, Ltd., London
6-5, American Museum of Natural History
6-6, iStockphoto
6-7, United Nations
6-8, American Museum of Natural History
6-9, Courtesy of Dean Birkenkamp
6-10, From Jacques Maquet, *Africanity, The Cultural Unity of Black Africa,* Oxford U. Press, 1972, p. 112

Chapter 7

7-1, From *Standard Cyclopedia of Horticulture,* Mac-Millan, 1916
7-2, Evans/Three Lion Photos
7-3, Courtesy of the Metropolitan Museum of Art, Museum Excavations, 1919–1920, Rogers Fund, supplemented by contribution of Edward S. Harkness
7-4, Courtesy of the Metropolitan Museum of Art, Museum Excavations, 1919–1920, Rogers Fund, supplemented by contribution of Edward S. Harkness
7-5, United Nations
7-6, Courtesy of Exxon Corporation
7-7, United Nations
7-8, United Nations
7-9, Courtesy of the Metropolitan Museum of Art, Bashford Dean Memorial Collection, Funds from various donors, 1929
7-10, iStockphoto

7-11, Paul Chesley/Tony Stone Images

7-12, Battle of gladiators against the wildcats, detail depicting a gladiator running through a wildcat, 320 AD (mosaic), Roman, (4th century AD)/ Galleria Borghese, Rome, Italy/Alinari/The Bridgeman Art Library

Chapter 8

8-1, United Nations

8-2, Pietro F. Mele/Photo Researchers

8-3, Paolo Koch/Photo Researchers

8-4, By Permission of Institut Français d'Archéologie, Beirut, Lebanon

8-5, Courtesy of the Metropolitan Museum of Art, Rogers Fund, 1906.

Chapter 9

9-1, AP Photo/Corpus Christie Caller-Times, Rachel Denny Clow

9-2, The Smithsonian Institution

9-3, © Bettmann/CORBIS

9-4, ENIAC (first computer), public domain

9-5, Edward L. Bafford Photography Collection, Albin O. Kuhn Library & Gallery, U. of Maryland, Baltimore Gallery

Chapter 10

10-1, Courtesy of Oxbo Corporation

10-2, Imaginechina via AP Images

10-3, Christopher Penler/Shutterstock

10-4, Copyright Bettmann/Corbis/AP Images

10-5, AP Photo/CHINATOPIX

Chapter 11

11-1, Courtesy of the New York Public Library, Astor, Lenox and Tilden Foundations

11-2, Independence National Historic Park Collection

11-3, Library of Congress

11-4, AP Photo

11-5, AP Photo/Suzanne Plunkett

Chapter 12

12-1, Steve Petteway, Collection of the Supreme Court of the United States.

12-2, 360b/Shutterstock

Chapter 13

13-1, Wellcome Library, London

13-2, © Reinhard Eisele/CORBIS

13-3, Rob Marmion/Shutterstock

13-4, Gerhard Lenski

Chapter 14

14-1, United Nations

14-2, © Kevin Carter/Sygma/Corbis

14-3, AP Photo/Greg Baker

14-4, United Nations

14-5, Corinne Dufka/Reuters/Corbis

14-6, Alfred/SIPA Press

14-7, AP Photo/D. Gray

Chapter 15

15-1, Cartoon, Frank and Ernest, copyright Newspaper Enterprise Association, Inc.

15-2, Courtesy of Ron Dear

15-3, Dusko Despotovic/Corbis

15-4, AP Photo/Frank Franklin II

15-5, China Features/Corbis Sygma

15-6, AP Photo/File